To my father, Dale, and brother, Ron, whose dancing was
undoubtedly curtailed, and who supported mine anyway

JENNIFER FISHER

To my dear friend Patrice Marandel, for all his support

ANTHONY SHAY

WHEN MEN DANCE

CHOREOGRAPHING MASCULINITIES ACROSS BORDERS

EDITED BY

Jennifer Fisher

Anthony Shay

OXFORD

UNIVERSITY PRESS

2009

OXFORD
UNIVERSITY PRESS

Oxford University Press, Inc., publishes works that further
Oxford University's objective of excellence
in research, scholarship, and education.

Oxford   New York
Auckland   Cape Town   Dar es Salaam   Hong Kong   Karachi
Kuala Lumpur   Madrid   Melbourne   Mexico City   Nairobi
New Delhi   Shanghai   Taipei   Toronto

With offices in
Argentina   Austria   Brazil   Chile   Czech Republic   France   Greece
Guatemala   Hungary   Italy   Japan   Poland   Portugal   Singapore
South Korea   Switzerland   Thailand   Turkey   Ukraine   Vietnam

Published by Oxford University Press, Inc.
198 Madison Avenue, New York, New York 10016

www.oup.com

Oxford is a registered trademark of Oxford University Press.

Library of Congress Cataloging-in-Publication Data
When men dance : choreographing masculinities across borders / edited by
Jennifer Fisher and Anthony Shay.
   p. cm.
Includes bibliographical references and index.
ISBN 978-0-19-538669-1; 978-0-19-538670-7 (pbk.)
1. Male dancers.   2. Male dancers—History.   3. Male dancers—Social conditions.
4. Masculinity.   5. Gender identity in dance.   6. Dance—Sociological aspects.
7. Dance—Anthropological aspects.
I. Fisher, Jennifer, 1949–   II. Shay, Anthony, 1936–
GV1588.6.W5 2009
792.8081—dc22   2008050034

Printed in the United States of America
on acid-free paper

ACKNOWLEDGMENTS

First and foremost, our thanks go to the men who dance, and then to the women who have taken a relative backseat when a topic like this becomes the focus. And, for that matter, to everyone who finds constriction in the labels that inevitably arise while the topic is being explored. In some way, the idea that "masculinity," in its many incarnations, can be defined and labeled as such is a condition of this volume, yet potentially its limitation, too. We thank our contributors and our readers for bearing with us on our journey to illuminating some of the many ways concepts of masculinity have existed in general and specific cases. Given that many of these concepts of masculinity have haunted our contributors of the "personal histories" that enliven and ground this book, we thank them especially for sharing aspects of their stories with us. They were a great gift. To the countless friends, acquaintances, and colleagues who shared even more anecdotes and experiences that involved the many facets of masculinity and dance, we apologize for not being able to follow every intriguing lead and include them all. We trust that many of their themes are found in our selections and that there are many more revelatory stories to come.

Our thanks go as well to the Congress on Research in Dance, which gave us the opportunity to present at an annual meeting the panel on dance and masculinity (with Fisher, Krishnan, and Shay) that eventually evolved into this volume. We are most grateful to all our essay writers, who often worked through revisions that enhanced their already cogent scholarship and provided us with timely responses that made our job easier. Their sometimes detailed help with illustration was also appreciated, especially in the case of Jill Nunes Jensen, whose enthusiasm and efficiency aided the project every step of the way. To the following, we also owe a debt of gratitude for providing photographs: British Library Board, Chris Campolongo, Aaron Cota, Timothy Fielding, Andrea Flores, El Gabriel, Stephanie Garcia, Joe Goode Performance Group, Lois Greenfield, Stephen Johnson, Leslie Klein, Sharon Kung, Donald McKayle, Brian Mengini, Richard Merrill, Artemis Mourat, Ryuichi Oshimoto, Bill Pack, Frank Peters, Thomas Rodrigues, C. P. Satyajit, Beatriz Schiller, Stephen Schreiber, Marty Sohl/Alonzo King's LINES Ballet, Davesh Soneji, David Street,

Richard Termine, Catherine Turocy, Sharon Vanderlinde at the National Ballet of Canada Archives, Cylla von Tiedemann, Bobby Ysias, the Ibrahim Farrah Archives, and Norton Owen at the Jacob's Pillow Dance Festival.

Jennifer Fisher thanks in particular her colleagues at the University of California, Irvine, for their constant support and suggestions; her intelligent dance major students and MFA candidates, who are always full of insight and opinion; her colleagues Thomas DeFrantz and Naomi Jackson for helpful scholarly and structural advice; and her family and friends for general support, in particular Lenna DeMarco, whose journey in dance has happily intertwined with hers ever since they were snowflakes who never questioned why the guys weren't snowflakes, too, back in the Louisville Ballet *Nutcracker* land. Fisher also thanks Tony Shay for his longtime friendship, patience, and ever-optimistic soldiering on when it came to collaboration. In relation to the men she has danced with, acted with, argued with, and written about, who often seemed cast in another world, she stands in awe of their maverick strain.

At Oxford University Press, we are grateful for the copyediting expertise of Susan Ecklund. And we offer thanks of the highest magnitude to Oxford editor Norman Hirschy for the intelligent and gracious shepherding of this manuscript into bookhood. His keen interest, patience, enthusiasm, and belief in the project's potential, fielding all questions and offering astute advice on all levels, strengthened the book and made the process a pleasure.

CONTENTS

WHEN MEN DANCE

Introduction

Because two of the seminal terms in this book's title are sometimes hard to pin down—Whose version of masculinity? What sort of dancing?—they seem to require some definitions at the start. Yet, as the working title "Dance and Masculinity" was used while we gathered contributions and explained the book to both insiders and outsiders for the past several years, everyone seemed to agree there is a lot to say about the topic, as if we all knew what we meant. In some ways that's true: a fairly common understanding of dance is that it's what occurs when the body moves in patterned or improvised ways that are different from the movements of the nondancing body; and that dance occurs onstage, in social life, and during celebrations. In this volume, we are careful to use the term "dance" only in reference to activities the participants themselves define that way, as opposed to movement forms that exist in rituals or trance, for instance. Because this book originates in North America, it often focuses on concert dance forms, with some mention of social dance and spectacle; but, significantly, there are also essays about popular and classical dance forms that originated in other parts of the world, especially in Asia and the Middle East.

A working definition of "masculinity" is trickier. It can be described in many ways to indicate variations in behavior that revolve around different cultures, experiences, and points of view. Given that acknowledgment of variation, a starting point here will be the fact that the term is so often associated with biologically defined males, and that it tends to be accompanied by notions of its presumed opposite, "femininity." Beyond that, the debates correctly begin, given what masculinity can mean in different contexts, and given the slippage that can occur between conceptions of "sexuality" and "gender." Still, a common reaction to this book's working title tended to be, "Dance and masculinity, yes, there's a problem—I could tell you stories . . . " Some of those stories appear here, in a selection of scholarly essays and personal histories that engage the history and theory surrounding issues of dance and *masculinities*, the plural term that more correctly describes the number of choices and paths that are taken.

When it comes to the intertwining valences associated with the terms "sex" and "gender," the feminist historiography of dance has featured prominent explorations from a number of perspectives, often highlighting "the relational value" presumed to dictate the categories of masculinity and femininity (Nordera 2007, 172). In other words, "femininity and masculinity are not built independently but by a reciprocal relationship through progressive adjustments that depend on culture, on social conditioning, and on the imaginary of a given time, as well as on the way in which individual desires and impulses take form" (172). How this might look in a dance performance is suggested by Mark Franko as he considers the "blended voices" evident in the boundary-breaking multivalent performances of Kazuo Ohno, an elderly Japanese artist whose male body is as visible as the feminine Victorian regalia he wears onstage in *Suiren*, for instance. For Franko, Ohno seems to embody all at once "nature, hackneyed femininity, and emotion" and become "a conceptual space of sexual splicing" (1995, 104). In his performance, the usual binaries regarding sex and gender are confounded not by throwing them over by means of subversive cross-dressing, a frequent strategy of the Western theater. Instead, suggests Franko, Ohno provides a "through-dressing" performance, not reliant on fixing identity according to old hermeneutic models (104–7).

Many authors in this collection reenvision old theoretical models by reconsidering the histories of stereotypes and prejudices, by turning over old meanings in the quest to understand and overturn them. The masculine quality known as "machismo," for instance, makes an appearance often, sometimes as a sociocultural value that audiences and choreographers seek or impose upon the male dancer. The fact that its embodiment in movement terms shifts from age to age, from culture to culture, and regime to regime should be a clue to its elusiveness and impermanence, yet new iterations of "acceptable" machismo arise regularly. The fact that machismo might reasonably be attributed to female dancers as well (Fisher, this volume) is not irrelevant, yet the binaries of male and female continue to be asserted in various dance contexts, as if they were ontologically secure. Both men and women suffer from narrow notions of who can dance and how, and who can lay claim to being masculine, feminine, or something less easily labeled. Women are not absent from discussions here, but the subject is men this time, providing a needed focus on relatively unexplored topics that relate to men's particular obstacles and challenges when it comes to dancing.

Dance studies, as a relatively new field, has been a bit slow off the mark to delve into what Ramsay Burt has famously called "the trouble with the male dancer" (1995). Burt's seminal study was part of a vanguard of exploration just now beginning to flourish (with Burt continuing to contribute here). There have also been stimulating new perspectives on dance and masculinities in the edited volume *Dancing Desires: Choreographing Sexualities On and Off the Stage* (Desmond 2001), in Kevin Kopelson's *Queer Afterlife of Nijinsky* (1997), and in Peter Stoneley's *A Queer History of the Ballet* (2007). These works have started "to explore an historical kinesthetics of sexuality" and to "make the invisible

visible" (Desmond 2001, 27). Yet today, in the first part of the 21st century, after significant shifts in both popular and scholarly definitions of masculinity, and after both stage and social spaces have been declared a safe place for men to dance in many contexts, there is still much to say regarding the stigma and challenges that regularly arise around the topic of men who dance.

Too often, scholars have not been able to break out of "the adulatory discourse that protects the dance field from investigative research."[1] Much of the dance field's reluctance to discuss issues revolving around masculinity can be seen to relate to its relatively low positioning in the arts world. Dance partisans and promoters, for instance, might have wanted to avoid the risk of being seen as dominated by women and gay men in order to protect reputations or the status of an art form still struggling for respect (Morris 2006, 32). The ballet world, Stoneley points out, has had a history of "discretion" when it comes to mention of homosexuality, for fear of being thought of as "only for 'lasses' and 'poofs'" (Stoneley 2007, 2). Very real fears of injurious discrimination, of course, kept many topics in the closet for both dance practitioners and scholars.

Although challenging stereotypes have been applied to both gay and straight men (and all variations in between), much of the recent literature on dance and masculinity focuses on the previously taboo topic of homosexuality in the dance world, both as it exists as a stigmatizing identity and, as queer studies has posited, as "queer viewpoints" become a way to explore how outsider status figures in scenarios of persecution and resistance. The sea change that promises refreshing breezes in dance studies can perhaps be glimpsed succinctly in the following book endorsement for *A Queer History of the Ballet*, from choreographer Mark Morris: "Queers in ballet? This shocking development is revealed by Mr. Stoneley in this very interesting book on the secret culture of ballet. As a homosexual choreographer, I was pleased and relieved to have the elephant in the room acknowledged" (from the back cover of Stoneley 2007). Couching revolution in campy irony, as he often does, Morris perhaps pinpoints an exact, liberating moment when the well-known fact of ballet's appeal to homosexual men went very public. In fact, it's tempting to see homophobia and the infamous closet that kept homosexuality both a hidden and a feared aspect of the dance world—even as it was an open secret privately—as the defining theme of a book about dance and masculinity. It certainly *is* "the elephant in the room" when it comes to not being discussed in depth. The topic thus appears here often, as one absolutely key element of a long history and complex present. It's still one worth focusing on, while remembering that a general denigration and suspicion of dance as an occupation also looms largely, as do the repercussions of colonialism, sexism, racism, and nationalism. This volume covers aspects of these themes, while acknowledging that there is much more to be written in the future by scholars and practitioners alike.

Our addition of personal histories—monologues that resulted when we asked men to tell their stories of the dance world, as they relate to masculinity themes—emphasizes the importance of the inclusion of dance practitioners in scholarly volumes.[2] It is also part of a theoretical approach that owes much to reception-based criticism that values the case history method, as well as the "horizon of expectations" each person brings to dance experiences. The personal histories here are placed between scholarly essays, relating directly to them on a few occasions, but more often providing in general what anthropologist Dorinne Kondo calls "the evocative voice." This is a "rhetorical/theoretical strategy" that can "call forth a world," in all its particular complexity and richness, and at the same time problematize that world by questioning the notion that the writer's account is a comprehensive worldview (Kondo 1990, 3–33). The evocative voice, Kondo says, in combination with an author's reflexive passages, can indicate the possibilities and limitations involved in a process during which researchers and people in their "fields" can seek "to understand each other within shifting fields of power and meaning" (8). The lives of individual people and the ways they participate in collective enterprises are complex, Kondo points out, and difficult to contain within theoretical structures. Therefore, she sets out to expand "notions of what can count as theory." For her, "experience and evocation can *become theory*, [and] the binary between 'empirical' and 'theoretical' is displaced and loses its force" (8). Furthermore, "in attempting to enlarge the boundaries of what counts as theoretical, I attempt to build on feminist scholarship that expands our definitions of what counts as political. Power can create identities on the individual level, as it provides disciplines, punishments, and culturally available pathways for fulfillment" (10).

In the ballet world, to take one world in which hierarchies abound amid disciplinary power structures, different men recall different levels of experience with the well-known prejudice about ballet being "not quite masculine." Some veteran ballet men describe torrents of physical abuse and merciless teasing from bullies and bigots, as well as less threatening aspersions cast on them by well-meaning but confused others (for instance, the familiar question that goes, "But what do you for a *real* job?"). Other male dancers, especially from a younger generation, claim they haven't really encountered that sort of thing, that people have become more tolerant, more educated these days. In the former Soviet Union, so goes the myth, there *was* no prejudice against male ballet dancers, a nice idea that turns out not to have been entirely true. Some reflections that reflect rampant prejudice against male dancers in Soviet-era Azerbaijan are found in the contribution of Namus Zokhrabov in this volume. For him, the Georgians provided an example of a culture that respected dance in general, yet sometimes, the taint of being a dancer varied only in degree throughout much of the old Soviet Union.[3] It's also often thought that men in modern dance might be less stigmatized—or perhaps not at all if they do tap, jazz, or hip-hop. But for many prejudicial parties, a male dancer is a male dancer is a sissy, no matter what the genre.

Examples of prejudicial male dancer stereotypes from movies and television are too numerous to mention, proving that knee-jerk reactions often reflect attitudes that are deeply woven into popular culture. Dance analyst Marina Nordera found such attitudes already couched in her five-year-old son when he laughed at male ballet dancers on television and asked why a man would wear "woman's tights" (2007, 172). For Nordera, this episode demonstrated "how, from early childhood on, knowledge and the images tied to it are structured around stereotypes that pass over the biological differences between men and women to become fixed in the category of gender" (173).

Is the male dancer always suspect? In many cultures, there is no stigma about dance being feminine or homosexual. This is particularly true in many parts of Africa, for instance, and at certain moments in the history of European and Asian courts, and in North American powwow culture, or sometimes in street dance culture today. Historically, dancing men have been celebrated as warriors or courtiers, as graceful, delicate tempters whose movements are praised in poetry, and as extraordinary creative forces and works of art. But in some eras, they have also been ridiculed, branded as prostitutes, and banned from the stage in an astonishing number of places around the world. This introduction will lay a little groundwork when it comes to the history and conceptual schemes that are part of the landscape of dance and masculinities today, including themes such as choreophobia, homophobia, effeminophobia, colonialism, and racism, which all appear more specifically in the essays that follow.

The themes surface as well in the series of personal histories of male dancers when they talk about the way they experienced issues of dance and masculinity. Not surprisingly, and always eloquently, they reveal the personal side of the political, speaking for themselves and undoubtedly for other men in dance. Once started, this project could easily have kept going for years, so rich, diverse, and revealing were their stories; our selection merely suggests the wealth of information to be had. Our contributors of these personal histories had some-times never spoken about the "masculinity issue" publicly in any meaningful way. More often, they had been called on to defend men's right to dance or to ignore any negative attitudes that came their way. Several of them, once they started, were reluctant to stop talking about it, so liberating was the feeling of finally thinking it through and having a listener. It seems as if there is a new age of memoir to come.

Men in dance have come a long way from the time when the question of being gay or straight was practically the only one that came up in many contexts—usually covertly, since until recent times the closet door was emphat-ically heavy and hard to budge without danger. Homosexuals, then, have felt the enormous weight of negative stereotypes about men in dance, but so have heterosexuals and all of those who aren't so easily defined as gay or straight. We acknowledge that prejudice against men who dance can be an equal opportunity oppressor, and that the bipolar habits of essentialization tend to arise in many, many locations. Male dancers have undoubtedly felt the societal pressure to state if they are gay or straight, since it has been "the elephant in the room" for so long, as if their performances always arose ineluctably from sexual preference. In this volume, sexual orientation of individual dancers is often irrelevant or else very relevant if it figures importantly to individuals in particular situations. On the other hand, the general topic of sexual orientation, confused as it is by "nature or nurture" debates and a tendency to admit only to socially received categories, has an impact on the whole discussion of how masculinity has been connected to men who dance.

Fitting into the Pink and Blue Genes

To what degree sexual orientation is genetic or culturally constructed is much in contention in the scientific community as well as society at large, and the body, as a locus where experiments are played out and attitudes performed, both replicates the status quo and provides challenges to it. The European and Anglophone world are deeply committed to a binary structure of biological sex, as symbolized by the well-known "pink-and-blue" syndrome, which assigns colors that represent an array of "correct" behaviors for girls and boys. As one basis for the contemporary suspicion of the male dancer, the mandate of having to choose pink or blue status is worth looking into. Pink, having become a symbol of ballet and femininity, has enjoyed great popularity in North America, especially since the mid-20th century. In *Shall We Dance*, the recent Hollywood movie that revolves around ballroom dance classes, the color shows up in a list of names one character was called ("Swish Butt," "Fancy Pants," and "Pinkie Boy") just for liking to dance to his mother's rumba records as a child. One of the more sinister uses in the history of pink was the pink triangle, which was used to brand homosexuality in the infamous days of Nazi Germany and has since been reappropriated as a symbol of gay rights. Pink has enjoyed various amounts of popularity as a fashion color for men while continuing to be suspect to many. A 2007 *New York Times* article on boys in ballet quoted one young man who described his frustration with being in the girls' class by saying, "I can't take the pink anymore."[4]

Not surprisingly, the pink-and-blue categorization scheme is irrelevant to many other places and time periods. Today, for instance, pale pink or mauve satin is rarely considered appropriate for men's power suits in North America, and yet it was considered perfectly masculine for leaders like the American president George Washington and Britain's George III. Whether or not dancing is considered masculine for world leaders has changed as well, of course. Today's political leaders in the West, for instance, would rarely be pictured slaving away with a dancing teacher in order to maintain supremacy on the dance floor, the way elites in 17th- and 18th-century France did.

When it comes to the scientific evidence that underpins the binary pink-and-blue system today, a few examples indicate the difficulty of considering male and female the only two "natural" categories. First of all, not all babies are born with a clear indication of which sex they are. Who decides in those cases? According to the studies of biologist Anne Fausto-Sterling, "Doctors may use only their personal impressions to decide that a baby's clitoris is 'too big' to belong to a girl and must be downsized" (2000, 60); and for an infant to be declared a boy, he must have a penis of "adequate size," or he ends up having it amputated and being assigned female status (57). Physical signs of masculinity and femininity in these cases become very crucial indeed. The process, according to Fausto-Sterling, "sometimes leads to unnecessary and sexually damaging genital surgery" (60). According to countless revelations that now occur in autobiographical literature, film, and television, the process can also lead to considerable gender confusion and agonizing choices as an adult, all in the name of fitting into a "natural" male and female scheme.

Both Fausto-Sterling and philosopher Edward Stein call into question many of the "experimental" biologically based programs that began at the start of the 20th century and were set up to determine the origins of human sexuality. Stein points out that "scientists interested in developing a theory of the origins of sexual orientation seem to appreciate that there are 'genuine' bisexuals but go on to ignore them for the purpose of developing their theories" (1999, 50). For Fausto-Sterling, the "biological truth" of experiments on fruit flies, seagulls, and rats is tainted by premises "based on preexisting cultural ideas about gender" (2000, 177). Both Stein and Fausto-Sterling rigorously demonstrate that the overwhelming majority of these tests and experiments are seriously flawed because scientists cannot distance themselves from the existing sex and gender structures to carry out value-free experimentation in this admittedly emotional context (Stein 1999; Fausto-Sterling 2000). Fausto-Sterling suggests how many different responses to gender indeterminacy there are when she reports that in the Dominican Republic and New Guinea, children born with a hormone (DHT) deficiency that causes male genitalia not to fully develop are recognized as a third sex, although in the United States they would be operated on immediately in an effort to fit into female status (2000, 109).

An entire edited volume of essays called *Third Sex, Third Gender* explores the question of whether or not "sexual dimorphism" is "natural" by investigating the attitudes, history, and science surrounding issues that have been previously neglected by historians and anthropologists (Herdt 1996). That volume includes thoughtful considerations of individuals who have confounded the categories of male and female in different cultures, among them the Native American berdache (Roscoe); the *māhū*, *fa'afāfine*, and *fakaleitī* in Polynesian societies (Besnier); and the *hijra* of North India (Nanda). Gender outsiders, who also include transsexual and transgendered individuals everywhere, often suffer persecution and marginalization, although there are societies in which difference is tolerated and sometimes even revered. There is ample evidence that these myriad categories have long histories, both in mythology and in written or oral history, yet the wealth of misperceptions about these categories and the fluid nature of what's called "gender liminality" indicate how little is really understood about territory that's off the map of traditional male-or-female land.

Experiments and studies that try to determine what is "natural" when it comes to sex and gender are often most telling in terms of revealing a society's rules, boundaries, and levels of tolerating difference.[5] The way these dictates of science and society devolve on the dance world is that men and women often must learn to fit into a standard performing style of masculinity and femininity. Just as boys are taught to "act like a man" and "not like a girl," whether they are sitting, walking, or gesturing, male dancers often face strictures about how to "dance like a man." And like the many rules of society that govern gender "norms," these performance rules are often difficult to define and embody, as seen in a story that contributor David Allan tells about how his ballet director once told him not to be so "sissified" onstage. His partner Michel Gervais tells his own version of learning to "perform masculinity" in the ballet world, as a separate but related project to deciding how to "perform" offstage. What becomes clear is that dance provides a particularly rich performance landscape from which examples can be drawn.

Theoretical Points of Viewing

The theoretical approach we start with as scholars in the cultural studies and performance studies tradition is that both masculinity and femininity are learned performances, affected but not dictated by genetics and societal expectations, with as many nuances and meanings as there are individuals who adopt, embody, or redesign them. Gender as a fluid, protean performance, not a biological given, has been explored in writing from Simone de Beauvoir to Judith Butler, finding its most recent iterations in much of the literature mentioned in the following. This perspective comes up in virtually all the essays that appear in this volume, as well as in the personal histories. Many of the dancers and choreographers interviewed for this volume struggled to fit into predefined rules about being masculine; some of them redefined perceived norms in a way that expanded previous notions. What the scholars and practitioners share is the acknowledgment of masculinity and femininity as ideals created, handed down, and embodied by particular societies. After a performer has learned the rules and opportunities available in different dancing roles and styles, it gets easier to assume that gender in daily life also has a performative component. Or, as Martha Graham imitator Richard Move is fond of intoning succinctly, "What's wrong with female impersonation? Some women have been doing it for years." Likewise, each dancer makes choices in terms of how he performs masculinity or femininity or some combination less easy to label.

We begin as well with a theoretical outlook heavily weighted in the direction of agency, following the postmodern ethnographic tradition that sees a struggle between the opposing forces of structure and antistructure.[6] That is, most of the male dancers and choreographers here are presented as subjects who both conform to societal pressures and struggle against them, sometimes striving for balance, sometimes courting disruption with pleasure. The authors in our collection use various theoretical approaches to unearth history and perspectives in ways that might illumine these issues in the dance world, using the various incarnations of dance analysis and tending toward the microhistory/case-history approach, with special attention paid to hermeneutic and ethnographic methods. Although the authors in this volume enjoy more freedom to explore sensitive issues than in the past, it might help to recall the darker societal forces that still circulate in some form when it comes to dance and masculinity.

The Dance Phobias: Choreo, Homo, and Effemino

It's been four decades since anthropologist Ray Birdwhistle, in an introduction to an edition of *Dance Perspectives* called "The Male Image," bravely stated that male ballet dancers were often stereotyped as feminine and "sissy." He even admitted that as a callow youth, he felt that "God and Darwin had so ordained" that men look strong and women fragile (1969, 9). Birdwhistle was somewhat singular in bringing up such a taboo topic before such things were very openly discussed. For a long time, acknowledgement of existing stereotypes did not show up in dance writing, perhaps because the dance world's struggle to become established as a viable art form was already deemed difficult enough without admitting that gender stereotypes existed as a barrier for men. In 1969, amid the liberation movements of that decade, Birdwhistle provided a somewhat enlightened opening for men to discuss existing prejudices, pointing out that differing cultural contexts often control the way behavior is judged appropriate for men and women. "The conviction that one's own society is 'natural' is pervasive and coercive," he wrote, concluding that "art is conventional and erroneous when it allows the binary logic of the primary sexual characteristics to determine the rhetoric expressing human interaction" (11).

Interestingly, none of the famous ballet men whose contributions followed Birdwhistle's introduction reflected these ideas. Instead, their first-person essays tended to illustrate the way ballet's sexual division of labor—never questioned, often endorsed—impacted their own struggles in the art form. In this way, they sketch out the fearsome set of challenges that were undoubtedly facing ballet men then and continue to do so now. To some degree, they were being asked to represent all men in dance and must have felt the burden of that task; a certain defensiveness in the tone of the first-person essays reflects the time. Some of the categorical clichés that appear, especially in the "he-man" statements of the senior dancer in the group, Igor Youskevitch, are not surprising, given the fact that these male dancers likely had to defend choosing such an unusual career. Terms were blithely thrown out, such as "natural sex instincts" and "inborn feminine instincts," and ideas abounded about men having to look positive and grounded, whereas women could be vague and languorous.

As well as reflecting the times, these comments and assumptions perhaps reflected the demands of classical ballet itself, in that all princes have to be clearly distinguishable from their princesses. Taking that bipolar mandate to great heights, Youskevitch stated his belief that certain "specifically feminine" movement traits "have been demonstrated from time immemorial in woman's walk" and that they became more pronounced "in the conscious effort to please the opposite sex" (Birdwhistle 1969, 14). It was all very "natural" for women to show off and to be temperamental and unreasonable, just as man's history as a hunter and fighter led male dancers to use logic and purpose to undergird their every strong, simple "masculine" movement.

From a younger generation, Helgi Tomasson wrote that the business of being masculine onstage was simple, in that "the man needs just to say, 'I know who I am, I know what I am'" (33). It would be nice if it always worked that way. Not surprisingly, New York City Ballet star Edward Villella, the poster boy for a streetwise, tough guy in ballet back then, identified part of being male onstage as having "a fantastic attack" (39); but he also showed a soft side by mentioning "the delicacy of the control" and how athleticism has to be "alive and beautiful" (48). Spanish-born Joffrey dancer Luis Fuentes wrote about the way "you have to express yourself through your eyes," and that "a man is always a man, and you don't have to build muscle to show it" (35). The challenge seemed to be how to make ballet masculinity look viable when overt strength had to be always tempered by the art form's mandates of refinement and delicacy.

Absent from this particular set of interviews was an acknowledgment of the homophobia inherent in the "sissy" stereotype that so many men in ballet faced as "the elephant in the room." The three interlocking themes of this section—choreophobia, homophobia, and effeminophobia—all contribute to this stereotype, which is pervasive in the history of Western concert dance forms and in many parts of the world. "Choreophobia" is the term coined by Anthony Shay to describe ambivalent and negative attitudes toward dance. The concept worked particularly well in describing the history and current attitudes toward dance in the Middle East, the first application Shay explored with his book of the same name in 1999, but it can apply equally to other locations and eras. Examples of selected choreophobia-related incidences in the 20th century alone include the outlawing of swing dancing as racially undesirable in Nazi Germany, the destruction of classical dance in Cambodia during the Khmer Rouge era, and the prohibition of dance and music in Taliban-ruled Afghanistan. Intertwined in these instances, of course, are agendas that relate to totalitarian regimes.

The history of North America provides numerous examples of choreophobic attitudes, many of which relate strongly to racism; they include the suppression of the African dance and music of slaves and the banning of Native American dance and ceremonies. As a result of self-appointed guardians of morality in the religious sphere, an "antidance" campaign was waged on moral grounds as early as the 17th century, perhaps peaking in rhetorical force in the late 19th and early 20th century. At various moments in history, Methodists, Baptists, Presbyterians, and Congregationalists advised from the pulpit that dancing would more or less take you "from the ballroom to hell" (Needham 2002, 99). In reprints of his famous sermons, the Reverend Thomas Faulkner traced the decline that would occur once a young woman allowed just any man to put his hands on her during the waltz. Her only alternative, once ruined by being too loose and loving on the dance floor, was to become a prostitute (Needham 2002, 112–18). Today, long after the waltz has lost its power to threaten, the gyrations of "freak dancing" or "dirty dancing" have been at the center of freedom of expression debates when high schools have banned school dances altogether.

Both men and women have suffered from choreophobic attitudes and laws; for men in Western culture in particular, dance has been suspect because of the mandate to take a leading role in society and support a family. As the 19th-century Parisian ballet critic Jules Janin so succinctly put it in the age of the female-dominated Romantic ballet, men should not "[caper] aimlessly" when they were so obviously "made expressly to bear a rifle, saber, and uniform," and to be "a community leader, an elector, a member of the municipal council" (quoted in Chapman 1997, 204). In that era of ogling and idolizing female dancers, perhaps the idea was to keep the male competition onstage to a minimum, but whatever the motivation, it's likely that Janin's sentiment—and those of other prominent ballet critics of the time—both reflected and created attitudes about men onstage in that era. The lack of sufficient remuneration and financial security in a dance career persists as a challenge for the male dancer. Even in cultures where a dancing man is admired, in African American circles, for instance, dancing is only okay until you get *too* involved in it as an adult, a point choreographer Rennie Harris reiterates in this volume. Still, if you start to make money dancing, Harris says, your masculine reputation is back on track.

In many societies of the past, there have been male performers who contravened or ignored the well-defined borders between masculine and feminine that seem so well patrolled in many parts of the West today. In both medieval Japan and the Islamic Iranian world, for example, male dancers deliberately created an air of sexual ambiguity and often became "stars" because of it. The category of "dancer/entertainer" in both these societies once included revered male performers who articulated both masculine and feminine aspects of behavior through movement, clothing, and demeanor. The lionizing of the handsome male dancer is found in Japanese and Persian literature, especially in poetry. Although the optimum age for such a performer was 12 to 16, the more witty, charming, and talented of these men carried their careers and admirers into old age. Gary Leupp, in his study of Japanese homosexualilty, notes that "male prostitutes and actors were often valued for their gender ambiguity" (1995, 177), describing the acclaim for the more popular male performers as follows: "Urban audiences expressed their enthusiasm for these actors in ways that would be familiar to fans of contemporary rock 'n' roll stars. They organized fan clubs, often on a ward basis; fiercely loyal, they would bar any member who patronized another actor's performances. They circulated posters bearing their thespian hero's image and attended his performances in groups, chorusing their devotion. They purchased 'actor-critiques' that publicized not only his dramatic skills but his physical charms as well" (130). Similarly, in the Iranian Central Asian world, male dancers were invested with what we might today call "star quality." In 1876, English adventurer Eugene Schuyler wrote: "These *batchas*, or dancing boys, are a recognized institution throughout the whole of the settled portions of Central Asia, though they are most in vogue in Bukhara, and the neighboring Samarkand. *Batchas* are as much respected as the greatest singers and *artistes* are with us. Every movement they make is followed and applauded, and I have never seen such breathless interest as they excite, for the whole crowd seems to devour them with their eyes, while their hands beat time to every step" ([1876] 1966, 70–71).

Many Westerners, as well as some postcolonial scholars with no personal experience of this type of performance in the Islamic Middle East, Central Asia, and North Africa, mistakenly assume that male dancers were copying or parodying female performances. In fact, this was not an attempt to disguise their maleness (with the exception of the female roles such as the *onnagata* in Japanese theater). Instead, male identity was shown through movement and aspects of clothing, such as a way of arranging the hair or a special headpiece. These male entertainers were specifically valued *because* they were male. Both men and women viewers might appreciate them (when women were allowed to view them), but most often they were considered available for same-sex activity. It is important to note that, unlike same-sex relationships in the West, those in Japan and the Iranian world in no way precluded marriage or sexual relationships with women. In fact, as Leupp notes, "they were corollary. The *iro* (sexual desire) of most Tokugawa men was bisexual" (1995, 199).

A connection between male homosexuality and dance (along with music and acting) had firm roots in these two societies, where even today a conflation of the words "dancer" and "prostitute" is found. The degree to which social categories were institutionalized differed, as did general perceptions regarding the individuals in these categories. Throughout most of Asia, however, the class of entertainer has historically been one of the lowest, often outcast, categories for both men and women. In the Iran of the 1960s, for instance, ethnomusicologist Laurence Loeb found that people largely believed that "music, accompanied by dance, frequently acted as a sexual stimulus . . . sometimes causing private gatherings to be transformed into sexual orgies" (1972, 8). In colonial India, outrage and misunderstandings about dancing traditions, especially as they related to the use of sexual metaphors to represent the union of humans and the divine, led to official acts that banned dancing in the temples (O'Shea 2007; Meduri 1988). Although the revived tradition of Indian classical dance is associated more with women in the popular imagination, male dancers have always been part of the various dance traditions in many parts of India (see Hari Krishnan's essay in this volume). Along with other dance forms (belly dance, hula), bharata natyam is now so attached to images of dancing women, many people are surprised to find out that men also perform in this tradition.

Although there have been significant variations in how much or how little choreophobia exists in various cultures over the years, it's not difficult to see that many societies have exhibited negative reactions to male dancing bodies, particularly when dance has been linked to homosexuality and effeminacy. The degree of choreophobia often depends on whether a cluster of elements intersect. First, there is the fact that dance is "perhaps the most highly complex and codified of kinesthetic practices" and "one of the most important arenas of public physical enactment," which is inevitably linked to "sex, sexiness, and sexuality" (Desmond 2001, 7). Then, there is the proximity of dancing bodies in a particular context, and how dancers are seen to contravene religious standards and values that relate to gender and sexuality. Local and global politics also figure in, as illustrated by the times when local male dancing traditions have been replaced to fit into colonial or nationalist agendas dictating macho representations of masculinity that came from the West (see Karayanni, Krishnan, and Shay, this volume).

A primary aspect of this process has been, and remains, homophobia and its correlate, effeminophobia, a term coined fairly recently to refer to a "generalized fear of effeminacy," which has afflicted even the gay community at times when the effort to erase stereotypes has led to marginalizing men who might fit into them (Gere 2001, 367–68). Ironically, until around the 18th century, the words "effeminate" and "effeminacy" referred not to homosexuals but to men who were too interested in women and were categorized as womanizers. An effeminate man, in order to attract women, affected "a narcissistic self-display through fashionable clothes, scents, snuff, and dance" (Jordan 2001, 132). Over the years, meanings, as well as wardrobes, have changed. Today, in "a culture that values testosterone gone amok" (Gere 2001, 374), the adjective "effeminate" is used to impugn a man's masculinity in no uncertain terms.

Connections between homosexuality, effeminacy, and dance had started to fall into place securely in the West by the early 20th century, when "all the arts [were considered] vulnerable to colonization by homosexuals" (Stoneley 2007, 94) and "expressiveness was identified with femininity" (95). This occurred despite the presence of popular male dancers with plenty of female admirers who thought otherwise. Even the sensational Ballets Russes star Vaslav Nijinsky and the tangoing movie icon Rudolf Valentino, with their cults of adoring female fans, were often pronounced not quite manly enough. Film scholar Gaylyn Studlar comes to the conclusion that America in the first half of the 20th century was even more virulently homophobic than today and uses these two men as examples. Male dancers at the time were often derided, Studlar says, and "Vaslav Nijinsky provoked special antagonism among the nation's male critics who dismissed him for his 'lack of virility' and 'unprepossessing effeminacy'" (1993, 24). "Omnisexual" is the word Stoneley uses to describe Nijinsky, because he combined muscular, powerful leaps and delicate beats and curving gestures in the same performance, as the Spirit of the Rose in *Spectre de la Rose*, for instance. The choreographer of that ballet, Michel Fokine, declared that Nijinsky's "lack of masculinity" made him suitable for some roles but not other "manly" ones (Stoneley 2007, 74). Valentino shared with Nijinsky an ethnic "otherness" that on the one hand garnered praise for being "exotic," and on the other inspired racial epithets.[7] Valentino's racially suspect Italian ethnicity and his previous profession as a paid dancing partner marked him as a particular target for the American press, which famously labeled him a "pink powder puff" and "a wop" (Studlar 1993, 24). At that time, male dancers were so suspect in American culture that even the popular ballroom dancer Vernon Castle couldn't escape slurs on his masculinity, although he was famously married and trained pilots in World War I (39).

Male dancing stars who followed Nijinsky, Valentino, and Castle perhaps fared better when it came to having their masculinity questioned—literary theorist Steven Cohan proposes that Fred Astaire and Gene Kelly were considered graceful but authoritative male presences in Hollywood musical films, managing to create a "new styling of masculinity" by embodying audacious personas in spectacular dance numbers full of visual excess (Cohan 1993, 65–66). Interestingly, some spectacular production numbers allowed the occasional female movie star (swimmer Esther Williams is his example), through lingering close-ups on a powerful physique, to transform the traditional showgirl image into one full of "physical strength, awesome muscularity, and disciplined athleticism" (66). Characters played by men in later mainstream Hollywood dance movies, such as *Dirty Dancing* (Patrick Swayze) and *Shall We Dance?* (the American version starring Richard Gere), encountered various aspects of choreophobia, alongside homophobic references in the latter's humor, which is firmly based on the male characters' awkwardness and embarrassment about dancing. Although Swayze's character in *Dirty Dancing* was a confident heterosexual presented as a muscular hunk, the theme of class difference, emphasized by his being a "hired dancer" patronized by an upperclass clientele, harked back to an era of class prejudice based on choreophobia and economic realities.

In Western culture, the era when "the noble, dancerly body was also a manly body" had long gone (Stoneley 2007, 9). For a brief period, peaking during the reign of Louis XIV, dancing was thought to keep a man in shape for battle, so the turned-out stance and controlled postures of ballet were seen as proper preparation to fence and fight (9). Ideas about desirable masculine behavior changed as courtiers were gradually replaced by professional dancers, especially when the Enlightenment thinkers began to critique aristocratic refinement as unsuitable artifice—unsuitable for a man, that is, whereas women could still be "frivolous and effeminate" (10). In a way, there was a shift back to finding powerful postures in a refined art form when gay men in the 20th century flocked to the ballet world, where ballet, Stoneley concludes, "seemed to establish an exclusive environment, in which homosexual men might feel as at home as anyone else" (115). Explaining playwright Jean Genet's attraction to the art form, he says that "ballet enabled him to envisage an attractive and powerful otherness within an otherwise intractable reality" (151). Stoneley proposes, "If being homosexual was a threat to one's social authority, this feeling might have been assuaged by conducting one's homosexual life in prestigious locales" where "homosexual dressiness could pass as upper-class behavior" (115).

In the modern dance world, as well as in ballet, a high percentage of homosexual men worked in all aspects onstage and backstage, as Gay Morris notes in her study of post–World War II dance and modernism. Like Stoneley, she suggests that gay men "found a haven in the dance field where they could garner support from like-minded individuals and where, too, they could gain power" (Morris 2006, 34). Women, she observes, dominated the field, which resulted in its "feminization" and in dance having "less stature than the other arts." Even the much-married George Balanchine, who made the "macho" argument that ballet sharpened skills the soldier needed, could not convince American boys to enter the field (34). Morris points out that it did not help that homophobia was rampant in the postwar years, fed both by the rise of religious figures like Billy Graham and Bishop Fulton Sheen, and by a kind of hysteria over the Kinsey Report's revelation that homosexuality was far more widespread than imagined (35).

It's not surprising that gay men's attraction to dance, their contributions, and an analysis and appreciation of this connection took a while to be documented in the Western world. Studies such as Stoneley's and Morris's illuminate many factors in the Euro-American context, but it might take even longer for similar studies to appear in many other parts of the world. Consider the fact that homosexuality didn't even exist during the era of the former Soviet Union— that is it did not *officially* exist, according to the regime, of course. At that time, the relative openness of homosexual life in the West was used in Soviet propaganda as proof of degeneracy. Ironically, American propaganda was linking homosexuality to Communism, so that political perversion became sexual perversion in an orgy of name-calling. American leaders kept up their role in homophobic discourse, like the time in 1946 when U.S. president Harry Truman went on record as worrying about "parlor pinks" and "soprano voiced men" (Morris 2006, 34–35). While American gays had much to fear from the homophobic hysteria of the time, the iron-curtain closet was perhaps more dangerous than most, in that homosexuality was a crime that could be punished by banishment to Siberia or death.

While dance was officially a manly profession in the former Soviet Union, many dancers who lived through that era have since spoken about being labeled effeminate and having their occupation denigrated as unserious. It was, however, a well-subsidized occupation, so the economic advantages often spoke louder than choreophobic voices. For the Soviet Union, as well as other countries that caught on quickly, dance companies constituted an important element of what came to be known as "cultural diplomacy" (Prevots 1998; Shay 2002). In an economy of scarcity, talented Soviet citizens could rise above financial and social deprivation once they were chosen for a state-conservatory dance education. What did it matter if there was some stigma attached to men who danced for a living if you got special privileges when it came to housing, food, consumer goods, and travel? Unlike the case of aspiring professionals in the West, a dance career in Soviet times equaled a major step up the social ladder. Wearing tights, therefore, perhaps was seen more as a uniform than as something that would automatically draw accusations of effeminacy.

Folk dance in particular suited the Soviet regime's promoting and exporting images of "the common folk," but the universal acclaim of Russian ballet also served the purpose of asserting national supremacy in the arts. Formerly connected to the interests of the aristocracy, ballet had been reenvisioned by early Soviets as a representation of the cultural achievements of "the people." Its dancers had historically come from working classes, after all, and ballet had a virtuosic athleticism and noble line that could easily support whatever political regime presented it. Viewers of Soviet-era films of classical dance can soon see the style considered appropriately masculine for the various ballet princes of the Bolshoi or Kirov stage: before the famously flamboyant Nureyev, male ballet dancers tended to keep leg extensions low and rose on their toes only a manly minimal distance from the floor.

Interestingly, Nureyev's more extravagant style, not beloved of conservative ballet hard-liners back in his homeland, continues to be suspect even today in terms of what is deemed appropriate for the male ballet dancer, at least in the view of some "expert" observers. In a review of a 2007 PBS documentary (Nureyev: The Russian Years), dance critic Lewis Segal couches his commentary in effeminophobic terms when he suggests Nureyev might as well have been called "Nureyevna," a feminization of his name.[8] Nureyev's style innovations are the problem for Segal, who calls him "an ever-smirking, feline creature, beyond the norms of real men and women" (2007, F12). Instead of perhaps noting the way styles change over time when it comes to ballet masculinity,

Segal chose to patrol the borders of acceptable macho dancing by making a joke at Nureyev's expense. In case you missed the point, Segal went so far as to compare Nureyev's classical style to the "parodistic mannerisms" of the comedic transvestite dancers of Les Ballets Trockadero de Monte Carlo. On the other hand, *New Yorker* dance contributor Joan Acocella, writing about the same documentary, places Nureyev's style, "notably the hyperstretched torso," in a wider historical context, without effeminophobe overtones. "It was considered effeminate when he introduced it," she writes about his postural extravagance. "Now it is standard" (2007, 18).

On another Russian front, Igor Moiseyev, who founded his popular eponymous folk company in the 1930s and toured widely during the cold war years (the company continues to tour today), provided a crossover point for folk forms and ballet, having trained in a classical conservatory. The appeal of his lively, colorful, and virtuosic choreographies guaranteed that theatricalized folk dance was heavily influenced by ballet from its start. Moiseyev's formula, widely influential for state-supported dance companies around the world, reflected not only his technical training and talent but also the puritanical official attitudes of the Soviet era when it came to sexuality and its regularization of gendered performances. In Moiseyev evocations of village dancing, everyone is heterosexual and happily flirting or ignoring sexual attraction altogether as they portray "happy peasants" or sturdy comrades.

Reflecting folk dance's first existence, Moiseyev's men and women tend to dance in separate ensembles (though there are some couple dances), with women's delicacy and lyricism emphasized, while men lift them and do the obviously athletic power moves. On the stage, the separation between men and women became even more institutionalized than in village dancing; women were chosen for pleasant, symmetrical features and cast in either a tall or a short girl ensemble; they dressed identically and often came onstage to provide background scenery for showy men's sections. Male dancers also dressed identically but showed more variation in height, weight, and features. In this way, masculinity either could be couched in relative androgyny, since clean-shaven, boyish males looked similar to female dancers, or it could emerge full force in a macho, mustachioed character like the soloists in the Ukrainian *Gopak*, whose large leaps are enhanced by emphatic low notes from instruments in the orchestra.

When such moments of hypermasculine folk dance did not occur in the history of village folk forms (as they did in many Soviet-era locations), they were often invented for state-supported companies that followed in the Moiseyev tradition. The fact that both male and female dancers did basically the same dance movements in areas of Egypt, Uzbekistan, Iran, and Turkey meant little to choreographers who were under pressure to represent their countries with male images that fit into a more macho style (see essays by Shay, Karayanni, and Krishnan in this volume). Not surprisingly, the fact that traditional dancers had also been professional sex workers disappeared as well, as many versions of wholesome, asexual behavior were created to represent aspects of national and ethnic identity in state folk dance companies in Poland, Ukraine, Belarus, and Rumania. Within some of these companies, ethnic pre-judices arose in terms of deciding which characters *could* show overt sexuality. As seen in the orientalized dances in Western ballets (the "Arabian dance" in *The Nutcracker* or temple dancers in *La Bayadère*), markers of overt sensuality were projected on characters considered "Other" in theatricalized folk dance com-panies. For instance, the men of Kolo, the Serbian folk ensemble, dressed up as "Gypsies" and lustfully carried off "wanton women" who had been sweltering with sensuality while cooking at the fire. In this way, the company provided some acknowledgment of sexuality but only by projecting wanton desire onto the "low Other" in Serbian society (Shay 2007). Notably, Amalia Hernandez, with her Ballet Folklórico de Mexico version of the state-supported dance troupe, did *not* eliminate sexuality as part of many theatricalized folk dances.

In this section, we have traced a few of the crucial elements that combine to produce the many challenges for men in dance, especially as they are seen to relate to aspects of choreophobia, homophobia, and effeminophobia, giving a few key examples and pointing to the wealth of others that may gradually emerge. The clichés and stereotypes that accompany these circulating "phobias" have often dominated the popular imagination and, until recent years, even dance literature. We have emphasized the way the stereotype of male dancers as "less than masculine" has dogged men in dance throughout many eras and locations, how essentialized notions of what men should be shadow the enter-prise, and how notions of masculinity have changed throughout the years. The belief that all male dancers are gay, so predominant in the West and perhaps elsewhere, is always "the elephant in the room," though it is not the only obstacle men face. The good news is that not all male dancers think of it as an obstacle anymore, in an age when more analysis, education, and discussion about the history and experiences of men dancing are seen to make a difference. This volume is intended to be part of that history, shining a light on various parts of a once-shadowy closet.

The Essays

Many of the essays that follow explore case histories and historical moments that relate to dance and masculinities; others sketch old attitudes, reveal hidden ones, and propose new ways of thinking. Part I, "Issues in the Pink and Blue West," highlights aspects of masculinity as they relate to ballet and modern dance. Addressing one of the ballet world's fondest ways of trying to make ballet "safe" for boys, Jennifer Fisher critiques this history in "Maverick Men in Ballet: Rethinking the 'Making It Macho' Strategy." Ballet is, after all, as demanding as football physically, but it *isn't* like football and never will be. How boys in ballet become marginalized through "heterocentric bias" and other gender norm demands is the topic of Doug Risner's "What We Know about Boys Who Dance: The Limitations of Contemporary Masculinity and Dance Education." From a sociological perspective, Risner references studies from the United States, Australia, the United Kingdom, and Finland, exploring the way boys and young males deal with biases founded on narrow definitions of masculinity in the ballet classroom and beyond. Maura Keefe "goes deep" into the relationship between sports and dance with analysis of examples that range from sports-themed choreography to Gene Kelly's 1958 television special *Dancing—a Man's Game*. Keefe, like Fisher, concludes that simplistic macho definitions have masqueraded as progressive strategies for too long.

How choreography can reproduce or resist normative gender ideologies is explored by the two concluding essays in part I. Jill Nunes Jensen looks at how the male dancing body can confound expectations and suggest multiple masculinities in progressive ballet pas de deux in "Transcending Gender in Ballet's LINES." Nunes Jensen focuses on San Francisco–based Alonzo King's renovations to ballet's duets and how they offer opportunities for the company's men to break out of the prince persona. For her, the LINES men literally show more sides of themselves in cooperation with their also-iconoclastic female partners, emphasizing cooperation and flow between male and female partners versus a "male-active, female-passive" ballet duet. In "The Performance of Unmarked Masculinity," Ramsay Burt analyzes Joe Goode's *29 Effeminate Gestures* and Pina Bausch's *Der Fensterputzer* and expands further the themes of his volume, *The Male Dancer: Bodies, Spectacle and Sexualities*. He again shows how dance can destabilize expectations and embody resistance to constraints, leading the spectator into brave new perspectives that have liberating possibilities.

Part II, "Historical Perspectives," includes three essays that explore very specific time periods in terms of the way masculinity and dance were intertwined. In "Pricked Dances: The *Spectator*, Dance, and Masculinity in Early 18th-Century England," John Bryce Jordan gleans what behavior was expected of men at that time from a popular urban periodical published daily in London. It turns out the man who danced at an 18th-century ball or assembly had to tread a thin line if he wished to escape being satirized—too carefully refined and he was pronounced a mincing fool; too energetic and he was called a country booby without appropriate, class-defined restraint. For the rare black man who ventured onstage in Europe more than a century later, Stephen Johnson reveals an odd exception to the usual gender norms in "Gender Trumps Race? Cross-Dressing Juba in Early Blackface Minstrelsy." Although William Henry Lane (Juba) did not make a career of cross-dressing, Johnson proposes that during one particular tour of England in 1848, his embodiment of "Miss Lucy Long" was a case of using gender confusion to distract from the presence of sexual content, as well as his being the single black performer among white men in blackface.

Concluding part II, Yvonne Hardt moves us forward to another century and European location when she links the political and dance agendas of two movements that proceeded the Nazi era in Germany in "*Ausdruckdstanz*, Workers' Culture, and Masculinity in Germany in the 1920s and 1930s." In addition to early modern "expressive" dance empowering women, men, too, were theoretically offered the chance to "rediscover" themselves in ways that could emancipate them from traditional gender roles. Yet the dance of the time could also reflect ideals of Socialist and Communist ideology, which reinscribed some old male-female divisions by emphasizing the physical strength of the male worker. Implicit in Hardt's analysis is the difficulty of embodying political ideals in dance in a clear way that acknowledges the multiple strands of complex gender identities.

The four essays in part III, "Legacies of Colonialism," deal with the way that Western powers influenced male dancers and dance genres that originated in the Islamic Middle East and India. Here, the practical effects of choreophobia plus orientalism emerge in some detail. Stavros Stavrou Karayanni, in "Native Motion and Imperial Emotion: Male Performers of the 'Orient' and the Politics of the Imperial Gaze," analyzes the performances of professional male dancers in Egypt and the colonial reactions to them. Because of the connection between professional male dancers and prostitution, and the dancer's use of ambiguous movement strategies, clothing, and costume, Westerners overwhelmingly found these dance performances scandalous—yet often irresistible, according to the evidence. Reactions ranged from European homophobic panic to the breathless critique of Gustave Flaubert, which contained a certain frisson of excitement.

The colonial gaze was a powerful force for social change in the Middle East and Central Asia, aided by the conversion of the Westernized intelligentsia among native populations. Ruling forces from the West and Russia coerced or forced people to exchange their relaxed attitudes toward ambiguous sexuality for ones reflecting strictly heterosexual identity and behavior. These changes had an impact on the way in which dance was viewed and practiced by males, a topic that both Anthony Shay and Hari Krishnan address. In "Choreographing Masculinity: Hypermasculine Dance Styles as Invented Tradition in Egypt, Iran, and Uzbekistan," Shay looks at the creation and development of supermacho dance styles for state-supported dance companies in Egypt, Iran, and Uzbekistan. Krishnan's "From Gynemimesis to Hypermasculinity: The Shifting Orientations of Male Performers of South Indian Court Dance" provides some of the little-known history of male dancers in 18th-century South India and compares those practices and attitudes with those of contemporary bharata natyam dance tradition.

In "Ibrahim Farrah: Dancer, Teacher, Choreographer, Publisher," Barbara Sellers-Young illuminates the life and career of a Lebanese American performer who came to terms with issues of masculinity in the shadow of a choreophobic culture. One of the most influential figures in the world of American belly dancing, Farrah was the publisher and editor of the nationally distributed journal *Arabesque*. Having faced significant prejudice against male dancers in a field widely perceived as only for women, Farrah managed to use the dance vocabulary formerly "owned" by both sexes to forge an identity that combined his American upbringing and his Lebanese heritage. Along with the other authors in this section, Sellers-Young foregrounds the way the forces of colonialism reshaped and recontextualized contemporary dance practices in the subcontinent of India and the Middle East, as well as in transnational contexts.

The Personal Histories

The lives of individual people and the ways they adopt or resist performances of masculinity or femininity are complex, to say the least, and therefore sometimes difficult to contain within theoretical structures. Following in the steps of ethnographers and others whose goal is to "keep our interpretations sensitive to concrete specificities, to the unexpected, to history" (Ang 1996, 52), we include here, between essays, a selection of personal histories of men in dance. They range from veteran professionals whose names are well known to dancers and choreographers who have toiled less famously. These personal histories were perhaps the most exciting aspect of editing this book, and we found it hard to end the discussions with our contributors to this part, realizing that almost every man in dance brings up the very themes our scholarly authors defined, and that each was powerfully individual in his articulation of them. We worked with each to fashion a monologue from our conversation. So often, what was theoretically proclaimed elsewhere—the fact that gender expectations are learned and performed, not "natural"; the mandate for men to "choreograph" their performances of gender both on and off the stage—emerged as an integral challenge in the lives of an individual dancer. Very often, both the age and the experience of these men had brought into focus these challenges, and their reflections poured out.

The impact of prejudice undoubtedly took its toll in many of the lives sampled; others choreographed their responses in ways that contributed to their elegant survival and triumph on many levels. From our youngest contributor, Aaron Cota (who combined his marine reserve duty in Iraq with a university dance major), to our most veteran, the modern dance icon Donald McKayle (whose talent and positive attitude led him to almost sail through potentially treacherous waters of prejudice against the male dancer as well as racism), the stories were never less than fascinating and informative. In the process of "crafting themselves" in the world of dance, each of these men undoubtedly suggests the experiences of many others.[9] Men in dance have tap-danced around conformity and expectations, learned to fit in and stand out by turns, and in the process embodied change that has the potential to enlighten and help liberate us all from narrow definitions of gender performances.

NOTES

1. This is a quotation from veteran dance scholar and critic Marcia Siegel, as she reviewed Lynn Garafola's book *Legacies of Twentieth-Century Dance* (Middletown, CT: Wesleyan University Press, 2004). Siegel, a senior dance scholar and critic, lauds Garafola for having the "sophistication to bypass the adulatory discourse" so frequently found in dance history publications in the past (*Dance Research Journal* 38, nos. 1 and 2 [2006]: 186–88).

2. The gathering of personal histories of male dancers was begun in 2007, after most of the essays in this volume were collected and edited. It was described to contributors as an inclusion of "voices" of men in dance to accompany a volume of scholarly essays about dance and masculinity. The men were interviewed mostly in Southern California, though many contributors were not based there but were visiting. With a few exceptions, the process always included a face-to-face interview, using guiding questions (see the appendix), and lasted from about an hour to several hours. Most of the interviews were conducted by Jennifer Fisher (with institutional review board approval at the University of California, Irvine) and Anthony Shay (then an independent scholar) with the exception of one interview by Jill Nunes Jensen (independent scholar). See the appendix for more specific information.

3. The idea that there was prejudice against men in ballet during the Soviet era is based partly on the observation and experiences of the editors, both on trips to Russia and the former Soviet Union and in conversation with émigrés who trained under the old Soviet system. One of those occasions occurred for one author (Fisher) during a preliminary series of interviews, highlights of which are worth recounting here. This first foray into interviewing male dancers several years ago was instructive in how best to meet and interview men in dance, as well as revealing the range of attitudes about prejudice against the male dancer. Because the interviews were arranged through a publicist for an internationally renowned ballet company, perhaps the dancers seemed up for the kind of conversation they were used to giving to newspaper writers. They provided ready phrases and rationales that revolved around the question "What's it like to be a man in a woman's art form?" Three dancers, randomly chosen, represented three very different experiences in the ballet world. One near-teenager, who came from an artistic university town and had gone from an elite ballet conservatory straight into a major company, seemed genuinely unscathed by prejudice against men in ballet. His nonballet schoolmates had been supportive about his going to ballet school, he said, and he had not encountered preconceptions about it being "unmanly or feminine." He mentioned that his girlfriend's parents did not find it all that odd that he was a ballet dancer. A 30-something soloist also talked about his personal life early on, mentioning his wife and children, and he was more experienced with the prejudicial stereotypes about ballet men in the popular imagination. Yes, he had encountered teasing and bigotry, but it wasn't all that difficult to deal with; it helped that he was in a prestigious company and was not gay. The third dancer had been trained in the former Soviet Union and seemed reluctant to the point of defensiveness when the talk turned to prejudice against the male ballet dancer. He admitted that men in his home country called ballet men "sissy," but he came from a theatrical family and never cared about such people, he emphasized—they were ignorant, and he knew who

he was. "It doesn't bother me at all," he said several times, dismissively and almost menacingly.

4. Joy Goodwin, "Keeping That Big 'Nutcracker' Party Coed," *New York Times*, August 19, 2007, AR27.

5. We are using the terms "sex" and "gender" throughout as being indicative of categories dictated by biology (sex) and by societal behavioral expectations (gender).

6. As emphasized succinctly by Lena Hammergren in her essay "Many Sources, Many Voices," in *Rethinking Dance History: A Reader*, ed. Alexandra Carter (London and New York: Routledge, 2004, 20–31), cultural studies has long emphasized "the tensions between structure and agency as explanatory and interpretative modes," which has been particularly well explored in studies of subcultures and popular culture (27). To understand how individuals find agency even in regulatory systems, then, it's necessary to "mediate between the two perspectives and be constantly aware of how they constitute each other. This mediation can be conceptualized in theoretical terms as a joining together of structuralism and hermeneutics" (28). Hammergren cites as an exemplar Nadine A. George's work on the Whitman Sisters, who were African American vaude-villians at the start of the 20th century. Among myriad other examples is Gay Morris's (2006) study of constraints, conformity, and limited agency of modern dance choreographers during the years of the cold war.

7. Nijinsky's exotic looks (high cheekbones, slanted eyes) were often simply called "Russian" when he toured in the West. In Russia itself, he had been derided for being of Polish ancestry.

8. The feminine form of "Nureyev" in the Russian language would actually be "Nureyeva," so perhaps Segal was playing with spellings in the spirit of fake names of Les Ballets Trockadero de Monte Carlo.

9. "Crafting selves" is a phrase and concept from anthropologist Dorinne Kondo, which refers to ways in which the fragmented, postmodern individual can "craft" identity. She reiterates regularly the fact that "the self" should be a plural concept and that selves are "potential sites for the play of multiple discourses and shifting, multiple subject positions" (Kondo 1990, 44).

WORKS CITED

Acocella, Joan. 2007. "Out of the East." *New Yorker*, August 27, 18.

Ang, Ien. 1996. *Living Room Wars: Rethinking Media Audiences for a Postmodern World*. London: Routledge.

Besnier, Niko. 1996. "Polynesian Gender Liminality through Time and Space." In *Third Sex, Third Gender: Beyond Sexual Dimorphism in Culture and History*, ed. Gilbert Herdt, 285–328. New York: Zone Books.

Birdwhistle, Ray L. 1969. Introduction, "The Male Image." In *Dance Perspectives* 40, 9–11. New York: Dance Perspectives Foundation.

Burt, Ramsay. 1995. *The Male Dancer: Bodies, Spectacle, Sexualities*. London: Routledge.

———. 2001. "Dissolving in Pleasure: The Threat of the Queer Male Dancing Body." In *Dancing Desires: Choreographing Sexualities On and Off the Stage*, ed. Jane C. Desmond, 209–41. Madison: University of Wisconsin Press.

Chapman, John V. 1997. "Jules Janin: Romantic Critic." In *Rethinking the Sylph: New Perspectives on the Romantic Ballet*, ed. Lynn Garafola, 197–241. Hanover, NH: University Press of New England.

Cohan, Steven. 1993. "'Feminizing' the Song-and-Dance Man: Fred Astaire and the Spectacle of Masculinity in the Hollywood Musical." In *Screening the Male: Exploring Masculinities in Hollywood Cinema*, ed. Steven Cohan and Ina Mae Hark, 46–69. London: Routledge.

Desmond, Jane C. 2001. "Introduction: Making the Invisible Visible: Staging Sexualities through Dance." In *Dancing Desires: Choreographing Sexualities On and Off the Stage*, ed. Jane C. Desmond, 3–32. Madison: University of Wisconsin Press.

Fausto-Sterling, Anne. 2000. *Sexing the Body: Gender Politics and the Construction of Sexuality*. New York: Basic Books.

Foster, Susan Leigh. 2001. "Closets Full of Dances: Modern Dance's Performance of Masculinity and Sexuality." In *Dancing Desires: Choreographing Sexualities On and Off the Stage*, ed. Jane C. Desmond, 147–207 Madison: University of Wisconsin Press.

Franko, Mark. 1995. *Dancing Modernism/Performing Politics*. Bloomington: Indiana University Press.

Gere, David. 2001. "29 Effeminate Gestures: Choreographer Joe Goode and the Heroism of Effeminacy." In *Dancing Desires: Choreographing Sexualities On and Off the Stage*, ed. Jane C. Desmond, 349–81. Madison: University of Wisconsin Press.

Herdt, Gilbert. 1996. Preface and Introduction to *Third Sex, Third Gender: Beyond Sexual Dimorphism in Culture and History*, ed. Gilbert Herdt, 11–81. New York: Zone Books.

Hopwood, Derek. 1992. *Sexual Encounters in the Middle East: The British, the French and the Arabs*. London: Ithaca Press.

Jordan, John Bryce. 2001. "Light in the Heels: The Emergence of the Effeminate Male Dancer in Eighteenth-Century English History." Ph.D. diss., University of California, Riverside.

Kondo, Dorinne K. 1990. *Crafting Selves: Power, Gender, and Discourses of Identity in a Japanese Workplace*. Chicago: University of Chicago Press.

Kopelson, Kevin. 1997. *Queer Afterlife of Vaslav Nijinsky*. Palo Alto, CA: Stanford University Press.

Leupp, Gary P. 1995. *Male Colors: The Construction of Homosexuality in Tokugawa Japan*. Berkeley: University of California Press.

Loeb, Laurence D. 1972. "The Jewish Musician and the Music of Fars." *Asian Music* 4 (1): 3–14.

Meduri, Avanthi. 1988. "Bharata Natyam, What Are You?" *Asian Theatre Journal* 5 (1): 1–22.

Morris, Gay. 2006. *Game for Dancers: Performing Modernism in the Postwar Years, 1945–1960*. Middletown, CT: Wesleyan University Press.

Nanda, Serena. 1996. "Hijras: An Alternative Sex and Gender Role in India." In *Third Sex, Third Gender: Beyond Sexual Dimorphism in Culture and History*, ed. Gilbert Herdt, 373–418. New York: Zone Books.

Needham, Maureen, ed. *I See America Dancing: Selected Readings 1685–2000*. Champaign: University of Illinois Press, 2002.

Nordera, Marina. 2007. "Gender Underway: Notes for Histories Yet to Be Written." In *Dance Discourses: Keywords in Dance Research*, ed. Susanne Franco and Marina Nordera, 169–86. London: Routledge.

O'Shea, Janet. 2007. *At Home in the World: Bharata Natyam on the Global Stage*. Middletown, CT: Wesleyan University Press.

Prevots, Naima. 1998. *Dance for Export: Cultural Diplomacy and the Cold War*. Middletown, CT: Wesleyan University Press.

Roscoe, Will. 1996. "How to Become a Berdach: Toward a Unified Analysis of Gender Diversity." In *Third Sex, Third Gender: Beyond Sexual Dimorphism in Culture and History*, ed. Gilbert Herdt, 329–72. New York: Zone Books.

Schuyler, Eugene. [1876] 1966. *Turkistan: Notes of a Journey in Russian Turkistan, Kokand, Bukhara, and Kuldja*. New York: Praeger.

Segal, Lewis. 2007. "Nureyev: Dancing around the Lies." *Los Angeles Times*, August 19, Calendar section, F1, F12.

Shay, Anthony. 1999. *Choreophobia: Solo Improvised Dance in the Iranian World*. Costa Mesa, CA: Mazda.

———. 2002. *Choreographic Politics: State Folk Dance Companies, Representation, and Power*. Middletown, CT: Wesleyan University Press.

———. 2005. "Dance and Jurisprudence in the Islamic Middle East." In *Belly Dance: Orientalism, Transnationalism, and Harem Fantasy*, ed. Anthony Shay and Barbara Sellers-Young, 51–84. Costa Mesa, CA: Mazda.

———. 2006. "Male Dancer in the Middle East and Central Asia." *Dance Research Journal* 38 (1 and 2): 137–62.

———. 2007. "Choreographing the Other: The Serbian State Folk Dance Ensemble, Gypsies, Muslims, and Albanians." In *Balkan Dance: Essays on Characteristics, Performance, and Teaching*, ed. Anthony Shay, 161–75. Jefferson, NC: MacFarland.

Stein, Edward. 1999. *Mismeasure of Desire: The Science, Theory, and Ethics of Sexual Orientation*. Oxford: Oxford University Press.

Stoneley, Peter. 2007. *A Queer History of the Ballet*. London: Routledge.

Studlar, Gaylyn. 1993. "Valentino, 'Optic Intoxication,' and Dance." In *Screening the Male: Exploring Masculinities in Hollywood Cinema*, ed. Steven Cohan and Ina Mae Hark, 23–45. London: Routledge.

PART I

ISSUES IN THE PINK AND BLUE WEST

I

Maverick Men in Ballet

Rethinking the "Making It Macho" Strategy

JENNIFER FISHER

On a new spate of "dance reality TV" shows at the start of the 21st century, the old specter of prejudice against men dancing emerges with absolute clarity from time to time.[1] Based to some degree on talent contests like *American Idol*, a number of these television series (*Dancing with the Stars, So You Think You Can Dance, Step It Up and Dance,* to name just a few) police the borders of conventional male and female movement styles in simplistic ways that echo lasting biases men in dance have faced. Female dancers are often allowed to display both softness and strength, but any male contestant whose limbs drift too languidly or curve into a form that might be interpreted as too

Figure 1.1 Juilliard graduate Anthony Bryant ran into trouble when his dancing with a ribbon was judged unmasculine on a popular dance reality television program in 2005. Photograph by Richard Termine. Used with permission.

soft or vulnerable may have his masculinity questioned in no uncertain terms. During the first season of *So You Think You Can Dance* (Fox TV, 2005), for instance, a young ballet-trained dancer who did an impressive solo holding a flowing ribbon was rejected roundly for lack of "masculinity."[2]

It's not coincidental that the dancer in question was well trained in ballet, given the fact that ballet (along with other so-called classical forms elsewhere in the world) is one of the most refined and suspect forms of dance in North America. Because many of the dance reality TV shows feature romantic couple dancing, the judges often reinforce conventional notions of who should be sturdy and who should be pliant. To be sure, these sensationalized television shows are more likely to highlight stereotypes of all sorts in the name of ratings and commercial revenue, but in the concert dance world, the demand for male dancers to fulfill conventional expectations in terms of masculine style has often been as severe.

In this essay, I explore one aspect of the prejudice against male dancers as it relates to the ballet world and is reflected in articles, books, documentaries, and conversations, both in the popular press and in the dance world in general. I focus on stereotypes and responses to them, on coded language and the power of labels. In the West, as well as other contexts where bipolar definitions of masculinity and femininity exist, boys and men who do ballet might reasonably be seen as exceptionally brave or foolhardy, or both, because of the art form's strong associations with a superfeminized world of women. In all but the most liberal of contexts, men often take abuse for not choosing a more conventional occupation. Tale after tale from anyone in the field reveals that a stigma about men in ballet still exists, long after that sort of thing might have been thought reasonably to have disappeared.[3] In a sociological study reported in 2003, male ballet dancers repeated a number of negative characterizations they had encountered: "feminine, homosexual, wimp, spoiled, gay, dainty, fragile, weak, fluffy, woosy, prissy, artsy and sissy."[4] It's quite a list. The dance contestant mentioned earlier, who was accused of being too feminine, then worked on strengthening and simplifying his style, trying to better "perform" the role of a manly dancer.

How has the official ballet world—teachers, critics, writers, dancers themselves—responded? How has it dealt with the polarizing cruelty of stereotype and misinformation? In general, the ballet world has answered its detractors with another polarizing tactic, by promoting dance as a macho activity. It has insisted that ballet is as tough as football, a "real" man's game, that it provides proximity to lots of barely clad women, wink, wink, and is, in short, a lot like the marines, only with briefer uniforms and pointed toes. Has it worked to insist that John Wayne might have felt at home in variations class if only he knew how macho it really was? Have beer-guzzling guys at the pub torn themselves away from watching football on TV to carry on the babe hunt in ballet class? Not noticeably, with the exception of one Argentinean beer commercial in which that very thing happens for comic effect.[5] It might be time to shed some light on the popular "making it macho" strategy and suggest other ways of conceptualizing the plight of boys and men in ballet.

A Short History of the "Making Ballet Macho" Strategy

Characterizing ballet as macho, in the sense of making it seem athletically masculine and resolutely heterosexual, has been a common attempt to counter effeminate stereotyping in the ballet world. The strategy might have coalesced most strongly in North America, where masculine types arose from the various pioneer/cowboy/self-made-man mythologies that circulated around nation-building.[6] But the roots of anxiety over male ballet dancing can be seen long before classical dance came to the New World, for instance, in the much-quoted pronouncements of 19th-century Parisian critic Jules Janin, who decided that the Romantic ballet stage should be graced only by women. How could "a creature made expressly to bear a rifle, saber and uniform" become the sensuous purveyor of passion? How could "men, ugly men" join the ballerinas they clearly worshiped? For Janin, men were clearly destined to make laws and govern, not to embody balletic ideals in a world where seeming ephemeral was clearly a women's job (quoted in Chapman 1997, 204). By the early 20th century in North America, male dancers clearly struggled with the idea of entering the profession. Could dancing be a manly activity for really manly men who engaged in virile pursuits and did not eat quiche or wear tights? I use the hyperbolic mode ironically here before mention of Ted Shawn and his bravely naive tactics when facing prejudice in the first half of the 20th century.

Shawn's attempts to ennoble the masculine aspects of dance are well documented and run along the lines of conjuring up handsome Greek statues, sporting bodies, and rugged outdoor camping adventures.[7] Early in life, he had to think fast when a fraternity brother warned him that "dance was all right for aborigines and Russians . . . but hardly a suitable career for a red-blooded American male" (Shawn 1979, 11). He entered the field anyway and became a seminal part of American modern dance beginnings with Ruth St. Denis in their glorious Denishawn years. After that, Shawn formed an all-male company, which took on the task of making dance safe for American men. They toured from 1933 to 1940, offering such hardy favorites as *The Dance of the Threshing Floor, Mule Team Driver's Dance*, and *Labor Symphony*. In other words, their titles often conjured up dance as work, not frivolous or feminine fun, and they might have had some luck changing hearts and minds about men in dance along the way. Or not. In Western concert dance, Shawn was at least the first prominent male to proclaim loudly that dance was not for sissies, doing us the favor of admitting that there were choreophobic[8] and homophobic tendencies circulating at a time when so many others avoided any suggestion of what Ramsay Burt has called "the trouble with the male dancer" (Burt 1995, 10).

Shawn's noble male dancers leaped like broad jumpers, ran like sprinters, and stomped in stern poses, but how much they did for the "normalization" of male dancing is unknown. Shawn himself hardly helped the cause of ballet, since he distanced what he did from ballet, calling Nijinsky, for instance, "decadent" and "freakish" and declaring that "America demands masculinity more than art" (Foulkes 2001, 113). But he might as well have cast his lot in with any male dancer, considering that such stereotypes tend to be applied across the board and have proved to be tenacious. Most men in his company really were hardy athletic types, who cleared the land and built much of Jacob's Pillow when they weren't rehearsing. But they were not actually threshers or mule team drivers, nor did they compete for prizes like other male athletes. They were all dressed up (or undressed, likely as not), ready to be looked at, not really accomplishing any manly task other than being admired for their physiques and muscular grace. For insiders, there has always been a certain amount of irony in Shawn striving so hard to be a conventional macho man because he was gay, although, of course, nothing prevents gay men from being macho. In the land of stereotypes, opposites become mutually exclusive only in the minds of those who buy into them.

Because early dance histories never mentioned the homosexual aspect of Shawn's life, he might be seen as a closeted male dancer who was protesting too much during his lifetime. In many of the old films—when Shawn poses like a Greek god on a pedestal, half-naked and buffed white, for instance—he might have looked manly to some, narcissistic and effeminate to others. This is because "different audiences picked up different messages," as Julia L. Foulkes succinctly puts it in an essay that productively shines new light on Shawn's embodied effects (2001, 130). What Foulkes usefully points out is that, no matter what Shawn intended to do, the dancing bodies in his all-male pieces proclaimed a space for "same-sex object choice for gay men," as well as "detach [ing] masculinity from heterosexuality" (129–30). In other words, by trying to be so macho and not a bit feminine, while actually being homosexual, Shawn's dancing body and his choreography stood for more than he might have suspected. Perhaps inadvertently, he pointed the way to a time when gender identity would become more acknowledged as a social construction and a choice.

Yet simplistic polarities that revolve around ballet and machismo continued to circulate in North America. In the dance boom of the late 1960s and 1970s, ballet stars such as Edward Villella and Jacques D'Amboise became poster boys for manly men in dance in a different way than Shawn. Their tough personas and working-class backgrounds were promoted seemingly to suggest they could convince streetwise New York kids to choose ballet over juvenile delinquency. Villella even appeared on an episode of television's *Odd Couple* series in a script that had him successfully competing with football players, presumably to show that ballet men were "regular" athletic guys. In 1958, Gene Kelly had also had a fling at making dancing masculine in a television special called *Dancing—a Man's Game*, which included guests from the sports world like Mickey Mantle and Sugar Ray Robinson.

Promoting ballet as manly in his own way, Rudolf Nureyev became a glamorous jet-setting hunk after his spectacular defection from cold war Russia in 1961. Photographs and stories of his liaisons with Margot Fonteyn and other women suggested he was a real ladies' man, despite the fairly common knowledge that he preferred men. Then, in the late 1970s, another Russian sensation, Mikhail Baryshnikov, projected a clearly heterosexual persona in movies like *The Turning Point*, in which one character speculated that "that horny little Russian will make ballet safe for boys." Did he make it safe? No surveys exist. And he wasn't the last ballet man to be trumpeted in this way. In the last few decades, many prominent male dancers from Latin America and elsewhere have inspired lots of newspaper and magazine articles with headlines that advertise "ballet's sexy new men." A 1996 article in the Toronto *Globe and Mail* by its then dance critic was titled "Ballet's New Men" and subtitled "Straight Talk: the stereotype of the gay dancer is fading as more and more athletic young men take up ballet."[9] The implication that gay men were not athletic evidently did not alarm any editors of the newspaper. The article read like an unabashed "hooray for heteros" diatribe and stirred up a certain amount of controversy. Letters to the editor tended to include the claim that "sexual preference doesn't matter," inadvertently leaning toward a kind of "don't ask, don't tell" doctrine.[10] Protesters took the position of saying it was insulting to connect ballet with sexual preference because sexual preference has nothing to do with art or talent—gay or straight, it's the dancing that counts. The more interesting revelation at the time was that ballet supporters could not find the rhetoric to counter one dance writer's simplistic claims, and that the writer conflated heterosexuality with stereotypes of "manliness," perhaps to bolster the reputation of ballet men in general.

Few would argue with the fact that negative stereotypes about men in ballet have disappeared in some places today—in the arts community, for instance, or among any number of people who simply don't subscribe to such prejudices. In some of my interviews and conversations with male ballet dancers, younger men have said they were never teased and never faced negative stereotyping. Anecdotally, I have noticed that these men are sometimes of large stature or menacing demeanor, but not always. Certainly, the standard associations between ballet and "less-than-masculine" men still pop up regularly in movies and television shows where innuendo and essentialized identities are the stuff comedy and anxiety are made of. Examples of how "he's a ballet dancer" becomes code for "he's gay," or simply "he's weak," are too numerous to detail.[11]

In the 1990s, the makers of the movie *Billy Elliot* had a go at making ballet macho by showing a working-class boy's triumph over stereotype, and within a few years, the Royal Ballet's lower school had so many male applicants that it admitted more boys than girls for the first time in its history. It was called "the Billy Elliot effect."[12] Various enlightened, optimistic dance commentators are always declaring that times have changed and the old prejudices don't exist anymore. As far back as the 1970s, on an *Eye on Dance* program (made for New York public television), host Celia Ipiotis declared the prejudice against male dancers at a definitive end. Everything had progressed nicely, she said while interviewing a few male guests, and nowadays, men in dance were accepted by everyone. But in the 1990s, I found that the male students of the National Ballet School in progressive Toronto had to be given permission not to wear their school uniforms on field trips because they were getting threatened too often by local toughs. It was thought that fisticuffs could be avoided if they were not wearing ballet school insignias.

But for all the difficulty boys and men face in terms of stereotype, they also enjoy certain privileges in the ballet world, most certainly because of their endangered status. For instance, boys may not be required to wear standard studio gear or keep hair out of their eyes if it is thought that such restrictions deter them from coming back to ballet class. In private studios as well as conservatories, boys sometimes receive more scholarship money than girls and are often given leeway when it comes to disciplinary infractions. Making ballet macho has been a time-honored strategy when recruiting male ballet dancers. In the 1970s, when Arthur Mitchell wanted to lure boys off the street for his school of the Dance Theatre of Harlem, he compared ballet to sports and promised them they didn't have to wear tights (Backlund 1988, 31–32). In this same vein, any director of a *Nutcracker* knows that you secure adolescent boys for the party scene by pointing out they get to be around girls in that scene. To get younger ones for the battle scene, you just mention that weaponry is involved. Once recruited, ballet men face less competition in terms of getting professional jobs and hold many so-called power positions as artistic directors and choreographers. But it's an odd supremacy, in that they often pay dearly for any preferred status advantages, facing prejudices that accompany their unusual career choice.

In the new millennium, the "making it macho" strategy made an appearance in a PBS documentary called *Born to Be Wild* (2002), which took its title from the Bruce Springsteen song and linked it to ballet star Ethan Stiefel's penchant for motorcycles. In an opening segment, Stiefel talks about the ballet world offering him the opportunity to be close to minimally clad, physically fit women all day with a sheepish grin that suggests a wholesome boy overcome by hormones. Poor Stiefel never suspected that his sexual preference, as natural to him as the color of his hair perhaps, would provide such an effective promotional tool for the "making it macho" ballet strategy, nor that he would look so naively partisan to dance analysts who probe issues of gender. More power to him and all the flirtation that goes on in any ballet class, but one can't help but notice that only the heterosexual men in the documentary have the romance in their lives acknowledged. The omission of what gay men do on a date—or any mention of sexual preference, even in passing—must still be considered part of the protective coloring the ballet world has tended to promote as part of the "making it macho" strategy.

This tendency to try to mark male dancing as not only masculine enough but *unquestionably* masculine, I suggest, was inherited in deluxe fashion by the young lyrical dancer whose rejection on *So You Think You Can Dance* began this essay. The Juilliard-trained dancer actually returned a few seasons after his initial audition with an attitude that he clearly hoped would establish his credentials as a manly dancer. Wearing camouflage combat fatigues, he announced (in a voice-over) that he was going to do a "more dynamic," "in-your-face" dance this time, with "acro-tumbling power," if that's what the judges wanted. But he couldn't win for trying; the judges still found him a "wonderful technician" but felt that, somehow, there was a "spark missing." Despite his clear technical skill and willingness to take direction, they eliminated him at the first stage. In Internet chat rooms, followers of the series were in general not fooled by the judges' statement that a spark was missing. Hetero-sexuality was the thing that was missing, one blogger indicated, and another said being talented but "too feminine" went against "the basic rules of engage-ment within dance [that] have been set since the beginning of time." Yet another comment began with, "I have nothing against gays but . . . ," continuing with objections to any dancer who looked feminine.

In the more conservative mid-1950s, demands for manly style—in both social dance and concert dance—might have been coded, with male dancers criticized at times as "not direct enough" or "not bold enough." But today, a new bluntness has crept into daily discourse, perhaps encouraged by commercial television's dissemination of colloquialisms and put-down speech, so that male dancers can be told to dance "like a man" or even to "butch it up," whether it's on the ubiquitous free-for-all Internet sites or even sometimes on camera. One openly gay contestant on the 2008 edition of a series called *Step It Up and Dance* (Bravo TV) recently paraphrased the judges' objection to his too-soft, preening style by saying, "Oh, was I too much of a fag?" He took note of the critique and successfully impressed them afterward with his deliberate performance of "manly" dancing.

A Girl's-Eye View

In the world of ballet, as opposed to the world at large, the "unmarked" category is female, and the "marked" category male, to use distinctions Peggy Phelan (1993) has delineated. In Freudian terms, the female dancer is the one whose body is the standard, so that her "lack" (lacking the male genitalia) becomes the "norm." That is, classical dancers are meant to have smooth bodies with no inconvenient bulges; they are bearers of a type of ideal beauty, strength, and form, and any secondary sexual characteristics are harnessed, shaved, or otherwise minimized. In this aesthetic universe, the male dancer becomes the one with the inconvenient "surplus"—inconvenient because, although classical dancers tend to play roles that are all strictly defined in terms of gender (either girly girls or manly men), they are not supposed to have sexual organs. In ballet, everything must be smoothed over and not get in anyone's way. In other words, there is no penis envy in ballet.

There is also no question of women not fitting in—women "own" the ballet world, or at least overpopulate it, and increasingly are taking their place as rulers of that world, though they still often face glass ceiling limitations as artistic directors and choreographers. But even in that realm, they are making progress, with the number of "power" positions in the ballet world being held by more women each decade. Women also have the advantage of being able to play with ballet's extreme version of femininity, taking it off at will and remaining relatively unsuspect in terms of their gender identity, in both onstage and offstage life. It's not so easy for men, who are rarely able to play with conventional markers of masculinity without being suspect.

Except in major urban centers, there is generally a shortage of ballet men, so that their numbers perhaps militate against their becoming more commonplace and known. Perhaps it isn't unusual, then, that as I grew up learning ballet in the United States, I had absolutely no interest in the fact that men were also involved. Unlike other realms, where it seemed that male privilege obtained, I thought of ballet as a woman's world, where men were useful mainly for holding up the ballerinas I admired. Who were Anna Pavlova's partners? Men whose names I could barely remember. The great Pavlova and Karsavina in the past, or Ulanova and Fonteyn as I grew up, were the main attractions to me. Even when Nureyev and Baryshnikov, the Russian sensations, came to overshadow them in the public imagination, the ballerinas were the figures who captured my attention. There were no boys in my ballet studio, and when male dancers showed up to dance the generic "Cavalier" and "Trepak" in my local ballet company's *Nutcracker*, they seemed to me shadowy characters whose lives I couldn't quite imagine. I did notice their positive attributes—they tended to be considerate, relaxed, and fun; and they knew how to talk to women, which is more than I could say for the boys at my school or the grown men who watched sports or sat stolidly around me at family affairs. Some of them were gay, I vaguely understood, but I had little knowledge about or interest in what that meant.

Later in life, as I did fieldwork in *The Nutcracker* world, I talked to many other girls and women whose ballet landscapes also seldom included the presence of men, with one exception—the mothers of boys in ballet. More than once, as I was focusing on the enfranchisement of women in the world of *Nutcracker* and ballet, a mother would say parenthetically, "You should really write about the boys, you know. Now *there's* an interesting story that should be told." Despite many fierce critiques that insisted male privilege and power still prevailed in the gender codes of the pas de deux, many women and men still saw ballet as a place where women ruled and the males took second place, always behind the tutu.[13] For me, *Nutcracker* season became an interesting place to notice a man's plight as a creature at the margin of the main event. Except in the largest ballet company productions, ballet boys and men were a seasonal occurrence, arriving only at *Nutcracker* time. In terms of being suspect sissy boys, as the stereotype would have it, they seemed to get a special dispensation each Christmas, due to the ballet's popularity and the fact that many of its male roles did not require much dancing.

Still, I could see that *Nutcracker* communities tended to be worlds of women. The ranks of regional ballets were dominated by women not only as dancers and teachers but as directors, backstage workers, board members, and other volunteers. In the *Nutcracker* world, women even dominated the ranks of choreographers. Come December, boys and men constituted a subcategory in many ballet communities, appreciated but marginal and often troublesome. The littlest male participants, for instance, needed more wrangling backstage than the girls; adolescent boys looked gawky next to their more technically schooled female partners; men backstage took orders from the women in charge; and male dancers got only a few moments to strut their virtuosic stuff, while Clara and the Sugar Plum Fairy caught the imaginations of so many in the *Nutcracker* audiences. For years, I was busy theorizing the ostensibly dichotomous image of the female ballet dancer, finding ways to hold together and accept the fact that she is skilled and strong but must appear conventionally feminine and acquiescent.[14] The ballerina is a woman of steel, I decided, who, in the service of art, must appear as mild-mannered as Clark Kent, unable to show that she is actually as macho as Superman. Who, then, was the male dancer?

With thanks to many men in ballet I have talked to and read about, as well as the work of scholars such as Ramsay Burt and Doug Risner, both represented in this volume, I started to focus on the stereotypes about men in ballet, many of which are nourished by representations in movies and on television. My comic book comparison for ballet men goes something like this, then: men in ballet not only have to appear as mild-mannered as Clark Kent but also—like Superman *and* the ballerina—have to overcome the dicey image of a man in tights.

The Gay Elephant in the Room

Relatively little has been written about homosexuality and ballet until recent years, with the subject opening up very, very gradually after feminist and gay "liberation" movements accelerated in the wake of the civil rights movement of the 1960s. Before that time (and even since), popular biographies of male dancers were full of omissions and innuendo, unless the definitive wife and children could appear. John Gruen's gossipy 1979 biography of Erik Bruhn, for instance, avoids personal pronouns almost obsessively—"there are certain people to whom I am drawn physically," Bruhn says, but he doesn't like being overwhelmed by "someone" in a relationship. Gruen makes much of supposed romances with famous ballerinas—Bruhn was gay, and for those in the know, the coded language becomes extreme: Bruhn says he has "loved people on many different levels" (97), and Maria Tallchief records that Bruhn was "elusive" in their relationship, and that he "comes to the brink of things and then, suddenly, something stops" (101). The answer to this mystery is then addressed when friend Sonia Arova notes the moment when Bruhn "began to relate more fully to Rudolf Nureyev" (115) and when Bruhn himself describes their relationship as "[going] through a great deal together, and on many different levels" (124). Levels, hmmm. Like sex? It's left to the active reader's imagination. It took a few more decades before a tell-all biography like Diane Solway's *Nureyev* would leave nothing to the imagination.

Considering the number of homosexuals involved in ballet, dance critic Horst Koegler wrote in 1995, "its 'coming out' has taken an unusually long time" (231), but he accurately predicted a sea change. One of the few North American dance writers who had approached the topic directly long before then was Toronto-based Graham Jackson, who wrote extensively about dance during the 1970s, often for small publications. His collected writings included an essay that is uncharacteristically frank about ballet's limitations—that it has a "straight" aesthetic, for instance; that gentleness is not recognized as a masculine quality in North America, though it sometimes was in England, he says, where danseurs like Anthony Dowell could be "somewhere in between" dainty and macho; that the status quo was preserved by gay choreographers and artistic directors who became conservative so as not to jeopardize their positions. He calls gay men to arms, stating that choreography won't ever reflect more than limited realities until they speak up by supporting, attending, and making more diverse dances for the ballet (Jackson 1978, 38–43).

Ramsay Burt reasonably suggests that the "widespread reluctance to talk about dance and homosexuality" might have been an attempt to protect the institution of ballet inasmuch as it might be threatened by taboos among corporate and individual donors (1995, 29). He points out that Judith Lynn Hanna's 1988 consideration of the topic suffers from a characterization of homosexuality as a "problem" for ballet men, as opposed to a problem existing as a result of the roiling sociopolitics surrounding Western society's homophobia (29). Burt's own book-length study of men and dance is one of the few written in a scholarly vein about popular perceptions of the male ballet dancer; in it, he says that prejudices against the male dancer in Europe did not exist until the 19th century (1995, 10), and he tells us that there was no pronounced association between ballet and homosexuality until the age of Diaghilev.[15] This statement is relatively undocumented, but few would doubt that, as Burt claims, bourgeois men of the 19th century may have felt that "to enjoy the spectacle of men dancing [was] to be interested in men," so that "the pleasures of watching men dancing became, in the mid-nineteenth century, marred by anxieties about masculine identity" (28), because of confusion between just being friends with men and the fear of being thought homosexual (28).

This anxiety can be documented in North American popular culture, especially in movies, where it's often addressed by stereotyping, on one hand, and reassurances of heterosexuality, on the other. In the early part of the 20th century, for instance, when Ted Shawn was warned that American men in dance were sissies, the association was not universal enough to prevent Fred Astaire from playing a famous ballet dancer in his film *Shall We Dance?* (1938). But it seems he did have to prove he was a skirt-chasing heterosexual within the first few minutes of the film by putting taps on his ballet shoes and ogling a photo of Ginger Rogers. And he never appeared in tights; instead, he wore the rehearsal pants male ballet dancers often wore back then. Perhaps when more revealing costumes became common for male ballet dancers later in the century, the stigma grew. "People think tights are like pantyhose," one ballet mother told me when discussing the negative stereotypes she encountered with a son in ballet. It's evidently okay for men to wear pantyhose only if they are worn under major-league football uniforms for warmth. I had always assumed the prejudice against men in tights had to do with being too exposed, which somehow conjured up unseemly vanity or vulnerability for men, and perhaps that association exists, too, but this mother's pantyhose association revealed another facet of the perceived "girliness" of ballet.

In virtually any film that features a male ballet dancer, the question of his sexuality comes up. If his character is meant to be heterosexual, this is made clear within a very short amount of time, usually by reference to his hankering for female companionship. I once pointed this out to a male student in one of my university classes, and he confirmed my observation by surveying a number of dance movies from the early days of Hollywood to the present. He recorded the time between the first appearance of a male dancer and a definitive reference to his heterosexuality, finding it ranged from about 30 seconds to 3 minutes, as I recall. In that respect, the ballet movie *Center Stage* (2000) made progress when it introduced both gay and straight male characters as such, making the identification a matter of useful information. When a group of incoming female dancers are staring at an attractive company member from a distance, for instance, they immediately ask which side he plays for, so they know whether their crushes will be figurative or literal. "Straight," they're told, and they send up a small cheer. No covert codes, no ostensible judgments, just practical facts. Notably, although gay characters are acknowledged in this movie, none of them are shown in relationships or intimate moments; dance movies perhaps have not come that far.

The assumption that all men in ballet are gay—a common stereotype despite research showing that about 50 percent are heterosexual (see Risner, this volume)—was virtually undiscussed during my *Nutcracker* research. In many interviews, I often sensed a veneer of politeness or political correctness in avoiding such a topic. Only a few frank souls spoke of the gay stereotype, such as one ballet mother whose husband wouldn't let their son be in *The Nutcracker*. Why? "Oh, I think he's homophobic," she said. The temptation to stress ballet's machismo quotient must arise from such encounters, but it seems a blunt one-pronged attack that needs rethinking.

The Maverick Strain in Ballet

Striving to make ballet macho is perhaps an expected strategy that well-meaning people have attempted to make ballet acceptable for men in the Western world. In the history of the United States, for instance, a "he-man" stereotype, nourished by various European tropes of masculinity, progressed from rugged individualist pioneers to cowboys to self-made men, and, eventually, to Rambo, the Terminator, Ronald Reagan, and George Bush. That's a lightning-round condensation of an evolution described with more nuance in histories of modern masculinity by George Moss and Michael Kimmel, among others.

Figure 1.2 Dancer and choreographer Eugene Loring, possibly the first ballet cowboy, in the title role of his 1938 *Billy the Kid.* Photographer unknown.

Kimmel uses particularly resonant images from popular movies and television series, most of which assure us that the selfish, sexy Rhett Butler (from *Gone With the Wind*) will always win out over the more sensitive, genteel Ashley Wilkes as a role model for American men (Kimmel 1996, 219–20); and that the new, sensitive man who started getting a toehold in the film *Kramer vs. Kramer* (1979) never took off like the Marlboro Man did (290). Put another way, the real identity crisis for contemporary men is choosing between two *Star Trek* role models—the rational alien Mr. Spock or the aggressive traditional man, Captain Kirk (290).

The fact is, North America does not have a national or folk hero or movie star who does ballet, so the more familiar stereotypes of ballet men as gay, sissy, or questionably sensitive still prevail. Supporters of Ballet Man continue to recommend he "up" his machismo quotient, but this constant pursuit of testosterone-charged images has its end point. Men in ballet *do* have to wear tights eventually, and they have to act as genteel as Ashley Wilkes and as precise as the nerdy Mr. Spock for much of their careers. Ballet is a refined art form, not a sport where athleticism is fueled by steroids, or ever looks like it is, nor will ballet ever be an athletic activity that results in six-figure salaries and enviable endorsement deals that are offered to the other macho guys.

Men in ballet have to cross a line into what is largely perceived as a feminized world. They have to come to terms with the color pink, because it will shadow their lives, whether they wear it or just come in frequent close contact with it.[16] They will wear tights, play princes, and point their toes in a careful fashion. So "making it macho" is not a strategy that will ever work, simply because ballet *isn't* conventionally macho and never will be. It's athletic, yes, manly, undoubtedly and of course, but Ballet Man will always be something the Terminator is not—light, precise, and more delicately attentive to the music and the muses than a strictly macho man could hope to be. What is Ballet Man to do? How can we intervene in "the realm of impressions and associations" that constitute a strongly stigmatizing stereotype? "The way to break the code is to examine it," so that a new reality can be constructed where a tired old one used to prevail (Dixon Gottschild 2003, 40). Having investigated the stereotype, we need a new definition of masculinity, scholars of its history tend to agree (Kimmel 1996, 333–35; Mosse 1996, 194; Burt 1995, 9, 30, 196). For Ballet Man, the uphill climb to diverse definitions of masculinity may be a long one, but he might take heart in the potential of making a significant contribution to the cause.

To this end, I propose an image that might replace the making-it-macho strategy with another "m" word, more appropriately applied to men in ballet—"maverick." The association between ballet men and mavericks is a logical one if you consider what all the brave men who can deal with the stigmatized world of ballet have in common. The anecdotal evidence, as well as that culled from the few studies that have been done, suggests that, not surprisingly, a range of men become involved in ballet, and they all have individual motivations, yet perhaps a few things in common.[17] In the interest of illustrating a few maverick beginnings, I suggest that several points of Ballet Men's common ground revolve around the following identifications:

- the athletic boy who accidentally finds he's good at ballet and likes the unique and secure position this usually gives him
- the boy in a large family who stakes out unusual territory because his brothers and sisters have already claimed many other potential professions
- gay or straight men who don't worry about putting a macho reputation at stake
- gay or straight men who find the arts a welcoming environment for many kinds of people
- secure men who don't worry what people think

No matter what the reason for identification with ballet, what men in ballet all must have in common, it seems to me, is a maverick strain, in the sense that "maverick" is defined as "a person who thinks and acts in an independent fashion, often behaving differently from the expected way" (Cambridge online dictionary) and "an irregular, a rebel, someone who is unconventional and unorthodox" (hyperdictionary.com). The word "maverick" has macho cowboy associations, as well, so the new strategy does not leave behind the old one entirely. A maverick can also mean "an unbranded range animal." And, of course, it became the name of the charming Wild West gambler played by James Garner in a television series and later by Mel Gibson in a movie version of *Maverick*. Interestingly, the word can also have a more sophisticated association, when used in a sentence the Cambridge dictionary suggests: "He was considered something of a maverick in the publishing world." It's a word with appropriate versatility.

Like the male ballet dancer, the maverick can be refined, but even when "tamed," he still may not follow the herd. Like the ballerina, the male ballet dancer is well advised to take the stereotypes of passivity and too much fairyland, if you will, and reinterpret them. The image of a maverick offers new rhetorical associations and is meant to shift perceptions. I don't think ballet will ever get more macho, for men *or* for women, although it's an athletic, tough endeavor for both of them and might reasonably be thought of as macho, in the classical sense of the word. I may be replacing one stereotype with another, but "making it maverick" seems to promise so much more scope than the dead-end strategy of "making it macho." For Ballet Man, it could be a brand he can live with.

NOTES

This essay appeared in a slightly different form and under another title in *Dance Chronicle* 30 (2007): 45–66.

1. "Reality TV" is an umbrella term that, in the first decade of the 21st century, includes a vast number of commercial programs that bear some relationship to documentary film but perhaps could be more reasonably seen as evolving from early television contests, "makeover" shows, and celebrity showcases of the 1950s and 1960s. Those that follow to some degree the formula of the wildly popular pop singing contest *American Idol* but focus on dance instead of singing, I am calling "dance reality TV shows." Reference to "reality" in these genres is perhaps understood best by comparing it to "structured improvisation" in the dance world. There is a formula, and the programs are shaped by strategic editing, but there are also nonprofessional participants and some leeway to improvise.

2. This dancer was Anthony Bryant, who was asked to make a cameo appearance at the end of the first *So You Think You Can Dance* season, as a kind of apology. Without any proof, I assumed at the time that perhaps that viewers had complained about his treatment by Nigel Lithgow, the executive producer and judge, who had said, "You didn't look like a masculine dancer." Bryant's return for the 2008 season audition provided extra drama as a "comeback" story. When he didn't get chosen to be on the show once again (although many less talented dancers did—Lithgow during the first season pointed out that they are "casting a show," not just looking for the best dancers), he provided a different kind of drama by cursing the judges as he stormed out and cameras followed him onto the street. Bryant, who had recently graduated from Juilliard, could be seen on youtube.com in 2008, as well as on his own Web site, anthonybryant. org. I thank him for helping me find a photograph of his ribbon dance.

3. A few illustrations will sketch territory that contains myriad testimonies to this effect. Former New York City Ballet dancer Edward Villella writes in his autobiography about growing up "a red-blooded American boy from an Italian working-class family in Queens," New York, during the 1940s that "kids who jeered [at him for doing ballet] never got a chance to finish their sentences. I just whacked them and left a string of bloody noses in my wake" (1992, 13). In 2006, a perusal of Internet posts, mostly from ballet mothers, reveals that both teasing and bullying of boys who take ballet still go on in the United States, although there are also some reports of more enlightened experiences. Various recent articles from around the world also echo familiar stereotypes. A *Los Angeles Times* article about ballet training offered to poor children in a South African township repeats warnings boys received from family and others that "ballet is for girls," and that it "would turn [them] gay" (Robyn Dixon, "On Their Toes for a Way Out," *Los Angeles Times*, November 15, 2005).

4. This was Amanda Berger's master's thesis in sociology at Boston College, dated April 1, 2003. Her fieldwork concentrated on interviews with 10 male ballet dancers whose experience includes dancing and teaching in the Boston area as well as other locations in the United States and other countries. Her research also included conversations and observation that put her in touch with the topic in other ways, as well as noting the statements of male dancers in documentaries. Although her fieldwork sample was

small, many of her findings are relevant in that they echo those of other researchers and my own, in relatively small fieldwork projects and in interviews I conducted during extensive research on *The Nutcracker*.

5. This beer commercial made the rounds on the Internet, featuring a young man drinking with friends who suddenly announces he must go off to ballet class. Oddly, he puts two pointe shoes tied together around his neck and leaves. His friends follow him and witness him in intimate poses in which his face is close to various female body parts. A few of these poses are reasonably close to everyday studio procedures; some are outlandishly unlike anything male and female partnering requires.

6. See, for instance, Mosse 1996, who explores the roots of modern masculinity, especially as they underpin stereotypes in Europe and the United States; and Kimmel 1996, in which images of American manhood are traced from the turn of the 19th century to the present, including stereotypes such as the "genteel patriarch" or "self-made man." Kimmel concludes, not surprisingly, that a new definition of masculinity needs to emerge for contemporary men to incorporate the virtues of both strength and compassion (334–35).

7. See historical accounts such as those by Shawn (1979), Sherman and Mumaw (1986), and Terry (1976). For a contemporary consideration of the issues surrounding gender and nationalism in relation to Shawn, see especially the essays of Julia L. Foulkes and Susan Leigh Foster in Desmond 2001.

8. The term "choreophobia" was coined by dance scholar Anthony Shay to describe feelings of negativity or ambivalence in relation to dance. He elaborates on aspects of choreophobia as it occurs in the Iranian cultural sphere in *Choreophobia: Solo Improvised Dance in the Iranian World* (Costa Mesa, CA: Mazda Press, 1999) but acknowledges the existence of the phenomenon in many parts of the world, including, of course, the United States.

9. Deirdre Kelly's article brings up many sensitive topics and perhaps was intended to open the ballet closet to frank dialogue. She claims a trend toward fewer gay men in ballet (she polls Canadian companies and lists statistics lower than the usual 50 percent found in scholarly studies) and also engages in "making it macho" strategies in the way they are outlined earlier in this chapter. Near the end, she states that "gay or straight, [men in ballet] can be as delicate or as strong as the role demands." But on the way to that conclusion, the text tends to conflate macho athleticism with heterosexuality, and heterosexuality with social acceptability—for instance, quoting a conservative director who says more and more boys are applying to ballet school, so that the absence of gays in ballet and its popularity with boys appear causal. The feature article appeared in the fall of 1996 in Canada's nationally distributed *Globe and Mail* newspaper, on the front of the Arts section, with a large photo of "three men who are proud of their profession," all of whom are bare-chested and identified in the article as heterosexual. The "continued" page includes two photos of Nijinsky, who is mentioned only in a sentence that offers famous names as examples of the fact that "for the first half of this century, gays did dominate the profession."

10. A letter to the *Globe and Mail* on December 21, 1996, calls Kelly's article an example of "sexual voyeurism and queasiness," while focusing mostly on the author's

"apparent need to still bring up the subject of homosexuality in dance," two statements that seem off the mark to me, though I appreciated the outraged tone of the letter. Kelly's prose style often seems breathless and gossipy, as when she enigmatically ties together Nureyev's machismo, his ability to "sex up" Fonteyn's dancing, and the fact that he was "promiscuously homosexual" and died of AIDS. But the letter writer's plea to ignore sexuality in favor of detached "technical and artistic merits" addresses only part of the problem.

11. Some examples of ballet stereotyping that relate to masculinity were detailed in my book *Nutcracker Nation* (New Haven, CT: Yale University Press, 2003), 159–62. Others appear in the introduction to this volume, in the personal histories, and in the essays by Jordan, Keefe, and Risner.

12. Catherine Milner, "More Boys Than Girls Join the Royal Ballet," News.telegraph. co.uk, April 24, 2002.

13. "Out from Behind the Tutu" is the title I once heard Canadian dancer Rex Harrington suggest for his memoirs. Harrington, who retired from the National Ballet of Canada in 2004, was known as a dramatic dancer and a gifted partner, not especially for his virtuosic feats.

14. The relationships of women to ballet constituted my first field of inquiry as a master's degree student at York University and then emerged further in small research projects during Ph.D. coursework at the University of California, Riverside. The dominating female presence in the *Nutcracker* realm, though not my original focus, also became a theme in my dissertation (1998) and the book that followed (2003). Culminating thoughts in this direction can be found in my essay "Tulle as Tool: Embracing the Conflict of the Powerhouse Ballerina," *Dance Research Journal* 39, no. 1 (2007): 3–24.

15. In this volume, John Jordan examines evidence to the contrary by noting negative associations associated with dance in the 18th century.

16. This history of pink is yet to be written, but here's a start: George Mosse refers to a "pink file" (1996, 98), in which names of homosexuals were kept at the start of the 20th century in Germany, where laws outlawing homosexuality had been on the books since 1871. Popular associations nowadays range from baby girl identification and fashion colors associated with femininity (though pink has been a somewhat accepted color for men's shirts since the mid-1960s), to political identifications such as pink ribbons used in breast cancer campaigns, and the pink triangle symbol for gay liberation.

17. My summation of these Ballet Man "types" is only a suggestion based on the following: informal observation and conversations with men in ballet, as well as ballet mothers and teachers during research periods focused on other ballet topics (from 1996 to 1998); one fieldwork study in 2003, which involved interviews and observation of a boys' ballet class during a Southern California summer intensive; browsing of Internet contributions on sites that revolve around boys and ballet; conversations with Deborah Williams, whose study (2003) of boys who take ballet revealed, among other things, that they often feel socially isolated and have a persistent love of dance (iii); and impressions from ballet autobiographies.

WORKS CITED

Backlund, Ralph. 1988. "From a Garage on West 152nd Street, a Ballet Company Soars to Moscow." *Smithsonian*, July, 28–40.

Burt, Ramsay. 1995. *The Male Dancer: Bodies, Spectacle, Sexualities*. London: Routledge.

Chapman, John V. 1997. "Jules Janin: Romantic Critic." In *Rethinking the Sylph: New Perspectives on the Romantic Ballet*, ed. Lynn Garafola, 197–241. Hanover, NH: Wesleyan University Press.

Desmond, Jane, ed. 2001. *Dancing Desires: Choreographing Sexualities On and Off the Stage*. Madison: University of Wisconsin Press.

Dixon Gottschild, Brenda. 2003. *The Black Dancing Body: A Geography from Coon to Cool*. New York: Palgrave MacMillan.

Foulkes, Julia L. 2001. "Dance Is for American Men: Ted Shawn and the Intersection of Gender, Sexuality, and Nationalism in the 1930s." In *Dancing Desires: Choreographing Sexualities On and Off the Stage*, ed. Jane Desmond, 113–46. Madison: University of Wisconsin Press.

Gruen, John. 1979. *Erik Bruhn, Danseur Noble*. New York: Viking Press.

Hanna, Judith Lynne. 1988. *Dance, Sex, and Gender: Signs of Identity, Dominance, Defiance, and Desire*. Chicago: University of Chicago Press.

Jackson, Graham. 1978. *Dance as Dance: Selected Reviews and Essays*. Scarborough, ON: Catalyst.

Kimmel, Michael. 1996. *Manhood in America: A Cultural History*. New York: Free Press.

Koegler, Horst. 1995. "Dancing in the Closet: The Coming Out of Ballet." *Dance Chronicle* 18 (2): 231–38.

Mosse, George L. 1996. *The Image of Man: The Creation of Modern Masculinity*. New York: Oxford University Press.

Phelan, Peggy. 1993. *Unmarked: The Politics of Performance*. London: Routledge.

Shawn, Ted, with Gray Poole. 1979. *One Thousand and One Night Stands*. New York: Da Capo Press.

Sherman, Jane, and Barton Mumaw. 1986. *Barton Mumaw, Dancer: From Denishawn to Jacob's Pillow and Beyond*. Hanover, NH: Wesleyan New England.

Terry, Walter. 1976. *Ted Shawn, Father of American Dance*. New York: Dial Press.

Villella, Edward, with Larry Kaplan. 1992. *Prodigal Son: Dancing for Balanchine in a World of Pain and Magic*. New York: Simon and Schuster.

Williams, Deborah. 2003. "Examining Psychosocial Issues of Adolescent Male Dancers." Ph.D. diss., Marywood University.

AARON COTA

Cota graduated as a dance major from the University of California, Irvine, in the spring of 2007, after taking some time off to serve in the Marine Corps Reserve in the Iraq War. His dance video Ya, We Were Bored, *which featured off-duty marines at Camp Fallujah, has been screened at the UCI Dance Film Festival. He earned a dance M.F.A. at UCI in the spring of 2009 with a concentration on dance for the camera.*

I became a dance major almost by accident, because I filled in my application to be a film major wrong. I went to the audition anyway, and once I was accepted, I thought, why not? I grew up with three brothers in Santa Maria, California, in a pretty artistic family—my mom likes to draw, and my brother was the dancer in the family, since he was six. I was into musical theater when I was younger, then I stopped doing that when I started playing football in high school. But I sort of missed it, and in my senior year, I enrolled in a beginning ballet class. When my brother's teacher found out I was taking ballet, I was thrown into an intermediate class with all these girls who had been taking ballet for 12 years. I had no idea what I was doing, but I was having a lot of fun. That was really why I started taking ballet—I saw the girls my brother was dancing with. It's an added bonus relating to girls at that age, because when they get to know you, they come to you with everything. Sometimes I've learned far too much information, but that just comes with the territory of being a male dancer. The good thing is that you learn the dos and don'ts as far as boyfriends are concerned—you hear the complaints, and you sometimes wonder why they're still with this person. Then you just kind of pick that up, and you know what not to do.

I tried out different kinds of dance, and I found I loved ballet more than jazz or modern, but I also found out I'm not the best ballet dancer. I think modern feels a lot better on my body. But for me, ballet seemed far more athletic for guys, that's why I liked it so much at first. In almost every ballet I've seen, it's so athletic for the guys, they do some insane, crazy jumps and leaps. It makes you wonder how the body moves that way, and how much stamina you must have to do some of that—like Mikhail Baryshnikov, he set the bar so high for male dancers, that

Cota in a snapshot taken after he left the marines to earn an M.F.A. in dance at the University of California, Irvine. Photograph by Sharon Kung. Used with permission.

everything you see after that has to be crazy and athletic. So the challenge of it all is what appeals to me. I watch it over and over again to see how they do this movement and how I would choreograph something like that. But for me, since I don't have the great ballet dancer body and I don't have the flexibility that it takes or the height of the jumps required, modern allows me to do what I can personally do. Modern can do whatever it wants to do, so I've come to appreciate it a little bit more.

For a while I was interested in becoming an officer in the Marine Corps after my reserves commitment, and then a helicopter pilot, then find work in special effects in film. But now I've discovered I can study dance for the camera in graduate school, and I decided to do that. On my mom's side of the family my grandfather is a retired lieutenant colonel in the Marine Corps—he was a pilot, and my uncle is a helicopter pilot for the Marine Corps. There's no pressure from them to stay with the marines, not even from the guys in my unit; they all think dance is really cool. I guess there was always some teasing in my unit—I got that all the time. But all the guys who made fun of it, they'd see the girls that we dance with, and then say,

"Oh, man, why don't I take dance?" And I'd say, "Well, you think it's for sissies or something, I don't know." [laughing] "You're the one who thought it was just for gay men." You just have to explain to them what it takes to be a dance major. Because it's not a regular major, it's not a basic 8 to 4 going to school. Some quarters I've been at school from 8 in the morning till 10 at night in rehearsals, and on weekends. And it's not a "you're only dancing" thing—you have to do dance history, you have to do a lot of writing, learn a whole language, Laban, a written language to record dance. And dancing all the time, it's so hard on your body, your knees, your back. It's a very physical major, not like sitting in a lecture hall all day. You're also hard on your body, so it's not a wimpy major, it's more a macho major.

One of the things my brother and I would always remind our friends about regarding men in ballet was that Barry Sanders—one of the greatest NFL running backs ever, in my opinion—attributed his skill and catlike reflexes to ballet, which he took as part of his training. There are a lot of professional and college football teams that now warm up using ballet, and there are a few martial arts stars that I've heard mention ballet as part of their training, like Jean-Claude Van Damme and Jet Li. Then there's the thing about wearing tights—when my friends rib me about having to wear tights, I tell them it's like wearing football tights. And if they want to make fun of me wearing tights, they should go up to a professional wrestler from WWF and make fun of him for wearing booty shorts. Heck, college wrestling uniforms are even more feminine-looking than tights. And if you need another example of scantily clad men, go see the movie *300*, in which the Spartans wear nothing more than Speedos and red capes. Granted, the Spartans kick ass and don't prance around onstage. But if some men are homophobic and think seeing men in tights might make them gay, then those men should not be watching any type of wrestling either.

I also want to bring up the whole gay men in dance thing. They know who's gay and who's not, and they don't come onto men who are straight. Like straight men, if they're interested in somebody, they usually find out first the critical information about being straight or gay, then whether they are seeing anyone or not. Once a gay guy knows you're straight, they don't bother you anymore, and most of the time they become great friends. My advice is that any straight man should have as many gay friends as possible—the stereotype exists for a reason, because they know a lot about women, they really know how to party, and they always have really hot female friends.

I wasn't a dance major when I first joined the Marine Corps, but you have to get a college degree to be an officer candidate. When they found out it would be a dance degree, they were like, "What? You're what?" They were just kind of confused. You just have to explain it to them. When the guys in my unit would see some of the things I've done, or they see videos of what other people dance, and they're like, "Holy crap, how can they do that?" I've gotten a couple of them to see a show, and they'll bring their wives or girlfriends, and they're like "Wow, that's amazing," and "That's kind of opened my eyes..." It's funny, one of the guys I met in my unit and I'm still friends with was one of the tough, macho marine guys, the epitome of the Marine Corps toughness. And up until last year when we were in Iraq, I never knew he was interested in becoming a culinary chef. He's going to a culinary arts school, and I would never have guessed that, no one did. That's not something you hear every day in the Marine Corps. I think me being a dance major might have helped him get accepted more—after all, being a chef is not a dance major.

In Iraq, our unit was paired up with some marines from Ohio and Iowa and others from the East Coast. I think I might have gotten more flack from them about dancing. Maybe it's because of where they grew up and they didn't have access to the arts that a lot of us in California or other places do. I think it was just that they just automatically assume that you're gay, and they make jokes about that even when they find out you're not. It's good-natured, but it's persistent. After a while, it's like, "Okay, I get it, you think I'm gay because I'm a dance major, okay." So you just kind of brush it off. But then they saw the music video my buddy and I made with some of the other marines over there, and they all thought it was hilarious. You know, they saw what dance could do for other people, help get their mind off not being at home, being away from their loved ones, what was going on, and just get their minds off the sheer boredom we had out there at times. There was a lot of downtime. So to bring dance over to Iraq there, it helped the guys forget about that life for a while and give them a good time for a while.

The funny thing about my marine unit is that it's a largely Hispanic unit, and most of the guys grew up in a culture where you either joined a gang, or ended up in jail, or join the military, or go to school and become very successful. So we have a whole range of guys, but the arts didn't seem to fit in there—now it kind of does. In time, they've just come to accept it, and they're all, "What's going on, are you still dancing?" or "Hey, when's your next performance?" So, things just kind of change over time. People just change their views about certain things in their lives that they might not have given any thought to before.

KRISTOPHER WOJTERA

Wojtera received his ballet training in his native Gdansk, Poland, at the National Ballet School during the Communist era. He graduated in 1995, by which time Poland was independent. He danced with the Baltic Opera in Gdansk, then with Wielki Theatre in Warsaw. After coming to the United States in 2001, he became a soloist with Columbia City Ballet in South Carolina, then joined the Louisville Ballet as a first soloist in 2003.

Nobody from my family knew about dancing—my father worked in the shipyards, my mother worked at a sweet factory. But when I was 10, a normal kid in elementary school, a lady came to our school—later I found out she was from the ballet school, but at that time, I didn't know what it was about. A few of us had to appear in our shorts and a T-shirt in a special room, where they showed us exercises to find out if our hips were open, how flexible we were, how rhythmic we were. She recommended that I take an audition for dancing school, and I got in. At that time, I wanted to be a soccer player. I was on a team and even after I went to ballet school, I kept playing soccer. After about a year, they told my mom that I had potential to be a good ballet dancer and asked me to quit soccer, because playing that was bad for your body, using different muscles. That was hard, but I didn't mind—I think it helped that everyone was so proud of me, that I could learn art, which nobody from my family ever did. So that was something different. We weren't wealthy, we were middle-class, so my whole family was kind of excited that I was there at ballet school.

Under the Communists, the arts were hugely important; the government gave a lot of money to the arts. The school was very nice, not like regular schools. And if I'd stayed in a regular high school, I don't know what I would have done after that, whether I could get a good job, or one I wanted. To be in the ballet school was something, a privilege. But that didn't keep boys from being teased about ballet, just like here. It was hard to talk to my friends in my neighborhood because they didn't understand what ballet was. I don't know if they'd ever seen it, if they'd ever been to the theater to see anything. I think they maybe thought that I was going to be a clown or something. They knew I had to wear tights, and maybe they questioned my sexuality.

Wojtera in rehearsal during the National Choreography Initiative, held annually in Irvine, California (artistic director, Molly Lynch), in the summer of 2008. Photograph by Aaron Cota. Used with permission.

I think because ballet school was so different, I didn't like it at first, but every year I liked it more and more. In the first few years, we were learning basic steps and how to stretch our bodies a lot, every day. I was in a lot of pain, but I found that somehow my body was flexible—I think it's genetics or something. I was living at home then, and my mother would help me as I tried to be focused more and more. Then each year I would pass the classical exams, and other students would get cut. When I started, there were two classes of about 30 dancers each. Out of those 60 students, only 10 girls and 5 boys ended up graduating.

We had a lot of Russian teachers and some Polish teachers, and the training we had every day was very strict. Everyday there would be people who were crying because the teachers were so demanding, wanting so much, and there would be disappointments. I don't know, maybe they were trying to make us strong people and strong dancers. They could be mean, not that they ever hit anyone, but they would push you, maybe get angry and disappointed because they wanted 100 percent every day. Sometimes, they were very hard on the girls, but I don't think there was a big difference in the way we were treated. Maybe the guys got told not to be too soft, not to dance like a girl. In the Russian training, I think you always have to be strong. It's never mellow, it's always very strong, never floating—very definite, for the girls, too. Only after I graduated did I understand more what the ballet means, what dance is all about. It's not only the positions and the steps, but you have to create it yourself.

I can see a huge difference here in the United States when it comes to teaching ballet. When I was in the ballet school in Poland, the teachers were allowed to correct our posture by touching our muscles. Touching a student was very common and normal—it was a way to better understand the technique and the feeling of the muscles. But when I got to the United States, in the classes I saw I noticed that the teacher never touched the students. Even if the student did not understand the correction, the teacher would not fix their posture physically—they can only explain the correction verbally. I know that there are precautions in America, but it's difficult for me to understand how to learn ballet without manual correction.

It's also different in that male dancers can always make good money here. There are hundreds of ballet schools, with millions of girls but no guys. So there are always jobs for male dancers and lots of guesting opportunities. In my country, it's more even—they are looking for girls as much for guys. Right now, Poland is still behind economically, and it's easier for ballet dancers to get jobs in other countries. But both here and back in Poland, people often don't understand what it's like for a guy to be a dancer. They ask what kind of dancing you do, what it looks like, what you wear. They don't even know what to call guys in ballet—you call the girls ballerinas, and the guys are danseurs, from the French.

When I was in school in Poland, because of my culture and traditions, homosexuality was not welcomed. There were gay people, for sure, but they had to hide it. Then when I was dancing in Warsaw, out of maybe 40 guys in the company, only 1 or 2 were gay. It's different here in America. In my whole life in Poland, I never knew a gay person—maybe they were there, but I never hung out with them; I never got to know one. When I came to dance in the United States, I met gay people, and it was hard for me at first to understand, but I found they are just like other people, except they are attracted to a partner of the same sex. I think my parents did a good job raising me, in that they never spoke wrongly about homosexuality—in fact, they never even spoke about homosexuality. Maybe they were scared because their son was in a ballet school. I just didn't have any experience with gay people, even in the ballet school. We were just guys who liked to hang out with the girls. Even with the teachers, I never knew if any of them were gay.

My parents would like me to go back to Poland, because I live so far away here, but I can learn a lot here and have a lot of opportunities. It's hard for girls to get a good job in the ballet here in the United States, but for men, it's easier. And there are so many good things about ballet—you get to travel, meet new people, learn new choreography. I'd maybe like to choreograph in the future. You learn so much, you want to share it with other people, and teaching is a definite possibility for me.

2

What We Know about Boys Who Dance

The Limitations of Contemporary Masculinity and Dance Education

DOUG RISNER

This essay explores dance education experiences of boys and young males in Western concert dance through a lens of dominant constructions of contemporary masculinity (Pollack 1999; Kimmel 2005) and the limitations these hegemonic discourses place on dance more broadly. Although research indicates that 50 percent of male dancers in the United States are gay or bisexual (Bailey and Oberschneider 1997; Hamilton 1998), the dance community has only recently begun to speak of the silence that surrounds gay and bisexual males in dance. Recent research on male youth in dance highlights various kinds of prevailing social stigma, including narrow definitions of masculinity, heterosexist justifications for males in dance, and internalized homophobia in the field. Those boys and young males in dance education provide an important vehicle for researchers interested in exposing dominant notions about masculinity, gender, privilege, sexual orientation, and the body.

From emerging research in the United States (Risner 2002a, 2002c, 2007; Risner and Thompson 2005; Williams 2003), Australia (Gard 2001, 2003a, 2003b), the United Kingdom (Keyworth 2001), and Finland (Lehikoinen 2005), I synthesize existing literature that documents the ways in which male youth in dance confront heterocentric bias, gender norms, and gendered bodies, as well as peer pressure and dominant cultural ideology in dance training and education. Key social questions of difference, pleasure, marginalization, and the larger effects and limitations of contemporary masculinity are explored within the dance world. I argue that a dance education that embraces all the experiences of its male students—straight, gay, and bisexual—has the ability to significantly impact homophobic prejudice, question dominant notions of masculinity, and more widely disrupt the social stigma of difference long associated with males in dance. I hope that confronting these issues within the dance education profession will be an important first step for broadening current limitations of contemporary masculinity.

Figure 2.1   Boys and young men training in dance walk a fine line when it comes to gender norms, heterocentric bias, peer pressure, and dominant cultural ideology. Photograph of Beau Hancock by Steven Schreiber. Used with permission.

Gender and Dance Education

Dance education and training have long been associated with gender and gender roles in world culture (Kraus, Hilsendager, and Dixon 1991; Sanderson 1996; Posey 2002; Stinson 2005). While dance in many cultures has been and continues to be viewed as an appropriate "male" activity, the Western European cultural paradigm situates dance as primarily a "female" art form and has done so since the 18th century (Hasbrook 1993). Moreover, research indicates that the overwhelming majority of the student population engaged in dance education and training is female.[1] Dance education researchers have gleaned considerable energy from the area of social foundations in education, especially in the realm of schooling and its impact on gender identity. With hybrid research agendas and methodologies from feminist thought, critical theory, gender studies, critical pedagogy, and most recently men's studies, dance education literature has begun to focus on the ways in which socially embedded assumptions about gender and dominant structural power relations produce unjust educational and sociocultural outcomes.[2]

Gender and its social construction play an important role in students' participation and attitudes regarding dance study.[3] Beginning as early as three years of age, girls, unlike boys, often grow up in dance as a taken-for-granted activity of childhood, adopting values "which teach that it is good to be obedient and silent, good not to question authority or to have ideas which might conflict with what one is being asked to do" (Van Dyke 1992, 120). Traditional dance pedagogy tends to school for obedience and emphasizes silent conformity in which dancers reproduce what they receive rather than critique, question, or create it. Stinson cautions that "there is a kind of freedom in obedience, the freedom from responsibility" (1998a, 118). To deal with this sense of powerlessness, Stinson says, some dance students escape "into a world of beauty. Others escape into the world of self, allowing the image in the mirror, or achieving one more inch of elevation (in a jump), to become the focus of existence" (120). Although males begin dance training much later in their lives, this kind of escape or silent conformity can affect them as well.

A key consideration for studying gender and dance education is understanding the "feminization" of theatrical dance in the west and the way males who dance are always at risk of being classified as effeminate, "alongside the denigrated female" (Thomas 1996, 507). Due in large part to dualistic thinking that separates mind from body, intellectual activity from physical labor, and to dance's close association with girls and women, dance is often perceived as part of women's domain, whereby its denigration for its dense female population is possible. Historical notions about the body often link the *feminine* with intuition, nature, the body, and evil; conversely, the intellectual, culture, and mind historically have been perceived as *masculine* (Risner 2001). Dance education scholar Edrie Ferdun summarizes: "The term 'dance' is usually associated with girls and feminine qualities by a significant portion of the dominant culture. Labeling dance as female prevents dance from functioning fully as an educational medium. It limits participation by anyone, male or female, who does not want to be associated with stereotyped gender images and practices" (1994, 46). Some approaches for confronting gender stereotypes in dance teaching and curriculum have been identified.[4] Central to most of these strategies is a concerted effort to make gender a conscious variable in all aspects of dance education (Ferdun 1994) and the affirmation of individual differences in gender and culture (Bond 1994; Kerr-Berry 1994).

Males in dance often benefit disproportionately because of their gender (Garber et al. 2006). Despite women's majority of the dance population, dance does not necessarily offer more opportunities to women than to men. Because of the seeming legitimacy men bring to dance, although they constitute a definitive minority, males often receive more attention and cultivation in their classes, training, and scholarship awards. Dance teachers often emphasize the need to make boys and young men in dance "feel more comfortable" by inviting them to actively contribute ideas for movement, music, costumes, and choreographic theme (Risner, Godfrey, and Simmons 2004); by developing lesson plans and movement (sports movement, vigorous actions) that allow boys a feeling of ownership (Baumgarten 2003); and by emphasizing the challenge and satisfaction of jumping higher, shifting weight faster, moving bigger, and balancing longer (Gard 2001).

To cultivate more male participation in dance, normalizing strategies over the past two decades have frequently centered on noteworthy heterosexual male dancers (Hanna 1988; Fisher, this volume), masculinist comparisons between sports and dance (Crawford 1994; Keefe, this volume), and minimizing the significant gay male dance population (Spurgeon 1999; Risner 2002a). Even so, male participation in Western European dance remains a culturally suspect endeavor for male adolescents, teens, and young adults (Sanderson 2001; Stinson 2001; Risner 2002a; Gard 2003b; Williams 2003; Lehikoinen 2005).

Dance Is for Girls: Rehearsing Masculinity

Current discourses in contemporary masculinity and gender, as well as the findings of leading researchers on boys and young males, show a direct correlation between postmodern masculine identity and homophobia (Kimmel and Messner 2001). Understanding more fully the experiences of boys who dance requires particular attention to the parallel relationship between masculinity and homophobic attitudes.

Noted dance scholar Ramsay Burt gives a rigorous explication of the cultural, social, and political history of masculine representation in dance, most notably the 20th-century construction of prejudice toward male dancers and the homophobia that today continues to surround gay or straight men in dance. In his seminal text, *The Male Dancer* (1995), Burt charts the development of homophobia as a means for males to rationalize their close attraction to one another. In this scheme, men can bond socially (which one would think is a reasonable human endeavor) only when homophobic attitudes accompany such intimacy. In other words, although men might enjoy watching other men dance, in order to do so, they must profess an absolute repulsion for homosexual desire or attraction. Straddling this important boundary between acceptable homosocial bonding and repressed homosexual attraction is the crux for the heterosexual male spectator watching men dance. This notion is a key element in understanding many men's culturally prescribed anxiety toward gay men. It is instructive for dance educators to realize that similarly uncomfortable boundary crossings might reasonably apply for many fathers, siblings, and friends attempting to watch or support male dancers. Without facing these foundational aspects of culturally defined masculinity (as narrow and destructive as they may be), there is little hope for any real progress. Recent research in men's studies reveals much the same conclusion; homophobia is a key defining element in contemporary, postmodern masculinity (Kimmel and Messner 2001).

As sociologist Michael Kimmel (2005) notes in the current politicized debate about boys' achievement and behavior in schools:

> We hear about boys failing at school, where their behavior is increasingly seen as a problem. We read that boys are depressed, suicidal, emotionally shut down. Therapists caution parents about boys' fragility, warn of their hidden despondency and depression, and issue stern advice about the dire consequences if we don't watch our collective cultural step. Though we hear an awful lot about *males*, we hear very little about *masculinity*. Addressing the issue of masculinity will, I believe, enable us to resolve many of these debates, and move forward in a constructive way to create equity in our schools for boys as well as girls. (220)

Although postmodern feminist theory has greatly expanded our understandings of multiple subject positions, as well as the notion of diverse femininities or ways of being female for girls and women, it appears that contemporary masculinity has become even more narrow, or like a "gender straightjacket" for boys and men (Pollack 1999, 6). In the pioneering *Real Boys*, William Pollack (1999) outlines the significance of a cultural reevaluation of prevailing ideas about boys, men, and masculinity:

> The boys we care for...often seem to feel they must live semi-authentic lives, lives that conceal much of their true selves and feelings, and studies show they do so in order to fit in and be loved. The boys I see in schools and in private practice often are hiding not only a range of their feelings but also some of their creativity and originality....The Boy Code is so strong, yet so subtle, in its influence that boys may not even know they are living in accordance with it. When they do [stray from the code], however, society tends to let them know—swiftly and forcefully—in the form of a taunt by a sibling, a rebuke by a parent or a teacher, or ostracism by classmates. (7)

The "gender straightjacket" and "Boy Code" have profound effects on more than just the lives of boys and young males (Kimmel 2005; Kimmel and Messner 2001; Pollack 1999; Katz and Earp 1999). Unchecked traditional values of masculinity—emotional detachment, suppression of feelings, feigned bravado and self-confidence, dominance, aggression, and valorized individual achievement—diminish all human experience. Katz and Earp (1999) describe this phenomenon as "the crisis in masculinity," in which "it is vital that we understand that the real lives and identities of boys and men often, if not always, in some ways conflict with the dominant 'real man' ideal. Behind the bravado and tough guy posturing, there is human complexity. In other words, behind the guise is the real boy and man, the results of a sensitive, nuanced experience of the world that rarely airs in public" (3). Sociologist Timothy Curry (2001) reminds readers of the socialization process in which boys learn to be masculine by avoiding all that is feminine, homosexual, or *unmasculine* to any degree, noting that "the reasoning may be seen as follows: (a) 'real men' are defined by what they are *not* (women and homosexuals); (b) it is useful to maintain a separation from femaleness or gayness so as not to be identified as such; (c) expression of dislike for femaleness or homosexuality demonstrates to oneself and others that one is separate from it and therefore must be masculine. Not only is being homosexual forbidden, but tolerance of homosexuality is theoretically off limits as well" (196). In an earlier study of male athletes, Curry (1991) notes that this kind of hegemonic masculinity can also manifest in more aggressive forms, fueled by defensive male athletes' physical contact in sport, as well as their closeness and nudity in the locker room. The coach in this 1991 study stated: "We do so much touching that some people think we're queer. In 37 years I've never for sure met a queer [athlete]. At [a certain college] we had a [teammate] that some of the fellows thought was queer. I said, 'pound on him, beat on him, see what happens.' He quit after 3 days" (cited in Curry 2001, 197).

When we consider seriously this mask of dominant masculinity that society imposes on boys and young males, we see more clearly not only the disruptive cultural resistance but also the overwhelming courage necessary for our male students to pursue dance study and consider a career in dance. Dance educators would do well to look more closely at the dominant social structures and cultural assumptions that guide our own practice and research, as well as the ways in which our actions wield the power to deplete or enrich an empowering common humanity. Obviously, additional complexities are involved in unpacking the social experiences, ethnicities, and gendered bodies of males in dance; it requires attention to the marginalization of male dancers in a culturally feminized field, which is combined with the privilege, benefit, and authority of being male in a patriarchal society.

What We Know about Boys Who Dance

While research on adolescent male dancers and their experiences is scant, what we do know is troubling, linked as it is to dominant notions of masculinity, pervasive homophobia, and boys' neglect and harassment (Gold 2001; Patrick 2001; Williams 2003). The most comprehensive social understanding of male adolescents in dance at this time emerges from a quantitative-qualitative doctoral dissertation, *Examining Psychosocial Issues of Adolescent Male Dancers*, by Deborah Williams (2003), whose research was conducted from a human development perspective. The study of 33 boys (12 to 18 years of age) enrolled in summer intensive dance training programs revealed three significant aspects regarding adolescent males in dance: that they experience severe social isolation; that they have perceptions of unmet needs; and that, despite lack of social support and negative experiences, they persevere in their dance study.

Williams notes the following aspects of social isolation among her subjects:

- a lack of same-gender peers and teachers in the dance environment
- a need to talk about issues but not having a supportive person to talk with
- in some cases, having family members who did not support or discouraged their desire to dance
- a need to keep their dance life a secret from academic peers
- fear of or actual teasing and harassment by peers
- perceptions of homosexuality regardless of the dancer's sexual orientation
- teachers, parents, and directors attempting to justify dance activities by relating them to sports (57)

What is particularly compelling about Williams's study is the accompanying qualitative data in which the boys' narratives clearly articulate their social isolation, frustration, and contempt for misguided efforts by teachers, parents, and directors to justify dance for males in traditionally masculinist ways. The study's participants were overwhelmingly negative in regard to this issue, as one boy chided: "I'm an artist, not a football player! Why does everyone keep insisting on comparing me to a sports star who takes ballet for exercise as though that should make it alright to dance?... That has nothing to do with being a dancer" (59). Another participant stated: "It feels like someone is trying to justify that men dance. As though it is only O.K. because some sport guy does it. Why isn't it O.K. just because it is what I want to do? It makes it embarrassing to admit that you are a dancer who doesn't do sports" (59). One boy relayed that his private studio, in an attempt to attract more males, changed the title of ballet class to Sports Movement for Boys. Acknowledging his disgust at what he termed "tricking" boys into dance, he noted, "Who are they trying to fool? Kids are smarter than that!"

In previous work, I have been critical of these kinds of hegemonic approaches (Risner 2002a, 2002b) and have advocated, with others (Crawford 1994; Gard 2001, 2003b), for more rigorous questioning and thoughtful strategies that focus on greater understanding of dominant notions of masculinity and societal stigma about males in dance. Williams's study provides ample evidence of the harmful and dehumanizing effects of reproducing hegemonic masculinity by compromising and devaluing male adolescents in dance programs, studios, and schools. As dance educator John Crawford suggested more than a decade ago: "Men have traditionally fulfilled roles as choreographers and managers, whereas women have been the prevalent performers and workers. Yet male dominance in dance has not led to an increase in male dancers, possibly because it conforms to, rather than challenges, the very structures that brought about the scarcity in the first place" (Crawford 1994, 40).

Male adolescents in dance clearly highlight the necessity of perseverance (in their words, "a love for dance") in confronting negative stereotypes and social isolation outside the dance studio. However, an internalized homophobia in dance education is powerful as well. Teachers, directors, and peers sometimes use homophobic language to emphasize the importance of adhering to strictly masculine behavior, gesture, and movement execution. For example, the male teacher who coaches a young male dancer to execute movement more strongly states, "You're a beautiful dancer, but you dance like a fag. We'll need to show you how to dance like a man" (Williams 2003, 71). For one of Williams's participants struggling to affirm his gay identity, the pejorative societal stereo-type of the gay male dancer looms largely in his consciousness: "I recently came out to my friends and family. It was a hard decision but what is even harder is how I feel now. I feel guilty because I let my fellow dancers down. I'm the stereotypical gay guy who dances. I'm exactly what everyone thinks male dancers are. I'm ashamed of that" (60).

Recent research in dance education and physical education has begun to explore the ways in which hegemonic masculinity, as an institution, can be challenged through the participation and experiences of boys and young males in dance (Gard 2001, 2003a, 2003b; Keyworth 2001; Risner 2002a, 2002b). Central to this work is the notion that dance education may serve as an important means for disrupting dominant cultural assumptions about accept-able ways of moving for males and for challenging cultural stereotypes about male dancers and nonheterosexual modes of sexuality. Obviously, this is not to say that all boys and young men in dance consciously enter the dance studio with the intention of challenging dominant paradigms of masculinity. Nor can it be denied that some males in dance reaffirm narrow definitions of masculinity and heterosexism through their actions and discourses. Rather, this area of research suggests that the experiences of males in dance education can provide powerful insights into hegemonic assumptions about dance, gender, and sexu-ality, as well as dominant codes that govern all the former.

Saul Keyworth (2001) notes significant feelings of isolation, both for himself and for the male dance participants in his physical education study, who acknowledge their pejorative status as the "dancing queens" on campus. Although participants enjoyed their dance experiences, many were reluctant to pursue further dance study away from the "safety" of a university sports and athletics program. While optimistic that more males in dance will be sensitized to "question and ultimately subvert their own gendered condition-ing," Keyworth concludes that the study's participants will "continue to carry their gendered legacy" (133). More simply, the power of narrowly defined masculinity continues to police the behaviors of young men, regardless of the joy and pleasure they experience while dancing.

Michael Gard's (2001, 2003a, 2003b) work focuses on the possibilities that dance education offers for "disruptive and discomforting experiences," as well as pleasurable ones, for students in schools and universities, more specifically, exhuming the taken-for-grantedness of gendered male bodies and heterosexual embodiment (Gard 2003a, 211). Gard notes: "While I have heard male students use words like 'weird,' 'stupid' and 'dumb' to describe dance movement, my research suggests that the association of dance *per se* and particular forms of dance movement with both feminine and non-heterosexual ways of moving and being remains strong. And yet it is this knowledge, the knowledge that bodies carry and construct gendered meanings, which we might address through dance" (2003a, 220). In Gard's 2003 case study, culled from a larger research project investigating male dancers, the notion of gendered investments (or committed ways of deploying the body) in dance education is explored. In a life history narrative of a professional male dancer named Ralph, Gard found an interesting correlation between the absence of "enjoyment" or pleasure and an acute awareness that "boys don't dance" (2003b, 109). This kind of love-hate relationship with dance stems from the idea that males are enculturated to manifest a particular kind of body and a specific way of moving that evidences a strict heterosexual regime (or set of governed practices). Although Ralph was a highly proficient professional dancer, his narrative account of dancing is one of repeated ambivalence, "bereft of any talk of bodily pleasure" (113). Gard argues that this kind of uncertainty hinges upon a struggle to reconcile enjoyment of dancing with other bodily investments more consistent with and characteristic of dominant male heterosexuality, such as Ralph's skills in rugby and surfing. Challenging dominant gender norms, whether intentional or not, obviously requires an intense internal struggle with external forces and expectations.

Previous research on sexual orientation and male participation of under-graduate students that I conducted with six introductory-level male dance students revealed five important themes that point to a deeper understanding of social stigmatization: homophobic stereotypes, narrow definitions of masculinity, heterosexist justifications for male participation, the absence of positive male role models (straight and gay), and internalized homophobia among male dance students (Risner 2002a). Three of the participants in this study self-identified as heterosexual; two self-identified as gay, and one as bisexual.

Resisting cultural norms for these young men (average age 19) began with confronting homophobic stereotypes held by their own families and peers, in which the participants' negative preconceptions of male dancers figured prominently as each contemplated and began dance study. At the same time, participants later spoke eloquently about the personal satisfaction they felt while studying dance. Similar to the work of Gard (2003b), Keyworth (2001), and Lehikoinen (2005), I am interested in understanding the ways in which young men in dance balance these powerful competing narratives. As I pointed out in an earlier essay: "On the one hand, their dance education is an important source of joy, satisfaction, and affirmation. While on the other, their masculinity and sexual orientation is repeatedly questioned and surveilled. Complicated meta-narratives require equally complicated coping mechanism for young men in dance" (Risner 2002a, 87).

Justifying their participation in dance emerges as an important arbiter of masculinity for young men who dance. Justification or "excuses," as Gard refers to them, frequently result in heteronormative half-truths, that is to say, that a "real male" would never actively choose dance study on his own volition. As AJ (pseudonym), whose degree program in theater requires course work in dance, acknowledges in his narrative: "If you *have* to take dance, rather than if you just chose to take it, it frees you up. By it being a requirement, you don't have to show that you're interested, but of course I am. I did use it [the requirement] as an excuse with my friends back home, my family" (Risner 2002a, 87). In a follow-up interview, AJ made clear that dance was required for his degree; he also felt compelled to tell me of his deep and profound attraction to both women and sports. Other respondents also emphasized the similarities between dance and sport in explaining to others their attraction to dance. For example, "Most people have misconceptions of dance, that only weak people take it so they won't have to play sports, that dancers couldn't play football. I let them know it's just as difficult as sports" (87).

As in Williams's study of male adolescents, many of the male students in my study described their frustration with the lack of positive male role models in dance, citing the need for more affirming examples of men as dance teachers and professional dancers, as well as popular media images of men dancing. Without strong role models to challenge narrow views of masculinity, some of

Figure 2.2   Research indicates that comparing dance to sports in order to justify it as a "masculine" activity has negative effects on young men pursuing dance seriously. Photograph of Beau Hancock by Steven Schreiber. Used with permission.

the participants suggested, homosexual stereotypes become so imbedded in the culture's association with dance that young males in dance accept the homophobic responses their dancing frequently garners (88).

Although I have little doubt that the physical nature of dance is commensurate with that of football or soccer, like Gard (2001), I have been concerned about discourses that colonialize dance in traditionally masculinist ways. With the intention of making dance more accessible for boys and more palatable to their peers, family, and culture, these discourses regularly position dance as sport. Nor do I doubt, for those participants who are straight, the ontological significance of their heterosexual orientation and the ways in which dancing may challenge some of their deepest feelings about what it means to be male. However, I do find it problematic that justifying male participation in dance requires testimonials that clearly serve not only to buttress homophobic stereotypes but also to erase the otherwise positive experiences of these young men in dance. First, why do these young men engaged in dance study—gay and straight—reaffirm some of the very stereotypes they repeatedly confront themselves? Second, why do these men feel it necessary to deny the presence of gay and bisexual men in dance education in order to legitimate their own participation? While we certainly acknowledge the enormous courage required of the young men like those discussed in these various studies, we must also recognize the myriad ways in which denigrating some people serves to privilege others—in this case, heterosexual males and dominant notions of masculinity.

Dominant Masculinity and Gay Males in Dance

For young gay males, the protection offered by the dance studio often carries the high cost of extreme isolation for a number of reasons (Risner 2002c, 68). First, young girls significantly outnumber their male counterparts in dance. Second, both gay and straight boys who suffer from negative stigma associated with males in dance often go to great lengths to display traditional heterosexual markers, often isolating themselves further from peers, family, and their own sexual orientation or questioning. Leaving the dance studio often means returning to the embarrassment, humiliation, and contempt of being labeled a pansy, fag, or queer. In addition, research shows that nonheterosexual males in dance receive far less parental and family encouragement and support for dancing than do their heterosexual peers (Bailey and Oberschneider 1997, Risner 2002a). As I have noted in previous research: "The lack of parental support and approval experienced by gay male dancers may be attributed to parents' more general disapproval of dancing, or to dance as a career choice for their sons. It may well be the case that larger fears of homosexuality inhibit parents from encouraging their male children to pursue dance study, especially if one or both of the parents harbor homosexual suspicions about their male child" (Risner 2002a, 90).

Young boys' avoidance of their homosexual orientation is facilitated by countless devices perpetrated by a pervasively heterocentric culture, especially when considering the overwhelmingly ridiculed status of "sissy boys" in American society. Education researcher Eric Rofes (1995) notes that the widely accepted sissy/jock paradigm operates as a key element in male youth culture, whereby traditional masculinity is narrowly described in highly misogynist ways. Boys in dance, unlike their male peers in athletics and team sports, are participating in an activity that already casts social suspicion on their masculinity and heterosexuality. For gay male youth in dance, coping with this double-bind situation (marginal in a marginalized field), it is a complicated dilemma.

Although there is vast individual variation, many young gay males tend to begin homosexual activity during early or middle adolescence; similar activity for lesbian females begins around age 20 (Anderson 1995, 18). Because adolescents are only beginning to possess the capacity for abstract thought or formal reasoning skills to cognitively integrate their sexual experiences, dance educators must realize that boys and especially young gay males in dance are extremely vulnerable to gendered criticism, homophobic attitudes, antigay slurs, and the absence of positive gay male role models. Young self-identified gay males in dance experience far more alienation in dance class than their straight male peers (Risner 2002a, 89).

Young gay males may also develop internalized homophobia, in which self-hate, low self-esteem, destructive behavior, and further confusion characterize their underlying attitudes and conduct. Many gays, incapable of resisting persistent heterocentrism and homophobic prejudice, internalize negative attitudes about homosexuality, themselves, and other gay people (Lehne 1976; Margolies, Becker, and Jackson-Brewer 1987). As Luke (self-identified as gay) told me in 2002: "I never talk to men in class. I prefer straight women because they're not as difficult to talk to as gay men . . . we [speaking for himself as a gay man] don't identify with other gay guys. This sounds stupid, but I really don't like gay people that often. And the ones I do like really get on my nerves. . . . I mean, who wants to talk to a bitchy male dancer?" (Risner 2002a, 89); or as Brett (self-identified as gay) in the same study told me: "I know many openly gay people in theatre, but in dance, many are closeted. I don't understand why. I get so frustrated with them. I mean, I know it's difficult and I don't judge them, but please, we're in dance . . . and these closeted guys try so hard. It's all about their girlfriends" (89).

Because at that time I found the phenomenon of internalized homophobia somewhat surprising, I asked the gay and bisexual participants if they felt dance was a supportive environment for gay men. Although the group uniformly believed that dance provides an open and supportive atmosphere for gays, each struggled to articulate how they experienced that support, telling me, "There's some sense of support in that nobody's calling you names. It's not hostile," or

"It's a big escape in the studio . . . when I come out of dance class I feel it all back on me," and finally, "There's no harassment from the other dancers and that feels extremely supportive" (Risner 2002a, 90). The interesting picture these young gay and bisexual men paint depicts a contradictory landscape character-ized by a strong sense of gay and bisexual support and affirmation, on the one hand, but a deeply internalized homophobia, on the other. This landscape, when combined with the homophobic attitudes characteristic of homosocial bonding, tends to isolate gay males from their straight male classmates, as well as from each other. What this small picture may be showing us is that some young males in dance—gay and straight—tend to distance themselves from gay males and homosexuality at all costs.

This kind of environment is stressful and often threatening for gay and bisexual male students, particularly because they are vulnerable young people who are struggling to claim and affirm their sexual orientation in an often hostile atmosphere of homosexual denigration. For closeted gay youth, the weight of this burden over a long period causes many other psychological and emotional hardships, though at the time, recognition of these dilemmas may be unacknowledged (Besner and Spungin 1995, 95). Deceiving others ultimately leads to deceiving one's self, a deception that goes well beyond sexual orientation.

Moreover, gay adolescents and teens often have far fewer resources available to them than adults do for understanding homosexuality in a balanced and unbiased manner. Because the field often suppresses candid and forthright discussion of gay issues in dance education, it rarely, if ever, addresses the sexual harassment and abuse that sometimes occurs (Risner 2002b). Hamilton (1998, 92) reports that, although there are far fewer males in dance overall, they are three times as likely to experience sexual harassment in dance than females, and that perpetrators of sexual harassment are more than seven times as likely to be male than female. In addition, male dancers in their teens are propositioned for sex by their dance teachers, directors, choreographers, and fellow dance students at a rate of three to one compared with female dancers, with the gender of the solicitor being male nearly 70 percent of the time (Hamilton 1998, 92).

The dance profession's silence surrounding sexual abuse is deeply worrisome and also relates to the unwritten preference the profession maintains for the *unspoken*. Dance educators should rigorously question the motivation and perpetuation of a silence that allows this kind of abuse to be perpetrated upon young dancers. When such issues are not addressed by dance educators, three grave dangers emerge: (1) male students rarely, if ever come forward about sexual harassment and abuse; (2) sexual abuse by male dance faculty is often trivialized or ignored; and (3) within the profession's muted discourse, sexual abuse and homosexual orientation are wrongheadedly equated with an-other. These kinds of disconcerting, if not incriminating, statistics reported by Hamilton (1998) certainly exacerbate the continued absence of serious discussion surrounding issues of masculinity in dance education. When faced honestly, these issues should compel dance educators to speak more openly and candidly about the "truth" of the matter in its entirety.

Gay men have been and continue to be an important part of the dance landscape. As a profession, we can counter society's negative message about gays only by answering it directly, not by avoiding it. Taking a critical stance about sexual harassment and abuse should not require that we deny the important presence and significant contribution of gay men to our field. However, all too frequently this has been the case. What is even more confounding, however, is the way in which the profession's silence and lack of response wrongly serve to equate homosexual orientation *with* sexual harassment and abuse, and thereby reproduce negative attitudes and stereotypes about gays and dance.

Conclusions: Supporting Boys in Dance Education

It is important to understand that dehumanizing discourses and their continued implications for boys who dance are part of a much larger cultural reevaluation, one, I believe, that compellingly requires participation by the dance community. Much of the prevailing societal stigma associated with boys in dance can be traced to powerful, long-standing metanarratives that, though sometimes well-intentioned, have reproduced a deleterious mythology about *all* males in dance, regardless of sexual orientation. Until recently, many of these narrowly defined heterocentric paradigms have gone unquestioned.

Although I have acknowledged the appeal of cultivating a larger male population and audience in dance, one that more closely resembles our communities, schools, and cultures, I continue to find it highly problematic to do so by denying the presence of gay and bisexual male dancers (Risner 2002a, 2003b). Within our current political, economic, and social climate, attracting more males to the profession might conceivably bolster credibility and generate greater financial support for dance. But if recruiting strategies ignore important issues of sexual orientation, gender identity, and homophobic attitudes, they will be pragmatic and shortsighted, forfeiting vast opportunities for educating the dance profession and our highly confused culture about its sexuality and discrimination. Even with the best of intentions, the profession's pragmatic attempts to encourage young boys and men to pursue dance frequently reproduce narrow derogatory stereotypes of gay dancers (Crawford 1994; Bond 1994) and, in so doing, demean the entire male dance population, its diverse contribution, and the field of dance as a whole.

Six strategies for forceful confrontation of gendered teaching and inequity in dance teaching and curriculum are offered by Ferdun: (1) make gender a conscious topic in all aspects of dance education; (2) do not reduce dance to the "body"; (3) consider and create carefully the contexts for dance performances; (4) teach a broad range of dance genres, and dance from different historical and cultural contexts; (5) promote empathy in dance experience by providing opportunities to practice and imagine how it is to move and feel like another; and (6) provide dancing experiences that promote gender equality (1994, 47). In addition, pedagogical approaches to dance that overlap with feminist approaches to teaching dance include choreographic exploration of the body as a living laboratory (Arkin 1994); use of African dance to encourage male and female students to express themselves through gender-flexible movements (Kerr-Berry 1994); openly discussing gender identification and the experiences of dance students (Risner 2002b); and exploring gender bias, sexism, homophobia, elitism, and power relations (Horwitz 1995).

Supporting Boys in the Studio and Classroom

I conclude with what I believe the dance profession can do today to improve the experiences and training of boys and young males in our programs and schools. Although each dance professional's environment is unique, with its own set of opportunities and constraints, these suggestions are presented for further contemplation and informed action in our own locales and individual contexts. It is also particularly important to understand the necessity of age-appropriate approaches to sexual orientation and alternative lifestyles. Some of these suggestions are adapted from sport studies scholar Pat Griffin's (1995) work addressing homophobia in athletics and the needs of lesbian, gay, and bisexual athletes; others are developed from practical implications derived from Williams's (2003) findings on adolescent males in dance.

Dance educators can inventory their own heterosexist beliefs, gender assumptions, and *taken-for-granted* actions that unintentionally create an environment of shame, humiliation, or embarrassment for males in the studio and classroom. I encourage teachers to understand more fully their authority and power as positive role models for dancers, and the respect teachers inherently garner from their students. It is important to contemplate seriously the fact that what you don't say is just as important as what you do. For gay, lesbian, and bisexual dance educators, try to be as open and candid as you safely can about who you are. *All* students need to know gay adults who are leading satisfying, productive, and meaningful lives. Heterosexual dance educators can give unwavering support to their gay and lesbian dance colleagues by speaking out against antigay attitudes, actions, and policies. Dance educators can also do the following:

- Identify teaching methods and in-class language that reinforce narrow definitions of femininity and masculinity. Understand that young males are particularly sensitive to gendered criticism, especially gay and bisexual males.
- Refrain from assuming that all dancers are heterosexual. Some probably are lesbian, gay, or bisexual. Others may be questioning their sexual identity.

- Realize that most dance programs are devised and administered by adults (many of whom are female) who base what they think boys need in adult thought processes; find ways for young males to connect in meaningful ways with peers who have similar aspirations, concerns, and questions; actively plan special master classes or study outings that feature strong male role models as teachers or performers.
- Explore and identify simple yet inclusive ways to incorporate gay, lesbian, and bisexual issues in the classroom and studio in a balanced and unbiased manner. For example, invite guest artists, former dancers, or current faculty members who are gay or lesbian to teach a master class, present a lecture, and speak in an open manner about themselves and their experience in dance.
- Be available and prepared to talk with male dancers (and/or their parents) who are questioning their sexual orientation or expressing overtly homophobic beliefs. Many closeted gays use homophobic slurs and antigay epithets to buttress an outwardly heterosexual persona.
- Provide performance opportunities that enhance male students' learning and self-image; monitor the casting of boys in multiple roles, which can set young boys up for fatigue, injury, and feelings of inadequacy.
- Identify and readily make available pertinent resources for students who need them, such as the Gay Straight Alliance (GSA), an extension of the Gay, Lesbian, Straight Education Network (GLSEN, www.glsen.org). Prominently display the pink triangle—universally associated with safe zones for gay, lesbian, and bisexual people.

Supporting Boys through School Leadership

Dance educators can encourage school and department administrators to (1) establish nondiscrimination and antiharassment policies that include sexual orientation, and (2) ensure that all teachers, parents, and dancers understand what actions are unacceptable, and what procedures are to be followed when the policies are violated. Dance administrators can provide dance teachers and staff with sexual harassment and abuse education focusing on asymmetrical power relationships between faculty and students. School directors and department heads can openly support gay and lesbian faculty and staff by nurturing an environment that is sensitive, supportive, and respectful of sexual orientation and of alternative lifestyles and family structures.

While it may appear difficult to include parents in these kinds of strategies, addressing their concerns and participation is equally important. At the outset, dance educators can encourage parents (1) to know their child's private dance school, public school dance program, or university department—its teachers and administrators, and (2) to discuss with their children, in an age-appropriate fashion, what constitutes sexual harassment and abuse. Dance educators can also facilitate and nurture candid dialogue between parents and children about their dance teachers, classmates, and dance classes and their child's progress in dance. Dance teachers can also help parents do the following:

- Challenge their own prejudices and biases about gay, lesbian, and bisexual people and evaluate how they condone or reaffirm antigay prejudice in their children. Help parents understand that a dance teacher's sexual orientation does not determine his or her ability to be an effective and respected professional.
- Understand that for all males, there is a great deal of social stigmatization for boys who study dance. Explore the ways in which parents support or discourage their child's dance training.
- Realize that the most current research on boys' emotional and psychological needs reports that boys are not receiving the level and quality of emotional attachment they actually say they need; though their son may exude confidence and independence, they should actively find ways to enter into meaningful dialogue with him about his dancing.
- Consider the very real possibility (given statistics in dance) that their son might be gay or bisexual, and if not, that their son most likely will experience the same discrimination and prejudice regardless of his sexual orientation.
- Support their son's dance performances as much as possible; attendance by family members is crucial for validating and affirming his work. Contemplate the arduous struggle a child endures as a gay, lesbian, or bisexual person. Show sensitivity and support, if their child comes out as gay, lesbian, or bisexual. Remember that sexual orientation is a leading and contributing factor to teen depression and suicide. Contact a local chapter of Parents, Families, and Friends of Lesbians and Gays (PFLAG www.pflag.org) for information and support.

NOTES

1. Though this is seemingly obvious, see, for example, Adair 1992; Van Dyke 1992, 1996; Sanderson 2001; Higher Education Arts Data Services/HEADS 2003.

2. The last decade or so's work in dance education scholarship and research in this area includes Arkin 1994; Clark 1994; Horwitz 1995; Marques 1998; Shapiro 1998, 2004; Smith 1998; Green 2000, 2002–3, 2004; Keyworth 2001; Schaffman 2001; Doi 2002; Risner 2002a, 2004a, 2005; Blume 2003; Gard 2003a, 2003b; Letts and Nobles 2003.

3. Social construction of gender in dance education receives interrogation in the following important works: Stinson, Blumenfeld-Jones, and Van Dyke 1990; Flinthoff 1991; Van Dyke 1992; Cushway 1996; Sanderson 1996, 2001; Stinson 1998a, 1998b, 2001; Gard 2001, 2003a; Green 2001, 2002–3, 2004; Risner 2006.

4. Readers may be interested in approaches for confronting gender issues and inequity in dance teaching and curriculum as articulated by Arkin 1994; Bond 1994; Crawford 1994; Daly 1994; Ferdun 1994; Kerr-Berry 1994; Risner 2002b; Clark 2004; Dils 2004; Stinson 2005.

WORKS CITED

Adair, C. 1992. *Women and Dance: Sylphs and Sirens.* New York: New York University Press.

Anderson, D. 1995. "Lesbian and Gay Adolescents: Social and Developmental Considerations." In *The Gay Teen,* ed. G. Unks, 17–30. New York: Routledge.

Arkin, L. 1994. "Dancing the Body: Women and Dance Performance." *Journal of Physical Education, Recreation and Dance* 65 (2): 36–38, 43.

Bailey J., and M. Oberschneider. 1997. "Sexual Orientation and Professional Dance." *Archives of Sexual Behavior* 26: 433–44.

Baumgarten, S. 2003. "Boys Dancing? You Bet!" *Teaching Elementary Physical Education* 14 (5): 12–13.

Besner, F., and C. Spungin. 1995. *Gay and Lesbian Students: Understanding Their Needs.* Philadelphia: Taylor and Francis.

Blume, L. B. 2003. "Embodied [by] Dance: Adolescent De/constructions of Body, Sex and Gender in Physical Education." *Sex Education* 3 (2): 95–103.

Bond, K. 1994. "How 'Wild Things' Tamed Gender Distinctions." *Journal of Physical Education Recreation and Dance* 65 (2): 28–33.

Burt, R. 1995. *The Male Dancer: Bodies, Spectacle, Sexualities.* New York: Routledge.

Clark, D. 1994. "Voices of Women Dance Educators: Considering Issues of Hegemony and the Education/Performer Identity." *Impulse* 2 (2): 122–30.

———. 2004. "Considering the Issue of Sexploitation of Young Women in Dance: K–12 Perspectives." *Journal of Dance Education* 4 (1): 17–23.

Crawford, J. 1994. "Encouraging Male Participation in Dance." *Journal of Physical Education, Recreation and Dance* 65 (2): 40–43.

Curry T. 1991. "Fraternal Bonding in the Locker Room: A Profeminist Analysis of Talk about Competition and Women." *Sociology of Sport Journal* 8 (2): 119–35.

———. 2001. "Fraternal Bonding in the Locker Room: A Profeminist Analysis of Talk about Competition and Women." In *Men's Lives,* ed. M. Kimmel and M. Messner, 188–201. Needham Heights, MA: Allyn and Bacon.

Cushway, D. 1996. "Changing the Dance Curriculum." *Women's Studies Quarterly* 24 (3–4): 118–22.

Daly, A. 1994. "Gender Issues in Dance History Pedagogy." *Journal of Physical Education, Recreation and Dance* 65 (2): 34–35, 39.

Dils, A. 2004. "Sexuality and Sexual Identity: Critical Possibilities for Teaching Dance Appreciation and Dance History." *Journal of Dance Education* 4 (1): 10–16.

Doi, M. M. 2002. *Gesture, Gender, Nation: Dance and Social Change in Uzbekistan.* Westport, CT: Bergin and Garvey.

Ferdun, E. 1994. "Facing Gender Issues across the Curriculum." *Journal of Physical Education, Recreation and Dance* 65 (2): 46–47.

Flintoff, A. 1991. "Dance, Masculinity and Teacher Education." *British Journal of Physical Education,* Winter, 31–35.

Garber, E., D. Risner, R. Sandell, and M. Stankiewicz. 2006. "Gender Equity in the Visual Arts and Dance Education." In *Handbook for Achieving Gender Equity through Education,* ed. S. Klein, 359–80. Mahwah, NJ: Erlbaum.

Gold, R. 2001a. "Confessions of a Boy Dancer." *Dance Magazine* 125 (11): 52.

———. 2001b. "Dancing around the 'Problem' of Boys and Dance." *Discourse: Studies in the Cultural Politics of Education* 22: 213–25.

———. 2003a. "Being Someone Else: Using Dance in Anti-oppressive Teaching." *Educational Review* 55 (2): 211–23.

———. 2003b. "Moving and Belonging: Dance, Sport and Sexuality." *Sex Education* 3 (2): 105–18.

Green, J. 2000. "Emancipatory Pedagogy? Women's Bodies and the Creative Process in Dance." *Frontiers* 21 (3): 124–40.

———. 2001. "Socially Constructed Bodies in American Dance Classrooms." *Research in Dance Education* 2 (2): 155–73.

———. 2002–3. "Foucault and the Training of Docile Bodies in Dance Education." *Arts and Learning* 19 (1): 99–126.

———. 2004. "The Politics and Ethics of Health in Dance Education in the United States." In *Ethics and Politics Embodied in Dance*, ed. E. Antilla, S. Hamalainen, and L. Rouhianen, 65–76. Helsinki: Theatre Academy of Finland.

Griffin, P. 1995. "Homophobia in Sport: Addressing the Needs of Lesbian and Gay High School Athletes." In *The Gay Teen: Educational Practice and Theory for Lesbian, Gay, and Bisexual Adolescents*, ed. G. Unks, 53–66. New York: Routledge.

Hamilton, L. 1998. *Advice for Dancers: Emotional Counsel and Practical Strategies.* New York: Jossey-Bass.

Hanna, J. L. 1988. *Dance, Sex, and Gender: Signs of Identity, Dominance, Defiance, and Desire.* Chicago: University of Chicago Press.

Harris, D. 1997. *The Rise and Fall of Gay Culture.* New York: Hyperion.

Hasbrook, C. 1993. "Sociocultural Aspects of Physical Activity." *Research Quarterly for Exercise and Sport* 64 (1): 106–15.

Higher Education Arts Data Services. 2003. *Dance Annual Summary 2002–2003.* Reston, VA: National Association of Schools of Dance.

Horwitz, C. 1995. "Challenging Dominant Gender Ideology through Dance: Contact Improvisation." Ph.D. diss., University of Iowa, 1995. Abstract in *Dissertation Abstracts International*, 56 (06), 2023. Abstract retrieved June 11, 2005, from Proquest UMI/Digital Dissertations database.

Katz, J., and J. Earp. 1999. *Tough Guise: Violence, Media and the Crisis in Masculinity.* North Hampton, MA: Media Education Foundation.

Kerr-Berry, J. 1994. "Using the Power of Western African Dance to Combat Gender Issues." *Journal of Physical Education, Recreation and Dance* 65 (2): 44–45, 48.

Keyworth, S. 2001. "Critical Autobiography: 'Straightening' Out Dance Education." *Research in Dance Education* 2 (2): 117–37.

Kimmel, M. 2005. "What about the Boys?" In *Critical Social Issues in American Education: Democracy and Meaning in a Globalizing World*, ed. H. Shapiro and D. Purpel, 219–25. Mahwah, NJ: Erlbaum.

Kimmel, M., and M. Messner, eds. 2001. *Men's Lives.* Needham Heights, MA: Allyn and Bacon.

Kraus, R., S. Hilsendager, and B. Dixon. 1991. *History of the Dance in Art and Education.* 3rd ed. Englewood Cliffs, NJ: Prentice-Hall.

Lehikoinen, K. 2005. *Stepping Queerly: Discourses in Dance Education for Boys in Late 20th Century Finland.* Oxford: Peter Lang.

Lehne, G. 1976. "Homophobia among Men." In *The Forty-nine Percent Majority: The Male Sex Role*, ed. D. David and R. Brannon, 66–88. Reading, MA: Addison-Wesley.

Letts, W., and C. Nobles. 2003. "Embodied [by] Curriculum: A Critical Pedagogy of Embodiment." *Sex Education* 3 (2), 91–94.

Margolies, L., M. Becker, and K. Jackson-Brewer. 1987. "Internalized Homophobia in Gay Men." In *Homosexuality and Psychotherapy: A Practitioner's Handbook of Affirmative Models*, ed. J. Gonsiorek, 59–69. New York: Haworth Press.

Marques, I. 1998. "Dance Education in/and the Postmodern." In *Dance, Power, and Difference: Critical and Feminist Perspectives on Dance Education*, ed. S. Shapiro, 171–85. Champaign, IL: Human Kinetics.

Patrick, K. 2001. "Speaking Out: More Male Dancers Tell It Like It Is." *Dance Magazine* 125 (11): 53–55.

Pollack, W. 1999. *Real Boys: Rescuing Our Boys from the Myths of Boyhood*. New York: Random House.

Posey, E. 2002. "Dance Education in Dance Schools in the Private Sector: Meeting the Demands of the Marketplace." *Journal of Dance Education* 2 (2): 43–49.

Risner, D. 2001. "Blurring the Boundaries: Hope and Possibility in the Presence of the Necessary Stranger in Gay Liberation." Ph.D. diss., University of North Carolina at Greensboro, 2001. Abstract in *Dissertation Abstracts International*, 62 (03), 1236.

———. 2002a. "Male Participation and Sexual Orientation in Dance Education: Revisiting the Open Secret." *Journal of Dance Education* 2 (3): 84–92.

———. 2002b. "Re-educating Dance Education to Its Homosexuality: An Invitation for Critical Analysis and Professional Unification." *Research in Dance Education* 3 (2): 181–87.

———. 2002c. "Rehearsing Heterosexuality: Unspoken Truths in Dance Education." *Dance Research Journal* 34 (2): 63–81.

———. 2004. "Dance, Sexuality, and Education Today: Observations for Dance Educators." *Journal of Dance Education* 4 (1): 5–9.

———. 2005. "Dance and Sexuality: Opportunities for Teaching and Learning in Dance Education." *Journal of Dance Education* 5 (2): 41–42.

———. 2006. "Critical Social Issues in Dance Education." In *International Handbook for Research in Arts Education*, ed. L. Bresler, 965–82. New York: Springer.

———. 2007. "Rehearsing Masculinity: Challenging the 'Boy Code' in Dance Education." Research in Dance Education 8 (2): 139–53.

Risner, D., Godfrey, H., and Simmons, L. 2004. "The Impact of Sexuality in Contemporary Culture: An Interpretive Study of Perceptions and Choices in Private Sector Dance Education." *Journal of Dance Education* 4 (1): 23–32.

Risner, D., and S. Thompson. 2005. "HIV/AIDS in Dance Education: A Pilot Study in Higher Education." *Journal of Dance Education* 5 (2): 70–76.

Rofes, E. 1995. "Making Our Schools Safe for Sissies." In *The Gay Teen*, ed. G. Unks, 79–84. New York: Routledge.

Sanderson, P. 1996. "Dance within the National Curriculum for Physical Education of England and Wales." *European Physical Education Review* 2 (1): 54–63.

———. 2001. "Age and Gender Issues in Adolescent Attitudes to Dance." *European Physical Education Review* 7 (2): 117–36.

Schaffman, K. 2001. "From the Margins to the Mainstream: Contact Improvisation and the Commodification of Touch." Ph.D. diss., University of California at Riverside, 2001. Abstract in *Dissertation Abstracts International, 62* (07), 2270. Abstract retrieved March 21, 2005, from Proquest UMI/Digital Dissertations database.

Sedgwick, E. 1990. *Epistemology of the Closet.* Berkley: University of California Press.

Shapiro, S. 1998. "Toward Transformative Teachers: Critical and Feminist Perspectives in Dance Education." In *Dance, Power, and Difference: Critical and Feminist Perspectives on Dance Education,* ed. S. Shapiro, 7–21. Champaign, IL: Human Kinetics.

———. 2004. "Recovering Girlhood: A Pedagogy of Embodiment." *Journal of Dance Education* 4 (1): 35–36.

Smith, C. 1998. "On Authoritarianism in the Dance Classroom." In *Dance, Power, and Difference: Critical and Feminist Perspectives on Dance Education,* ed. S. Shapiro, 123–46). Champaign, IL: Human Kinetics.

Spurgeon, D. 1999. "The Men's Movement." Paper presented at Congress on Research in Dance, Pomona College, Claremont, CA, December.

Stinson, S. 1998a. "Places Where I've Been: Reflections on Issues of Gender in Dance Education, Research, and Administration." *Choreography and Dance* 5 (1): 117–27.

———. 1998b. "Seeking a Feminist Pedagogy for Children's Dance." In *Dance, Power, and Difference: Critical and Feminist Perspectives on Dance Education,* ed. S. Shapiro, 23–47). Champaign, IL: Human Kinetics.

———. 2001. "Voices from Adolescent Males." *DACI in Print* 2, November: 4–6.

———. 2005. "The Hidden Curriculum of Gender in Dance Education." *Journal of Dance Education* 5 (2): 51–57.

Stinson, S., D. Blumenfeld-Jones, and J. Van Dyke. 1990. "Voices of Young Women Dance Students: An Interpretive Study of Meaning in Dance." *Dance Research Journal* 22 (2): 13–22.

Thomas, H. 1996. "Dancing the Difference." *Women's Studies International Forum* 19 (5): 505–11.

———. *The Body, Dance and Cultural Theory.* New York: Palgrave Macmillan.

Van Dyke, J. 1992. *Modern Dance in a Postmodern World: An Analysis of Federal Arts Funding and Its Impact on the Field of Modern Dance.* Reston, VA: American Alliance for Health, Physical Education, Recreation, and Dance.

———. 1996. "Gender and Success in the American Dance World." *Women's Studies International Forum* 19 (5): 535–43.

Williams, D. 2003. *Examining Psychosocial Issues of Adolescent Male Dancers.* Unpublished doctoral dissertation, Marywood University. UMI 2090242.

DAVID ALLAN AND MICHEL GERVAIS

Allan was raised in St. Louis, Missouri, and went to the National Ballet School of Canada in Toronto when he was 14. He became a choreographer while dancing as a soloist with the National Ballet of Canada from 1977 to 1989, during the years Erik Bruhn and Rudolf Nureyev were associated with the company. Now a professor at the University of California, Irvine, he has had his works performed by many companies, among them the National Ballet of Canada, New York City Ballet, and Rome Opera Ballet. Hong Kong Ballet has recently staged his evening-length Cinderella, *which was filmed for television.*

Gervais grew up in northern Ontario and pursued a career as a dancer with many companies, among them Theatre Ballet of Canada, Les Ballets Jazz de Montréal, Feld Ballets/NY, California Riverside Ballet, and Ballet Pacifica. He has worked widely as a teacher and ballet master, often assisting David Allan and staging his ballets. He has been a popular choreographer for the American Ballet Theatre's Southern California summer intensive program and has had works performed by California Riverside Ballet and Festival Ballet Theatre (California).

Allan and Gervais met when Allan was a guest choreographer for Theatre Ballet of Canada in the late 1980s and have been together ever since. They are based in Irvine, California, and continue to work both together and separately in the dance world.

DAVID: Our experiences with the whole masculinity thing were so different as we were growing up—I feel like I was very lucky not to be tortured by that whole question like Michel was. I knew I was gay at an early age, and I knew I wanted to be a dancer, and nothing anyone said bothered me. Not that I didn't have trouble along the way, but Michel had a very different experience.

MICHEL: When I got into dance at about eight or nine back in Sudbury, Ontario— the nickel-mining capital of the world, by the way—I felt I had to keep it a secret. I first did gymnastics, and that was okay, but when that place closed down, I did tap.

Gervais in a 1984
studio snapshot, just
before joining Les
Ballets Jazz in
Montreal. Used with
permission.

I didn't enjoy that, but I think it was because I didn't feel challenged—I felt like it
was way too easy. And my tap teacher, Miss Buffy, was blond and so sweet
I couldn't quite take it. I didn't like being spoken to as a child in the cutesy tones she
used, so that was a turn-off. I quit tap. What I really wanted to do was to be an
actor. During recess, I would write plays with a few girls in my class, and we'd
sometimes present them to the class.

   Then I got inspired to dance again from watching the June Taylor dancers on
The Carol Burnett Show. I said, "I want to do that," so I started taking jazz at 11.
My sister took ballet, and I wasn't a huge fan, but my jazz teachers said to be a good
dancer I had to take ballet. It wasn't really good training. Back then, I only seemed
to have those ballet teachers who were too stiff. I wanted to move and dance, and
I felt constrained by ballet, just stuck, and I didn't enjoy that at all. I wasn't serious
about ballet for a long time; I just took it to help me improve my jazz. My dream
was to be on Broadway. I took voice lessons, I did musical theater, I was singing
Latin masses when I was eight years old.

I used to play superheroes with another guy I ended up at the same studio with, and I'd always be Cat Woman and Bat Girl—I liked doing the female roles because they always had the better costumes and cooler powers. I found them more appealing. And I always liked Mr. Spock better than Captain Kirk—out of all those television characters. That macho hero, "solve things with your fists" kind of image was always a big, big turn-off. Even in ballet, I always thought the swan was more appealing than the prince, so much more interesting. Except I wish I had gotten to play the prince in Matthew Bourne's *Swan Lake* because he's so flawed, and I love flawed characters, because to me that's so much more real. In that version, the swan is probably too macho and butch and heroic for me, oddly enough. That doesn't suit me. Although I did like the character of Don Juan in *Carmen*—to get to murder somebody onstage, that was a fun challenge, one of the best roles I did, but he was also a very, very flawed character.

There was a huge stigma about taking ballet or dance at the time and place where I was growing up. But even before I started dancing, I got teased a lot at school. I was an extremely effeminate boy, so much so that people would mistake me for a girl. Actually, ballet butched me up—it made me physically stronger. I got sick a lot as a kid, and I was weak. School was an absolute nightmare, my whole life. Whether it was because I was gay and was slightly effeminate—or very effeminate, depending on who you talked to—I don't know. My parents tried to change me while I was growing up. They were like, "You can't walk around with your hands like this" [broken wrist]. They tried to teach me how to be more masculine, saying, "If you behave like that, the boys are going to tease you," and all that. And in church, my father was very, very Catholic. I used to tease him when he made certain comments and say, "That's very Catholic of you but not very Christian."

My mother confronted me one time when she found some magazines I'd been hiding. She said, "You're reading the wrong magazines. Boys should want to see girls." My reaction was, "Surprise, surprise!"—I was a little flippant at the time. Basically, she asked if I wanted to talk to the priest, which I didn't—what could be done? They ended up saying, "We don't approve of that lifestyle, but we love you, we just don't want to talk about it." I knew the subject would be taboo. Eventually, when I came home late and my mother asked me where I'd been, I'd say, "You don't want to know." David's reaction from his mother was very different; she gave him confidence to be who he was, because she never made him self-conscious of how he came off to other people—it was completely unimportant to her. For me, it was different. I was brought up to feel ashamed of what I did.

DAVID: I got into dance because when I was nine in St. Louis, Missouri, I saw Margot Fonteyn and Rudolf Nureyev in *Romeo and Juliet* in 1969, and that was it. I think I levitated off my seat when I saw Nureyev, and after five minutes, I turned to my mother and said, "Where can I do this, I have to learn how to do this." I went home and tried to do all his jumps, and I kept bugging my parents to take me to ballet for six months. My stepfather was an ex-marine, black belt in karate, and let's just say he didn't care for this—he used to scream at me about it! But I didn't even like him, so I didn't care what he thought. I really was a mischievous brat who had his own destiny—I wasn't good as Puck in Ashton's *Midsummer's Night's Dream* later for nothing. I was going to be a dancer and that was it.

I did get into some trouble at one point, when I was about 10 or 11 years old, after I'd taken ballet a while, practically every day of the week, once I started. I was so proud of what I could do—I could turn, I could jump, I was getting muscles in my legs—I wanted to dance at talent day at my school. It was a junior high school in St. Louis, where everyone was more or less middle to lower-middle class. I was so excited about doing "A Dance from David," my first choreography. So, when I came out in my pretty white tights, there was a big roar of laughter. I didn't know why, but I just thought, "Well, they must like me." I didn't remember people laughing at the ballet, but it was a response I could hear, and I took it as encouragement. They'd get quiet during my leaps or turns, but when I did the other steps, there was this roaring laughter again. It never occurred to me to be insulted or discouraged. It wasn't till later that I met some guys in the hallway of my school who were making rude comments, that it was anything negative. Even then, I didn't get that "You're that dancer guy" would turn into being thrown down the stairs. But fortunately, that only happened that once. I don't know why it didn't bother me that much—it's like I was operating in a bubble of self-confidence and their opinions of me never really sunk in.

When I was 14, I got the opportunity to take a ballet class with the Stuttgart Ballet when they were touring—that was when Richard Cragun and Marcia Haydée were there, and they asked me if I wanted to go back to Stuttgart to go to school. But going to Germany was not even considered for a little Jewish boy from St. Louis. So then they suggested School of American Ballet in New York and offered to phone them to recommend me for a scholarship. But they had no academic program there. My parents couldn't afford New York, and they were very interested in my having a good education. So then, they thought of the School of the National Ballet of Canada, which does have its own academic classes, so they called there. The director, Betty Oliphant, paid for a ticket for me to come to audition the next day, and I went on my own. It was the second day of the summer session, and my first teacher was Erik Bruhn—his picture was on my wall at home, and there I was in his class, I couldn't believe it. I was mesmerized. After that class, Erik called me over and asked where I was from. He had this really low voice, and he said, "You did really well. I'll see you sometime again." I didn't see him again for another few years at the school, but I did end up working with him when I joined the company.

When I first got to Canada, it was all very strange to me. When I went up to the residence hall, there was my first roommate, Gaétan, hanging out of the window stretching his leg on the ledge and playing his guitar, singing in French. It was so international—a guitar-playing dancer! I played the saxophone; it was like I found another home. I was the only boy in school who danced back in St. Louis, and all of a sudden I was in the middle of boys who all became professional dancers. Some of them became my best friends, but there was one guy who reminded me of the bullies who threw me down the stairs—he had a kind of gruff, butch thing. He was always pushing the fact that he could jump the highest, and I said the wrong thing early on, just tossing it off without thinking—"You don't jump any higher than anyone else, you just take off slower—you don't do it with the music." I mean, he grabbed me and shoved me up against the locker and said in this tough voice, "Nobody asked your opinion." I apologized—"I'm sorry...I didn't mean to offend..." And all of a sudden, I thought, "Oh my god, he wears tights and he could kill me." So you've got bullies at the ballet—I had a South American dancer once later try to kill me! Eventually, I just learned to avoid the macho tough guys like that.

So I became aware that there were both feminine and masculine guys in the ballet. I knew I was gay from an early age, and it never seemed like a problem to me—I thank my mother to this day for not putting it in my head as a problem, not like the Catholics who were telling Michel, "You're going to go to hell." As my relatives found out I was going to have this career—and later I was dancing with my idol, Rudolf Nureyev—they just wanted tickets; they were just proud of what I was doing. They never had time to worry about my sexuality or masculinity; they just knew I was being successful and they were proud of me. I never worried about maybe being effeminate—until one occasion I'll never forget, when the company was on tour in Ottawa.

I was 18 and a half years old, and I was in the ballroom scene of John Cranko's *Romeo and Juliet*, that dramatic scene where the men carried pillows with long things hanging off their costumes, all very formal. I thought it was the frou-frouest thing I had ever seen in my life. I kept stepping on these trailing bits with the beads

Allan as Alain in Frederick Ashton's
La fille mal gardée, in the mid-1980s,
when he was dancing with the
National Ballet of Canada.
Photograph by David Street,
courtesy of the National Ballet of
Canada Archives.

on them, so I started flipping the tails around and evidently I wasn't staying in line or kneeling in a straightforward enough fashion—I was always flicking the costume. So afterward the director at the time, Celia Franca, came to our dressing room, said good evening to everyone in her very formal voice, then switched to a stern kind of shout when she said, "David Allan, come here!" She only came to the corps dressing room when she was pissed. She said, "Come here, now!" She'd never really scared me before, but it was like there was froth coming out of her mouth. She just looked down at me, standing there in my little towel, and almost shouted, "Don't be so sissified! Pull yourself together!" And I went, "Okay, sorry." [small voice] All of a sudden I just collapsed.

When she left and I turned around, the other guys were all, "Ooo-oo-oo-oo, you're in big trouble." At first, I got all huffy and said, "Well, I've never been called a sissy before." And everybody in the dressing room said, "But you *are* a sissy." [laughing] This is the first time I was ever made aware that's what they thought—all the gay and straight men, all recited it at the same time. I didn't have a comeback joke. It was the first time I thought, "Oh my god, I look like a faggot onstage." I left the theater and felt really depressed. I was up till 4:30 in the morning, mortified that everybody thought I was a sissy. Because I never thought of myself that way—I could turn, I could jump. Boys coming up in my era, we were outdoing men from the previous generation, we were getting that "new world" technique. For me it was a kind of defining and devastating moment. It was the first time since I got into the company that I reexamined how I was doing everything. I'd think, "Oh my god, in *Swan Lake* I looked like this or that." I was taken out of that *Romeo and Juliet* scene and never did it again. So I actually did try to redefine myself and my masculinity at that moment when Celia Franca humiliated me. I looked at every role I did, I thought through every step I did—I realized that as a peasant, I let my foot flip up, or my eyes were looking the wrong way. I was all of a sudden like a dancer being observed through one of those one-way mirrors, like I was being investigated by a cop—or Celia Franca—patrolling the borders of masculinity.

MICHEL: I felt that way my whole life.

DAVID: I never realized anyone felt that way—I never felt that way. She made a statement that was horrifying to me, that I could possibly look like that in any ballet. And in that way, it made me realize that in some roles, I needed to be a bit more manly, and in others, I could be more flamboyant—either way, it had to be a choice. I couldn't just be David Allan in every role, that wasn't good enough anymore. It wasn't really about my sexuality—or, I guess it was, but only about my sexuality onstage, not as a person in life. And everybody thought, "Oh, you're taking this thing really well." I just took it as a learning experience in my career. I had a lot of learning experiences back then—being in the company, getting new roles, traveling all over the world. Everything was about my dancing. I wasn't interested in anything else in the world but dancing. So it actually helped me redefine what I looked like. It helped me realize, too, that I couldn't live just on natural talent anymore. I had to be a thinking dancer and think about my portrayals of a role. Everything about what I looked like became very important. It helped me as a dancer, and it didn't change me on the street. It didn't touch my personality; it didn't make me different as a person.

MICHEL: Because it was a dance critique, it wasn't a personality critique. I took it that way, too, eventually, but it took a while. I kind of got criticized on all fronts, and I felt that even in my dance career, everyone was trying to butch me up—my family, my friends, in the arts as well. I got told how to dance, like "You can't let your arm go flowing so much or so high. You have to control it or place it." But that's also part of technique, being in complete control of your body. I heard, "Don't dance like a girl, you have to dance like a man," absolutely all the time, my whole career. But not usually when I was doing choreography, only in class. Because in class I would let myself be very exaggerated and have a blast by being over-the-top, having fun with it. But getting the style of the choreography—that was probably my greatest gift as a dancer. I can't recall any choreographer who felt I didn't adapt to their style, in modern, in ballet or anything.

DAVID: I always felt that throughout his career, it was so much easier when he was with a choreographer with a specific style and specific movement he could emulate. He could be inspirational to that choreographer, finding ways to move. But when he was learning something that was already set, it took longer to find a way of doing it, a voice. So that was something that made him more insecure. Whereas choreographers like Lynn Taylor-Corbett or Juan Antonio or me, we've always been attracted to Michel because he doesn't come with a preconceived idea of himself when he comes into the studio. It's kind of vague—even the sexuality is kind of vague, hard to peg as a choreographer. So in that way, he's extremely flexible and you can mold him in a ballet.

MICHEL: But if someone asked me to "be myself" in a ballet, that was always a problem. I'd get told to dance like a man, not like a girl, but it didn't translate sometimes. What really worked for me was something Lynn Cox [a ballet mistress at Marin Ballet and at Riverside Ballet] said, one day when I was working on a solo in David's ballet *Etc!*. There was a point when I turned my back on the audience and ran to prepare for a *manège* [a series of jumps and turns], and when it wasn't right, she said, "You just have to be wide and big, so you take the audience with you." And suddenly, it was more about communication with the audience, it's about what you're saying physically, and sometimes with the flitty, mushy kind of thing, you lose the audience because you're not projecting enough, you're not being big and solid enough. And it finally clicked for me, the way she approached it. It wasn't about being butch or feminine, it was really about using your full energy to draw the audience in and keep them there. So it would be kind of selfish to remain in yourself—it was about communication.

For me, I always had to play the roles—I always had to be in love with a woman onstage, and I had a theater background that was very, very helpful. I've always been very empathic, so I'd just put myself into the character, so I could look at the girl—even if she drove me crazy and I wanted to throw her across the room if we didn't get along—and like Method acting, I could put myself in a state of becoming that role and making yourself have those emotions. I did have the ability to do that. And through dance, through ballet, I got so much stronger physically, I got control

Allan and Gervais celebrating Gervais's retirement from dancing in June 2001. Photograph by Leslie Klein. Used with permission.

over my body. So I also grew in confidence. I think the main thing that made me a more masculine man is my confidence. When I stopped worrying about what everybody else thought about me, I started to find myself, and I found that my self was not supermacho—I'm a very soft person, friendly, outgoing. But I didn't feel like I had to pretend anything.

When people don't know that I'm gay, I'm shocked—anytime during my life, because I think everyone knows. Of course in the 80s, when I was dressing more flamboyantly, it wasn't hard. But, you know, the more outlandish and crazy I looked, the more people left me alone. It made me feel safer—because I scared them back then, whereas they had always scared me. To some degree, I was paranoid, but, you know, when I stopped being paranoid, people didn't come to the conclusion that I was gay as quickly anymore. When I first came out, I went, "Oh, I'm gay, so I have to be flamboyant, I have to be bitchy, I have to make sarcastic jokes all the time." To me, that was part of gay culture, and I had to fit in. But I was so uncomfortable. I was 17, so I didn't have any idea who I was anyway. I started dating David when I was 22, so already being in a committed relationship at that age, I didn't have to be "out there" anymore, trying to find a mate. So in a lot of ways, I could just find myself.

DAVID: He didn't feel like he had to be in the gay culture anymore—I was never in the gay culture, ever, ever in my life. I mean, like "gay life in the city." I was in gay life as a dancer in a way when I was in the National Ballet of Canada, but I always had a lot of heterosexual friends, too. If I had just gone out with the gay guys in the company, I wouldn't have felt like an individual. My best friends from the company for years have been both gay and straight, as many of each. My friends are made because of our relationships, not sexual preference. I think everyone in ballet companies has a different experience, so it would be hard to generalize about who hangs out with a subgroup and whether it's gay or straight.

MICHEL: Even at 22, I was still trying to discover myself, and as I became more comfortable in my skin, I became more masculine. Because I got to the point that I could accept the fact that I was a gay man. And I realized, just because you're attracted to men doesn't mean you have to put on these airs and "act gay." It was hard for me—growing up I had no role models—my father is extremely effeminate

DAVID: We're talking Armand in *La Cage aux Folles* here.

MICHEL: He was always attracted to men, I later found out, but he had never acted on it. He swears he just fell in love with my mother. But when she left him, because she came out of the closet—

DAVID: That's a story for the Oprah Winfrey show—after three children, three grandchildren, and 27 years of marriage, *both* of his parents eventually came out of the closet. You know, they could have helped the son who wanted to join *The Carol Burnett Show* when he was growing up a little more. His mother was hiding her masculinity, and his father was hiding his femininity, so who was he supposed to follow?

MICHEL: It's a strange story, especially after the way I grew up. As a family, when we watched TV, we would criticize everyone, and if you saw a man who was suspect, it was talked about—they were constantly gossiping and criticizing people. It was always "You can't behave like that." They made me so aware of how people perceived me. You know, when I see father-son scenes on TV when they express love for each other, I cry like a baby. My father always loved me, kissed us good night, but I have a feeling, probably, that as much as he said he loved me, he didn't accept me, who I was. I didn't realize at the time—it was because we were so similar, and he wasn't accepting himself. When he came out of the closet, he came running to me, and I was angry. I found it hard to forgive him.

DAVID: I was shocked. I said, "You can't forgive him?" This is when I found how truly tormented he was as a teenager. We had talked about it, but I don't think I had an understanding of it till then.

MICHEL: It was hard for me. But my whole theory is, when you're coming out and you're troubled with it, it takes you a long time to accept it. When I came out to everyone, there were different responses—my brother said he wasn't mad I was gay, but he felt deceived, that I had lied to him. It takes everyone some time to accept it—they know you as someone, and all of a sudden that reality changes for them, as it does for yourself when you come out. It's understandable; I've never been angry it took people a while. And I even got over it with my parents. We were close again after I came out and before they did. At first, I blamed myself for their coming out because I figured if I hadn't come out—if I stayed closeted, they would have stayed closeted. I felt that somehow I made them aware of this possibility—which was complete garbage, but you go through these things. I never told them this, and I never talked to them about how they hadn't made it easy for me; I didn't want to lay a guilt trip on them. It was okay.

DAVID: One night when I came late from rehearsal with Douglas Becker, who was staging some [William] Forsythe at UCI, we came into the living room to find Michel sitting in his boxer shorts, eating potato chips, playing his Game Boy, and watching wrestling at the same time, with his beer in a cup holder. Douglas, being in his lofty European mode now, turns to me as we come in and puts his hand on my chest to stop me and says in a low voice, "Oh my god, David, your boyfriend is a closet heterosexual." [laughter]

MICHEL: That's been the thing with me all the time, really—I felt I didn't fit in anywhere. I like the Barbra Streisand, Liza Minnelli, and show tunes thing and whatever, musical theater, opera; I like that whole side of the world. Growing up I would play with Barbies, but I also have the other side—I love rock and roll, hard rock, sometimes heavy metal stuff, it's such a great release and outlet; I like certain sports, even wrestling, which is more entertainment than sport. I like certain things that are considered very masculine or "straight," but it's always upset me that when I was trying to pretend to be straight, I wasn't accepted, then when I came out, in the gay community, it was "How could you like that music?" or whatever.

DAVID: Like there were prerequisites for being a homosexual.

MICHEL: It felt like no matter what I did, I never fit in.

DAVID: And the problem is that he cares; I never cared if I fit in, it didn't matter to me.

MICHEL: Well, I don't care so much now, but it took a long time. And I still have trouble with that, not caring. When it comes to talking about our relationship, for instance, I move it slowly—it depends so much on the situation. I moved around a lot in my career, and I used to worry about board members of a ballet company or people I don't know. And when I mention it, it's always quickly, in passing—"Oh, my partner's doing this or that," very matter-of-factly, not announcing, "My boyfriend does this or that…"

DAVID: We've worked together a lot in many places, he's been a ballet master, then a choreographer, and he's assisted me when I was staging ballets in Hong Kong and at New York City Ballet; he was a dancer and assistant both when we worked with Riverside Ballet. I think we've succeeded in working as individuals in that situation, having a working relationship when we were working. Michel's more of a fact person, and I'm not—I think we're a very nice balance together.

MICHEL: I've had a lot of parents of students who've suggested that David and I should adopt because we'd make such good parents. We've gotten more of that kind of thing than the bigoted response. And we've had some dancers who are maybe just coming out who tell us they'd like to have a relationship like ours someday. It's very nice of them, very sweet.

DAVID: I don't think we've felt that anyone feels any kind of weirdness about us in that way, the opposite actually.

MICHEL: But I've always been very cautious, mostly with parents, I think. I've met some strongly religious families, and no one's ever said, "You're a sinner, you're going to hell" or anything like that, and I haven't encountered any open animosity—I think if they've thought those things, they keep it to themselves. I don't think we're very threatening. I've had uncomfortableness come from dancers more than outsiders, actually, like rehearsing a duet with a guy who thinks I might come on to him or something, and I have to put him at ease. You actually get more criticism from the gay dancers when it comes to being masculine—like they'll say, "Oh my god, you're such a queen when you do that." But as far as real prejudice, it's not that serious. That's maybe why I chose dance over other art forms. I thought, "Well, maybe I can be myself there." Because I thought it was okay to be gay and be a dancer. With acting or singing it wasn't that way, somehow, even though there are gay-friendly communities in theater. If you were heading toward a film or television career, for instance, you didn't want to seem gay. Maybe that, subconsciously, played a small role in why I ended up in dance.

I don't think David and I have ever been in a situation where we've actually had to hide our relationship—I'm just shocked by that, really. But I think there is a difference when it comes to how free gay men can be versus heterosexuals. They can be very casual mentioning a wife or husband right away, whereas I wait about a month for you to get to know me and feel like I can mention that I have a partner.

DAVID: Michel is much more aware of things like that than I am. When we're in San Francisco, for instance, if we're in the Castro, we can hold hands, but if we're near the Opera House or in Marin County, and I reach for his hand, he'll pull away. I get mad because I don't get it.

MICHEL: I have a friend who was stabbed, I've had experiences that make me cautious.

DAVID: See, I don't get that, why don't I get that?

MICHEL: You're lucky, I think, you're very, very lucky.

3

Is Dance a Man's Sport Too?

The Performance of Athletic-Coded Masculinity on the Concert Dance Stage

MAURA KEEFE

Mickey Mantle, 5 feet 11 inches, 195 pounds. New York Yankee. Home run hitter, Hall of Fame 1974. Johnny Unitas, 6 feet 1 inch, 195 pounds. One of the greatest quarterbacks of his and possibly all time. Seventeen years with the Baltimore Colts. Pro Football Hall of Fame, 1979. Sugar Ray Robinson, lifetime record, 128 wins, 1 loss, 84 knockouts.

I could tell you more about these three men. I could tell you the locations of Robinson's fights, how many passes Unitas completed, or the number of at bats that Mantle had. These kinds of statistics and histories are readily available for athletes. On the other hand, we're not certain how tall Gene Kelly was; we don't talk about how much Ted Shawn might have weighed; nor do we know how many turns, leaps, or jumps Vaslav Nijinsky successfully completed.

I will, of course, explain why that list of athletes is relevant to concert dance at all, so far from the field, the ring, the ballpark. But before I do that, I point out that the men on that list, Mantle, Unitas, and Sugar Ray, are figures who suggest to many a kind of "authentic masculinity," not only because of their physical skills but also because of their connection to sports in the United States.

In this essay, I argue that choreographers in the United States have again and again drawn inspiration from both athletic themes and the athletes themselves for works on the concert dance stage in order to give their dances a sense of validity. Further, I suggest that the genuine presence, or "realness," of the athletes works to counter long-held anxieties about the effeminacy of the male dancer. I have organized my thoughts about a selection of dances chronologically, starting with Vaslav Nijinsky's *Jeux* (1913) and then tracing a repeated, unchanging, and I think heretofore unexamined use of male athletes in dance. First, I discuss Ted Shawn's *Olympiad* (1936); second, a television documentary, *Dancing—a Man's Game* (1958), written, directed by, and starring Gene Kelly; and, finally, Twyla Tharp's *Dancing Is a Man's Sport, Too* (1980).

Why bring dance and sports together for comparison? Obviously, they differ in the cultural value placed on them. Concert or theatrical dance is thought of as "high art," and sports as popular culture. Dance is about art, and sports are about winning. Despite these differences, in many ways athletics and dance honor the same things. They are embodied practices, studied, trained for, rehearsed, and performed. Observers talk about the physical beauty of athleticism and the artistry of both dancers and athletes.[1] Critics acknowledge that live performances are the best way to view both. Fans discuss technique, virtuosic performances, and the grace, strength, endurance, power, subtlety, and sweat of both dancers and athletes. As sport and culture historian Michael D. Giardina writes in his *Sporting Pedagogies*, "Sport is thus every bit a part of our trans/national landscape, a place inhabited by heroes and villains . . . bold and beautiful, a history of the present told through box scores and movie scripts. . . . It is one of the strongest ties that bind us to previous and future generations."[2]

This is certainly not the first discussion of dance using sports or of sports using dance. For example, in their book *Sport, Dance and Embodied Identities* (2003), coeditors Noel Dyck and Eduardo Archetti draw on scholars from both dance and sports. In their introduction they write:

Bringing together sport and dance as ethnographically distinctive but analytically commensurable forms of body culture and social practice represents a departure from previous ways of thinking about these two fields within anthropology and other disciplines. Sport and dance are conventionally viewed in the West as residing within separate and even opposed cultural realms. Yet they share not only a common status as techniques of the body (Mauss 1973), but also a vital capacity to express and reformulate identities and meanings through their practised movements and scripted forms. Sport and dance spark widespread participation, critical appreciation and endless interpretation by performers and their audiences. Indeed, the embodied practices of athletes and dancers afford not merely pleasure and entertainment but powerful means for celebrating existing social arrangements and cultural ideals or for imagining and advocating new ones.[3]

While the collection proves very useful in updating the seminal essay by Marcel Mauss mentioned by these authors, for the most part the 12 essays consider dance and sports as separate but equal bodily practices. The bodies playing the sports discussed, such as handball, badminton, and football, are not the same bodies that salsa or tango. Further, none of the essays focuses on sports or dance in the United States, where I would contend there remains a particularly strong anxiety about men in dance. Even if the editors of the collection are more concerned with sports on the one hand and dance on the other, without any overlap, no discussion is raised about overt or even subtle homophobia in the dance world or the sports world.

Many people in the United States have a relatively sophisticated literacy about sports. People deal with a variety of sports as both spectators and participants. Growing up, Americans play them in school and as extracurricular activities. Even when people drop their participatory relationship with sports, sports continue to play a major role in the popular imagination. Many Americans watch them on television, attend amateur and/or professional sporting events, and read about them in newspapers and magazines. The literacy learned early continues to be put to use and further develops as fans discuss a great game or player. Even people who are not invested in sports often display familiarity with famous sports figures.

Dance, on the other hand, has long been considered challenging and threatening to many people. Not everyone grows up participating in it or watching dance, especially not the predominant theatrical forms of modern dance and ballet. A majority of students at any given dance studio will probably be girls and women. Rarely does a dancer enter the popular imagination, except perhaps someone like Mikhail Baryshnikov, and in his case, long after his high-profile ballet career, it is probably for his role as a paramour on *Sex and the City.*

To set up my discussion of the use of athletes and athletic themes on the concert dance stage, I begin with an examination of Vaslav Nijinsky's *Jeux* (1913), which translates from the French as "game" or "play." *Jeux* may or may not have been about athletes and sports, although its costumes and props definitely suggest tennis, and audiences then (and now) may have termed the performers "athletes." Nijinsky, the Russian dancer and choreographer perhaps best known for his *L'après-midi d'un faune* and *Le sacre du printemps*, abandoned *Jeux* after only eight performances. Despite its lack of popularity at the time of its short performance life, there is quite a bit of historical evidence about the dance, including anecdotes by performers, several sketches of the dance in performance, a series of black-and-white studio photographs, and considerable published criticism. Dance historian Barbara Barker, who lamented the overshadowing of *Jeux* by *Sacre*, remarked that *Jeux* was new and significant in that "it was the first ballet to use modern man as a theme."[4] In *Jeux*, Nijinsky used sports as a metaphor for the personal interaction among the three performers—Nijinsky himself and two female dancers. Dressed in stylized tennis clothes of the time and occasionally armed with tennis rackets, the three dancers appear in different combinations, their angular movements punctuated with fragmented gestures and stillness. The dance begins and ends with a tennis ball bouncing across the stage.[5]

The content of the dance was highly experimental. Ballets had long explored themes of fairy tales and otherworldly creatures. Whose idea was it, and what does it represent? Who suggested this more modern theme, to be of this world and not the other? Dance historian Lynn Garafola cites this account, long attributed to Nijinsky: "The close study I have made of polo, golf, tennis, has convinced me that these sports are not only a healthy form of relaxation, but that they are equally creators of plastic beauty."[6] This statement, which may not have been made by the shy choreographer, does suggest that he looked at the movement practices around him and saw more than the game; he saw the possibility of art.

Nijinsky recorded another perspective of *Jeux* in his diary: "The story of this ballet is about three young men making love to each other. . . . I told Diaghilev my idea. Diaghilev likes to say that he created the ballet, because he likes to be praised. . . . The *Faun* is me, and *Jeux* is the life of which Diaghilev dreamed. In the ballet, the two girls represent the two boys and the young man is Diaghilev. I changed the characters, as love between three men could not be represented on stage."[7] Another opinion about *Jeux*'s creation comes from one of Nijinsky's biographers, Françoise Reiss, who writes: "Nijinsky dreamt of expressing in the ballet the essence of that athletic lyricism, whose future he foresaw in the modern world."[8] Finally, in his lavish coffee-table book *Nijinsky Dancing*, Lincoln Kirstein, writer, arts patron, and cofounder of the New York City Ballet, recounts this version of the impetus for *Jeux*:

> Diaghilev asked the portraitist Jacques-Émile Blanche to suggest an archetype for Nijinsky that would canonize him as modern man. A Marxist might have chosen the mechanic, but this was for the future. Blanche selected the leisure-class sportsman. Revival of the Olympic Games in the 1890's, their recent presentation in Stockholm in 1912, gave fresh meaning to the idea of sports on a semiheroic level. Bakst in designing the décor first imagined Nijinsky as a soccer player, but this was too specific. In the performance Nijinsky leaped onstage in pursuit of a big tossed ball, but wearing his own uniform, a dancer's practice-dress, and white rather than black trousers. The racket, held as a symbol on his entrance, never came into play.[9]

Kirstein's understanding of the role of the athlete as "an archetype" for the future is of particular interest. The trope of the athlete as modern man is important because it's dramatically different from the princes of ballets of the past. There is no doubt that the image of the male athlete persists as a key iconic representation of masculinity.

I have read with interest reports that Nijinsky became obsessed with tennis, going to courts near the rehearsal space to study not only the movement but also the way to best hold the racket. Nijinsky's fascination with tennis might have led audience members and critics to expect a kind of verisimilitude. There is a frequent and, to me, surprisingly disparaging tone used not only by reviewers in Nijinsky's time but even by one of his biographers about his lack of understanding of the real game of tennis.

A review published in France in May 1913 seemed to lampoon the ballet for its stylization of tennis: "Summer sports. A number of readers have enquired about the rules of Russian tennis." A brief description of the dance follows, and the review concludes, "The purpose of this sport is to develop suppleness of the neck, wrist, and ankles."[10] These comments are startling because at the time of the premiere of *Jeux*, no one expected any authenticity or realness in dance-making.[11] This comparison of the real game of tennis and *Jeux* continued when Nijinsky biographer Richard Buckle wrote parenthetically in 1971, "In fact, since tennis-players use one hand and not two, this movement was more like golf—but Nijinsky hardly knew the difference between the two games."[12]

An aside here. Although I think none of us should tell the Williams sisters that tennis players use only one hand, not two, it's worth noting that tennis movement vocabulary changes, rendering moot Buckle's criticism of Nijinsky's lack of familiarity with the game. Buckle gives no indication that he knows how tennis players moved in 1913.[13] Returning to the multiple criticisms of Nijinsky's performance, what is particularly intriguing is the complaint issued both in 1913 and in 1971 that the movement vocabulary was not accurate: the tennis game was not replicated in action on the concert dance stage. This valuing of the "real," the sport movement vocabulary over the artistry of the choreography, led me to think about questions of accuracy and how they might relate to masculinity. For example, if Nijinsky failed to convince critics that he had successfully transferred the movement vocabulary of sport to that of choreography, perhaps he just wasn't the right performer to pull it off. He was a dancer, not an athlete. Some of his successors took the concept of the iconic athlete and ran with it—only they used athletes, not dancers, to do it.

In 1933, Ted Shawn left his professional dancing partner and wife Ruth St. Denis to try to build an identity for the American male dancer. Although Shawn and St. Denis had toured successfully for years as Denishawn and had dance schools in New York, Los Angeles, and Boston, Shawn was still dissatisfied with audience responses to male dancers. He wanted there to be an air of respectability associated with men on the U.S. concert dance stage. Shawn was particularly well situated to address concerns about men dancers. He came of age during a time when concerns about white middle-class male identity in the United States were heightened. In her book *Manliness and Civilization*, historian Gail Bederman explores turn-of-the–20th-century constructions of manhood and describes middle-class men of the time as being "unusually obsessed with manhood."[14] Bederman does not agree with other theorists that this obsession equaled a crisis, as "there is no evidence that most turn-of-the-century men ever lost confidence in the belief that people with male bodies naturally possessed both a man's identity and a man's right to wield power."[15] While Bederman's time frame ends in 1917, it sheds light on the notions of masculinity and manliness in circulation when Shawn was first dancing, exemplified by figures such as Theodore Roosevelt and his Rough Riders and Tarzan. Bederman doesn't discuss dancers, but she does stress that by 1890, "an ideal male body required physical bulk and well-defined muscles" and, further, that "strenuous exercise and team sports had come to be seen as crucial to the development of powerful manhood."[16] This attention to physicality and manliness is something that Ted Shawn certainly drew on in developing his dancers and his choreography.

Dance historian and gay theorist David Gere writes that part of Shawn's project was to state unequivocally that "dance was not for sissies," severing the connection between "male dancers and compromised masculinity."[17] Shawn had been working on this project for years, writing in his 1926 book: "The false idea clings that dancing is an effeminate expression for men. This can be corrected only with the correcting of the whole fundamental conception in regard to the importance of the art of dancing in general."[18]

Shawn was not the first male dancer to be called a "sissy" for dancing, nor is this stereotype uniquely American. Dance writer Ramsay Burt, in his book *The Male Dancer*, argues that men in the 19th century were uncomfortable viewing male dancers on the stage.[19] Dance scholar John Jordan, in this volume and elsewhere, has compellingly argued that the labeling of the male dancer as effeminate can be traced back to the 18th century. By looking at essays published in the British newspaper the *Spectator* and in etchings by William Hogarth, Jordan identified mocking and labeling by dancing masters as effeminate.[20] No matter where one marks the beginning of the stereotype of the effeminate male dancer, one thing is certain—it was in full force in the 1930s when Shawn founded what was to become a popular touring company called Ted Shawn and His Men Dancers. The company was housed at the site of the present-day dance festival Jacob's Pillow in western Massachusetts. Before starting to tour, Shawn first had to find men for his company. He located men he felt he could train as dancers at nearby Springfield College, a well-known institution for physical education.

More than two decades after the Men Dancers company disbanded, Shawn wrote an autobiography, *One Thousand and One Night Stands*. No matter that the company had been quite successful, one sees in reading about his search for male dancers that Shawn was still engaged with his clear political agenda about men dancing. He first comments that he realized it would be difficult to persuade men at Springfield College to dance, saying, "I would be up against five hundred young men, all set for careers in physical education and athletics, the hardest, toughest group I could have tackled."[21] Despite the assembled group of tough athletes, Shawn was obviously successful. He continues: "The students [at Springfield College] found that the fundamental dance exercises, which looked effortless and easy when I did them, were more strenuous than basic training for football, basketball, and wrestling."[22] Of particular interest in this statement is the relative difficulty of the fundamental dance exercises when compared with football, basketball, and wrestling.[23]

Shawn appreciated the men's sports training not only because it resulted in physical prowess but also for the content it provided him. In the summer of 1936, three years after founding the company and training the dancers, Shawn used the experience of his athletes-turned-dancers for a new work, *Olympiad*.

Figure 3.1   Ted Shawn and His Men Dancers in rehearsal at Jacob's Pillow in 1936, with Shawn at left. Photograph by Richard Merrill, courtesy of Jacob's Pillow Dance Festival Archives. Used with permission.

The 1936 Olympics loomed large in the popular imagination, with African American track star Jesse Owens setting records and Adolf Hitler refusing to acknowledge him. This was the context in which Shawn had the idea for his work. Barton Mumaw, a leading member of the Men Dancers and Shawn's long-time life partner, wrote about *Olympiad* in his self-titled memoir. As Mumaw describes it, Shawn asked each of the men to contribute sections to the work. The men, Mumaw reports, drew on their experiences as athletes at Springfield College, with sections devoted to, for example, basketball, boxing, and fencing.[24] Mumaw, the only trained dancer and non-sportsman in the group, performed a solo called *Banner Bearer*, which paid tribute to the Olympic opening ceremonies.

This was the first time that Shawn had solicited creative input from his dancers. I would argue that it was not their development as artists that led Shawn to give them artistic license but their past as athletes and their physical familiarity with that "real" movement vocabulary, which Shawn wanted to bring to the stage. *Olympiad* (originally called *Sports Dances*) was enormously popular with audiences. Shawn wrote about it in a letter to Lucien Price: "The boys, this being their first big job, nearly tore themselves to pieces working and rehearsing—and it is all extremely vigorous—today there is a collection of bruises, blisters, and charley-horses such as never before."[25] The language that Shawn uses to describe the efforts of the men dancers is anything but sissified. They "nearly tore themselves to pieces," and it was all "vigorous," resulting in numerous injuries.

Olympiad was documented on silent black-and-white film in the 1930s.[26] Although a variety of dancers choreographed the different sections, a sense of wholeness connects the sections of the dance. Each section is easily identified by the sport that served as inspiration, such as decathlon, fencing, basketball, and boxing. Although not strictly pantomimic, the movements are not abstract either, as they were 20 years earlier in Nijinsky's *Jeux*. Neither do the sports stand as a metaphor for anything as grand as the modern man. If anything, they serve as an equation: athletes plus dance subtracts effeminacy from the standard stereotype, leaving as a remainder an aura of authentic masculinity. Shawn's project of using male athletes to create a "safe" identity for male dancers seems to have been persuasive to audience members and critics alike. In 1936, a full-page photo essay from the *Boston Post* presented several action photographs of the men dancing, mostly in midair. The accompanying caption reads:

> DANCING
> The most strenuous profession of all! Here are members of the Ted Shawn group in rehearsal at Shawn's farm atop Jacob's Ladder in the Berkshires. These lads, besides doing all the work on the farm, train five hours daily. They're more rugged and better fit physically than any other athlete in the world and this dancing business, though it may seem simple, is more hazardous than any he-man sport.[27]

Shawn was calculating in his use of male athletes, knowing that it would help him achieve his mission of creating an acceptable identity for the American male dancer. He writes in his autobiography: "I was sure that when people saw young American athletes going through masculine dances, prejudice would be overcome and dancing as a career would take its place with other legitimate professions."[28] Dance critic and Shawn biographer Walter Terry seemingly concurs with this strategy when he notes: "It was part of Shawn's shrewd plan to publicize the fact that his boys were mainly university lettermen excelling in such masculine sports as boxing, wrestling, swimming, decathlon."[29] Terry elaborates by describing a kind of public relations campaign Shawn conducted, keeping members of the press informed about what other members of the press or audience were saying about the Men Dancers. "Not long after I came to know Shawn, he began to send me clippings of reviews, or in his letters, quotes from the press. A writer, assigned to cover a performance on the first tour, said in advance, 'Must be a bunch of pansies.' But after an interview and a look at the performance he wrote, 'No pansies they—these men, their work being of a most difficult type . . . demands the respect of even the most accomplished athlete.'"[30] Terry acknowledges Shawn's deliberate construction of the Men Dancers as athletes, a conclusion similarly drawn by sports and gender studies scholar

Michael Gard. In his recent book, *Men Who Dance: Aesthetics, Athletics and the Art of Masculinity*, Gard argues that there has been a deliberate construction of the male dancer as an athlete starting with Shawn: "My central argument is that the male dancer as athlete has come to occupy a dominant *discursive* position in constructions of who the male dancer is, and what kind of skills a male needs in order to become a professional dancer."[31] Gard goes on to compare Shawn with Nijinsky: "Unlike Nijinsky, Shawn's dancers were not simply vigorously athletic. Shawn was also at pains to explicitly associate them with sport."[32] While Gard's reading of both the rhetoric and the reviews of the so-called athletic male dancer is illuminating, overall he is less interested in the dancing bodies and the choreography they perform than in the reasons that men dance.

Some 20 years later, Gene Kelly would similarly draw on the implied masculinity of athletes in writing and producing a documentary for *Omnibus*, an NBC television program with a serious and positive reputation. Kelly, unlike Ted Shawn and Nijinsky, had had aspirations of becoming an athlete as a young man in Pittsburgh. In high school, Kelly played football and hockey and did gymnastics. In the biography *Gene Kelly*, Alvin Yudkoff recounts an anecdote from early in Kelly's life that foregrounds exactly the stereotype that Shawn sought to eradicate two decades earlier. Evidently Kelly, at age 10, was walking to dance class with his two brothers and two sisters. According to Yudkoff, "The Kellys heard 'sissies' and 'fags' and worse taunts surrounded by curses. Gene clenched his fists....He was ready. They formed a line facing the Kellys, and now, unbelievably, they were placing hands on hips and wiggling their asses, tongues extended for some reason. 'Pussy...pussy.' Gene was only ten years old, but he guessed a crude and challenging evocation of femininity when faced with it."[33] Even allowing for hyperbole in the retelling of a story from Kelly's youth, what remains is that Kelly as a dancer was called sissy, and he struggled lifelong to combat that association. Although Kelly was referred to as an athletic dancer, especially compared with the lighter grace and class of Fred Astaire, he was most able to directly counter the stereotypical association of dance and effeminacy with the production of the television special *Dancing—a Man's Game* (1958). Kelly intentionally linked sports and dance from the opening shot. The soundstage looks like a gym, although it is theatricalized. We see a basketball player dribbling a ball through gymnastic equipment; we see a heavy bag hanging from the ceiling right next to a ballet dancer giving himself a ballet barre. Kelly walks among a group of men, identifying them by name and sport association as he goes through the room. Johnny Unitas is there, Bob Cousy, Mickey Mantle, Sugar Ray Robinson. All the athletes were at the height of their popularity, and their place in popular imagination ensured the success of the documentary.

In her essay "Dancin' in the Rain," film studies professor Carol J. Clover argues that Kelly had "a political agenda in [*Singin' in the Rain*], one that he would spell out three years later in...*Dancing—a Man's Game*, in which he showed how the moves of male dance matched the moves of sports (baseball, football, boxing, and basketball) in hope of dispelling [what Kelly biographer Clive Hirschhorn called] the 'stigma of effeminacy that has always clung to the art of dance.'"[34] Kelly's use of professional athletes, rather than simply doing the movement vocabulary associated with each of the sports practices, was deliberate. It imbued the film about dance with a sense of masculine authority tied to the bodies of the "real" athletes. Peter Wollen, in his intensive examination of *Singin' in the Rain* published by the British Film Institute, makes a similar observation about Kelly's understanding of the male dancing body: "For Kelly, obsessed with the validity of the male dance, the presence of the body was all-important, a male body that is acceptably exhibitionist in its athleticism."[35] In *Dancing—a Man's Game*, Kelly made explicit the connection between his exhibitionist body and the athletes' bodies.

After panning across the gym, the camera focuses in on each athlete in turn, giving each a "solo." Each man executes a hallmark action from his sport; for example, Mantle mimes hitting a home run. Then Kelly performs a stylized version of the same action. As Kelly throws an imaginary ball with the momentum leading him into a turn, fakes a jump shot that turns into a leap, and swings a phantom golf club, he says again and again, "It's the same thing." To quote again from Yudkoff: "Gene directed stop-motion vignettes featuring . . . stadium heroes . . . and luminaries of the sports pages to underscore his theme: athletics is competitive and dance is creative, but both are rooted in the same balletic movements."[36]

In 1980, Twyla Tharp offered another variation on the theme of combining athletes and dancers, sports and dance. She paired New York City Ballet dancer Peter Martins and football player Lynn Swann in a piece called *Dance Is a Man's Sport, Too*. At that time, Martins was at the height of ballet popularity and acclaim as a principal dancer with the New York City Ballet, and Swann was a renowned player with the Pittsburgh Steelers.

Swann was a likely choice for Tharp for two reasons. He was an incredibly popular athlete (Howard Cosell said of Swann: "Maybe the most perfect wide receiver of all time," while Curt Gowdy called him "the Baryshnikov of football").[37] But Swann was also well known for having studied ballet, modern dance, and tap as a child.[38] Even after starting football, he continued to study ballet to enhance his athletic skills.[39] In his Football Hall of Fame induction speech, he joked: "You try leaving football practice with a pair of tights—named Lynn—at an all-boys Catholic school. You'll find yourself learning a few moves."[40] The implied threat of violence and questioning of Swann's masculinity aside, Tharp had an athlete who had been trained in dance to pair with Martins.

In the piece, choreographed specifically for television, Martins and Swann compete in a series of athletic and dance endeavors, with the physical challenges emphasized through filmic techniques. The set is minimal, with white lines against a dark background demarcating the space, reminiscent of chalk lines on a football field. Tharp, Martins, and Swann huddle, run in place, and feint dodging and ducking around each other. For Tharp to include herself in what is essentially a duet for the two men can be read as an instance of what Eve Kosofsky Sedgwick termed a "homosocial triangle."[41] Tharp's presence, her female body, inserted between the two men, keeps the relationship heterosexualized, even though Martins as a refined dancer suggests the possibility of effeminacy and homosexuality. In keeping with Sedgwick's theory, that the woman is less important than the relationship between the two men, Tharp exits and the dance continues, with a competition beginning between the two men.

They sprint from one white line to another, bending over to touch the line before setting off again. They run, slide, and do a full body roll. They leap into the air, one at a time, Martins with a beautiful *tour*, Swann as if catching a football. The camera freezes them at the apex of their jumps, making it possible to compare form, execution, and height. Dance writer Marcia Siegel described the duet in her biography of Tharp: "This curiosity was another compare-and-contrast duet, for New York City Ballet star Peter Martins and Pittsburgh Steelers linebacker Lynn Swann, joined briefly by Tharp. It had aired on the ABC *Omnibus* series 15 June 1980. According to Don Mischer, who cocreated the segment with her, they marked out yardlines on a black floor to simulate a football field, and Tharp gave the men jumping and throwing movements that each would do in his own way."[42] Tharp, like Kelly and Shawn before her, is a savvy artist and entertainer. All three were committed to making serious art, while at the same time concerning themselves with the reception of the work by the public.

Nijinsky studied tennis as inspiration and used the rules of the game as a metaphor for human relationships. He was criticized in his own time and 60 years later for having no sense of the real game or the real movement associated with it. Despite being the sole male with two women, his lack of success in presenting authentic athletic movement made his dance suspect. Ted Shawn recruited athletes to become dancers and let them explore their choreographic vision as it specifically related to the sports they had played before becoming dancers. The dual status of dancer and athlete assured that the movement of Men Dancers would be read as authentic and, therefore, masculine. Gene Kelly placed himself amid a sea of athletes at the height of their popularity and demonstrated again and again the sameness between the athletes' performances and his own. His masculinity was heightened by association with athletes. Tharp, the only woman I discuss here, placed a dancer and an athlete in a friendly competition, showing them leaping and turning within the vocabulary of their specific movement practice.

What, then, is the result of this choreographic use of sports? As I said earlier, anxiety surrounding male dancers and effeminacy is not new. Even in the naming of their works, Kelly with *Dancing—a Man's Game* and Tharp with

Dancing Is a Man's Sport, Too, the choreographers propose something that is decidedly not effeminate, while obliquely referring to long-held stereotypes and accusations that it is. It seems, then, that again and again choreographers in the United States have worked to counter that association by dipping into one of the most assuredly masculine practices—that of sports. One might assume that as the 20th century unfolded there would be less need to continue to promote the acceptability of men dancing. But that assumption does not prove true when looking at the works I have mentioned here. However, the concert dances I look at are all more than 20 years old. Does this suggest that masculinity, femininity, and effeminacy are all now equally welcome on the concert dance stage? Beyond the dances I've discussed here, there are examples of dancers who trade on their prior status as athletes to build their reputations as performers—such as Edward Villella and David Dorfman. Choreographer Peter Pucci aggressively markets his *Pucci: Sport* as "a showcase for professional dancers and athletes, bringing together national talents from both worlds in a celebration of the joy of making sport."[43]

Perhaps the most telling recent eruption of athlete-branded masculinity for dance has been on the popular culture phenomenon *Dancing with the Stars,* a television series on ABC TV. In *Dancing with the Stars,* celebrities famous for a variety of reasons partner with professional dancers to compete in ballroom dancing and are judged by both professional judges and television viewers. From the first season, with the selection of boxer Evander Holyfield as one of the celebrities, athletes have had a prominent presence on *Dancing with the Stars.*[44] Other athletes have included football players Jerry Rice and Emmitt Smith, basketball player Clyde Drexler, female boxer Laila Ali, and speed skater Apolo Anton Ohno. Certainly there is a vast difference between the concert dance stage and the reality TV world. However, it is a new site where clear examples about the long-held anxieties about dancing lacking masculinity can be found.[45]

When Emmitt Smith, former Dallas Cowboy and Super Bowl champion, took to the *Dancing with the Stars* stage, his performance and eventual victory of the third season were not about his dancing ability. Rather, they seemed to reflect his charm, his style, and, I would argue, his overwhelming popularity as a football player. When Dallas Cowboys owner Jerry Jones was interviewed about Smith's victory on *Dancing with the Stars,* he had no comment about Smith's dancing. Instead, he said: "Emmitt Smith is one of the great competitors that I have ever been around. Regardless of the competition, and regardless of the stakes, he always plays to win." Similarly, former teammate Roger Staubach also commented on Smith's fierce competitiveness.[46] Bob Cook wrote an opinion piece for MSNBC.com called "Opinion: Emmitt Shows Men It's Okay to Boogie. Manly men don't have to act hard, just work hard, even if it's at dancing." Cook reiterated long-familiar stereotypes: "But despite any trepidation, from the first episode, Smith stood out. 'Man, you are the king of effortless cool!' swooned judge Bruno Tonioli, who is, shall we say, *the more flamboyant type men tend to associate with dance.*"[47]

It appears to me that the work of Shawn, Kelly, and Tharp—to make dancing a man's game—is not yet done. The same strategies of employing athletes to dance not because of their physical skills but for the assured masculinity tied to their athlete stature, persist on television and on the concert dance stage.

NOTES

An earlier version of this essay appeared in *The Gay and Lesbian Review Worldwide,* Harvard University Press (November/December 2006), ed. Richard Schneider Jr., PhD., Publication Date 01-NOV-06.

With thanks to James Latzel, Mark Witteveen, and especially Jenny Showalter, an athlete turned dancer, for their helpful suggestions.

1. In his book *In Praise of Athletic Beauty* (Cambridge, MA: Harvard University Press, 2006), Hans Ulrich Gumbrecht provides an excellent consideration of the training of spectators to appreciate the aesthetics of athleticism. He poses the question, "What makes athletic beauty so addictive?" (55). Gumbrecht discusses a range of possibilities for responding to the viewing of athletics. He looks at what he terms "high culture" responses in the writings of literary figures such as Norman Mailer and Joyce Carol Oates, theoretical responses in the works of cultural theorists Norman Bryson and Pierre Bourdieu, and the everyday responses that one reads in the newspaper or hears in conversation.

2. Michael D. Giardina, *Sporting Pedagogies: Performing Culture and Identity in the Global Arena* (New York: Peter Lang, 2005), 13.

3. Noel Dyck and Eduardo P. Archetti, "Embodied Identities: Reshaping Social Life through Sport and Dance," in *Sport, Dance and Embodied Identities,* ed. Noel Dyck and Eduardo P. Archetti (Oxford: Berg, 2003), 1.

4. Barbara Barker, "Nijinsky's *Jeux,*" *Drama Review* 26, no. 1 (1982): 60.

5. In 1996, dance historian and choreographer Millicent Hodson collaborated with art historian Kenneth Archer on a reconstruction of Nijinksy's *Jeux* for the Verona Ballet, with subsequent restagings by the Royal Ballet, London, in 2000, and the Rome Opera Ballet and Joffrey Ballet of Chicago. http://www.fulbright.org/cohenfund/Hodson_2004 .pdf (accessed September 15, 2007).

6. Lynn Garafola, *Diaghilev's Ballets Russes* (New York: Oxford University Press, 1989), 59.

7. As quoted by Lincoln Kirstein, *Nijinsky Dancing* (New York: Knopf, 1975), 137.

8. Françoise Reiss, *Nijinsky: A Biography,* trans. Helen Haskell and Stephen Haskell (New York: Pittman, 1960), 114.

9. Kirstein, *Nijinsky Dancing,* 137.

10. From an article signed simply "Swift," in *Bulletin de la Société Musicale Indépendante,* as quoted in Richard Buckle, *Nijinsky* (New York: Simon and Schuster, 1971), 289.

11. For example, as Anthony Shay pointed out to me, reviewers at the time did not find fault with the folk dances in *Le sacre du printemps* or question whether they were danced "properly."

12. Buckle, *Nijinsky*, 276.

13. Athlete turned dancer and choreographer Bill T. Jones noted the changing movement style or vocabulary of sports. He remarked on the changes over time to movements that athletes use, and suggested that the differences mark specific eras: "A range of gestures, more than fashion, defines obvious periods of time. There's a radical difference between the way Babe Ruth ran around the bases and the way people do it now, in the way Jesse Owens and Carl Lewis run. Gestures are very contemporary indicators." Elizabeth Zimmer and Susan Quasha, eds., *Body against Body: The Dance and Other Collaborations of Bill T. Jones and Arnie Zane* (Barrytown, NY: Station Hill Press, 1989), 84.

14. Gail Bederman, *Manliness and Civilization: A Cultural History of Gender and Race in the United States, 1880–1917* (Chicago: University of Chicago Press, 1996), 11.

15. Ibid., 11.

16. Ibid., 15.

17. David Gere, "Foreword," in Jane Sherman and Barton Mumaw, *Barton Mumaw, Dancer: From Denishawn to Jacob's Pillow and Beyond* (Middletown, CT: Wesleyan University Press, 2000), xiv.

18. Ibid., xiv.

19. Ramsay Burt, *The Male Dancer: Bodies, Spectacle and Sexuality* (New York: Routledge, 1995).

20. See also John Bryce Jordan, "Light in the Heels: The Emergence of the Effeminate Male Dancer in Eighteenth-Century English History" (Ph.D. diss., University of California, Riverside, 2001).

21. Ted Shawn with Gray Poole, *One Thousand and One Night Stands* (Garden City, NY: Doubleday, 1960), 242.

22. Ibid., 243.

23. For a discussion of the relative difficulty of dancing, see Jennifer Fisher's essay, "Maverick Men in Ballet: Rethinking the 'Making It Macho' Strategy," in this volume.

24. Sherman and Mumaw, *Barton Mumaw: Dancer*, 283.

25. As quoted in Sherman and Mumaw, 138.

26. In 1986, Norton Owen, now director of preservation at Jacob's Pillow Dance Festival, directed a project to add sound to many of the 16mm silent films from the 1930s. Original composer and Men Dancers' accompanist Jess Meeker served as musical director. The archives at Jacob's Pillow and the Dance Collection at the New York Public Library both have copies of *Olympiad*, with sound added, in their collections.

27. "Farm Work Limbers Up Dance Muscles," *Boston Post*, October 25, 1936, 4.

28. Shawn with Poole, *One Thousand and One Night Stands*, 242.

29. Walter Terry, *Ted Shawn: Father of American Dance, a Biography* (New York: Dial Press, 1976), 144.

30. As excerpted by Terry in *Ted Shawn*, 142.

31. Michael Gard, *Men Who Dance: Aesthetics, Athletics and the Art of Masculinity* (New York: Peter Lang, 2006).

32. Ibid., 60.

33. Alvin Yudkoff, *Gene Kelly: A Life of Dance and Dreams* (New York: Back Stage Books, 1999), 2.

34. Carol J. Clover, "Dancin' in the Rain," *Critical Inquiry* 21, no. 4 (Summer 1995): 726.

35. Peter Wollen, *Singin' in the Rain* (London: British Film Institute, 1993), 57.

36. Yudkoff, *Gene Kelly*, 236.

37. Retrieved from Lynn Swann's biography on Keynotespeakers.com.

38. In an interview with *Playbill*, the magazine that is distributed along with program information in theaters throughout New York City, white dancer John Selya refers to Swann's identity as dancer turned athlete when he responds to questions about how he got into dance. Selya, former American Ballet Theatre dancer and Twyla Tharp company member, became a Broadway star in Tharp's *Movin' Out*.

[Interviewer] Wayman Wong: . . . I hear you never got any grief as a kid [for dancing]. True?

John Selya: Yeah, I was never ridiculed. My friends were very open minded. Plus, I was a jock and played soccer. . . .

Q: Were you influenced by the ballet movie "The Turning Point"?

Selya: No, my own turning point was seeing a news program about Lynn Swann, a wide receiver for the Pittsburgh Steelers. He took ballet to improve his coordination and athletic prowess.

Wayman Wong, "THE LEADING MEN: *Movin' Out* and Movin' Up," *Playbill*, February 1, 2003, page unknown.

39. While the subject is outside the scope of this essay, it is interesting to note that the two athletes with dance training prior to beginning their professional athletic careers are Swann and Sugar Ray Robinson. Before returning to boxing as a career for the third time, Robinson, who had studied tap as a child, tap-danced in nightclubs. Swann and Robinson, both African American, were raised to accept dance as a part of male physical embodiment that is arguably typically absent from the childhood of white men.

40. Retrieved from http://www.npr.org/programs/npc/2003/030115.lswann.html (May 21, 2007).

41. Eve Kosofsky Sedgwick, *Between Men: English Literature and Male Homosocial Desire* (New York: Columbia University Press, 1985).

42. Marcia B. Siegel, *Howling Near Heaven: Twyla Tharp and the Reinvention of Modern Dance* (New York: St. Martin's Press, 2006), 165–66.

43. Retrieved from http://www.pucciplus.com/sport.html (September 15, 2007).

44. Holyfield became widely known beyond the boxing world in 1997 when Mike Tyson bit off part of his ear in a Las Vegas boxing match.

45. See also Jennifer Fisher, this volume, with regard to *So You Think You Can Dance*.

46. Retrieved from http://www.dallas cowboys.com/docs/EmmittWins_111506.html (May 16, 2007).

47. Bob Cook, "Opinion: Emmitt Shows Men It's Okay to Boogie. Manly men don't have to act hard, just work hard, even if it's at dancing," http://www.msnbc.com/id/15740306, emphasis added.

WORKS CITED

Barker, Barbara. "Nijinsky's *Jeux*." *Drama Review* 26, no. 1 (Spring 1982): 51–60.

Bederman, Gail. *Manliness and Civilization: A Cultural History of Gender and Race in the United States, 1880–1917*. Chicago: University of Chicago Press, 1995.

Buckle, Richard. *Nijinsky*. New York: Simon and Schuster, 1971.

Burt, Ramsay. *The Male Dancer: Bodies, Spectacle and Sexuality*. New York: Routledge, 1995.

Clover, Carol J. "Dancin' in the Rain." *Critical Inquiry* 21, no. 4 (Summer 1995): 722–47.

Dyck, Noel, and Eduardo P. Archetti, "Embodied Identities: Reshaping Social Life through Sport and Dance." In *Sport, Dance and Embodied Identities*, ed. Noel Dyck and Eduardo P. Archetti. Oxford: Berg, 2003.

"Farm Work Limbers Up Dance Muscles." *Boston Post*, October 25, 1936, 4.

Garafola, Lynn. *Diaghilev's Ballets Russes*. New York: Oxford University Press, 1989.

Gard, Michael. *Men Who Dance: Aesthetics, Athletics and the Art of Masculinity*. New York: Peter Lang, 2006.

Gere, David. "Foreword." In Jane Sherman and Barton Mumaw, *Barton Mumaw, Dancer: From Denishawn to Jacob's Pillow and Beyond*. Middletown, CT: Wesleyan University Press, 2000.

Giardina, Michael D. *Sporting Pedagogies: Performing Culture and Identity in the Global Arena*. New York: Peter Lang, 2005.

Gumbrecht, Hans Ulrich. *In Praise of Athletic Beauty*. Cambridge, MA: Harvard University Press, 2006.

Hodson, Millicent. Summary of the Selma Jeanne Cohen Lecture "Nijinsky's Bloomsbury Ballet, Jeux." http://www.fulbright.org/cohenfund/Hodson_2004.pdf.

Jordan, John Bryce. "Light in the Heels: The Emergence of the Effeminate Male Dancer in Eighteenth-Century English History." Ph.D. diss., University of California, Riverside, 2001.

Kirstein, Lincoln. *Nijinsky Dancing*. New York: Knopf, 1975.

Reiss, Françoise. *Nijinsky: A Biography*. Trans. Helen Haskell and Stephen Haskell. New York: Pittman, 1960.

Sedgwick, Eve Kosofsky. *Between Men: English Literature and Male Homosocial Desire*. New York: Columbia University Press, 1985.

Shawn, Ted, with Gray Poole. *One Thousand and One Night Stands*. New York: Doubleday, 1960.

Sherman, Jane, and Barton Mumaw. *Barton Mumaw, Dancer: From Denishawn to Jacob's Pillow and Beyond*. Middletown, CT: Wesleyan University Press, 2000.

Siegel, Marcia B. *Howling Near Heaven: Twyla Tharp and the Reinvention of Modern Dance*. New York: St. Martin's Press, 2006.

Terry, Walter. *Ted Shawn, Father of American Dance: A Biography*. New York: Dial Press, 1976.

Wollen, Peter. *Singin' in the Rain*. London: British Film Institute, 1992.

Wong, Wayman. "THE LEADING MEN: *Movin' Out* and Movin' Up." *Playbill*, February 1, 2003, page unknown.

Yudkoff, Alvin. *Gene Kelly: A Life of Dance and Dreams*. New York: Back Stage Books, 2001.

Zimmer, Elizabeth, and Susan Quasha, eds. *Body against Body: The Dance and Other Collaborations of Bill T. Jones and Arnie Zane*. Barrytown, NY: Station Hill Press, 1989.

FRED STRICKLER

> *Strickler has been dancing professionally since 1961. He was a founding member of the Jazz Tap Ensemble and Eyes Wide Open Dance Theatre, as well as his own group, Fred Strickler & Friends. He has also been a featured artist with Rhapsody in Taps and the Bella Lewitzky Dance Company. Since 1983 he has performed his choreographic version of the* Tap Dance Concerto. *He is Distinguished Professor Emeritus at the University of California, Riverside, where he taught dance for 40 years.*

My earliest memory of dancing was spinning on the front porch of our small house in Columbus, Ohio. I couldn't have been more than three years old when I discovered that if I put on my mommy's skirt, which must have dragged on the ground beneath my tiny body, the skirt would billow and flutter as I turned faster and faster. Of course, at the time, I was unaware that for centuries men halfway across the world in Turkish Sufi centers had been whirling in long-skirted clothes, achieving altered states of consciousness. Later I learned that I was good at spinning, and it became a motif in many of my choreographic works throughout my life. For as long as I can remember I loved to dance. Another of my favorite early memories was performing a Dutch dance in kindergarten.

I used to accompany my mother and my sister, Ruth, who was two years younger than I, to the Jimmy Rawlins Dance Studio, where she took tap lessons. I loved that dance studio. To me, it was altogether glamorous, with a long row of framed photos of famous dancers and entertainers mounted at eye level above a red-carpeted staircase that led us into a world utterly unlike the drab, poor neighborhood I came from. I had found my new home. When I was 10, I asked my mother if I could take tap lessons. It must have been a hard decision for her, because we had so little money. She must have sacrificed a lot for us kids. Mom agreed, however, that I could take tap dance lessons if I promised to stick to it for at least a year. No problem here. I was hooked from the get-go, and I practiced in our kitchen constantly. There were a few other boys in my classes, but it never occurred to me as odd or out of balance. I was in my own world. I also studied other genres of dance: ballet, ballroom, and a bit of jazz. I think that excelling in tap dancing provided me a place in a large family where I often felt invisible and

Strickler in a studio improvisation. Photograph by Lois Greenfield. Used with permission.

physically awkward, especially among my three older brothers, all of whom were into sports, which I wasn't.

In my family, positive male role models barely existed. My father had left the family when I was four. I don't recall feeling anything particular about that, except that he was not there. I also had uncles—my mom's brothers—who came and went. Nearly all of them helped with expenses, but they were also alcoholics. Working or drinking, they were not available. So for me, adult men did two things: they left and they got drunk. Worthless. I certainly didn't want to be like any of them, except for my Uncle Pete, who was caring, clever, funny, and sober. Otherwise, I grew up in a household dominated by women: my grandmother, mother, and aunts. My Uncle Gene and I shared a room from the time I was seven or eight, which must have been difficult for him. No privacy. Me too. He thought I was a sissy, a little queer-brat, and a smart aleck. I thought he was a macho, drunken boor and a know-it-all. We were both right, and we both missed the point. Neither of us was the man we imagined the other ought to be.

In elementary school I learned about what we now call gender. In the first grade, I remember on show-and-tell day, one of the boys brought his doll to school. Dolls were for girls. The other kids laughed and branded him a sissy. I realized I had better not bring a doll to school or do anything else that might be humiliating. Another early incident: I was lying on the couch nose to nose with Patty, a girl my age, with bad breath. We weren't even kissing, just curious about what grown-ups do. My aunt came into the room and instantly went into a rage, yanking us apart. From that, I guessed that kissing girls was wrong, wrong, wrong. In junior high school I learned that there were many things that boys didn't do. You had to "act like a man" and not cry. Don't put your hands on your hips. Learn to swear. One day, in seventh-grade gym class during roll call, the coach received a note calling me to the principal's office. As I walked across the gym to leave, the coach walked behind me, mocking the way my hips swung side to side, and all of the boys burst into laughter. I never forgave him for that humiliation, but I started to walk straight (in both senses of the word): no swinging of the hips, feet pointed straight forward—like a man. Because I had already been dancing for a few years, I had the discipline and skills to successfully learn that masculine walk. It became clear to me that I *had* to learn all of the proper boy/man behavior or I would be shunned by friends and disowned by my family, so I worked hard at reinventing myself as a real boy. I was also studying ballet by that time but kept it a secret from the schoolmates. Tap dancing was okay, but ballet was strictly a girl thing. Even into my college years, I was afraid of saying publicly I was a dancer, terrified that people would call me a sissy.

With plans to be a teacher of English and mathematics, I studied at Ohio State University in Columbus. (I was the first of my siblings to graduate from college.) On my first day at OSU, I ran into a friend who told me that I could sign up for a modern dance class to satisfy my physical education requirements, so from day one I was dancing. By the end of my sophomore year, it was clear to me that math was not for me. So I changed my major to dance and never looked back. Dance has lots of room for masculine behaviors that don't fit our Euro-American stereotypes.

My family, like all the others in our neighborhood, pushed their children to go out on their own as soon as possible, and I got out as soon as I could. My grandmother told me emphatically, "Your talent is in your feet," meaning that dancing was my ticket out of the neighborhood. She and my mother reveled in my dancing success, and today I am grateful for their unflinching support. It was difficult financially. I worked part-time teaching dance to kids, modeling for art classes, and taking innumerable tests as a research subject for psychology projects. During summers, I was a dancer-singer in musical theater touring companies in Ohio and New England.

In the 60s, it was assumed that if a guy was a dancer, he was gay. The stereotype was someone who was fey, quick, light, graceful, well-mannered—in other words, a gentleman. This was especially true in ballet, where the role of the male dancer was to frame and glorify the ballerina. Males and females, regardless of age, were called boys and girls. As a partner, the boy was there to hoist the girl and otherwise support her dancing. She was the focus, not he, except for brief solos in which he could show off his male prowess in fast, energetic, flashy steps designed to wow the audience. In partnering, the boy/gentleman/prince could show emotional tenderness, or anguish, but nothing like the range of emotions a ballerina would be expected to express. Male dancers in those days wore a specially designed jockstrap/thong, called a dance belt, under their tights. The dance belt smoothed out—erased even—the shapes of the genitals, though not the size of the bulge. While it was considered altogether proper to see the male body revealed for the aesthetic purposes of line and form, it was unspoken that everyone was also looking at asses and crotches. That a male dancer thus exposed himself undoubtedly contributed to the notion that he was not fully a man. In those days, only women were supposed to be objects of desire, not men. Men who did that were, well, not *real* men.

Nevertheless, there are, of course, many straight men in dance, but the ways they move are visually different. Even in the dance environment, there were ways of being masculine. To be openly gay was (still is somewhat) taboo, and I learned "to dance like a man" and wear a "mask of straightness." I erased my visible sexuality as much as I could. I remember in the Broadway musical *Kismet* I wore balloon pants and a vest over my bare chest. The director shouted at me: "Swell out your chest." It was absurd because I was skinny as a rail. I could never appear athletically manly because I never had a muscular body. But I pushed out my chest, stood with legs wide apart, fists on hips, and tried to glare darkly. I can't say any of that was particularly effective, but it was all I could do to look like a man.

As a kid I was aware that there were male dancers because I used to haunt the huge old Carnegie library in Columbus and read every book they had about dance. So I was aware of Rudolf Laban, Vaslav Nijinsky, Kreutzberg, Jooss. I loved Nijinsky. Daniel Nagrin influenced me; he came to perform one of his early solo concerts in Columbus. I was completely mesmerized by his work. His performance was very passionate. Physically, he was wiry, compact, muscular—very butch. But, for all his obvious maleness, his humanity trumped his gender. Even now I feel his influence. As a young man looking for male role models, it was transforming to realize that male dancing could be real and powerful. Nagrin did things that amazed me; I think it was his certainty that moved and inspired me. After the performance, he was very generous, spending time backstage talking to a group of us young dancers. As a man, he was fully present with us, sharing his views of art, free, passionate, fully self-expressed, hiding nothing. At last, this was a man I could want to be like. He was himself. I was inspired to dance like myself.

In 1967, after graduation from Ohio State, I was offered a job at the University of California, Riverside, where I taught for 40 years. By that time, I was essentially a modern dancer, heavily involved in the modern dance world on the West Coast. I began to tap dance professionally when I was 37 or 38, very late in life, at a time when I was thinking about giving up a performing career. As a tap dancer, even when I was young, I was frequently and favorably compared to Gene Kelly and Fred Astaire, then Gregory Hines. Flattering though that was, I was not interested in looking like any of them because I have no interest in imitating anyone else's style. Over the years, I have come to deeply respect their styles. Currently, with the rise of the remarkable Savion Glover, tap dance is currently dominated by a decidedly hard-hitting, masculine, black style of moving. I am considered an old-style tap dancer now. Watching his work is informative. He is an absolutely wonderful dancer, but I don't want to dance in his style. I'm gay, white, and a generation older than him. Copying him would be absurd.

Gender and tap is interesting. Tap dance is a male-dominated dance tradition. In the old days, besides Bill Robinson, the Nicholas Brothers, Donald O'Connor, Gene Kelly, and Fred Astaire, the outstanding women were Ruby Keeler, Eleanor Powell, Ginger Rogers, and Ann Miller. They were all very feminine, and Powell was a particularly fine technician. During the tap renaissance of the mid-1970s and 1980s, women like Brenda Bufalino, Camden Richman, and Lynn Dally had to dance like men, in flat-heeled shoes and wearing trousers, doing complicated rhythms—like the men—just to be noticed, because the prevalent notion among male tap dancers was that female tap dancers couldn't dance as well as men. The male style, which Savion Glover epitomizes today, is heavy, hitting the floor, aggressive, percussive, ultrafast, and dazzling. The feet are generally placed wider than the hips. Contemporary male dancing has a "boxerliness" that is unsuitable for a "girl" dancer, who "should be" pretty, sexy, long-legged in high heels: eye candy and not much else. It's the men, with their strength, speed, and agility, who can and do carry the show. But even that is already being challenged by Savion's female contemporaries, like Roxanne Butterfly, Chloe Arnold, and Dormesha Sumbry.

As I look back, I did not experience any problems of harassment as a male dancer. When I'm on the stage, there's no question I am a man, even though I do not fit male stereotypes. I have found that dancers tend to be intelligent and articulate because they're artists, and artists have to be intelligent. Men who dance are exactly like men who do anything else. You can find the full range of sexuality, physicality, intelligence. They are really part of the larger inquiry of what it is to be a human being. To be a dancer means that you participate in one of humankind's oldest communal activities. I say that we're not there to be sexy or to display our virtuosity, or even to be admired. All that may be present, but we are dancing to express ourselves as human beings. Inside that expression, we can be who we say we are, not who others say we ought to be.

I sometimes asked myself: "What and whom do I represent?" I can't really say that I'm a representative of gayness; rather, I am an *instance* of gayness. Only a few times have I used specifically gay themes in my work. Nor do I really want to put myself forward as a representative of masculinity. Both, I think, are in my work, but they don't define my work. I can say now that at my age I challenge and break the rules about what it means to be masculine. The tools that I use in my performance stem from who I am as a person. If my dancing is feminized, it's probably because I grew up in a matriarchal household and dance is dominated by women, so we are exposed to the feminine psyche and points of view. I'm far more interested in being human than being a man. While I'm certainly not a woman, I am willing to dance with all the tools of expression, including anything that might ordinarily be understood as feminine. I remember at the New York City Center, there was a concert of Martha Graham's work, and these two male dancers—one of them was Steve Petronio—showed up in miniskirts. Even in a dance environment, many people were shocked at that gender-bending display. I remember thinking that, while not for me, what they were doing was terrific.

Now I do what I want, what interests me. The rules of masculinity, after all, are constructed—works of fiction made up by communities of people who have invented them as ways in which their culture should/must be expressed. The result is that now there is (apparently) insurmountable confusion about what's true and what's not about being masculine. We "bought" these stories from our fathers, uncles, boys around us, and from the girls and women who passed them along, too. My goal in dancing has been to forward humanity in the best ways possible. Given that, the breaking up of a bunch of old and very weird rules about manliness is a must.

RENNIE HARRIS

| *Harris is a dancer, choreographer, and teacher who has combined*
| *elements of his hip-hop background to make dance for the concert stage.*
| *Founder of Rennie Harris Puremovement in 1992, he is based in*
| *Philadelphia and has toured widely with acclaimed stage productions*
| *such as* Rome and Jewels *and* Facing Mekka.

I never thought of myself as "a dancer" when I was growing up, because dancing was such a part of my community—it wasn't an extracurricular activity, everybody accepted it. A guy could not even do much on the dance floor, but just the way he did it made people just love it—he was the man. All the guys around him would want to imitate him—I mean, you see a guy who can dance, people are just naturally attracted to that. So in that way, there weren't negative stereotypes about men dancing, at least not most of the time. But there's a perception about a man in the black community, that if you're still spending a lot of time dancing at a certain age, maybe after you're 18, I think you'll get questioned, like "Why don't you have a job? You can't dance all your life." So when I started making money, that took the pressure off about getting a job. People in the neighborhood were beginning to see that, "Hey, Lorenzo's doing something"— they'd see my name in the paper or see me in a video, and they started making the connection, like, "Hey, man, you're really doing this." Then it was, "Wow, you bought a house from dancing? Really?" Interestingly, they really don't know what I do, they just know I do something that gets me in the paper for a few days. They can't make the connection between dance and theater, so they say, "I haven't seen you in a video for a while, are you still in videos?" I'm saying [laughing], "There haven't been videos for a while for me, there ain't going to be any now."

I didn't know anything about dance in the theater when I grew up either—I didn't even know people took classes to learn how to dance. The only reason I'd even seen a ballet class was when I was 14 or 15, and there was this white priest who thought I was a good dancer—the only white people in our neighborhood [North Philadelphia] were with the church back then. He saw me dance and said, "Let me take you to a dance class," and I was like, "Really? People go to school to learn how to dance?" I had never heard anything like that in my entire life. I didn't

Rennie Harris improvising. Photographs by Brian Mengini. Used with permission.

even know there was a performing arts high school. If I'd known, I would have gone, and I'd probably be doing something very different today. But when I went into that one ballet class, it was like a major culture shock. I saw all these guys with tights on, and I was, like, "Hmmmm..." [laughing at his young self]. Like, there was stuff hanging, I don't know.... I wasn't a sports guy, so I wasn't used to being with other men changing clothes. So many things were going around in my head at that time, and I was thinking, "I don't know about this." But I went in and got at the barre, going through the motions with people around me saying, "Your neck, your neck should be like a swan! Ahhhh, like a swan!" And we'd be in these positions [tilting forward], and I'd be looking at the guy in front of me to figure out what to do, but those tights were something really distracting—there was this guy's butt in front of me, it was nasty, man [laughing]. It was like taking this kid out of a culture, the only thing I'd ever known, and I'd never seen something like that. At that time, I didn't even know there were black dancers in ballet. I didn't even know what gay was at the time—I was more just thinking, "Hey, that's not right." Even though the dancing was interesting, I was never inspired to go back.

The kind of dancing I was doing as a teenager was called GQ, sometimes referred to as jeeking, Iking, or steppin', not to be confused with fraternity step dance. After GQ, I was a popper, then a B-boy. Back then, I got a lot of flack sometimes—not because I was dancing, particularly, but because of the way I dressed. It was okay to wear a white T-shirt when you danced, but if you wore leather pants or designer sneakers, people might say you were gay. I didn't know leather pants were something gay people wore [laughing]—they cost a lot of money, I thought they were dope, you know? But when you were a strong individual, I think people didn't challenge your gender preference so much. Maybe if you did ballet or modern or jazz dance in my community, that was a sign you were gay, but if you were a social dancer, that was okay. And I was always protected from all the gangsters and drug dealers or whatever. If you were a dancer, you got a pass; you could walk from one neighborhood to the next and have no problem, because the guys who ran the streets were like, "That's a dancer, he's okay." The only problem with that was that you had to dance anytime they asked you to [laughing]. They'd be like, "Yo, yo, go ahead, man, show them what you do." And you had to do it, because that guy ran the block. You didn't say, "I'm not feeling good right now, man," because they'd end up buying you clothes, buying you shoes, buying you stuff so you could perform and do your thing. They'd also let us know when something was about to break out—they'd say, "Yo, Rennie, you need to get up against the wall," and you didn't ask any questions, you got up against the wall. Sure enough, there would be mayhem. In my experience, once they realized you were a dancer, you got protected.

In terms of prejudice, it comes down to what peoples' perception of masculinity is. In hip-hop, I think as long as a guy can contract back and forth when he's dancing, it's okay. But anytime he moves side to side, it's not okay. It's a sexual thing—it's control, you have to be in control, you're the man. Out of all hip-hop, House is probably the one dance that allows you to be feminine and masculine at the same time, and you're not considered anything less than a man, because it's such a freestyle dance, a different aesthetic. I think with men, in general, the only way they can kind of address feminine movement in social dance is to play with it, so it's just cute, and everyone likes it. With the Campbell Lockers, for instance, they would "clown around play" with whacking gestures as a spoof when they were battling the Outrageous Whackers. There was Shabba Doo (Adolfo Quiñones), who incorporated whacking in his arsenal of Campbell Locking vocabulary. Don Campbell, the creator, spoofed feminine movement, which was inspired by the Whackers. One of Don's signatures was when he'd blow you a kiss and then flap his hands as if he was trying to fly—which, of course, gave the impression that he was suggesting that he was a fairy or feminine-soft. In Adolfo's case, he used the movement as part of his vocabulary, and in Don's case, he used it as a spoof. When the Outrageous Whackers would go up against Don, their movement technique would come from the same basis, and from the heart, but it was also different. So what happened was as they battled, they started to pick up each other's movement 'cause they became friends. They were all cool together, and they'd take all these movements from each other—so you see some movement in Campbell-locking that comes from Outrageous Whackers and vice versa. A style and a technique begins to be a hybrid.

With some guys who whack, it's a feminine style. They still play with the whole masculine/feminine thing sometimes. Some guys whack straight—I think there's still a fear of being too feminine sometimes maybe, but less fear in the House movement. That's because of the fact that House came about in a place where everyone mixed—gay, white, straight, black, ballet dancers, jazz dancers, everybody was partying, Studio 54, that whole era. So you can imagine afterward they realized, when you can party together, it's a different culture—remember, in the 60s there were still people riding at the back of the bus. So you can imagine the freedom of that next generation—it opened things up, everything was okay. House aesthetic came out at the time of women's liberation, the sexual revolution. House dancers to me are like beatniks, they're like peace, they're hippies, they're just free about their movements, and it's interesting. They're just different from hip-hop dancers who are hard-core, when they do hip-hop as an exhibition or an exchange or a circle. When you're doing hip-hop as a party dance, it's just a celebration.

4

Transcending Gender in Ballet's LINES

JILL NUNES JENSEN

In 1982, Alonzo King's LINES Ballet premiered in San Francisco.[1] At that time, the predominantly female company consisted of dancers who found latitude and transformation in King's approach. This committed group had left various professional ballet companies where they perceived their individuality to be stifled by the genre's conventionality. King's way of working provided an alternative—particularly because he did not ask women to reproduce the gendered protocols familiar to the world of classical dance. This is something that the men who eventually joined them would also discover. In the pages that follow, I situate King's philosophies and choreographic process as the foundation for a flexible understanding of gender in dance—one that is conspicuously fixed in most other ballet-based companies in the United States. Moreover, I use King's dances, and the effects his strategies have, to anchor the idea that his work for LINES offers an evolved kind of ballet with respect to current constructions of masculinity and femininity. Through a framework based on the phenomenological privileging of experience that offers dance scholars a chance to discuss the practice of dancing, this essay interweaves choreography, commentary, and current critical discourse to foreground the assertion that Alonzo King's LINES Ballet not only is physically transforming gendered relationships but also is transcending tropes that have become just as commonplace in the genre as the technique itself.[2]

Point of Entry

Alonzo King's own dance training and performing career made him all too aware of the gender specificity of ballet, where boys learn to become princes and girls their princesses. He attended the School of American Ballet, the Joffrey School, Dance Theater of Harlem, and Harkness—yet as a dancer he performed with modern companies (Bella Lewitzky, Donald McKayle, and Lucas Hoving), where much of ballet's courtly division of labor did not exist. From this somewhat divergent background, King assumes a novel approach to directorship, making pieces that strive to extend ballet's core vocabulary, all the while infusing it with modernist tenets. When asked about the genesis of his inspiration, King does not credit one specific teacher or any choreographic principle as primary. Instead, he explains: "I think training comes from living life. From the wheel of mistakes and successes, and observing in others what works and what doesn't work. A large part of what was placed in me came from my parents. They encouraged me to develop myself according to a design based on honesty. The largest contribution to my 'training' came from my father who introduced me to yoga and meditation and the teachings of Paramhansa Yogananda."[3] King also says his "main training" came from "hours of dancing alone in private spaces with no one watching and from observing nature."

In the works that he makes for LINES, King uses pointe shoes, impressive extensions, and recognizable ballet steps, but these components are often twisted and redirected in ways that visually contradict what mainstream companies present. Some hallmarks of his aesthetic include curved arms that morph into angularity, bodies tilted in unexpected directions, continual movement, and a sense of groundedness. King's dancers slide rather than float, are pulled and pushed instead of carried or placed, direct their focus inward, and find center just off ballet's vertical axis. The dancers do not strive for stillness in

Figure 4.1   Hallmarks of King choreography include curved arms that morph into angularity and bodies tilting in unexpected directions. Dancer: Ricardo Zayas in Alonzo King's *Sky Clad* (2006). Photograph by Marty Sohl. Used with permission of Marty Sohl/Alonzo King's LINES Ballet.

balanced poses; alternatively, they emphasize motion, flow, effort, and transitions. His ballets do not include a rigidly symmetrical corps, and therefore they allow dancers greater freedom than would be tolerated in most classical troupes. The company members are not really expected to perform in exact unison; instead, they are given the chance to embody each step as if it were an experience, not a task to complete. This does not mean that the choreography shifts into improvisation, but it does mean that King's process compels his dancers to develop their own idiosyncratic interpretations in a way that results in an especially powerful lived experience.

Within seven years of the company's formation, King established the San Francisco Dance Center (SFDC) with the help of Pam Hagen and Robert Rosenwasser. Though LINES and the Dance Center were meant to remain separate (i.e., the center was never intended to be an exclusive training facility for LINES), SFDC's consistent financial profit proved welcome as the company struggled to broaden its touring circuit and reach new audiences.[4] The relationship proved successful, and during the 1990s, critics and artists alike began to take note of King's innovations, as well as to speculate about how they might affect the form. For instance, in 2000 Karen Campbell of the *Boston Globe* contended: "The future of ballet lies not only with the careful preservation of great classics, but in the ground-breaking invention of those brave and talented choreographers willing to test the art form's limits and stretch the boundaries of centuries-old tradition. Though he is not especially well-known on the East coast, Alonzo King has been trying to bring a fresh look to contemporary ballet in San Francisco and elsewhere for almost two decades with a stylistic aesthetic that takes ballet into the realm of hard and fast with nary a trace of French court dance" (C11).

Moreover, in 2006, *San Francisco Chronicle* critic Rachel Howard noted the complexity and uniqueness of King's ballets by marking his dancers "alien" within the current scene: "Watching a King ballet is like alighting in a distant, unknown country and observing the rituals of an alien culture with curiosity and a sense of eerie recognition. Who are these strange creatures with these unspooling limbs, liquid musculature and jutting hips?" (E5). Adding to these comments, William Forsythe, a choreographer who is no stranger to boundary-breaking, has said that "Alonzo King is one of the few true Ballet Masters of our times. His intimacy with ballet's multiple histories has made his choreography rich with the complex refractions that demonstrate a full command of the art's intricacies."[5]

King's choreography for women was an initial distinguishing feature, as it manipulated more than the "lines" of dancing bodies. Yet time after time, movement descriptions were eclipsed, and the company dancers were depicted in reviews and articles in terms that played up physical strength. This stemmed from the fact that the women have appeared taller and sometimes more muscularly defined than the men since early on in the company history. In

1990, dance historian and critic Janice Ross noted in the *Oakland Tribune* that Summer Rhatigan[6] "easily dominated" her male partner Enrico Labayen[7] in one of King's pas de deux "because she is at least a foot taller," and "One's feeling in watching this *pas de deux*, which some viewers regarded as controversial because of the extreme contrast in their sizes, shifted from amusement and disbelief to pleasure at the *un*expectedness of this odd pairing"[8] (C1). Also in 1990, Rita Felciano, writing for the *San Francisco Bay Guardian*, declared, "Lines [*sic*] has a very distinct look: The women tend to be quite tall … assertive, with strong ballet training" (34). This would still prove noteworthy 15 years later as Ann Murphy pronounced in the April/May 2005 edition of *Pointe* magazine, "Since the creation of San Francisco–based Alonzo King's LINES Ballet 23 years ago, its dancers have been a tall, leggy bunch" (34).

While calling attention to the dancers' heights, reviewers have additionally pointed out their muscularity, particularly in works like *Lila* (Joffrey Ballet commission 1991) and later *Who Dressed You Like a Foreigner?* (1998) and *Koto* (2002). European critic Marie-Christine Vernay wrote about LINES' 2004 performances in Lyon, France, that *Koto* and *Who Dressed You Like a Foreigner?* demonstrated "the choreography and technique of an ensemble that is classical at its base" through work that "is more muscular than the majority of American companies." Vernay's observations echo New York critic Anna Kisselgoff's earlier commentary that positioned King as an artist capable of infusing ballet with stalwart "modern-dance idioms." As Kisselgoff wrote in 2000, "Mr. King knows how to exploit classical technique to the maximum. Yet every arabesque is struck with muscular tension, not exhibited for the noble line" (E5).

Because there were no ballets with fairy-tale or storybook plots, the men who joined LINES in the late 1990s found they did not have to fit into the gender-specific ballet roles of the prince and swan variety. As King's repertory evolved with both sexes, men continued to support ballerinas *en pointe*. But even though they still held the women at the waist and pivoted their smaller frames, the choreography was moving away from the courtly version of ballet masculinity so prevalent over the centuries. This meant the LINES men would not become *porteurs*, lifting their posed female partners above their heads as if on display, or dance as virtuosos in the familiar masculine style that often seems to be concerned only with completing multiple pirouettes and spectacular leaps. Correspondingly, by conceiving pas de deux as an exploration of "qualities," not characters, King choreographed sections where the men of his company were frequently "supported" in promenades by ballerinas rather than being required to initiate action as is typical of ballet danseurs. Through the continued disregard of some gender tropes, King's duets began to allow the dancers to form relationships and explore space with less inhibition.

I first became familiar with LINES after seeing the company in 1999. The dancers immediately transfixed me as they moved on and offstage in a way that created a sense of flow and continual motion. I had never seen a U.S.-based ballet company traverse space like that, and when it came time to choose a dissertation topic, I did not hesitate to situate LINES as the centerpiece of my investigation into contemporary ballet.[9] After viewing LINES' performance videotapes and rehearsals and attending fall seasons at the Yerba Buena Center for the Arts (the company's home theater in San Francisco), I selected a cross section of pieces to read through the lenses of race, gender, and sexuality. I positioned King as a pioneer, because he re-forms ballet so overtly.[10] I argued that his choreography is groundbreaking because it allows ballet to be put into contemporary critical discourse. While working on that project and during the years that have followed, I have spent time interviewing King, his current and former dancers, LINES administrators, and its guest artists in order to write the first critical analysis of the company.

My primary work, then, focused on King's unconventional approach to femininity in ballet. I had wanted to recast the image of the dependent ballerina as a powerful force and knew the dancers of this company were poised for the job. Though the scope of my work has remained purposefully limited to LINES, I found early on that King's aesthetic shares certain qualities with the work of William Forsythe—perhaps the best-known artist working in contemporary ballet—and it would be impossible to ignore their relationship in my ongoing analysis.[11] For this reason, I include a brief analysis of Forsythe in this essay. Still, near the conclusion of my initial project I realized King was doing much more than entering into choreographic discourse with other well-known artists. He was doing more than reinvigorating preconceived notions of femininity. King was changing the dynamic of ballet partnerships. In so doing, his oeuvre stands to expand the movement potential for both female and male dancers.

Evolution in the Pas de Deux Line

Gender distinctions in ballet invariably start during the training process. Historically these divisions arose from social guidelines, cultural practices, and value systems esteemed by Parisians in the 18th and 19th centuries. Such codes then became part of the dancers' understanding of how ballet technique should be executed. The genealogies of these and other balletic constructions are unpacked in dance scholar Susan Leigh Foster's *Choreography and Narrative: Ballet's Staging of Story and Desire*. In this study Foster examines the way separate roles for male and female dancers originated from one's placement in a specific societal milieu. By staging a narration complete with period librettos, Foster's analysis illustrates how dancers were positioned both literally and historiographically. She asserts: "*Pas de deux* offered the female dancer considerable visibility but relatively little autonomy. During her solos, dancing on her own and by herself, she commanded the viewer's attention as an independent character with a particular temperament and set of accomplishments. Dancing with her partner, prominent as she was, her movements depended upon and were guided by his support" (205). The images that Foster describes in relation to pas de deux would become astoundingly persistent—so much so that today's training requires a dancer to internalize identifiable gender constructions in which the female is often marked as vulnerable and powerless to the will of the male.[12]

King's early works cultivated an alternative position and reception for the female dancer, and she became associated with characteristics deemed masculine, such as overt strength, command, and power.[13] Yet in order to embody and develop this new lexicon of femininity, the LINES ballerinas had to forsake some of their foundational training. Though seemingly counterintuitive, in this instance forgetting does not imply the negative idea of loss. In fact, "undoing" can actually produce gains for the dancer who seeks to work in ways counter to presumed balletic norms. In *Undoing Gender*, performance theorist Judith Butler contends that "undoing" can facilitate gender theorizations by allowing the possibility for alternatives. In light of this, she problematizes the assumption that agency cannot exist if the surrounding circumstances appear prohibitive. As Butler further explains, with respect to this constitution of gender, "That my agency is riven with paradox does not mean it is impossible. It means only that paradox is the condition of its possibility" (3). For the LINES dancers, finding a way to work within ballet's rigidity and create movement that paradoxically suggests autonomy has proved a necessary part of the creative process. This very type of "undoing" permits the dancers to interject their individual personalities, subsequently diversifying the vocabulary and making the act of doing ballet more meaningful.[14] The dancers of this company develop a heightened sense of control by ignoring some of the technique's specific codifications about form and performance. Eventually, this translates into a feeling of efficacy for those who dance with LINES.

In the same way that Butler considers paradox a site for opportunity, LINES' repertory encourages agency in a genre that has traditionally sought to restrain it. Throughout history, ballets have depicted male dancers who stand behind graceful, lithe females for support. Although dances and artists have presumed to challenge this idea through homogeneous pairings, innovative lift sequences, or transgendered costuming, many of these endeavors have simply reified gender binaries in another (still aberrant) way, and in so doing solidified the belief that there is an identifiable norm from which one can deviate or choreograph an opposite. LINES, however, has purposefully avoided such reductive approaches by presenting work in which gender is undone, transversed, and reenacted. Ultimately LINES finds its niche by transcending femininity and masculinity. This is seen not only through the aesthetic that these particular bodies have cultivated but also through King's creative process—one that insists the dancers' own subjectivities should contribute to the formation of each piece. Because King believes all dances are about relationships, a comment he often emphasizes in interviews and discussions about his work, it is not surprising that his ballets choreographically move through the power struggles inherent therein.

As gender theorist Michael Gard points out in *Men Who Dance: Aesthetics, Athletics and the Art of Masculinity*, treatments of gender can never be removed from the socially constructed matrix of power within which they originate. Gard's conceptualization of masculinity is one that centralizes relationships in order to suggest that the individual corporealizes subjectivity through interaction. I contend that this occurs in the dances King makes. Gard draws heavily on feminist discourse (with some reservations), because "it remains the only area of scholarship in which both the symbolic and material dimensions of gender relations have been systematically questioned and challenged" (28–29). At the same time, he explains the need to emphasize the experience of the body so that gender is not a term for something that happens "outside the body"; rather, it is the "arena in which gendered identities are constructed" (30). By relying on the work of several theorists from a wide array of disciplines to suggest that subjectivity and, consequently, gender identity are "shaped, though not determined, by the form and capacities (such as for sensation) of our bodies," Gard develops an approach to discussing masculinity not as a construction that can be teased out of its context but rather as a "process" that is directly linked to the body (28, 31).[15] I include Gard's analysis here because it has some parallels with the theory of gender I offer in regard to King, the main difference being that even though Gard presumes to "transcend biological/cultural divides" in his study, the role of women is conspicuously absent (29). In King's aesthetic, masculinity and femininity are qualities that transform as they interact with one another. Consequently, neither can be constructed in opposition to one another, or without the presence of both. For King, it is this balance of gender that brings harmony and transcendence to his work.

In terms of suggesting an alternative position and reception for male and female ballet dancers, I maintain King's ballets forsake and therefore challenge gender distinctions rigidly adhered to throughout cultural history. Because King does not construct the pas de deux in a predictable way, but instead as an exploration of how masculinity and femininity can coalesce, his works disrupt the notion that males must control females in danced partnerships. In the majority of his duets, dancers are not asked to play the parts of men and women—they are invited to demonstrate qualities that "examine the male and female sides of the individual," "the balance between reason and logic," or the "light and darkness within" that manifests itself through "struggle and harmony," says King. Former LINES dancer Nora Heiber explains, "The gender of the person doing it is not really the point—it's more the quality that he [King] is trying to represent, and whether or not the individual that he is going to use can represent that quality. So the ideas of masculine and feminine are more aligned with energetic qualities as opposed to anatomical characteristics."

Because King believes ballet training teaches males and females about how their bodies should look while dancing, he thinks that unlocking fixed understandings can broaden the scope of the classical paradigm. In light of this, he encourages dancers to disregard what they have been taught about how to use space differently: where to place legs, arms, and feet; whether or not their elbows should bend, or if their wrists should move. To him, these practices are the result of a gender-specific instruction system, and they produce dancers who perform in accordance with sociologically created understandings of masculinity and femininity.[16] For King these ways of moving are really only "ideas," and consequently they can be manipulated through the course of the pas de deux.[17] Thus, he strives to avoid the reiteration of narratives wherein strong, supportive male dancers are in back of pliable females, and he presents work in which such categorizations are undone, erased, reenacted, and traversed.

This new approach is not always obvious to viewers, since most of the time the ballerinas dance *en pointe* alongside male partners who often seem to position their limbs. Yet the difference here is that the men are not posing the women in the classical sense but rather working with them to facilitate movements that could not be accomplished by either dancer independently. What is more, in King's pas de deux the women—not men—tend to initiate and guide movements in a way that tends to even out the responsibilities of each. Finally, the fact that the dancers reinterpret stock staging protocols, so that they rarely face full front, helps refocus attention on the act of moving, not presenting. This ultimately distances LINES' pas de deux from those in which the female appears to be a puppet controlled by the male. Due to these revisions, I argue this company has found its niche transgressing popular notions of gender—despite holding on to certain rules of pas de deux—so that masculinity and femininity are not pitted in conflict but become segments of the same socially constructed matrix.

Every dancer who has come to work with King speaks of having previously embodied the role-playing that persists in the classical ballet idiom. They join LINES hoping to take their love of ballet in another direction. In terms of gender, King's emphasis on the exploration of qualities over any fixed idea of characterization facilitates a certain amount of liberation. As he explains: "If a role demands a particular kind of power, I will look for who can exemplify that power regardless of sexual distinction. It is absurd to think that a woman couldn't play Hamlet or a man Ophelia. In essence these are ideas, and actors have the potential to be whatever the role demands. It isn't the sex but the artistry that I am interested in. In the vast panoply of energies, masculine and feminine are merely two tones." Because King rarely distinguishes between male and female dancers in rehearsal, it is not surprising that the men and women of the company share a more similar movement vocabulary than in many other ballet companies. King's choreography asks dancers, regardless of sex, to barge through space one minute with tremendous force and effort, then to shift into lightning-quick footwork accompanied by flyaway arms and downward glances, only to once again transition into graceful hyperextensions and off-center balances.

When developing a new work, it is not uncommon for King to ask a man to perform an undulating arm sequence that he had originally set on a woman, nor is it unusual for him to urge his female dancers to let go of contrived notions of ballet beauty—holding the head at a certain angle or curving their elbows in a particular way—to heighten the intensity of their dancing. Former LINES dancer Maurya Kerr explains how during the creative process King has been known to say "stop being pretty."[18] According to Kerr, this is "because we're so conditioned, being women in ballet, to be dainty and pretty and to actually get by with that and to use that instead of strength... it [King's philosophical approach] is very 'anti' the conventions of ballet. But in terms of trying to be part of the process of helping people grow, it's such a great aspect—especially for women, to claim their space and also to claim your body as powerful."

Although LINES' pas de deux do adhere to some identifiable ballet rituals, they are distinct from traditional partnerships in key ways. This is perhaps most evident as King, like many contemporary ballet choreographers, swaps imagined narratives for nonlinear works that encourage gender (as customarily understood) to be transcended. Without "stories" the masculine/feminine dyad can be blurred, and neither the male nor the female has to follow prescribed guidelines dictating how to move. Still this does not mean masculinity and femininity are erased; rather, they are enhanced and embodied by the dancers irrespective of sex.

Former San Francisco Ballet dancer Kimberly Okamura,[19] who performed with LINES as a guest artist, said about King's understanding of gender: "If anything, he recognizes the strengths in his dancers, and that might be that not all of the women have a feminine quality and not all of the men have a masculine quality....Summer [Rhatigan] was an incredibly powerful dancer so she would always get these really tough, really hard roles... and then there's Greg [Dawson], who is not your danseur noble kind of guy; he has a kind of catlike, almost a feminine quality."[20] Okamura's comments in regard to King's fluctuating use of masculinity and femininity are a testament to his unorthodox pas de deux stagings. Because King does not privilege frontal spacing and the male dancers are not placed directly behind the women to pose, maneuver, or present, traditional ballet lifts are transformed. Because movements in which the woman is held and centered by the man are replaced by phrases that emphasize intricate entanglements of the legs and arms, connection, unification, and a shared partnership are continually reinforced. This directly contrasts with classical pas de deux that highlight difference, just as it also gives the audience a new perspective from which to view the relationship between masculinity and femininity in ballet.[21]

Figure 4.2   Ballet pas de deux in which women are held, centered, and presented by male partners are re-placed in King's choreography by phrases that emphasize the intricate entanglement of limbs and a shared sense of journey. Dancers: Keelan Whitmore and Caroline Rocher in King's *Irregular Pearl* (2007). Photograph by Marty Sohl. Used with permission of Marty Sohl/Alonzo King's LINES Ballet.

Once uncomplicated costuming is added to these already irregular duets, paradigmatic ideals of what ballet dancers should look like are further dispelled. The typically monochromatic costumes (often designed by Robert Rosenwasser and/or Colleen Quen) frequently differ for the men and women, yet they always emphasize the lines of the dancers' long, bare legs. It is not unusual for the men to wear soft, flowing skirts or the women to wear nothing but simple earth-toned leotards. Rather than dress each dancer in the same unitard-style outfit, the costuming also draws attention to the fact that LINES is a company of men and women—while playfully questioning and sometimes reversing their customary attire. This is especially important because it confirms that King's dances are not trying to circumvent or ignore constructions of masculinity and femininity; instead, the ballets, in all facets of their design, overtly query gender.

King also has new ideas about pointe work that compel a changed image for the female dancer. He uses the shoes not to convey weightlessness or fragility but to elongate the lines of the dancers' legs to the fullest possible extent. Contrary to their original intent—to make female dancers appear light enough to levitate, therefore potentially diminishing their status and subjecthood—the LINES dancers wear pointe shoes to become larger and take up just as much stage space as the men. This challenges Ann Daly's declaration, that the ballerina *en pointe* can never gain parity with a male partner, on two counts.[22] First, the LINES women tend to dance alongside the men when *en pointe*—they do not wait for the latter to facilitate maneuvers or initiate movements in the pas de deux. Second, the females do not rely on the male dancers to achieve moments of unspoiled steadiness while *en pointe*; more accurately, they dance on the tips of their toes to extend their reach and emphasize the power of movement. By appearing stronger, more solid, and sometimes in command of their male counterparts, the LINES ballerinas contest preconceived notions of masculinity and femininity in ballet.

As Rita Felciano's 1996 *Dance Magazine* review of the company's New York season at the Joyce Theater sums up, "Few have explored the intricacies of pointe work as extensively as King. Yet even *en pointe*, his dancers always stay firmly grounded" (23). This observation locates the LINES ballerinas as earthbound and agency-laden rather than ephemeral. Moreover, because the women stabilize themselves, the LINES men are not asked to anchor them. This not only unrestricts the role of the male but also removes quintessential pas de deux roles in order to make duets that are about the relationship of bodies and energies rather than the ability of one partner to steady the other.

Redirecting the Masculine Line

Because the role of the male dancer is expanded beyond stock characterizations in King's pieces, the LINES men dance in ways that look different than other male ballet dancers—even those performing contemporary work. Part of this has to do with the fact that King's choreography accentuates transitions over tricks. The men seem to float more, to arch backward with grace, and undulate through their upper bodies. They tilt their heads diagonally down so as to look at their shoulders, and they show high extensions in a seamless way. This is not to say that the LINES male dancers lack commanding jumps or are technically inferior to others—just the opposite at many moments. But they are charged to explore all ranges of movement, as opposed to focusing on displays of bravura.

King's choreography does not lend itself to the way masculinity has been marketed in the world of big ballet at the beginning of the 21st century. For instance, the PBS documentary *Born to Be Wild: Leading Men of American Ballet Theatre* (2004), the stage show *Kings of the Dance* (presented in Orange County, California, and New York City in 2006), and the movie *Center Stage* (2000)

Figure 4.3   The LINES aesthetic emphasizes transformation over tricks. Men as well as women must float, undulate, and demonstrate lyricism. Dancer: Brett Conway in King's *Migration* (2006). Photograph by Marty Sohl. Used with permission of Marty Sohl/Alonzo King's LINES Ballet.

highlight the virility of ballet men in a stereotypical way, calling attention to such things as motorcycle riding, unruly behavior, multiple turns, and punching leaps. The LINES men do have something in common with the male dancers featured in those roles; they all blend grace with strength, are quiet and yet bold, and execute powerful movements with refinement. Nonetheless, there is something distinctly different about the way they are presented and how they look when dancing. According to the men of the company, this has everything to do with King's approach to movement. Veteran company member Gregory Dawson describes the process as learning to "flow with what comes" and "to really go inside" when working with King, so that the technical feats are deemed secondary to the experience one has with the dance.

When this philosophy is corporealized, masculinity takes on different qualities. The LINES men say that they learn to reprioritize and redirect their dancing, choosing to accent fundamentals other than the volume, height, or impressiveness of "tricks." King asks them to use their heads and arms more fluidly than in ballet proper. He also provides sections of unison lyrical dancing that convey a sinuous quality customary to female corps in conventional ballet. While maintaining aspects of the princely refinement common to male dancers, the LINES men display lyricism and a polyrhythmic understanding of the music, form asymmetrical shapes, and seem secure in "off-balance" balances; these ways of moving combine to yield a new kind of embodied masculinity.

When King's company expanded in 1998 to include more male dancers than ever before, he was inspired to create two ballets that called attention to the men: *A Long Straight Line* and *Who Dressed You Like a Foreigner?*[23] After these works, King continued to explore what male dancers could offer, ultimately changing the persona of what was once a primarily female company. Dawson remembers that *Foreigner* was "a step in another direction" for LINES; it was the first time King had a "really strong core group of men" who could "feed off of each other." What is crucial for the purposes of this analysis is that King did not alter his process when the men joined the company, and as a result, his ballets did not become more masculine in the traditional sense. Instead, the men (having all come from classical ballet backgrounds) went through the same transition as the ballerinas before them, learning to deconstruct what they had previously thought to be the most important things about being male ballet dancers and to investigate what it meant to move without preconceived notions or imagery. Because of this, *A Long Straight Line* and *Who Dressed You Like a Foreigner?* are not "testosterone pieces." They do not perpetuate the construction of masculinity in which strength triumphs, nor do they reconstitute the familiar tropes of gender and sexuality so often seen in concert dance. Instead, these ballets question the presumption that fluidity should be exclusive to female performers and strong actions left to the men. Although working more intensely with male dancers might seem like a normal progression in accordance with what was going on in the dance world at the time (i.e., a period of increased notoriety for danseurs), for the men of LINES this was a significant moment. In their opinion, it meant that King was taking his work in a new direction—one that would not only permit increased artistic freedom but also augment performance opportunities.

My assertion that King's dances rework fixed ideologies by interrogating masculinity can be correlated to the points made in dance theorist Ramsay Burt's book *The Male Dancer: Bodies, Spectacle, Sexualities*. As one of the few pieces of dance scholarship devoted to the investigation of male dancing bodies (this volume notwithstanding), Burt's inquiry is of special relevance here.[24] He questions the dominant norms of patriarchy, as well as the techniques through which gender binaries are reproduced and represented in the dances of "reformers and innovators" (5). Through a series of descriptions about the "subversive," "denaturalizing," and "destabilizing" realizations of masculinity in performance, Burt posits that societal assumptions about maleness are habitually revealed in theater dance. It should be noted, however, that despite unpacking Nijinsky's masculinity and subsequent legacy, the majority of Burt's movement examples fall within modern or postmodern territory. Nevertheless, using the choreography of Martha Graham, Merce Cunningham, Trisha Brown, Steve Paxton, and Pina Bausch to foreground the contention that "masculinity is a socially constructed identity" with the potential to be subverted, his analysis has set a standard for research on masculinity and its embodiment (9).

Taking Burt's study in a different direction, I argue that King's choreography for LINES has broadened the range of male ballet dancing by not forcing dancers to perpetuate patriarchal structures and not giving in to token representations of masculinity. By utilizing a shared movement vocabulary for LINES' men and women, King's works allow the former to avoid clichés often employed in male ballet dancing. At the same time, it is important to point out that the dancers still adhere to certain protocols that are rooted in gender division (having only women *en pointe* is one) because King accepts such conventions if they stand to investigate qualities he wants to explore in a particular ballet. Even though the men and women of this company do not dress or dance identically, they do sometimes take on costumes, qualities, and movement often reserved for the other sex. In this way, the LINES dancing bodies stand to alter perceptions of gender in the ballet world.

Diagonal Lines

Many ballet pas de deux appear to examine romantic relationships between men and women, with only the occasional dance about friendship, swordplay, or familial interactions. King, like other choreographers, has created duets that explore various permutations of love, yet the pieces are always understood by him to have a spiritual connection. The idea that something divine is present in his ballets is at the root of King's rhetoric and practice—so much so that each dancer with whom I have spoken has mentioned the importance of spirituality in both the creation and performance of his works. For LINES alumna Debra Rose, these ideas are manifest in the spatial design of King's choreography.[25] She feels his approach is especially poignant because there is not a contrived "resolution," but rather an overwhelming sense that "everything is a continuum," or that dance is a "process that doesn't end." Her understanding of spirituality echoes that of King, who uses diagonals as staging patterns in an attempt to reference the angle of ascension from this world up to the next.

King is one of seven choreographers profiled in critic Janet Roseman's *Dance Masters: Interviews with Legends of Dance*.[26] In this study, King is quoted as saying that his work strives to make up for the two things he felt were consistently missing from his own dance training: spirituality and "the concept that 'it [the spirit] is within you'" (113). King's way of working with dancers contrasts with most Western dance pedagogy in that it prioritizes "being" rather than "doing." Thus, this choreographer sees movement not as a concept he brings to the dancers but, rather, as something they have inside themselves that he must find a way to uncover. King believes it is imperative for dancers to understand this distinction because it reframes the idea of creation as craftsmanship and in turn generates ballets with which the dancers feel personal connections. This is confirmed by former LINES dancer Marina Hotchkiss, who remembers her role in *Who Dressed You Like a Foreigner?* as providing the "extraordinary opportunity to inhabit the Divine." In fact, Hotchkiss felt so moved by the work that many years later she continues to consider it an "experience that still nourishes me in some way."

Former LINES dancer Christian Burns agrees that *Foreigner* was not only "the most satisfying dance of my life" but also "the most extraordinary experience."[27] Calling to mind the rarity of the event, Burns struggled for the right words, revealing how he often performed the duet with his eyes closed, and how liberating it felt to be able to "get really deep in a public form." He says this ballet offered him a sense of intimacy that has been impossible to replicate. These and other company dancers agree that *Who Dressed You Like a Foreigner?* marked a change in the repertory, instigating a significant transformation not only for each performer but also for the company's overall perception and image.

Although King does not ask the dancers to talk about their feelings toward choreography, or to improvise per se, he does create phrases based on their individual interpretations of his ideas. This means that the company members choose moments to emphasize; consequently, they feel a close relationship to the ballets that are made. Although he prioritizes individuality in a way that the dancers consider spiritual, it is important to point out that King does not label his ballets as such; instead, he believes spirituality is a concept that must be encountered, not explained. At the same time, he feels that it is something concert dance, regrettably, does not often centralize.[28] "The experience of the Spirit is so personal," he says in his profile in Roseman's collection, "and for the most part secretive, and understandably so. It's an inner experience, and to talk about it is to lessen it" (127). King's unwavering belief in "the spirit" is also what prompts him to denounce claims of authorship or celebrity: "Technically, everything comes from a higher source. . . . All great thoughts, all invention, is acquired through the superconscious mind. The world's greatest composers, inventors, saints, scientists, and reformers acknowledge tapping into that source. It is accessible to everyone; there is no ownership of ideas. It takes place by being still and entering a place of keen interest with deep concentration, or by great faith" (125). For King, the true work of the artist is to find that place where predilections and ego fall away, and the spirit has a chance to enter.

This dialogue is of the utmost importance when it comes to gender because it is this very type of deep exploration that prevents King's ballets from becoming surface-level love stories destined to reinforce the masculine/feminine dyad. By emphasizing spirituality as part of the dancers' internal engagement to the movements, King's aesthetic undermines ballet's historic relationship with

Figure 4.4   Strength, power, and quickness are tempered with asymmetry and a willingness to be open in King's choreography. Prince Credell, former dancer with LINES Ballet, in King's *Before the Blues* (2004). Photograph by Marty Sohl. Used with permission of Marty Sohl/Alonzo King's LINES Ballet.

opening up ("turning out") and presenting oneself to an audience. His dancers do not move in ways that they think might look pretty or powerful. They do not adjust their execution of a phrase to match the dancer next to them, nor do they look at themselves in the mirror. (Even though there are mirrors in the studio, the dancers rarely seek affirmation from their reflections.) Instead, they take a technique in which they are all well versed and use it as a tool to explore undiscovered facets of ballet. From this internal and individual way of working, LINES has forged new ways of thinking about masculinity and femininity that arise from qualities and feelings rather than the presentation of archetypes.

Of course King is not the only one to work with contemporary ideas through inventive means in today's ballet world; in fact, when it comes to streamlined renovations of the form, William Forsythe has been a driving force for many years.[29] Because both Forsythe and King uniquely approach ballet, while not abandoning its key protocols (partnering, pointe shoes, and vocabulary), a comparison between the two is valid on many levels.[30] Over the past few decades the two artists have had various interactions. In 1986 King created a pas de deux for Forsythe's wife, Tracy Kai Maier, while she was dancing with the San

Francisco Ballet.[31] A few years later, King was commissioned to choreograph for Forsythe's Ballett Frankfurt. Differences in style and content notwithstanding, both choreographers create idiosyncratic ways of moving, exploring off-kilter balances and unusual partnering in pas de deux.

Forsythe and King have been linked by both national and international critics, who also evoke Balanchine when describing the major precedent for contemporary choreographic trends. For example, in 1998, reviewer Rita Felciano explained, "For those who can define ballet by geometry—lines and planes—and play with gravity, King fits right into the modernism of, let's say, Balanchine's *Agon* or the explorations of his contemporary William Forsythe" (64). In Paris, *Liberation* critic Marie-Christine Vernay described King's choreography by writing, "In the footwork we could evoke William Forsythe." In *Le Figaro*, René Sirvin positioned King as an artist "unknown in France" whose work "like Forsythe . . . venerates Balanchine." Sirvin also mentioned that the LINES "dancers with long legs . . . remind us of New York City Ballet" as they execute work that is "sensuous and feline."[32]

Even though Forsythe and King create work that can be seen to challenge traditional gender roles, I suggest that the results tend to look quite divergent. Neither choreographer adheres to the 19th-century prince-swan archetypes in any obvious way—indeed, the fairy tale is long gone—so that both male and female dancers initiate movement, have strong and weak moments, and often defy stereotypes. Yet for me, a Forsythe pas de deux, for instance, reflects his emphasis on movement design, text, and structural organization of the body and of bodies in space.[33] Men still frequently support women, and the relationship can end up looking conventional in terms of gender differentiation. King's dancers, on the other hand, seem prayerful, contemplative, and sometimes trancelike in a pas de deux, embodying a relationship that looks more like a mutual journey to somewhere beyond themselves. It could be that each choreographer's approach reflects priorities that offer different opportunities when it comes to gender portrayals. After talking to a few dancers who have worked for both, I found some clues as to emphasis in each process—Forsythe with his (at times mathematical) formulas and reframing devices that create shapes, patterns, and lines; and King, who asks his dancers to feel energies, essences, and qualities and often puts forth ideas that connect and subvert gender notions. I suggest that it is the process that leads to a heightened sense of possibility in King's work, and this is likely due to the fact that he espouses concepts of masculinity and femininity differently than Forsythe.

When specifically asked about the roles of male and female dancers in the development of new works, former Forsythe dancer Maia Rosal recalls that gender was "not an issue" when it came to the creation of ballets.[34] Instead, one of the main things that seemed to inspire Forsythe was the "classical form." Although the classical form is also important for King as he makes ballets that celebrate "lines," his dancers rarely mention form as one of his inspirations.

Instead, the LINES dancers talk of spirituality and experience. Whereas Rosal was careful not to speak for Forsythe, she explained that the way the dancers worked "as a team, improvising, evolving, establishing, re-imagining," set his choreography apart from the stylized role-playing and gender specificity that she had previously known ballet to be.[35] In Forsythe's pieces (at least those she had the chance to dance in), Rosal recalls roles that "are clearly female, such as the women wearing big gowns in Act I of *Impressing the Tzar*" (1988), but at the same time there "are also pieces where it makes absolutely no difference if the performer is male or female." For instance, "Act IV of *Impressing the Tzar* has the entire company dressed identically as Catholic schoolgirls: wigs, blouses, pleated skirts," and "*Skinny* [1986] had interchangeable parts with all performers dressed in shorts, t-shirts, and tennies." In addition, she clarifies that there is "a third type of role, where it is neither of the two types described above," examples of which are seen in *Enemy in the Figure* (1989) and *In the Middle Somewhat Elevated* (1987). With this in mind, Rosal concludes that gender distinction is often performed, but not "because the movement is specifically male or female." Instead, it is because there is "something in the quality or interpretation of movement [that] calls for that part to be done by a man or woman."

This description suggests that King and Forsythe both test gender as depicted in traditional ballet. Nevertheless, Rosal's assertions still support the observation that Forsythe's eye-catching translations place primacy on carrying out a structure. As a result, his dancers understand that the work is not about them but rather about how they relate to the form. Unlike the process Rosal describes, my study of King's dances shows that he uses masculinity and femininity as fundamental sources for movement. Because King believes gender to be a social construction that has produced particular ways of dancing ballet, his choreography attempts to question traditional mind-sets through demonstrations of feminine strength, masculine fluidity, and the myriad of possibilities that exist between these extremes. When King chooses dancers to work with, the selection is based on his understanding of the dancer's energy and whether he or she can reveal a specific quality. In Forsythe's ballets, dancers are also challenged to rebel against established standards, yet their impetus to do so is described by those who have worked for him as well thought out and strategic, not cathartic.

In an essay from 1993, performance theorist Heidi Gilpin, who worked as a dramaturg for Forsythe, maintains that his chief concern is to disrupt balletic principles; Forsythe does this by uncovering "forms of division and moments of instability that are actually the joints of movements" yet regularly considered failures in ballet (107). Like King, Forsythe expects dancers to investigate movement as a means of generating permutations within the ballet vocabulary. Still, a major discrepancy between the two choreographers is brought out when Gilpin describes Forsythe's ballets as enactments of "these disturbing moments of (lost) attention," "disequilibrium," and "the process of disappearing," so that the ensuing dances do not accentuate the qualities of an individual performer but instead highlight how a dancer responds when positioned in a challenging or risk-laden situation. These occasions of loss are what Gilpin suggests most ballets force viewers to overlook. Because Forsythe uses non-movement-based textual and philosophical theories to bring life to these "failures," his choreography redirects the spectator's attention away from the dancer and toward the context of the dance.[36] Even though King's choreography also tries to strip away ballet's rules to re-form movements in an edgy way, he unfailingly draws on its customs to confirm subjectivity rather than to accentuate instances of breakdown.

Former LINES dancer Katherine Warner said, "When working with Alonzo, as work was being developed, I felt as if I was doing my own work—rather than putting on movement given by the choreographers. I was so inspired by the concepts we were working with, that it felt as if the work was just me."[37] Nora Heiber also reinforced that in King's rehearsals the dancer is always paramount: "Alonzo responds to energy. . . . When he is creating a piece it's like he's cooking, and he'll have a smell or a taste that he wants to put in, or a color that he wants to add to the meal, and a person comes out and offers him that color or that smell, and it's either in keeping with the idea that he already had, or it's offering something that he hasn't thought of . . . it's like 'oh that could be interesting, let me try that.'" Like Warner, Heiber always felt that cultivating her own understanding of movement was of greater importance to King than designing phrases or corporealizing theories. Both of these accounts directly contrast Rosal's depiction of Forsythe's rehearsals in which the dancers were sometimes told to "forget that it was about us at all," as well as Gilpin's observation that the context, not the dancer, is the source for investigation in Forsythe's ballets.

Dancers Kimberly Okamura and Christian Burns have at one time danced for both King and Forsythe (Burns with both companies; Okamura, guesting for LINES and more briefly with Forsythe when he set a piece on the San Francisco Ballet). In general, Okamura saw more differences than similarities between Forsythe's and King's respective approaches to dance-making and interaction with dancers. For her, the parameters through which each choreographer urged dancers to make movements "their own" were notably dissimilar. In Okamura's experience, when Forsythe asked dancers to improvise, it was within the narrowest of circumstances. There were set qualifications that included time constraints, framework guidelines, and the required insertion of specific gestures. On the other hand, she found King to purposefully leave directions nebulous, forcing the dancers to find "their way." Although Okamura saw masculinity and femininity as more clearly addressed in King's pieces, she attributed this to the fact that she had worked longer and more intensely with LINES.

Burns spent five months dancing for Forsythe in 1997 (before joining LINES), at a time when he was seeking "a place where I could continue to work improvisationally without leaving my ballet base."[38] When I asked him to speak about the two choreographers with respect to the process that Okamura commented on, he noted meaningful variances despite the fact that both are innovators: "I have heard people say that they [King's and Forsythe's dances] look so similar and wonder who was influenced by whom. I am not so sure if they were necessarily influenced directly by one another, but if you come from a deep understanding of what Balanchine was on to, and simply pull it out a bit farther, you will end up with a faster, higher, edgier, more dangerous form of ballet. They came to the same place from very different places. They have arrived at an inevitable place." Nevertheless, by classifying Forsythe as an "intellectual" who "may use references from Foucault to architecture to analyze a phrase" and King as "very spiritual, very concerned with feeling and emotion," Burns concluded that the two "couldn't get more different actually." Though reticent to generalize about Forsythe's interpretations of gender, Burns underscored King's unique ability to encourage dancers to investigate movement in ways that might be deemed transgressive when measured against common notions of masculinity and femininity.

From these discussions of the rehearsal and creative process, it becomes clear that Forsythe and King are often inclined to begin their experimentations from different points. Another choreographer who has recently begun to deconstruct the conventional U.S. ballet aesthetic in ways that could potentially be seen as similar to those of King and Forsythe is Dwight Rhoden for Complexions Contemporary Ballet.[39] Rhoden, an African American ballet-based choreographer and artistic director, has engaged former LINES dancers as guest artists.[40] I bring up Complexions here because its repertory has been compared to King's in terms of its reliance on spirituality in concert dance. In an article entitled "Ballet of Transcendence" that appeared in *Ballettanz* in 2003, Coleen Payton connects these choreographers (along with Alvin Ailey, Bill T. Jones, and Ballethnic's Waverly Lucas) based on the fact that each has a company performing "ritualistic and celebratory works that employ the mixed vocabularies of African dance and ballet" (28). On the other hand, Ann Daly has noted differences between Complexions and other contemporary choreographers. In her review of the "Altogether Different" series at the Joyce in 1997, she suggested that, rather than being innovative, the Complexions style consists of "men's puffed-up chests, women's long legs, and more awkwardly labyrinthine limb-limning and butt shots than I've ever seen on a legitimate stage. I want to call it 'muscle ballet'" (18).[41] Daly's comments were echoed by Roslyn Sulcas writing for *Dance Magazine*, who observed, "Rhoden confects a sexy mix of Ailey-style muscular virtuosity, slam-bang momentum, and acrobatic partnering (interestingly, in these politically correct times, almost exclusively heterosexual) infused with a little nineties New Ageism and stretchy, ab-and-thigh-baring costumes" (86).

Former LINES dancer Tanya Wideman-Davis (who has also performed with Complexions) proposed the only similarity between LINES and Complexions is that they both employ ballet dancers.[42] In her opinion, Rhoden and Richardson's work is "very sexual and funky." I include these remarks not to further critique Complexions or to suggest Rhoden's work is subpar to that of King and Forsythe, but rather because these observations point out how Complexions' pas de deux have been seen by critics and dancers alike as reinforcing standardized protocols that, instead of focusing on spirituality or reconstruction of the form, often reify gender roles by centralizing heterosexuality. Even though Complexions does use similar costuming and off-vertical movements that might remind some viewers of King's ballets, the outward focus of the dancers, the repetitive patterning of phrases, and the emphasis on the peripheral over the internal are just a few of many differences.

Rearticulation

Because King encourages his dancers to explore qualities of humanity without preconceived notions of how ballet men and women should move, his pas de deux depart from existing norms. This is evident not only when women lead men but also as the men exhibit smoothness and undulation. Ballets like *Lila* and *Koto* seem to reassign conventionally masculine qualities to female dancers, just as *Who Dressed You Like a Foreigner?* and *A Long Straight Line* permit men to perform movements in ways that might be deemed feminine by some. For King, the sociologically created understandings of masculinity and femininity are not compulsory in pas de deux, but neither are they taboo. This means he is not interested in making dancers look the same, or radically different from previous standards, just to prove a point. Instead, his approach and the beliefs underlying it provide the freedom to simultaneously refuse and correspond to ballet's gender models relative to the ideas foregrounding the dance.

King's choreographic transgressions are not always obvious to the viewers, especially when ballerinas still dance *en pointe* alongside male partners who seem to position their limbs. Nevertheless, I suggest that subtle differences, variations in the dancers' intent, their lived experience of the movement, and changes in their relationships toward one another, are enough to make a big impact—so much so that King's ballets defy present categorizations. By allowing his dancers the chance to move and flow in ways that may signify masculinity and femininity, but not necessarily in accord with their maleness or femaleness, King has rearticulated the role that gender plays in ballet. As a result, LINES' repertory challenges audiences to see something other than elegant ballerinas manipulated by manly men.

In this essay I have discussed a company that corporealizes nontraditional approaches to gender by confusing the boundaries that currently separate what male and female dancing bodies are directed to do in conventional U.S. ballet. By transgressing such norms, Alonzo King's choreography encourages men and women to reevaluate concepts that have historically determined how they should move, and such alterations have set the stage for a transition in the genre. For nearly three decades, King has viewed gender as a concept rather than a constraint. That is to say, if he needs a dancer to play a part that is princely, he will not look for the male dancer with the nicest hair or the biggest jump; instead, he ponders what it means to be a prince and selects the individual whose movement best personifies those characteristics. King explained it to me this way: "We are drenched in clichés and stereotypes. We are told, a prince must be tall and blond, no—a prince has to be noble. Nobility is a soul quality, and has nothing to do with money, race, or culture."

When choreographing, King asks female dancers to take on princelike roles that demand a commanding focus, while the men are invited to be disciples, to show frailty, or to exude affection. This practice aligns his opinions with current theorists who regard masculinity and femininity as beliefs, constructions, or made-up notions that socialize men and women into acting and moving in specific ways. By creating ballets that complicate gender, King's work does not ignore standard portrayals. It does something much more innovative: it offers choice.

NOTES

1. LINES, a Dance Company, was the group's original name. This was officially changed twice: first to LINES Contemporary Ballet and once more to the current title, Alonzo King's LINES Ballet. The company is best known as LINES within the dance community.

2. I first interviewed Alonzo King in April 2003. This was the beginning of many conversations I would have with him while writing my doctoral dissertation about LINES. The quotations that appear throughout this essay are all from personal communiqués with King that have transpired as part of my continuing research on his work. His help has been invaluable. I also thank dance scholar Jennifer Fisher for her thoughtful editing and support in seeing this essay through to publication.

3. Paramhansa Yogananda (also spelled Paramahansa Yogananda, 1893–1952) was a yoga master and spiritual teacher from India who sparked great interest in meditation and spiritual awakening by touring widely in the United States, starting in the 1920s. His memoir, *Autobiography of a Yogi* (1946), has been translated widely, enjoying particular popularity in the 1960s and 1970s. Spiritual centers and retreats founded by disciples still carry on his teachings.

4. Although the company is now also associated with the LINES Ballet School and the LINES/Dominican College B.F.A. program, neither was created specifically to feed the company.

5. LINES associate artistic director Robert Rosenwasser received this quote in an e-mail communication from William Forsythe. The quote now appears in the Alonzo King biography section of the LINES Web site. See http://www.linesballet.org/lines/alonzoking/ (accessed August 14, 2008).

6. Summer Rhatigan danced for LINES from 1988 to 2001.

7. Enrico Labayen left LINES to form his own dance company in San Francisco. The group, known as the LAB Projekt, was established in 1990.

8. Height differences like this are most frequently used for humor in traditional ballets, as exemplified by the works of Les Ballets Trockadero de Monte Carlo.

9. I thank Susan Leigh Foster for her suggestion to consider LINES as the primary subject of my dissertation, as well as her guidance throughout the writing process.

10. See Jill Nunes Jensen's *Re-forming the Lines: A Critical Analysis of Alonzo King's LINES Ballet.*

11. I was initially disturbed by the fact that each time I told someone about my research, they countered by asking a question about Forsythe. I quickly realized this meant I would have no choice but to locate King's work in relation to Forsythe's.

12. In "The Balanchine Woman: Of Hummingbirds and Channel Swimmers," dance scholar and critic Ann Daly explains that in Balanchine's *Four Temperaments*, "Pointe work often frames the ballerina as needy of her partner's help," so much so that the male dancer appears "linear and stable" next to a ballerina who is "curvaceous and inconstant" (285). In "Classical Ballet: A Discourse of Difference," Daly further argues, "Male and female—'power' and 'fragility'—are 'equal' only insofar as they maintain the asymmetrical *equilibrium* of patriarchy—which does not offer equality at all" (291).

13. In 1989, Rita Felciano noted in the *San Francisco Bay Guardian*, in a review of King's 1988 ballet *Ligeti Variations*, that ballerina Nora Heiber (a LINES company member from 1987 to 1998) was "a tall, heroic dancer" capable of "dominating her two partners" (33).

14. As Shona Innes writes, it is a "fallacy" to presume that the "ballet trained dancer has the greatest potential versatility and range for a choreographer, that they could do any style of dancing well, that they could do anything that was asked of them by any choreographer, modern or classical" because "ballet trains people to do ballet" (39). She continues by asserting: "The held state of the body produces a corresponding fixity of the intellect and emotion which is almost pubescent in a lot of cases. For choreographers who are interested in individuals and what happens on the inside of a person while they are dancing, pure ballet trained dancers present many difficulties" (39). Following Innes helps clarify why the LINES dancers have had to "undo" some of their ballet training in order to tap into their individual dancing personae in the way King demands.

15. Many contemporary theorists engage and challenge gender as related to the body. Teresa de Lauretis, for example, in her work *Technologies of Gender: Essays on Theory, Film, and Fiction*, problematizes gender as routinely understood. De Lauretis plumbs the work of other scholars ranging from Louis Althusser and Jacques Lacan to Wendy Hollway and Kaja Silverman to arrive at the postulation that "gender is the representation of a relation" (4). Taking this further, she dismisses the notion that gender is linked to just one idea, a single body, or an individual relationship and explains that the construct(ion) of gender is "both the product and the process of its representation" (5). A complete analysis of de Lauretis and other significant contributors to the gender discourse is well beyond the scope of this essay.

16. As dance scholar Cynthia Novack explained in "The Body's Endeavors as Cultural Practices," the relationship between dance and culture is intertwined so that "dance may reflect *and* resist cultural values simultaneously" (181). It is because of this that "groups

of people may, through dancing, construct and separate themselves from others" in a way that "their dance becomes associated with gender and age" (181).

17. For more on King's understanding of "ideas," see Rita Felciano, "His Ideas"; Allan Ulrich, "Breathtaking LINES: 25 Years of Alonzo King's Vision" (34); and Nunes Jensen, "OutLINES for a Global Ballet Aesthetic" (375, 381).

18. Maurya Kerr danced for LINES from 1994 to 2006.

19. Kimberly Okamura danced for LINES in 1996 and 1999.

20. Gregory Dawson danced for LINES from 1987 to 2005.

21. Daly's "Classical Ballet" problematizes society's immutable viewpoint that femininity is masculinity's token counterpart ("or difference"). With this, Daly solidifies not only the difficulty of performing a gender analysis on ballet but also the reluctance many have toward such balletic re-visions. For this reason, King's conception of the pas de deux dancers as striving toward a single line, rather than opposing displays of masculinity and femininity, is all the more revolutionary.

22. See Daly's "The Balanchine Woman" on this point.

23. *Who Dressed You Like a Foreigner?* was reintroduced for the company's 2004 tour and fall season and has become a signature work. The piece is divided into six sections: "Duty," "Silence," "Faith," "Time," "Wave," and "Ma."

24. Michael Gard confirms this in *Men Who Dance*, writing, "Little scholarly attention has been paid to the experience of male dancers" and going on to cite a series of dance theorists whose work either centralizes the "experiences of women" or relies heavily on "feminist perspectives" (5). He cites Burt's work as one the "few" models for his own exploration of men in dance (4).

25. Debra Rose danced for LINES from 1984 to 2000.

26. The others are Edward Villella, Merce Cunningham, Mark Morris, Catherine Turocy, Danny Grossman, and Michael Smuin.

27. Christian Burns danced for LINES from 1999 to 2002.

28. King wrote the foreword to another work by Janet Roseman—a book on modern dance and spirituality entitled *Dance Was Her Religion: The Spiritual Choreography of Isadora Duncan, Ruth St. Denis and Martha Graham.*

29. As dance historians Nancy Reynolds and Malcolm McCormick explain in *No Fixed Points: Dance in the Twentieth Century,* Forsythe was so lauded in Europe in the early 1990s that "in addition to acquiring cult status, Forsythe took on something of a mystical persona, no longer calling himself a choreographer, but claiming to be only one of many collaborators on a new ballet (the others were his dancers)" (594).

30. Because I have not observed Forsythe's creation process in the way that I have King's, this analysis relies on the testimony of former Forsythe dancers, scholars who have written on his work, critics, and my own observation of his ballets in performance. In so doing, I focus on Forsythe's earlier works in accordance with the dancers herein interviewed. However, it is important to note that the desire to compare Forsythe and King is still quite present, as is indicated by the number of European reviewers who do it despite the fact that much of Forsythe's current choreography abandons pointe shoes and codified ballet vocabulary.

31. Both Kai Maier and Christopher Boatwright, the two dancers who originally performed King's ballet *Stealing Light* in 1986, are now deceased. LINES reintroduced the work, danced by Laurel Keen and Brett Conway, as part of its 2003 San Francisco season.

32. Even though Balanchine's aesthetic touted *female* dancers with long legs, Sirvin does not make gender-based distinctions when using this description in regard to LINES.

33. In addition, critical accounts of Forsythe's work continually point to form as a primary source for inspiration. According to dance historian and Forsythe scholar Ann Nugent, his duet *From a Classical Position* (1997) "demonstrates how classically based movement can serve as a basis from which to discover new harmonies. Its score, again by Thom Willems, includes passages of Bach-like (Johann Sebastian) music in which the choreography (and filming) supports the classical style in the elegant posing of its two dancers (at least in this particular sequence). Legs then 'shoot' into arabesques, and bodies bend courteously forward, but the movement takes on a changed trajectory and dynamic, and the forms become alien, emphasizing not the expected 'turn-out' and finish but the 'underside' of classical positioning. Wrists are flexed and, led by the elbow, caused to revolve inwards. Hips, traditionally minimized by turn-out, are deliberately rounded" (84). Although the use of the term "alien" here can be likened to Rachel Howard's aforementioned observations about LINES, Nugent emphasizes it is the form and not the dancers that can be so likened in a Forsythe ballet. This further bears out Forsythe's and King's allegiances to structure and dancing bodies, respectively, within their avant-garde choreographies.

34. Maia Rosal danced for Pacific Northwest Ballet and then for Forsythe from 1988 to 1992. Her quotes herein come from a personal conversation held with the author.

35. Says Rosal of Forsythe: "Individual performances were absolutely riveting in a way I had never seen. It was not pirouettes or jumps but absolutely still moments timed perfectly, or monologues, or fantastic improvisations in which you could not even tell which limb went where how [*sic*]. There is so much that ballet dancers in general cannot do, like be still, walk, talk, and gesture without self-consciousness. We were all expected to bring notebooks during creation of a new work, to keep notes on sections, ideas, and 'tasks.' Bill would have us try different combinations of actions that required note taking and quick thinking beyond knowing the steps."

36. In "Static and Uncertain Bodies: Absence and Instability in Movement Perfor-mance," Gilpin gives the following example as further clarification of Forsythe's process: "Often textual material is created as a source of movement research: for *Limb's Theorem* [1990], a production I worked on as dramaturg, we were working with a number of ideas for both conceptual and physical enactment, including but by no means limited to: circles and spirals, the shape of the letter U, Archimedes' principle of displacement, and the architect Aldo Rossi's idea of the fragment as an object of hope. With these ideas as background noise, I combined mathematical, architectural, and physical terms with terms of action and motion, change, form, order, dimension, quantity, relation, differ-ence, and time to construct an extensive series of directives called 'U-lines.' These short phrases were then given to the dancers to be applied as operations onto various movement material in a virtually infinite number of ways" (110).

37. Katherine Warner danced for LINES from 1982 to 1997.

38. Burns was awarded a McKnight Fellowship for Dancers that subsidized this time in Frankfurt.

39. Rhoden and Desmond Richardson are the co-artistic directors of Complexions. Despite a collaborative choreographic process, Rhoden alone is credited as the company's choreographer.

40. King worked with Rhoden on Lisa Niemi and Patrick Swayze's film *One Last Dance* (2003). It is also worth noting that this film's narrative is supposed to depict the contemporary dance scene, and the four choreographers who were selected by Swayze and Niemi to represent that landscape were King, Rhoden, modern dance choreographer Doug Varone, and Swayze's mother, Patsy.

41. Daly continues by noting that it was instantly recognizable that "somebody had seen too much William Forsythe," as the Complexions pieces were "long on postmodernish styling (smart costuming, pseudo-smart texts, fragmentation, hip attitude, white-noise 'music', and hyper-classicism)" (19). Her critique is somewhat bolstered by Richardson's own claims that working with Forsythe while dancing at Ballett Frankfurt instilled in him a better understanding of improvisation that would impact his contributions to Rhoden and Complexions.

42. Tanya Wideman-Davis danced for LINES from 2002 to 2004.

WORKS CITED

Banes, Sally. *Dancing Women: Female Bodies on Stage.* London: Routledge, 1998.

Berman, Janice. "World Premiere Dance 'Vibraphone Quartet' Shows Lines in Fine Form." *San Francisco Chronicle,* October 18, 2003, D1, D6.

Bordo, Susan. *Unbearable Weight: Feminism, Western Culture, and the Body.* Berkeley: University of California Press, 1993.

Burt, Ramsay. *The Male Dancer: Bodies, Spectacle, Sexualities.* London: Routledge, 1995.

Butler, Judith. *Gender Trouble: Feminism and the Subversion of Identity.* New York: Routledge, 1990.

———. *Undoing Gender.* New York: Routledge, 2004.

Campbell, Karen. "Alonzo King Bends Ballet in Unique Ways." *Boston Globe,* August 25, 2000, C11.

Complexions Dance. Home page. http://www.complexionsdance.org/ (accessed April 1, 2007).

Daly, Ann. "Finding the Logic of Difference." *Dance Theatre Journal* 13, no. 3 (1997): 18–21.

———. "The Balanchine Woman: Of Hummingbirds and Channel Swimmers." In *Critical Gestures: Writings on Dance and Culture,* 277–88. Middletown, CT: Wesleyan University Press, 2002.

———. "Classical Ballet: A Discourse of Difference." In *Critical Gestures: Writings on Dance and Culture,* 288–93. Middletown, CT: Wesleyan University Press, 2002.

De Lauretis, Teresa. *Technologies of Gender: Essays on Theory, Film, and Fiction.* Bloomington: Indiana University Press, 1987.

Driver, Senta, ed. *William Forsythe.* A Special Edition of the journal *Choreography and Dance.* Vol. 5, part 3. OPA (Overseas Publishers Association) N.V., 2000. Reprinted by Routledge in 2004.

Dunning, Jennifer. "Trysts and Battles with Long Sleek Lines." *New York Times,* August 21, 2002.

Felciano, Rita. "Space Problems: Theater Artaud Defeats Lines Dance Company." *San Francisco Bay Guardian,* May 17, 1989, 33.

———. "Lining Up to Dance." *San Francisco Bay Guardian,* April 4, 1990, 34.

———. "Philosopher King at the Joyce." *Dance Magazine* 70, no. 6 (1996): 23.

———. "Lines Contemporary Ballet." *Dance Now*, Spring 1998, 60–65.

———. "His Ideas." *San Francisco Bay Guardian*, October 17, 2001.

———. "The Foundry." In "25 to Watch," ed. Cheryl Ossola. *Dance Magazine* 77, no. 1 (2003): 52.

Foster, Susan Leigh. "The Ballerina's Phallic Pointe." In *Corporealities: Dancing Knowledge, Culture and Power*, ed. Susan Leigh Foster, 1–24. London: Routledge, 1996.

———. *Choreography and Narrative: Ballet's Staging of Story and Desire*. Bloomington: Indiana University Press, 1996.

———. "Closets Full of Dances: Modern Dance's Performance of Masculinity and Sexuality." In *Dancing Desires: Choreographing Sexualities On and Off the Stage*, ed. Jane C. Desmond, 147–207. Madison: University of Wisconsin Press, 2001.

Garafola, Lynn, ed. *Rethinking the Sylph: New Perspectives on the Romantic Ballet*. Hanover: NH: Wesleyan University Press, 1997.

Gard, Michael. *Men Who Dance: Aesthetics, Athletics and the Art of Masculinity*. New York: Peter Lang, 2006.

Gilpin, Heidi. "Static and Uncertain Bodies: Absence and Instability in Movement Performance." In *ASSAPH Studies in the Theatre*, no. 9, 95–114. Tel Aviv: Department of Theatre Arts, Tel Aviv University, 1993.

———. "Aberrations of Gravity." *Architecture New York*, no. 5, March/April (1994): 50–54.

Gladstone, Valerie. "Desmond Richardson: The Role of a Lifetime." *Dance Magazine*, 71, no. 5 (1997): 42–44.

Howard, Rachel. "Lines Ballet Steps Into Wondrous, Foreign World with Favorite Work." *San Francisco Chronicle*, April 15, 2006, E1, E5.

Innes, Shona. "The Teaching of Ballet." In *Writings on Dance* 3, 37–47. Armadale, Australia, 1988.

Kealiinohomoku, Joann. "An Anthropologist Looks at Ballet as a Form of Ethnic Dance." In *Moving History/Dancing Cultures: A Dance History Reader*, ed. Ann Dils and Ann Cooper Albright, 33–43. Middletown, CT: Wesleyan University Press, 2001.

Kisselgoff, Anna. "Offering a Vibrant Challenge with Visual and Kinetic Impact." *New York Times*, December 4, 2000, E5.

Lines Ballet. Alonzo King. http://www.linesballet.org/lines/alonzoking/ (accessed April 1, 2007).

Munger, John, and Libby Smigel. *Dance in the San Francisco Bay Area: A Needs Assessment*. Washington, DC: Dance/USA, 2002.

Murphy, Ann. "Dancing outside the Lines." *Pointe*, April/May 2005, 34–35.

Novack, Cynthia J. "The Body's Endeavors as Cultural Practices." In *Choreographing History*, ed. Susan Leigh Foster, 177–84. Bloomington: Indiana University Press, 1995.

Nugent, Ann. "Seeking Order and Finding Chaos in the Choreography of William Forsythe." In *Society of Dance History Scholars Conference Proceedings*, 81–85. Stoughton, WI: Society of Dance History Scholars, 2001.

Nunes Jensen, Jill. *Re-forming the Lines: A Critical Analysis of Alonzo King's LINES Ballet*. Ann Arbor, MI: University Microfilms, 2005.

———. "OutLINES for a Global Ballet Aesthetic." *Dance Chronicle* 31, no. 3 (2008): 370–411.

Payton, Coleen M. "Ballet of Transcendence: Ailey, King, Rhoden, Jones, and Lucas." *Ballettanz*, April 2003, 28–31.

Reynolds, Nancy, and Malcolm McCormick. *No Fixed Points: Dance in the Twentieth Century*. New Haven, CT: Yale University Press, 2003.

Roseman, Janet Lynn. *Dance Masters: Interviews with Legends of Dance*. New York: Routledge, 2001.

———. *Dance Was Her Religion: The Spiritual Choreography of Isadora Duncan, Ruth St. Denis and Martha Graham*. Prescott, AZ: Hohm Press, 2004.

Ross, Janice. "Alonzo King's Shapely Works Close Series." *Oakland Tribune*, April 9, 1990, C1, C2.

Sirvin, Réne. "Alonzo, Le 'King.'" *Le Figaro*, December 3, 2004.

Sulcas, Roslyn. "What's New?" *Dance Magazine* 71, no. 4 (April 1997): 86–87.

———. "Dance: Using Forms Ingrained in Ballet to Help the Body Move beyond It." *New York Times*, December 9, 2001, 11.

Thom, Rose Ann. "Reviews, New York City: Complexions." *Dance Magazine* 69, no. 5 (1995): 90–91.

Ulrich, Allan. "Breathtaking LINES: 25 Years of Alonzo King's Vision," *Dance Magazine* 81, no. 11 (2007): 34.

Vernay, Marie-Christine. "Alonzo King, Droit au Chœur." *Liberation*, December 7, 2004.

Wulff, Helena. *Ballet across Borders: Career and Cultures in the World of Dancers*. Oxford: Berg, 1998.

CHRISTIAN BURNS

Burns has choreographed, taught, and performed a wide range of contemporary dance for various companies, schools, and art centers around the United States, Europe, and Asia. A former dancer with Alonzo King's LINES Ballet and a guest artist with William Forsythe's company in 2007, he has won awards as a director in the dance for the camera genre. In 2005, Burns established a base in Holyoke, Massachusetts, near where he grew up and where he is renovating and developing a multidisciplinary "projectspace" meant to serve visual and performance artists, as well as researchers.

I was never good at multiple pirouettes or the virtuosic bravura technique that male dancing is supposed to be about. I'm only five foot eight. I was not the marketable type. In ballet, conventionally, there are typecasts. For example, classically speaking, if a male is my height or shorter, he would have to be an extremely virtuosic dancer—multiple turns, multiple *tours en l'air*, et cetera. On the other hand, if a male is tall, then he would be the "partner guy," doing the pas de deux roles which require a sensibility of a "leading man"—big, strong, tall, good partnering skills, enough technique to get through the variations. In my case, I was average-to-short height, as well as having less-than-ideal proportions for classical types—long spine, not long legs—and I wasn't the virtuoso type. I was more of a partnering guy type. I was a very sensitive partner, and that was one of my strengths.

I was 7 when I started ballet. My mom took me to Pioneer Valley Ballet School in western Massachusetts. It was a pretty hard-core studio. I really liked performing and did several *Nutcrackers*. I think I did every child role in *Nutcracker*. I left dance because there came a point when I realized that I was just not terribly into weekly classes. At age 14 a performance lured me back to Pioneer Valley. I received a lot of affirmation about being there—probably because I was the only boy at the school most of the time. Rather than being faced with stereotypes, being a dancer in such a small minority gave me some kind of cool cachet.

By the time I turned 16, I knew I would not go to college and wanted a career in dance. I moved to New York and the School of American Ballet. At SAB, there was

Christian Burns in *Capacity from Shallowness*, created in 2001 by The Foundry (Burns and co-choreographer Alex Ketley). Photographer, Andrea Flores. Used with permission.

constant competition with 30 other equally, if not more so, talented young men. Classes were segregated so that the men could train differently from the women, and the groups would only meet in the afternoon for pas de deux or rehearsals. The environment was extremely competitive, high-strung, and hyperfocused, so much so that the bar was continually being lifted and things like getting in a quick 200 sit-ups before going to sleep were simply the norm. Although thriving on the competition, there was always a desire to find another way to approach ballet. Today, I personally cannot work with dancers trained exclusively in ballet. Classical technique is inherently important, yet it is based upon physical abilities which are just parameters of how conversation can be expressed. When developing new work, choreography should emerge out of the dancers' responses to one another.

Much of the discussion of masculinity pertains to the classical virtuosic tradition. It is difficult for me to address potential prejudices in the male ballet dancer without looking at the context of the culture that has informed how a male feels he can "be" in ballet, and in turn how he is perceived/discriminated against from outside the culture. From the perspective of the general public looking into the ballet culture, then yes, there will always be resonances of prejudice pointed in the directions of all minorities, until eventually enough is argued against such narrow-minded outlooks. Our idea of what men should be like within Western culture is always shifting and will usually be in conflict with some of our ideas about masculinity and femininity within gender. I think most people would acknowledge the fact that the gender paradigm isn't as rigid as society dictates, and that human beings aren't only one-dimensional—that's a myth.

The culture of classical ballet has been beholden to the lure of this ideal, from the court, the prince and princesses, poets and tales of the Romantic era, followed almost a century later by the neoclassical works, wherein the male still lifts the female in order for her to be relevant. These images, even within the abstract perspective that Balanchine would bring to the pas de deux form, hold to the same ideal and culturally reaffirm this mythology—that man is the strong support and woman worshiped as an icon through his actions, whether it be lifting, placing, promenading or choreographing. Balanchine, of course, shifted this; in the ballet vernacular he really made extraordinary shifts in what it meant to dance as a male. The choreography was driven by much more sophisticated and, for its time, modern forces: musicality, dynamic structures and shades, details to the footwork, and even a sense of an American style—maybe appropriated from the likes of Gene Kelly and others.

But stereotypes are deeply embedded within the culture of ballet because they are still reflected in mainstream culture, the primary audience for ballet. Because ballet is a business, the question of how masculinity is performed has a very tangible connection to commerce. Like big blockbuster Hollywood films that play out traditional models of male and female roles in order to reach a mainstream audience, ballet in America has adopted a similar structure. This informs both the dancers' ideas about how they should be "men," as well as how an audience sees, or more accurately wants to see, men dance. Masculinity in ballet becomes a side effect or something that is performed and created to meet certain specifications.

I have been lucky enough to work with very open-minded dance makers—James Sewell, Alonzo King, and William Forsythe—men who are interested in asking questions and developing how masculinity can be more than a one-dimensional caricature. Dancing for Sewell, and King's company LINES Ballet, I was given the opportunity to question preset gender roles. King's work in particular allowed me to experiment with ways of embodying both strength and grace; this is largely because he works from the idea that masculinity and femininity are merely two points on a universally accessible continuum.

Does mainstream culture put pressure on men to be "manly"? Yes. Are the lead roles for men in the classical ballet repertory geared toward an idealized masculine model? Yes. Are men in today's culture free to express the many complex layers of masculine and feminine traits simultaneously? I would say certainly not, by looking at the picture through a binary-minded lens. What is problematic about ballet today is when classical dance is viewed as relevant simply because it is still performed. If audiences realize classical ballet is old, the stereotypical clichés of masculinity will be seen as such. Adding a historical perspective to the form in this way will allow contemporary artists the freedom to break away from themes and gender portrayals prevalent in ballets from over a century ago. Since what it means to be masculine has changed over time, it is stifling for ballet to ignore those shifts. Great masculine ballet dancing is not about role-play and restraint, it is about becoming awake and delivering lessons about how to be, through a creative process that preserves certain aspects of ballet technique while releasing others.

There are a growing number of ballet-based dance artists who are working in very interesting ways, who are looking at broader landscapes of how the human experience can be expressed within presentational contexts, infused by an enormous trickle-down effect of postmodern and new dance practices from a previous generation. These contexts are, in my opinion, an indication that perhaps ballet will continue to develop and mature and transform. That is what any form needs to do in order to assert some shred of relevance to future generations.

5

The Performance of Unmarked Masculinity

RAMSAY BURT

When I look now at my book *The Male Dancer*, published more than a decade ago, one thing disappoints me: that I didn't know or hadn't at the time really understood two books that appeared while I was writing it. These are Judith Butler's *Gender Trouble* (1990a) and Peggy Phelan's *Unmarked* (1993). I still subscribe to the central thesis of *The Male Dancer*, that there is nothing wrong with being a man. The problems start with the way normative gender ideologies maintain inequalities between the sexes by reinforcing the idea that masculinity, but not femininity, is an unproblematic norm. There are ways in which Butler's and Phelan's ideas can contribute to an investigation of the anxieties surrounding male dance, which, I have argued, are a consequence of social structures that police gender norms.

The Male Dancer told a story of radical, experimental choreography during the 20th century that sometimes found chinks in the armor of normative gender ideologies that could be opened up and exploited to stage alternative masculinities. Such stagings are not just useful to the dancers themselves and to those who may identify with them but are beneficial to society in general. Men and women, straight, gay, or lesbian, as well as intersex and transsexual people, all suffer as a result of limited, normative definitions of masculinity. Troubling these normative ideas therefore has an ethical value. With help from theoretical perspectives, including those of Butler, Phelan, and the art historian Mieke Bal, my aim in this essay is to define the nature of this project and its ethical dimensions more clearly. In doing so I consider some possibilities not covered in *The Male Dancer*, through a discussion of Joe Goode's *29 Effeminate Gestures* (1987) and a solo by Dominique Mercy from Pina Bausch's *Der Fensterputzer* (1997). Both, as I shall explain, trouble norms through exploiting the power of unmarked masculinity.

If one's gender and sexuality are social constructions, as *The Male Dancer* argued, this means that one's body interfaces and mediates between one's individual experience and one's place within society. Gender and sexuality are attributes of one's body that seem to be fundamental to one's sense of self but whose meanings are determined by norms that come from outside oneself. Dance is an area through which, as embodied beings, we negotiate the social and cultural discourses through which gender and sexuality are maintained. As

150

Judith Butler has pointed out: "The body has its invariably public dimension: constituted as a social phenomenon in the public sphere, my body is and is not mine. Given over from the start to the world of others, bearing their imprint, formed within the crucible of social life, the body is only later, and with some uncertainty, that to which I lay claim as my own" (2004, 21).

There are a number of different practices through which one can lay claim to one's body, but, because dance is a performing art, it is, I suggest, a particularly useful area in which to consider the ways in which gender is performed. For Butler, "gender is an act which has been rehearsed, much as a script survives the particular actors who make use of it, but which requires individual actors in order to be actualized and reproduced as reality once again" (1990b, 277). One cannot refuse to perform the gender that is ascribed to one, but as one lays claim to one's body, one lays claim to the means through which one responds to and interprets this demand.

If one way in which one lays claim to one's body is through an involvement in the dance world, this is not only through performing but also through watching theater dance. In an analysis of the training processes through which dance techniques construct the body, Susan Foster has argued that dancing bodily consciousness is formed "within Western assumptions about the body, the self, and the expressive act" (1997, 236). She has argued that, through daily repetition in dance class, "the images used to describe the body become the body" (239). These images mediate traditions that are particular to the kind of dancing that is being learned but are also carriers of social and cultural values. Through learning a dance technique, therefore, the dancer becomes aware of what Foster calls "the rhetorical relations that bind body to self and to community" (253). Watching theater dance is accessing a privileged space within which these rhetorical relations operate. Foster's account of the process of learning a dance style and Butler's account of the social construction of embodied experience both therefore locate the body in an intermediary position between the individual and society. If circumstances sometimes cause the nature of this intermediary position to become visible, the normative limits of these relations to self and to community are tested.

Men within the Western dance profession have, for the last century, been a source of social anxieties because dance performance can sometimes make visible a correlation between the way men relate to their bodies and the way male power is preserved. Rosalind Coward's observation in 1984 is still true today even if circumstances may have changed. "Somewhere along the line," she observed, "men have managed to keep out of the glare, escaping the relentless activity of sexual definition" (227). White, heterosexual, middle-class masculinity remains largely invisible and is generally assumed to be an unproblematic norm and therefore not in need of testing. Without needing to think about it, men generally avoid drawing attention to themselves because, as Peggy Phelan has observed, "visibility is a trap . . . it summons surveillance and the law; it provokes voyeurism, fetishism, the colonial/imperial appetite for possession" (1993, 6). Although underrepresented communities can be empowered by an enhanced visibility, Phelan points out that "there is real power in remaining unmarked" (6). The spectacle of male dancers, however, is a source of anxiety where it threatens to draw attention to the otherwise invisible power that enforces inequalities of gender and sexuality. While these norms are therefore maintained through the unmarked nature of masculinity, what interests me about *29 Effeminate Gestures* and the solo in *Der Fensterputzer* is the extent to which they permit Joe Goode and Dominique Mercy to perform their masculinities in ways that remain unmarked without, as I shall show, reinforcing restricted definitions of masculinity.

In drawing attention to the advantages of remaining unmarked, Phelan acknowledged her disappointment at the way in which work on the gaze by feminist film theorists during the 1970s and 1980s was being forgotten. If the idea of the male gaze has not been well received by many dance scholars, this is in part because it gives an empowering role to the spectator that is incompatible with conventional ideas about dance appreciation. In the conventional view, a dance work's value and significance derive solely from its choreographer while the spectator is no more than a passive recipient of a choreographed message. The art historian Mieke Bal, explaining her semiological approach to analyzing visual images, has suggested that neither an approach that is purely concerned with authorial intention nor one that focuses exclusively on voyeurism can provide a satisfactory account of the process of visual analysis. She points out that each model "can only account for ideal, totally successful communication" (1995, 148), whereas the artist (as sender) does more than transmit a clear message: "the package contains other, subliminal and unconscious messages" (148). In turn, the spectator (as receiver) approaches the work within her or his own preoccupations. Bal therefore argues that "the receiver manipulates the sender, by being whom she or he is and by the affective, political and intellectual relationship between receiver and sender. Manipulation is not only an instance of (ideological) agency, but also of the historical embeddedness of that agency. Rather than the assumed (but in fact projected), authorial intention, the interaction between work and audience should be the object of a genuine historical inquiry" (148).

By calling this process manipulation, Bal conveys the idea that the artist's work is not complete without a spectator, but the spectator does not actually add anything to it by interpreting it. Where dance analysis is concerned, this situation is further complicated by the fact that dancers perform an intermediary role between choreographer and spectator. Where Bal proposes that the receiver manipulates the sender in the way he or she interprets the message, I suggest that in live performance, where the performer senses the audience's response, dancer and spectator both interact through manipulating the message. The spectator responds to the performance itself, while the performer frames the material in ways that limit and direct the kinds of interpretative manipulations the spectator can make.

Bal's proposition that one takes the interaction between work and audience as the object of inquiry has important implications for dance studies. It means focusing on the dancer-spectator relationship during the moment of live performance and not treating the performance as merely a projection of the choreographer's intentions. This means shifting from the study of choreography to the analysis of performance, and this shift, I suggest, is a prerequisite for an understanding of how dancing bodies perform gender. Who is performing and what kind of affective, political, and intellectual relationship is created between dancer and spectator are crucial to the ideas about gender that are brought into play during a performance.

Butler and Phelan have both emphasized the importance of the activity of performance. Phelan has made us aware of the specificity of performance as a live, unique event: "Performance's only life is in the present. Performance cannot be saved, recorded, or otherwise participate in the circulation of representations of representations" (1993, 146). She points out that it is the presence of the living bodies of the performers that cannot be saved or recorded. For Ann Daly, this is the core of the pleasure of watching dance: "Presence is the silent yet screeching excitement of physical vibrancy, of 'being there.' It is one of the thrills of watching dance, to see someone radiate pure energy, whether it is in stillness or in flight" (1989, 25). Ann Cooper Albright has argued that it is through creating a powerful physical presence that dancers like Isadora Duncan and Yvonne Rainer were able to resist being objectified as women by a voyeuristic male gaze. Her contention is that Duncan had an extraordinary ability to share with her audience her experience while dancing, and that Rainer was able to draw her audience's attention to the process of "making and remaking the self through movement" (Albright 1997, 19). Because Duncan and Rainer were both "conscious of the stakes involved in performing their female selves, their dancing traveled back and forth across the dual loops of representation and experience to create powerful physical presences" (19).

In other words, Albright is arguing that strong women performers can challenge women's disempowerment through asserting a powerful physical presence. Both Albright and Daly, then, see presence as the affective relationship between dancer and spectator and view strong presence as more desirable and valuable than weak presence because it can affirm gendered identity. This, however, does not address Phelan's point that "there is real power in remaining unmarked" (1993, 6). In Phelan's view, performance's ontology is its disappearance, which teaches us "to learn to value what is lost, to learn not the meaning but the value of what cannot be reproduced or seen (again)" (152). Presence and absence are not binary opposites. In Phelan's view there are always presences and absences in operation during performance. The implications of this become clear when Phelan applies it to the work of feminist performance artists like Adrian Piper, Sophie Calle, and Angelica Festa. All these artists have used absence and disappearance to create a space for the performance of aspects of women's experience that cannot be represented within cultural representation because this only permits the reproduction of male sex and gender and is therefore, as Phelan puts it, "hommo-sexual" (151). Absence and disappearance can therefore be powerful in troubling or uncanny ways where they draw attention to gaps and limitations within normative cultural representation. As I shall show, male dancing bodies can also sometimes produce these kinds of troubling and uncanny affects.

André Lepecki has pointed out that, where dance is concerned, presence is not necessarily an attribute of body, and there is a need to distinguish between the two: "Neither just presence (of the body) nor just (the presence of) body, dance announces itself as an interstitial imbrication of one into the other by the means of a dialectic of difference taking place in an empty space" (2004, 3). Presence is therefore an element within performance that contributes toward the way a dance signifies difference: it can mark or unmark a dancing body. Lepecki proposes that "critical theories of dancing practices must consider how it is that 'presence' challenges the very stability of 'the body'" (6).

I take this to mean that, by troubling and undoing the simple binary or presence or absence in order to realize a multiplicity of presences, dance performance can challenge the processes of social and cultural construction that render some bodies marked and others unmarked. The kinds of presences that dancers project and the absences they call to mind determine the points of view that spectators can take up in relation to the performance. Point of view both enables and restricts the ways in which embodied memories and histories, that are shared by performer and spectator, are evoked during performance. The kinds of memories and histories that are evoked have the potential to either reinforce or destabilize "hommo sexuality"—the constricting cultural discourse of gender and sexuality. For example, Martin Hargreaves (2000) has argued that the male swans in Matthew Bourne's version of *Swan Lake* (1995) are haunted by the absence of the bodies of the female swans in the classic, late 19th-century ballet. Casting male dancers in these roles would not be significant if the swans in *Swan Lake* had not up until then been feminine. This suggests that ghosts (emanations that are simultaneously both present and absent) from past performances and of past performers are often a factor brought into play as spectators watch and interpret live performance. These ghosts create a dialectic of difference between present and past that impacts on the performance of gender. In this way both male and female dancing bodies have the potential to destabilize norms, and I have been arguing that the potential for male dancing bodies to do this underlies anxieties about the male dancer.

In *The Male Dancer*, many of the examples I discussed staged alternative masculinities by drawing attention to the spectacle of male dancing bodies. By doing so, they invariably lost the privilege of being unmarked. What I want to do in the rest of this chapter, through discussions of *29 Effeminate Gestures* and a solo in *Der Fensterputzer*, is to explore instances where Joe Goode and Dominique Mercy, by destabilizing conventional expectations about performative presence, have been able to evoke embodied memories and histories that address broader and more open kinds of experiences than those generally permitted by "hommo-sexual" cultural representations.

Ghosts, Violence, and the Politics of Camp

Initially choreographed in 1987, Joe Goode's *29 Effeminate Gestures* remained in his company's repertoire over a long period; Goode was still performing it in the early 2000s. Lasting 11 minutes, it consisted of a choreographed sequence of 29 gestures repeated five times in different variations that, as the title suggests, signified effeminate male behavior. The label "effeminate" has often been used against gay men in a derogatory and injurious way to suggest their failure to behave like proper men. Michael Scott, reviewing Goode's piece in 1991 in Vancouver, remarked, "The content, for anyone who has ever felt society's disapproval, is deeply moving" (1991). The solo referred to the kinds of gestures that a drag queen might perform. One could perhaps call them camp; however, their use in the piece was not primarily entertaining but, as Scott suggests, created a sense of community between performer and spectators through its evocation of shared memories and histories of a kind that are normally denied. By doing so, it enacted a powerful argument that gay identities are no less viable than straight ones.

The title's use of the word "effeminate" therefore signaled a political stance. Goode's deliberate reappropriation within this solo of these kinds of gestures and their associations was equivalent to the contemporary reappropriation of the term "queer": the solo's reappropriation could be read as a political act within the context of what Judith Butler called an "increasing politicization of theatricality for queers" (1993, 233). However, to say that Goode's piece did no more than communicate a gay political message would be reductive and would not account for the enduring success that its long run implies. I shall argue that the piece's fascination lay in the tensions it created between elements of the material it brought together. There was a tension in the piece between dance, spoken or sung words, and gestures; there was also a tension between Goode's performative declaration, by dancing these effeminate gestures, that he is a gay man, and his use of many signs of normative heterosexual masculine power that would ordinarily render him unmarked. It is more productive, therefore, following Mieke Bal, to consider that, rather than transmitting a clear message, these tensions within Goode's piece were a sign that it "contains other, subliminal and unconscious messages" (1995, 148), and this formed the basis for performer and spectator to interactively interpret the material performed. Through this, the piece enacted a reinscription of queer folk within society, and it can therefore be seen as a ritual healing of violent and traumatic exclusions.[1]

The performance started in the dark as Goode, unseen onstage, muttered a droning chorus of "He's a good guy," the adjective "good" being a homonym of his own name. As the lights came up, the audience saw that he was wearing a blue boilersuit and a protective face mask on his head. He switched on an electric chain saw and proceeded to cut into a cheap, rather kitsch, gilt chair. Leaving the saw running on the now trashed chair, and stripping his boilersuit off his upper body, he walked upstage to announce the piece's title, shouting it above the chain saw's piercing whine, and then proceeded to take up each of a series of 29 gestures.

This was the first time the series was seen, but the gestures would be repeated four more times in different forms. Goode himself said they had an "extreme, lavish, grander-than-thou, queenly quality" (Goode in Shank 1994, 73). David Gere, in an excellent analysis of the piece, to which my own discussion is indebted, provides admirable descriptions of the sequence, such as the following: "He lowers his gaze and places his hands dramatically on the chest, as if to feel the shape of his breasts" (2001, 353); "The hands sweep up in a flicking gesture to frame the face, which is tilted towards the light, a Renaissance virgin captured at the instant of the annunciation: rapture" (354); "The head tips back slightly, lips smiling coyly; the arm previously thrust in the air is now broken at the wrist, fingers fluttering in a perky 1940s wave" (357); "The hand pulls back to cover the mouth, which is distended now in an attitude of mock horror, the body and head dropped forward in fear and revulsion" (363).

Gere suggests that this last gesture evoked a stereotype of a fearful, effeminate gay man, illustrating it with a description of a scene from the mainstream Hollywood movie *The Rock* (1996). In this scene, Sean Connery, who plays the role of a dangerous convict, is having his hair cut by an effeminate hairdresser. Suddenly Connery makes a bolt for freedom, "nearly murdering a man by throwing him off a balcony," (363) and runs for the lift. When the lift door closes, he finds himself inside with the now terrified, cowering hair dresser, who eventually moans: "OK, I don't want to know nothing. I never saw you throw that gentleman off the balcony. All I care about is, are you happy with your haircut?" (363).

Goode's performance cited such stereotypical gay roles and framed them in a way that was both critical and camp. A video that the Joe Goode Performance Group gave me documents a live performance in San Francisco in 1992. Occasionally during the performance, a member of the audience laughed in recognition or appreciation. Generally, however, the audience seemed to be watching quite soberly. Campness is notoriously difficult to define or characterize. It is a metropolitan, gay subcultural style that assumes a common appreciation of the value of artifice and subversion, of surface rather than depth. Richard Dyer sums up the defensive value of such subcultural solidarity when he says,

Figure 5.1   Joe Goode can be both critical and camp, suggesting a contradictory overlay of meanings in his solo *29 Effeminate Gestures* (1987). Photograph by Bill Pack, courtesy of Joe Goode Performance Group. Used with permission.

"It's being so camp as keeps us going" (1992). The serious response of Goode's gay- and queer-friendly audience suggested that they recognized the camp quality of the gestures as a marker of an acknowledged, politicized gay identity.

Switching off the chain saw, Goode repeated the set of gestures more or less identically, accompanying each with a spoken commentary—"If you talk too much . . . if you feel too much . . ." without ever completing the sentence. By failing to match an "if" with a "then," Goode seemed to be telling his audience, which he addressed directly in a second-person narrative, that he knew they knew the consequences of such transgressions. For one gesture, he did not even name the offense. He started by saying, "If you . . ." and then in silence fluttered his fingers while glancing coyly over his shoulder at the audience, completing the part-verbal, part-gestural phrase by saying "too much." It was as if words here were insufficient. The third time the complete sequence was repeated, Goode accompanied the gestures with vocal sounds—explosions, gunfire, sirens—that seemed like those of a small boy playing with toy soldiers or a toy gun. (Were these the unnamed consequences, the "then" clauses that the preceding list lacked?)

Taken together, these verbal and nonverbal commentaries in effect proved how much dance movement can convey that cannot be put into words. But at the same time, dance is invariably hard to see and is not particularly good at conveying precise information or specific narrative content: the phrase "dancing all over the place" suggests evasion. Dance is a time-based art that often reveals processes of change and transformation. Goode clearly wanted to convey very specific information in this solo, and this is why the initial sequence of 29 gestures was repeated three times in a row without choreographic variation.

It was only when Goode was sure that the sequence was established in the spectators' minds that he began to develop it in two more variations. He pulled up his yellow T-shirt to bare his torso, catching the shirt on his head and twisting it into a headdress. His appearance now recalled Nureyev's swashbuckling pirate solo from *Le Corsaire* or perhaps Nijinsky's Golden Slave from *Schéhérazade*—the improvised turban exotically framing his desirable male body. To an upbeat, Latin-inflected drumming track he performed a bravura solo that still incorporated many of the 29 gestures, now incongruously combined with vigorous break dancing or aikido rolls and wheels on the floor and slicing arm movements. It was a solo whose energy and confident expansiveness and whose martial arts references might otherwise be considered unproblematically masculine.

The solo and music ended. Goode shrugged off the T-shirt headdress and started to sing, unaccompanied, a queered version of a line from the song "Sunrise, Sunset" from the musical *Fiddler on the Roof* (1969)—"Is this the little boy I carried?"—while running, one last time, through the sequence of effeminate gestures.[2] David Gere has pointed out that much of Goode's work in the early 1990s seemed to be haunted by ghostly figures, which Gere links to the traumatic loss, from AIDS-related illnesses, of so many gay men, and male dancers in particular, in metropolitan gay communities like those in New York and San Francisco. Goode's song functioned as a melancholy lament. As he sang, a power drill was lowered from the lighting grid. Goode turned it on and aimed it at the audience as if it were a revolver, and then disturbingly pointed it toward his own mouth. Kneeling, he turned it farther, so that the drill was pointing at his shoulder with the side of the motor housing facing his cheek. He folded his upper body forward, as if hugging the drill, pressing his face against its housing. As the lights faded, his foghorn voice was still competing with the drill's grating whine.

Gere's reading of this piece largely concentrates on the way Goode's 29 gestures interrogated and challenged stereotypes of gay behavior, and he argues that Goode used camp as a political marker with which to performatively declare a strongly affirmative gay identity. It is essential to recognize and underwrite the importance of gay dance works, and what interests me about Goode's performance is the effect on normative gender discourses of its contradictory overlaying of different meanings. It overloaded an already overdetermined economy of signs with tensions, contradictions, and troubling absences. Goode's 29 gestures signified a gay identity, but his mechanic's blue boilersuit and familiarity with tools suggested working-class status,[3] a "good guy" who is perhaps a potentially violent one. The noise of the tools was violent, and the relief when they were switched off palpable: violence is an attribute of "proper" masculinity.

Goode also showed off a solidly muscular and desirable body to create a homoerotic charge through evoking the ghosts of former, desirable male dancers that belied the abject state associated with effeminacy. And, if camp is an elaboration of surface that denies the possibility of depth and is a glittering, unstoppably excessive display of unfixable signs, then the clash of camp subversion with melancholia and mourning was particularly disturbing. Spectators saw the same body performing in all these seemingly incompatible ways and became aware of other ghostly presences—seductively homoerotic dancers, the lost boy.

Following Bal, spectators manipulated the piece in order to try to find some coherence within its discontinuities and fragmentation. Goode, as performer rather than as choreographer, used his sense of the audience's response to make it as difficult as possible to read a coherent subjectivity into his performative presence and the ghosts he evoked. In Lepecki's terms, his presence challenged "the very stability of 'the body'" (2004, 6). It is around the question of the stability and instability of the masculine body that performer and spectator therefore interacted. What was at stake in this interaction is the limit of normative masculine identity. By mixing and confusing effeminate gestures with the actions of a good guy, the piece allowed Goode as performer to trouble and subvert the homosexual/heterosexual binary. There would be nothing good about good guys if there were no effeminate queens to define the limit beyond which guys become no good. Homosexuals are thus essential to the continuation of heterosexuality; as Leo Bersani has put it, homosexuals are "the internally excluded difference that cements heterosexual identity" (1995, 36).

By trying to find a coherent subjectivity within material that is discontinuous, spectators necessarily try to fit its fragmentary parts together inside the boundaries of the same body. Through trying to make the spectator's task as difficult as possible, Goode forced his audience to recognize the fragility of the limit dividing straight inside from gay outside. Without this boundary, differences between straight and gay collapse, sucking the meanings out of signs and making them available for resignification. To try and say what the final, disturbing image of Goode singing while cradling the electric drill meant would be futile. But the anger and violence within this image—its affective power—rather than confirming normative masculinity seemed instead directed against the very constraints that defined and normalized it.

By erasing the limit for himself and his audience at this particular historical juncture and within the privileged time-space of a theater, Goode destroyed the means through which gay behavior can be marked as different. His piece therefore showed what it would be like if the constraints of normative ideologies of gender and sexuality did not exist. By destabilizing known possibilities, the piece offered its audience an opportunity to find new ways of interpreting gender and sexuality, showing them that it does not have to be like this.

Fragmentation and the Problematics of Memory and History

My discussion of Dominique Mercy's solo in *Der Fensterputzer* has nothing to do with AIDS or gay politics, but I will show that there are nevertheless similarities in the way Goode's and Mercy's solos summon ghosts and engineer the collapse of signifying structures. When I initially decided to put these solos together in this chapter, I thought of them as very different pieces. I was therefore a little surprised, when I read more about Goode's work, to find a few critics had specifically compared it with Bauschian *tanztheater*. Indeed, Goode himself has admitted to feeling a "kinship with Anne Teresa de Keersmaeker and Pina Bausch. I feel that there's a theatrical element at work there, a desire to expose the raw bone and nerve of something, and I'm very attracted to that" (Goode in Shank 1994, 76). Goode qualified this by saying that, in his opinion, a lot of their work was very balletic and "very derived from an almost classical form. . . . I think that is a difference between the European and American" (76–77). From my own European point of view, I of course agree that Goode's approach to movement is very different from Bausch's, but I suggest the reasons for this are more complicated than a straightforward distinction between classical and modern dance.

The relationship between Bausch's generation of contemporary dancers and the German modern dance of the first half of the 20th century is a far more complicated and difficult one than the relationship between U.S. postmodern dancers and historical figures like Isadora Duncan, Ruth St. Denis, and Martha Graham. In the 1930s, Graham insisted on the Americanness of her dance, around the same time that Mary Wigman was asserting that there were essentially German qualities in her own dancing. The American dance world has not had much incentive to reflect on the rhetoric of American exceptionalism that sometimes informs discussions about modern dance. But the undeniable acquiescence by Rudolf Laban and Wigman with nationalistic discourses about German national identity made their modern dance, in the postwar period, incompatible with the new spirit of European internationalism. It was the shocking realization of the Holocaust that inspired the drafting of the European Convention of Human Rights in 1948, and this itself initiated the political process of integration that eventually became the European Union. Modern dance went underground in a divided Germany that found its own histories and memories traumatic. The metaphysical vision to which dancers like Wigman and Harald Kreutzberg aspired in the 1920s and 1930s subsequently lost its credibility at a time when the philosopher Theodor Adorno was asking whether, after Auschwitz, it was still possible to reconcile metaphysical speculation with experience.

What can make Bausch's pieces hard work to watch is the way they refuse to offer any transcendence. This suspicion of nationalism contributed to Bausch's decision to use for her company's daily company class the neutral internationally practiced movement form, ballet. For similar reasons she selects dancers from all over the world for her polyglot company. Where Bausch has exposed what Goode calls raw bone and nerve, particularly in her earlier pieces, this needs to be understood in the context of the problematics of European memory in the public sphere. This politics of history and memory is essential to an understanding of Mercy's performance of masculinity in *Der Fensterputzer*.

When Bausch's piece *Palermo, Palermo* (1989) began with a large breeze block wall that filled the proscenium arch, falling backward onto the stage, some connected this with the fall of the Berlin Wall, which had taken place a few weeks before the premiere. Peter Pabst, the scenographer who has been Bausch's long-term collaborator, has insisted that there was no connection, and that technical plans for the falling wall had begun months before the climactic events of reunification.[4] That he felt a need to say this is in itself significant because it demonstrates the way some people wanted to interpret or, as Bal puts it, manipulate this piece. Gabrielle Cody has argued that "Bausch's mediating ideology is precisely that there is no mediating ideology. For her to provide one would be to succumb to the very myths of transcendence she is deconstructing" (1998, 122).[5] In the cases of *Palermo, Palermo* and *Der Fensterputzer*, this suggests a refusal to satisfy a desire for an easy and reassuring mediation of current social and political concerns.

Der Fensterputzer, a coproduction by the Goethe-Institut Hong Kong and the Hong Kong Arts Festival Society,[6] was first performed in Hong Kong a few weeks before the former colonial power, Britain, handed the island and its territories back to China. At the level of cultural diplomacy, a recently reunified Germany was therefore contributing to an artistic celebration of Hong Kong's reunification with mainland China. Commissioned to celebrate a particular historical event, it therefore set up an expectation that it would provide some sort of commemoration. As Irit Rogoff has pointed out, there was a marked tendency in Germany during the 1980s and 1990s to use art to memorialize recent German history, exemplified by Jorg Immendorf's *Café Deutschland* paintings and several Holocaust memorials. "Spectacular history," Rogoff observed, "serves as a device for establishing a cohesion, a myth of nation and a unifying narrative in terms of which everything is interpreted" (1995, 116). She went on, however, to suggest that women artists like Rebecca Horn and women writers like Christa Wolf "have chosen to fragment concepts of totalizing history and its concomitant memories, in the name of difference and through an insistence on multiple, concurrent histories which embrace the mundane quotidian and the obliquely subjective" (117). Much of this is applicable to Bausch's work. Rather than presenting a unifying, cohesive narrative, her work often focuses obsessively on the mundane and trivial to insist on the coexistence of multiple, seemingly incompatible subjectivities. Mercy's solo in *Der Fensterput-zer* exemplified this fragmented approach to memory and difference. As I shall show, his performance of masculinity evoked multiple, discontinuous presences and uneasy ghosts that troubled and disrupted the desire for a totalizing history.

Der Fensterputzer was a sumptuous and spectacular production that never-theless refrained from offering a cohesive narrative of the events taking place around its premiere. The decor was dominated by a 20-foot-high, movable mountain covered in red silk bauhinia flowers that spilled off it to spread across the stage.[7] Photographs of Hong Kong were projected onto the stage, over-loading it with rich color, giving the piece a fittingly tropical feeling for a teeming, tropical city. Suspended above the front of the stage, a man washing windows from a hanging cradle cleaned one large suspended sheet of clear plastic after another. Below and behind him, a cast of 23 dancers acted out small and large scenes in a fragmented, revuelike format, occasionally breaking proscenium to offer drinks and fruit to the audience. Each dancer had several sumptuous changes of clothes and a profusion of props and extras, including Pekingese dogs, large electric cooling fans, and a lots cigarettes. Mercy's solo was one among many that the dancers perform during the piece. After creating a solo for herself in *Danzon* (1995), Bausch's work seemed to contain more and more solos where very individual movements were set to music that was often interpreted in a lyrical, almost romantic way.

This kind of solo was one sign of the way Bausch's work was changing during the 1990s. Critics in the United States suggested that it was becoming mellower and more benign. Ann Daly commented on *Danzon*'s "lighter touch, its lyrical music, delightful humor and joyful dancing" (1999). Alice Naude said the humor in *Der Fensterputzer* "is more delightful than cutting. This piece has more actual dancing than any Bausch work in recent memory" (1998, 101). They could perhaps say this because they had been watching Bausch's work for a long time, but the company also kept older, darker pieces in repertoire. In any one year it could be seen performing both some of the mellower recent works and revivals of older, more harrowing and painful ones. Ghostly memories of the past thus haunted the newer lighter pieces. Some critics picked up on hints of a darker undercurrent. Reviewing *Der Fensterputzer*, Anna Kisselgoff commented: "If Ms. Bausch is concerned with the futility and hope of human experience, then she has not done badly with her metaphor of a window washer faced with miles of glass skyscrapers in Hong Kong. [But] when the characters rush around offering drinks and fruit to the audience, they do so because they come from one huge duty-free shop of a city where the sellers aim to please" (1997, B5).

In *Der Fensterputzer*, as in all her work, Bausch was sending not one clear message but a complex package of conscious and unconscious associations that fragment what Rogoff calls concepts of totalizing history. Unlike Goode's piece, where the interaction between performer and spectator concerned the partial exclusion of gay men from society, what was at stake in *Der Fensterputzer* were the possible points of entry into unresolved, traumatic narratives of past events. Mercy's solo consisted of vigorous movements and urgently emphatic gestural material; it was extremely fragmented, with very asymmetrical and disturbingly uncentered dance phrases that marked out complex, syncopated rhythms. While movement seemed to be initiated from a neutral center, one side of Mercy's body often appeared to make an involuntary response as the other pulled sideways against it. Like Nijinsky's performance in *Petruschka*, he seemed tossed about like a rag doll by the incoherent violence of material over which he seemed to be only partially in control. More than once his movements led him to collapse on the flower-covered floor, from which he had to pull himself back up to continue dancing.

My description here might seem to evoke a vigorous and energetic display of virtuosic dancing, the kind of bravura solo that affirms normative ideas about masculinity. This, however, was not the case. Despite the clarity of his execution, Mercy seemed very self-absorbed, rarely looking at the audience. When he did so, his eyes had an almost frightened expression, though this was no doubt in part due to the concentration necessary to perform such difficult material. Alice Naude said Mercy looked "heart-breakingly vulnerable" (1998, 101), while Deborah Jowitt wrote about Mercy's "demented dancing and entrancingly numb 'little man' persona" (1999, 73). While he danced, a group of other male dancers peered surreptitiously at him from behind the movable hill of flowers, slowly pushing it so that it appeared to follow him around the stage. Although Mercy did travel during his solo, the fact that the hill traveled with him made it appear that he wasn't getting anywhere.

The solo ended when Mercy became lost in a crowd of frolicking dancers who, seemingly oblivious of him, rushed onto the hill and rolled around in the flowers, playfully throwing handfuls of them into the air. The music for the solo was Dizzie Gillespie's celebrated live recording of his piece "Swing Low Sweet Cadillac."[8] This piece begins with an exciting, extended drum solo during which Gillespie and fellow musicians engage in largely nonverbal calls and responses before eventually beginning the song. Mercy's solo took place during the extended introduction while the crowd of dancers rushed past him onto the hill when the song itself started.

While there were traces of ballet vocabulary in Mercy's solo, these simultaneously both hinted at and undermined conventional notions of balance and order that ballet generally exemplifies. At the same time, the gestural material suggested the expression of a character, personality, and feelings. The fragmentation within the choreography, however, problematized this. Mercy's solo deflected the spectator's focus, canceling the effect of thrusting movements and avoiding logical or instinctive recoveries. Fragmentation, deflection, and cancellation in Mercy's solo had the effect of disturbing and troubling the otherwise automatic, conventional associations of both classically harmonious shapes and dynamically forceful expressiveness with masculine rationality, order, and control. These affective qualities were present in Mercy's solo, but rather than being privileged signifiers of unmarked, normative masculinity, they seemed unhinged, available, albeit in a somewhat anxious way, for different significations.

I have suggested that Bausch's solos in the 1990s seemed lyrical only because they evoked the ghostly presence of her older, darker pieces. Around the time Bausch and her company were working on *Der Fensterputzer*, she and some of her longer-serving company members, including Mercy, were teaching her piece *Le sacre du printemps* (1975) to dancers at the Paris Opéra.[9] There are surprising similarities between Mercy's solo in *Der Fensterputzer* and the final sacrificial solo by the Chosen One in Bausch's *Sacre*, a role created by Marlis Alt.[10] Both solos include the challengingly uncentered and asymmetrical movements and the falls to the floor; the loose, dry peat on which the Chosen One dances herself to death corresponds to the loose silk flowers onto which Mercy falls; even the drumming and syncopated, almost ritualistic calls and responses of Dizzie Gillespie and his band bear some correspondence to the complex, syncopated rhythms of Stravinsky's famous score.

As soon as these correlations are highlighted, however, the differences between *Der Fensterputzer* and *Sacre* become apparent. Compared with the rich variety of costumes in *Der Fensterputzer*, the community uniformly dressed dancers in Bausch's *Sacre* seem undifferentiated. The women in *Sacre* are evidently subordinate to and in fear of the men who harass them, until one of them gives up and becomes the sacrificial victim. The whole community witnesses her suicide. Incidentally, Mercy was not a member of the original cast of *Sacre*. His solo in *Der Fensterputzer* seemed an intimate affair, one that just happened to take place and did not need to be solemnly witnessed. Although its fragmentation and the disorienting qualities of its movement material resembled Alt's 1975 solo, Mercy performed it without any sign of violence or self-harm. Bausch's *Sacre* showed a community that was falling apart; everyone appeared to be on their own, unable to trust anyone. In *Der Fensterputzer*, the dancers who peered at Mercy around the side of the mountain did so only to adjust its position, and later no one seemed to notice him as they rush past to play with the flowers.

Mercy was attempting to perform his solo in an invisible way and thus remain unmarked while reflecting critically on the performance of violent, threatening masculinity by the male dancers in *Sacre* and in many of Bausch's pieces during the 1970s. Bausch's earlier pieces had shocked some audiences through showing physical and psychological violence inflicted on female bodies. Bausch was, in effect, using strong masculine presences to mark as abnormal and unacceptable what was generally considered to be normal and unexceptional. I have shown that although in 1997 Mercy performed the same kinds of fragmented and disorienting movement material that had been danced by a woman in 1975, his invisibility and the memories he evoked had the effect of distancing his performance from normative though violent and aggressive masculine behavior. In doing so, it challenged assumptions about which masculine bodies are marked and which unmarked. Through the way it drew on history and memory, it showed that masculinity (singular) is not a timeless ideal but that masculinities (plural) are social and cultural performances that are contingent and undergo continual processes of change. In this way it troubled and destabilized the boundaries that determine which male bodies to mark and which to leave unmarked.

Conclusion

Both *29 Effeminate Gestures* and Mercy's solo in *Der Fensterputzer* problematized the limits and boundaries that men encounter as they lay claim to their bodies. Goode's performance undermined the limit dividing straight inside from gay outside, while Mercy's performance cast doubt on what kinds of masculine behavior are normal and unexceptional. Each solo used fragmentation, and each evoked problematic and violent histories and memories that in their singular contexts were difficult for their audiences. For Goode, violence and injury were the price that gay men paid for a sometimes partial and conditional acceptance within hostile and homophobic society. His dance therefore made a plea for unconditional acceptance of gay people: this, I suggest, might have positive consequences for all those who are marked as different or who may find themselves so marked at some point in the future. In Mercy's case, an inability to acknowledge violent and aggressive memories and histories was a restriction and limitation. His dance in turn revealed the necessity for greater self-reflection and, I suggest, self-acceptance, since violence against others is often the result of not wishing to admit one's own vulnerability.

While *Der Fensterputzer* may have been mellow and benign, Mercy's solo did not suggest that things were any better in the 1990s. It merely indicated that things were different. Bausch's vision may have been less bleak in the 1990s than it had been two decades earlier, but her insistence on showing the coexistence of multiple, seemingly incompatible subjectivities, and her refusal to reduce their differences into a single, coherent unifying narrative remained constant. Goode's solo promised his audience the possibility of a future in which experiences that made the present unbearable might no longer exist. But in doing so he also undermined expectations about the entertaining or sentimental nature of queer performance.

Both Goode's and Mercy's solos, therefore, invoked an alternative resource of histories and memories that were grounded in the body and gender. Such resources permitted different, less familiar kinds of access to past experiences and offered possibilities for realizing new perspectives and insights into the otherwise imprisoned meanings of a traumatic past. To quote Peggy Phelan again, Mercy and Goode taught their audiences "to learn to value what is lost, to learn not the meaning but the value of what cannot be reproduced or seen (again)" (1993, 152).

NOTES

1. Goode studied theater at Virginia Commonwealth University, where, as Allan Ulrich notes, he "fell under the spell of a professor who was a disciple of Polish avant-garde director Jerzy Grotowski" (1989). The function of theater as ritual is a key concept in Grotowski's work.

2. When Goode was just starting out as a young dancer in New York, before he moved to San Francisco, he got a part as a tap dancer in a long-running Yiddish musical, *The Big Winner.* "I still recall those little old ladies from New Jersey coming back stage to see their favorite stars, wagging their fingers at me, saying, 'You can't fool us. We know you're gentile'" (Goode in Ulrich 1989).

3. Much of the politicized, queer community, including gay members of Goode's 1992 audience in San Francisco, is middle class.

4. Peter Pabst, interview with Valerie Briginshaw and Ramsay Burt during a study day on Pina Bausch, Sadlers Wells Theater, London, February 2, 2002.

5. Note here that Bausch's work is therefore in agreement with Adorno's pessimistic account of the problem of metaphysical speculation in a way that dominant discussions of Laban and Wigman's prewar dance were not.

6. According to Barbara Newman, "For Bausch, co-production means a three week residency ... during which the co-producer supports her company. The dancers then return to Wuppertal, where Bausch filters their impressions and improvisations through her own process of discovery to complete the piece" (1997, 1070).

7. The bauhinia, or tree orchid, which has a red flower, is the emblem of Hong Kong and appears on the city's flag.

8. On the 1967 Impulse record AS 9149 *Swing Low Sweet Cadillac.* As Thomas J. Sugrue has pointed out, Gillespie's song was a telling comment on the place of the car in black popular culture, where car ownership was a powerful status symbol, and Cadillac cars had assumed iconic status among the black elite. See Sugrue 2004.

9. A documentary by Christiane Gibiec shows him working with Bausch at the Paris Opéra; the film also shows Bausch, Pabst, and other company members in Hong Kong during the residency to make *Der Fensterputzer.*

10. I am grateful to Lena Hammergren, who pointed this out to me when I presented an early draft of some of the material in this chapter at a symposium organized by Cristina Caprioli at Stockholm Danshoegskollen in 2002.

WORKS CITED

Albright, Ann Cooper. 1997. *Choreographing Difference.* Middletown, CT: Wesleyan University Press.

Bal, Mieke. 1995. "Reading the Gaze: The Construction of Gender in 'Rembrandt.'" In *Vision and Textuality,* ed. Stephen Melville and Bill Readings, 147–73. Basingstoke: Macmillan.

Bersani, Leo. 1995. *Homos.* Cambridge, MA: Harvard University Press.

Butler, Judith. 1990a. *Gender Trouble.* London: Routledge.

Butler, Judith. 1990b. "Performative Acts and Gender Constitution: An Essay in Phe-nomenology and Feminist Theory." In *Performing Feminisms: Feminist Critical*

Theory and Theatre, ed. Sue-Ellen Case, 270–82. Baltimore: John Hopkins University Press.

———. 1993. *Bodies That Matter*. New York: Routledge.

———. 2004. *Undoing Gender*. New York: Routledge.

Cody, Gabrielle. 1998. "Woman, Man, Dog, Tree: Two Decades of Intimate and Monumental Bodies in Pina Bausch's Tanztheater." *The Drama Review* 42 (2): 115–32.

Coward, Rosalind. 1984. *Female Desire*. London: Paladin.

Daly, Ann. 1989. "To dance is 'female.'" *The Drama Review* 34 (4): 23–27.

———. 1999. "Mellower now, a resolute romantic keeps trying." *New York Times*, October 31.

Dyer, Richard. 1992. "It's Being So Camp as Keeps Us Going." In *Only Entertainment*, 135–48. London: Routledge.

Foster, Susan. 1997. "Dancing Bodies." In *Meaning in Motion*, ed. Jane Desmond, 235–57. Durham, NC: Duke University Press.

Gere, David. 2001. "29 Effeminate Gestures: Choreography by Joe Goode and the Heroism of Effeminacy." In *Dancing Desires*, ed. Jane Desmond, 349–81. Madison: University of Wisconsin Press.

Hargreaves, Martin. 2000. "Haunted by Failure, Doomed to Success: Melancholic Masculinity in AMP's *Swan Lake*." In *Dancing in Millennium: Conference Proceedings*, 235–39.

Jowitt, Deborah. 1999. "Lingering as Metaphor." *Village Voice*, November 16, 73.

Kisselgoff, Anna. 1997. "Man as a Window Washer and a Metaphor for Futility." *New York Times*, October 6, B1, B5.

Lepecki, André. 2004. *Of the Presence of the Body*. Middletown, CT: Wesleyan University Press.

Naude, Alice. 1998. "Reviews, New York City: Pina Bausch Tanztheater Wuppertal." *Dance Magazine*, January, 100–101.

Newman, Barbara. 1997. "Pina Bausch in Frankfurt and Paris." *Dancing Times*, September, 1069–71.

Phelan, Peggy. 1993. *Unmarked*. New York: Routledge

Rogoff, Irit. 1995. "The Aesthetics of Post-history: A German Perspective." In *Vision and Textuality*, ed. Stephen Melville and Bill Readings, 115–40. Basingstoke: Macmillan.

Scott, Michael. 1991. "Disaster Looms as a Landmark Fusion of Theatre and Dance." *Vancouver Sun*, October 31, C6.

Shank, Theodore. 1994. "Joe Goode's Performance Lifestyle: An Interview with Theodore Shank." *TheatreForum* 5 (September): 71–77.

Sugrue, Thomas J. 2004. "Driving While Black: The Car and Race Relations in Modern America." http://www.autolife.umd.umich.edu/Race/R_Casestudy/R_Casestudy1.htm (accessed January 19, 2006).

Ulrich, Allan. 1989. "The Master of Disaster." *San Francisco Focus*, July, n.p. (Joe Goode Performance Group press pack).

DONALD MCKAYLE

*Named one of America's first 100 "Dance Treasures" by the Dance
Heritage Coalition, McKayle has been choreographing for nearly 60 years.
He began dance classes at the New Dance Group in New York City, later
dancing for such luminaries as Merce Cunningham, Sophie Maslow,
Martha Graham, Anna Sokolow, and Charles Weidman. He made his
name as a choreographer on the concert stage, on Broadway, and in
movies. His masterworks include* Games, Rainbow Round My Shoulder,
and Angelitos Negros, *among many others. He is also a professor in the
dance department of the University of California, Irvine. His prize-
winning autobiography is called* Transcending Boundaries: My Dancing
Life.

When I was growing up in New York City, I never went to the theater or a dance concert, but of course I went to the movies. I saw Bill Robinson dancing there, with Shirley Temple, tapping up all those steps. When I found out he lived not too far away, I used to wait for him with a few other little friends, in the inner courtyard where he lived, in this well-to-do Harlem residence. When he came home, we'd beg him, "Please, Mr. Bill, dance up the steps for us." And he was so nice, he'd smile, and even though there were only a few steps, he'd dance up them—de-dup, de-dup, de-dup—and he'd go in the door, touching his bowler hat. We'd wait for him again and again, hoping for a repeat performance.

That was what I knew as dancing, but of course we went to social dances—that was very important in my family. I saw men dance, but it never entered my mind that you could be a dancer for a living. My mother was a little shocked when she saw that was what I was going to do. As far as she was concerned, dance was what you did to "lively up yourself," it wasn't ever thought of as a profession. She knew about Bill Robinson, and her brother's wife was a showgirl at the Cotton Club, but those were "special people." Dancing was never discussed as a career, and I never thought of it, until I saw Pearl Primus dance. Then, I wanted to do it. That very night, I went home with one of my friends in a social club I was in—she took dance classes at the New Dance Group—and I wanted her to show me all these

McKayle in his work
They Called Her Moses
in 1954. Photograph by
Esta McKayle. Used
with permission.

steps I'd seen, so we pushed back the furniture and we danced. That weekend,
I choreographed my first dance, not knowing that there was any process to it; I just
did it. After that, I started taking classes at the New Dance Group.

You know, I never got all that prejudice about it not being a masculine thing to
do—all I heard was that it wasn't a profession that you could make a living in. It just
didn't make any sense to my parents at first. In fact, my mother was well into her
senior years, she would still ask, "You still dancing?" Yes, Mother. Then she would
say, "You still teaching? You got nice students?" Yes, Mother, "Are they a mixed
group?" She meant boys and girls. She was happy it was a mixed group. But they
never had that problem of thinking dancing meant homosexuality. It wasn't part of
the way they thought. When I think of it now, many men's experience of being
called feminine because they danced—that's very different from my experience.

Now I know the troubles a lot of boys have from my students here [at the
University of California, Irvine]. It's still a problem for boys in the United States, and
I think in a lot of places in the world. But it wasn't a problem, I remember, back
when I was touring with Martha Graham in 1955 in Indonesia. I met this dancer
who gave a wonderful performance of a Javanese *Slendang*, and he was a colonel in

McKayle teaching in the dance department at the University of California, Irvine. Photograph by Frank Peters. Used with permission.

the army—that was a real confirmation of dance as a real profession. And, of course, there are so many places in Africa where men dance so powerfully, like the Masai, with their high jumps.

I don't know if my being trained around all those great modern dancers made a difference in how I thought about masculinity and femininity—I never thought about it that way. But the people I grew up around in the dance world were all these proletarian choreographers—people were people, whether they were in the street, in the fields—[he sings heartily to demonstrate], "I ride an old paint, I lead an old dam, I'm going to Montana to throw the holihan," or "Old Bill Jones had two daughters and a son; one went to college, the other went wrong." Those are the people I knew in all those old songs used by Sophie Maslow and Bill Bales. And I knew a lot of other folk songs, all about human beings who had to leave home, work, and live a rough life. Modern dance then didn't have the background of the ballet, which came from the courts, none of that—all of that was news to me later. I took ballet class for a while, but I didn't know much about it. I never considered it for a career—I knew there were no black people in the ballet, that was very clear to me. Later, of course, there were some, but I just never considered it.

Part of being strong as I grew up was that you had to "transcend boundaries," you know, you had to get somewhere. A lot of times when men couldn't get jobs, a woman could always get a job and bring home the money. A strong woman was always part of the black American community. Men had to allow their women to do that. Also, women were in charge at the home—my mother and Aunt Alice were very particular about the way things were—there was no doubt about who ruled the roost at home. The men accepted a woman who was strong, but they also expected a woman to be beautiful. My mother and all of them had a vanity, where they would make up and everything. And I would go and watch, I was very interested, that's how I knew about all of that, to put in dances later. I grew up very involved with the women and men of my parents' generation.

My interest in folk music and black culture, even before I went to the New Dance Group, led me to discover lots of strong characters, which eventually led to making dances like *Rainbow Round My Shoulder*, to work songs. This was part of what I decided I could create in dance. I never thought about what were appropriate masculine or feminine movements, not in those terms. But with *Rainbow*, for instance, I was thinking of these men on a chain gang, and they were thinking of freedom. For them, the idea of freedom comes in the guise of a woman. There were the different characters—this young boy chasing a girl, for instance. So the movements were very much those of a boy [he indicates lurching forward with a gleam in the eye] after this girl, who does things like [prancing, arms back] showing off her bosom with the guy after her like, "Hey, good looking." She fusses with her nail polish, like the girls that I knew, who were much more mature than the boys, very girly girls.

And with *Games*, because it's about children at play, there were just girls' games and boys' games, because girls were girls, and boys were boys—I never thought of it in any other way back then. It was later on when I was older that I began to see different things when it had to do with the sexes. I made these solos for strong women, like the ones in *Blood Memory* and *Angelitos Negros*—this was the eternal woman, woman the creator. You know, you heard "God is a man," but when I teach *Angelitos*, I tell the dancer for her entrance that each step she takes is like creating a world, powerful and in charge.

I never considered whether it was the man or the woman who was strong or weak, not as a general thing. But it came up, I guess. I was just listening to an introduction I did for a performance of *Blood Memory*, in which I describe female dancers as portraying the waterways, with "the fluidity of their body movement masking the tremendous strength of their musculature," while the male dancers had to "press against the awesome powers of the waters in unison." So it's always there, I guess, but there are so many ways you see power and vulnerability with both men and women.

I'm lucky in that I was never harassed for dancing—that was never a problem for me. It may be true that stereotypes about men being sissies were reserved for the ballet world—they wore tights more, and ballet was considered a lot of flitting around. Whereas modern dance was grounded, and characters like the ones in *Rainbow Round My Shoulder* were definitely not fooling around—they were breaking rock, and their bodies were used as tools. And my family never had that kind of mentality—they never thought dancing had that kind of "sissy" stigma. At first my mother warned me that dancing is a short life, but finally she said, "If you really want to do this, you have our support." And my father built the set for *Games*. They were both just wonderful. That was the thing he talked about most after that premiere, that he liked the way the bricks looked—he was mostly into his set [laughing]. They wanted me to be very successful, that was all.

If I hadn't had supportive parents, that would have changed a lot of things. My mother said to me, anything you want, you can do. Her father was an English Jew, her mother was West Indian, so she was from a mixed background racially, and when something happened, like not being rented an apartment, some kind of prejudice, she always told me, "We're as good as anyone else." That's all she said, and that I could do anything I wanted to do. So when you grow up with that kind of protection and support, it's a gift.

JOHN PENNINGTON

A modern dancer and choreographer, Pennington was a senior member of the Bella Lewitzky Dance Company for 14 years, touring widely with Lewitzky repertory he now sometimes stages. He is currently artistic director of Pennington Dance Company, based in Los Angeles, and teaches contemporary dance at Pomona College in Claremont, California. In 2009, he received his MFA in Dance from the Hollins College/American Dance Festival program.

I was born in Detroit, and we lived in a real working-class neighborhood. My father was a mechanic who rode and raced motorcycles with a blue-collar "gang." He was a hard-drinking, über-macho man, and by contrast my mother was a churchgoing Southern Baptist. I attended church every Sunday, and in many ways church was a positive experience. I learned discipline, which later on taught me to attend rehearsals with regularity, and in the turmoil of my family setting, the church gave me some stability. Neither of my parents finished high school; I was the first in my family to attend and graduate from college.

An example of culture in my house was watching the televised *Lawrence Welk Show*, where I sat eagerly waiting for the featured dance routines of Bobby and Sissy. My first memories of seeing live dance are of my older brother and sister, who were social dancing in our basement in the late 60s. They were in their teens, and I was only five, watching them do the mashed potato, the frug, the watusi, and the swim. In the seventh and eighth grades I had my first exposure to other types of dance through arts in the schools programs.

My high school years were spent in Phoenix, Arizona, where my family moved to improve my father's failing health. It was there in the desert I learned to rebel. I became a social dancer, an activity that was forbidden by the Southern Baptist Church, and in an ironic twist, dance also became my profession. In my first year of high school, I discovered musical theater. I thought there was something wonderful about theater people; they were more authentic, demonstrative of their feelings, and I bonded with them. When my father died in my freshman year, it was the presence of my theater family that comforted me. They became my second family.

Pennington in his piece *Cuirass* (2001). An old French term for a leather breastplate, *cuirass* is used by Pennington to refer to the barrier that shields "the emotional heart." Photograph by Chris Campolongo. Used with permission.

In high school I had the great fortune to know Joanne Blase, an ex-Broadway dancer who took interest in young people. She choreographed our high school musicals and also taught the first ballet class I took. Joanne was an amazing first encounter with professionalism. She was nurturing but also demanded discipline. She gave me the first inkling that dance was an art form. But it wasn't until college that I encountered modern dance, when I was on a voice scholarship at Northwestern University. For my physical education requirement I took modern dance from Melissa Nunn, who taught Cunningham technique. She's the one who opened my eyes to what dance could be—that what theater could say in words, dance could express in movement. The 70s were an era of generous dance funding, so I attended many performances of touring companies that came through Chicago. Dance was so popular that it found its way into mainstream magazines like *Time* and *Vogue*. It was as if dance had been elevated to celebrity status.

I would say I struggled with issues of masculinity through most of my early life. In my family, appearance was of great importance—what the neighbors might think was critical, and it was absolutely necessary to appear masculine. While struggling to define my sexuality in college, I was happy to know that Mikhail Baryshnikov, the most prominent male ballet dancer of the era, was very fond of women, which made it more permissible for "straight" men to dance professionally. I knew I could always use Mikhail as an example of hetero virility, while my own identity was in question. At some level I worried about the stereotypical image of the male dancer as effeminate, overly emotional, and even unrestrained sexually. Baryshnikov provided a "model" for me to aspire to, as well as a convenient mask to escape the stereotypes I feared.

The familial hetero coding extended so far that my mother would never publicly admit that I was a professional dancer. Even later, years after I'd been successful with the Lewitzky Company, she would tell people I was in theater arts and privately ask me when I might be returning to acting, because she was more comfortable with that.

As I developed into a dance artist I wondered, "Where do I fall on the masculinity scale?" "What is the masculine role?" Cultural masculine coding was everywhere, and it was clear what I *should* do as a man. I realized that gender rules created tension in me, but dance ended up liberating me by challenging my beliefs and allowing room for the fluidity of gender and sexual roles. That happened later, but in 1980, my girlfriend and I moved from Chicago to California and attended California Institute of the Arts, because we were seeking a conservatory environment for training. I came to Cal Arts as an actor and continued to take dance as an elective within the program. After my first year, I was faced with a financial crisis of having no tuition money. The dance department, in need of male students, offered a full scholarship, which I eagerly accepted. It was a fabulous time to be there. Those were halcyon days when the roster of exceptional instructors included Donald Byrd, from the Twyla Tharp Company; Nicholas Gunn, who had danced with Paul Taylor; Sandra Neels, who had been with Merce Cunningham; Rebecca Bobele, who was with Bella Lewitzky; and Tina Yuan, who had danced with Alvin Ailey. I immersed myself in dance and graduated with a B.F.A. from Cal Arts.

The day after graduation I got married, and a month later my wife and I moved to New York, where I had a short apprenticeship with the José Limon Company. After much discussion about careers, we moved back to Los Angeles, where I heard there was an opening with the Bella Lewitzky Dance Company. I had previously taken workshops from Bella, and I was familiar with her work and her style, so I auditioned and joined the company in April 1983. Bella was not only an accomplished choreographer but also a progressive feminist. Her politics colored her work, and it was through her choreography that I began to challenge my views of gender roles and typical assumptions about the physical capabilities of male and female bodies. I began to explore new ways to think about male identity and how they applied to my life.

I remember one dance, *Inscape*, in which Rudi Gernreich, through his costumes, attempted to erase male and female physiognomy with unisex costumes that flattened the women's chests and erased the men's genitals as much as possible. Of course, it was physically impossible, but he tried. In the dance, the choreography explored the tension between and within gender: women lifted women, men partnered men, while masks, skullcaps, and makeup concealed the "true" gender of the dancer. The piece was created in the mid-70s, when unisex ideas of gender were in the public realm.

In general, Bella's work was less focused on gender and more on design—the body's architecture and relationship to the space in which it existed. The connection between male and female dancers was reflective. I found that what attracted me to Bella's choreographies was the de-emphasis of gender-specific roles. The line between classically assigned gender roles was many times smudged and redefined.

It was in the artistic hothouse of dancing professionally and being exposed to the likes of Mark Morris's male-male partnering and the gender-bending displays of Ballets Trockadero that my constructed straight masculinity began to crumble and I found the courage to step toward something different. Not willing to deny my true identity, I came out of the closet after five years of marriage, confronting a lifetime of my own mixed messages.

Even today, I don't always say I'm a dancer. This hesitation comes from the past when I engaged in conversations about what I wasn't—I wasn't a ballet dancer although I took ballet class, or a Vegas performer, or a Broadway gypsy, even though I also spent many years in musical theater. Sometimes I would say I was a "movement architect." That description seemed to stop the conversation cold. Fred Astaire and Gene Kelly had stamps of approval, but modern concert dance is alien to the majority. Even today men in dance are not always considered to be making wise choices for career longevity, stability, and well-being. About 20 years ago I was selected to be on a game show filmed in Los Angeles and was told not to admit my profession was dance. "It wouldn't play well in Peoria" was the reason given. Of course, television executives and the sponsors were afraid of audience assumptions about a male dancer, and I was told to say "teacher," which was not a lie but not quite the whole truth either.

Now, I continue to refine my explanation of what I do as a dancer, choreographer, and teacher. Through education I want to make inroads to counter those often-held narrow attitudes about male dancers. I'm still aware of appearances and expectations, and how I might be viewed is a lingering concern, but less as time goes by. Now I think less of being defined by my male chromosomes, and more by my work. People have remarked, "You are so masculine on stage!" often coded to mean "not gay," and I am at once flattered and confused by the statement. In my journey to know my true self I found my authentic identity as a gay man that on one hand shifted my self-perception and on the other provoked great confusion in the groundwork I had laid for my life. All my cultural coding was up for examination, and a comment from an audience member about my masculinity had to be viewed through a new lens.

What defines masculinity? Or femininity? That list of requirements, I suppose, changes from viewer to viewer. But I realized I had to disengage from the perception of what constitutes male and female in dance movement. Right now, being a man or woman means many things as many definitions are up for grabs. For example, in my own choreography I recently premiered a suite of 14 solos, each solo double cast with a male and female dancer. I was interested in how the same movement danced by different genders would be understood by dancer and audience alike, creating "body politics" in the performance.

Within the form of dance there is great capacity for expression. Dance allows me the space to escape previously scripted gendered constraints. My journey in dance has led me to this point, knowing that gender expression is fluid, mercurial, unpredictable, and surprising, and that many masculine and feminine traits are culturally constructed through the eyes of the observer and the observed. While anatomical differences in male and female will prevail in the "outer," I will continue to investigate possibilities of the "inner," both in myself and in my choreography. Dance has the power to integrate the disparate aspects of the physical, emotional, and spiritual in life—and just as I pursue the elusive goal of "perfect technique," which is always several strides ahead, I continue to reach for deeper integration of all elements, with movement as my guide.

PART II

HISTORICAL PERSPECTIVES

6

Pricked Dances

*The Spectator, Dance, and Masculinity in Early
18th-Century England*

JOHN BRYCE JORDAN

From 1711 to 1714, Joseph Addison and Richard Steele published the *Spectator*, one of the first and best-known examples of the modern urban periodical.[1] This daily London publication not only was widely read in its own time but also continued to be reprinted and recommended throughout the 18th century. Rather than having the format of a modern newspaper, the *Spectator* was a daily essay, often supplemented by letters from readers. Each issue was only a few pages long. The paper addressed a wide variety of topics, ranging from current fashions to the pleasures of country life, as well as more serious subjects such as the nature of mourning. Most of the issues were written by Addison and Steele on alternate days, though other authors contributed occasionally. Regardless of their actual authorship, all the issues were written in the voice of "Mr. Spectator," a fictional narrator who prided himself on his quiet but observant temperament. His silent watchfulness allowed him to serve as a "fly on the wall," reporting and commenting on contemporary events.

Two topics that appear frequently in the pages of the *Spectator*, either for their own sake or in the context of other discussions, are gender and dance. While the *Spectator* does not use the modern term "gender," the paper does, over the course of its run, map a complex terrain of social possibilities for men and women, depicting and evaluating a variety of male and female social types. In certain issues, masculinity and femininity are examined in relation to one another, whereas in other issues only one gender receives attention. In the present study, male behavior and the concepts of masculinity and effeminacy expressed in the periodical are the focus, and thus most of the articles examined here center primarily or exclusively on men.

Somewhat less frequent, though still notable, are the references to dance and dancers in the essays and letters. The characteristics ascribed to these dancing figures help elucidate period understandings of dance as a socially meaningful, gendered practice. Taken together these discussions offer an important resource for the study of the intertwined histories of dance and masculinity as they developed together in early 18th-century England.

One such discussion bringing together dance and a particular male type is *Spectator* number 475, from September 4, 1712. In it, Mr. Spectator uses a letter from a young female reader to expound upon the hazards of giving honest advice on matters of love. He includes a letter from "B.D.," a girl who reports her age as 14, setting the stage for her passionate and naive tone. She writes to ask for Mr. Spectator's opinion about a "Mr. Shapely," of whom she is clearly in favor. In the process B.D. draws particular attention to Mr. Shapely's abilities as a dancer: "Now, Sir, the thing is this: Mr. Shapely is the prettiest Gentleman about Town. He is very Tall, but not too Tall neither. He Dances like an Angel. His Mouth is made I don't know how, but 'tis the prettiest that I ever saw in my Life. He is always Laughing, for he has an infinite deal of Wit. If you did but see how he rowls his Stockins! He has a thousand Pretty Fancies, and I am sure, if you saw him, you wou'd like him" (4:184). B.D. goes on at length with her gushing description, which inadvertently undermines her own credibility as a reasonable judge. She also unwittingly damns the man she intends to praise. Already in these opening lines, she pays great attention to Mr. Shapely's looks, using the word "prettiest" or "pretty" three times, concluding "if you saw him, you wou'd like him." To B.D., Mr. Shapely can be rightly judged by his appearance. Mr. Spectator agrees; however, he draws the opposite conclusion. Rather than speak in his favor, Mr. Shapely's prettiness argues against his suitability as a husband. It is not that men are supposed to be unconcerned with their appearance, but that excessive attention bespeaks a whole complex of behaviors and priorities geared not toward appropriately masculine ends but toward pleasing women.[2] And these priorities are implicitly opposed to those that the *Spectator* considers truly important.

Mr. Shapely's merit is then further called into question by other telling details. His primary explicit problem, the only obstacle B.D. acknowledges, is that he lacks an estate. Perhaps a younger brother who will not inherit or from a family that has fallen on hard times (B.D. does not elaborate), Mr. Shapely offers no financial security. As a result, B.D. can find little support among her friends and family for her desire to marry him: "Every Body I advise with here is poor Mr. Shapely's Enemy." Normally this would be enough to prevent the match, since without her father's support the girl would bring no money to the marriage, leaving the couple destitute. While Mr. Spectator does at times condemn the practice of arranging marriages based purely on the financial suitability of the partners (the *Spectator* is an early advocate of marriage as romantic companionship), neither is he willing to completely ignore the pragmatics of financial security.[3] However, B.D.'s situation is more complicated. She writes that she has a "portion," probably inherited from her mother or some other relative, and as a result, she has a degree of financial independence. While this fortune may alleviate concerns about the couple's financial survival (we are not told exactly how much money B.D. has), this only casts further doubts on the character of Mr. Shapely. Now in addition to his suspect personal appearance and his lack of financial self-sufficiency, the possibility is raised that Mr. Shapely is interested in B.D. only for her money.

Shapely's qualifications as a dancer should be understood in this negative context. One of the first qualities B.D. praises in Mr. Shapely is his dancing ability. She then returns to dancing two more times in her short letter. The final line in the body of her letter exclaims, "I heartily wish you cou'd see him Dance," with the expectation that if Mr. Spectator could see him dancing, surely he would be as persuaded of Mr. Shapely's desirability as she herself is. To B.D., the man's skill at dancing is an important qualification. However, the *Spectator*'s use of this letter makes it clear that the paper does not share her opinion. B.D.'s account is presented as an example of mistaken judgment in love, impervious to the warnings of friends. Consequently, the *Spectator* intends the reader to find suspect all that B.D. finds persuasive. Because she values dancing skill in her prospective male partner, the *Spectator* implicitly does not, and thus, at least in this instance, dancing is not a trait recommending a man for matrimony.

Even apart from this logic of reversal, though, Mr. Shapely's attributes raise suspicion in themselves. Praised almost entirely on the basis of looking good, Mr. Shapely lacks other more weighty qualifications for marriage: seriousness, intelligence, reputation, and financial security. In the absence of these, dancing, good looks, and charm alarm the reader by their frivolous inconsequence. Mr. Shapely's dancing provides one more example, perhaps the most telling, of his misplaced priorities and dangerous lack of substance. Dancing is precisely that skill that is of no real value, particularly when, as here, it appears the possessor has cultivated dancing ability to the exclusion of other, more practical skills. To the *Spectator*, to dance well is a talent that sometimes impresses but should rightly be of little importance in the serious matter of choosing a husband. Rather than an accomplishment for a man to flaunt, a facility at dancing is depicted here as something that gives rise to suspicion and potentially discredits.

The Woman's Man

Mr. Shapely offers one illustration of a category of man that figures heavily in the *Spectator* and is known by a few different but related terms, including the "beau" and the "woman's man." Multiple issues of the *Spectator* are devoted to discussing these men in some detail, though not always in a consistent manner, and it will be useful to examine a few more of these accounts for the assumptions about dance and gender they reveal. One of these discussions takes place in *Spectator* 128 (July 27, 1711), which attempts to analyze the nature of gender difference and to address certain problems of cross-gender attraction. Because of its general, theoretical scope, this discussion lays out some important ideas that help explain the *Spectator*'s attitudes toward different types of men and toward dancing as these are expressed elsewhere in the publication's run. In this theorization, men and women each have certain inherent predispositions that differentiate the sexes in body and, more important, in temperament: "Women in their Nature are much more gay and joyous than Men; whether it be that their Blood is more refined, their Fibers more delicate, and their animal Spirits more light and volatile; or whether, as some have imagined, there may not be a kind of Sex in the very Soul, I shall not pretend to determine. As Vivacity is the Gift of Women, Gravity is that of Men" (2:8). Women are innately cheerful, delicate, and exuberant, whereas men are grave, sturdy, and practical. Such definitions foreshadow the paper's understanding of dance in gendered terms, with dance's energetic physicality and gay sociability aligning it more easily with femininity than with the weighty, taciturn masculinity described here.

Though admitting his uncertainty about the causes of these gender differences, Mr. Spectator is nonetheless confident about their consequences. Left unchecked, these innate tendencies will lead individual men and women away from a desirable moderate rationality: "They should each of them therefore keep a Watch upon the particular Bias which Nature has fixed in their Minds, that it may not draw too much, and lead them out of the Paths of Reason" (2:8). Nature here is not something to be embraced and obeyed directly but rather something that presents difficulties or liabilities to be managed. Both men and women are essentially unbalanced, and without appropriate intervention, their natural tendencies will have undesirable personal and social consequences. Mr. Spectator's analysis therefore quickly leads him to deduce and advocate an obvious solution for neutralizing this apparent problem: cross-gender partnership: "By what I have said we may conclude, Men and Women were made as Counterparts to one another, that the Pains and Anxieties of the Husband might be relieved by the Sprightliness and good Humour of the Wife. When these are rightly tempered, Care and Chearfulness go Hand in Hand; and the Family, like a Ship that is duly trimmed, wants neither Sail nor Ballast" (2:9). In this simile, smooth sailing requires both masculine gravitas and feminine vitality. When the innate qualities of a man or woman are matched with those of a partner of the other sex, each member of the pair moderates and enriches the other, improving them both as individuals and as a family unit. Mr. Spectator thus articulates here a theory of male and female as complementary opposites, each possessing qualities that can not only moderate negative excesses in their partner but also combine to form a positive collaborative whole. Notably, the overt dichotomy articulated here is not between a masculine reason and a feminine emotion. Both the masculine and the feminine biases are described as a kind of unreason. True reasonableness requires moderation, and in this construction both the masculine and the feminine left unchecked tend toward an indulgence in certain qualities rather than a temperate equanimity.

Despite this seeming equivalence in the male and female tendencies away from desirable balance, however, Mr. Spectator devotes more attention in this essay to the failure of women to effectively moderate themselves than he does to the failures of men in this regard. After laying out his model of gender difference and heterosexual complementary opposition, Mr. Spectator addresses the second third of his essay to the lack of interest and respect women show toward properly masculine men in favor of other, less appropriate love objects: "It has been an old Complaint, That the Coxcomb carries it with them before the Man of Sense. When we see a Fellow loud and talkative, full of insipid Life and Laughter, we may venture to pronounce him a female Favourite: Noise and Flutter are such Accomplishments as they cannot withstand" (2:9). Thus what leads many women astray from a complementary match is one or more types of improper man.

At first this man is described in terms that to modern readers may not seem particularly feminine: boisterous, talkative, noisy. The last word used, "flutter," is perhaps most easily recognizable as a suspect masculine attribute and hearkens back to one of the most famous fops of Restoration comedy, Sir Fopling Flutter, from George Etherege's *Man of Mode* (1676). The term "fop" is typically used both in the period and in modern scholarship to describe a ridiculous male figure affected with extravagant tastes and manners. Loud, self-important, and foolish, fops are frequently also depicted as unmanly in that they often fail to demonstrate the masculine-coded traits of courage and sexual aggressiveness. Like the fops, the men Mr. Spectator is concerned with in *Spectator* 128 also violate the standards of desirable masculinity, at least according to the system of gender difference and female desire that he is attempting to lay out. However, unlike most Restoration fops, it is these men's supposed attractiveness to women that helps to mark them as suspect.

This attractiveness is a problem because of the innate tendency on the part of women to desire not what is good for them but what is like themselves: "If we observe the Conduct of the fair Sex, we find that they choose rather to associate themselves with a Person who resembles them in that light and volatile Humour which is natural to them, than to such as are qualified to moderate and counterbalance it" (2:9). Thus the men in question are not just loud and boisterous but are in some important sense like women in their nature or character. "Loud" and "boisterous," along with "light" and "volatile," signify femininity here. This chain of reasoning leads Mr. Spectator, paraphrasing Dryden, to make a remarkable assertion: "The Passion of an ordinary Woman for a Man, is nothing else but Self-love diverted upon another Object: She would have the Lover a Woman in every thing but the Sex" (2:10). Cross-gender desire here is far from straightforward. According to Mr. Spectator, a woman's natural, if problematic, desire is primarily for herself, which can be generalized as a desire for women, and then to those men who are most like women. In this attempt to account for female desire, Mr. Spectator thus also theorizes a type of man who, by virtue of his success in courting women, is defined by the *Spectator* as practically a woman in a man's body, "a Woman in every thing but the Sex."

This intermediate, one could even say transgender, male type therefore becomes a necessary part of the social landscape, helping to account for (and condemn) women's taste, while laying the groundwork for a system to evaluate men and male behavior as appropriately masculine or perilously womanlike.[4]

According to the *Spectator*, the misguided desires of women, in combination with these womanlike men, threaten disaster to women and society: "This is a Source of infinite Calamities to the Sex, as it frequently joins them to Men who in their own Thoughts are as fine Creatures as themselves; or if they chance to be good-humoured, serve only to dissipate their Fortunes, inflame their Follies, and aggravate their Indiscretions" (2:10). Reiterating the femininity of these men "in their own Thoughts," the *Spectator* predicts that the woman's man will leave his female partner financially destitute, both through indulging the woman's costly desires and through the man's own irresponsible expenditures. These are in effect the same concerns expressed toward Mr. Shapely, discussed earlier, those of misdirecting energy toward inessential, superficially attractive activities such as dance while failing to provide financial security, understood as a proper masculine duty.

These dangers are not confined to unmarried girls. Under the negative influence of these male tempters, married women are also at risk, since they may begin to dislike their "faithful prudent" husbands and long for "the fine gay Gentleman that laughs, sings, and dresses so much more agreeably" (2:10), and who, one suspects, dances more agreeably as well. Lastly, this errant female desire also puts a woman's children at risk, in that "she admires in her Son what she loved in her Gallant; and by that Means contributes all she can to perpetuate herself in a worthless Progeny" (2:10). Thus the womanlike man perpetuates himself indirectly by way of these misguided women, who shape their sons after his image. To stop this dangerous cycle, the *Spectator* believes society must exert a policing function against the desires of women. Though discussed as natural to many or even all women, these desires are nonetheless treated as mistaken and even perverse by Mr. Spectator's analysis. Women's attractions must therefore be actively redirected to promote other more balanced and socially functional relationships and behaviors.

This model depends upon an idea of a nonstandard man, the womanlike man, to whom women are wrongly attracted. Once this theoretical framework is in place, the elaboration of this feminized male type and the assignment of some men to fulfill this theoretically necessary, if disparaged, male role become inevitable. In *Spectator* 128, however, these womanlike men are not discussed as individuals worthy of attention or correction in themselves. And unlike the women who are prone to love them, these problem men are not encouraged toward any sort of balancing alliance. How could they be? The only logical options would be for the unmasculine men to align themselves with masculine women or other more masculine men, neither of which would be an acceptable solution to Mr. Spectator. The womanlike men are thus left largely outside the discussion, appearing only as a dangerous temptation to ordinary women, but irrecuperable themselves within Mr. Spectator's system.

The characterization of these men as undesirable "other" serves instead to warn away "regular" men from having or appearing to have the derided characteristics. As will become clear, many issues of the *Spectator* contribute to this implicit condemnation of certain behaviors and characteristics in men through the depiction of discredited male figures who possess them. These satirical portrayals articulate and reinforce a model of gender difference, which leaves little acceptable space for men and women who do not conform to the ideals of temperament, physical type, and areas of interest that have been assigned to the respective genders by Mr. Spectator and the broad segment of English society that he represents.[5] Importantly, dance plays a prominent role in defining many of the discredited or suspect male types in the essays of the *Spectator*, demonstrating the historical span of the effeminate connotation of dance within English culture and the relevance of dance to constructions of English masculinity.

The Beau's Head

For all their various imputed faults, the womanlike men of the *Spectator* are not usually depicted as straying from standard cross-gender desire. Just as many women are drawn to the womanlike man as outlined earlier, making him also a "woman's man," so too are these men actively attracted to women. In most of the issues in which they appear, these men are clearly depicted as engaged in the pursuit of women. For instance, *Spectator* 275 (January 15, 1712) uses as its conceit a dream brought about after a day spent listening to a discussion of the scientific dissection of human bodies. In his dream, Mr. Spectator imagines the dissection of the head of a "beau," a virtual synonym for woman's man in the *Spectator*. This dream allows the paper to catalog the various (dubious) attributes of the beau by supposedly finding evidence of these qualities and activities in the physical anatomy of this male type.

The "discoveries" are comic and cutting. The beau's pineal gland, reputed to be the seat of the soul, smells of cologne and is surrounded by a mirrorlike substance. Thus at the most fundamental level, the beau is vain and perfumed. The cavities in the beau's brain are filled with a variety of fashionable materials, including snuff, ribbons, and lace, as well as less tangible, more symbolic ingredients such as "flattery" and "froth." One compartment of the skull "was stuffed with invisible Billet-doux, Love-Letters, pricked Dances, and other Trumpery of the same nature" (2:571). "To prick," as the editor's footnote explains, "is to set down music by means of pricks or notes," which suggests to the modern editor that Mr. Spectator is alluding to sheet music to accompany dances (2:571 n. 4). It seems at least as likely that these "pricked dances" are instead a reference to Beauchamp-Feuillet dance notation, which had been

Figure 6.1   An illustration of the passacaille step combining dancing bodies and dance notation. From *The Art of Dancing Explained by Reading and Figures*, by Kellom Tomlinson (London, 1735), book 1, plate 13.

introduced in England in the previous decade. This notation system recorded dance steps and spatial paths as well as accompanying melodies.[6] In either case, dancing, whether through written dance music or dance notation, is one of the defining elements of the beau figure in this mock dissection. Interestingly, these pricked dances are grouped with love letters and other unspecified items called "trumpery of the same nature." To the *Spectator* both the letters and the dancing share something in common as "trumpery" or worthless finery, and probably more specifically, as tools for wooing women.

Another discovery during the dream dissection confirms that the *Spectator's* version of the beau is sexually active, unlike the asexual fops of Restoration comedy. Along with the other fantastical ingredients, the anatomist discovers mercury, the common treatment for venereal disease, flowing through the beau's brain. We are also told that the beau died from a blow to the head from a shovel wielded by a citizen, while the beau was "tending some Civilities" to the citizen's wife (2:573). The term "citizen" referred to the merchant class of

London, who were routinely portrayed as cuckolds at the hands of more rakish gentlemen. Thus the *Spectator* represents the beau as vigorously sexually motivated by an attraction to women resulting in his infection with venereal disease and ultimately his death at the hands of the jealous husband of one of his mistresses.

The beau's connection to dance is reasserted later in the essay through a description of him before his death. We are told that he "had passed for *a Man* above five and thirty Years; during which time he Eat and Drank like other People, dressed well, talked loud, laught frequently, and on particular Occasions had acquitted himself tolerably at a Ball or an Assembly; to which one of the Company added, that a certain knot of Ladies took him for a Wit" (2:573). Despite the ironic, understated tone of the writing, the reference to the beau's "tolerable" skills at balls and assemblies draws attention once again to his connection with dancing, using the trait to help define this male type. Dancing adds to the beau's showy, attention-getting qualities as a fancy dresser, loud talker, and frequent laugher, qualities familiar from the descriptions of Mr. Shapely and the Woman's man discussed earlier, whose reappearance here reasserts the unmasculine association of these traits in the period.

The *Spectator* understands these attention-getting characteristics of the beau, including dance, as compatible with, and motivated at least in part by, a sexual desire for women. However, this sexual motivation is not enough to secure the man's masculinity. The quote above begins by saying that the beau "had passed for *a Man*," that is, he was not really a man, only looking like one. This same principle is evident from the beginning of the essay, such that the beau's head "appeared like the Head of another Man" on the surface, but upon closer inspection the anatomists discovered "that the Brain of a Beau is not real Brain, but only something like it" (2:570–71). These teasing remarks use the new discoveries of anatomists, made possible by recently developed magnifying technologies, to set the beau in opposition to a true man, with the beau's manlike appearance undermined by his very different constitution. The beau is thus neither masculine nor perhaps even human in this comic analysis, but is instead a creature only superficially resembling a man.

Importantly, this false man is both a dancer and a lover of women, reiterating a model of disparaged masculinity whose failings do not depend on a lack of cross-gender sexual drive but are in fact largely motivated by an excessive pursuit of women. This exaggerated sexual motivation leads to, or is compounded by, a narcissistic self-display through fashionable clothes, scents, snuff, and dance, in the pursuit of a self-glorifying conquest of women's hearts and bodies. But whereas these sexual conquests were one of the hallmarks of the masculine rake-hero in restoration comedy, understood in opposition to an asexual effeminate fop, in the pages of the *Spectator*, these sexual escapades are ridiculed as themselves emasculating, and they result in men who are vain and filled with insubstantial trumperies like love letters and dancing. The *Spectator* thus intervenes in received cultural categories, reassigning the gender characteristics of certain behaviors to further its own emergent middle-class moral agenda. The stigma of effeminacy is used here to discredit excessive womanizing in favor of a bourgeois marriage based on opposite and complementary roles for men and women. In the process, dance is lumped together with other suspect activities and materials as something that real men (as distinct from beaux) avoid.

Dick and Tom

Another episode in the *Spectator* further elaborates the typology of the beau or woman's man, detailing some possible variations within the category. And once again, the authors convey the male type in part through the inclusion of dancing. This issue also offers an example of a common rhetorical strategy used in the *Spectator*, explained in the issue's introduction: "I cannot forbear inserting the Circumstances which pleased me in the Account a young Lady gave me of the Loves of a Family in Town, which shall be nameless, or rather for the better Sound, and Elevation of the History, instead of Mr. and Mrs. such a one, I shall call them by feigned Names" (1:384). Many of the issues of the *Spectator* are cast as retold stories. Also common is the use of obviously fictional names. In addition to Mr. Spectator and the source of the story, who remains nameless, this account from *Spectator* 91 (June 14, 1711) features Lady Honoria and her 15-year-old daughter, Flavia. We are soon also introduced to their respective suitors, Dick Crastin and Tom Tulip. As in the case of Mr. Shapely, this avoidance of the name of the supposed source of the story and the use of fictional names for the characters, as though to protect the anonymity of the persons involved, works to blur their status as real or fictional.[7]

The story focuses on the matter of age. Honoria, though 40, acts like a girl of 20. However, Honoria's girlish coquetry is undermined by her daughter, Flavia, who makes a point of drawing attention to Honoria's age in front of the mother's potential suitors. Both women seek to attract the romantic attention of men, and each resents the other for interfering. The *Spectator* criticizes both for their inappropriate behavior. Honoria is held to blame for acting younger than she is, while Flavia is condemned for her disrespectful actions toward her mother.

After acquainting us with these women's competitive relationship, however, the focus of the issue shifts to their two male admirers, Dick Crastin and Tom Tulip. Though the two women do not compete for the same man's affections, the *Spectator* explains that each nonetheless tries to show her man's charms to be superior to those of her relation's suitor. We are told that the two men were "purposely admitted together by the Ladies, that each might show the other that her Lover had the Superiority in the Accomplishments of that sort of Creature, whom the sillier part of Women call a Fine Gentleman" (1:386). The *Spectator* clearly holds neither man in good stead, alluding to a distinction between the "good" and the "fine" elaborated elsewhere, in which the latter is aligned with affectation rather than truly desirable qualities.[8]

Following the difference in age between Honoria and Flavia, Dick Crastin and Tom Tulip represent, respectively, the older and younger generations of beau: "As this Age has a much more gross Taste in Courtship, as well as in every thing else, than the last had, these Gentlemen are Instances of it in their different manner of Application. Tulip is ever making Allusions to the Vigour of his Person, the sinewy Force of his Make, while Crastin professes a wary Observation of the Turns of his Mistress's Mind. Tulip gives himself the Air of a resistless Ravisher, Crastin practices that of a skilful Lover" (1:386). Here the distinction between the two men is understood in large part to be a function of their difference in age. The younger Tulip is more physical and overtly sexual, whereas the older Crastin is more subtle and romantic. More specifically, then, the difference between the two suitors turns on each man's relationship to sex. As the principal example of their rivalry given by the *Spectator,* Tom Tulip recites a verse from Ovid extolling his sexual potency: "'Tis I can in soft Battels pass the Night, / Yet rise next Morning Vigorous for the Fight" (1:386). Dick Crastin responds with a more subtle verse "which at once spoke Passion and Respect," leading Honoria to "cast a Triumphant Glance at *Flavia,* as exulting in the Elegance of *Crastin's* Courtship and upbraiding her with the Homeliness of *Tulip's*" (1:387). The women thus serve as audience, judges, and scorekeepers for the performances of their respective suitors. Stung by his rival's success in the previous round, Tulip responds by hinting at Crastin's impotence, continuing his strategy of contrasting his own youthful sexual vitality against Crastin's older, allegedly less functional sexual abilities: "*Tulip* understood the Reproach, and in return began to applaud the Wisdom of old amorous Gentlemen, who turned their Mistress's Imagination, as far as possible, from what they had long themselves forgot, and ended his Discourse with a sly Commendation of the Doctrine of *Platonick* Love; at the same time he ran over, with a laughing Eye, *Crastin's* thin Leggs, meager Looks and spare Body" (1:387). Tulip not only accuses the older man of sexual incapacity but also anchors this charge by drawing attention to Crastin's scrawny body.

This attention to the physical differences between the two men sets up the role of dancing in this story. After Tulip's insult, Crastin leaves the room in disorder. Then, celebrating his victory, "*Tulip* sung, danced, moved before the Glass, led his Mistress half a Minuet," and hummed a song. Here dancing and singing appear on the side of youth, and more significantly on the side of sex. Unlike the dancing fops of Restoration comedy, depicted as effectively asexual, here the dancing man is characterized by a youthful, almost vulgar boasting about sexual prowess in opposition to a more refined, less sexual rival. Male dancing and a strong cross-gender sex drive go together rather than opposing one another, even for a beau, which thereby activates another set of associations for dancing circulating in the *Spectator:* dancing as a site of flirtation and as sexual metaphor.

But this reversal of the earlier pattern to align dance with virility rather than sexual insufficiency is itself further complicated by the final events in this issue. After his celebratory dancing and singing, Tom Tulip receives a note from the absent Dick Crastin. In it, Crastin challenges Tulip to a duel in response to Tulip's innuendo regarding Crastin's impotence. Tulip blanches, then leaves town, never meeting Crastin at the appointed location for the duel. As a result, Flavia, disenchanted by her lover's cowardice, renounces Tulip and becomes her mother's rival for the love of Crastin. Despite his youthful vigor and sexual boasting, Tulip's manhood is compromised by his refusal to participate in a duel, which brands him a coward. In contrast, Crastin, despite his age, refinement, and impugned sexual potency, nonetheless proves his masculinity in this most important arena, upholding his honor and demonstrating the courage to fight. These two generations of beaux therefore avoid a simple characterization as wholly effeminate or wholly masculine, combining within each of them unique mixtures of masculine and unmasculine qualities.

Interestingly, dance is associated only with Tulip in this story. Given the men's identification as beaux, one might expect dance to have been associated with both Tulip and Crastin, perhaps with each man assigned a distinct style of dance. Dance could easily have been one of the arenas of their competition to impress their respective ladies. But it is not. Only Tulip dances, and his connection to dance is reinforced by a triple repetition: Tulip "danced, moved before the Glass, [and] led his mistress half a Minuet." Notable here is the limited involvement of his female partner. Tulip first dances by himself and in front of a mirror before eventually dancing with Flavia in an incomplete minuet. These dances are less about courtship than about celebrating himself and his apparent victory over Crastin, and this narcissistic display fits comfortably within the English tradition of fops and beaux.

More curious than the link between Tulip and dance is the absence of such a link for Crastin. However, assigning dance to only one of the men furthers the intended contrast between them. Age offers one explanation of the choice of Tulip as the dancer in this case. Because dance is typically associated more often with youth than with age, either as something young characters do or as something older characters remember doing in their youth, it makes sense that Tulip is the dancer here.[9] This pairing also implicates dance in the final, defining contrast between the two men. Tulip is in the midst of his dancing and singing when Crastin's challenge arrives, cutting short his celebrations. Whereas Tulip is the dancer, Crastin is the fighter. Though both men are clearly romantically interested in women, it is the coward who dances. Even as dance is insulated from implications of unmasculine sexual deficiency, it remains opposed to masculine courage and honor.

Mr. Fanfly

The examples of Tulip, Shapely, and the beau's head rely on the understanding that this type of man would be actively attracted to women as well as attractive to them. However, at least one account in the *Spectator* presents a different version of the woman's man, excluding him from any real participation in cross-gender desire. *Spectator* 515 (October 21, 1712) prominently features the dancing of "Mr. Fanfly" as part of its comic message. In this case the context is a letter from a coquette named Gatty, who describes her romantic intrigues to her friend Jenny in the country. As with the earlier letter from B.D. regarding Mr. Shapely, the reader is meant to distance him or herself from the perspective of the letter writer; however, this does not result in any recuperation of Mr. Fanfly's besmirched reputation.

In her letter, Gatty recounts a particularly satisfying evening at a recent ball in which her skills as a coquette were put to effective use. She first describes a country-dance in which she carefully arranged whom she would dance with: "I chose out of my Admirers a Set of Men who most love me, and gave them Partners of such of my own Sex who most envy'd me." She reports with malicious glee, "The wildest Imagination cannot form to it self, on any Occasion, higher Delight than I acknowledge my self to have been in all that Evening" (4:332). While this carefully choreographed manipulation of the feelings of those around her brings her the most delight—and makes plain to the reader Gatty's scheming character—the wicked pleasure enacted through dancing also sets the stage for a second, more targeted dance stratagem that turns on the assumed opposition between dance expertise and masculinity.

Gatty next explains her method. She will make one of her suitors jealous by pretending to be interested in another man, and she will humiliate the hapless suitor in the process. She does this, she claims, because the suitor "pretends to give himself Airs of Merit" (4:332), that is, she uses her beauty and allure to humble those men who are so forward as to expect respect from her rather than approach her as a supplicant. For her decoy Gatty chooses "the most insignificant Creature" she can find to receive her feigned affections. Enter the male dancer: "At this Ball I was led into the Company by pretty Mr. Fanfly, who, you know, is the most obsequious well-shap'd well-bred Woman's Man in Town. I at first Entrance declared him my Partner if I danced at all; which put the whole Assembly into a Grin, as forming no Terrours from such a Rival" (4:332). "Pretty," "obsequious," "well-shap'd": Gatty's description of her dance partner collects many of the key words used to signify compromised masculinity, anchored most clearly by the term "woman's man." Even "well-bred," normally a positive term indicating a polite education and gentlemanly good manners, in this context contributes to the picture of Mr. Fanfly as overrefined, unmanned by an excessive attention to the niceties of polite behavior.

Gatty announces that Fanfly will be her only dance partner for the evening, which, rather than suggest the special favor she holds him in, instead amuses the others at the ball. Whether because of particular details in his appearance or because they are already familiar with his character, the other men present can tell immediately that Mr. Fanfly poses no real threat to them as a rival. For her ploy to be successful, however, Gatty must convince the targeted suitor that her interests in Fanfly are sincere, thus making the suitor jealous. She soon reports that she heard the gentleman "say with an Oath, There is no Raillery in the thing, she certainly loves the Puppy" (4:332). His swearing and his use of the disparaging term "puppy" betray the would-be suitor's irritation, demonstrating the effectiveness of Gatty's ploy. That everyone else present could tell immediately that Fanfly was never a serious contender for Gatty's affections only adds to the humiliation of the jealous and now gullible suitor.

The battle then intensifies over who will "plague the other most," as the unnamed male suitor in turn attempts to make Gatty jealous by pretending affection for another woman on the dance floor whom Gatty says she "love[s] most to outshine." In response, Gatty deploys the final indignity: "I made Fanfly, with a very little Encouragement, cut Capers Coupee, and then sink with all the Air and Tenderness imaginable. When he performed this, I observed the Gentleman you know of fall into the same Way, and imitate as well as he could the despised Fanfly. I cannot well give you, who are so grave a Country Lady, the Idea of the Joy we have when we see a stubborn Heart breaking, or a Man of Sense turning Fool for our Sakes; but this happened to our Friend" (4:332). Convincing Fanfly to incorporate flashy jumps in his dancing, she thereby motivates her hapless suitor to jump in imitation and competition. According to Gatty, this turns her "man of sense" into a fool, fulfilling her aim of publicly humiliating and humbling him, with dance serving as both the context for and the mechanism of this humiliation.

But while the suitor is made ridiculous by the skillful manipulations of the coquette, Mr. Fanfly's ignominy is less directly attributable to Gatty. Instead, his status as a "most insignificant creature" has more to do with his own tastes and skills. Gatty reports that it took "very little Encouragement" to convince Mr. Fanfly to caper in front of the assembly, suggesting that he was all too willing to do so, waiting only for a bit of prompting. Thus we have reason to believe that Fanfly likes to dance and has put extra effort into mastering difficult dance steps. Using the word "sink," Gatty also describes Fanfly as either landing his capers, or possibly bowing, "with all the Air and Tenderness imaginable," again suggesting a carefully practiced execution. "Air" had many meanings, but the one that fits best here is the impression created by a person's demeanor, particularly suggesting a refined or elegant composure. The combination of "air" and "tenderness" suggest a gentle, delicate finish to Fanfly's virtuosic display, simultaneously indicating his skills as a dancer and attributing to him a dainty style. We are meant to sympathize with the predicament of Gatty's suitor, propelled by her petty manipulations into making a fool of himself; however, Mr. Fanfly has no such excuse. He remains despised for the qualities he voluntarily exhibits through his personal choices and style of self-presentation. He is therefore more intrinsically a fool and not at all a man of sense in Gatty's schema of assessment.

Though Mr. Fanfly is called a "Woman's Man," this version of the type obviously differs significantly in one crucial dimension from other portrayals such as that of Mr. Shapely, discussed earlier. Shapely was also polite, pretty, well-bred, and, one assumes, "well-shaped." He was also a good dancer. However, Shapely was depicted as something of a sexual predator. We are meant to suspect Mr. Shapely's motives and to consider the possibility that his charm, good looks, and dance ability are in the service of dazzling the young girl B.D. in order to get her money. Mr. Fanfly, on the other hand, poses no such threat to anyone. From his first appearance, virtually everyone discounts his candidacy for the romantic affections of the woman in question. Gatty expresses an utter lack of interest in him and contemptuously labels him the most insignificant creature she could find. Fanfly's pretty, well-shaped appearance and dancing skills, far from marking him as a sexual threat, instead serve to undermine his masculine authority and sexual agency. Shapely and Fanfly, along with the other beaux and women's men discussed earlier, illustrate the ambiguity of the idea of the woman's man as articulated in the *Spectator*. At times signifying a determined effort to win the hearts of women and at others implying a complete lack of romantic interest or potential, the good looks, refined manners, and keen attention to self-presentation that characterized the woman's man failed to fall into a stable relationship with the norm of cross-gender sexual interest. Nevertheless, both the woman's man as sexually motivated and the woman's man as erotically void are consistently critiqued or satirized. Whether by simply exceeding the bounds of acceptable effort and attention to certain styles and behaviors or by engaging in activities understood to be more fundamentally at odds with proper manhood, the woman's man violated the rules of masculinity and thus was in danger of being understood as no man at all. And notably, one of the recurring features used by the *Spectator* to establish this category of suspect man was a marked interest in and facility for dancing.

John Trott

The *Spectator* makes use of a number of continuing characters to convey its advice and opinion on current events and the conduct of life. The most important of these is, of course, Mr. Spectator, the fictional narrator of the entire series. In addition to Mr. Spectator and the other characters planned for and introduced by the authors at the outset of the series, numerous minor characters crop up in subsequent issues representing particular types of people. Some of these appear in real or supposed letters from readers. These letters supply a large percentage of the material in many of the issues of the *Spectator*, and they frequently also include the name or pseudonym of the author at the end. This named figure is then available for reference in subsequent issues. One instance of this type of recurring minor character is John Trott, whose name appears in five separate issues, an unusually large number of occurrences. And every time Trott is mentioned, it is in relation to dancing.

Trott's name probably derives from the Restoration comedy *The Man of Mode; or, Sir Fopling Flutter* by George Etherege, first performed in 1676 but repeatedly revived, including a production in 1711.[10] Thus Trott's character would have been familiar to many of the *Spectator*'s readers. In the typical manner of Restoration comedy, the character's name alludes to his defining feature, in this case an inelegant movement style. In the play, Trott is the only Englishman in a retinue of six dancing servants attached to the title character. Fopling, in love with all aspects of French aristocratic culture and manners, brings back a group of servants from France to serve as his "dancing equipage," to entertain at social events, and, he believes, to add to his reputation as a man of style and sophistication. Instead, they only serve to further exemplify Fopling's ostentatious bad taste and relentless self-promotion.[11] Fopling explains that he has hired Trott as a replacement for one of the French servants who has "miscarried," and this provides the opportunity for some comically bad dancing as Trott fails to keep up with the other dancers during a brief demonstration of their skills.[12]

Unsatisfied with the sound of Trott's monosyllabic name, Fopling at one point renames him "Hampshire" after Trott's home region, in imitation of a similar French practice of referring to servants by where they are from.[13] Trott thus represents not only England but more specifically a country rustic, and therefore the antithesis of the French sophistication Fopling aspires to. While not mentioning the play overtly, the *Spectator* invokes these social qualities for those readers familiar with Etherege's famous comedy. However, the accompanying descriptions make Trott's character clear enough even for those who are unaware of the literary allusion.

Trott first appears in *Spectator* 296 (February 8, 1712). This issue is composed entirely of short letters supposedly from readers, lacking even the short introductory paragraph in the voice of Mr. Spectator common to many other issues. The only theme uniting these diverse letters is their appeal to Mr. Spectator for advice, which he supplies in an especially pithy style. The letter purportedly from Trott is the last of six. He writes:

> Sir, I am a great Lover of Dancing, but cannot perform so well as some others: However by my Out-of-the-Way Capers, and some original Grimaces, I don't fail to divert the Company, particularly the Ladies, who laugh immoderately all the Time. Some, who pretend to be my Friends, tell me they do it in Derision, and would advise me to leave it off, withall that I make my self ridiculous. I don't know what to do in this Affair, but

am resolved not to give over upon any Account till I have the Opinion of the SPECTATOR. Your humble Servant, John Trott. (3:57)

Despite his relatively positive self-assessment, Trott's letter makes clear that he is something of a buffoon, whose dancing amuses by its absurdity rather than its skill. In this respect he fits well with Etherege's Trott, whose bumbling while dancing supplies much of the comedy in the scene in which he appears.[14] However, the *Spectator*'s Trott is not simply a hired servant compelled to dance but is a "great Lover of Dancing" and, despite cautions from his friends, generally understands himself to be a successful comic dancer. Indeed, he has become somewhat like Fopling himself in his naive self-confidence and belief in the affection of those around him, particularly the ladies. But unlike Fopling, he does at least admit that he "cannot perform so well as some others," and he is willing to submit to the more neutral authority of Mr. Spectator regarding the suitability of his continuing to dance.

Eager yet of limited skill, and presenting a comic spectacle rather than an impressive display, Trott exemplifies a different version of the English male dancer than the ones discussed here so far. While not ruling out the possibility of mastery, portrayals such as Trott advance a more ironic relationship between Englishmen and dance. Under this model, Englishmen may enjoy dancing, but they are unlikely to ever be truly expert and are perhaps more likely to end up looking at least a little ridiculous. While the allusion to Etherege's Trott associates the character with the non-urban and the unsophisticated, the *Spectator*'s Trott is initially less precisely defined in terms of place and class than the play's version. This ambiguity leaves it unclear to what degree Trott is meant to represent the "typical" Englishman as opposed to the "country booby." His dancing, his grimaces, and his buffoonish self-comedy nevertheless clearly set him in opposition to the more moderate and more savvy character of Mr. Spectator, locating Trott outside the embryonic bourgeois class position that the *Spectator* helps to construct.[15]

In his response to Trott's letter, Mr. Spectator ignores Trott's references to "grimaces" and his implied slapstick buffoonery and instead concentrates specifically on the issue of dancing: "If Mr. *Trott* is not awkward out of Time, he has a Right to dance let who will laugh: But if he has no Ear he will interrupt others; and I am of Opinion he should sit still. Given under my Hand this Fifth of *February*, 1711–12" (3:57). Aside from the mock-serious conclusion, Mr. Spectator lays out a suitably egalitarian criterion for assessing Trott's behavior. In line with English self-perceptions as a culture particularly valuing freedom tempered by civility, Mr. Spectator endorses Trott's dancing as a legitimate choice for a man to make so long as he can keep time and therefore does not "interrupt others." Given a certain basic level of skill, he has "a Right to Dance."

However, this in no way circumvents the problem of appearing foolish. Trott's initial query was initiated by his friends' advising him to desist because people were laughing at him. Mr. Spectator instead almost assumes he will be laughed at for his dancing: "He has a Right to dance let who will laugh." In other words, you are free to dance, even though others are just as free to laugh at you for it. The *Spectator* articulates a position that does not rule out the possibility of dancing for men, while simultaneously acknowledging the likelihood that others will treat the dancing man as a buffoon. Permissible, yet inherently posing certain threats to a man's credibility, dance demands careful handling.

The York Assembly

John Trott returns to the paper 12 issues later in *Spectator* 308 (February 22. 1712). In an issue again devoted entirely to letters from (probably fictional) readers, Trott appears as the subject of complaints from others in his community, now identified as located in York. The signatory, Eliz. Sweepstakes, writes to request that Mr. Spectator revise his earlier opinion and speak out against John Trott's dancing, which has become a nuisance as a result of Mr. Spectator's previous endorsement (however limited). An "Assembly" provides the setting for the problem: "The Privilege you have indulg'd *John Trot* has prov'd of very bad Consequence to our illustrious Assembly, which, besides the many excellent Maxims it is founded upon, is remarkable for the extraordinary Decorum always observed in it. One Instance of which is, that the *Carders*, (who are always of the first Quality) never begin to play till the *French* Dances are finish'd and the Country-Dances begin" (3:112).[16] These introductory comments establish their assembly as a recurring social gathering featuring dancing and gambling at cards. They also reference the standard early 18th-century practice of beginning balls with one or more French dances before proceeding on to the less technically demanding English country-dances. This introduction makes clear that some or all of the more sophisticated participants (including Miss Sweepstakes, one presumes) participate only in the French dances at the start of the event before retiring to play cards. They normally forgo the English country-dances.[17]

However, a new problem has disrupted their pattern: "*John Trot* having now got your Commission in his Pocket, (which every one here has a profound Respect for) has the Assurance to set up for a Minuit-Dancer" (3:112). Mr. Spectator's printed defense of Trott's right to dance in *Spectator* 296, his "commission," has encouraged Trott to participate in the French dances in the first part of the ball, in particular the minuet, much to the dismay of the local gentry. The problems posed by Trott's dancing are decidedly different here than in the first letter from Trott. His transgression in this second letter is not simply his love of, and engagement in, dancing in general, but his participation in the French dances, more specifically the minuet. Compounding the problem, Trott has persuaded his extended family to participate as well: "He has brought down upon us the whole Body of the *Trotts*, which are very numerous, with their Auxiliaries the Hobblers and the Skippers; by which Means the Time is so much wasted, that unless we break all Rules of Government, it must redound to the utter Subversion of the *Brag-Table*" (3:112).

The sheer number of new participants is one part of Miss Sweepstakes' complaint. Trott and his family's participation in the staid French dances slows down the sequence of events at the ball so much that the gamblers are prevented from ever getting to "Brag," their card game. One important difference between French dances and English country-dances is that the latter can be performed by large numbers of dancers at once, while the former are performed by fewer dancers at a time, possibly as few as one couple at a time if French court tradition were strictly followed.[18] Increasing the number of participants in the French dances would necessarily prolong that section of the ball significantly. Miss Sweepstakes writes to request that Mr. Spectator clarify the permission he gave to Trott, hoping to reverse the disruption of the assembly: "We are pretty well assur'd that your Indulgence to Trot was only in Relation to Country-Dances; however we have deferred the issuing an Order of Council upon the premises, hoping to get you to joyn with us, that Trot, nor any of his Clan, presume for the future to dance any but Country-Dances, unless a Horn Pipe upon a Festival Day" (3:113). Sweepstakes proposes as a remedy to her dilemma that Trott and his family be confined to certain kinds of dances. Miss Sweepstakes wants Trott and his family excluded from the French dances and allowed to participate only in country-dances and the occasional hornpipe.

For the humor of this issue of the *Spectator* to be successful, however, something more than the sheer number of participants at a rural assembly must be at play here. Why write to Mr. Spectator for advice specifically about Trott, if the problem is simply too many participants attending a dance? Instead, the narrative implies Trott's unsuitedness for the French dances. This unsuitedness could be a lack of the necessary dance skill, but Miss Sweepstakes never comments directly on his abilities. And by broadening her complaint to include Trott's relatives, she implies that they all have something in common that disqualifies them from participation. Social class provides a likely explanation, since this is a feature Trott and his family might all share.

By identifying her friends as "always of the first Quality" and telling us that they opt out of the country-dances to play cards after the French dances are completed, Miss Sweepstakes associates the French dances with the local elites. The impression created is that the elites consider the French dances as properly their own and, perhaps, that participation in the French dances is one way these people perform their special place within the community.[19] In contrast, the names of Trott and his relations the "Trotts," the "Hobblers," and the "Skippers" all suggest a common rather than genteel social status, as well as an accompanying inelegant movement style. Based on her comments, it seems safe to surmise that Miss Sweepstakes does not consider Trott and his family to be among the people of the "first quality."[20] As such they are entitled to participate in some dances, but not others, and by encroaching on the French dances, these implicitly lower-class participants violate the class boundaries enacted by the different dance types.[21] In this letter, Trott is not merely an overenthusiastic dancer, he is a provincial, lower-class man who ignores or is unaware of the rules of polite behavior and the rituals of social distinction enacted at social gatherings such as a provincial assembly.

Significantly, this letter does more than simply reference the class hierarchies within the assembly described; it also specifically identifies the letter as originating in York, a region relatively distant from London. The "people of quality" described thus represent the landed gentry as opposed to the urban upper class of London. Though perhaps technically of the same class level as many of London's gentlemen and ladies, by living so far from the capital, these people of quality necessarily run the risk of losing touch with current fashions and thus appearing ridiculous.[22] Interestingly, the *Spectator* takes pains to shore up their credibility. In the comments introducing this letter, Mr. Spectator describes the person delivering the letter as having "a polite Discerning hiding under a shrewd Rusticity: He delivered the Paper with a Yorkshire Tone and a Town leer" (3:112). While not denying the regional identity of the deliveryman, he likewise attributes discernment, manners, and shrewdness to him, thereby implicitly attributing them to the letter's authors as well. There is no obvious indication in the letter or in Mr. Spectator's reply that the paper is holding the Yorkshire gentry up to ridicule, except perhaps in the most gentle way for their being troubled by something as minor as an overly enthusiastic dancer. If this criticism falls anywhere, it falls on the supposed author, Miss Sweepstakes, the spokesperson for the community, or at least the one bothered enough to write for advice.

If the letter is indeed entirely fictional, constructed by the authors of the *Spectator*, it makes sense that they would choose to make the letter's purported author a woman. For a man to take such an interest in the protocols of dancing would draw too much attention to him. He would be marked as overly interested in dance, just like the problematic John Trott, which would confuse the distinction being drawn here and require further explanation. Having a woman be concerned with dancing and the etiquette of a ball is far less remarkable in the world of the *Spectator*. It requires no further explanation. The (fictional) female correspondent remains a more neutral representative, signifying, if anything, the position of the regional gentry and its members' interest in maintaining social hierarchies.

In his reply, Mr. Spectator sides with Miss Sweepstakes and "clarifies" his permission to Trott, recommending that "Mr. Trot should confine himself to Country-Dances: And I further direct, that he shall take out none but his own Relations according to their Nearness of Blood, but any Gentlewoman may take out him" (3:113). Mr. Spectator resegregates Trott (and presumably his extended family) out of the French dances, returning these to the exclusive possession of the local elite. Responding particularly to the concluding line of the letter, he also prevents Trott from asking any woman to dance except his own relatives, further partitioning Trott away from others at the ball to help contain his clearly irritating enthusiasm. Thus the *Spectator* itself, and not just its fictional contributors, comes out in favor of maintaining social divisions enacted through access to dance types. Dancing itself is not directly attacked, and the assembly implicitly includes other male participants. But these men dancers go carefully unmentioned in the account. Only the ridiculous Trott and his ungendered relatives receive negative attention as foils to the stuffy yet endorsed group of upper-class card players.

Danced Out of Favour

The next installment in this debate over Trott's dancing takes the form of a short letter signed by him in *Spectator* 314 (February 29, 1712). In it, Trott complains of a disastrous consequence that his propensity for dancing has brought about, which took place just before the *Spectator* published its reply to his first letter. Again at the York assembly introduced in *Spectator* 308, Trott was observed dancing by "an old Gentleman" who turned out to be the father of a girl Trott was romantically interested in. After seeing Trott dance, and once apprised of Trott's interest in his daughter, the father calls Trott "an insignificant little Fellow" and takes steps to confine his daughter to her room and otherwise keep her away from Trott. Trott complains to Mr. Spectator that he is "ready to hang my self with the Thoughts that I have danced my self out of Favour with her Father" and begs for advice on how to "cheat the old Dragon and obtain my Mistress" (3:137). Coming as it does after the previous two letters, this account reinforces and compounds the *Spectator*'s negative portrayal of Trott. As constructed in the earlier letters, this English male dance enthusiast is a ridiculous nuisance, but he is tolerated within certain limits. With this third letter, however, the *Spectator* abandons whatever sympathy might have remained for Trott and his situation. Trott's capering has cost him the respect of another man, and Mr. Spectator treats this as a fit reward for Trott's behavior.

While dancing is the explicit cause of Trott's problem, the comments of the *Spectator* redirect attention to Trott's manners or personal style, particularly a lack of proper respect and restraint. The *Spectator* expresses these sentiments in the comments preceding Trott's reprinted letter, explaining: "I cannot comply with the Request in Mr. *Trott*'s Letter; but let it go just as it came to my Hands, for being so familiar with the old Gentleman, as rough as he is to him. Since Mr. *Trott* has an Ambition to make him his Father-in-Law, he ought to treat him with more Respect; besides, his Stile to me might have been more distant than he has thought fit to afford me" (3:137). Mr. Spectator takes issue with the casual tone of Trott's letter and the disrespectful attitude Trott expresses toward the father (Trott calls him an "old Dragon"), and this lack of proper respect confirms what was written about Trott in *Spectator* 308. Specifically, it demonstrates Trott's lack of manners and even his lack of awareness of these conventions. Trott seems oblivious to his mistakes, and his failure to perform appropriate civilities in his speech corroborates Miss Sweepstakes' complaints about his invasion of the genteel French dances. One can easily imagine Trott riding roughshod over movement conventions in the same way that he ignores the polite tone set in the *Spectator*.

Whether a reflection of his personal ineptitude or his lower class status, both the letter and the complaints about Trott's dancing suggest a lack of "class," a lack of training in, and sensitivity to, the conventions of social interaction that would signal a polite education and a social class higher than that of a laborer or tradesman. This letter thus solidifies the characterization of Trott as cloddish and unsophisticated. Almost the direct opposite of the excessively mannered city dancing-master, Trott is an insufficiently mannered country man. He loves dancing and dances to impress the ladies, but is too imperceptive to realize that in doing so he makes himself ridiculous. His enthusiasm for dancing inconveniences those around him, and he does not seem to realize that he is an unwelcome guest at the party.[23] His eagerness also leads him to overestimate his abilities, and he inserts himself into dances whose subtleties completely escape him. As a result, he disrupts the social hierarchy of his town and alienates the father of the woman he is romantically interested in. Although Trott at first believes his dancing will further his romantic intrigues with women, it serves instead to further block his chances, first through the laughter it provokes among the women, then through his being prohibited from asking women unrelated to him to dance at the assembly, and finally by so alienating the father of his beloved that she is placed out of Trott's reach. Dancing, though ostensibly in the service of cross-gender pairing, ends up obstructing it.

This image of the male dancer as country booby plays an important complementary role to the image of the male dancer as overrefined and effeminate. The image of the effeminate male dancer fits well with the refined French noble style and its accompanying rules of deportment, but other forms of dance with different sets of associations, such as the country-dances and hornpipes, require different modes of satire. Similarly, some men are simply immune to accusations of overrefinement and delicacy. The obviously crude, the uneducated, the unsubtle, the dense—these types of men are in little danger of being associated with the mincing, officious, effeminate stereotype of the male dancer. Trott's version of the English male dancer as foolishly unsophisticated serves to regulate male behavior from the opposite end of the social spectrum, providing an alternate mode of satire applicable to these different types of men.

Trott the Dancing-Master

These two complementary depictions of the male dancer appear together in a later issue of the *Spectator*, where they present an unsatisfying choice between two equally undesirable alternatives. In *Spectator* 376 (May 12, 1712), Trott is referenced for the last time by "Rachel Watchfull," a woman in charge of "the Government and Education of young Ladies" (3:414). Interestingly, Miss Watchfull has previously not allowed her girls to study dancing. But after reading the *Spectator*'s (qualified) endorsement of dancing in an earlier issue, and feeling that "there is something very wanting in the Air" of her young charges relative to the appearance of "fine bred Women," Watchfull resolves to add dance training to her curriculum (3:415).[24] Unsure of whom to employ for this service, she writes the *Spectator* for advice on selecting a dancing-master. Her choice is made more difficult by the parents of the girls, who have strong feelings on the matter. Watchfull describes two contenders for the post, the first suggested by Colonel *Jumper*'s Lady (a parent): "She recommends Mr. *Trott* for the prettiest Master in Town, that no Man teaches a Jigg like him, that she has seen him rise six or seven Capers together with the greatest Ease imaginable, and that his Scholars twist themselves more ways than the Scholars of any Master in Town" (3:415). More than two months after his penultimate appearance, Trott returns to the pages of the *Spectator*, but now in the unlikely role of dancing-master. Despite his troubles in York and his chastisement by the *Spectator*, Trott has continued his dancing, and (according to the fictional narrative) his mis-placed confidence in his own abilities has inspired Trott to set himself up as a dance instructor.

Several clues indicate that he continues to dance in the same unrefined style that got him into trouble in the first place. First, he is recommended by Lady Jumper, whose name indicates her greater interest in showy springs than in tasteful poise. Likewise, her praise of Trott emphasizes his ability at capers, that class of flashy jumping kicks that Trott referenced when first introducing his situation in *Spectator* 296. Lady Jumper also praises Trott's ability at "Jiggs." While gigues were certainly part of the French noble style, the English jig form also preexisted the importation of the French dance style into England in the late 17th century, and so to some extent the jig functions like the English country-dances and the hornpipe as an identifiably native dance form. Jigs and ability at jigging are commonly referenced in connection with early Resto-ration drama as a form performed as part of or alongside stage comedies for the entertainment of audiences.[25] Jigs were also associated with amateur perfor-mances at social gatherings and festivals.[26] By describing Trott as a teacher of jigs and capers, the *Spectator* constructs a non-elite English analogue to the French noble style that was more typically taught by a dancing-master. Jigs, a dance type, and capers, a category of dance steps, were both more performance-oriented than the participation-oriented country-dances, and the reference to jigs and capers suggests a focus on the mastery of flashy steps. But whereas even the showy beaten jumps and turns of the male repertoire within the French noble style are still meant to convey a noble ease and gentlemanly control, the hops and kicks of jigs and capers instead tend to invoke a rustic boisterousness and a cocky exuberance.[27] Excluded from the French dances at the York

Figure 6.2 Dancing masters taught skills relevant both to dancing and to everyday deportment. From *Le Maître à Danser*, by Pierre Rameau (Paris, 1725), page 17.

assembly, Trott comes to stand in for an alternate English tradition. But rather than advancing an acceptable English alternative to French dance culture, the *Spectator* uses the lowbrow English dances to further ridicule the figure of Trott and the type of unsophisticated English male dancer he represents, leaving the hierarchical relationship between the distingué French dances and the less refined English dances firmly in place.

Mr. Prim

This contrast of styles is heightened by the other dancing-master Miss Watchfull considers hiring for her students, Mr. Prim: "A very extraordinary Man in his way; for besides a very soft Air he has in Dancing, he gives them a particular Behaviour at a Tea-Table, and in presenting their Snuff-Box, to Twerl, Slip, or Flirt a Fan, and how to place Patches to the best Advantage, either for Fat or Lean, Long or Oval Faces; for my Lady says, there is more in these Things than the World Imagines" (3:415). This description devotes most of its attention to the nondance elements of Mr. Prim's instructions, which cover a variety of polite skills. Aside from referencing the many matters of courtesy that fell under a dancing-master's purview beyond the specifics of dance technique, the particular skills listed here were frequently discussed in relation to the negative quality of "affectation" and were understood as behaviors prone to excessive embellishment. The *Spectator* in particular had devoted several previous issues to the handling of fans and to the placement of beauty patches, developing elaborate parodies of their supposed meaning and importance.[28] Mr. Prim's specialties, then, include some of the most mocked behaviors representing the extremes of feminine affectation. The contributor's remark that "there is more in these Things than the World Imagines" references both the low regard with which these skills are held by most (the "World") and their high value to Mr. Prim and his students, with the *Spectator*, through its ironic distance, implicitly siding with the former. The tea table, while not necessarily a sign of affectation, was nonetheless typically coded as feminine. Frequently set in contrast to the male-dominated coffeehouse, the tea table was a site of female interaction, and thus Mr. Prim's expertise with tea table behavior, while understandable for a teacher of etiquette, also links him with the feminine realm.[29]

The only direct discussion of Prim's dancing style confirms his association with feminine or effeminate characteristics. His dancing is described as having "a very soft Air." Softness is not uncommonly used in gendered contexts in the period, usually aligned with women and the feminine in opposition to a masculine hardness. While love could soften a man, leading him away from the masculine context of war to the arms of a woman, over the 18th century softness was also increasingly used as an adjective for effeminate men, as for instance a boy raised too indulgently by his mother, resulting in a soft and unmasculine man.[30] Taken together with his attention to fans and face patches and his knowledge of the tea table, Mr. Prim's soft air in dancing signals his suspect masculinity and locates him within the familiar model of the effeminate male dancer.

Miss Watchfull's choice between Mr. Trott and Mr. Prim as to who will serve as dancing-master to her students therefore demarcates two opposite possibilities for the dancing Englishman. On one extreme, Trott, with his lack of sensitivity to the protocols of polite behavior, depicts a type of male dancer that retains a kind of masculinity or at least avoids charges of effeminacy but is nonetheless mocked for his lack of refinement and social discernment. At the other extreme is the figure of Mr. Prim, whose familiarity with the niceties of social interaction is the direct opposite of Trott's social cloddishness. Prim represents the expected characteristics of a dancing-master, polite to the point of affectation and effeminacy, and consequently his character requires far less elaboration in the *Spectator*. A few clues, and the readership can call to mind any number of overrefined characters from dramatic comedy or other early portrayals to fill in this model of the dancing man. Adding the model of John Trott has the advantage of accounting for another group of male dancers, including lower-class participants in country festivals and social events, not normally addressed by the effeminate male dancer image. The *Spectator* still pokes fun at this other group of male dance enthusiasts for their excessive interest in dance and lack of subtlety, but unlike the more typical dancing-masters, these men escape with their masculinity (if not their good sense) intact. While not eliminating the familiar stereotype of the male dancer as effeminate, with this series on Trott the *Spectator* broadens the range of male dancer types it depicts by developing alternate modes of comic disparagement.

Dance and Englishmen

Dancing men play a notable, recurring role in the pages of the *Spectator*, usually, though not exclusively, representing various types of problem men. In some cases the man is depicted as defectively masculine because of his particular involvement in cross-gender attractions, as with Mr. Shapely and the "beau's head." In the case of Mr. Fanfly, however, the man associated with dance is assumed to have no erotic potential whatsoever. Messrs. Prim and Trott present another pair of opposites. While Mr. Prim is unmanned by his overfamiliarity with courtesy and other female-coded activities, Trott is discredited by his blindness to the rules of social decorum. The relationship between dance and men in the *Spectator* is therefore not a simple one, including as it does so many conflicting examples. In all these cases, however, the dancing man is the butt of satire. The *Spectator* conveys a fairly consistent uneasiness with male dancing. This discomfort does not provoke an outright proscription against dancing but rather encourages a cautious restraint. Proper manhood necessitates a careful relationship with dancing in order to avoid the potential hazards it presents.

The *Spectator*'s recurring attention to dance reveals dance's significance as a contributor to the conception of the bourgeois Englishman in this period. Rather than a marginal, irrelevant activity, dance functions as a meaningful embodiment of cultural ideology. Alongside other social practices, dance participates in the development and enforcement of period understandings of gender roles, serving as a site for the performance of the appropriate and inappropriate behaviors and interests of men. As such, dance and representations of dancers should be included in any thorough analysis of masculinity and effeminacy in early 18th-century England. Conversely, a thorough investigation of the stigmas associated with men who dance must take into account the long-standing history of such negative attitudes, which the *Spectator* reveals to be at least 300 years old.

NOTES

1. *The Spectator*, ed. Donald F. Bond, 5 vols. (Oxford: Oxford University Press, 1965). All references are to volume and page number in this edition.

2. See my discussion of the "woman's man" later in this chapter.

3. The *Spectator* treats marriage on numerous occasions. For a few examples, see *Spectator* 261 (December 29, 1711), 2: 514–15; *Spectator* 437 (July 22, 1712), 4: 35–37; and *Spectator* 236 (November 30, 1711), 2: 419.

4. In the *Spectator*'s analysis, there is still no indication of homosexuality per se; same-gender bodies are not engaged in sexual physical contact. However, there is, at least for women, an inherent same-gender desire of the soul, if not of the body, which must be policed, discouraged, and redirected toward more appropriate ends. Proper cross-gender desire is neither natural nor assured. The *Spectator* does not seem to realize or at least does not acknowledge the possibility of actual same-gender sexual desire or behavior invoked by this model. This is despite the reports of a group of men in London who apparently engaged in same-sex activities and who, in their adoption of a number of female-coded behaviors, offer a different model of the womanlike man. The new visibility of these "mollies" in London, sodomites reportedly adopting female nicknames and meeting in special taverns to dance and have sex while in female clothes, offered a kind of proof that bodily gender and sexual behaviors do not have to align in the socially sanctioned configurations. Discussions of the apparent development of a subculture of effeminate sodomites or "mollies" in London at the turn of the 18th century include Randolph Trumbach, "The Birth of the Queen: Sodomy and the Emergence of Gender Equality in Modern Culture, 1660–1750," in *Hidden From History: Reclaiming the Gay and Lesbian Past*, ed. Martin Duberman, Martha Vicinus, and George Chauncey Jr. (New York: Meridian, 1989), 129–40; Alan Bray, *Homosexuality in Renaissance England* (London: Gay Men's Press, 1982); and the more recent and more nuanced discussion by George Haggerty in "Gay Fops/Straight Fops," in his *Men in Love: Masculinity and Sexuality in the Eighteenth Century* (New York: Columbia University Press, 1999), especially 53–59. Unlike the womanlike men that Mr. Spectator is concerned about, however, the effeminate mollies were primarily sexually interested in each other and were, therefore, not luring women away from the moderating cross-gender pairing that Mr. Spectator advocates.

Although there has been relatively more academic work investigating the history of male same-sex desire in the 18th century, recently female same-sex desire has also begun to be studied in more depth by a number of important scholars. In *Passions between Women* (New York: HarperPerennial, 1996), Emma Donoghue presents a history of British lesbian culture from 1668 to 1800. In *Dangerous Intimacies* (Durham, NC: Duke University Press, 1997), Lisa Moore proposes a Sapphic history of the English novel. Susan Lanser has examined accounts of lesbianism in a variety of western European contexts. See her "Befriending the Body: Female Intimacies as Class Acts," *Eighteenth-Century Studies* 32, no. 2 (Winter 1998–99): 179–98.

5. In *The Politics and Poetics of Transgression* (Ithaca, NY: Cornell University Press, 1986), Peter Stallybrass and Allon White offer a succinct account of the *Spectator*'s relationship to its varied readership, which merits quotation here at length:

> It is clear and relatively uncontentious that the early periodicals such as *The Tatler* and *The Spectator* had a central role in this respect, negotiating a cultural alliance between the gentry, the Court and the town through the formation of an inclusive, refined public gently coerced with a mixture of satire and example, into the ways of tolerance and good manners. Naturally this mixture, in which aristocratic values and leadership were combined in a complex and uneven manner with the conservative

desires of the squirearchy and the aspirations of the bourgeoisie in the City and the professions, could never be an homogeneous one. . . . Yet the containment of dispute, its restriction to discursive expressions of nominally free critical judgement, was undoubtedly carried through in and by the public sphere. (83)

While the "public sphere" is routinely called "bourgeois," as described by Stallybrass and White this construct actually also encompasses the upper classes into a larger, not purely class-defined grouping. Nonetheless, I take this blurring of class boundaries to be related to the middle-class values of social equality and class mobility, and thus the public sphere remains in some sense a "bourgeois" structure, even as it includes people of multiple class positions. In the *Spectator*, this inclusive understanding of the paper's readership can be seen in Mr. Spectator's easy shifts between addressing the issues of the landed gentry, represented by Sir Roger de Coverley (e.g., 1: 439–45), and discussing the merits and concerns of urban merchants and tradespeople (e.g., 1: 296, 2:463).

6. Although it is a source from some decades later, Lord Chesterfield's famous *Letters to His Son* includes a similar use of the word "pricked," providing some support for my reading: "He acts as awkwardly as a man would dance, who had never seen others dance, nor learned of a dancing-master; but who had only studied the notes by which dances are now pricked down as well as tunes." LETTER CLXV LONDON, April 30, O. S. 1752.

7. When one remembers that Mr. Spectator himself is a fiction created collectively by the multiple authors of the *Spectator*, the literal truth value of a secondhand story told to him by an unnamed source must certainly be called into question. This ambiguous status applies equally to the letters supposedly from readers that are reprinted in other issues. While some of these were likely based on actual submissions, others were probably complete fabrications. In either case, all were edited and presented for their instructional and entertainment value. Regardless of their actual authorship and their status as literal fact or constructed fiction, however, all the accounts in the *Spectator* are nonetheless indicative of the concerns and conceptions literally in circulation in early 18th-century London. In each case it can be interesting to speculate whether the account in any given issue is based on real events or is entirely invented, just as the original readership of the *Spectator* must also have done. This process of curious assessment invited by the format is one of the paper's charms. However, the content of the papers and their cultural effect are in large part independent of the exact origin and authorship of the stories told in its pages. In *Men in Love*, George Haggerty has recently articulated a similar stance toward fictional and semifictional sources: "For the historian of sexuality, what is said about what is done is often more important than any independent 'fact,' even if such a thing could be imagined. The account is, after all, the product of the cultural imagination in which any kind of identity is given shape. The account, then, not any actual event, is the fact that interests me" (54). Such an approach seems useful and appropriate when dealing with a complicated resource such as the *Spectator*.

8. See, for example, the references to fine gentlemen at 1: 323–24 and 3: 511.

9. *Spectator* 301 begins with a discussion of older men and women inappropriately clinging to youthful activities, including dancing (3: 75). See also the older gentlemen remembering dancing in his youth in Thomas D'Urfey, *Madam Fickle; or, The Witty False One* (1676), in *Two Comedies by Thomas D'Urfey*, ed. Jack A. Vaughn (London: Associated University Presses, 1976), 3.1.108–13.

10. Bond, *Spectator* 65 (May 15, 1711), 1: 278 n. 2.

11. See my discussion of Fopling and his relation to dance in "'Is He No Man?' Toward an Appreciation of Male Effeminacy in English Dance History," *Studies in Eighteenth-Century Culture* 30 (2001): 201–22.

12. George Etherege, *The Man of Mode*, ed. John Barnard (London: Ernest Benn, 1979), 4.1.286–92.

13. See the editorial note "Hampshire" in ibid., 83.

14. I am not, of course, arguing for the existence of any real person named John Trott, alive since the 1670s. This is simply one of the more clear examples of a letter supposedly from a reader fabricated by the authors of the *Spectator* for comic (and prescriptive) ends.

15. Grimaces, or facial expressions, are the subject of *Spectator* 173, which gives an account of a country contest to make the most amusing or bizarre face (2: 181–85). For the *Spectator*'s contribution to an emergent bourgeois identity, see Stallybrass and White, noted earlier.

16. The *Spectator* is inconsistent in its spelling of Trott's name (either "Trott" or "Trot"). I have retained the original spelling in all quotations, but I have chosen to regularize my references to "Trott," following the spelling of the first letter.

17. Alternately, the Carders may simply watch the French dances before beginning their gaming. The wording is ambiguous on this point. Regardless of their physical participation, the important distinction is their choice to associate themselves with the French dances and to avoid the English dances.

18. To be more precise, after the couple dances, the French courtiers would have moved on to contredanses, a French style based on English country-dances. See Wendy Hilton, *Dance of Court and Theater: The French Noble Style, 1690–1725* (Princeton, NJ: Princeton Book Company, 1981), 14.

19. John Brewer's *Pleasures of the Imagination: English Culture in the Eighteenth Century* (New York: Farrar, Straus and Giroux, 1997) offers further information on the development of assemblies across England, particularly in the provinces, over the 18th century. Though focusing on sources from the later 18th century, his description mirrors many of the features described in the *Spectator*: "The assembly brought together the leading members of the provincial community, demarcating 'the quality' from others, providing their children with opportunities for courtship and affording the occasion for collective admiration" (548).

It is not arbitrary that the French dances would be the markers of upper-class status. In addition to these dances' association with the French court, the performance values of elegance and restraint called for in the French noble style and the specialized training it requires both served to reinscribe the participants' higher class position and social standing. Access to a dancing-master to learn the French style of dance, in terms of both the time to devote to the training and the money to pay for the lessons, also signaled the dancer's relative wealth and leisure. Over the 18th century, the increasing affluence of the merchant class began to put stress on this meaning of dance ability, as access to dance training spread beyond the traditional upper classes to include the families of wealthy businessmen. Nonetheless, in the early part of the century when this issue of the *Spectator* appeared, French dancing apparently still retained enough symbolic capital to serve as an attribute properly available only to the upper echelons of York society.

In contrast, country-dances have a more ambiguous class status. Despite their name, they had long been enjoyed by urban as well as rural social groups of multiple class positions. See Margaret Dean-Smith, *Playford's English Dancing Master, 1651* (London: Schott, 1957), xvii–xviii. In this account, however, they are assigned a lower position than the French dances, and Miss Sweepstakes sees no conflict in having Trott and his family participate in them. A number of differences between the country-dances and the French dances could have contributed to this assignment of lesser prestige to the former. Country-dances were performed by many dancers at once, unlike the French, which featured one couple at a time. The French dances focus all eyes on two people, who thereby have a chance to distinguish themselves from the rest of the assembly. The group country-dances, in contrast, emphasize the shared participation of many, and thus do not highlight distinctions among dancers. In addition, many country-dances are structured such that couples work their way down the entire line of participants, eventually dancing in turn with every other couple, and this more egalitarian structure also works to level rather than shore up distinctions among the participants.

In terms of their movement vocabulary, country-dances place far less emphasis on particular steps than the French dances, perhaps allowing some choice on the part of the dancer as to which step to perform. The country-dances instead focus on floor patterns and movements of the dancers toward and away from one another. French noble-style dances also incorporate elaborate floor patterns, but their step vocabulary places more emphasis on precise footwork, which demands a greater degree of control and balance. The French dances thus pull the dancer's effort and attention inward toward the center of the body, while the country-dances invite movement outward through space in relation to the other dancers. Country-dance choreographies are also significantly less elaborate than those of French noble style dances, featuring many repetitions of a short pattern. The longer, through-composed choreographies of the French dances would have to be learned and practiced in advance of a ball or assembly, while new country-dances could be learned relatively quickly at the event itself. All these differences contribute to a different tone in the two dance forms, with the country-dances inviting a more relaxed, sociable interaction than the more technically demanding, performance-oriented French dances. These differing qualities could have contributed to the distinction Miss Sweepstakes is trying to maintain in *Spectator* 308 between the two dance types and the "quality" of people who participate in each. One of Brewer's primary sources on the assemblies is the memoir of a man who prefers "more boisterous country dances to the formal minuets" (548), indicating the continued difference in connotation and tone of the English and French dance forms into the later 18th century.

20. Brewer recounts a similar episode of upper-class members of an assembly objecting to the participation of a lower-class "Organist ranking in their opinion with the Tradespeople." See *Pleasures of the Imagination*, 549.

21. Miss Sweepstakes also references the hornpipe, a musical form and dance type native to England. The hornpipe has a long and complex history, and the term covers a variety of dance and music forms. From the sixteenth to the 18th century, dances identified as hornpipes feature significant differences in meter, in the number and social class of their participants, and in their performance contexts. According to Martha Curti, in the early 18th century, the hornpipe was "still danced by country people, but also by members of the upper level of society; sometimes duple, sometimes triple; sometimes as a step or clog dance and sometimes as a country dance." See Curti, "The Hornpipe in the Seventeenth Century," *Music Review* 40, no. 1 (February 1979): 18. Unfortunately,

hornpipes are mentioned in *Spectator* 308 but nowhere else in the paper, preventing a comparison of the use of the term in other examples. Based on its usage in this letter, the hornpipe seems to be a dance performed at rural festivals, perhaps by the lower classes, and this fits with some period uses of the term. Attempting to account for the overlapping references to jigs, hornpipes, and country-dances in texts from Renaissance England, Charles Baskervill suggests their shared performance context as one connection between the dance forms: "Another natural link for these dances is to be found in the May game, which included a great deal of what might be called semi-social dancing around the May pole or about the arbor of the May lady. The terms morris, hornpipe, and jig all occur in connection with such dancing." See Baskervill, *The Elizabethan Jig and Related Song Drama* (1929; reprint, New York: Dover, 1965), 363.

In her article for the *New Grove*, Margaret Dean-Smith describes three types of dance using the name "hornpipe": The first is "a solo dance executed by one person, or by two or more people dancing simultaneously but independently," which existed in England since at least the 16th century. The second version is "a rustic round dance for both sexes in hornpipe tempo" found primarily in the fifteenth through seventeenth centuries. The third version is "a longways country dance of the late 17th century in syncopated 3/2 time, created by dancing-masters for the assembly rooms or for private patrons." See *The New Grove Dictionary of Music and Musicians*, 2nd ed., s.v. "hornpipe."

The *Grove* fails to note a fourth category, or perhaps subsumes it within the first. These are theatrical hornpipes, some of which have been preserved in Beauchamp-Feuillet dance notation, a system developed to record dances in the French noble style. Two examples are *The Richmond* and the second section of *The Union* (1707), two dances composed by Mr. Isaac for the birth-night celebrations of Queen Anne and later published in notation by John Weaver. See Richard Ralph, *The Life and Works of John Weaver* (New York: Dance Horizons, 1985), 289–355. These are difficult dances; *The Union* was originally performed by professional dancers (Ralph, *Life and Works*, 339). This type of hornpipe features a distinctive rhythmic pattern, fitting three dance step-units into two musical measures, rather than the typical one-to-one correspondence between step-units and measures. See Carol Marsh, *French Court Dance in England, 1706–1740: A Study of the Sources* (Ann Arbor, MI: University Microfilms, 1985), 243–58.

The only other hornpipes for which notations exist are the country-dance type. Examples of country-dance hornpipes begin in the late 17th century (e.g., *Mr. Eaglesfield's New Hornpipe* [Playford, *The Dancing Master*, 9th ed., 1695]) and continue into the 19th century (e.g., *Astley's Hornpipe* [T. Wilson, *The Treasures of Terpsichore*, 2nd ed., 1816]). In his chapter discussing the dance forms of different countries, Giovanni-Andrea Gallini references both theatrical and country-dance hornpipes. See his *Treatise on the Art of Dancing* (1762; New York: Broude Brothers, 1967), 182–84. He presents hornpipes as distinctively British, though he also indicates that foreign theatrical performers were coming to England to learn to perform them.

Some of these possibilities make more sense than others in the context of the *Spectator* 308. Desiring to shore up boundaries between social groups, Miss Sweepstakes requests that Trott be excluded from the French dances and be restricted to country-dances only. She allows the one exception of "a Horn Pipe upon a Festival Day," indicating that this too would be an appropriate outlet for Trott's participation in her opinion. This assignment makes sense if she understood the hornpipe as a rustic form. Trott's rough enthusiasm for dancing and even his tendency toward "grimaces" and other comic displays discussed in his first letter to the *Spectator* fit comfortably within the festival context suggested by Baskervill, *The Elizabethan Jig*, despite the significantly later date of this example. The country-dance version of the hornpipe also makes some sense, since Miss Sweepstakes permits Trott to participate in these dances. However, this fails to account for the distinction she implies between hornpipes and country-dances when she lists the occasional hornpipe as an exception to Trott's confinement to country-dances only. Even less likely here is a reference to the hornpipes that used the step patterns of the French noble style. This type would make little sense in this context, running counter to the primary distinction Miss Sweepstakes poses between French dances and country-dances. French noble-style dances, while still physically demanding, cultivate a performance affect of calm control and easy grace, very different from the semi-skilled antics of Trott.

The location of the assembly in York also supports the rustic hornpipe interpretation. In her *Grove* article, Dean-Smith indicates, "As a folk dance the hornpipe was centered in Derbyshire, Lancashire and Nottinghamshire," counties neighboring the Yorkshires. Interestingly, Dean-Smith also specifically references assemblies in her article: "At country assemblies [hornpipes] were performed both as solos and collectively, the dancers advancing in a row, each performing a sequence of steps jealously regarded as exclusive personal property." Therefore, when Miss Sweepstakes relegates Trott to the occasional hornpipe on festival days, she could refer to dances that take place at the assembly itself and not just at some outdoor festivity. Unfortunately, this possibility in itself does not clarify the intended connotation of the hornpipe one way or the other. Nonetheless, I would argue that the usage in *Spectator* 308 does clearly distinguish the hornpipe from the French noble style dances and relies on the difference in dance types as a way to sort or classify different types of participants.

22. *Spectator* 119 discusses the tendency for people in the country to be out of date in their fashions and manners (1: 486–89).

23. Here I am speaking somewhat figuratively. Assemblies were not exactly parties; participants often paid admission to attend. See again Brewer, *Pleasures of the Imagination*, 547.

24. She could be referring to *Spectator* 334, which argues on behalf of performance and training, and which Bond and Richard Ralph attribute in large part to John Weaver. See Bond, *Spectator*, 3: 236 n. 3; and Ralph, *Life and Works*, 375. Ms. Watchfull seems not to have noticed the less flattering issues of the paper devoted to the dancing of John Trott.

25. See my discussions of English jigs in "Light in the Heels: The Emergence of the Effeminate Male Dancer in Eighteenth-Century English History" (Ph.D. diss., University of California, Riverside, 2001), 43–44, 53, 62, 87.

26. See again Baskervill, *The Elizabethan Jig*, 16, 363.

27. My intention here is not to deny the possible differences within the jig category. Native English dances such as the jig, the hornpipe, and the various kinds of morris dancing were subject to the same range of variations of style and quality as other dance forms. These dances also often called for a high degree of specialized skill to execute their fast, precise, and intricate footwork. Instead, what I am arguing is that the references to jigs and capers in *Spectator* 376 are meant to activate a whole class of associations perceived as opposite to the associations attached to the French dancing. Here we are

dealing more with the deployment of stereotypes than with precisely accurate portrayals. It is in this sense that I am proposing that jigs would have called to mind a provincial, exuberant, lower-class connotation as distinct from the restrained, urbane elegance of the French noble style.

28. Although commonly misunderstood as a form of makeup or "paint," beauty marks or "patches" were frequently made of small pieces of silk or other fabric applied to the face, sometimes cut into hearts or other shapes. They originally were designed to cover pimples and other facial blemishes such as those caused by venereal and other diseases but came to be applied for purely aesthetic reasons. The *Spectator* makes multiple references to them, including numbers 50 (1: 214–15) and 81 (1: 346–49). On fans, see *Spectator* 102 (1: 426–29).

29. On the feminine associations of the tea table, see Elizabeth Kowaleski-Wallace, *Consuming Subjects: Women, Shopping, and Business in the Eighteenth Century* (New York: Columbia University Press, 1997), 25.

30. A number of examples that set softness opposite to masculinity are reproduced in Ian McCormick, ed., *Secret Sexualities: A Sourcebook of 17th and 18th Century Writings* (London: Routledge, 1997). For instance: "They had women singers and eunuchs from Asia, at a vast price: which so softened their youth, they quite lost the spirit of manhood" ("Reasons for the Growth of Sodomy in England" [1730], in McCormick, *Secret Sexualities*, 141); and "the Gentleman turn'd lady; that is, female softness adopted into the breasts of a Male, discovering itself by outward signs and tokens in feminine expressions, accent, air, gesture and looks" ("The Pretty Gentleman: or, Softness of Manners Vindicated . . . " [1747], in McCormick, *Secret Sexualities*, 154).

SETH WILLIAMS

> *Williams received degrees in comparative literature (Latin) and dance at the University of California, Irvine. He has worked primarily with the New York Baroque Dance Company, the Mark Morris Dance Group, and the Sean Curran Company and has taught residencies and master classes at studios and colleges across the country. At present, he is the senior operations analyst at the derivatives brokerage firm Creditex Group.*

I've read a lot of narratives that explore the difficulties of being a man in dance. They sometimes relate the identity crises men experience as they navigate the ambiguities of conflicting gender codes and wayward masculinities. This has not been my experience. If you ask me, it's a fairly cushy job.

I grew up in the college town of Davis, California, and enjoyed the predictable taunt of "dance-fag," but thanks to the city's broad liberality it never amounted to anything particularly pervasive or dispiriting. I started dancing because my high school offered dance classes for PE. Changing into a leotard in the locker room was somewhat less than fun, but it went far better than it might have. The major hump for male dancers in America is overcoming any social disincentives to pursue the field in the first place; once involved in the field, I'd say that guys have it pretty easy: since many don't get over said hump, male dancers are a sought-after commodity. But then, having it easy in a tough field isn't necessarily an enviable position.

As a contemporary dancer who also specializes in "baroque" ballet, I'd have to say that on balance the 18th century was probably as good a time to be a male dancer as it is today. That might not be saying much, but the point is that from the perspective of social acceptance, I'd rather be a male dancer in 17th-century Paris than in, say, 1930s Atlanta. But let me back up to how I even started doing baroque ballet, a fringe field of dance that's even smaller than its related movement, early music. When I was a teenager—right around when I started dancing, in fact—I discovered baroque music on the local classical radio station and was instantly devoted. Rameau and Purcell were the chief reasons for that affection. When running errands in the family car, if a particularly nice cantata came on the radio and it didn't seem likely to end soon, I tended to swerve off onto a country road to extend the trip. By contrast, I rarely minded getting out of the car in the middle of Ravel or Strauss.

Williams in a dress rehearsal with Catherine Turocy's New York City Baroque Dance Company. Used with permission.

In college, in addition to my dance studies at the University of California at Irvine, I did a degree in comparative literature, writing in part about classical Roman dance—a fairly exasperating line of inquiry, incidentally, as there are few surviving sources. So when I found out, at a conference, that baroque ballet could be faithfully reconstructed, I was immediately interested and got in touch with Catherine Turocy, a prime mover in the field. When I moved to New York in 2001, I started doing projects with the modern choreographers Mark Morris and Sean Curran, but I also got very involved with Catherine and her New York Baroque Dance Company. She's a much-honored person for very good reasons and has pioneered a multisource, multidisciplinary approach to re-creating baroque ballet. She's been an important mentor to me and to many.

Baroque ballet is the direct forerunner of classical ballet, and though it shares a lot of the same principles, it has a unique vocabulary of steps and ornaments, is vigorously musical, and is characterized by fleet footwork and a florid use of the arms. The theatrical repertoire is harder than you're probably thinking. It survives fairly intact, thanks to a thorough system of notation first published in 1700, now known as Feuillet notation. John Jordan's essay in this volume describes some of the social "types," like the fop and the cad, that were affiliated with men in dance even in the 18th century. We still summon those images today, often in combination with a poor historical conception of the era, so that our impression of men in baroque ballet is a notably effeminate one. But then that has to do with our broader stereotypes of the time period as a whole: the baroque era is regarded as one when men in general were fairly fey. Admittedly, baroque ballet does have a certain drag queen quotient to it. I've had to learn to maintain wigs, to do heavier makeup, and to get about in large, heavy, and frilled costumes. It's what men wore then, and it does absolutely affect how one dances. The weight of the flared jackets and the high-calf cut of the pants change one's center of gravity and bring out a different approach to legwork. And if you think it's a bit excruciating for a guy to confess to his non-theatergoing relatives that he does ballet for a living, try confessing to doing ballet from the *18th century*.

To do baroque ballet properly, I've had to learn about gender etiquette from the time period. All duets (which dominate both the social and theatrical repertoire) start with the man to the left of the woman. Why? Because the sword was worn on the left-hand side and had to be kept out of a woman's skirts. That convention endured even in the absence of a sword. Men and women bow differently, they do some different steps (the men have harder footwork), they specialize in different musical styles (for example, the *passacaille* tends to be done by women), and have very different approaches to posture and movement quality. It's interesting that being a male dancer of the 18th century requires, to some degree, shedding the gendered conventions of today's bodily comportment and adjusting one's notion of masculinity. For example, a soft and sinuous use of the hands that might be considered effeminate today would have been standard fare for men in some baroque ballets. What's more, the baroque era involved a lot of dance *en travestie*, that is, in drag. I even did one ballet—a version of *Les Charactéres de la Danse*—in which I played a man of the 18th century doing a comic impersonation of female gestures, which proved something of a cognitive "tongue-twister."

Dance in the 18th century was, in general, quite centered on men, especially in comparison with the subsequent focus on women that was developed in the Romantic ballet. This is due in part to that great impresario, Louis XIV. Ironically, today's field of baroque ballet tends to be both led by and focused upon the repertoire of women. The first two generations of baroque researchers and reconstructors have been almost entirely female. This might in part be because it's considered an even *more* effeminate field to pursue than classical ballet, and so men are discouraged. It might also be because leadership opportunities for women in classical ballet are limited, and this happened to be an avenue for professional exploration that was more open to women assuming authority. Romantic, classical, and neoclassical ballet are largely traditions focused upon a female repertoire but crafted chiefly by men. So, baroque ballet is anomalistic in that it offers a notably rich masculine repertoire and has chiefly been revivified by women.

That we live, still, in a strikingly sexist society can't be brushed aside. This deserves special mention, since the state of affairs was of course similarly imbalanced in the 18th century. Any mention of masculinity in baroque ballet is cast against this fundamental backdrop. Not that the 18th century lacked for women of genius—witness, among others, Marie Camargo and Marie Sallé. And as with the persistence of sexism, I'm often struck by the similarities between today and the 18th century in terms of the social expectations for men in dance. In some ways, it was an extremely respected career: skills in dance were indispensable at court, and male dancers like Claude Ballon and Louis Dupré enjoyed celebrity status. On the other hand, as John Jordan makes clear, male dancers also faced some of the same bromidic scorn that they do today (and, I can vouch, that they did in the 2nd century—see Lucian's De Saltatione). I see the same contradictions today: we have the pop culture status of Baryshnikov, and we have the "dance-fag" taunts.

I've had countless conversations on this subject with audiences, colleagues, and patrons during post-show cocktails. My own sense, in dancing this diverse repertoire and talking to people about it, is that we fail to do the male dancers of the 18th century justice. This is strange, since we are today more interested in the idea of "identity" by several orders of magnitude. We linger over questions of personality and selfhood and yet approach historical dance with a myopic lack of nuance. People tend to expect that I must surely feel silly dancing in such clothes, and doing such twee gestures. Other contemporary dancers, sometimes drawing brisk conclusions about the outmoded gender conventions of baroque ballet, seem to imply that there is value in these dances only as artifacts, and not as art. I'll be honest: I do sometimes feel silly, and some of the dances do strike me as a bit parochial. And that's the point where I need to man up and keep working. Whether performing or watching, the great blessing of experiencing these revived dances is working through our preconceptions to reach the subtleties: moving from merely seeing types—be they fops and cads or heroes and gods—and into seeing characters.

I should also say that the baroque repertoire for men often strikes me more favorably than the bland generalizations of Romantic ballet or the hypermanly overcompensations found in some of today's ballet roles. It's too bad that, at present, we mostly look at baroque ballet and see a bunch of prissy, flouncing men;

when we do, we are misapprehending the substance of these dances and are making dismissive generalizations rather than valid criticisms. There's a diverse repertoire, with some great moves that are elegant and difficult. In the absence of a live performance, you might seek out the (too sparse!) filmic work of, for example, Carlos Fittante, Ken Pierce, and Tom Baird. In watching their work it's easy to move beyond the lace and wigs and see a dynamic strength. The sinuous use of the arms in baroque ballet becomes not a cliché of limp wrists but living evidence of an obsolete masculinity.

I'm often asked just *how* accurate our reconstructions of baroque ballet actually are. My answer is: fairly but not entirely. There's a lot of preparatory work, even before one enters the studio. I've learned to read the Feuillet notation, but even after several years of proficiency I still have to puzzle over the occasional passage and keep in mind that the notation is a means toward an end, and not the end itself. Just as I may struggle to decipher a step, someone else (always a man, judging by surviving publications) struggled to capture it in notation.

A similar process takes place in reconstructing a period sense of masculinity. In addition to a sense of period etiquette, one looks to journals, opera lyrics, contemporaneous descriptions, and paintings to get a sense not only of the steps but of how they were done by men as opposed to women. A lot can be inferred; some things can't. And the bodies, conventions, and social sensibilities of masculinity varied considerably between, for example, France and England, gentry and aristocracy, ballrooms and stages. An understanding of how a man moved, and what those movements meant, is part history and part conjecture. In doing one of the celebrated ballroom duets, I have to restrain my comportment within the bounds of aristocratic etiquette; when dancing the same steps in a peasant pantomime inspired by the commedia dell'arte, they become brusque and bawdy.

As I mentioned, the bulk of commentary about men in dance today, insofar as it's expressly concerned with the idea of gender, often dwells on stuff like getting taunted as a kid and how brave it is for men to assume a career that's counter to cultural norms—that is, how being a man in dance can be difficult. True enough. But even truer is the simple fact that the overwhelming majority of successful dance companies are run by men, and the overwhelming majority of successful choreographers are men. While it might be challenging to be a man in dance sometimes, by my appraisal it's challenging to be a woman in most other careers most of the time. So that's my disclaimer. It isn't to say that we oughtn't discuss the peculiar experiences of men in dance—just that a little context never hurt, and that I tend to arch an eyebrow when these discussions of masculinity flirt with a sense of victimhood.

My experience has been unusual because of when and where I grew up (California, and with a supportive family). I've probably faced less gender stigma than many other male dancers, even while involved in a subfield that's viewed with greater suspicions of effeminacy. I consider it my good fortune to admit that gender prejudice has played a minor role in my professional worries, especially compared with the worry of, say, affording a secure standard of living. To the degree that I've dealt with apprehensions about my career, I'd say that those have had more to do with my sexuality, being in a stereotypically gay career. Introducing my profession is, in some settings, equivalent to a declaration of sexual orientation. That's admittedly awkward at times, but rarely consequential. I'm more preoccupied with the struggle of trying to make good art and to be a good person than with sorting out a working definition of masculinity. That might sound a bit blasé, but there you have it. I play dress-up and do flamboyant ballets to old music: big deal.

7

Gender Trumps Race?

Cross-Dressing Juba in Early Blackface Minstrelsy

STEPHEN JOHNSON

On October 18, 1848, the *Manchester Guardian* published a review of a performance by a touring American minstrel troupe then appearing in the Free-Trade Hall.[1] The review describes a group of six young men "in possession of nigger-like physiognomies"—that is, in blackface makeup—performing a combination of grotesque comedy and sweet harmony, in an (alleged) authentic depiction of plantation life in the southern United States, all before a mixed-gender, middle-class audience that clearly reacted warmly. In fact, the reaction was at times *too* warm for this eyewitness, causing "a most undignified unbending of the facial muscles," with many "handkerchiefs employed to conceal the smothered laughter of their fair owners." The troupe—the Ethiopian Serenaders—was performing a blackface minstrel show, an evening's entertainment from America that, during the 1840s, proved a particularly popular export to Britain. In its general praise and "purple" prose, this description is typical of the times; what is not typical is that the focus of the description moves quickly to one performer, called "Juba"—a "real nigger," and not a "sham" like the others. He is, apparently, not in blackface.[2] His appearance is described in unusual detail—including the size of his head, his height, his build. There is an uncharacteristic precision in the description of his dance that historians long for in other documents. And he is wearing a dress: "With a most bewitching bonnet and veil, a *very* pink dress, beflounced to the waist, lace-fringed trousers of the most spotless purity, and red leather boots,—the ensemble completed by the green parasol and white cambric pocket handkerchief,—Master Juba certainly looked the black demoiselle of the first ton to the greatest advantage." Juba's presence in this document makes it particularly troublesome, and difficult to read as a cultural artifact. He embodies and exposes a dizzying array of contradictions: an aggressively racist and segregated form of entertainment shares the stage with a young black performer; descriptions of wild abandon alternate with a sense of extraordinary precision and control; a clownlike performance idiom is juxtaposed with appeals to ethnographic accuracy. And at the center of the description is the image of a young

Figure 7.1 Juba dancing at Vauxhall Gardens. From the *Illustrated London News*, August 5, 1848. Used with permission.

male dancer of color, in drag, dancing to a song ("Lucy Long") performed by a group of young white males in blackface, for the entertainment of a middle-class mixed-gender polite audience—the whole advertised as an authentic depiction of the slave culture of the American plantation. The purpose of this essay is to attempt to understand this image, by looking first at minstrelsy and its depiction of gender in the cross-dressing "wench dance," and then at the peculiarities of the dancer, Juba.

Race, Gender, and the "Wench" in Early Blackface Minstrelsy

The American blackface performer was not new to the American and British stage in 1848, but the idea of a "minstrel show" was.[3] A number of individuals, most notably T. D. Rice, had been successful on the variety stage in both countries from the 1830s. In their "act," these white performers appeared in blackface, in the alleged costume of a southern plantation slave and speaking with an (again, alleged) authentic dialect, in a performance combining song, dance, comic monologue, and parody. It was, in some ways, an Americanized version of the much earlier Elizabethan "jig," chaotic, clownlike, topically political and salacious, and in this case (unsurprisingly) intensely racist. Rice in particular had a large following on both sides of the ocean, and many imitators. From 1843, however, a variation on this entertainment took hold with the formation of the Virginia Serenaders in New York, a group of four solo artists who booked a small venue and presented a stand-alone full evening's entertainment, previously unheard of for blackface performance, and relatively uncommon in popular entertainment generally. Although this event may seem a minor development, it was in fact notable. In effect, the act of booking a venue and advertising a full evening's entertainment set the minstrels, typically clown-like mainstays of the circus, saloon, and theater, in opposition to these other business enterprises, their former employers. Their immediate and unqualified commercial success in New York and other urban areas set them up in direct competition, and ultimately, blackface minstrelsy became among the most popular genres of entertainment in 19th-century America, persisting as a major commercial vehicle until the 1920s, and in amateur cultures much longer.[4] But in the 1840s, it was a rebel form.

Although in its early years minstrelsy had no set structures or rules, there were some common attributes.[5] Performers were white, generally Anglo-Amer-icans, who "blacked up" with burnt cork or by other means. They purported to be imitating (or "delineating") the authentic culture of southern plantation slaves, in dress, speech, song, and dance. Despite this claim, strong vestiges of an earlier circus clown culture persisted, in such elements as long, oversized clown shoes, or extravagant collars that could hide the entire head. Early minstrel dress was typically rural or ragged, with outlandish colors and patches described as "authentic" to slave culture, but more often suspiciously harlequin-like. In general the performers sat in a line or semicircle, playing an array of instru-ments. The two "endmen" were the most essential feature, one who played the tambourine (which was more like an Irish *borrin*), and one who played the "bones" (related to the Spanish castanets and Anglo-folk "spoons"). The third essential instrument was the quite new and exotic banjo—recently commercia-lized from an instrument common in southern slave culture, and in this early incarnation unfretted and consisting of five strings. Other instruments included the fiddle and (less often) the accordion. The program included a range of popular songs in the stage dialect of the southern plantation slave. The songs might be topical, sentimental, highly sexual, or entirely nonsensical; they were interrupted or accompanied by raucous dances, comic monologues, burlesques, and dialogues dependent on the bad pun. In the sense that the troupe appeared to be out of control during performances, and through their "black" personae incapable of formal structure, the genre might be said to have parodied the polite concert format of, for example, the Hutchinson Family of American concert singers popular at the time.[6]

A number of excellent studies have been written about the complexities of the early history of this new performance genre, by Eric Lott, W. T. Lhamon, William Mahar, and Dale Cockrell (among others), all emphasizing the difficult-to-read attitudes toward race, class, and gender, often contradictory and embedded in the same imagery.[7] The minstrel show can be read as racist bile, creating a set of stereotypes that remain embedded in American and European culture, designed to segregate, to define difference by inferiority. It can also be read as a purveyor of skills—clog and tap, versions of American folk song, the triumph of the nonsense dialogue, the dialect monologue, and the pun. And it can be read as a political force to be reckoned with—a strong venue for satire, primarily intended for a dispossessed rural male workforce just arrived in the city. No doubt all these interpretations are true, more or less and at the same time. Most inclusive of this range of attitudes toward the form is the work of W. T. Lhamon. Admitting the inherent racism—it is difficult to deny—he argues that minstrelsy as we know it is in fact a manifestation of the working-class popular culture of an Atlantic diaspora, co-opted by middle-class show business. Lhamon argues that, obscured beneath the commercial form—the alleged depiction of "authentic" slave culture, the sentimental depiction of slavery—we should still be able to see vestiges of another culture. This street culture, including dance, speech, humor, a carnivalesque attack on "the man," was fed by a variety of folk cultures—Anglo, Irish, European, South American, and African, all of which had been displaced to an urban industrial landscape, all endangered. He argues that these folk traditions commingled and coalesced on the street and in public and private spaces, among a disparate and almost completely invisible group that left little record except through those who suppressed their culture, or co-opted it. For Lhamon, commercial minstrelsy is a partially successful attempt to manage and commodify this street culture. He persuasively argues for complexity with respect to the role of "blackface" in this early form.[8] As William Mahar phrases it in *Behind the Burnt Cork Mask*: "The instantly recognizable representations of overlapping racial, sexual, national, ethnic, economic, social, political, and religious categories . . . convey enormous amounts of cultural information in an extremely condensed form" (203).

It comes as no surprise that recent discussions of minstrelsy focus on race; almost as much critical attention, however, has been paid to the form's attitude toward sexuality. Minstrelsy was, during its early years, a decidedly working-class male performance idiom, for audiences as well as for performers; its obsessions and attitudes followed suit. Mahar's study cogently and persuasively shows the extent to which gender relations and the display of masculinity predominated. "Maleness itself," he writes, "became a subject for blackface parody as minstrel comedians recognized the potential hypocrisy in all social behaviours and sought to exploit them for humorous ends" (202). Women were imagined—in a chapter Mahar titles simply "Misogyny"—as "objects of male desire, as dominating personalities or complaining shrews, as defenceless victims of abduction or early death, and as ideal subjects for sentimental veneration" (269). He emphasizes the equation of the women portrayed in song and skit on the early minstrel stage with mixed-race, ostracized women, and with the prostitution surrounding the performance venues.

However ambivalent the working-class audience may have been toward the image of race—by turns condescending toward a perceived natural inferiority and identifying with a dispossessed culture—on the face of it there appeared to be no such ambivalence toward women. Eric Lott, in his influential work *Love and Theft* (to which Mahar's work is in part an answer), further emphasizes the sexual nature of the minstrel show, though he ties it much more closely to race. In his view, the minstrel performance was a furnace of sexual intensity, fueled by the depiction and reception of an image of the black male body, viewed with a "combined fear of and fascination . . . [which] cast a strange dread of miscegenation" (25). The minstrel man displayed a "bold swagger, irrepressible desire, sheer bodily display; in a real sense the minstrel man was the penis" (25). Subsequent writing about early minstrelsy has taken issue with Lott's view, but such statements reinforce a general agreement that early minstrelsy was unkind toward women,[9] "dramatized," Lott writes, "with a suspiciously draconian punitiveness, . . . usually in . . . grotesque transmutations" (27), with "fat lips, gaping mouths, . . . big heels, huge noses, enormous bustles; here is a child's eye view of sexuality" (145).

Discussions of sexuality in the early minstrel show take as a starting point the assumption of a social construction of gender. They also speak to the complex of cultures and subcultures brought to bear by audiences of a particular time and place in that construction. A spectator of course may have reacted toward depictions of gender and sexuality onstage in any number of ways—Mahar and Lott between them suggest the diversity, from the sentimental idealization to the dehumanization of women, and from the erotic to the repellent body in performance. It seems clear, however, that a particularly virulent misogyny was reserved for women of color, however attractive the specific imagery—or so it seemed.[10]

All such depictions in the early minstrel show, with the exception of Juba, were portrayed by blackface performers in drag—one small piece of the rich historical puzzle of performance cross-dressing. There has been much good work on this subject—Laurence Senelick's study *The Changing Room* and Marjorie Garber's *Vested Interests* are representative. Garber, for example, traces the uses of cross-dressing as a means to disrupt, question, and attack the stock definitions imposed by society and to explore—or to reinforce—the limits of gender definition and, by association, class and race. The critical work on the association of cross-dressing with blackface minstrelsy has been contentious. Popularly known as "wench" dancing, it seems a clear borrowing from other popular commercial performances, though there are also references to it in folk culture—men in dresses and in blackface during Irish carnival-like activities, for example.[11] The depiction of the woman's body in the minstrel show has been examined as a vivid reinforcement of its misogynism, doubly demeaning race and gender stereotypes—equating inadequacies, incompetencies, uncontrollable and unreasonable natures, or alternatively reinforcing a submissive, powerless placement in society. It has been argued that such depictions invented and then reinforced stereotypical attitudes toward African American women, while at the same time attacking a feminizing Victorian morality, a newly empowered women's movement, and—in Eric Lott's work—providing an outlet for masculine homoerotic fantasy. If there are redeeming features to blackface depictions, these in no way seem to temper the misogynist imperative of the cross-dressed characterizations, which took three forms in particular: parodic imitation of the entertainments of the audience's "betters" (Fanny Elssler's Cachucha dance, Jenny Lind's operatic concerts)—part of a broader parodic agenda in minstrelsy; songs of sentimental loss and death, in which objects of affection are kidnapped or sold or die; and mock courtship songs and scenes.[12]

Research on the "wench" performances of early minstrelsy argues for a common pattern: the cross-dressed performer remains silent, dancing while another performer sings. The lyrics to "Lucy Long" reinforce the aforementioned misogyny, as in this exemplary set:

Oh, I just come out before you
To sing a little song
I plays it on de banjo,
And I calls it Lucy Long.
      Take your time, Miss Lucy.
      Take your time, Miss Lucy Long.
      Take your time, Miss Lucy.
      Miss Lucy, Lucy Long.
Oh, Miss Lucy's teeth is grinnin'
Just like an ear ob corn
Her eyes dey look so winnin'
Oh, would I'd ne'er bin born.
Her teeth look like tobacco pipes,
Her skin as bright as soot,
Her eyes just look like two coach lamps,
Like a pickaxe is her foot.
She leaves a strong impression,
Whenever she does go.
Her foot steps mark the gravel,
as easily as snow.
I asked her for to marry,
And she's to be my bride.
Oh, she's a lubly creature,
Tho' her mouth is rather wide.
So soon we're going to marry,
Oh, what a happy day—
But mind you this old darkey
Won't let her have her way.

And if she prove a scolding wife,
I'll whip her sure yer born,
And I'll take her down to New Orleans
And sell her off for corn![13]

The singer is attracted to the ugliness of Lucy and, depending on the roughness of the version of the song, wants immediate sexual gratification, complains about her shrewish nature and refusal to submit, and threatens to "sell her off for corn" as so much chattel if she does not submit. The misogynist "lesson" of the lyrics is clear enough; there is a critical consensus that this is the epitome of the "mock courtship" song, and the most popular number in early minstrelsy. As with all popular culture, however, a text such as this is only pre-text; the meaning generated by the performer—and received by the audience—is transformed through performance.

The eyewitness description of Juba in Manchester provides a potentially richer understanding of this complexity, if we can "unpack" it. I note that there are two crucial differences in this description from the typical portrait of early minstrelsy: the audience belongs to the British middle classes;[14] and the dancer is not in blackface but is black, and perceived as such. Each of these differences will be addressed in turn.

Class, Touring, and the Eyewitness in England

The "making up" of their leader was extremely ludicrous. With literally a yard of shirt collar and frill, it was scarcely possible to witness his extravagant grimaces, without a most undignified unbending of the facial muscles, and many were the handkerchiefs employed to conceal the smothered laughter of their fair owners. The party have some good voices among them, and they harmonize well together; indeed, the melody of several of the chants, and other concerted pieces, was so pleasing to the ear, that they were loudly encored.

Minstrelsy was manifestly hated by middle-class white culture when it first appeared in America; it was seen as dangerous, allied with populist political movements, immorality, and a loss of control. Early success, however, led to a proliferation of troupes and greater competition. This in turn initiated an effort to broaden the audience. To some extent this was an act of reclamation: minstrels had performed at circuses frequented by children; and variety houses had at least some women audience members. Most important, however, was the effort by minstrelsy to accommodate the middle classes.[15] During the first 10 years of minstrelsy, we can see a stabilization and gentrification of the venues leased and rented, from basements and saloons to "mechanics halls" and legitimate (if lesser) theaters. The entertainments, though still raucous, were self-censored; for obvious reasons, the references were less sexual, and the lyrics more sentimental. If the minstrel performer still defined the body out of control, and the roots of the form were still clearly from urban streets, ports, and levees, ways were found to make that body safe.[16]

Nowhere is this shift more evident than in the early tours to England. British culture held a strongly ambivalent place in the heart of American culture, at once resented and imitated. American performing arts—even among the working classes—relied heavily on British imports, and American performers traveled to Britain frequently for financial gain, and because it carried a critical cachet back home.[17] Early minstrel performers were no exception. The Virginia Serenaders traveled to Britain only months after they "invented" the stand-alone minstrel program, and for the next 10 years dozens of imitators landed at Liverpool and Dover. The press regularly announced a glut of such "delineators" and a (hoped-for) decline in their appeal, but they kept coming until finally they were both accepted and thoroughly Anglicized.[18]

The Ethiopian Serenaders are perhaps the clearest example of this effort to "legitimize" minstrelsy, during two tours of Britain beginning in 1846.[19] On the face of it they exhibited the basic traits of the genre. A group of young white men in blackface makeup, they sang songs in dialect and created imitations of the sounds of the city, sometimes with every instrument and a kind of whole-body playing and dancing at once.[20] G. W. Pell, in particular, the much-praised star of the troupe, embodied the popular traditions of minstrelsy as the (clearly) out-of-control clown, with a huge collar and bow, a frantic manner, "bad" puns, and an extraordinary skill at percussion (he played the "bones"). But the changes from its working-class and street culture were apparent. Instead of appearing in a saloon, or as part of a variety bill, the Ethiopian Serenaders played the St. James, a concert hall that also booked a French-language theater company, amateur theatricals, and concerts. By association, they were just another alternative but respectable performance idiom, exotic but only slightly suspect. Instead of the ragged or garish costumes of other minstrel troupes, the Serenaders dressed in formal wear, apparently starting what became a standard feature of the genre, emblazoned with a bright yellow waistcoat, for a neat, if sporting, appearance.[21] They attracted the attention of a range of classes—appearing privately for the minor aristocracy and, late in 1846, for Queen Victoria. They performed for a mixed-gender audience and held special morning concerts for children. On their return visit in 1848, they performed for the entire summer at Vauxhall Gardens, a popular outdoor resort that attracted a clientele of a broader-than-usual range of class and gender; then they toured to venues around England and Scotland that would attract a "suitable" audience, in particular those associated with the educational lecture and exhibition.[22]

The Manchester description exhibits the complex negotiation between the new middle-class audience and the minstrel show. Women are present, but there is a sense of discomfort with their response to the humor. A pedagogical defense of the performance is made through an appeal to authenticity and the exhibition of other cultures. Singing is praised in terms of control, harmony, and the pure exhibition of skill. On the other hand, there remain strong vestiges of the circus, in the costume and description of "grotesque" movement, and there is something incomprehensible and dangerous, if attractive, in Juba's dance.

Dance, Juba, and the Exception to the Rules

Promenading in a circle to the left for a few bars, till again facing the audience, he then commenced a series of steps, which altogether baffle description, from their number, oddity, and the rapidity with which they were executed. The highland fling, the sailor's hornpipe, and other European dances, seemed to have been laid under contribution, and intermixed with a number of steps which we may call "Juba's own," for surely their like was never before seen for grotesque agility, not altogether unmixed with grace.

The idea that early blackface minstrelsy contains vestiges of an Atlantic street culture speaks directly to the long-standing historical arguments concerning its dance forms—and in particular the potential influence of an Africanist aesthetic.[23] At the root of the discussion is whether dance in minstrelsy was a creative and empowering melting pot or a gross example of exploitation. W. T. Lhamon's argument, in contrast, is that all culture is local, and that the reality was not simply a matter of a single, monolithic African or Africanist culture co-opted by a monolithic European culture. Instead, he posits a polyglot dance culture that traded steps, styles, and rhythms from, for example, Yoruban and North Kerry folk idioms.[24] In this scenario, Atlantic street culture was a richly creative meeting of dance styles—an integrationist, syncopated conflagration of clogs, jigs, hornpipes, and reels, of *giouba* dances and ring shouts, of rude parodies of every kind of elite dance—that remained embedded deep in the racist and segregationist commodity culture of the minstrel show and has persisted, under the radar of show business, occasionally resurfacing in explosions of tap, of jazz, and of hip-hop.[25]

The complexities of dance in blackface minstrelsy are corroborated and intensified by the presence of Juba—in microhistorical terms an "exceptional normal," a dancer of color who should have been ostracized and yet was embraced by the early minstrel show.[26] It is no simple culture that would allow for his presence, and I believe the argument for minstrelsy as a manifestation of a hybrid street culture is strengthened by his presence. Juba, whose real name (by tradition) was William Henry Lane, was a fixture of the concert saloons and dance halls of New York City and had performed with early minstrel shows in the northeastern United States.

He was a dancer of working-class renown, who had been involved in a series of competitions in the mid-1840s. Fortunately for his career, and for the dance historian, he was seen by Charles Dickens during the writer's first tour to the United States in 1842 and described in Dickens's *American Notes*. This association was put to good use when, in 1848, the Ethiopian Serenaders made their second tour to England, during which Lane was billed as "Boz's Juba" (Dickens first published under the pen name "Boz"). Dickens's description typically accompanied all advertisements, establishing the speed, grotesquerie, and implausible skill of Juba's performance that found its way into many other eyewitness accounts of his dance: "Single shuffle, double shuffle, cut and cross-cut; snapping his fingers, rolling his eyes, turning in his knees, presenting the backs of his legs in front, spinning about on his toes and heels like nothing but the man's fingers on the tamborine; dancing with two left legs, two right legs, two wooden legs, two wire legs, two spring legs—all sorts of legs and no legs—what is this to him?"[27]

Two contrasting characteristics in particular were prevalent in the descriptions of Juba's performance, both of which can be seen in the Manchester review. The first was the precision of his performance. It was a percussive dance related to the clog, and generally considered to be a precursor to what we know as tap, but an unusual emphasis was placed on the attribution of control, and the frequent admonition in advertisements for silence from the audience during his performances. The second common characteristic in descriptions of his dance, in contrast, was the incapacity of language to describe it. Reviewers resorted to extraordinary rhythms and rhetoric in their prose, and to a range of analogies—including "dervishes" and the "wilis"—in an effort to capture the event, though they typically admitted defeat and declared his performance sui generis.[28]

There is in these descriptions a strong sense of a loss of control, if not by Juba himself then by the critic in his capacity as one who understands and interprets what he is watching. For the most part this was experienced as an exciting confrontation between the "indescribable" and the ordered, though not all responses were benign. There are reviews warning Juba that he "jumps too fast," and that he "would be wise to jump in time"—an apparent warning about the nature of his dance.[29] A reviewer at Vauxhall, describing Juba as diligently as the Manchester writer, but to different purpose, says this:

Juba's talent consists in walking round the stage with an air of satisfaction and with his toes turned in; in jumping backwards in a less graceful manner than we should have conceived possible; and in shaking his thighs like a man afflicted with palsy. He makes a terrible clatter with his feet, not owing so much to activity on his part as to stupidity on the part of his boot-maker, who has furnished him with a pair of clumsy Wellingtons sufficiently large for the feet and legs of all the Ethiopians in London:

besides this, he sometimes moves about the stage on his knees, as if he was praying to be endowed with intelligence, and had unlimited credit with his tailor. As a last resource, he falls back on the floor.[30]

This description is no less precise in its physicality than the Manchester review, and it betrays the potential danger of the performance, the vestige of the working-class, saloon-oriented, and male-oriented roots of the form. The Manchester reviewer, writing about this same performance in a more polite venue, concentrates on its value as an exhibition of exotic culture for pedagogical purpose, and on the measured portions and precision of the dance. The Vauxhall reviewer, watching Juba in a somewhat less edifying setting—the circuslike "rotunda" of Vauxhall Gardens—can see through to the street culture, and he disapproves. The Dickens description and this Vauxhall review illustrate the complex reaction to Juba that finds its way into the Manchester account; but in Manchester this is exacerbated by the fact that he is cross-dressed—or, at least, it seems reasonable to assume so.

At first glance, the Manchester description of Juba as Lucy Long corroborates the misogynist agenda of the minstrel show: "Promenading in a circle to the left for a few bars, till again facing the audience, he then commenced a series of steps, which altogether baffle description, from their number, oddity, and the rapidity with which they were executed. The highland fling, the sailor's hornpipe, and other European dances, seemed to have been laid under contribution, and intermixed with a number of steps which we may call 'Juba's own,' for surely their like was never before seen for grotesque agility, not altogether unmixed with grace." Lucy's dance bursts into extremes of unladylike movement, described very much in the manner of Juba's dances later in male costume (and in the previously quoted negative review). The lyrics to the song quoted earlier suggest that there was a clumsiness and ugliness to these cross-dressed performances best expressed through the exposure of the masculine beneath the costume. If we accept for a moment that the primary singer was the other "star" of the troupe, G. W. Pell, then Juba's costume, partly taken from the circus, argues for a particular performance style: "With literally a yard of shirt collar and frill, it was scarcely possible to witness his extravagant grimaces, without a most undignified unbending of the facial muscles." His shoes were (most likely) the long clown shoes still seen in the circus—so long, for example, that another Pell-like performer wore candles on the end of his (as "foot lights"). If Pell, the uncontrollable trickster and clown of the troupe, was the featured singer, it only makes sense that Juba's performance played on that fact. Lucy's costume is garish—one might argue distasteful, certainly comic.[31] So if we take Juba's performance to be as clownlike as Pell's certainly was, the lyrics become literal, except that the male lover becomes as incompetent in his masculine stereotype as Lucy is in hers. In effect, the gender types are reinforced by showing how unfortunate the exceptions are—doubly reinforcing the type through race prejudice. The man is a weak buffoon in performance, the woman is powerful, masculine, and unattractive; but then, they are only clowns, and anyway "black," so they are bound to be comically incompetent as they attempt to imitate the misogynist status quo.

The Polyvalent Image of Juba: Rereading the Dress and the Drag

There are other ways of reading the evidence, however—not to dispute the prejudices but to complicate them. The depiction of the wench dancer in the minstrel show ranged along a continuum from complete illusion at one extreme—surprising, impressing, and upsetting the audience with the skill at imitation—to the "dame" roles famous in English pantomime at the other extreme, in which the male type is so visible, the imitation so "poor" (or "theatrical," if you like), that gender becomes satirical commentary (whether to reinforce or disrupt conventions varies with context). I emphasize that these two extremes rest on a continuum, and in blackface minstrelsy I am convinced (despite some arguments to the contrary) that the full range existed on the same stage from minstrelsy's earliest days, drawing from all other forms of entertainment. Circus equestrians and acrobats leaned toward the illusionist in their use of cross-dressing, as did the early minstrel performer George Christy. Others were clearly and overtly clownlike, "clad in some tawdry old gown of loud, crude colors, whose shortness and scantiness display long frilled panties" and sporting "Number 13 valise shoes."[32]

Figure 7.2   Wench act on a working-class stage in New York City. Note the clown shoes and simple garment. From the *New York Clipper*, March 14, 1874. Used with permission.

Figure 7.3   Wench dance, probably G. N. Christy. From a sheet music cover for Edwin P. Christie's Minstrels, published in Boston, circa 1848. C. British Library Board. All rights reserved. [H.1652.SS/3]. Used with permission.

In addition, the shape and color of the clothing can be traced to at least two sources, each of which would complicate an audience reading of the dance. The first is the image of the plantation slave wearing her mistress's cast-off clothing; the colors are mismatched both because the clothes are cast-offs and because the wearer has no "taste." The second is the contemporary urban working woman—working both in factories and in brothels—whose fashion (argues Eric Lott) was garish and flew in the face of "bourgeois decorum." A contemporary description (by George Foster) of such women on the street of New York City highlights, in phrases clearly reminiscent of the descriptions of Juba's costume, "a light pink contrasting with a deep blue, a bright yellow with a bright red, and a green with a dashing purple or maroon" along with "ankle-length skirts, and painted faces."[33] These women were a noisy and visible presence on city streets—in contrast to their middle-class counterparts. It has been argued—effectively, in my opinion—that the presentation of fashion in minstrelsy is a parody of middle-class prudishness and the muted, modest costuming just then being promulgated.[34] But this is a two-edged sword. On the one hand, figures of the slave and the working woman conflated might be read as demeaning, expressing an incompetent sense of taste to go with other forms of incompetence, ugliness, and distasteful behavior. On the other hand, "attitude" in performance can turn this message on its head. The working women of the Bowery expressed pride in these fashions; and the southern slave culture was noted for its mockery of the dominant culture, through dance as well as fashion. If so, then the depiction of "Lucy Long" might become that of a proud and arrogant woman of the street, certainly when placed next to a male clown.

I personally favor the idea that Juba created a Lucy Long that stood in contrast to Pell's grotesque, comic suitor—a strong, skillful dancer in defiance of custom, and in defiance of control. The Manchester critic does not describe his appearance as ugly, or even particularly comic, and he is clearly impressed with the dance. This positive reading may be a hopeful imposition—but as evidence, I note a difference in the footwear. Juba is not wearing the typical grotesque "Number 13 valise shoes" but, on the contrary, elegant red leather boots. These are Juba's trademark dancing boots, seen in the only image of Juba in performance, described as making a "terrible clatter" in the negative criticism of him, and remembered in the first posthumous reference to him (by a Cockney blackface street performer): "Juba was along with Pell. Juba was a first class—a regular A1—he was a regular black, and a splendid dancer in boots."[35] I will not argue that they were delicate, or that Juba was attempting the illusion of the feminine; however, I do argue that he was exposing himself *as Juba* and *as a dancer* from underneath the dress. As such, "Lucy" was displaying "her" impressive, attractive, original skills, "not altogether unmixed with grace," thereby giving her the upper hand over the "men" around her.

The description of movement in this account further complicates a reading of the dance. One or more of the minstrels sing while Juba dances. "Lucy" slowly circles on the stage, then breaks loose with quick steps that are clearly impressive to the eyewitness, and not unlike the dances in male attire that come later in the evening. "Lucy Long," however, was no ordinary song and dance. It was a mainstay of organized minstrelsy from its inception, and appears to have been an extended dance scene; it has been argued that it was an early form of the minstrel "walk-around," in which members of the troupe circled the stage and took turns performing individual specialities and competitions. There is evidence that in this earlier form all performers were involved in clapping, keeping rhythm, shouting vocal encouragement, and improvising patter between verses.[36] Admitting here the apparent focus on one dancer, I would argue that there was more going on in Manchester than a clown singing "I just come out before you." Just as there were potential sources for the costuming of the wench dancer, there were potential models for this more improvisatory, noisier definition of the wench dance—and like the costuming, one is steeped in slavery, the other in class.

On the one hand, these early "walk-arounds" have been tied to the African "ring shout," a form of circle dance interrupted by individuals improvising in the center to the rhythmic encouragement of the group. One writer calls this form the "pivot," by which "black dance radiated outward in America to become a formidable presence"; another suggests the walk-around is its "secular parody."[37] There is evidence here of the "authenticity" of the plantation culture advertised by early minstrelsy—and a defense of Juba's Africanist contribution to dance in this context, here in the performance of Lucy Long.

On the other hand, there is evidence that dancing in this style took place on the streets of America, and by women—again, working and working-class women. *The Libertine*, in 1842 (the same year that Dickens saw and described Juba), depicts and describes a dance competition on the streets of Boston between two "gals," to minstrel-like tunes played by a black fiddler:

> The first dance on the list was a hornpipe, and the one who took the most steps was to come off victor. It was Bryant's first turn, and as she entered the ring, she made three courtesies to the spectators who formed three sides about her. The word was given; the negro fiddler struck up Fisher's Hornpipe, and Susan commenced—and the way she put in the big licks was a "sin to Moses." Shouts of applause rent the air, whenever she changed a step. Every move was grace, her limbs moved as if guided by machinery. She now came to the heel and toe business—and done it to a nail, with which she wound up the hornpipe.... Every step the Bryant took Nancy repeated—and all [conceded] that it would be hip and thigh between them, which is a tie.... The negro struck up the Camptown Hornpipe and the gals struck the wharf. It was hard to decide who was to come off victor notwithstanding that the knowing odds were offered in favor of Bryant. From the Camptown the tune was changed to the Grape Vine; yet both went it, as the change had no effect on them. From this they changed to "Take your time Miss Lucy," and the way they went at it was a caution—even the change to "Where did you come from knock a nigger down," and "Jenny get your hoe cake done my lady," did not affect them—the sweat run down their faces, as if all within was on fire; perhaps occasioned by the gin taken in the recess. But now came the tug of war—the tune was changed to one of Sandford's jigs—"Go it Nancy," "Go it Suze," came in from all sides. They danced—the sweat poured.[38]

This description is notable because it describes women dancing, and because it is clearly indebted to minstrel performance—except that this predates its rise as a popular commercial form. The presence of the African American fiddler and the use of dialect folk songs give credence to the existence of a carnivalesque street culture that included a full range of cultures, races, and genders. These women compete to the tune of "Lucy Long," as if the wench dance performed onstage was directly imitative—or, more likely, that stage and street were mutually influential. If true, then this description of street dancing becomes further evidence of the kind of performance that took place on the minstrel stage. This is not to say it is a positive portrayal of women; the issue of the *Libertine* from which this description comes is filled with reports of abuse, rape, murder, "white slavery," and prostitution, a kind of print voyeurism under the guise of reform. This competition, according to the writer, follows a fistfight between two other women; thus violence and dance are closely linked. There is certainly nothing sentimental or submissive about the description; but by the same token, there is nothing weak or incompetent. It is robust, skilled, aggressive, and controlled—not an entirely negative image of race, class, or gender.[39]

If these precursors and influences are embedded in the minstrel show—the southern plantation slave in her mismatched wardrobe and the working-class woman's exuberant fashion sense, the walk-around and the street dance competition—what associations might Juba's Manchester audience have made? The description of the wench dance differs from the norm in two respects. First of all, the audience was not working-class and American but middle-class and British. As such, spectators could not reasonably be expected to understand the references to a street culture where women danced competitively, and certainly not to an alleged connection to African "ring shouts." It is perhaps more likely that they made a connection with the southern plantation slave mismatching her mistress's cast-off clothing; it is also possible that a local connection to the culture of working-class women could be made. The reception to Juba's performance must have been generally positive, in part because it persisted throughout his tour with the Ethiopian Serenaders, and in part because there is some evidence that it was only recently added to the program. The Ethiopian Serenaders did not include the wench dance in their first tour to England, although it was a ubiquitous feature of all such shows in the United States, and the troupe included a known wench dancer (F. C. Germon). One wonders why, unless there was too much of the street culture and working class in "Lucy Long" to make the transition to performances for the middle class; the presence of cross-dressing on the English pantomime stage notwithstanding, an American form just on the edge of respectability may not have felt it could sufficiently censor this particular aspect of its improvisatory performance. This begs the question, then, why wench dancing was introduced when the Ethiopian Serenaders returned to London in 1848; the only substantial difference in the composition of the troupe was the presence of a performer of color.

If, as the description seems to indicate, Juba was not in blackface, this must have changed the way audiences witnessed his performance in general, and it would be doubly true of his performance as "Lucy Long."[40] The wench dancer in blackface reinforces the artificiality of the depiction of both race and gender. The blackface persona emerging from underneath the dress is just as artificial as Lucy Long herself. But this is not the case when Juba performs. What emerges from beneath the dress, when he leaves the "promenade" for his "grotesque" dance, is his well-advertised authenticity. Would this have been read as a parody of a plantation slave or a working-class woman—or is something else going on? I note that, just as the Ethiopian Serenaders seem to have waited for Juba before exposing middle-class audiences to "Lucy Long," Juba seems to have waited as well. There is no evidence of Juba cross-dressing prior to his run at Vauxhall Gardens in London in 1848—and then only halfway through that run—and he stopped the practice after he left the troupe in 1850 to perform in working-class music halls and saloons across Britain. "Lucy Long" was a staple feature of minstrelsy from its inception—but for Juba, it was a performance strictly for middle-class, mixed-gender British audiences. Was there a reason?

Juba's cross-dressed performance might have been entirely demeaning; that is, however skilled the dancer under the skirt, the contextual disparagement of women in the minstrel show would have become attached (literally) to the authenticity of his color, the sexual energy clearly evident in his dance diminished as he is feminized. If true, he can be seen as an unfortunate precursor to Topsy, introduced in the following passage from Uncle Tom's Cabin: "In a wild fantastic sort of time ... producing in her throat all those odd guttural sounds which distinguish the native music of her race; and finally, turning a summerset or two, and giving a prolonged closing note, as odd and unearthly as that of a steam-whistle, she came suddenly down on the carpet, and stood with her hands folded, and a most sanctimonious expression of meekness and solemnity over her face, only broken by the cunning glances which she shot askance from the corners of her eyes."[41] W. T. Lhamon argues that this passage shows the extent to which blackface minstrelsy had already entered (American) middle-class culture, whether Harriet Beecher Stowe had seen a minstrel show or not, prior to the invention of this character. The description is tellingly similar to the descriptions of Juba in Britain four years prior: the "native music of her race"; the use of vocal sounds (Juba's laugh while dancing was noted with enthusiasm); the syncopation; the acrobatics; and the strange "bow" at the end, seeking favor but with a "cunning glance," as if considering some more radical action. Topsy had a long subsequent history as a stage character, performed in blackface by a white woman, with strong ties to the minstrel stage and to the wench dance. Topsy as a character in the narrative of Uncle Tom, however, existed solely to perform for her white owners; if this was perceived as an authentic depiction of southern plantation life, then this is also one possible "reading" of Juba by the middle classes.[42]

I would like to advance a more positive view. Consider the image, printed in the *Illustrated London News*, of Juba dancing at Vauxhall Garden—a summer meeting place where, to some extent and with some controls, class and gender met in a freer environment than normal. Juba and the Ethiopian Minstrels appeared in a circuslike setting, the Rotunda, mixed in with equestrian acts and acrobats. The spectators depicted in this image are all women, which may be an accident of engraving but may be significant, particularly in the context of reviews that are so glowing, so excited, so engaged with Juba's moving body that they tend to support Eric Lott's argument that minstrelsy was a locus of intense and complex sexual attractions—even allowing for puffery. Even the negative reviews emphasize the roughness and rudeness of the movement as inappropriately out of control—dangerous to know. Perhaps we should consider the prospect that Juba, to young British middle-class spectators in 1848, was a very attractive performer. "[Many] were the handkerchiefs employed to conceal the smothered laughter of their fair owners," writes the Manchester reviewer. The minstrels were "hot"; perhaps Juba was hotter.

Unquestionably this stretches the bounds of a provable thesis; however, before dismissing the idea completely, it is worth returning to Marjorie Garber's work in *Vested Interests*. In her chapter on the relationship between cross-dressing and race in America, she quotes the following performer: "We were breaking through the racial barrier.... The white kids had to hide my records coz they daren't let their parents know they had them in the house. We decided that my image should be crazy and way-out so that the adults would think I was harmless. I'd appeared in one show dressed as the Queen of England and in the next as the Pope."[43] The writer is Little Richard, who is used as an example of Garber's idea that, in effect, gender confusion trumps racism. By her argument, cross-dressing might be used to confuse, distract, and displace the prejudice against color, allowing the performance to continue while the "parents"—the enforcing agents of the status quo—scratch their heads.

It would be impossible to prove that Juba, halfway through the summer of 1848, put on a dress to distract the moral arbiters of Victorian society from the sexual nature of his dance, and from the exceptional circumstances of his presence on this segregated stage. On the one hand, the act was a standard of minstrelsy, and he was a headliner; his performance of it may be as simple as that, and the extraordinary skill of his performance sufficient to explain his continued appearance—the only performer of color on the minstrel stage during this period. On the other hand, it may be that Juba was not as easily accepted on these middle-class stages as the positive press and puffery made it appear. If we return, one last time, to the Manchester description of the minstrel show, there are signs of distress: the "smothered laughter" of the women in the audience; the reference to a "grotesque element," to physical exertion, and to the "oddity" of dances that "baffle description"; the precise, almost ethnographic description: "He is apparently about eighteen years of age; about 5 feet 3 inches in height; of slender make, yet possessing great muscular activity. His head is very small." The writer repeatedly emphasizes with admiration those elements of the dance that are most controlled, noting that to him "the most interesting part of the performance was the exact time, which, even in the most complicated and difficult steps, the dancer kept to the music." He also consistently removes Juba from the other members of the troupe in the descriptions, in this way critically segregating him as if he was on exhibition, something authentic to be contained and understood directly by the audience, and not enjoyed in the same way as an entertainer in blackface. We might read the negative feedback in other, less articulate references to his performance—that he "jumps too fast" and tends to create a noisy reaction among "the gallery crowd"—back into this review, the firm politeness of the tone in fact an effort to control through writing. In this respect the extended, precise description of Juba's dress and his dance as Lucy Long takes on a new significance—it was a relief and a distraction. A drag act was something the writer could understand, and for a time he could forget about the uncommon presence of a black body dancing in an incomprehensible manner. When Juba danced as Lucy Long, it signified in a very different manner than for any other performer who put on the dress.[44]

NOTES

1. The review reads as follows, in full:

FREE-TRADE HALL.—"Juba" and the Serenaders.—A party of serenaders, under the leadership of Mr. G. W. Pell, late of St. James's Theatre, gave one of their peculiar exhibitions on Monday evening in the Free-trade Hall. They are six in number, and are mostly happy in the possession of nigger-like physiognomies. The "making up" of their leader was extremely ludicrous. With literally a yard of shirt collar and frill, it was scarcely possible to witness his extravagant grimaces, without a most undignified unbending of the facial muscles, and many were the handkerchiefs employed to conceal the smothered laughter of their fair owners. The party have some good voices among them, and they harmonize well together; indeed, the melody of several of the chants, and other concerted pieces, was so pleasing to the ear, that they were loudly encored. But the great feature of the entertainment, and that which we imagine attracted the large and respectable audience present, was undoubtedly "Master Juba," the immortalized of Boz. This "phenomenon" (as the bills describe him) is a copper-coloured votary of Terpsichore,—the Monsieur Perrot of Negro life in the southern states; and possesses the additional attraction of being a "real nigger," and not a "sham," like his vocal associates. He is apparently about eighteen years of age; about 5 feet 3 inches in height; of slender make, yet possessing great muscular activity. His head is very small, and his countenance, when at rest, has a rather mild, sedate, and far from unpleasing expression. His first performance was "Miss Lucy Long, in character." With a most bewitching bonnet and veil, a *very* pink dress, beflounced to the waist, lace-fringed trousers of the most spotless purity, and red leather boots,—the ensemble completed by the green parasol and white cambric pocket handkerchief,—Master Juba certainly looked the black demoiselle of the first ton to the greatest advantage. The playing and singing by the Serenaders of a version of the well-known negro ditty, furnished the music to Juba's performance, which was after this fashion:—Promenading in a circle to the left for a few bars, till again facing the audience, he then commenced a series of steps, which altogether baffle description, from their number, oddity, and the rapidity with which they were executed. The highland fling, the sailor's hornpipe, and other European dances, seemed to have been laid under contribution, and intermixed with a number of steps which we may call "Juba's own," for surely their like was never before seen for grotesque agility, not altogether unmixed with grace. The promenade was then repeated; then more dancing; and so on, to the end of the song. His other performances were called the "marriage festival" and "plantation dances," in which, in male costume, he illustrated the dances of his own simple people on

festive occasions. They were even more extraordinary than the first,—the grotesque element, in the character of the steps, largely predominating, and the
physical exertion apparently much greater. The same peculiarity, of the alternate
promenade and dance, was observable in both. To us, the most interesting part of
the performance was the exact time, which, even in the most complicated and
difficult steps, the dancer kept to the music. He appears to be quite an enthusiast
in his art, and every round of applause he received seemed to stimulate him to
fresh exertion. Altogether, Master Juba's Terpsichorean performances are well
worth a visit.

2. Arguments can be made for and against this statement. Juba was pervasively
advertised as an "authentic" performer of color, not to be confused with the "sham"
performers in blackface; and a major factor in reviews was his "blackness." On the one
hand, this seems to suggest the importance of presenting Juba without the "sham" of
makeup. On the other hand, the insistence of this advertising may have been in compen-
sation for that makeup—that is, that despite the "burnt cork," he was in fact black.
I personally believe the former: that Juba was so unusual to the minstrel show, the
minstrel show was so new and unsettled in its ways, and this performer was advertised so
insistently as different (including completely separate advertisements) that he was a
complete exception to the norm (or "exceptional normal"—see note 26).

3. Crucial research for both these articles was conducted by Alexis Butler, Beth
Marquis, Diana Manole, and Birgit Schreyer through the University of Toronto's Graduate Centre for Study of Drama.

4. Blackface as a theatrical convention was still in use on American and British
television in the 1960s. From personal experience, I know that service clubs in North
America still used the form as a feature of fund-raising events in the 1980s.

5. A three-part structure developed over time, including an urban black character in
dandy costume, an "olio" or variety entr'acte, and a rural plantation finale.

6. The Hutchinson Family was an American concert troupe that, while advertising its
cultural origins, performed a range of skilled vocal harmonies. The *Court Gazette and
Fashionable Guide*, February 14, 1846, advertises the Hutchinsons and the Ethiopian
Serenaders contiguously, clearly meant as comparative American performances.

The history of early minstrelsy has been written with enthusiasm almost from its
inception. T. Allston Brown published what amounts to a (surprisingly accurate) documentary history in the *New York Clipper* in series from 1876, revised and expanded in
1912. An abundance of newspaper articles can be found in files and scrapbooks in the
New York Public Library and the Harvard Theatre Collection, among other archives; by
their existence and content it appears that minstrelsy had a strongly loyal and long-lived
fan base, which was keenly interested in the origin of the genre and its change over time.
For later narrative histories, see Carl Wittke's *Tambo and Bones*; Harry Reynolds's
Minstrel Memories; Edward Le Roy Rice's *Monarchs of Minstrelsy*; and especially Hans
Nathan's *Dan Emmett and the Rise of Early Blackface Minstrelsy*, and Robert Toll's
Blacking Up.

7. Eric Lott's *Love and Theft* examines the complex psychology and politics of that
first, working-class audience; Dale Cockrell's *Demons of Disorder* and William Mahar's
Behind the Burnt Cork Mask examine its roots in folk and popular tradition, and its
transition into a commercial form; W. T. Lhamon's *Raising Cain* explores the genre's

long-term legacy. A range of periodical literature also exists in what has been a rich field of research over the past 15 years.

8. T. D. Rice, who from the 1830s was the best-known exponent of blackface clown, exemplifies the breadth of this street culture; the singing and dancing of his highly politicized Jim Crow "persona" were the subject of adoration in both the United States and Britain, with both working and middle-class audiences. See Lott, *Love and Theft*, 68; Lhamon, *Raising Cain*, 69. He was, significantly, a favorite of London's (black-faced) chimney sweeps.

9. Mahar's work is in part a rebuttal to Lott's. Laurence Senelick also expresses strong reservations in *The Changing Room*: "It is hard to find any point at which sexual desire can gain purchase on the loose-limbed scarecrows of early minstrel drag" (297).

10. The work of Judith Butler on the social construction of gender is at the root of all such study, and it is important to emphasize the influence of time in that "social" construction. In a brief discussion such as this, it is easy to conflate past and present; but the mid-19th-century male audience member had a wide range of sexual preferences, identities, and misogynies available to him, inextricably commingled with a similarly heterogeneous complex of race(s) and class(es) (see note 14). Of the many useful works on sexuality for this period, three provide an immediate context for this essay. G. J. Baker-Benfield's *Horrors of the Half-Known Life: Male Attitudes toward Women and Sexuality in Nineteenth Century America* posits a particularly homosocial strain in American culture that in some respects takes precedence over potential divisions of age, class, and family. Jonathan Katz's *Love Stories: Sex between Men before Homosexuality* expertly distills the range of recent research into this subject (its bibliography is recommended), foregrounding the shifting definitions and classifications of sexual intercourse over time, class, and subculture. It includes a striking description of the trial of a cross-dressing black male prostitute in New York, who was the subject of derisive laughter in the courtroom—a good example of the "exceptional normal" in the study of the past (see note 26). Finally, a particularly unsettling depiction of sexuality, race, and gender during these years can be found in the compendium of diary entries, letters, and court proceedings reproduced in Thomas P. Lowry's *Story the Soldiers Wouldn't Tell: Sex in the Civil War*—with its eye-opening suggestion of the ubiquity of sexual intercourse as commerce, and the concomitant commodification and dehumanization of women of a perceived "lesser" class—or race. The distinctly offhanded character of physical intercourse with "raced" bodies is striking. In general, there is a good deal more research to be done to address the sexual zeitgeist surrounding the early minstrel show.

11. Cockrell, *Demons of Disorder*, 55: "No mumming play is without a female impersonator."

12. For the critical literature on minstrel cross-dressing, see, among others, Mahar, *Behind the Burnt Cork Mask*, 311–16; Lott, *Love and Theft*, 159–68; Garber, *Vested Interests*, 274–78; Annemarie Bean reviews the literature in her thesis on cross-dressing, by way of introduction to her own study.

13. Lyrics for "Lucy Long" abound in early minstrel publications. Samples and discussion can be found in Nathan, *Dan Emmett and the Rise of Early Negro Minstrelsy*; Mahar, *Behind the Burnt Cork Mask*, 307–11; and Lott, *Love and Theft*, 160–61 (and passim). These lyrics are from sheet music found in the British Library.

14. I use the plural of "class" where it will not confuse the argument, in an effort to avoid the tendency to simplify this complex word, as if easily defined, monolithic, homogeneous, and discrete. Even if the singular is used, however, my understanding is as follows: individuals are "members" of a range of cultures and subcultures, some of which may be defined through class. See, with respect to this study: Hugh Cunningham's *Leisure in the Industrial Revolution*, which outlines three popular cultures expressing hedonism, methodism, and radicalism (37–41); Bluford Adams's *E Pluribus Barnum*, which follows Barnum's tactics for appealing to and manipulating a cross-class culture of "respectability"; and Karen Haltunnen's *Confidence Men and Painted Women*, which explores with elegance the phenomenon of the middle classes as a culture "in social motion" (29). These arguments inform this study.

15. Besides the works already noted, Robert Winans particularly explores the shift in audience through the corresponding shift in song repertoire during this crucial first 10 years. See Lhamon, *Raising Cain*, 44; and Lott, *Love and Theft*, 63ff., 138–39, all of which discuss class consciousness and the early minstrel show.

16. I am indebted specifically to Michael Sappol's work on the 19th-century anatomical museum for the idea of the minstrel as a body out of control in a society for which this was both captivating and troublesome. He in turn cites Eric Lott's work.

17. P. T. Barnum defined this ambivalence, traveling with Tom Thumb to Britain with an aggressive campaign to "pitch" him to the middle classes and to the aristocracy—while at the same time writing regularly published letters home "pitching" American values and skills at the expense of the British. Adams, in *E Pluribus Barnum*, assesses Barnum's rise through the "classes" of America through his writing. See especially pp. xiii; 11 (on his letters from Britain to the *New York Atlas*); 16 (on his own increased "respectability" in New York society after his British tour); 76 (on a "respectable" culture that crossed class lines); and 94 (on the sometimes vulgar tastes of the so-called middle class). Bruce McConachie also discusses Barnum's relationship with class and audience in "Pacifying American Theatrical Audiences, 1820–1900," in Butsch's *For Fun and Profit*, 47–70.

18. See Hans Nathan's study of Dan Emmett, one of the original Virginia Serenaders. This information exists as well in a range of fugitive clippings in the New York Public Library and the Harvard Theatre Collection. For an example of the reference to a "glut" of minstrels, see *John Bull* (October 24, 1846): "So many things of this kind have been brought forward lately, by Henry Russell, the Hutchinson Family, the Ethiopian Serenaders, and we do not know how many others, that they are getting quite stale; and any further attempt of the sort must have some wholly new features in order to become attractive."

19. The members of the first Ethiopian Serenaders were Frank Germon, Moody Stanwood, George Harrington, Gilbert Pell, and W. White. James A. Dumbolton was the "agent," though his relationship with the troupe is unclear, since Pell was clearly the most prominent member, and Germon seemed to handle the press. See *New York Clipper*, March 30, 1912.

20. A popular feature was the "celebrated railroad overture," in which all instruments imitated what was then a new technology.

21. G. W. Pell seems to have been the exception to this change, adapting his new apparel to the needs of his clowning.

22. A number of London and provincial newspapers were surveyed as part of an ongoing study of the Ethiopian Serenaders. See, for example, the *Observer*, May 16, 1847, for reference to regular morning concerts, to private performances, and a more self-serving reference to the "vulgar imitations" of other blackface minstrels. See the *New York Clipper*, October 7. 1876, for a reprinted program of a performance by the Serenaders at the duke of Devonshire's birthday party (May 30, 1846). See the *Observer*, June 27, 1846, for a review of the performance for the royal children; and the same newspaper for June 7, 1846, for their appearance at "The Horns, Kennington" on a dark night at the St. James. Particularly telling is this report from *John Bull*, April 11, 1846, describing their appearance at a Covent Garden fund-raiser: "The royal Duke was so much pleased with them, that he sent to request them to repeat one of their pieces; and afterwards permitted them to sing in the more immediate presence of the ladies, where they were again encored." Their appearance at Arundel Castle for the royal family occurred in early December 1846.

For appearances by the Serenaders at Vauxhall Gardens, see the *Morning Advertiser*, June 13 and 20, 1848, for descriptions. The *Morning Chronicle*, July 8, 1848, describes a fund-raiser for the Distressed Needlewomen's Society, attended by the lord mayor and other dignitaries and aristocrats. The same paper August 30, 1848, and September 4, 1848, reports discounted tickets and large attendance figures (6,000 and 20,000, respectively, though these cannot be trusted). See the *Observer*, July 31, 1848, for an advertisement by the Vauxhall listing the range of dukes, lords, marquises, and viscounts who had visited that summer. Other information may be found in a dedicated file on the Vauxhall in the Harvard Theatre Collection.

23. See Dixon Gottschild, *Digging the Africanist Presence in American Performance*, and Thompson, "An Aesthetic of the Cool," on the idea of an Africanist aesthetic in American dance.

24. This "range" was driven home to me at a lecture in Limerick, Ireland, in June 2003, when, watching Catherine Foley's videotapes of an old village dancer in Kerry, I was struck by the similarity to performances by the tap dancer Chuck Green in his later years.

25. The best works on minstrel dance are in Nathan, *Dan Emmett and the Rise of Early Negro Minstrelsy*, 70–97, as well as Stearns and Stearns, *Jazz Dance*. See Lott, *Love and Theft*, 256 n. 10, for the idea that, of all elements of street culture that found their way onto the minstrel stage, dance was the least changed in the transition.

26. "Exceptional normal" is used by Edoardo Grendi (quoted in Levi, "On Microhistory," 109). Other related terms include "an opaque document," in Robert Darnton, *The Great Cat Massacre*, 5; a "dissonance," in Carlo Ginzburg, *The Cheese and the Worms*, xix; and a "contradiction of normative systems," in Giovanni Levi, "On Microhistory," 107. See also Carlo Ginzburg, "Microhistory: Two or Three Things That I Know About It."

27. This is the full quotation used in numerous publications and can be found in *American Notes*, 90–91.

28. Most writers on early minstrelsy include a discussion about Juba. Most of these are based on the essential article by Marian Hannah Winter, which is based on a very few documents. Many more are now available for study. See http://www.utm.utoronto.ca/~w3minstr/. The following are useful examples.

Era, June 18, 1848: "It is the most wonderful conglomeration of every step that was ever thought of, and reminds the spectator more of one of the 'dancing dervishes,' or fabled willis, than anything else he can think of."

Manchester Examiner, October 17, 1848: "Surely he cannot be flesh and blood, but some more subtle substance, or how could he turn, and twine, and twist, and twirl, and hop, and jump, and kick, and throw his feet almost with a velocity that makes one think they are playing hide-and seek with a flash of lightning! Heels or toes, on feet or on knees, on the ground or off, it is all the same to Juba; his limbs move as if they were stuffed with electric wires. . . . His legs must be of India rubber; his feet of jointed iron: how else the former can have so much elasticity, and the latter can bear so much beating on the floor, we know not."

Morning Post, June 21, 1848: "His pedal execution is a thing to wonder at, if his flexibility of muscle did not confound us. He jumps, he capers, he crosses his legs, he stamps his heels, he dances on his knees, on his ankles, he ties his limbs into double knots, and untwists them as one might a skein of silk, and all these marvels are done in strict time and appropriate rhythm—each note has its corresponding step and action. Now he languishes, now burns, now love seems to sway his motions, and anon rage seems to impel his steps."

The Mirror and United Kingdom Magazine, July 1848: "We fancied we had witnessed every kind of dance, from the wilds of Caffraria [*sic*] to the stage of the Academie at Paris; but all these choreographic manifestations were but poor shufflings compared to the pedal inspirations of Juba. Such mobility of muscles, such flexibility of joints, such boundings, such slidings, such gyrations, such toes and such heelings, such backwardings and forwardings, such posturings, such firmness of foot, such elasticity of tendon, such mutation of movement, such vigour, such variety, such natural grace, such powers of endurance, such potency of pastern, were never combined in one nigger. Juba is to Vauxhall what the Lind is to the Opera House."

29. These admonitions are from a later appearance in Manchester, noticed in the *Era*, August 4, 1850: "[Juba is] jumping very fast at the Colosseum, but too fast is worse than too slow, and we advise [Juba] to be wise in time. It is easier to jump down than to jump up"; *Era*, August 11, 1850: "Juba has jumped away—by the way of an earnest yet friendly caution, let us hope that he will not throw himself away. Be wise in time is a wholesome motto." See also the *Huddersfield Chronicle and West Yorkshire Advertiser*, November 30, 1850: "The performances of Boz's Juba have created quite a sensation in the gallery, who greeted his marvellous feats of dancing with thunders of applause and a standing *encore*. In all the rougher and less refined departments of his art, Juba is a perfect master." This review damns by faint praise, a far cry from the rapturous reviews of 1848–49.

30. From *The Puppet-Show*, August 12, 1848, in a Harvard Theatre Collection folder devoted to Vauxhall Gardens. The full quotation follows:

The principal feature in entertainments at Vauxhall is Juba: as such at least he is put forth—or rather put first—by the proprietors. Out of compliment to Dickens, this extraordinary nigger is called "Boz's Juba," in consequence, we believe, of the popular writer having said a good word for him in his *American Notes*: on this principle we could not mention the Industrious Fleas as being clever without having those talented little animals puffed all over London as being under the overwhelming patronage of the *Showman*. Juba's talent consists in walking round the stage with an air of satisfaction and with his toes turned in; in jumping backwards in a less graceful manner than we should have conceived possible; and in shaking his thighs like a man afflicted with palsy. He makes a terrible clatter with his feet, not owing so much to activity on his part as to stupidity on the part of his boot-maker, who has furnished him with a pair of clumsy Wellingtons sufficiently large for the feet and legs of all the Ethiopians in London: besides this, he sometimes moves about the stage on his knees, as if he was praying to be endowed with intelligence, and had unlimited credit with his tailor. As a last resource, he falls back on the floor.

31. Other descriptions of Juba as Lucy corroborate and elaborate on this costuming. For example: *Era*, August 27, 1848:

VAUXHALL GARDENS.—On Monday night the famous Juba appeared in a new character at these gardens. The part was that of "Lucy Long," and was a most favourite one with our neighbours across the "broad Atlantic." Juba makes his appearance on the stage attired in the habiliments of a stylish lady: pink muslin dress, blue bonnet, green parasol, and, as a kind of foundation to this gaudy gear, a pair of red morocco boots. Juba is accompanied by Pell, suitably equipped as a Broadway dandy; this latter sits and sings to the accompaniment of the banjo, violin, and tambourine, the well-known ditty of "Lucy Long," while Juba is executing the most difficult pas, introducing double-shuffles, pirouettes, and every imaginary step to be achieved by the nimble foot. The dance was encored, as is usual with the saltatory efforts of this agile performer. The dance was preceded by a most excellent performance of the equestrian troupe, in which were introduced many very surprising and cleverly-executed feats; among these were the impersonation of the passions, by Mddle. Macarte, and the excellent exercises of several well-trained and sagacious steeds, and others. After the performances of these in the Rotunda theatre, the second portion of the concert was given, with the grand pyro-technic display, and the exhibition of the model of Constantinople. The gardens were very well attended.

32. A number of writers have commented on the range of cross-dressed perfor-mances in early minstrelsy. As examples: Laurence Senelick in *The Changing Room* notes the use of cross-dressing among acrobats and equestrians, and George Christy's elegance as a "wench" in early minstrelsy is noted by him, though in general he argues that the image was grotesque during these years (296–99). See also Garber, *Vested Interests*, 275–78. The quotation comes from Olive Logan's essay "The Ancestry of Brudder Bones," 698.

33. See especially Christine Stansell, *City of Women*. The George Foster quotation is from *New York in Slices*, quoted in Stansell, *City of Women*, 94. Lott makes good use of both works (*Love and Theft*, 159ff.).

34. The relationship of the Bowery "g'hal" is discussed in Lott, *Love and Theft*, 80–86 (though the entire study focuses on issues of class formation); and Mahar, *Behind the Burnt Cork Mask*, 277–82, and in Stansell, *City of Women*.

35. "It must be eight years ago...since the Ethiopian serenading come up—ay, it must be at least that time, because the twopenny boats was then running to London-bridge, and it was before the 'Cricket' was blown up.... I used to wear a yellow waistcoat, in imitation of them at the St. James's Theatre.... The first came out at St. James's Theatre, and they made a deal of money.... Pell's gang was at the top of the tree. Juba was along with Pell. Juba was a first class—a regular A1—he was a regular black, and a splendid dancer in boots." Henry Mayhew, *London Labour and the London Poor*, 191.

36. For the origin of the "walk-around," see Nathan, *Dan Emmett and the Rise of Early Negro Minstrelsy*, 234–42 (on the "walk-around") and 130–33 (on "Lucy Long" and improvised patter), as well as a note on p. 93 on the alternation of rapid and slow movement. See also Stearns and Stearns, *Jazz Dance*, 29–31.

37. See P. Sterling Stuckey in DeFrantz, *Dancing Many Drums*, 52; and H. E. Krehbiel, *Afro-American Folksongs* (1914), quoted in Stearns and Stearns, *Jazz Dance*, 31.

38. See *The Libertine*, June 15, 1842, in the archive of the American Antiquarian Society. This image and description are discussed in Cockrell, *Demons of Disorder*, 8–11.

39. I personally believe that the description of this event is too precise for it not to have taken place, but it must be admitted that the event could be a fabrication. If it happened, it speaks to a relationship between street and minstrel culture; if it did not, then it may in fact represent a theatrical event imagined on the street.

40. See note 2. The premise of this essay remains valid whatever the makeup, but it does act as further argument against Juba's use of blackface.

41. See *Uncle Tom's Cabin*, 207.

42. Lhamon discusses Topsy's relationship with minstrelsy in detail; see *Raising Cain*, 141–42. *Uncle Tom's Cabin* and its relationship with minstrelsy in the novel and onstage is well covered by Lott, *Love and Theft*, 211–38. See also Haltunnen, *Confidence Men and Painted Women*, and Ann Douglas, *The Feminization of American Culture*, on a shift in perceptions among the middle classes, which would have included attitudes toward race.

43. Little Richard, quoted in Charles White, *The Life and Times of Little Richard* (New York: Pocket Books, 1984), 66, in Garber, *Vested Interests*, 302.

44. Juba never returned to the United States. From the time he left the Ethiopian Serenaders, he toured solo and with various individual (white) performers, playing in saloons and as an entr'acte at provincial theaters. There is no evidence that he performed as Lucy Long, or otherwise put on a dress except for his appearances with the full-fledged evening's minstrel show in 1848–49. By 1852 Juba/Lane had disappeared from the documentary record. In more than one later history of minstrelsy, he is said to have died in England; in one report, his skeleton was on display in Sheffield.

WORKS CITED

Adams, Bluford. *E Pluribus Barnum: The Great Showman and the Making of U.S. Popular Culture*. Minneapolis: University Minnesota Press, 1997.

Baker-Benfield, G. J. *Horrors of the Half-Known Life: Male Attitudes toward Women and Sexuality in Nineteenth-Century America*. New York: Routledge, 2000.

Bean, Annemarie. "Transgressing the Gender Divide: The Female Impersonator in Nineteenth-Century Blackface Minstrelsy." In *Inside the Minstrel Mask:*

Readings in Nineteenth-Century Blackface Minstrelsy, ed. Annemarie Bean, James V. Hatch, and Brooks McNamara, 245–56. Hanover, NH: Wesleyan University Press, 1996.

———. "Female Impersonation in Nineteenth-Century American Blackface Minstrelsy." Ph.D. diss., New York University, 2002.

Bean, Annemarie, James V. Hatch, and Brooks McNamara, eds. *Inside the Minstrel Mask: Readings in Nineteenth-Century Blackface Minstrelsy.* Hanover, NH: Wesleyan University Press, 1996.

Burke, Peter, ed. *New Perspectives on Historical Writing.* Cambridge, UK: Polity Press, 1991.

Butsch, Richard, ed. *For Fun and Profit: The Transformation of Leisure into Consumption.* Philadelphia: Temple University Press, 1990.

Cockrell, Dale. *Demons of Disorder: Early Blackface Minstrels and Their World.* New York: Cambridge University Press, 1997.

Cunningham, Hugh. *Leisure in the Industrial Revolution, c. 1780–c. 1880.* London: Croom Helm, 1980.

Darnton, Robert. *The Great Cat Massacre.* New York: Random House, 1984.

Day, Charles H. *Fun in Black; with The Origin of Minstrelsy by Col. T. Allston Brown.* New York: DeWitt, 1893.

DeFrantz, Thomas, ed. *Dancing Many Drums: Excavations in African American Dance.* Madison: University of Wisconsin Press, 2002.

Dickens, Charles. *American Notes for General Circulation.* 1842. New York: Penguin, 2000.

Dixon Gottschild, Brenda. *Digging the Africanist Presence in American Performance: Dance and Other Contexts.* Westport, CT: Greenwood Press, 1996.

Douglas, Ann. *The Feminization of American Culture.* New York: Knopf, 1977.

Emery, Lynne Fauley. *Black Dance: From 1619 to Today.* London: Dance Books, 1988.

Ferris, Leslie, ed. *Crossing the Stage: Controversies on Cross-Dressing.* New York: Routledge, 1993.

Foster, George G. *New York by Gas-Light: With Here and There a Streak of Sunshine.* New York: DeWitt and Davenport, 1850.

Garber, Marjorie B. *Vested Interests: Cross Dressing and Cultural Anxiety.* New York: Harper Perennial, 1993.

Ginzburg, Carlo. *The Cheese and the Worms.* New York: Penguin, 1982.

———. "Microhistory: Two or Three Things That I Know About It." *Critical Inquiry* 20, no. 1 (1993): 10–35.

Hall, Catherine. *White, Male and Middle Class: Explorations in Feminism and History.* Cambridge, England: Polity Press, 1992.

Halttunen, Karen. *Confidence Men and Painted Women: A Study of Middle-Class Culture in America.* New Haven, CT: Yale University Press, 1982.

Johnson, Stephen. "Past the Documents, To the Dance: The Witness to Juba in 1848." In *The Performance Text*, ed. Domenico Pietropaolo, 78–96. Ottawa: Legas Press, 1999.

Katz, Jonathan. *Love Stories: Sex between Men before Homosexuality.* Chicago: University of Chicago Press, 2001.

Katz, Jonathan Ned. *The Invention of Heterosexuality.* Chicago: University of Chicago Press, 2007.

Levi, Giovanni. "On Microhistory." In *New Perspectives on Historical Writing*, ed. Peter Burke, 93–113. Cambridge, England: Polity Press, 1991.

Lhamon, W. T. *Raising Cain: Blackface Performance from Jim Crow to Hip Hop.* Cambridge, MA: Harvard University Press, 1998.

Logan, Olive. "The Ancestry of Brudder Bones." *Harper's New Monthly Magazine* 58, no. 347 (1879): 687–98.

Lorimer, Douglas A. *Colour, Class and the Victorians.* Leicester: Holmes and Meier, 1978.

Lott, Eric. *Love and Theft: Blackface Minstrelsy and the American Working Class.* New York: Oxford University Press, 1993.

Lowry, Thomas P., M.D. *The Story the Soldiers Wouldn't Tell: Sex in the Civil War.* Mechanicsburg, PA: Stackpole Books, 1994.

Mahar, William J. *Behind the Burnt Cork Mask: Early Blackface Minstrelsy and Antebellum American Popular Culture.* Urbana: University of Illinois Press, 1999.

Mayhew, Henry. *London Labour and the London Poor.* Vol. 3. London: Griffin, Bohn, and Co., 1861–62. Reprint, New York: Dover, 1968.

McConachie, Bruce A. "Pacifying American Theatrical Audiences, 1820–1900." In *For Fun and Profit: The Transformation of Leisure into Consumption*, ed. Richard Butsch, 47–70. Philadelphia: Temple University Press, 1990.

Nathan, Hans. *Dan Emmett and the Rise of Early Negro Minstrelsy.* Norman: University of Oklahoma Press, 1977.

Reynolds, Harry. *Minstrel Memories: The Story of Burnt Cork Minstrelsy in Great Britain from 1836 to 1927.* London: A. Rivers, 1928.

Rice, Edward Le Roy. *Monarchs of Minstrelsy, from "Daddy" Rice to Date.* New York: Kenny [c. 1911].

Sappol, Michael. *A Traffic in Dead Bodies: Anatomy and Embodied Social Identity in Nineteenth-Century America.* Princeton, NJ: Princeton University Press, 2002.

Senelick, Laurence, ed. *Gender in Performance: The Presentation of Difference in the Performing Arts.* Hanover, NH: University Press of New England, 1992.

———. *The Changing Room: Sex, Drag and Theatre.* London: Routledge, 2000.

Stansell, Christine. *City of Women: Sex and Class in New York, 1789–1860.* New York: Knopf, 1986.

Stearns, Marshall, and Jean Stearns. *Jazz Dance: The Story of American Vernacular Dance.* New York: Macmillan, 1968.

Stowe, Harriet Beecher. *Uncle Tom's Cabin.* Ed. Elizabeth Ammons. New York: Norton, 1994.

Thompson, Robert Farris. "An Aesthetic of the Cool: West African Dance." In *The Theater of Black Americans: A Collection of Critical Essays*, ed. Errol Hill, 99–111. New York: Applause Theatre Book Publishers, 1987.

Toll, Robert C. *Blacking Up: The Minstrel Show in Nineteenth-Century America.* New York: Oxford University Press, 1974.

Winans, Robert B. "Early Minstrel Show Music, 1843–1852." In *Inside the Minstrel Mask: Readings in Nineteenth-Century Blackface Minstrelsy*, ed. Annemarie Bean, James V. Hatch, and Brooks McNamara, 141–62. Hanover, NH: Wesleyan University Press, 1996.

Winter, Marian Hannah. "Juba and American Minstrelsy." *Dance Index* 6, no. 2 (1947): 28–47.

Wittke, Carl. *Tambo and Bones: A History of the American Minstrel Stage.* Durham, NC: Duke University Press, 1930.

PAUL BABIAK

Channeling Juba's Dance—a Rehearsal Journal

> *The following rehearsal journal excerpts are from actor and dramaturg*
> *Paul Babiak, who observed as a short play was created from historical*
> *material about William Henry Lane ("Juba"). The "collective creation"*
> *evolved from the research of Juba scholar Stephen Johnson and the*
> *improvisatory work of three female actor/dancers.* Channeling Juba's
> Dance *was presented by Handmade Theatre at the Festival of Original*
> *Theatre (FOOT) at the Drama Centre of the University of Toronto, in*
> *Ontario, Canada, in March 2004. Invited to observe by Johnson, who was*
> *the dramaturg for this play, Babiak reflects on the process, his*
> *preconceptions, and what he imagines about Juba.*

Wednesday, February 18, 2004

When I arrive for a rehearsal of *Channeling Juba's Dance*, I see Stephen Johnson and
a diverse trio of young dancers (Jennifer Johnson, Kathleen Salvador, and Elizabeth
Dawn Snell) musing over scattered photocopies, reading to each other,
underlining and highlighting. They are apparently sorting through a lot of reviews
about some sort of entertainer, now and then reading out brief snatches of phrase:
"such toes and such heelings," and, "His pedal execution is a thing to wonder at."
A dancer of some kind, then? "He trills, he shakes, he screams, he laughs." Sounds
like an interesting sort of dancer. I pull out my clipboard and start making notes on
a yellow pad: it's a conditioned reflex, a strategy for coping with the bizarre.

Self-consciousness forbids my asking what's going on. But while Jennifer,
Kathleen, and Elizabeth are in discussion, Stephen comes over to me and asks if I've
ever heard of Juba. I confess I haven't. Stephen picks up a black paper folder
containing a set of photocopies and hands it to me: this is the dramaturgy package
for *Channeling Juba's Dance*. It includes the handbill for an engagement of Pell's
Serenaders at the Theatre Royal, Birmingham, on Thursday, December 21, 1848.
The company of G. W. Pell apparently performed a standard "Nigger Minstrel"
show, as it was unfortunately called then, a form that survived in the United States
into the 1920s. There are some contemporary pictures, including one of Pell's
Serenaders as a banjo orchestra, seated on chairs in a semicircle, with Pell in

blackface at one end playing the bones. At the other end sits a character with a tambourine, identified by a subscript as Juba. Inset are portraits of both Juba and Pell: the former is a broodingly handsome young black man. Other pictures include a couple of 19th-century-style caricatures: a black man, wearing leather high boots with pointed toes, usually lifting one knee in terpsichorean frenzy, yet with a strangely contemplative expression on his face.

As I leaf through the package, Stephen sits beside me and narrates some of what we know, or think likely, about William Henry Lane, a.k.a. Juba, London's performing sensation of the late 1840s. He was an American, probably born in the Five Points area of New York. He enjoyed several years of celebrity in England as an interpreter of specialty dances based on the traditions of the Deep South; at one point he performed as a headliner in the famous park at Vauxhall. Later in his career he was to be seen in numerous less distinguished venues. Finally, in the early 1850s, he disappeared.

There are some biographical materials in the dramaturgical package—two "posthumous reports" drawn from recollections preserved by social historian Henry Mayhew and early theater historian T. Alliston Brown. These evoke a story, with an almost fairy-tale structure, of a "regular black" who, success having gone to his head, aspired to ride "in his own carriage," married a white woman, and died miserably for his presumption, to have his skeleton put on display at the Surrey Music Hall, Sheffield. Stephen has gone to a great deal of trouble trying to verify or disprove these reports, without success either way.

It has been surmised that Juba's dance incorporated elements of southern American festival and plantation dance (the Birmingham handbill says so)—these having possibly derived in turn from African tribal dance. He is also thought very likely to have been an early exponent of tap. In any case, he must have been a highly versatile performer: he apparently also did female impersonation in the character of "Miss Lucy Long," sang songs like "Come Back Steben" and "Jenny, Put de Kittle On," and played the tambourine. The package includes pianoforte sheet music for some of the songs listed in the handbill: Juba's songs, as published at least, call for a tenor voice with an extremely broad range—from D above middle C to D two octaves above. Finally, there are a number of excerpts from contemporary reviews. It is these reviews, for the most part extravagantly laudatory, that will form the basis for this collectively composed performance.

None of the reviews appear to be written by or for technical experts on dance: in consequence, no precise descriptive record of Juba's dance method is contained in them. Instead, the pieces attempt—in 19th-century journalistic language—to evoke the impressions left on one who has seen and heard Juba's performances in another who has not. A recurrent motif is that of the incapacity of all possible language adequately to evoke Juba's dance:

> The manner in which he beats time with his feet, and the extraordinary command which he possesses over them, can only be believed by those who have been present at his exhibition.[1]
>
> We must confess that we were never more struck with any performance, and, were we to attempt a description, we should have to surrender in despair.
>
> Single shuffle, double shuffle, cut and cross-cut; snapping his fingers, rolling his eyes, turning in his knees, presenting the backs of his legs in front, spinning about on his toes and heels like nothing but the man's fingers on the tambourine; dancing with two legs, two right legs, two wooden legs, two wire legs, two spring legs—all sorts of legs and no legs— what is this to him?[2]

Many of the descriptions the reviews contain are highly rhythmic, employing bursts of short phrases in succession, which accumulate and gradually lengthen out into long streams of excited language. For example:

> In his pas, cuts, shuffles, double-shuffles, pirouettes, in every motion of his limbs or body, he keeps the most exact time, and executes some of the most astonishing effects that ever were witnessed in the dancing phenomenon. . . .
>
> Surely he cannot be flesh and blood, but some more subtle substance, or how could he turn, and twine, and twist, and twirl, and hop, and jump, and kick, and throw his feet almost with a velocity that makes one think they are playing hide-and-seek with a flash of lightning![3]

Stephen has removed these quotations from their specific contexts and organized them, without citations, into sections under subject headings according to the qualities of Juba's dance to which they testify: authenticity, analogy/imitation and reference to other choreographies, precision, wild abandon, and so on.

I think I'm getting the idea: there will be tap dancing, an 1840s minstrel show— COOL! My mind's ear begins to swarm with melodies from *Showboat*. It only remains to see how this group will go about bringing it off. After quite a bit of time musing, underlining, and highlighting, Stephen persuades the dancers to select a single passage and put it on its feet. Standing in a circle, they read to each other from their selections of phrases; the air fills with a collage of exclamations: "exquisite time," "he bounds, whirls and astonishes," "indescribable activity of body." The dancers begin to move in a circle and cross around each other, moving across the stage. It's good; it's very expressive. It's not quite Bojangles Robinson, but it feels like it could lead to something. They do the same thing again a couple of times, elaborating, trying to reproduce the patterns in which the words fell, the way they crescendoed together, how they might end a phrase. Jennifer and Elizabeth sit down again while Kathleen continues tap-dancing softly in her running shoes. Each of the dancers will have a solo. Suggestions are made and rehearsal continues.

During a break over cookies and soda, Stephen and the dancers fill me in on what took place at the first two rehearsals, which I missed. At the first meeting, the reviews were read out loud and discussed. Each of the performers began making a selection of the passages that were most suggestive to her. At their second meeting the group discussed in greater detail what had really impressed them in the dramaturgical package. They wrote down images and series of words and began talking over rough ideas for creating a dance out of the words elicited from these white male Victorian reviewers by the exertions of this young African American man.

I'm delighted and intrigued, and instantly get the wrong idea. Of course! We use the language to inspire us to invent tap dancing! We retrace the descent of jazz from minstrelsy! Re-creationist theater as a form of social anthropology!

Fortunately, I haven't time to express this lunacy before Stephen explains the real concept of the show to me. The goal of the collective is *not* to attempt re-creating Juba's dance—it is to let the language that has arisen in response to Juba provoke a reciprocal dance response in Jennifer, Elizabeth, and Kathleen. Consequently, there will be no music: the movement will arise in direct response to the words, which will be selected from among the excerpts—or supplied by analogy with them—to accompany the piece.

No banjos, then? No *Showboat* medley? I become quiet and concentrate on my cookie.

This is the second theatrical incarnation of Juba. In an earlier play written by Stephen, a Historian narrates Juba's story as the documents, personified in two other actors and introduced in antithetical pairs, squabble over the silent figure of a single dancer, Jennifer, whose movements instantiate the speakers' words. In the play, the dance is contained within a structure of language and never breaks free of it; this time the language will be broken up and function as ancillary to the movement.

After the break, Stephen suggests that one of the combinations they might try is three different interpretations of the same text. Everybody is feeling comfortable after their cookies and soft drinks. They start to work on one particular sentence from a review of Juba: "He jumps, he capers, he crosses his legs, he stamps his heels; he dances on his knees, on his ankles, he ties his limbs into double knots, and untwists them as one might a skein of silk; and all these marvels are done in strict time and appropriate rhythm."[4]

The strategy in developing the piece will be to build up this central phrase and then subdivide it by solos. Some alternative means of mining the text for further movement ideas are talked over. A recurrent pattern of words in Juba's reviews suggests a series of antitheses (quick/slow, high art/folk art, happy/furious), which in turn suggest various forms of dance. These can be mirrored in a series of "Circles of Contradiction" in which two dancers at a time will manifest contrasting energies. A couple of the reviews include evocative references to classical dance with an implicit comparison of Juba to the Wilis—vengeful female apparitions—of Giselle.[5] This suggests there might be a moment at which Elizabeth may don her pointe shoes and execute a pas de bourrée across the back of the stage as Jennifer performs a modern phrase up front. There's the possibility for another contrast between Elizabeth's pointe work and Kathleen's tap. Finally, one of the reviews consists of a series of parallel ejaculations, each beginning "Such . . . !" "Such . . . !"[6] The climactic structure of that passage suggests that it might somehow be useful as a climax, or as a final cadence for the piece.

Notes are made to develop these notions further at the next full group rehearsal on Sunday. Saturday's rehearsal will focus instead on the solos. Stephen exhorts the group to think about their solos before coming in.

Saturday, February 21, 2004

Jennifer is lying on the floor trying to wrench a concept for her solo out of a page of prose. Kathleen has brought her tap shoes and is clattering across the stage, working on her solo. Her virtuosity is really impressive. She taps with a natural ease and gracefulness, lunging suddenly into jazz moves with almost feral vigor. Relapsing into playfulness, she experiments briefly with a series of hand claps to her elbows, knees, and feet of the type that Stephen notes used to be called ham-bone. Watching Kathleen experiment with sequences of steps, I imagine various possible suggestions I might make, all of which have to do with speech rhythms found in the reviews and patterns that could suggest a particular contemporary dancing style. I think about my unfulfilled longing for a blackface banjo orchestra, replete with bones and tambourine. Nowadays, such a performance couldn't be received as other than abominably racist. I don't want people to think I'm abominably racist. I just like tap dancing. And banjos. I can live without burnt cork.

Almost as if he knew what I was thinking, Stephen comes over, sits down beside me, and we talk about the reasons for not using Kathleen's ham-bone routine. The point is not re-creation. "You can go, 'He [Juba] did this, this, and this' based on your knowledge of what tap dancers do today. But Juba did other things as well: he did imitations of people; he did a drag role as Miss Lucy Long, he parodied people. Pell's entire orchestra used to use their musical instruments to replicate the sound of a train."

"This is a really romantic image," says Stephen. "But I can see him, walking down the street, and hearing all the sounds; the sound of trains—which were new at that time; of the telegraph, which was new—and wanting to re-create them in his performances."

Juba, like Stephen Foster, may never even have seen a plantation. (Stephen Foster never saw a plantation? I didn't know that.) The odds are that he grew up in Five Points in New York—where Dickens saw him—where he learned to be a professional entertainer and picked up an idiom that would sell. But Stephen's idea seems to be that that idiom turned out to be more than just a cash cow. It apparently became a very subtle mode of expression. That's the whole working assumption of Channeling Juba's Dance: like Falstaff, who was so witty that he made others witty, Juba was so expressive that the reverberations he set off in his contemporaries can stimulate new performances today.

Jen, in the meantime, is looking for ideas to fill out the group section. Stephen goes over to sit with her, and they discuss the options. The Circles of Contradiction can be developed out into full-blown dance duels, contrasting the styles of each pair of dancers—these duels can grow out of transitions from the collective numbers based on simple antitheses that evoke paradoxes drawn from what reviewers' descriptions lead us to imagine about Juba's style—for example, the sense of communion a performer can have with his audience ("integration") as opposed to the solitude of a black American performing for houses of white Britons ("isolation").

This rehearsal ends without anything definite being set. Once at home, I fortuitously stumble across Stephen's essay "The Witness to Juba in 1848" in a book I picked up: The Performance Text,[7] edited by Domenico Pietropaolo. It gives a full account of the scholarship Stephen has already done on Juba's dance and explains the ideas behind the dramaturgical method he's employing on the show.

I'm particularly interested in the fifth of his observations on "Provisional Historiographies":

> Some historians, in the (vain) effort to "get to" the subject-event, attempt reconstructions of the performance from the documents. One class of Shakespearean scholar does this, and it is a particularly strong practice among dance historians.[8]

Crushed again.

> I have been researching this, along with a dancer, with respect to Juba, and offer, as one last provisional historio-graphy, the sight of one contemporary body imitating (reading) graphic images that are themselves imitations (readings) of another body dancing.[9]

Hey, look, there are pictures of Jen!

> I add that this means of "getting to" the dance is predicated on the assumption that the images are based on firsthand viewing, and the intention of accurate recording; this assumption is questionable.[10]

I hadn't thought of that.

> Does the imitation help? I cannot answer that. But as imitation with difference, it may be a kind of useful parody. At the very least, imitation with the "difference" of modern dress may draw analogies with contemporary dance styles. Such similarities may be serendipitous, the result of the limits and tendencies of the human body in motion. However, they may also manifest the legacy of an oral-performative tradition—the main tenet of which is imitation with difference.[11]

It reads almost like a manifesto for the work we're doing on the show.

Sunday, February 22, 2004

Tonight, rehearsing in Robert Gill Theatre—the space the company will actually be performing in—Jen announces we're going to focus on contradictions and Juba descriptions. Stephen proposes an additional exercise: each of the dancers will perform a solo while the other two describe what she's doing, just as Juba's critics described his performances out of their impressions. After much fascinating experimentation with speaking and dancing out antithetical terms, Jen tries placing herself side by side with Kathleen and drawing an imaginary line across the stage between them.

Jennifer Johnson and Elizabeth Dawn Snell look for a way to embody in dance the idea that Juba might have felt both "isolated" and "integrated" in the minstrel show. Photograph by Stephen Johnson. Used with permission.

"Abandoned," Kathleen exclaims, and performs a wild jeté.

"Precision," says Jennifer, and executes a series of restrained robotic motions.

Kathleen steps across the line directly behind Jen and adopts movements like hers while speaking her word. Hearing her, Jen steps across the line, so she is beside Kathleen again; she repeats the word "abandoned" and delivers a series of judo kicks to the air. The pattern works—there is just the right combination of sameness and otherness between the two performers and their motions. Working the same way, Kathleen and Elizabeth see what they can do with "graceful" and "grotesque," "genuine" and "artificial," "classical" and "popular," and so on. None of these works for them, but Jen gets an idea and sells it to Elizabeth before trying it out. On the one hand, she explains, Juba was fully integrated into the minstrel show—he was Mr. Tambo to Pell's Mr. Bones, and so on—and yet once he became a featured performer he must have become alienated from them. He would have come on, done his specialties, and then gone off again. They work with the contrast between "isolated" and "integrated," and this time they produce something they enjoy doing, that Stephen and I enjoy watching.

Now that I'm watching these three really talented dancers work with such intensity, I'm gradually forgetting the banjos and the bones. My own essentially reactionary tastes in dance are gradually being seduced by this company's flair for experimentation—and particularly by the way they're using language. The dancer's silence is a convention for which I always entertained an unquestioning respect— but I'm questioning it now, watching these performers work on their solos. As Elizabeth executes a particularly graceful turn, Jen and Kathleen sit watching her and improvise descriptions of her, addressed to nobody in particular: "She's coming toward me, red hair, red dress, the stripes; now she's bending, turning. . . . " The language is inadequate to contain the beauty of Elizabeth's gesture and instead accompanies it, sets it in relief. I feel how Juba's critics must have been beguiled, as one is always beguiled by a skillful performer: the way Fred Astaire made you feel it was easy to tap, that all you had to do was wish hard and you could do it. I feel Juba's reviewers danced along with him across stages built of words.

There's plenty of material for the performance now; all that needed is an order. They discuss options for finding moments when Elizabeth can get up en pointe and when Kathleen can put on her tap shoes. It could happen right at the very beginning, after which the specialty shoes could come off for the duration of the show. On the other hand, the whole idea might wait until just before Kathleen's solo, almost at the end of the show. In either case it's decided, the verbal reference to the Wilis ought to be used and somehow associated with Elizabeth.

At the end of the rehearsal I go home, thinking about a dancer's silence and about Juba's laugh. What did it mean, that laugh? The reviewers singled it out as one of his distinguishing marks: "There never was such a laugh as the laugh of Juba—there is in it the concentrated laugh of fifty comic pantomimes; it has no relation to the chuckle, and least of all to the famous horse-laugh: not a bit of it—it is a laugh distinct, a laugh apart, a laugh by itself—clear, ringing, echoing, resonant, harmonious, full of rejoicing and mighty mirth and fervent fun." I imagine the laughter of a young black man, growing up in a bad neighborhood in the United States before the Civil War, emancipated by the rhythms of popular songs, finding a voice for his rage and his exultation in the stamping of his boots, becoming celebrated by crowds of white men whose praise was the sincerest expression of their contempt, prospering by the public performance of his independence and his defiance. Perhaps that is what is expressing itself through that expanding structure in all the reviews: the cry of a soul in its mad dash toward freedom.

NOTES

1. For further information about reviews, as well as further history and illustration, search for "The Juba Project" Web site (through the University of Toronto and Stephen Johnson), where a previous version of this diary was posted.

2. Charles Dickens, *American Notes* (London: Oxford University Press, 1957), 90–91.

3. *Manchester Examiner*, October 17, 1848.

4. *Morning Post*, June 21, 1848.

5. *Era*, June 18, 1848; *Manchester Examiner*, October 17, 1848.

6. *Mirror and United Kingdom Magazine*, July 1848 ("Such mobility of muscles, such flexibility of joints, such boundings, such slidings, such gyrations, such toes and such heelings, such backwardings and forwardings, such posturings, such firmness of foot, such elasticity of tendon, such mutation of movement, such vigour, such variety, such natural grace, such powers of endurance, such potency of pastern").

7. Domenico Pietropaolo, ed., *The Performance Text* (Ottawa: Legas, 1999).

8. Stephen Johnson, "Past the Documents, to the Dance: The Witness to Juba in 1848," in *The Performance Text*, ed. Domenico Pietropaolo (Ottawa: Legas, 1999), 86.

9. Ibid.

10. Ibid.

11. Ibid.

WORKS CITED

Bly, Mark, ed. *The Production Notebooks.* New York: Theatre Communications Group, 1996.

Channeling Juba's Dance. Unpublished dramaturgical materials, assembled by Stephen Johnson, University of Toronto.

Johnson, Stephen. "Past the Documents, to the Dance: The Witness to Juba in 1848." In *The Performance Text*, ed. Domenico Pietropaolo, 78–96. Ottawa: Legas, 1999.

8

Ausdruckstanz, Workers' Culture, and Masculinity in Germany in the 1920s and 1930s

YVONNE HARDT

This essay focuses on issues of masculinity in the context of Germany during the *Ausdruckstanz* (expressionist dance) era and the workers' cultural movement in the 1920s and 1930s. Illuminating the interrelatedness of these two movements allows for an interesting analysis of the political dimensions and the gendered implications of this heterogeneous, modern dance form that developed at the turn of the 20th century and blossomed significantly in the democratic era of the Weimar Republic. While *Ausdruckstanz* has often been regarded as an abstract art form closely related to other contemporaneous expressionistic cultural productions, and thus been situated strongly within a bourgeois cultural milieu, there actually existed many ties between these two reformatory movements.[1] Most significantly, both were influenced by the life reform movement (*Lebensreformbewegung*), which envisioned that a different society could be achieved by a new body culture (*Körperkultur*). I explore the reasons modern dance could become so interesting for the workers' cultural movement. This demands a shift in gender perspective. So far, *Ausdruckstanz* has been predominantly discussed as a sign for an increasing emancipation of women in dance and society in general.[2] However, *Ausdruckstanz* also provided a chance to "rediscover" dance for men. Not only was one of its major protagonists a man, Rudolf Laban, but modern dance offered also an alternative to classical ballet, which in the eyes of the contemporaries had made "cheesy, wimpy figures out of men on stage."[3]

Issues of masculinity were especially paramount in the context of the workers' cultural movement because they were vehemently negotiated within a milieu that associated the fight for emancipation closely with the male worker and his physical strength. This explains why there was continuous emphasis on strong and stereotypical images of masculinity in the modern dance scene. As such, looking at dance can also provide a critical analysis of how some of the emancipatory beliefs in regard to gender issues that were articulated within the context of the Socialist and Communist movement were highly ambivalent when put into physical action. I do not want simply to insinuate an argument for the lack of challenging gender perceptions within the dance culture. Rather, I want to elucidate the way this endeavor was tried despite a setting of continuous social pressure.

While the reliance on a strong male body and a distinction between what is considered female and male movement continued to exist within the modern physical and dance culture in the 1920s and 1930s, one also needs to consider the acts of appropriation on the side of the workers as these new movement forms of modern dance imbued them with the power to act in a new cultural setting. In the same way that an analysis of gender issues complicates any linear interpretation of modern dance in terms of concrete (political or emancipatory) meanings, the interrelatedness between modern dance and the Socialist or Communist workers' culture does not necessarily imply that modern dance participation signified exclusively a modern or progressive political worldview. However, *Ausdruckstanz* did provide new forms of physical agency to the worker and the ability to contest an elitist art conception.

The fact that neither masculinity nor the political dimensions of moving bodies have played a significant part in the historiography of *Ausdruckstanz* is not based on a lack of sources. Quite the contrary, due to the constant need for justification, many publications featuring male dancers and critiques appeared, which are an invaluable source for this essay and any discussion about issues of masculinity.[4] To limit this essay in scope I will focus predominantly on thematic aspects that are evoked by the work and writings of three very different male dance protagonists of the time: Rudolf Laban, Martin Gleisner, and Jean (Hans) Weidt. Although Laban, one of the most important figures of *Ausdruckstanz*, was not explicitly political in the 1920s, he was highly influential in the modern dance scene, including members who were politically active. For instance, he was a teacher of Martin Gleisner, who eventually promoted and developed Laban's movement choirs throughout Germany in the context of the Social Democratic workers' cultural movement. Even more radical in terms of political visions was the Communist dancer Jean (Hans) Weidt, who worked with his dance collective both on showing the physical suffering and the strength of the worker's body and on discovering/exploring the body as a site for liberation as well as for artistic creation.

Right from the beginning, *Ausdruckstanz* not only signified a revolution of artistic dancing but was closely linked to a critical perspective on an increasingly mechanized world. In the context that led to the disastrous First World War, there was a general feeling of crisis in the Weimar Republic, the falling apart of a system that engendered feelings of instability in the individual; *Ausdruckstanz* symbolically embodied this feeling of crisis by generating movements that were based in an unconscious realm and showed dark, heavy, rhythmic, ecstatic movements. At the same time, it was seen as a site for liberation and the source of a more "natural" or "archaic" access to the body. Dancers wanted to swing freely and be united in that way within a community of people of shared beliefs. As such, *Ausdruckstanz* did not happen predominantly on the stages of theaters; dancers found new venues, many of them in nature in order to sense the liberating effect of their art, which could also be closely associated with a "return" to nature.[5]

Giving up the codified movements of ballet in favor of movements that played with relaxation, tension, and weight, *Ausdruckstanz* inevitably meant to some extent to challenge gender norms. Major female dance figures in *Ausdruckstanz*, such as Mary Wigman, Valeska Gert, and Vera Skoronel, broke away in quite different ways with the ideal of the beautiful, lighthearted, ephemeral dancing woman. In contrast to the first generation of modern dancers (e.g., Isadora Duncan, who also significantly influenced modern dance in Germany), they now added into the dance vocabulary rhythmical stepping and staccato movements (Wigman), grotesque physical endeavors (Gert), or geometrized forms (Skoronel). This never became a mainstream conception of dancing, but it opened possibilities for women to enter the dance stage as a "universal subject," both in how and what they could represent and also as actively creating their own dances. Accordingly, *Ausdruckstanz* has been often identified as a female artistic revolution.[6]

By the turn of the 20th century and also in the more liberal Weimar Republic, dancing was clearly encoded as a feminine art. Even those who championed the modern dance or the new expressionistic culture (*Ausdruckskultur*) had a very dichotomous conception of what constituted female and male movements. For instance, Hans Fischer, who published several books on body cultural movement, postulates: "Almost everywhere one considers beautiful the strong and able man who exposes at first sight his ability for fight, work and reproduction. Beauty in a man is always linked to a task."[7] In contrast, he perceives the beauty in women as having no specific purpose and physical labor as something that hardly renders a woman beautiful. He concludes: "Because the dance is the art of physical expression, as sports is the domain of strength, and it is for this reason that man has a greater but not an exclusive part in sports, so, too, in the area of dance it is the woman."[8] This distinction was commonly shared by many activists of the movement culture, and it was the context in which men had to negotiate and find ways to conquer dance without being challenged in terms of their masculinity.[9] Many of them saw a great chance in *Ausdruckstanz* both to allow "masculine" movement to exist in dance and to challenge implicit gender norms.

Men needed to contest the presumption that dancing was a feminine art and found different strategies for this. One of these men was Rudolf Laban. Born in 1879 in the Austrian-Hungarian Empire into a wealthy family, he rejected the military career that was envisioned for him, studied art and architecture, and finally became interested in dance.[10] His summer schools at Monte Veritá (1913–15), a small village in Switzerland close to the beautiful Lake Maggiore, established the format for his improvisation-based dancing and teaching. While the rest of Europe was enduring the horror of the war, this little retreat functioned as a refuge for many expressionistic artists and those inspired by the life reform movement. Dancers were often nude, and besides their daily exercises, participants also worked in the fields trying to establish an autonomous lifestyle apart from the industrial, metropolitan centers. The borders between life and art were supposed to be challenged.[11]

Laban belonged to those who believed in the power of natural flowing body movement, imbuing it with an almost religious meaning. There was even an egalitarian approach to what constituted dancing. He conceived of all movements as part of a larger cosmic swinging, and this was the basis of all dancing. It would allow everybody to be a dancer if only he or she connected to this universal pulsation. As was the case for many of his contemporaries, "swinging" was a major aspect of his practical and theoretical understanding of dance. Swinging (*Schwingung*), which in German signifies both swinging and radiating, was the central term to contest the metric rhythm (*Takt*) that was associated with mechanization. It also described (in the sense of radiating) a form of communication that would bypass intellectual understanding and function directly via a form of "muscular sympathy." Philosophers like Ludwig Klages and prominent members of the body cultural movement like Rudolf Bode saw swinging as an antidote to rationalization because it meant a continuous movement that could not be separated into single analytical entities.[12] However, Laban classified, structured, and described the different pathways of swinging quite analytically in his so-called swinging scales, even while believing in their anatomical plausibility and naturalness.[13]

In general, Laban was very analytical and interested in a structural approach to the understanding of dance. In the period between 1920 and 1950, starting with his enormously successful book *Die Welt des Tänzers* (*The World of Dancers*), he published the most comprehensive analysis of movement and dancing up to this point.[14] Starting in Hamburg in 1923, he began successfully establishing schools throughout Germany, systematically spreading his analytical method of dancing with the help of his eager students. Inevitably, there is ambivalence about Laban's believing in the freeing of movement expression that resists intellectual analysis, on the one hand, and the undertaking of a precise analysis of movement and an attempt to impose his teaching method as the proper form to learn dancing, on the other hand.

Increasingly, the analysis of movement in regard to anatomical plausibility, to space (*choreutic*), rhythms, and also to its expressional value (*eucinetic*), became central to Laban's work. This was accompanied and fostered by his interest in notating dancing. It required a systematic analysis of dance in order to make precise decisions about which elements should be included in the notation. Notation was also a means to render the dance independent of the dancer and to make it last, thus freeing it from both the ephemeral and the physicality that were closely linked to femininity at that time. Dance has always been seen as ephemeral and thus without the stable, universal, and lasting qualities that were assigned to other art forms, such as writing or painting or music, with its strong affiliation to mathematics. The tendency to give more credit and standing to the art of dancing through notation had already had a long history at that point.[15] Laban's attempts to develop a dance notation and a means of creating dances on an analytical basis appear to have strategic reasons because of gender conceptions. While Laban relied heavily on his female assistants, starting with Mary Wigman, and later on Lisa Ullmann, he nonetheless argued that there was an essential difference between men and women in dancing. For Laban, women provided the emotional and sensational dimension of dance; men had an analytical focus on the art.[16]

Other aspects in Laban's conception of dance also allowed for an acquisition of dance by men without challenging their masculinity. Laban distinguished between different types of dancers and declared that each individual should dance according to his or her physical constitution. He differentiated between "low," "middle," and "high" dancers. Although these types were not exclusively linked to certain genders, there was nonetheless a tendency to perceive most male dancers as belonging to the category of "low" dancers, meaning that they kept their movements low to the ground. Energetic stamping and walking with bended knees became central to the new movement vocabulary of *Ausdruckstanz*. Power was centered in the legs and abdominals. The movement never seemed light, instead showing a great deal of effort, in contrast to "high" dancers, who were ostensibly light, dancing on their toes, deriving their source of movement from the solar plexus and using the arms lightly to enhance a feeling of flowing. This was, in a sense the movement quality of the classical ballerina but could also be found in *Ausdruckstanz*. This was definitely "charged" as a feminine art of moving. The possibilities of integrating these different types of dancers were ideally realized in the form of movement choirs.

Movement choirs were Laban's most striking development in the Weimar Republic, and they played a significant role in successfully integrating men into his work, as well as attracting the workers' culture movement to modern dance. Basically, movement choirs were group improvisations by lay dancers based on Laban's movement analysis.[17] A constitutive element was the interrelatedness of dancers to each other. Although the main focus was on following the leader of the group, improvisational structures were developed that emphasized spatial and dynamic patterns: moving toward each other or apart, reaching up while others crawled close to the floor, or moving slowly while others ran. This allowed for some individual freedom in executing the movements because the emphasis was on the relation to one another and not predominantly on synchronization. For instance, the whole group might be moving downward, but the way they moved differed from dancer to dancer.

As such, the movement choirs could ideally incorporate and make use of different types of dancers, as Fritz Böhme, one of the best-known dance critics of the time, pointed out: "By putting individual dancers of the choir into different functions according to their own preference of moving, Laban broke the coherence of the corps de ballet and created a living ensemble that was at one moment characterized by contrast and then by closeness. This created the illusion of a flood of movement."[18] Other critics also noted that "low" dancers were well integrated, although they did not always share Böhme's sympathy for grounded and deep movements, which they often described as barbaric (*hottentotisch*). An ostensible lack of synchronization and the untidy image of the choirs were actually off-putting to some audience members. Therefore, while it seemed on the one hand a typically gendered movement vocabulary, it nonetheless challenged contemporaneous perceptions of what constitutes dance. The leniency in regard to synchronization was possible because the main purpose of the movement choirs was not to perform onstage for an audience but to have an experience within a group.[19]

Yet another reason for the successful integration of men and nondancers had to do with the elimination of the star system. The dancing in a movement choir did not aim at the solitary presentation of a single body; thus it deviated from presenting one to any voyeuristic gaze that was associated with the position of the star dancer, especially the sexualized ballerina at that time. Movement choirs were conceptualized as a community event, which not only made them extremely attractive for male dancers—and most of the men involved in the modern dance movement were dancing in choirs—but also related to the belief of sharing and creating a community on physical grounds that was fostered within left-wing circles.

In this context, movement choirs became relevant because they could both symbolically express the newly envisioned social community and make it happen performatively for the participants. Thus, movement choirs were part of the extensive debate about the meaning, quality, and purpose of the social community that dominated Weimar thought. In the construction of multiple discursive models of "community," the Cultural Socialists played a significant part. This group of Socialists, which was mainly associated with the Social Democrats (SPD), understood Socialism as a political, economical, and cultural movement.[20] In the light of Weimar reality that had neither realized the desired revolution nor created better living conditions for the workers, the Cultural Socialists wanted to anticipate a better future, at least in part, by a "cultural uplift" of the working class.[21] They also believed that the body was a central vantage point for the reform of the worker's life and his or her liberation. Anna Siemsen, Max Adler, Valtin Hartig, and many others associated with the Cultural Socialists believed that even more problematic than the low wages was the detachment (*Entfremdung*) of the worker's body by reducing him or her to a pure object of work. Therefore, it was a proclaimed goal to fight this physical abuse.[22]

Martin Gleisner was the most prominent man at the meeting point of modern dance as it was promoted by Laban and the workers' cultural movement. Born in 1897 in Berlin as a Slovakian citizen of Jewish parents, he first

Figure 8.1   A moment from the movement choir *Götzendienst* by Albrecht Knust. Women on the ground reach and kick upward with their legs while the men tower above them. From Martin Gleisner's book *Tanz für alle* in 1928.

studied acting and then dance with Laban. Eventually he became one of the leading protagonists in establishing and promoting movement choirs, in the context of both the modern dance culture and the workers' cultural movement. Being an active member of the Social Democratic Party and believing that culture was a necessary part of imbuing workers with a sense of hope and vision for the future, he vehemently tried to integrate worker youth into his movement choirs and believed that this group activity could simultaneously create and represent the strength of the worker's community. He offered dance training in the context of Socialist youth clubs, thus providing easier access to dance for those who were not familiar with private dance schools and could not afford them. Gleisner also established movement choirs as a key element in huge mass pageants of the Social Democratic Party. His *Tanz für alle* (*Dance for All*) not only was one of the most successful and highly praised books on modern dance for the lay public, explaining both its function and its workings, but also offered a distinctive Socialist interpretation of dance and its political purposes.

According to Gleisner, who was central in articulating and developing a proper view of dance for the Cultural Socialist, *Ausdruckstanz* and especially its lay version of the movement choirs fit into an ideal of an art that focused on physical sensation and group improvisation. In this way, dance could activate and mobilize the body while simultaneously rejecting the competition characteristic of sports and capitalistic performance standards. In comparison, folk dancing was associated with being backward, and ballet symbolized bourgeois decadence by focusing solely on virtuosity while simultaneously arousing the sexual fantasies of male viewers. Even worse, Gleisner argued, ballet developed originally at the royal courts, thus making any relevance of this art form for the working class impossible.[23] In contrast, movement choirs not only were a new and thus yet historically unspoiled art form but also could be seen as the enactment of a specific understanding of an idealized social community.

The Cultural Socialists fostered the idea that the integration of the individual into the community should enhance individuality and not abolish it; therefore, the movement choirs were considered an ideal physical and social training method. In the improvisational process, one not only had to react to others and understand that the group could function only when everybody worked together, but simultaneously every dancer could move in an individual way. Albrecht Knust, a well-known student of Laban who also participated in the realization of movement choirs for the Socialist Youth, wrote: "It is a fact that nothing is more adequate to develop the capacity to act socially within a community than movement games. One has to comprehend in every moment what function one has to play in the context of the whole group. Doing too little is as harmful as doing too much."[24] When commenting on Jenny Gertz's work with children, Ilse Loesch illustrated this idea as follows: "The children learn within the group that when they stop the others cannot move."[25] Thus, the movement choirs were considered to train sensibilities that enabled a better integration into a group, as well as providing preparation to lead it. Moreover, Gleisner argued that it was necessary to learn from individual difference in order to work in groups: "By becoming aware of one's self and the challenge of a different movement type one gains a lot . . . the strengthening of one's own disposition and the taking on of that which is lacking, so that one's own base is challenged but rather enhanced."[26]

Dancers constantly focused on each other in order to follow the movements of their peers; they also believed that their dancing would generate a form of group spirit that would gather strength within the group as much as performatively creating it for the audience. The act of doing was at least as important as the goal of representing a specific content. Gleisner was very skeptical about the idea that movement choir performances could communicate explicit political ideas, even as he integrated them into huge mass pageants like the one for the Party Congress (*Parteitag*) of the Socialists in Magdeburg (1929).[27] He believed that their meaning was rather more symbolically and closely linked to the movement and its qualities. Movements could show force and suffering, the joining of groups and energies, and desired acts of unification. They could evoke uplifting spirits by physically engaging the onlookers.

Nonetheless, these movement choirs needed justification in the context of the workers' culture movement, which was still defined predominantly in a masculine sense. There was one group, especially interested in culture, that vehemently contested the competition associated with sports, but others in the workers' movement wanted to show off the physical prowess of the workers and, most of all, to defy any image of the worker as worn out, drunken, and uncivilized, a concept widely held by the public in the Weimar Republic. In reaction to that negative image, many political activists favored order, manliness, and cleanness as symbols for the emancipation and strength of the worker.

The movement choirs did not provide this on an overt level because they did not show virtuosic movements or clear lines. In addition, they were to a great extent based on improvisation, even when set more precisely for mass events that included up to 2,000 participants. This makes it understandable why Gleisner was always eager to explain that movement choirs were not just "improvisation" in the sense that it could be interpreted as a bunch of people coming together and having fun, without exposing any artistic merit. As Susan Foster has pointed out, in Western culture improvisation brings with it a connotation of being not deliberate and not artistically shaped, as well as being unstable. All these were traits that were associated also with femininity. Being aware of such criticism of improvisation, as well as the potential to be considered feminine in any way, Gleisner emphasized the structural and formalist qualities of the choirs.

Improvisation in the sense it was used in the movement choirs was not geared to overthrow orders but was designed as a means to envision a new society, a new order that was based on collective understanding.[28] Thus, Gleisner contested an image of improvisation as being arbitrary or purely individual. He showed that choirs were composed of structured improvisation, most often based on a score and the notation of an advanced and creative dancer, and that even those dancers not in charge needed a clear sense of the structure of the dance. Before anybody could join Gleisner's choirs, they needed to take a course in dance based on Laban's movement principles. The movement choir, even if formed by lay dancers, was in Gleisner's eyes an advanced group of movers. They required a sensual awareness of the dancers around them, as well as an analytical understanding of dancing, including a sense of dynamics, space, levels, and effort. Moreover, he was extremely critical of other dance groups, which featured what he called "chaotic" images and "ridiculous self-explorations" that had no formal dancing qualities. In order to distinguish his work from others and enhance the status of the movement choirs as being rational and artistically worthy, he often wrote biting critiques of such endeavors, but always suggesting what to do better.[29]

Some of Gleisner's movement choirs showed forceful male protagonists that fit well into the image of the strong, trained, and well-tanned man that was preferred by both Socialists and Nationalists. Gleisner's *Männertanz* (*Men's Dance*), which was originally only one of three parts of a movement choir's composition, illustrates this need for strong male protagonists. This might not have been his intention because he unified women and men in the last sequence, but the scene of the men was shown separately at some festivities. His

Männertanz, performed by a Socialist youth group, is characteristic of the way men were integrated into the choirs. It also exemplifies how the dancers worked with an awareness of oppositional spatial movements and how this might be used to express the double-sided image of the male worker's body. Dancing in nature, dressed only in tunics, the men pay tribute to an idealized body image. Their curved backs and bent knees make them recognizable as so-called low dancers. There is tension in the movement of the curved back, which could suggest the weight and force from outside, as much as an active resistance to it, because the curve is supported by a strong center. The use of the abdominal muscles not only avoids the collapsing of the body but also enlarges the curve and gives the illusion of taking space. This strong appearance is supported by the arm movements that not only indicate the position of defense but widen the back even more. One could assign a certain symbolic meaning to this: expressing through movement the idea that the worker's body is oppressed by outside forces but that he simultaneously is hard and strong at his core and will fight his enemies. Occupying space and having a strong center are major ideas in the context of the Socialist movement and are apparent in movement patterns, and they were primarily danced by men in most of the movement choirs, not only those of Gleisner.

However, segregation within the movement choirs should not be read as having one fixed meaning in regard to gender roles. While one should point out that despite the often proclaimed coeducational impetus within the ideals and practice of the socialist cultural movement, women and men stayed in different groups; this did not always, especially within Gleisner's movement choirs, prescribe stereotypical gender difference in the quality of movement. A precise analysis of the movements will render some situations more complex than the segregation might suggest. In a photo of *Götzendienst* (*Service to a Shrine*)— again a dance performed at activities of the Socialist youth movement—one clearly recognizes the separation into a female and a male group. Moreover, there seems to be a hierarchical structure implied by the spacing that assigns the young women the place at the bottom. However, it is important to look precisely at their movements; while the young women are on the ground, placed below the men, they kick and do not seem at all as weak as this position might imply. Additionally, critics remarked that this dance had an ironic presentation of this separation as it exposed "in humorous ways the pretense of the weakness of girls and the roughness of men,"[30] suggesting that these were not natural gender traits but rather socially acquired, and that these new young groups and comrades wanted to resist them and create alternatives. Even if separation existed along gender lines, the choirs did not subscribe exclusively to a stereotypical understanding of the genders. As such, the movement choirs were believed to allow for both: to obliterate differences in regard to gender and class, because everyone was united in a collective movement that also accommodated and nurtured differences.

The presentation of the group as a physically strong entity was even more paramount in the work of the Communist dancer Jean (Hans) Weidt and his dance collective the Red Dancers.[31] To look at his work allows one to investigate in more detail how it was possible to believe in the potential freedom that could be achieved through dance while simultaneously initiating a training that was designed to show the strength of the worker. Weidt was a fascinating figure in the world of *Ausdruckstanz*. Due to his politically motivated and very explicit narrative and mimetic dance style, he often has been placed at the margin of this modern dance development.[32] However, I would like to argue that he explicitly used the aesthetic movement possibilities of *Ausdruckstanz* for developing his political dance style. He could draw on the movement qualities of *Ausdruckstanz* because it allowed for the inclusion of men performing activities resembling physical work. While he shared many ideas about the empowering function of dance for the working class with the Cultural Socialists—and as such cannot be situated politically so simply as a Communist dancer as his membership in the German Communist Party might suggest—he was imbued with a far more combative and rebellious energy, which made him foster a strong dancing body as a source of empowerment.

Born in 1904 to a poor working-class family in Hamburg, Weidt was forced to financially aid his family from an early age. He began dancing only after finishing his training as a gardener at the age of 19 and took his first and very influential modern dance classes with Sigurd Leeder, the future collaborator of Kurt Jooss (yet two more prominent male figures of the *Ausdruckstanz* movement). For Weidt, the dancer's body played a major part in the political understanding of his dances, despite his focus on content and narration in his pieces with such telling titles as *Der Arbeiter* (*The Worker*), *Morgens-Mittags-Abends* (*In the Morning-At Midday-In the Evening*), and *Passion eines Menschen* (*Passion of a Human Being*). He believed that his work was simultaneously a formation and (re)presentation of the living conditions of the worker, which were significantly shaped by physical labor.

This was in line with the thinking of other Socialists and the value they assigned to the body in the act of emancipation. It makes understandable why Weidt focused so intensely on a strong, almost stereotypical male physicality. However, I will suggest that the gendered aspects in his work were more complex and challenged stereotypes on three different levels. First of all, Weidt's exposition of his body did not yield to any conception of a beautiful dancing body, even in terms of masculine gender. Second, he did not distinguish in his group of dancers according to gendered norms; the women were equally trained to perform strong movements. Finally, he chose to present onstage both the suffering and the strength of the worker's life, incorporating the more provocative movements of tensions, weight, and distortions of *Ausdruckstanz* next to vividly bursting movements of strength.

Weidt believed that the worker had a natural link to dance culture and should promote it. As another contemporary left-wing dance activist noted: "We do want the culture of the body. With its care and honouring the worth and value [*Achtung*] of physical work must rise and also the standing of the worker."[33] Because the body was perceived as natural, it was positioned outside the domain of socially constructed class differences. Otto Zimmermann, a politically active leader of movement choirs and a passionate nude dancer, remarked in this context: "The new dance culture has a deep relationship to the future culture of workers, for the simple reason that it gives back the needed meaning and admiration to the human body [*Leib*], which everybody shares—without class difference—without giving the capitalist any extra rights to it. The beautiful nude human body will have the right to explore itself in the new world of dance."[34]

Consequently, Weidt's collaboration with his dancers constituted more than a performance group. Members of the Red Dancers came predominantly from a group of organized workers' youth called Fichte-Arbeiterjugend (Fichte's Workers' Youth). They were all active, political young men and women who practiced sports, but they had almost no prior contact with dance. Rehearsals with Weidt could take place only on Sundays or sometimes during the week in the evenings. This rehearsal process was as important as the performances for Weidt because he wanted to transform the workers into dancers, into those who had agency over their lives and bodies. Similar to those engaged in the bourgeois life reform movement, he took strolls with them and offered nude gymnastic classes (*Frei Körper Kultur*, or FKK).[35] Weidt's dancers never achieved a systematic dance technique in the classical sense (which also was the case for many other modern dancers of the time). They were often quite the opposite of virtuosic. Nonetheless, they acquired and created a movement and dance vocabulary that was clearly artistic in its orientation, challenging even more than other modern dancers the contemporary understanding of what bodies are allowed to do and represent onstage. Even if they incorporated movements that looked like work activities, their movement vocabulary was clearly stylized as dance in terms of use of space and abstraction, and could not be used outside the dance context. Thus, while they argued for empowerment through dance, they did this in the context of a primarily artistic field. Unlike gymnastic movements, their moving was not aimed primarily at the regeneration or enhancement of physical labor capacity. They achieved a personal reward by discovering new movement practices and by perceiving themselves as active agents in this process, as being literally on the move. This also included being empowered to implement dance movements as much as various kinds of ordinary movement activities familiar to them from their daily life. By doing this, they challenged the elite prerequisites for dancing and presented dance as a form of labor rather than a mystical experience.

For the workers' cultural movement of the Weimar Republic, physical education and the presentation of strength were interwoven with a symbolic sense of emancipation for the worker. This gradual development from an oppressed to a liberated worker was a general theme in the workers' movement and also influenced Weidt's choreographic practice. For instance, for his dance *The Worker* (*Der Arbeiter*), Weidt created 12 different versions until he achieved one that suited him: "I worked at it until I had reached the point where the worker is not to be presented with his head down and hanging, but full of pride and secure about his future."[36] The representational dimensions of a dance were linked to a physical practice that actually helped to evoke this strength.

In this context, it is no surprise that there are many strong and dynamic movements in the photos of Weidt's work. The slender and muscular bodies are presented almost nude. Weidt's differentiated physical regimes allowed performers to acquire technical and physical abilities, resulting in an increase of energy that made it possible to present a new ideal of the worker. At the time, life reformers, gymnasts, and dancers shared strong disciplinary tendencies, although they usually would have denied that and talked about a natural training or regaining natural movements. One should also note that the energies of this social movement that created a new and independent movement style can be seen in a productive light. The term "discipline" should be freed from a solely negative connotation because the dancers courageously challenged conventional ways of presenting the body and usual restrictions on who has the right to dance. This crossing of borders is rooted in the close interaction between body and art in dance and is not only of an aesthetic order. As Laurance Louppe remarked (in writing about the *Ausdruckstanz*), "Because the gestural element is an important part of the source for generating identity as much for the individual as for the community, this movement revolution [of *Ausdruckstanz*] touched far more sensitive areas than those of the performing arts. The dancer as subject risks situations in which s/he crosses certain norms of behavior or isolates him/herself through them."[37]

Weidt himself had a striking physical appearance that was exemplary for the ambivalent image of the worker's body. It did not suit the notion of what is commonly considered a beautiful dancing body and, as such, illustrates what sort of risks were taken. Photos of Weidt show a person who appears slim and worn out, evoking the impression of someone close to starving. His facial features were hard, and his hands were enormous, shaped by working manually as a gardener and coal shipper to be strong and physically able. His act of presenting his body onstage was both an artistic and a political revolution. Even though modern dance had challenged aesthetic conventions, Weidt's physicality was still a provocation within the context of modern dance, even if it was made possible only in this avant-garde dance practice.[38] The political climate of the Weimar Republic provided the space for such experimentations. The only existing film excerpts of him in Max Reinhard's *Der Zauberlehrling* (1935) show an enormously expressive mover, yet one that is also rough in the transitions and slightly stiff in the joints. In contrast, other photos of Weidt show a man with clearly developed muscles, who controls his body in precise movements and energized jumps. Taking up a great deal of space, he generates an almost heroic image in these shots. They show a striking resemblance to those jumping images of Ted Shawn and His Male Dancers.[39] There might even have been an influence and exchange of ideas between Shawn and Weidt, as they met in Germany in the choreography of *Orpheus* (1929) by Margarete Wallmann, a student of Mary Wigman.[40] Definitely the photos show that men found similar movement vocabulary attractive across national borders. For instance, Shawn described his dancing as being close to the act of work, a feature of Weidt's dances as well. However, in Weidt's case it is not only linked to issues of masculinity but more closely tied to the political goals.

Weidt was not afraid to also embody the weak, elderly people, or suffering women, doing so in a way that completely submerged his physical prowess and also his male identity. Viewers seeing him dance his *Eine Frau* (*A Woman*) noted how one totally forgot that a man was behind the mask in this dance. In this sense, it was not a masquerade that would symbolize something while simultaneously marking the difference between the performer and the symbolized. Rather, Weidt merged completely with the identity suggested by the mask and the movements of a suffering woman. He bent extensively inward, with his hanging, his arms twisted, and his hands distorted by effort and tension. While it should be mentioned that the role of the victim was most often assigned to the elderly or the women, and in contrast the portrait of the fighting worker was a man, as in his already mentioned dance *Der Arbeiter*, all these characters meant a real challenge to the belief of what dancers' bodies should and could do onstage. While other *Ausdruckstanz* dancers, especially Mary Wigman in her *Witch Dance* and Valeska Gert in her grotesque dances, had challenged the perception of the beautiful female body, and for that reason Weidt can be place within that tradition, he differed in that he also exposed weaknesses that were closely linked to his own identity.

Laban, Gleisner, and Weidt thus worked within the categories of conventional male gender norms as much as they challenged them. Depending on their cultural milieu and their political standpoints, they found different interpretative strategies for the integration of men into dance. However, all of them believed that *Ausdruckstanz*, with its possibility of integrating different types of dancers—especially those featuring raw, energetic, bound, and grounded movements and the focus on the group—offered an advantage for that endeavor. Analyzing masculinity asks one to ponder the gendered meanings and dichotomies that arise in analysis of bodily movements and thus question some of the utopias of modern dance as a source for a more authentic and universal understanding.

NOTES

1. See Hedwig Müller and Patricia Stöckemann, " . . . *jeder Mensch ist ein Tänzer.* " *Ausdruckstanz in Deutschland zwischen 1900 und 1945* (Giessen: Anabas, 1993). If political issues are treated at all, most often the focus lies on parallels to National Socialist ideology because of the dancer's ideals, including a strong belief in an idealistic community. See Laure Guilbert, *Danser avec le IIIe Reich* (Paris: Editions Complexe, 2000); Horst Koegler, *In the Shadow of the Swastika: Dance in Germany, 1927–1936* (New York, 1974); Lilian Karina and Marion Kant, *Tanz unterm Hakenkreuz, Eine Dokumentation* (Berlin: Henschel, 1996). For a more detailed political reading of dance in the Weimar Republic, see Yvonne Hardt, *Politische Körper. Ausdruckstanz, Choreographien des Protests und die Arbeiterkulturbewegung in der Weimarer Republik* (Münster: LIT, 2004).

2. See Susan Manning, *Ecstasy and the Demon: Feminism and Nationalism in the Dances of Mary Wigman* (Berkeley: University of California Press, 1993); Amelia Soyka, *Tanzen und tanzen und nichts als tanzen. Tänzerinnen der Moderne von Josphine Baker bis Mary Wigman* (Berlin: Aviva, 2004).

3. Martin Gleisner, *Tanz für alle. Von der Gymnastik zum Gemeinschaftstanz* (Leipzig: Hesse und Becker Verlag, 1928), 90 (all translations are mine).

4. For instance, writings by Fritz Böhme, Rudolf Laban, Rudolf Bode, Martin Gleisner, Otto Zimmermann, Jean Weidt, Hans Fischer, Hans Brandenburg, Werner Suhr, and many more (see Works Cited).

5. See Hardt, *Politische Körper*, 35–41.

6. Gabriele Mittag, "Wunderbares Reich des Tanzes. Der Ausdruckstanz der dreißiger Jahre," in *Zwischen Aufbruch und Verfolgung. Künstlerinnen der zwanziger und dreißiger Jahre*, ed. Denny Hirschbach (Bremen: Zeichen und Spuren, 1993), 187–90.

7. Hans Fischer, *Körperschönheit und Körperkultur. Sport, Gymnastik, Tanz* (Berlin: Deutsche Buchgemeinschaft, 1928), 7.

8. Ibid, 11.

9. For instance, Bode, H. Fischer, Laban, Winther (see references in this chapter).

10. For a biography, see Valerie Preston-Dunlop, *Rudolf Laban: An Extraordinary Life* (London: Dance Books, 1998).

11. See Horst Koegler, "Die Tanzfarm von Monte Verità," *Ballett* 4 (1979): 44–51.

12. See Ludwig Klages, "Vom Wesen des Rhythmus," in *Künstlerische Körperschulung*, ed. L. Pallat and Frank Hilder (Breslau, 1923), 94–137; Fritz Winther, *Lebendige Form. Rhythmus und Freiheit in Gymnastik, Sport und Tanz* (Karlsruhe, 1920); Rudolf Bode, *Rhythmus und Körpererziehung* (Jena: Diederichs, 1923).

13. See Rudolf Laban, *Choreographie* (Jena: Diederichs, 1926).

14. Rudolf Laban, *Die Welt des Tänzers. Fünf Gedankenreigen* (Stuttgart: Seifert, 1920).

15. The attempt to give more value to the art of dance can be traced back to the first ballet notations at the courts. See Sibylle Dahms, ed., *Tanz* (Kassel: Bärenreiter, 2001), 63ff.

16. According to his student and longtime collaborator Kurt Jooss, Laban stated that men were more analytical in dancing and women provided the emotional expressiveness to the art.

17. For a more extensive description and analysis of movement choirs, see Yvonne Hardt, "Relational Movement Patterns: The Diversity of Movement Choirs and Their Social Potential in the Weimar Republic," in *Proceedings of the Society of Dance History Scholars*, Limerick, 2003, 64–69.

18. Fritz Böhme, *Rudolf von Laban und die Entstehung des modernen Tanzdramas* (Leipzig: Ed. Hentrich, 1996), 137ff.

19. See Rudolf Laban, "Vom Sinn der Bewegungschöre," *Schrifttanz* 3, no. 1 (1930): 25.

20. Valtin Hartig, "Über die Möglichkeit proletarischer Kunst," *Kulturwille* 1: 1.

21. See Walter Guttsman, *Worker's Culture in Weimar Germany: Between Tradition and Commitment* (New York: St. Martin's Press, 1990).

22. See, e.g., Anna Siemsen, *Politische Kunst und Kunstpolitik* (Berlin: E. Laubsche, 1927; V. Engelhardt, *An der Wende der Zeitalters. Individualistische oder sozialistische Kultur?* (Berlin: Arbeiterjugend-Verlag, 1925); Max Adler, *Die Kulturbedeutung des Sozialismus* (Wien: Wiener Volksbuchhandlung, 1924); Valtin Hartig, "Über die Möglichkeit proletarischer Kunst, " *Kulturwille*, no. 1 (1924): 1–2.

23. Gleisner, *Tanz für alle*, 137.

24. Albrecht Knust, "Die Quellen des neuen Laientanzes," *Der Tanz* 5, no. 3 (1932): 12ff.

25. Ilse Loesch, "Kinder im neuen Geist," *Der Tanz* 5, no. 9 (1932): 4.

26. Gleisner, *Tanz für alle*, 91.

27. For a detailed discussion of this event, see Hardt, *Politische Körper*, 286–98.

28. For a discussion on improvisation and the distinctions between those who saw improvisation mainly as a means to overcome structure and those who envisioned a new community within an American setting, see Susan Leigh Foster, *Dances That Describe Themselves: The Improvised Choreography of Richard Bull* (Middletown, CT: Wesleyan University Press, 2002).

29. Martin Gleisner, "Wie man es nicht machen soll," *Jungend-Volksbühne* 6 (1932): 92ff.

30. "Freikörperkultur in der FTGB. Der Beweis für die Notwendigkeit," *Der Abend* 10, no. 4 (1929).

31. In 1933 Weidt fled from persecution in Germany to France. The French being unable to pronounce Hans properly, he named himself Jean and kept this name for the rest of his life.

32. See Nils Jockel and Patricia Stöckemann, *Flugkraft in weite Ferne... Bühnentanz in Hamburg seit 1900* (Hamburg, 1989), 52–55. This has also been encouraged by his writing. Especially in the context of the GDR, which later on rejected the aesthetics of the *Ausdruckstanz*, he was eager to portray himself as different from the other "bourgeois" dancers.

33. *Arbeiterbewegung und Körperkultur, Kulturwille* 3, no. 5 (1926): 81.

34. Otto Zimmermann, "Gymnastik und Tanz vom Standpunkt des Arbeiters," *Kulturwille* 5, no. 1 (1928): 5.

35. *Frei Körper Kultur*, which is called most often by its abbreviation FKK, became a widespread phenomenon in the Weimar Republic, where activities at the beach, in clubs, and sport contexts were done without clothes. This belonged to a wider trend for a more "natural" form of life. See Jean (Hans) Weidt, *Der Roter Tänzer. Ein Lebensbericht* (Berlin: Henschel, 1968), 16–18.

36. Ibid., 10.

37. Laurance Louppe, "Der Körper und das Unsichtbare," in *Tanz in der Moderne. Von Matisse bis Schlemmer*, ed. Karin Adelsbach and Andrea Firmrich (Cologne: Wienand Verlag, 1996), 271.

38. Several critics remarked that he forced the audience into witnessing embarrassing moments. And one of his dancers, Dominique Dupuis, remembers that it was not the political implications that often aroused criticism but his lack of physical dancing qualities.

39. See the essays on Shawn in this volume.

40. Ted Shawn also once possessed copies of these photos of Weidt, which he later donated to the Library of Performing Arts in New York.

WORKS CITED

Adelsbach, Karin, and Andrea Firmenich. 1996. *Tanz in der Moderne. Von Matisse bis Schlemmer*. Emden: Ausstellungskatalog. Kunsthalle Emden.

Adler, Max. 1924. *Die Kulturbedeutung des Sozialismus*. Wien: Wiener Volksbuchhandlung.

Baxmann, Inge. 2000. *Mythos: Gemeinschaft. Körper- und Tanzkulturen in der Moderne*. Munich: Fink.

Bode, Rudolf. 1923. *Rhythmus und Körpererziehung*. Jena: Diederichs.

Böhme, Fritz. 1926. *Tanzkunst*. Dessau: Dünnhaupt.

Burt, Ramsay. 1995. *Male Dancer: Bodies, Spectacle, Sexualities*. London: Routledge.

Dahms, Sibylle, ed. 2001. *Tanz*. Kassel: Bärenreiter.

Engelhardt, V. 1925. *An der Wende der Zeitalters. Individualistische oder sozialistische Kultur?* Berlin: Arbeiterjugend-Verlag.

Fischer, Hans. 1928. *Körperschönheit und Körperkultur. Sport, Gymnastik, Tanz*. Berlin: Deutsche Buchgemeinschaft.

Foster, Susan Leigh. 2002. *Dances That Describe Themselves: The Improvised Choreography of Richard Bull*. Middletown, CT: Wesleyan University Press.

Gleisner, Martin. 1928. *Tanz für alle: Von der Gymnastik zum Gemeinschaftstanz*. Leipzig: Hesse und Becker Verlag.

———. 1929. "Tanzvergnügen und Tanzfeier." *Leib und Seele. Monatszeitschrift für deutsche Leibesübungen*, no. 5: 114.

———. 1932. "Wie man es nicht machen soll." *Jungend-Volksbühne* 6:92ff.

Guilbert, Laure. 2000. *Danser avec le IIIe Reich. Les danseurs modernes sous le nazisme*. Paris: Edition Complexe.

Guttsmann, W. 1990. *Worker's Culture in Weimar Germany: Between Tradition and Commitment*. New York: St. Martin's Press.

Hardt, Yvonne. 2003. "Relational Movement Patterns: The Diversity of Movement Choirs and Their Social Potential in the Weimar Republic." In *Proceedings of the Society of Dance History Scholars*, 64–69. 26th Annual Conference at the University of Limerick, Stoughton.

———. 2004. *Politische Körper. Ausdruckstanz, Choreographien des Protests und die Arbeiterkulturbewegung in der Weimarer Republik*. Münster: LIT.

———. 2005a. "Ausdruckstanz und die Ästhetisierung des Arbeiterkörpers." In *Leibhaf-tige Moderne. Körper in Kunst und Massenmedien 1918–1933*, ed. Michael Cowan and Kai Marcel Sicks, 245–63. Bielefeld: transcript.

———. 2005b. "Der Moderne Tanz in den kultursozialistischen Publikationen der Weimarer Republik." In *Tanz im Kopf/dance and Cognition*, ed. Johannes Birringer and Josphine Fenger, 47–62. Jahrbuch Tanzforschung 15. Münster: LIT.

Hartig, Valtin. 1924. "Über die Möglichkeit proletarischer Kunst." *Kulturwille* no. 1: 1–2.

Howe, Diane. 1996. *Individuality and Expression: The Aesthetics of the New German Dance, 1908–1936*. New York: Peter Lang.

Jockel, Nils, and Patricia Stöckemann. 1989. *Flugkraft in weite Ferne . . . Bühnentanz in Hamburg seit 1900*. Hamburg.

Karina, Lilian, and Marion Kant. 1996. *Tanz unterm Hakenkreuz. Eine Dokumentation*. Berlin: Henschel.

Klages, Ludwig. 1923. "Vom Wesen des Rhythmus." In *Künstlerische Körperschulung*, ed. L. Pallat and Frank Hilder. Breslau.

Koch, Adolf. 1928. "Arbeitergymnastik." *Kulturwille* no. 1: 5.

Koegler, Horst. 1974. *In the Shadow of the Swastika: Dance in Germany, 1927–1936*. New York: Dance Perspectives.

———. 1979. "Die Tanzfarm von Monte Verità." *Ballett* 4:44–51.

Laban, Rudolf v. 1920. *Die Welt des Tänzers. Fünf Gedankenreigen*. Stuttgart: Seifert.

———. 1926. *Choreographie*. Jena: Diederichs.

———. 1929. "Alltag und Fest." *Schrifttanz* 2 (3): 57.

Manning, Susan. 1993. *Ecstasy and the Demon: Feminism and Nationalism in the Dances of Mary Wigman*. Berkeley: University of California Press.

———. 1995. "Modern Dance in the Third Reich: Six Positions and a Coda." In *Choreographing History*, ed. Susan Leigh Foster, 165–76. Bloomington: Indiana University Press.

Mittag, Gabriele. 1993. "Wunderbares Reich des Tanzes. Der Ausdruckstanz der dreißiger Jahre." In *Zwischen Aufbruch und Verfolgung. Künstlerinnen der zwanziger und dreißiger Jahre*, ed. Denny Hirschbach, 187–90. Bremen.

Müller, Hedwig, and Patricia Stöckemann. 1993. *". . . jeder Mensch ist ein Tänzer." Ausdruckstanz in Deutschland zwischen 1900 und 1945*. Giessen: Anabis.

Preston-Dunlop, Valérie. 1998. *Rudolf Laban: An Extraordinary Life*. London: Dance Books.

Siemsen, Anna. 1927. *Politische Kunst und Kunstpolitik*. Berlin: E. Laubsche.

Soyka, Amelia, ed. 2004. *Tanzen und tanzen und nichts als tanzen. Tänzerinnen der Moderne von Josphine Baker bis Mary Wigman*. Berlin: Aviva.

Suhr, Werner. 1936. "Männlicher, weiblicher und kultischer Tanz. Um die Festkultur Labans." *Der Tanz* 9 (6): 1–4.

Weidt, Jean (Hans). 1968. *Der Roter Tänzer. Ein Lebensbericht*. Berlin: Henschel.

Winther, Fritz. 1920. *Lebendige Form. Rhythmus und Freiheit in Gymnastik, Sport und Tanz*. Karlsruhe.

Zimmermann, Otto. 1928. "Gymnastik und Tanz vom Standpunkt des Arbeiters." *Kulturwille* 5 (1): 5.

HELLMUT GOTTSCHILD

> *A dancer and choreograper, Gottschild taught for many years at Temple University and founded two dance companies in Philadelphia, Group Motion and ZeroMoving. Before leaving Germany in 1968, he had been with Mary Wigman for 10 years, first as a pupil, then her assistant.*

My Heroic Lament

> Heroic lament
> Heroic lament,
> Heroic,
> Heroic,
> Heroes, offsprings of gods with mortal women,
> Semi-gods, titans that challenge the heavens.
> Monumental super beings!

These lines and all other quotes in this essay are extracted from *Mary's Ark, Blue Eyes, and the Inability to Dissolve*, a performance work I made in the early '90s, in which I recall and comment on my time as a beginning dancer at the Mary Wigman Studio in Berlin. My studies there began 50 years ago; I was 21, and Mary was in her early 70s.

"So, my boy, you want to dance. Well, let's see. I want you to improvise. Here is your theme: 'Heroische Klage' [heroic lament]." These were Mary Wigman's words for the final section of my entrance exam at her studio. The first part had consisted of my participation in a class taught by her, and since it was a Saturday that class was Spinning, which meant that, for the length of the class, we would spin. Imagine me, a young man of 21 in a pair of cotton tights with buckling knees, shirtless—for I expected my bare, already somewhat hairy chest to appear impressively masculine—falling all over the place among all those young women, advanced dancers who never seemed to stagger away from their spot when whirling in place and who spun in a perfectly straight line when taking the turns across the floor. The contrast between them and me was heightened by the fact that they all wore skirts that, by concealing the moving legs, made their rotations appear incredibly smooth and harmonious. A most humiliating experience for me, and I considered giving up right there. Luckily the second part was to come, the

Gottschild in 2000, evoking the spirit of Mary Wigman's *Witch Dance* in his piece *Mary's Ark, Blue Eyes, and the Inability to Dissolve*. Photograph by Beatriz Schiller. Used with permission.

improvisation, which, as I soon realized, was what really counted. But: "Heroische Klage?!"

> Heroic lament,
> Heroic lament,
> Beloved
> Old woman,
> Do you really believe I can find within me, today,
> After all we have seen, an image like this, a pathos
> That rebounds in me back and forth between laughter and tears.

At the time I was still studying fine arts, was up-to-date on who was the avant-garde in painting and sculpture, and listened to music by Cage, Stockhausen, and Kagel. "Heroic Lament?" Didn't that sound a little old-fashioned, a little too much like the language that had led Germany into the disaster of 1933 through 1945? So much for the response of my left brain (after all, we who had grown up after the fall of Hitler's Third Reich had been tagged the "skeptical" generation).

Fortunately, my desire to dance was stronger than my doubts. I accepted the task and—promising myself that it would just be for the time being—blindfolded my critical faculties and submerged myself into what I felt might be heroic movement. In the course of it my left brain must have taken a nap because suddenly there was space in my head for . . . pathos. ("Pathos, that's not me," I thought briefly, but danced on, feeling better by the minute.) In the second improv, "Freedom Fighter," I exhibited revolutionary fervor by dancing over invisible barricades, swinging invisible flags, and directing my gaze mostly upward (whereas in the "Heroic Lament" my eyes had been focused chiefly inward and toward the ground). After that I was sent out of the room. The faculty remained to discuss my talent and, of course, my fate. There must not have been much discussion, for just about three minutes later Til Thiele, the teacher with whom I had taken one year of weekly lay classes, came out and revealed to me: "You know what Mary said? She said 'This boy *must* dance.' "

That was Mary. To *have to* dance was the only valid criterion for her. If the germ was present, it would invariably sprout and grow and find its unique form, possibly, probably, and hopefully a form that would be totally itself, unique, and different from forms other students might grow into. She, the teacher, would function as a gardener, providing the sapling with the space and nourishment needed for it to grow into itself, into *its* self—a rather romantic notion that, at times, I rejected because it put only secondary emphasis on movement skill and thus made it difficult for Wigman students to compete for summer jobs or theater positions with dancers who had a solid training in ballet and could care less for our striving for inner values. I still have those misgivings, but today I am able to accept and appreciate what I was given at the Wigman Studio. However, I was incapable of recognizing it until I came to the United States, where I realized, from the responses of colleagues and students, that I had received—and, as a teacher, had to give—something that was special and different from the approach generally taken in this country.

Back to my entrance exam. The themes Mary Wigman gave me to improvise were, of course, topics she would only give to a man. A woman might merely have lamented, but a man would have to lament "heroically." And then the "Freedom Fighter"!? Quite obviously this sapling was expected to grow up to appreciate and measure up to gender images that my postwar generation had great difficulties accepting. Too many of them had been misused and led to harm. This great woman and artist who had succeeded in escaping many aspects of a bourgeois pre-turn-of-the-century upbringing and who herself had lived a rather independent and liberated life was past the point where she would be able or willing to detach herself from a value system in which she had been safe, creative, and successful. For her, women receive, endure, even suffer while bearing the weight of an unpredictable and—at least as far as a woman is concerned—unchangeable fate. Men were assigned the opposite role. They were supposed to be initiators, movers, and shakers, and, because boys will be boys, it was all right to excuse their occasional blunders with a forgiving smile. After all, weren't all our lives largely determined by forces of nature—or even higher ones—that none of us mortals could influence?

> Heroic lament,
> Heroic lament,
> Dark clouds
> in the skies!
> The war she sees as a *natural* force, catastrophic,
> ferocious, and evil, innocent victims we all,
> playthings for moody gods of fate.

At the time the wounds of World War II were still visible all over the then-divided city of Berlin. They were less visible but painfully present in most Germans' minds. Even my generation, who had grown up and come into consciousness after the war, had been molded by the recent past. There was in us a healthy distrust toward the word "natural." We doubted events that seemed to originate in some inaccessible "unknown," had problems with heroism, and dismissed all symbolism, from hymns to flags to certain emblematic constructs. In contrast to our revered teacher, we understood war to be a disaster created by people. We, females as well as males, had learned to think politically. On the other hand, the most engraving experience for me was that, as I had begun to taste the sensation of dancing, I could give myself permission to unfold what might be called my feminine side along and in dialogue with the masculine. My dance did not have to shout "Look at me!" but could whisper and confess, "I want to give myself." Mary had called it "sich verstrahlen, sich verströmen, sich verhauchen" (to radiate oneself away, to flow out of oneself, to breathe oneself away). For a man of the mid-20th century this was a very unmanly statement. Yet it felt right and essential to me. This was exactly what I had yearned for, and this, I realized, was why I danced.

To not be misunderstood, I am not talking about sexual preference. I was far from being or dreaming of being gay. On the contrary, I have always been fascinated with women and have to admit that, early on, homosexual men had often been the objects of ill-conceived jokes by me and my friends. For us, the gay man was an Other who became a victim, since there was no place for him in the prevailing value system. Considering that the outside world saw virtually every male dancer as gay, and people, even within my own family, looked at me with suspicion, I felt I had to make every effort to come across as a "real man." Part of that effort was to demonstrate my superiority by theorizing and intellectualizing in verbal exchanges. My entire demeanor said: "I'm not one of you." This reveals another misconception held by me before I became a dancer: that gay as well as female dancers were intellectual lightweights, their interests limited to knitting and fashion magazines. Here I had fallen into the trap most of society was ensnared in (and from which it still has not totally freed itself): that man lives mainly above his neck, while woman dwells in the nether regions of the body (the same mistake is repeated over and over between white males and people of color).

> I wanted to dance. But where?
> In the penthouse of the head with the white, Aryan males and occasionally
>   lamenting heroes?
> Hm, that's where I come from . . .
> Down there in the dungeons [*hands on genitals*] with the exotics; the
>   drum beating, saxophone playing and oversexed primitives, Semites?
> Well I would not mind . . .
> In the middle levels of romance, purity, and unfulfilled dreams [*hands on
>   chest*] to which we had confined our women?
> Yes, yes, yes, I wanted it all!

In a rather harmless retaliation (of course it was harmless for me, because in my position as a member of a privileged group, I was invulnerable), I more than once heard my gay co-dancers talk, behind my back but loud enough for me to hear, "Normale können nicht tanzen" (normals can't dance). I am convinced they believed what they said, but I knew it was not true and could laugh with them. The tragic part is that, by calling me normal, they unintentionally designated themselves to be deviants, which established in me an even stronger a sense of superiority. How could they relinquish all their power to me? Fortunately, the same dance world that in those early days seemed to confirm my biases gave me the chance to learn and revise my views much faster than had I remained outside. Seen as located way below the controlling head in the body's unspeakable regions, dance has been the stepchild of the arts for centuries. In the Eurocentric Christian world it was taken seriously only in that it was a threat to order and morality. It has itself been looked upon as the woman among the arts, sensual, seductive, sinful, and not very intelligent. This is perhaps one reason why so many males have shied away from it. The notion of a bodily intelligence, well known to us dancers, still has to percolate through the general public.

There was a another generational gap between our "Meisterin" and us. She and, as far as is known to me, other early modern dancers had exclusively danced roles the gender of which was identical with their own. In contrast, we, a renegade group of Wigman students, turned to movement itself as the heart of our work, to its rise and fall, its values and qualities. We allowed ourselves to be informed by phenomena we could observe in the world around us: animals, plants, inorganic matter, light, but also the many new ways of moving suggested by film and electronic music. We boldly declared that we were creating the New Dance. In 1962, I and two female dancers who were also former Wigman students formed a dance collective we named after our agenda, Gruppe Motion (Group Motion). This was new in German modern dance, which, several decades earlier, had been named *Ausdruckstanz* (expressionistic dance), a designation we rejected. Reviewers, confronted with our work, found themselves helpless. The only term they could find to describe it was "abstract." They erred. Granted, our dance did not portray a known human situation, but, as we saw and felt it, it was quite concrete. Each dance was a living, breathing entity, a new reality created and formed by *sensing* rather than *designing* our way through its progression. And since they were realized by human bodies, those entities became human and spoke to the human experience. It was not the "non-emotional," albeit quite motional, abstract—and, as I see it, very male—movement of a Merce Cunningham whom I had had the chance to see in 1960 and who had impressed me so much that, for a while, I had tried to find a way into his cool way of dancing and making dances. But my movement came from a different place; it was too tactile rather than visual, too hot, as it were (perhaps too feminine?), and I always wound up making Hellmut Gottschild dances. I and my partners had remained Mary's children even though, at the time, we were not aware of it, and even though she herself had difficulties acknowledging that we were working from the same motional place she had. She could never warm up to our nonexpressive work.

Clearly, in this new dance, gender distinctions would be rendered meaningless. Now each of us could be anyone or anything. Looking at it today, I see it as a kind of liberation, men's as well as women's. Yet we did not think in programmatic terms. We simply did what we felt like doing and saw ourselves in line with contemporary artists in other fields. Also, it was the 1960s, and the movements in and of society itself had a great influence on us and our work.

After several years of making and performing relatively short—and, I would say, pure—dances of the kind critics had called "abstract," Gruppe Motion Berlin took on a project that led us to deal quite literally with the male-female relationship. It was 1967. For the first time we expanded our group to create a piece that included film, slides, original music, and text. At the center of the large-scale collaboration was the Orpheus myth, which we felt touched on many issues that moved us. Among other questions, we were puzzled by Orpheus being permitted to lead his wife, Euridice, back from the world of the dead into life, on condition that he not look at her. What did that say to us in the 60s? Well, for us it was that he, representing every artist and every man, must never gaze at his wife or any female the way women had been looked at by men before, as subordinates whose purpose it is to serve the male's needs and pleasures. In the myth he had failed, and we concluded that in order to make the new way of relating possible, Orpheus himself (the individual artist) had to die in order to give way to the new Orpheus (which for us, at the time, was the collective). His death was the "liftoff" moment following a countdown throughout the piece that we called *Countdown for Orpheus*.

> Heroic lament,
> Heroic lament,
> Everything
> crumbles.
> Fall forty-four: the bomb destroys our home.
> My father sheds tears. Oh, how can he do that?
> Cowboys and Indians would never have cried.

I set out to write about masculinity and the role it played in modern dance in my home country but ended up writing mainly about myself and Mary Wigman. Let me explain. When I began my studies, the so-called German Dance had virtually disappeared. I did not experience the great years of *Ausdruckstanz*; I was born when Mary's star had begun to decline and in a time when Germans did not look for pathos or emotionality. Instead, there existed considerable suspicion toward everything that reminded us of the Germany of the previous decades. Only a few dancers, almost exclusively female, still gave solo performances for dwindling audiences. The most eminent of them was the great Dore Hoyer, whose dance deserved to be seen and celebrated worldwide. Instead, there was a boom of classical dance, largely inspired by the powers who had occupied our country and supported by Germans' distrust of experimentation, which spelled insecurity. The only truly influential male figure in modern dance was Kurt Jooss, who had found a way to integrate classical and modern dance. From his Folkwang School, Pina Bausch and the Tanztheater movement would grow a few years later.

About 15 years ago I made a semi-autobiographical performance piece about that time, and I just had to make "Mary's Ark" part of its title. In many ways the Wigman studio had become an ark, floating and waiting for the flood of forgetfulness to recede and the world to change back to the way it had once been. I doubt that Mary herself believed that that could happen, but the studio kept operating as if it would. To me it was clear it wouldn't. The surroundings had become too alien, if not hostile. Often when I told nondancers that I was a student at the Mary Wigman Studio, the response was, "Wigman? Is she still alive?" Or, even more humiliating, "Who is she?" Dancers, on the other hand, especially the younger ones, simply laughed. In their eyes the "Wigmänner" (Wig-men) were covered with layers of dust from years past. However, even after completing my formal studies, I stayed at the studio, where, despite all my misgivings, I felt at home. Five years after my "Heroische Klage" improvisation, Mary asked me to teach for her. I became her youngest teacher, the only male, and the only one still alive.

Why place Wigman into the center of this article? Well, she was the only one of her generation I had a chance to meet intimately. So she became my window through which I could try to observe but mostly imagine the glorious time of *Ausdruckstanz*. As I get older and can let go of my apprehensions, I discover that a great deal of it is in my body, received through the mother's milk, so to speak. Underneath all the layers of another time a treasure was hidden: an approach to movement that I feel has enriched me tremendously and which, in my view, is sorely needed in today's dance environment. The more I find, the more my understanding and love for the great woman increase, as does my respect for her era. I began with and interspersed quotes from *Mary's Ark, Blue Eyes, and the Inability to Dissolve*, in which I attempt to recall and comment on my time as a beginning dancer at the Mary Wigman Studio. I will end with its opening lines: As the foot leaves the dirt, for one instant, we see a clear imprint. At the same moment, imperceptibly first, then more and more rapidly, the print begins to deteriorate, the trace to fade. It becomes increasingly difficult and eventually impossible to match its outline to the foot that made it. At the very rate it vanishes, memory of it becomes a construction." I wonder whether my attempt to match the imprint left 50 years ago with my foot of today is an act of retracing, reshaping, or destroying. Perhaps a little of each.

PART III

LEGACIES OF COLONIALISM

9

Choreographing Masculinity

Hypermasculine Dance Styles as Invented Tradition in Egypt, Iran, and Uzbekistan

ANTHONY SHAY

In the latter half of the 20th century, individual choreographers and government agencies made several attempts to create "proper" images for male dancing bodies for the state-sponsored dance companies of Egypt, Iran, and Uzbekistan, and their teaching institutions. The creation of these new hypermasculinized choreographic forms was related to pressures by both colonial administrations and the newly emerging postcolonial Westernized elites and middle classes to counter negative historical stereotypes of male dancers in these regions.

Forcible colonization had taken place in Egypt and Uzbekistan by the British and Russians, respectively, and Iran underwent considerable political and cultural pressure by the British and Russians, and later the Americans, without actually becoming a colony, although it was occupied by those three powers throughout World War II—a bitter memory for those who endured it.[1] Other regions of the Iranian world such as Afghanistan were established as a kind of no-man's-land between the English and Russian political spheres, and thus managed to preserve aspects of their traditional culture longer.[2] Nevertheless, throughout the entire region, colonialist attitudes and pressures were keenly perceived and felt by the local populations. England, France, Russia, and the United States, directly and indirectly, asserted their moral and religious values throughout the Middle East, North Africa, and Central Asia for three centuries, a process that continues today through the recent missions of democratization and nation-building in Iraq and Afghanistan.

Historically, the movement vocabularies of professional male and female dancers tended to be very similar in the various dance traditions that existed in these regions before the era of colonization, and even after. The movement vocabularies of the traditional dance often featured highly articulated torso, arm, hand, and facial movements. As I have suggested elsewhere (1999), the dance traditions throughout this region are an abstraction of calligraphy, one of the most important art forms in this region.[3] "This is kinesthetically realized in a dance vocabulary inclined toward small intricate movements of the head, hands, torso or hips. The legs are used to augment the movement of the head and torso; the arms to frame the movement. The dance's structure is based on improvised movements which evolve into a series of mini-crescendos reflecting the musical accompaniment" (Shay and Sellers-Young 2005, 5). Descriptions of these dance traditions in Egypt from the 19th century by authors such as Gustave Flaubert and Edward Lane and a short film clip of an Egyptian belly dancer made by Thomas Edison in the late 19th century compared with those seen in Aisha Ali's film *Dances of Egypt* make clear that the basic movements changed little within that period.[4] Edward Lane in the 1830s observed of Egyptian dancing girls: "Their dancing has little of elegance; its chief peculiarity being a very rapid vibrating motion of the hips, from side to side" (2003, 377); of the male dancers: "As they personate women, their dances are exactly of the same description as those of the Ghawazee [*sic*] and are, in like manner, accompanied by the sounds of castanets: but, as if to prevent their being thought to be really females, their dress is suited to their unnatural profession; being partly male, and partly female" (382–83).

Only in the 1920s, under the influence of Hollywood films, did Egyptian dancers in Cairo begin to significantly change and expand belly dance for cabaret appearances and for the expanding Egyptian film industry, which often featured elaborate dance sequences.[5] The cabaret style coexisted with that of the older style, as seen in Ali's film, and which I saw in Egypt in 2000. Women in the harems, who were able to watch the performances of young professional male dancers in courtyards, frequently emulated the professional dancers in their domestic versions of solo improvised dance.

But these old dance traditions underwent evolution, ostensibly for the honor of the homeland, driven by colonial disapproval and exacerbated by choreophobic attitudes, a term I coined to address the well-known negative attitudes toward dance, especially in its professional form, in the Middle East that existed historically in these regions. When it came to men in particular, state-sponsored choreographers responded to the considerable social and political pressure from colonial powers and Westernized native elites to create new "proper" images, a tradition that become embedded in postcolonial classes who craved respect from the West. Historian Afsaneh Najmabadi states: "In the early nineteenth century, Iranian men had become acutely and increasingly aware that Europeans considered Iranian older man-younger man love and sexual practice a vice.... Same-sex practices were often linked with young male dancers" (2005, 33–34). She adds: "This anxiety over Europeans' judgment of Iranian sexual mores and practices remained a preoccupation throughout the nineteenth century" (37). Even for female dancers the movements of the previous professional dancers, both male and female, were frequently sanitized.[6]

It would be wrongheaded, as well as an intellectually Orientalist strategy, to portray the populations of these regions simply as passive recipients of Western pressure. As Najmabadi cogently points out, Iranians at the end of the 19th century, still smarting from two large wars with czarist Russia in which they lost large geographic territories, often eagerly embraced Western values, including sexual mores and gender construction, as important elements of becoming modern (2005, 105–6).[7] In other words, despite often considerable Western pressures for social and moral change, important and influential elements among native populations, especially the elite and the intelligentsia, frequently exercised considerable agency and influence on local attitudes because, while paradoxically hating the West, they perceived Western modernity as the most important way of achieving political and social parity with the West.

Farida Fahmy, a longtime soloist with the Reda Troupe of Egypt, sister-in-law to Mahmoud Reda, and Reda Troupe choreographer, commented: "The elite and upper classes of Egypt typically expressed embarrassment toward their native dances in general and towards belly dancing in particular. One of the causes of this embarrassment is the impact the West has had on Egyptian culture" (1987, 12).

Egyptian dance ethnologist and historian Magda Saleh adds that Egyptian folklore, especially dance, is disdained among the elite classes, "where native arts do not have any cachet but are regarded as primitive and nonaesthetic. The theatricalized versions are, however, considered a substantial improvement in the drive toward refinement" (1998a, 496). "Refinement" signifies the acceptance of Euro-American aesthetic and intellectual values. In this process, native dance directors and choreographers created for men a new vocabulary of what I call "hypermasculine" movements, sometimes developed from elements most frequently derived from classical ballet, because of its acceptance by Westernized elites as a "refined" art form, but often influenced by, or claimed to be influenced by, various native sports such as polo and *zur-khaneh* exercises, work motifs, and, most often, the lively imaginations of various choreographers who create movements out of whole cloth.[8]

In this essay, I suggest that these invented traditions demonstrate how populations succumbed to and frequently embraced European attitudes toward sexuality and gender that directly provoked individuals in the field of dance to create these artificial choreographic styles. Thus, homophobia serves as an important subtext of these choreographic projects. It is difficult to assess what types of choreographic development might have emerged without this process of intervention, but in Iran and Uzbekistan, in particular, an entire genre of professional male dancing disappeared. I will address the specific types of changes that these choreographers crafted when they created an entirely new movement tradition for newly created, ballet-influenced stage choreographies, sanitizing and erasing perceived effeminate elements from past and contemporary dancing practices.

Postcolonial attitudes, particularly toward sexuality and gender, became powerful engines of change in all three of these areas—Egypt, Uzbekistan, and

Iran. It is simplistic to think, as many do, that once the colonizers have left or have been driven out, everything returns to the precolonial state. This phenomenon was particularly notable when the English, Russian, French, and American forms of colonialism instilled attitudes associated with Victorian prudery and the Christian-inspired "civilizing mission."

Culture clashes resulted in centuries of Orientalist attitudes from the West, from which negative stereotypes of Muslims were created in travel journals, novels, and paintings. These inevitably revolved around a presumed lasciviousness, rampant libidos, and "unnatural" sexual practices, a trope created by European travelers to the Middle East as early as the 15th century. These romantically decadent sexual and alluring Orientalist images were reinforced in the West in films such as *The Sheik* and in 19th-century Orientalist paintings like those by Jean-Léon Gérôme.

Seen in this light, it is no wonder that Muslims constituted a particular target for the colonial civilizing mission. Sanjay Srivastava notes of the British rule in India that "those investigated for 'unnatural acts' tended mainly to be Muslims" (2004, 31). The object of the civilizing mission was to "convert" dominated populations, so that they learned to think and act as proper Christian Europeans: this was, above all, a colonization of the mind. As I outline here, it was also, it turns out, a colonization and disciplining of the body. I address specifically the invented masculinity that was imported and adapted to colonized and postcolonial landscapes.

Historical Context: The Ambiguity of the Male Dancer

In the Middle East and Central Asia, past and present attitudes toward male dancers to some degree overlap, since contemporary attitudes are always historically situated. My focus here concerns what impact the intervening occurrence of colonialism and Westernization had in terms of dramatically altering the position of the male dancer in these regions; his image became a contested field of representation. I will describe and analyze the performance of male dancers, address key theoretical and conceptual issues that affect their image and positioning, as well as suggesting the artistic ramifications of this phenomenon of both colonially and locally inspired "masculinization."

In many ways, it is not difficult to understand how dancers became the vulnerable target of misunderstandings, censorship, and "re-choreographing" both during the era of the colonial powers, as occurred in Uzbekistan and Egypt, and during the postcolonial period, as occurred in Egypt and Iran. Throughout most of Asia, the class of professional entertainer, for both men and women, has historically been one of the lowest, often outcast, social categories; thus colonial intervention was made easier. Middle East historian C. E. Bosworth notes that entertainers were regarded as part of the *banu sasan*, the medieval Islamic underworld (1976, 1).

However, as cultural studies scholar Stavros Stavrou Karayanni notes: "Their performances were considered essential at celebrations such as wedding parties, festivals, and circumcision ceremonies" (2004, 70). Nearly every historical source, as well as contemporary ones, equates public dancers and entertainers, male or female, with prostitution.[9]

These choreophobic attitudes largely proceed from widely held perceptions of loose morals and effeminacy in connection with dance activities. Both historically and today throughout this vast region, which of course has myriad regional, linguistic, and ethnic groups, many of the public performances of these entertainers were indigenous Iranian theater, in which sex constitutes a fecund source of political and social comedy and dancing often formed an important part of theatrical skits.[10] Sex is not talked about publicly in these regions. Rather, sex is acted out through movement in the satire. Most European observers failed to note such sequences as comedic or satiric because of their lack of linguistic skills and their lack of cultural literacy. Following the Orientalist concepts with which they were familiar, they saw instead lewd and lascivious behavior in the movement practices they witnessed. They frequently mistook performances that were being played as a joke for native audiences as serious portrayals of the sex act. The male dancers and other performers in the Iranian indigenous theater genres *siyah-bazi* and *ru-howzi* frequently employed sexual gestures and situations in their dancing to lampoon society.

It was not that Europeans were ignorant of bawdy and raunchy performances, but these were enjoyable only if the performers were women. In the Middle East, Europeans were scandalized because the performers were frequently men, and in the homophobic atmosphere that obtained in Europe, where men caught in homosexual encounters were jailed, tortured, and executed, the sight of male dancers performing articulated movements of the torso and pelvic areas offended Westerners who believed movements of the pelvis and breasts to belong solely to the movement domain of women.

Eighteenth-century French traveler Vivant Denon recorded a typical European observation of male dancers: "The dance which followed was of the same description with the singing: it was not the expression of joy, or of gaiety, but of an extravagant pleasure, which made hasty strides toward lasciviousness; and this was the more disgusting, as the performers, all of them of the male sex, presented in the most indecent way, scenes which love has reserved for the two sexes in the silence and mystery of the night" (quoted in Berger 1961, 30–31).

Although solo improvised dance, including what is popularly called belly dance, can sometimes be characterized as sensual and seductive, in addition to its graceful aesthetic, it can also be comedic, both in private locations, such as the harem, and in the performances of professional dancers. Iranian writer Sattareh Farman Farmaian recalls from her youth: "My mother was too strict to clown, but she enjoyed watching the others' horseplay, especially one of Ezzat-doleh's maids, who could paint her naked buttocks to look like two eyes and, dancing with them to the onlookers, would roll them so that the two eyes crossed" (1992, 37). Historian Rudi Matthee cites the historical example from the Safavid court where a dance in the 1630s was "performed by a woman who at times lay on her stomach with a Persian turban on her ass, which she managed, through specific body movement, to throw up to the height of a man, thereby merrily accompanied by the music makers" (2000, 141). Given that Western eyes were used to the formal movement vocabularies of the minuet and the contredanse, we should not be surprised that observing solo improvised dancing in the Middle East by Europeans led to choreographic culture clashes and misunderstandings, even though bawdy dance performances were not unknown in Europe in commedia dell'arte, brothels, and other venues in which males were overwhelmingly spectators rather than performers.

Because belly dancing as experienced in the West has created widespread Orientalist images of sexy dancing girls, many Westerners, as well as native postcolonial scholars and writers, have had no personal experience seeing male performers; they think that solo improvised dance in the Middle East is the sole province of women, and that it constitutes a uniquely female form of dance. Many Western men think that only women should perform movements of the pelvis and torso. Overwhelmingly, Western observers and writers mistakenly assume that the appearances and performances of males were, and are, perforce, copying or parodying female performances because they use torso and pelvic movements.[11] Despite this mistaken apprehension, the contemporary YouTube Web site features several male dancers in the Middle East who demonstrate the movement vocabulary in the same way or similar to female dancers. One can see traditional Afghani dancing boys (see particularly Omar of Egypt for a fabulous example).

In his film *Afghan Village*, anthropologist Louis Dupree comments on an Afghan dancing boy: "The absence of women performers long ago led to the practice of female impersonation" (1976, 15). In fact, there was never any attempt by male dancers to disguise their maleness—their customers attended their performances *because* they knew that the dancer was male. Many of the dancers, however, did cultivate an ambiguity in dress and performance mannerisms that was attractive to their male audiences. Homosexual attraction throughout this region was often based on older male's attraction to young males of androgynous appearance—a look that was frequently cultivated by male dancers. Male identity was shown through certain movements, for instance, or the frequent practice of mixing styles of grooming or clothes. Dancers frequently wore items of both men's and women's clothing, such as a special headpiece or hair arrangement. For example, in the film of the Afghan male dancer, he wears a woman's robe but also retains a man's hat and the short hairstyle of men. The male dancer/entertainers were specifically valued because they *were* male, because in almost all cases they were assumed to be available for same-sex activities, a fact that Dupree specifically notes for the male Afghan dancer he filmed in the 1970s (1976, 16).[12] This sexual and gender ambiguity in many ways reflected the ethos and aesthetics of the premodern societies of medieval Islam, especially as expressed through literature. At least in urban areas many males were normatively bisexual in behavior and found younger males sexually attractive.[13] Rudi Matthee, referring to Iran during the Safavid period (1501–1725), observes: "Public dancing was therefore never done by 'respectable' women, or indeed by anyone of standing, male or female, but only by boys and courtesans.... According to Chardin [French traveler in 16th-century Persia] dancing was only done by prostitutes and public women. In reality public dancing was done by Georgian boys as well—who commonly served as male prostitutes" (2000, 139).

Using examples from the Iranian world, I will suggest that male dancer/entertainers constituted discrete, named social categories of persons and/or institutions, both historically and, in some areas such as Afghanistan, well into the latter part of the 20th century, with a resurgence today in post-Taliban Afghanistan, which may be viewed on YouTube. The degree to which these social categories were institutionalized differed, as did general perceptions regarding the individuals who made up these classes of performers throughout the area. Sometimes institutionalization through a special vocabulary and a set of both spoken and unspoken rules seems to have characterized this network, detailed by Baldauf (1990) and Shamisa (2002).

In sum, I want to put several Orientalist and historical assumptions about dancing boys to rest. First, historically in Iran and Egypt, as in many other areas of the Middle East such as Ottoman Turkey, in spite of prevailing Western images of sensuous female belly dancers, boy dancers were popular as entertainers; groups of both male and female entertainers were available for customers and clients to entertain at weddings and other celebrations. Thus, clients had their choice of either male or female groups of entertainers.[14] Second, both male and female dancers in these regions basically performed the same dance movements and styles. They also acted, performed acrobatics, sang, and played musical instruments.

The male dancer/entertainers were handsome youths of 12 to 16, but this was only an ideal, as reflected in medieval Turkish, Arabic, and Persian literature, especially in poetry.[15] In fact, these performers, particularly those who were engaging, charming, witty, or exceptionally talented, often carried their careers, and their admirers, into old age, a phenomenon I observed in the Iranian community in Los Angeles.

The historical record makes clear that these young dancers constituted a group of highly admired, sought-after entertainers. The dancer, called *raqās* in the Arab world and Iran, and *bacheh* in Afghanistan and Central Asia, constitutes a kind of person, not solely a characterization of homosexual behavior. I would characterize the individuals who occupied the categories of dancer/entertainers by a cluster of characteristics, all used in both poetic and popular descriptions, one aspect of which was that of the role of passive homosexual. Other characterizations of the male dancer included conflicting attributions: He is undependable. He is fickle. He is frivolous. He is flirtatious. He is cruel toward the faithful older lover. He is a member of the demimonde. He is a feminized male. He is a social outcast. And yet, he is at the same time an object of desire and ambiguity. He is both famous and infamous.

Taj Al-Sultana, a princess of the Qajar court, described one of the famous dancers of turn-of-the-century Tehran: "That night 'Abdi Jan's troupe had been called so that the harem occupants could watch the show. Of course, you remember 'Abdi well. Let me, nonetheless, give you a description of his looks. He was a lad of about twelve or thirteen, with large black eyes, languid and incredibly beautiful and attractive. His face was tanned and good-looking, his lips crimson, and his hair black and thick. Renowned throughout the town, the boy had a thousand adoring lovers. Being a dancer, however, he was unworthy of being anyone's beloved" (1993, 163). Her description encapsulates widespread native attitudes toward dancers as both desirable and inconstant.

Colonialism and Its Impact

Colonialist and postcolonial attitudes largely resulted in the destruction or displacement of the categories and practices of traditional performers. In some areas, such as Egypt and Central Asia, scandalized homophobic European colonial authorities took active steps to ban their activities and performances. These dancers and the homosocial milieus in which they entertained became tropes for the Oriental backwardness that offended those intellectuals in Iran who actively engaged in changing gender roles and sexual behavior.[16] After World War I with the overthrow of the six-century-long Ottoman dynasty, and later the deposing of the Qajar dynasty in 1925, by the Pahlavi dynasty, the new leaders of Turkey and Iran resolutely turned to the West for inspiration, cutting off patronage for traditional performers and creating new artistic genres or copying Western forms like ballet.[17]

In spite of Westernizing pressures, as late as the 1970s professional male dancers of traditional genres could still be observed in areas such as Afghanistan, Egypt, and to a lesser degree rural Iran.[18] As Magda Saleh observes of present-day Egypt: "The popularity of such dancing youths is rooted in ancient times, and the practice survives" (1998b, 495). As Najmabadi points out for Iran: "This profound heteronormalization of sensibilities was never fully 'accomplished' at the level of either gender or sexuality.... It took a century for many of these sensibilities to change" (2005, 55).

In the late 19th and early 20th centuries, the colonial powers—Great Britain, France, and Russia (and later the Soviet Union)—applied immense pressure on the local Muslim populations to conform to European standards of sexual behavior. Through the establishment of new educational, communications, and cultural systems, as Michel Foucault (1979) and later Timothy Mitchell (1991) and Bruce William Dunne (1996) tellingly analyze, the colonial practices of the Europeans became forcefully embedded in the minds of the colonized Muslim populations, particularly the elite. Many individuals among the Iranian elite, as well as those of Egypt, fervently embraced European behavior and attitudes as a means of achieving modernity and, thus, economic, social, and military parity with the European powers.

It must be stressed that there exist multiple forms of colonialism, and this phenomenon has not been thoroughly theorized because scholars like Edward Said and many after him have for too long focused on the imperialist enterprises of the West, particularly those of France and Great Britain, with passing reference to the United States, and no mention of the colonial projects of Russia and its successor state, the Soviet Union, in Central Asia. This is an error because the Russian/Soviet colonial enterprise was as brutal as that of Great Britain, France, and the United States. The Russian attitudes toward their Muslim populations were equally as disdainful as those of the Western powers.

One of the Orientalist tropes that symbolized "the degenerate Muslim" was the presence of dancing boys, a feature of Muslim cities throughout the Middle East and Central Asia. But, as Turkish scholar Metin And points out, the European observers could not "hide from their descriptions the breathless interest that they took in these performances" (1959, 24). In urban centers like Cairo, the fastidious British and French set about to rid the Egyptians of this moral plague through the educational, military, and penal systems. While sometimes the colonial authorities simply made the practice of professional male dancing illegal, characterizing it as prostitution, the larger colonial enterprise and civilizing mission was to create self-disciplined individuals who came to regard any manifestation of homosexuality as abhorrent.[19] The ideal colonized subject was one who became self-disciplined through exposure to Western ways and then passed on their colonialized mind-set to future generations. The object was to have the subject peoples adopt Western morals and values and propagate those values long after the colonizers had returned to where they came from. For this project they co-opted the elite classes, who often colluded with them, and they largely succeeded in inculcating their moral system, so that one finds many postcolonial subjects now adhering to Victorian models of propriety and views of sexuality, long after the former colonizers abandoned such attitudes.[20]

Over more than a century, the bisexuality that once constituted normative behavior in most of the Middle East and Central Asia came to be identified as deviant, and heterosexuality as normative.[21] These changes in sexual attitudes and practices dramatically demonstrate that both sexuality and gender constitute socially constructed spheres of activity and that sexuality and gender roles are malleable. Nevertheless, both gendered behavior and sexuality constitute deeply ingrained behavioral patterns, largely regarded as "natural" by those who

Figure 9.1   Dancing boy in Bukhara (today's Uzbekistan), circa 1890, in costume and hairstyle reflecting both male and female dress. Photograph by L. S. Barshchevsky. From the collection of Artemis Mourat. Used with permission.

follow cultural practices, and attitudes toward gender and sexuality take generations to change, as Najmabadi has demonstrated in her important study.

The Creation of Hypermasculine Dance Styles in Postcolonial Uzbekistan, Iran, and Egypt

The phenomenon of creating hypermasculine dance styles that arose due to the puritanical attitudes of the new elites is an example of the concept of "choreographing masculinity," a distinctive by-product of the colonializing project and civilizing mission. Choreographing masculinity is vividly demonstrated in the artificial creation of a masculine style of dancing that would prove acceptable to Western and Westernized elite tastes, sensitive to the already shady reputations of dancers, both male and female. This invented tradition was part of a wider but unconnected impulse among postcolonial choreographers throughout the

Middle East and Central Asia to distance male dance styles from what became increasingly regarded as exclusively or "naturally" feminine dance styles, seen from a Western or postcolonial point of view. At the same time, even before colonization and modernity, the dance profession—and even the word for "dancer"—constituted an insult and signified the lowest class of person. Nevertheless, the dancer and other entertainers, such as singers, actors, and musicians, who occupied a similar low status, were sought after and considered indispensable for celebratory occasions. After modernity, elite, Westernized populations sought new forms of entertainment.[22] In order to distance themselves from the traditional classes, in cities like Tehran and Cairo they moved to new Westernized suburbs.[23] When it came to attracting middle-class individuals in Egypt and Iran, and working-class children in Soviet Uzbekistan, to dance in newly formed, state-supported companies, as well as in amateur and private companies, the new hypermasculine style served to create a new cultural space, where one could safely dance, theoretically without stigma.

In Iran, the Persian neologism *raqsandeh* is a neutral term that came to replace the disdainful terms *raqās* (male dancer) and *raqāseh* (female dancer); it theoretically provided a neutral space for middle-class individuals seeking a career in state-sponsored dance companies.[24] In choreographic terms, stilted and banal hypermasculine dance movements, for "real men," were in fact alien and intrusive. This new style of dancing in Egypt, Iran, and Uzbekistan had two characteristics: it clearly drew heavily from Western classical ballet, and it was accompanied by choreographers' claims that their sources were actually indigenous sports, martial arts, and work movements.[25]

In Iran, choreographers like the early Armenian teachers and, later, the English choreographer Robert de Warren, who directed the Iranian State Folk Ensemble (Mahalli Dancers), claimed to use stylized movements based on such activities as *zur-khaneh* (indigenous Iranian martial arts) exercises and horseback riding.[26] Similar claims were made by Egyptian and Uzbek choreographers concerning inspiration from sports, masculine work movements, and martial arts, but a close analysis of these ersatz dance styles rarely shows any connection to polo, archery, or horseback riding that is not mediated by a Western ballet vocabulary.

The newly invented movement vocabularies for male dancers in all three areas tend to the simplistic, even parsimonious: the males skip and hop with huge steps, covering large spaces; they frequently stamp; and the hand and arm gestures are very broad and frequently ungainly, in contrast to the female dancers' graceful, more delicate arm and hand movements. Sometimes men's arms are employed like windmill blades, propelled by a strong wind and with the elbows locked, the arms making large sweeping movements. The dancers often appear rigid on the stage. In every way, the male movements are created in a culturally negative space to constitute a contrast to the movements that were historically shared by both men and women—that is to say, what Westernized elites now perceive as "female" movements. One of the major differences that occurs in the new style of male dancing in all these areas is that the torso is held immobile, unlike the previous forms of traditional dance; nor are there any shoulder shimmies or articulated pelvic movements. The hands and head also remain stiff and unyielding, in contrast to the intricate arm and hand movements, and lively facial expressions and head gestures, that formerly characterized these traditions.

In the new hypermasculine style, the males frequently serve as a backdrop for a female soloist or a female chorus. Their choreographic duties consist of standing in a row clapping, kneeling in a row as female dancers circle about them, or assuming a "masculine" pose as the women execute figures in front of them. They often carry staves or sticks to represent male martial activities or perform theatricalized martial arts. Because these hypermasculine styles were created to negate native movement traditions common to both sexes, they come with an extremely limited vocabulary that has not developed into a viable movement tradition over the past 50 years since hypermasculinity was invented.[27] This trend has also had the effect of attracting fewer male dancers to a style that emphasizes female artistry. As in the development of 19th-century Romantic ballet, the female dancer has become the main focus of spectacle.

Egypt and Mahmoud Reda's New Male Dancer

Through the colonizing process, the Egyptian elite came to despise their own "illiterate masses," as well as belly dance, a genre of undoubted sensuality, which was equally performed by both men and women. It became, in the words of Morroe Berger, "something of an embarrassment to the cultural and political custodians of the East, who began to consider themselves above their own popular arts.... [T]he government encourages instead the performance of a sort of folkloric dance that only vaguely resembles the belly dance" (1966, 43), and that was permitted only for the female dancers.

After 1950, with the fall of King Farouk and the formal departure of the British as the colonial rulers from Egypt, the Soviet Union exercised enormous political and social influence in Egypt and other regions of the third world, and this included the field of choreography. From the 1950s to the present, choreographers such as Mahmoud Reda and other Egyptians, with the aid of choreographers from the Moiseyev Company in the former Soviet Union, or at least influenced by Moiseyev's performances, created new hypermasculine dance styles that would be acceptable to Westerners, and the now Westernized, elite classes. Magda Saleh notes that "the artistic directors of the performing group of the [state-sponsored] Firqa al-Qawmiyah were initially Soviet specialists, and the first was Boris Ramazin. Since 1979, this troupe has been headed by Egyptians" (1998a, 496).

So important was this need to erase any traces of homoeroticism, especially in dance, which particularly served the Soviet Union as a politically safe icon of ethnic identity, that the Soviet Union sent Russian "advisers" and "brothers" to Egypt and Uzbekistan, and other Muslim republics, such as Turkmenia and Kazakhstan, to oversee this process throughout the 1940s, 1950s, and 1960s.[28] Homosexuality was a taboo subject in the former Soviet Union, where it was considered a sign of decadent capitalism.

In her study of Mahmoud Reda's choreographic innovations and practices, his main soloist, Farida Fahmy, claims that Reda was not influenced by Western forms: "In his formative years as a choreographer, Mahmoud Reda understood the dangers of allowing himself to succumb to Western influences, especially in the content of his art medium" (1987, 16). But dance historian Lois Ibsen Al-Faruqi disagreed and stated in her study of Middle Eastern dance: "In the Middle East, recent attempts at programmatic dance by companies like Firqah Reda of Egypt are obvious attempts to imitate an alien tradition (European dance) rather than one native to Egypt" (1987, 7).

Whatever the influences, it is clear even from Reda's account of his process that he was attempting to create a new style intended to replace older traditions. In 2000, Mahmoud Reda stated: "The men in the north had no dance of their own [i.e., they performed a domestic form of belly dancing], so I had to create a dance tradition for them for the stage" (personal interview, January 21, 2000). When I was in Egypt in 2000, the male dancers under the direction of Reda, the founder of the Reda Troupe, and the Firqah al-Qowmiyyah, which functioned as Egypt's state folk dance companies, did not perform anything resembling the belly dancing that I saw elsewhere, in several events from elite parties in Cairo to rural performances in the villages around Luxor. Outside Egypt's "official" theaters, both male and female dancers performed domestic versions of belly dance.[29]

Uzbekistan and the Creation of a New Masculine Dance Style

In Uzbekistan, as in the other Soviet republics, the creation of a new masculinized dance technique was crucial because dance was a centerpiece of representational strategies for the Soviet government. Dance was used to portray the happy workers (in the cotton pickers' dance, prominent in the repertoire of Bahor, one of the Uzbek state folk dance companies) and also was central to the portrayal of a rainbow of ethnic diversity. It was particularly important for use in cultural ambassadorship: the state folk dance companies were among the most popular attractions sent to the third world, where the former USSR was attempting to win hearts and minds. Moreover, in the heavily choreophobic environment of the Muslim populations in Central Asia, a new dance style, not tainted with prior allusions to prostitution and homosexuality, had to be created for both male and female dancers in order to attract young children from working-class families to undertake dance studies in the government-sponsored dance schools.

In her study of Uzbek dance, Mary Masayo Doi also sees it "as a commodity produced during the Soviet periods" (2002, 93). Uzbek choreographers created a new movement tradition for men, while for the female performers they elaborated the dance practices of professional boy dancers.[30] Historically, female performers in religiously conservative Central Asia were not permitted to dance in public. Thus, in Uzbekistan a new generation of female dancers relied on the professional practices of the *batchas* as the basis of the new "classical" style that choreographers like Mukarram Turgunbaeva and Tamara Khanum developed for the new state-supported dance ensembles. They elaborated and classicized this *batcha*-based style into a new theatrical medium that is now rather distant from its origins, in the same way that Riverdance has been elaborated and distanced from Irish step dancing.

Doi recognizes that this classical tradition is invented, created from the format in which ballet is taught and fusing it with native movement practices. But, even though she states that "in the pre-Soviet period, most professional dancers were boys who wore women's clothing" (2002, 44), she does not further explore this fact. Because of the lack of historical sources in her study, Doi fails to see that the primary sources for the Uzbek element in contemporary classical dance for women are the movement practices of professional boy dancers. Numerous European travelers to Central Asia in the 19th century described the movement practices of these boy performers, among them Eugene Schuyler, who wrote about the boy dancers doing the *katta uyin*, a dance that later became a staple in the repertoire of Bahor, the all-female Uzbek state dance company.

Doi describes the newly created male dance style taught in the Uzbek dance conservatory as follows: "The boys stood tall, stomped their feet with resounding thumps, slashed the air with arms like blades, jumped high in the air, or spun quickly into a drop to one knee" (2002, 89). Such movements constitute an invented movement tradition, in Hobsbawm and Ranger's (1983) terms, that is one performed only in theater settings and stands in stark contrast to the traditional movement styles still seen elsewhere in traditional dance in both social and professional contexts. The movements that Doi describes correlate exactly with the films that I took of the male dancers in the dance classes in Tashkent in 1987 and saw in concerts in 1976, 1987, and 1989.

Doi documents the way in which Uzbek native artists, under the aegis of the Soviets, who were attempting to create an "Uzbek" identity, created a new, Uzbek classical dance tradition. They did this through the establishment of government dance schools, known in the Soviet period as *koreografski institut*, and later simply as *maktab* (school). In these schools, a named vocabulary of movements was codified and taught in the 1930s and 1940s and showed up in the works of Roziya Karimova (1973, 1975, 1977) and a canon of classical dances created by artists of the stature of Tamara Khanum and Mukarram Turgunbaeva, the prolific choreographer and founder of the leading professional company, Bahor. The instructional books by Karimova graphically demonstrate my point that the number and description of movements for men is only a fraction of those for female dancers.[31]

In addition, the government supported five professional dance companies, some of which feature only female dancers, that are located in Tashkent, and smaller companies in provincial cities. Doi accurately describes and analyzes the way Uzbek classical dances are taught, using the parallel practices of Western ballet, which all professional dancers in Uzbekistan learn, and the new Uzbek classical tradition (2002, 133).

Compared with the technique and performance of the former boy dancers, the new masculine style developed by the contemporary Uzbek dance figures constitutes a sorry spectacle. This stiff, artificial style, created out of whole cloth, with limited movement possibilities, attracts few men to the ranks of professional dance. Most of the major companies in Uzbekistan have only female dancers. When there are male dancers, they stomp and flail in a hypermasculine style that renders them inappropriate for participation in traditional dance choreographies, which feature graceful movements of the arms, hands, and head.

Iran and the New Choreographed Male

In Iran, postcontact attitudes resulted in embracing those performances and performers who comfortably fit into the images of propriety internalized by the new, Westernized middle classes. In the early Pahlavi period (1925–79), the new Pahlavi regime felt the need to disavow the previous Qajar regime. As historian Afsaneh Najmabadi observes: "Anti-Qajar stories depended for their political work on accusing Qajar women of fantastic sexual improprieties and on marking Qajar masculinity with the desire for penetratees and for young adolescent males" (2005, 212). The emerging middle classes followed the lead of the early Pahlavi government: rather than patronizing traditional performance genres that had become a national embarrassment, they sought Western forms.

Historically, boys and women danced in the same style in Iran as well as Egypt and Uzbekistan; however, Iranian choreographers were influenced to use a new hypermasculine style. It started in the 1930s and 1940s with Armenian teachers, all of whom had been trained in Russia and other areas outside of Iran, who felt the need to create separate male and female styles, such as those that existed in Armenian traditional dance. Although these ersatz male dance styles may have achieved a certain political correctness among Iranian Westernized elites, they never achieved sufficient aesthetic levels to ensure their continuation. In *Chehel-Setun*, a dance choreographed by Robert de Warren for the Iranian National Dance Company (based on wall paintings from a 16th-century palace in Isfahan, Iran), the male dancers skipped awkwardly and gamboled about the stage waving handkerchiefs and performing an occasional jeté in order to provide a role for male dancers that never existed in any historical context but rather reflects a strong ballet influence and, in fact, constitutes an invented tradition based solely on ballet.[32]

In the process of creating these new, sterile dance forms, the possibility of recovering the former dance practices, with their spectacular gymnastic elements, has been lost.[33] The hypermasculine, invented dance styles constitute a choreographic dead end. In Iran, for example, the hypermasculine dance style died when Ayatollah Ruhollah Khomeini closed down all dance activities following the revolution of 1979.

And, as demonstrated in social dance practices in all these regions, the love for the old "degenerate" style continues among many individuals of all classes and can be seen in celebrations such as weddings and simple evening gatherings in which both men and women, boys and girls perform within the same style. In fact, in Iran, Afghanistan, Egypt, and the United States, many more male dancers are appearing who dance in the old style. This can be seen in the profusion of dance performances, amateur and professional, that can be found on YouTube.

Clearly, the figure of the dancing boy, the *amrad* (beardless youth), with his deep-seated cultural resonance and rich movement tradition, still haunts the political and social landscape with his timeless dance.

NOTES

An earlier version of this essay appeared in *Dance Chronicle* 13, no. 2 (2008): 211–38.

1. The history of colonialism in these states is beyond the scope of this essay. For those interested in a history of colonialism in Uzbekistan, see Allworth 1994; for Egypt, see Dunne 1996 and Mitchell 1991; for Iran, see Cottam 1979 and Keddie 2003.

2. I recently (December 6, 2007) saw an Afghani dancing boy on YouTube; he was performing before a large male audience in Ghandahar, who watched his performance with rapt attention. It was similar to a performance that I saw in Bamyan, Afghanistan, in October 1976. Also see Baldauf 1990; Koepke 2003.

3. See Shay 1999, especially 16–55.

4. See Karayanni 2004, for Flaubert's descriptions of Egyptian dancing, and Lane 2003, 377–82. Lane gives an account of the public dancers, both male and female, with a description of their movements. Ibrahim Farrah's film *Rare Glimpses* (1998) shows Thomas Edison's short film clip of the dancer Fatimah, who performed at the World's Columbian Exposition of 1893, in Chicago. Her dance is exactly the same as the extended filming of the Egyptian *ghawazi* dancers in *Dances of Egypt* ([1991] 2006), filmed 80 years later by Aisha Ali in 1973, and accurately described by Lane in the 1830s.

5. For a description of the numerous changes made in belly dance movements and choreography in the 1920s through the 1940s, see Shay 2008.

6. See 'Ameri 2003; Dunne 1996; Fahmy 1987; Najmabadi 2005; Saleh 1998b; Shay 2002; Tkachenko 1954.

7. The issue of homosexual practices in the Middle East and Central Asia is highly contested and charged with emotion. It is also dynamic. The best sources for a general overview of attitudes in the Middle Eastern Islamic world are Stephen O. Murray and Will Roscoe's *Islamic Sexualities: Culture, History, and Literature* (1997; the title is unfortunate, since "Jewish" and "Christian" sexualities do not exist, per se); Murray's article (1997b); Schmitt and Sofer 1992, which deals with contemporary societies and contains more personal, anecdotal material; and Najmabadi 2005, which is the most significant study describing changing practices and views of gender and sexuality in Iran.

8. Many Westerners perceive Middle Eastern countries as having an upper and a lower class. In fact, there are frequently two or three upper-class elites, who frequently do not interact. In Iran, for example, a class of extremely rich merchants from the bazaar (called *bazari* in Persian), who as a group followed a devout and traditional lifestyle, existed side by side but rarely interacted with the traditional landowning class (*zamindar*), who sent their children to the West for their education; the intellectuals from this class largely spearheaded the movement to modernity. In addition, a new class of prosperous, very secular individuals sprang up after World War II, and they took advantage of the propitious economic circumstances to create fortunes in manufacturing and construction. Like the landowning class they attempted to emulate, they preferred Western ballet as a refined, acceptable art form and abandoned the traditional forms.

9. Patlagean notes: "This empress, Theodora, ... seems once to have been a *scenica*, a show-girl, in other words a prostitute" (1989, 153). As I have stressed in other essays (Shay 1999), Byzantine and Sasanian attitudes held by the majority of inhabitants, who later became Islamized, continued into the Islamic period.

Also see, for example, Dupree 1976 for his discussion of dancing boys as prostitutes in Afghanistan.

10. See Beeman 1981, 1992; Beiza'i 1965.

11. See Shay and Sellers-Young 2005; Shay 2006.

12. I use the term dancer/entertainer because in this vast region dancing was only one of the aspects of their performance; they frequently also sang, acted, played musical instruments, and performed acrobatic feats. Typically the younger, most attractive youths danced; as they grew older, however, they tended to become musicians.

13. See Najmabadi 2005; Schmitt and Sofer 1992.

14. This was not, however, the case in Central Asia, where the politically powerful Muslim clergy forbade the public appearance of female entertainers. Also see And 1959, 24–32; Matthee 2000, 149–40.

15. For a more detailed description of the historical male dancer, see Shay 2006. Upon reaching maturity, primarily shown through the growth of a beard, a young man was no longer considered beautiful or sexually desirable. Of course, this was a cultural ideal, and young men frequently plucked their facial hair, or else the older partner looked the other way. Persian poetry is filled with the disappointment experienced by the older lover at the arrival of facial hair of his paramour. See Shamisa 2002, 51–52. Also see And 1959; Mashhun 2001; Murray 1997a; Shamissa 2002; Shay 2006; Southgate 1984; Wright and Rowson 1997.

16. See especially Najmabadi 2005.

17. See And 1959; Öztürkmen 2003; Saleh 1998a.

18. See the DVD *Dances of Egypt* ([1991] 2006); *Afghan Village* (1976); Mortensen 1993; Shay, personal observations, 1958–59, 1976, 1987.

19. See Dunne 1996.

20. See especially Dunne 1996; Mitchell 1991.

21. See Baldauf 1990; Dunne 1996; Najmabadi 2005; Schmitt and Sofer 1992.

22. See Fatemi 2005 for a description and analysis of how the Westernized Iranian elites turned away from traditional music and dance forms, while the traditional elites continued to patronize traditional dancers, albeit in much straitened circumstances. Fatemi also mentions the disappearance of male dancers.

23. Fatemi discusses the process by which the Westernized elites moved to the north of Tehran and patronized newly established nightclubs, theaters, and the radio and television that all featured newly Westernized forms of music and dance. The patronage formerly extended to traditional dancers and musicians was withdrawn except by the traditional elites and newly evolving criminal bosses centered in the southern part of Tehran.

24. So insulting and low is the term *raqās* that even male children who show an interest in playing music are discouraged by parents using the dreaded term for dancer (Jamal, personal interview, July 11, 2007). Lotfallah Mansuri, the celebrated director of the San Francisco Opera, told an audience that his father, upon finding that his son had abandoned his medical studies to pursue classical music, called him a *raqās* and refused to speak to him for years (public address, November 2004, San Jose, California).

25. For detailed descriptions of movements, see 'Ameri 2003; Fahmy 1987; Tkachenko 1954, the section on Uzbekistan. For Uzbek dance movements, see also Karimova 1973, 1975, 1977.

26. In the late 1920s and early 1930s, three Armenian dance teachers, Madame Yelena, Madame Coronelli, and Sarkis Djanbazian, moved from the former USSR to Iran and opened dance schools, teaching ballet and character dance. Their classes were largely attended by the sizable Armenian community in Tehran, but some Muslims, Jews, Baha'is, and Zoroastrians also attended. The best account of their activities and careers can be found on the Web site of Nima Kiann, which also furnishes other information and articles about dance in Iran. For a more personal account of the early period of the activities of the Armenian teachers, see Ramazani 2002.

27. I used the following films for the movement observations: *Egypt Group of Folk Dance* (n.d.), *Gharam fi al-Karnak* (n.d.), *Raqs-ha va Avaz-ha-ye Mahalli-ye Iran* (n.d.), and personal films taken in Uzbekistan in 1986.

28. See Fahmy 1987; Saleh (1998a), Tkachenko 1954, especially the sections on "Tajikistan" and "Uzbekistan".

29. *Gharam fi al-Karnak*; Shay 2002, chapter on Egypt.

30. The Caucasian Soviet Republics, Azerbaijan, Georgia, and Armenia of the former USSR also have a highly masculine dance tradition; however, it is one among many dance traditions in which men participate. In Azerbaijan, boy dancers historically performed like those in Iran. However, the so-called academic style—that is, highly stylized folk dance, in which the males wear the Circassian coat (*cherkes*) and depict warriors and choreographically display hypermasculinity—is the only dance tradition depicted in the dance performances of the national companies, except for a few rural line dances (Namus Zokhrabov, personal interview, July 28, 2007).

31. For a detailed movement analysis, including illustrations, see Karimova 1973, 1975, 1977.

32. See 'Ameri 2003 for a detailed description of the movements; also see video *Raqs-ha va avaz-ha-ye mahalli-ye Iran* (n.d.).

33. In the late 1960s and early 1970s, a wave of nostalgia for Qajar-era performing and decorative styles swept through Tehran, where a number of cafés sprang up in which former boy dancers, now elderly, but still capable performers, appeared. A detailed study of these earlier performers would have permitted some degree of historical reconstruction, but unfortunately this was not done (personal observation, October-November 1976).

WORKS CITED

Aldrich, Robert. 2003. *Colonialism and Homosexuality.* London: Routledge.

Allworth, Edward, ed. 1994. *Central Asia: 130 Years of Russian Dominance, A Historical Overview.* 3rd ed. Durham, NC: Duke University Press.

'Ameri, Azardokht. 2003. "Raqs-e 'amianeh-ye shahri va raqs-e mowsum be klasik: barrasi-ye tatbiqi dar howze-ye Tehran." *Mahour Music Quarterly,* no. 20 (Summer): 24–28.

And, Metin. 1959. *Dances of Anatolian Turkey.* New York: Dance Perspectives, 3.

Baily, John. 1988. *Professional Musicians in the City of Heart.* Cambridge: Cambridge University Press.

Baldauf, Ingeborg. 1990. "Bacabozlik: Boylove, Folksong and Literature in Central Asia." *Paedika* 2 (2): 12–31.

Beeman, William O. 1981. "Why Do They Laugh?" *Journal of American Folklore* 94 (374): 506–26.

———. 1992. "Mimesis and Travesty in Iranian Traditional Theatre." In *Gender in Performance,* ed. Laurence Senelick, 14–25. Hanover, NH: University Press of New England.

Behdad, Ali. 1999. "Sevruquin: Orientalist or *Orienteur?*" In *Sevruguin and the Persian Image: Photographs of Iran, 1870–1930,* ed. Fredrcick N. Bohrer, 78–98. Washington, DC: Arthur M. Sackler Gallery and Smithsonian Institution; Seattle: University of Washington Press.

Beiza'i, Bahram. 1965. *Namayesh dar Iran* [Theater in Iran]. Tehran: Keivan Press.

Berger, Morroe. 1961. *A Curious and Wonderful Gymnastic: The Arab danse du Ventre.* New York: Dance Perspectives, 10.

———. 1966. "Belly Dance." *Horizon* 8 (2): 41–49.

Blunt, Wilfrid. 1966. *Isfahan: Pearl of Persia.* New York: Stein and Day.

Boone, Joseph. 2001. "Vacation Cruises; or, the Homoerotics of Orientalism." In *Postcolonial Queer: Theoretical Intersections,* ed. John C. Hawley. Albany, NY: State University of New York Press.

Bosworth, Clifford Edmond. 1976. *Mediaeval Islamic Underworld: The Banu Sasan in Arabic Society and Literature.* Leiden: Brill.

Brown, Carl, ed. 1996. *Imperial Legacy: The Ottoman Imprint on the Balkans and the Middle East.* New York: Columbia University Press.

Cottam, Richard W. 1979. *Nationalism in Iran.* Pittsburgh, PA: University of Pittsburgh Press.

Diba, Layla, ed. 1998. *Royal Persian Paintings: The Qajar Epoch 1785–1925.* New York: Brooklyn Museum of Art.

Doi, Mary Masayo. 2002. *Gesture, Gender, Nation: Dance and Social Change in Uzbekistan.* Westport, CT: Bergin and Garvey.

Dunne, Bruce William. 1996. "Sexuality and the 'Civilizing Process' in Modern Egypt." Ph.D. diss., Georgetown University.

Dupree, Louis. 1976. "Afghan Village." Essay accompanying film. Washington, DC: National Science Foundation/American University Film Service.

Fahmy, Farida (Melda). 1987. "Creative Development of Mahmoud Reda, a Contemporary Egyptian Choreographer." M.A. thesis, UCLA.

Falk, S. J. 1972. *Qajar Paintings: Persian Oil Paintings of the 18th and 19th Centuries.* London: Sotheby.

Farman Farmaian, Sattareh. 1992. *Daughter of Persia.* New York: Doubleday.

Al-Faruqi, Lois Ibsen. 1987. "Dance as a Form of Islamic Expression." *Dance Research Journal* 10 (2): 6–17.

Fatemi, Sasan. 2005. "La musique legere urbaine dans la culture iranienne: Réflexions sur les notions de classique et populaire." Ph.D. dissertation, University Paris X-Nanterre.

Foucault, Michel. 1979. *Discipline and Punish: The Birth of the Prison.* New York: Vantage.

Hillmann, Michael C. 1990. *Iranian Culture: A Persianist View.* Lanham, MD: University Press of America.

Hobsbawm, Eric, and Terence Ranger, eds. 1983. *Invention of Tradition.* Cambridge: Cambridge University Press.

Hopwood, Derek. 1992. *Sexual Encounters in the Middle East: The British, the French and the Arabs.* London: Ithaca Press.

Jonas, Gerald. 1992. *Dancing: The Pleasure, Power, and Art of Movement.* New York: Abrams.

Karayanni, Stavros Stavrou. 2004. *Dancing Fear and Desire: Race, Sexuality, and Imperial Politics in Middle Eastern Dance.* Waterloo, ON: Wilfrid Laurier University Press.

Karimova, Roza. 1973. *Ferganskii tanets.* Tashkent: Literatura i Iskusstvo.

———. 1975. *Khorezmiskii tanets.* Tashkent: Literatura i Iskusstvo.

———. 1977. *Bukharskii tanets.* Tashkent: Literatura i Iskusstvo.

Keddie, Nikki R. 2003. *Modern Iran: Roots and Results of Revolution.* New Haven, CT: Yale University Press.

Koepke, Bruce E. H. 2003. "Covert Dance in Afghanistan: A Metaphor for Crisis?" In *Asian Music,* ed. Mohd Anis Md Nor, 92–107. Kuala Lampur: Asian Pacific Dance Research Society.

Lane, Edward W. [1836] 2003. *An Account of the Manners and Customs of the Modern Egyptians.* Cairo: American University in Cairo.

Lansdell, Henry. [1887] 1978. *Through Central Asia: Diplomacy and Delimitation of the Russo-Afghan Frontier.* Nedeln, Liechtenstein: Kraus Reprint.

Loeb, Laurence D. 1972. "Jewish Musician and the Music of Fars." *Asian Music* 4 (1): 3–14.

Mashhun, Hasan. 2001. *Tarikh-e musiqi-ye Iran* [A History of Iranian Music]. Tehran: Farhang-e nashr-e now.

Matthee, Rudi. 2000. "Prostitutes, Courtesans, and Dancing Girls: Women Entertainers in Safavid Iran. In *Iran and Beyond: Essays in Middle Eastern History in Honor of Nikki R. Keddie*, ed. Rudi Mathee and Beth Baron, 121–50. Costa Mesa, CA: Mazda.

Mitchell, Timothy. 1991. *Colonizing Egypt*. Berkeley: University of California Press.

Mortensen, Inge Demant. 1993. *Nomads of Luristan: History, Material Culture, and Pastoralism in Western Iran*. London: Thames and Hudson.

Murray, Stephen O. 1997a. "Corporealizing Medieval Persian and Turkish Tropes." In *Islamic Homosexualities: Culture, History, and Literature*, ed. Stephen O. Murray and Will Roscoe, 132–41. New York: New York University Press.

———. 1997b. "Will Not to Know: Islamic Accommodations of Male Homosexuality." In *Islamic Homosexualities: Culture, History, and Literature*, ed. Stephen O. Murray and Will Roscoe, 14–54. New York: New York University Press.

Murray, Stephen O., and Will Roscoe. 1997. *Islamic Homosexualities: Culture, History, and Literature*. New York: New York University Press.

Najmabadi, Afsaneh. 2005. *Women with Mustaches and Men without Beards: Gender and Sexual Anxieties of Iranian Modernity*. Berkeley: University of California Press.

Öztürkmen, Arzu. 2003. "Modern Dance Alla Turca: Transforming Ottoman Dance in Early Republican Turkey." *Dance Research Journal* 35 (1): 38–60.

Patlagean, Evelyne. 1989. "Empire in Its Glory." In *Cambridge Illustrated History of the Middle Ages: 350–950*, ed. Robert Fossier, 148–77. Cambridge: Cambridge University Press.

Ramazani, Nesta. 2002. *The Dance of the Rose and the Nightingale*. Syracuse, NY: Syracuse University Press.

Said, Edward. 1978. *Orientalism*. New York: Vintage Books.

Saleh, Magda. 1998a. "Egypt: Contemporary Dance Companies." *International Encyclopedia of Dance*, 2: 495–99. Oxford: Oxford University Press.

———. 1998b. "Egypt: Traditional Dance." *International Encyclopedia of Dance*, 2: 486–95. Oxford: Oxford University Press.

Schmitt, Arno, and Jehoeda Sofer, eds. 1992. *Sexuality and Eroticism among Males in Moslem Societies*. Binghamton, NY: Harrington Park Press.

Schuyler, Eugene. [1876] 1966. *Turkistan: Notes of a Journey in Russian Turkistan, Kokand, Bukhara, and Kuldja*. New York: Praeger.

Shamissa, Sirous. 2002. *Shahed-bazi dar Adabiayyat-e farsi* [Sodomy in Persian Literature]. Tehran: Entesharat-e Ferdows.

Shay, Anthony. 1999. *Choreophobia: Solo Improvised Dance in the Iranian World*. Costa Mesa, CA: Mazda.

———. 2002. *Choreographic Politics: State Folk Dance Companies, Representation, and Power*. Middletown, CT: Wesleyan University Press.

———. 2005. "The Male Oriental Dancer." In *Belly Dance: Orientalism, Transnationalism, and Harem Fantasy*, ed. Anthony Shay and Barbara Sellers-Young, 85–113. Costa Mesa, CA: Mazda.

———. 2006. "The Male Dancer in the Middle East and Central Asia." *Dance Research Journal* 38 (1 and 2): 137–62.

————. 2008. *Dancing across Borders: The American Fascination with Exotic Dance Forms.* Jefferson, NC: MacFarland.

Shay, Anthony, and Barbara Sellers-Young. 2005. "Introduction." In *Belly Dance: Orientalism, Transnationalism, and Harem Fantasy,* 1–27. Costa Mesa, CA: Mazda.

Shoberl, Fredric. 1828. *Persia, Containing a Brief Description of the Country; and an Account of Its Government, Laws and Religion, and the Character, Manners and Customs, Arts, Amusements, etc. of Its Inhabitants.* 3 vols. London: R. Ackermann.

Southgate, Minoo S. 1984. "Men, Women, and Boys: Love and Sex in the Works of Sa'di." *Iranian Studies Journal* 17 (4): 413, 451.

Srivastava, Sanjay. 2004. "Introduction: Semen, History, Desire and Theory." In *Sexual Sites, Seminal Attitudes: Sexualities, Masculinities and Culture in South Asia,* ed. Sanjay Srivastava, 11–58. New Delhi: Sage.

Taj Al-Sultana. 1993. *Crowning Anguish: Memoirs of a Persian Princess from Harem to Modernity.* Edited with an introduction and notes by Abbas Amanat. Translated by Anna Vanzan and Ali Neshati. Washington, DC: Mage.

Tkachenko, Tamara. 1954. *Narodny Tanets.* Moscow: Isskustvo.

Wafer, Jim. 1997. "Vision and Passion: The Symbolism of Male Love in Islamic Mystical Literature." In *Islamic Homosexualities: Culture, History, and Literature,* ed. Stephen O. Murray and Will Roscoe, 107–31. New York: New York University Press.

Wagner, Ann. 1997. *Adversaries of Dance: From the Puritans to the Present.* Urbana: University of Illinois Press.

Wright, J. W., Jr., and Everett K. Rowson. 1997. *Homoeroticism in Classical Arabic Literature.* New York: Columbia University Press.

FILMS

Afghan Village. 1976. Hanover, NH: American University Field Services.

Dances of Egypt. [1991] 2006. Los Angeles: Araf Discs.

Egypt Group of Folk Dance. N.d. Los Angeles: Saut wa Soora Co.

Gharam fi al-Karnak. N.d. Cairo: Gemal Elleissi Films.

Ibrahim Farrah Presents Rare Glimpses. 1998. New York.

Raqs-ha va avaz-ha-ye mahalli-ye Iran. N.d. Tarzana, CA: Pars Video. No. 125.

JAMAL

> *Born in Tehran, Iran, Jamal is a visual artist, designer, choreographer, and the artistic director of AVAZ International Dance Theatre, a Los Angeles–based dance troupe that specializes in traditional and contemporary dance of the Iranian world. He immigrated to the United States in 1976 and became a citizen in 1990.*

When I was a child, I used to see the women relatives dancing and singing in the theatrical games known as *bazi-ha*. I remember my sister, with whom I was very close, put a scarf around my hips to dance. She was two years older than I, and I remember her helping me learn to move my hips. That is my first memory of dancing. I came from a middle-class family. My father and brothers traveled widely throughout Iran on business; my father dealt in produce, which means he went throughout the countryside to bring it back to Tehran, and one of my brothers was in the air force, so I traveled a great deal in every part of the country with both of them, and to Luristan and Kurdistan to visit family members. We attended weddings in tribal areas with people my father did business with, and on all of these occasions I saw and participated in folk dancing.

There was no one that I knew in any of the middle-class neighborhoods that I lived in who participated in the arts. Children were actively discouraged from even thinking about participating in any artistic activities in a number of ways. When I was around 10, someone gave me a violin. I truly wanted to learn to play music. It disappeared from my room. If any of us drew pictures, our families would complain that we were not spending enough time on schoolwork. They could not envision their child as the next Monet or Picasso, because crafts are more prevalent in Iran, and art is associated mostly with crafts. No one wanted their child to become a craftsman. As a child, I was one of those who drew pictures. There were no art classes in Iranian schools, but I was fascinated with drawing and spent hours at it. I knew that my family would not approve, so I hid my drawings.

Dance lessons for people of our class did not exist. Anyone who wanted to act in the theater, play music, or dance, especially the boys, they called *raqas*, which means a male dancer, which is considered an insult or, at the least, a lightweight or unimportant person. Even though *raqs* [dance] symbolizes elegant movement and

Jamal beside a series of his Southwest paintings in 1990. Photograph by Anthony Shay. Used with permission.

grace, in conversation it can be very insulting. I remember once when I sat singing, not even moving, my father said, "Raqas-bazi dar naiar" ["Be quiet, don't act like a dancer"]. It is the greatest possible insult. That is not to say that there were not a few families who allowed their children to enter music or dance—people already involved in the arts, upper-class people who could afford dance lessons for their daughters or music lessons for the boys, or people who were involved in theater. These were mostly people who had contact with, or been educated in, Europe or the United States. But there were very few of these people. Of course, people danced in domestic settings for fun and for weddings. My sister-in-law was a fabulous dancer and taught her daughters to dance, but they did not dance in public. I learned a lot just by watching her.

I had no formal training in dance. There were no role models in dance in Iranian society. The few performances of state-supported companies, both those supported by the Iranian government and several companies that came from abroad, were for the elite. Most people in Iran did not attend concerts of any kind. They were expensive, and people were not used to going to theaters and museums as they do in the West. Most of the entertainment and recreation took place in family gatherings. I realize now that it wasn't that people were bad, but rather it was our environment. In school there were no field trips. I never saw live performances of music and dance. If I had seen Baryshnikov or Nureyev I might have had a different future, but our image of the West was all John Wayne. None of my friends entered the arts. If you entered either the visual or performing arts it was shameful.

To be masculine in Iran, you had to be a *molla* [Muslim cleric], butcher, or mechanic. And yet, these are the very types of men who approached me sexually as a young boy. So behavior that was valued in Iranian society as masculine had nothing to do with sexuality. And if you were young and played the guitar, or sang or acted, or participated in art in any form, it always raised the question of your masculinity. You were considered *mamush* or *susul* [sissy]. Iran is a society in which people judge the book by its cover. Of course, another way that families discouraged their kids from being in the arts was by saying that there was no financial future in it.

As a kid, like almost every other boy in my neighborhood, I was mad for soccer. It was my consuming passion, and I made it on the national youth team and traveled widely throughout Asia as a member of the soccer team.

Discos were popular in Iran, and we all did *baba karam* [a type of improvised dance associated with working-class men of Tehran]. We were very shy, and we would all look down as we danced, but we went to the disco to meet girls. After I graduated from high school, like everyone else, I went into the army. Isolated in our barracks, we danced and played music to entertain ourselves almost every night. Friday night was performance night, and we did everything from stripping to dancing on our toes. It was all a great deal of horseplay. My friend Hamid would try to dance on pointe like a Georgian dancer. He did it barefooted. We also performed comic dances, some of which were explicitly sexual, like the women's *bazi-ha*. Usually a few drinks helped. These performances were ultra-out-of-control performances. A few drinks would lead you down a path you had never been on before. But, like all such dance performances among Iranians, we let ourselves go because it was a "safe" environment, behind closed doors.

Naturally, with that image of dance as out-of-control behavior done behind closed doors, parents are not going to encourage their children to dance. It's bad enough for girls, but for boys it was even worse. So the environment for dance in Iran was very bad. People did not recognize it as an art, but only as disreputable, sleazy behavior. And this was only aggravated by the depictions of dance in the

Iranian cinema. I never dreamed that years later I would dance and choreograph a command performance for Farah Pahlavi, the former empress of Iran. [This was with AVAZ International Dance Theatre in 1998 in New York.]

In 1976, I came to the United States to study. I had dreamed of becoming a doctor, but higher education in Iran was limited to the few from the elite who had influence. There were so few universities that even those with the best grades could not find a place. My first opportunity in the United States to study was in Oklahoma, in the small town of Yukon. In a place where Pizza Hut is the highlight of the town, we Iranian students found ourselves going to church events to meet girls, and we attended barbeques and did line dances with the local people, many of whom came from Eastern Europe. These dances seemed very similar to the Iranian line dances I was familiar with. But still, soccer was my main activity and focus. We created a team in Yukon with the local Americans and the Iranian students. I love movement in all its forms, and in many ways soccer has many movements that are very graceful and dancelike. So soccer fulfilled that desire.

In 1978, I came to California and studied design, both architectural and fine art painting. I earned my B.A. and M.A. in the art department of California State University, Los Angeles. After graduating, I was first hired as a senior designer in an architectural firm, but ultimately, I felt the need to escape. I had been in America for 10 years, and I knew American society. I went into fine arts painting. I had several shows, and my work was exhibited in galleries nationwide.

In 1990, after seeing an AVAZ concert, I volunteered to serve on their board. It was a company making a crucial move away from a repertoire that covered the Middle East, North Africa, and Eastern Europe to a repertoire that focused on the Iranian world. I began to see the stage as a blank canvas for my expressive ideas. I designed backdrops, sets, and costumes for the company, and then I created my first choreography. By this time, I had gained the trust of the artistic director, the board of directors, and, most of all, the dancers. In the beginning, I only wanted to do one dance. I took all the elements of *shateri/jaheli*, a very sensual dance genre associated with lower-class men in Tehran, which also has stylized work movements of traditional bakers. It was one of the dances that we did in the barracks in the army, but this time it was without the drinking. It was an immediate hit with the Iranian American community because, without eliminating the sexuality and sensuality that is inherent in the tradition, I created a classicized dance genre— abstracting and stylizing the movements and placing it in the tradition of Iranian solo improvised dancing.

After that, I really went back to my past and created a series of tribal and classical Persian dances that were based on my visual and somatic memories. I created a complete set of Iranian folk dances. And then my title changed—people called me a choreographer. That really felt good. As I created new dances, I discovered that like all art, choreography is a variation of transitions, objects in space, which is the body as a medium, understanding the basic aesthetic elements, such as color, form, and contrast. I discovered that my formal training in art and design gave my choreographic work a unique look. Choreographing bodies, I am now more aware of dealing with masculine images with my male dancers and even for the female dancers. After many years of creating a body of work, and seeing multiple examples of Iranian dance on YouTube and in concert, I realize that my approach to choreographing Iranian dances is a masculine style, compared to the work of other Iranian choreographers.

You asked me if I wasn't afraid of what people would say about my masculinity. Well, in the beginning I was, because after all one is a product of one's culture and the attitudes from there. But, I didn't hesitate very long. I discovered that I truly loved dance, and I was good at performing it and creating it. I envision myself using choreography and dance to make a social statement now—dance is the most controversial art medium in the Iranian world. If I can shift the creation of dance to a more serious direction, I can challenge the choreophobia that characterizes Iranian society. Then I am making a contribution to my society and the art of dance.

10

Native Motion and Imperial Emotion

Male Performers of the "Orient" and the Politics of the Imperial Gaze

STAVROS STAVROU KARAYANNI

Musical performance, as well as the acts of listening, dancing, arguing, discussing, thinking and writing about music, provide the means by which ethnicities and identities are constructed and mobilised.

—Martin Stokes, *Ethnicity, Identity and Music*

The dance which followed was of the same description with the singing: it was not the expression of joy, or of gaiety, but of an extravagant pleasure, which made hasty strides toward lasciviousness; and this was the more disgusting, as the performers, all of them of the male sex, presented in the most indecent way scenes which love has reserved for the two sexes in the silence and mystery of the night.

—Vivant Denon, *Travels in Upper and Lower Egypt*

During the 20th century (especially the second half), the Greeks of Cyprus felt it imperative to excise anything that they marked as "Eastern," sounds and customs included. A Greek Cyprus aspiring to modernity yearned to cleanse itself of any possible remnants of centuries of Ottoman occupation. Belly dance itself, which captivated my childhood imagination with its promise for kinesthetic expression, was the object of derision and remained inaccessible to me because of ethnicity and gender. This very denouncement is what makes the *çifteteli* (the Greek and Turkish versions of belly dance) a personal site of reconciliation for what my identity as a Greek Cypriot man does not allow. Within this site, this particular dance form enacts a certain resistance to imperialism and an artistic claim for cultural and social territory that remains disputed and inaccessible. No other dance in the Greek or Greek Cypriot tradition has been Orientalized to the extent of the *çifteteli*. And, of course, Orientalization rarely comes unaccompanied by the accoutrements of abuse, abject feminization, and appropriation. In the popular Greek or Greek-affiliated

314

imagination, the *çifteteli* is an Eastern (Turkish) dance performed only by women in order to evoke great pleasure in the watching male. This severely limited misconception has determined the reception of this art. Investigating this dance and its linkage to sex and sexuality has intriguing connections with the history of sexual fashioning in Cyprus but also elsewhere.[1] If men perform it with some fervor, their sexuality will immediately come into question. Social norms will not permit a choreographic interpretation that attempts more than the standard steps rendered with solemnity and control, while hip swaying must not appear overindulgent. This dance is, therefore, a kind of frontier of masculine performance.

This frontier is strongly connected with colonization (the actual administration of faraway lands) and cultural imperialism. Colonization directs the scripting of national manhood, what it means to be a "man" according to the nation's definition. It is significant to decipher how the process of such scripting gives all forms of conquest and colonization access to and control over every individual subject's body. For the grand and magniloquent narratives that determine the gender character and sexual politics of a nation-state traverse culture and society as they run their course through peoples' bodies at every moment. Each subject negotiates her everyday affairs with movement and gestures that are sometimes inherited from parents but always learned through the context of the socially adopted and accepted body politic. Dance, in both its social and its cultural manifestations, serves as the fulcrum of my investigation. If our bodies are organic vessels that carry our personal history, our idiosyncrasies, our emotions and frustrations, signs that mark our national, gender, and class identity, then when we set that body in motion, the entire microcosm of the individual is on display; a microcosm replete with contraries such as control and resistance, compliance and oppression. In other words, in the condition of dance, the body resonates with its history, thus becoming a site where various meanings manifest themselves and cross paths with each other.

I have opened this article with reference to Cyprus, the eastern Mediterranean island where I was born and raised, since my investigation into belly dance springs from my own subject position. Such has been my passion for belly dance and so adverse was my environment that my position necessitated theoretical understanding of the complex issues that surround the various traditions of this controversial dance and my own involvement. My exploration yields some theoretical understanding of how gender and sexuality figure in its present-day context and how the contemporary performance of this dance is influenced by European colonization and Western imperialism. The two epigraphs, the first from Martin Stokes and the second from Vivant Denon, mark the trajectory of my exploration. I examine how dancing provides the means by which ethnicities and identities are constructed and mobilized, as Stokes puts it, and how the East-West interaction, evident in Denon's passage, has affected this construction. I discuss movement in terms of body memory, as if movement gestures (literally and figuratively) reveal not only prescribed behavior but also that which is proscribed, and with the confidence—as Stokes seems to suggest—that gender, meaning, sexual as well as ethnic identity, is constructed and mobilized through the medium of movement, making dance a prime site for investigating how we perform our compliance and defiance of our various identity embodiments.

My discussion begins with a historical investigation of the gender politics of public performers of 19th-century Egypt. This investigation occasions a broad examination of the male public performer as an Eastern cultural institution, something that provoked the sensibility of visitors from western Europe. Then I look at Mousbah Baalbaki, a contemporary male performer in Lebanon, and I conclude with comments on contemporary notions around ethnic, gender, and sexual identity and the male performance of belly dance.

Rich Performances and Poor Impressions

Cairo, early June 1834: Edward Lane informs us in a footnote to his chapter on Egypt's public dancers that the city's famous—infamous for many—dancing girls receive the portentous order to abandon their residence in Cairo. The *ghawazee* are to exile themselves to Upper Egypt with Essna, Qenah, and Aswan designated as their only possible residence options ([1860] 1963, 384). Issuing this edict is Egypt's pasha, Muhammad Ali, an Albanian-born soldier in the Ottoman sultan's army, who came to power in 1805, nominally under Turkish suzerainty. Ali was motivated by a keen commitment to modernize Egypt. Describing his endeavors, Leila Ahmed underlines the emphasis he placed on utilizing resources and passing reforms that would ultimately secure economic and administrative independence for Egypt: "Intent upon making Egypt independent, Muhammad Ali set about modernizing his army and increasing revenues. He introduced agricultural, administrative, and educational reforms and attempted to establish industries, his initiatives in these areas giving impetus to economic, intellectual, cultural, and educational developments important to women" (1992, 131).

Examined in the context of colonial discourse, a non-Western ruler's ambition to "modernize" his "Oriental" state implies—almost invariably to me, a Cypriot who has seen it happen in his own country—some sort of genuflection to the imposition of the technological and cultural superiority of western Europe. Modernization further indicates a willingness to allow, even invite, colonial influence, involvement, or dependence. Indeed, Muhammad Ali proceeds to make his reforms following the propositions of European advisers brought especially to lend their expertise in constructing a new, Westernized, industrialized, and fortified Egypt. As Ahmed indicates, these developments made, in their immediate impact, Western economic advances, but "Muhammad Ali's policies adversely affected some women, particularly lower-class urban and rural women" (1992, 131). However, neither here nor elsewhere does Ahmed make reference to the dancers of Cairo, so their social position and the nature of their profession remain undiscussed and, therefore, completely absent from an otherwise thorough and well-researched project. What emerges from Ahmed's (problematic) silence on the issue is that the fate of the *ghawazee* became entangled in Muhammad Ali's "eagerness to acquire the technologies of Europe, which was an important catalyst" (133) in Egyptian affairs of this time. The edict that banished dancers and courtesans to Upper Egypt was, perhaps, a measure to alleviate the pasha's embarrassment at his country's popular arts and customs, as Morroe Berger suggests, and to appease religious authorities: Muhammad Ali "became ashamed, I suppose, not only of his domain's economic backwardness but of its popular arts as well. Partly because of the bad impression they made on foreigners and partly because of pressure from religious leaders, Muhammad Ali barred the public dancing girls from the Cairo area in 1834" (1961, 30). Berger's syntax here is ambiguous: it seems to make the disturbing suggestion that the Egyptian leader's domain was indeed economically "backward," an interesting enactment of the kind of imperialism that the pasha had to contend with in the early 19th century. Indeed, if shame was Muhammad Ali's motivation, then his edict relied on an attempt to shift the territory of these artists' influence away from the bustling, cosmopolitan metropolis of Cairo.[2]

However, I am inclined to believe that more than religious authorities, the principal motive for banishing the *ghawazee* was to appease the Europeans, since the poor impression that many foreign visitors claimed to have about the dancers had become legendary. Vivant Denon's 1798 description of female dancers is one of the early examples of imperial dismay over the production of Oriental kinesthetic art:

> They were seven in number. Two of them began dancing, while the others sung, with an accompaniment of castanets, in the shape of cymbals, and of the size of a crown piece. The movement they displayed in striking them against each other gave infinite grace to their fingers and wrists. At the commencement the dance was voluptuous: it soon after became lascivious, and expressed, in the grossest and most indecent way the giddy transports of the passions. The disgust which this spectacle excited was heightened by one of the musicians . . . who, at the moment when the dancers gave the greatest freedom to their wanton gestures and emotions, with the stupid air of a clown in a pantomime, interrupted by a loud burst of laughter the scene of intoxication which was to close the dance. ([1803] 1973, 232–33)

By 1845, James Augustus St. John voiced a generally accepted opinion that "many travellers affect to have been much disgusted by the performances of the Ghazeeyeh" (270). In fact, even though the Orientalist (as Edward Said uses the term) sources do not make the point explicitly, some important facts point to

Muhammad Ali's European advisers as the main agent in securing the prohibition. For example, the very economics of the dancers' occupation manifest their indispensability. Again, according to Lane, because of their popularity, the *ghawazee* were numerous and enjoyed very high incomes, thus making a significant contribution to the Cairo-area income tax revenue (1963, 388). Apparently, following their exile, the sultan had to levy heavier personal taxes to compensate for revenue sacrificed to moral zeal. However, apart from the economics of the situation, the *ghawazee* were significant as an evidently established cultural institution. Their performances were considered essential at celebrations such as wedding parties, festivals, and circumcision ceremonies. Clearly, their artistic contribution to such events must have been important.[3] Directly associated with the Western gaze's effect was the opprobrium perceived to mark the dancers' performances, which scandalized some travelers and stimulated their negative accounts. In other words, the lasciviousness of the dance is an attribute that came to exist during scopic intercourse with the Western gaze.

Apparently, following Muhammad Ali's edict and the departure of large numbers of dancers and courtesans to Upper Egypt, the Cairo scene became inundated with *khawals*, dancing boys called *gink*, or *çengi* and *köçek* in Turkish. Rather amusingly, the *ghawazee* were sent away so as not to offend morals, yet as Berger informs us, the male dancers who came to prevail in their wake presented an even more relentless challenge to Western mores: "The number of male Oriental dancers increased, and they, as Flaubert found, were often more audacious and salacious than the girls. The male dancers were already famous before the banishment of the *almées*" (1961, 30).[4] These are enticing pieces of information that titillate, yet they undermine Berger's intentions to offer an objective and constructive appraisal of Middle Eastern dance.

This is clearly a moment when his article lapses into Orientalist banter that fails to offer an honest or engaging interpretation of male dancing in 19th-century Egypt. But I am still intrigued by the question of who exactly found the *khawals* more audacious and salacious. By whose standards were their performances more "lascivious" than the women's, and to what extent did the performers' gender affect the Western tourists' assessment?

My purpose in this essay is to examine the dynamics of Western interaction with the Middle Eastern male dancing body and the ways in which the questions of audience and moral standards affect the larger issues of colonial interaction and the colonial discourse that resulted from it. A force that propels this project derives from my personal involvement in Middle Eastern dance and my effort to deal with the variety of responses to my performance. Participating in an art form that, in the minds of most people in the West, is exclusively female, I often have to contend with attitudes both from audiences and from dance instructors. That is, most attempts to recuperate modern belly dance have relied on reconstructions of this dance as the remnant of women's fertility rites associated with

Figure 10.1   Turkish dancing boys, like the ones in this lithograph, moved in large numbers from Istanbul to Cairo in the 19th century. While Egypt was an Ottoman possession, the elites and those who served them wore high Ottoman clothing fashions. From the Artemis Mourat collection. Used with permission.

primeval goddess worship.[5] For some decades now these views have circulated as confident convictions developed under the rubric of feminism but regarded with mistrust within feminism itself, although performance of this dance can be, and is for many, a valuable service to women's liberation.[6] While this service is entirely agreeable, such a reconstruction of Oriental dance is nonetheless so widespread that it is not merely part of the West, in the geographic and cultural specificities that define the West today (primarily North America and Western Europe), but has established itself internationally. I think that globalizing the "femininity" of this art is disconcerting because it predicates itself on certain romantic notions that have distorted crucial aspects of this dance's traditions. For example, constructing modern Oriental dance as a female fertility ritual silences the widespread custom of male dancers in the East. Moreover, the legacy of colonial dynamics and Western imperialism plays itself out in those individual European and North American instructors and performers of contemporary interpretations of Oriental dance. Many see themselves in the role of "rescuers" of this tradition, yet in this rescue operation they fail or refuse to acknowledge the history of colonialism and the biases or privilege that their Western position bestows upon them. Especially problematic is the conviction, encountered frequently within the belly dance community, that if it were not for dance schools and instructors in North America, this dance would not have survived into our present time.[7]

I do not mean to reassess male involvement in Middle Eastern public dancing with the ultimate purpose of reclaiming male dominance (ubiquitous in most aspects of society and art anyway) in this artistic tradition. Such a purpose would be extreme and even spurious. Instead, I wish to explore gender politics whose multifarious complexity emerges mainly from native kinesthetic expression before the imperial gaze. This gaze is, in fact, the main province of my investigation, with my interest extending to the female performers as well as the male, since the dynamics of the female performance are inextricably linked with those of the male, especially in the imperial context. The processes that molded Western attitudes toward dancers in the Middle East in the latter age of European imperialist and colonial expansion have effectively defined contemporary attitudes as well. Regarding these perspectives, Anthony Shay (2002) has been urging us to recognize significant complexities in the politics that determine dance. These attitudes, Shay argues, are not the prerogative of "foreign" Western audiences but also are held by "native elites"—those individuals from colonized countries where imperialism has taken deep roots. These are people, artists among them, who had and continue to have vested interests in replicating the Western worldview and perpetuating the colonial project mainly, but not exclusively, because of economic investments or political interests.

One example of this kind of imperial interference in indigenous traditions has figured in the introduction to this essay. The *ghawazee* were banned because, under the Western gaze, the quality of their art was questioned, thus turning their dancing into cultural embarrassment. If Berger is indeed accurate in assessing the influence of Egyptian religious leaders and European advisers in Egypt, then both these factions shared concerns that seem to have coincided in effecting this development that pushed the dancers' cultural activity into the space that Anne McClintock defines as "anachronistic." Under the new measures for the implementation of a "new" Egypt, the dancers become the "inherently atavistic, living archive of the primitive archaic" (1995, 41), incompatible with progress. Europeans moved into Egypt with their bourgeois moral pretensions serving as a fulcrum to implement policies that would civilize, educate, and refine its "savage" inhabitants. These pretensions became, in fact, a perfect means for policing human behavior abroad. Of course, such intentions were unsettled by the European experience of polymorphous "Eastern perversity," which fueled the efforts for reform and set in motion the circular process required to sustain assumed imperial responsibility. Eastern excess and its resistance to representation, let alone containment and control, came to be embodied in the Middle Eastern dancer's performance. Both the physical embodiment and the theoretical implications of the dance became a metaphor for much of what the West perceived as "Oriental." By physical embodiment I am referring to the actual dance moves, which provided a

somatic articulation unlike any that Western eyes were used to or could culturally accept as public spectacle. Choreographies of Middle Eastern public performers, male and female, largely consisted of suggestive contortions: writhing,
undulating, swaying the body with side twists, isolated muscle quivering, and
rhythmically elaborate hip articulations (Azizeh's "furious jerking of the hips"
[Flaubert 1972, 122]). The theoretical implications of such choreographies for
the Western spectators were overwhelming, as Flaubert's and Curtis's travel
accounts illustrate in relation to Kuchuk Hanem, a famous *ghawazee* dancer.
Europeans' conventional expectations of corporeal, gendered behavior were
contravened dramatically. Generations of cultural dogma confined the hips,
shoulders, and lumbar region to a controlled attitude that signaled a state of
embarrassed silence. By contrast, in Middle Eastern dance these body parts
acquired an expression enunciating a carnal sensuality and desire even to the
uninitiated, unaccustomed, and undiscerning European eye.

Viewed as text, a choreographic sequence of Oriental dance spelled out a
hieroglyphics of uninhibited sexual desire and wantonness. As Lady Mary
Wortley Montague writes from Adrianople in 1717: "This dance was very
different from what I had seen before. Nothing could be more artful, or more
proper to raise *certain ideas*. The tunes so soft!—The motions so languishing!—
accompanied with pauses and dying eyes! half-falling back, and then recovering
themselves in so artful a manner, that I am very positive the coldest and most
rigid prude upon earth, could not have looked upon them without thinking of
something not to be spoken of" ([1838] 1971, 163). Evidently, Montague's text
revels in the erotic posturing of the dance. The details she chooses to describe
gesture strongly toward an exhibition of sexuality that clearly challenges her
racial and social identification. Nevertheless, Montague's assessment of the
dance is kindly devoid of vehement disapproval or emphasis on excess and
lasciviousness. This generosity is perhaps predictable if one considers that her
views were radical for her time, marking a departure from the stereotypical
representations of Oriental society instituted by travel writers who preceded her.
Drawing from her special involvement with Turkish female society, Montague
challenged and criticized these earlier writers' published misconceptions and
sought to represent a revised view of Turkish culture. Nonetheless, in accordance with the norms of her time, she brackets overt sexuality from the
performance of the dance, its manifestation confined to silence—"not to be
spoken of."[8]

If a "lady" traveler had to confine sexuality to the unspeakable, European
men had equivalent difficulties. To the average Western male gaze, Middle
Eastern dance epitomized the aberrance believed to be innate in Eastern culture
as a whole and dictated the assumption of a detached, critical stance. As an
othered topos, the dancer's body was a site too fluid and evasive, articulating a
meaning that was deemed unreachable when its obvious significations were too
threatening to dwell upon. Dance was, therefore, impossible to naturalize or

institutionalize even when deciphered as desire. Desire, in fact, was the domain of potency, since quite often the male Western spectators felt themselves hovering in that perilous space just past the edge of their imperial virtue and just before the surrender to the semiotics of the dance, which invoked the inexorable urge to possess the dancer's body.

Lane's description of the *ghawazee* in *Manners and Customs of the Modern Egyptians* is quite revealing of this profound ambivalence toward the Eastern dancer as a trope of the East in general: "The Ghawazee perform, unveiled, in the public streets, even to amuse the rabble. Their dancing has little of elegance; its chief peculiarity being a very rapid vibrating motion of the hips, from side to side. They commence with a degree of decorum; but soon, by more animated looks, by a more rapid collision of their castanets of brass, and by increased energy in every motion, they exhibit a spectacle exactly agreeing with the descriptions which Martial and Juvenal have given of the performances of the female dancers of Gades" (1963, 384).

Gades, otherwise known as Cadiz, was a Phoenician colony and subsequently a Roman conquest. It enjoyed a great reputation for its dancers, who were celebrated by several Roman writers. Juvenal described dancers who "sink to the ground and quiver with applause...a stimulus for languid lovers, nettles to whip rich men to live" (quoted in Buonaventura 1989, 43). Martial, a Roman satirist, records a special characteristic of these dancers' moves in a dinner invitation that details exotic pleasures that his guest will not experience: "Nor will girls from naughty Gades, endlessly prurient, vibrate their wanton thighs with sweet trembling."[9] Apart from exhibiting his erudition, Lane is also reiterating the romantic notion of the Orient as a seamless continuation with a distant past and presenting it, in effect, as a rich kaleidoscope of primeval scenes unfolding before the European gaze. Moreover, his brief yet apathetic analysis of the dance is an unpersuasive attempt to feign a lack of interest. Further in the same chapter he betrays his fascination and disdain: "I need scarcely add that these women are the most abandoned of the courtesans of Egypt. Many of them are extremely handsome; and most of them are richly dressed. Upon the whole, I think they are the finest women in Egypt" (1963, 386).

The availability and promise of these women are the very qualities identified with the East and paradoxically the qualities that generate anxiety in the Western traveler. This anxiety arises from a complex matrix of responses. In travelers' accounts, there is a feeling of being implicated in Eastern depravity through the gaze itself, a guilt obfuscated by the often repressed desire for the dancer and the perceived pressure to perform in response to the Oriental performance. Indeed, the argument that defines the Oriental subject as the abject object of the Occidental gaze has to be reconsidered in light of the agency of the Oriental dancer's body and choreography, both of which provoke a complex interaction with the viewer. In discussing a video clip by the female

African American pop group TLC, Susan Foster addresses precisely what I infer from the *ghawazee*'s performance:

> The dancers repeatedly invite the camera and, implicitly, the viewer toward them, gesturing the body's sensuality and desire. Masterfully they rebuff, refocus, and reorient the gaze so as to control access to intimacy. Standing firm, they mock the objectification of the female body. Slipping deftly out from under the gaze's scrutiny, they illuminate pathways of desire whose directionality and accessibility they have crafted. By choreographing such a complex relationship to the gaze, these women artists embody the tense dynamism of their identities as Afro-American and feminist, as members of an oppressed and marginalized social group, and as leaders in an international avant-garde aesthetic. (1988, 16)

Albeit without the advanced technological means of contemporary video clip creation, the *ghawazee*'s choreography also gestures the body's sensuality and sexual promise. Masterfully, their bodies rebuff, refocus, and reorient the gaze "so as to control access to intimacy." Especially in this dance idiom where the moves have to be isolated, this isolation takes the place of the camera focus. Through deft moves executed under the male gaze's scrutiny, the dancers "illuminate pathways of desire whose directionality and accessibility they have crafted." By choreographing such a complex relationship to the Western gaze, the *ghawazee* embody their own tense dynamism and potency as well as that of the East. Therefore, they must be banished if order is to prevail over sexual anarchy in the emerging, modernized, Westernized Egypt.

It was through this very complex configuration of contraries—desire and disavowal, control and abandon—that the female dancers "increasingly came to be fetishized into an isolated female sign of the Orient's erotic and passionate potential" (Lewis 1996, 173). There is an imperative in this sign: the *ghawazee* had to be contained in this image so that passion, an imperial emotion projected onto the native performer, could proceed with its circulation and yield desire. The *ghawazee* became the sign on account of their sex. If European Orientalists resisted them, then the contestants for this sign would be male dancers, who were perceived to engender further vilification of European sensibility and morals. Passion and desire engaged in their magnetic courtship dance on the colonial field would cease to be heterosexual, turning, instead, homoerotic. In the eyes of travelers, male performance was similar to the *ghawazee*'s in technique and style except that their gender posed a far more formidable threat to European sexual ethics. What is important to point out, however, is that these male dancers were indispensable as well as threatening. Their dance set in motion those mechanisms that regulated the emotional capital of the empire. Thus, they engendered anxiety and fear framed by desire.

The Poetics of Male Dancing

Male dancers' presence and popularity, not only in Egypt but also over the entire Middle East and as far as Central Asia, had a long and strongly felt presence. Their survival, however, has depended largely on the narratives of Western visitors to the East. In Turkey at least, the "early Turkish sources offer little information" on dancers (male and female) because "dancing was regarded by many writers of the past as an improper and wicked sport, especially when indulged in by professional women and boys" (And 1976, 138). A selection of these narratives might assist in envisioning their activities and bodies as sites that have generated sexual meanings for the empire. It is especially significant that these sites helped hypostatize the European man's heteronormativity.

As early as 1675, Dr. John Covel's diaries describe "a delicate lovely boy, of about 10 yeares old," and, dancing with him, "a lusty handsome man (about 25) both Turkes. They acceded all the roguish lascivious postures conceived with that strange ingenuity of silent ribaldry" (Covel 1962, 214). Although Covel's account of these dancers is succinct and circumspect, it firmly sets the tone of ambivalence. As it emerges here, their choreography, enacted in "lascivious postures," supposedly displays an innate, intelligent, and inspired vulgarity—a near oxymoron that aptly conveys the seduction but also the indecency embodied by the male dancer of the East in the eyes of the bourgeois traveler.[10] Vivant Denon was less subtle in his disapproval. In 1810, Lord Byron and John Hobhouse enjoyed performances by transvestite boys in the coffeehouses of Galata, a Constantinople suburb famous for its tavernas. Apparently Hobhouse found the demonstration "beastly" (Garber 1992, 418), but Byron's reaction is unrecorded (Murray 1997, 24). Dating from the same period (the first quarter of the 19th century) is Lady Augusta Hamilton's account of these singing and dancing boys, with its delightful and appetizing details. She wrote in 1822, "They are dressed like girls, and accompany words adapted to the purpose, with wanton looks and gestures, which will often so please their employers, that they will almost cover the boys' faces with ducats, sticking them on with their spittle; and the boys, in their turn, have the dexterity, in the course of the dance, to slide them almost imperceptibly into their pockets" (49).[11] In the early 19th century, fights in these coffeehouses broke out frequently among the Janissaries, the sultan's soldiers, who were fervent admirers and competed for the attention of these boys (who were also known as köçek). According to Thijs Janssen, "It was generally assumed that koçek [another name for çengi] could be buggered. This explains much of the excitement of the male spectators, many of whom courted the koçek" (1992, 84–85). The period that Hamilton writes about, approximately the time when Byron was in the taverns of Galata, must have seen the apogee of the male dancers' popularity.

Another Western source testifying to the popularity of dancing boys, but also pointing out their salaciousness, was Eugene Schuyler, who journeyed through

Turkistan. Schuyler was the U.S. consul in Russia, an office he held before he embarked on his travels in Central Asia in 1867. In the places he visited, especially in Uzbekistan, he found that Mohammedan prudery did not allow women to dance in public; therefore, their role came to be fulfilled by "boys and youths" called *batchas*. "The moral tone of the society of Central Asia is scarcely improved by the change" (Schuyler 1966, 70), he adds. He gives an account of their enthusiastic reception by audiences and their esteemed status as artists: "These *batchas*… are a recognized institution throughout the whole of the settled portions of Central Asia, though they are most in vogue in Bukhara, and the neighbouring Samarkand. *Batchas* are as much respected as the greatest singers and *artistes* are with us. Every movement they make is followed and applauded, and I have never seen such breathless interest as they excite, for the whole crowd seems to devour them with their eyes, while their hands beat time to every step" (70).

A few paragraphs later, in an attempt to fulfill his responsibility as an informed exponent of the exotic culture, Schuyler makes what seems like an honest and serious attempt to assess responsibly these boys' art for his readers: "The dances, so far as I was able to judge, were by no means indecent, though they were often very lascivious" (71). The oddness of this comment lies in the distinction Schuyler expects his readers to make between decency and lasciviousness. If the dancers were decent, how then were they lascivious? Whatever the referents are for the terms, what is important to note is the anxiety and the excitement that generate their use and the anxiety and the excitement that this use in turn generates.

Edward Lane is also graphic but not as elaborate when providing information on the dancing boys on the Egyptian scene, especially Cairo:

As they personate women, their dances are exactly of the same description as those of the Ghawazee; and are, in like manner, accompanied by the sounds of castanets: but, as if to prevent their being thought to be really females, their dress is suited to their *unnatural* profession; being partly male, and partly female: it chiefly consists of a tight vest, a girdle, and a kind of petticoat. Their general appearance, however, is more feminine than masculine: they suffer the hair of the head to grow long, and generally braid it, in the manner of the women; the hair on the face, when it begins to grow, they pluck out; and they imitate the women also in applying kohl and henna to their eyes and hands. In the streets, when not engaged in dancing, they often even veil their faces; not from shame, but merely to affect the manners of women. *They are often employed, in preference to the Ghawazee*, to dance before a house, or in its court, on the occasion of a marriage-fête, or the birth of a child, or a circumcision; and frequently perform at public festivals. There is, in Cairo, another class of male dancers, young men and boys, whose performances, dress, and general appearance are almost exactly similar to those of the Khawals;

but who are distinguished by a different appellation, which is "Gink"; a term that is Turkish, and has a vulgar signification which aptly expresses their character. They are generally Jews, Armenians, Greeks, and Turks. (1963, 389, my emphasis)

Having committed himself to providing an account of the manners and customs of the Egyptian people, Lane acts as if he has little choice but to include this description of the *khawals*. He does not spend many lines on them, his chapter focusing mostly on the *ghawazee* even though it is entitled "Public Dancers." Apparently, he finds their numbers small enough that he prefers to dedicate more space in his account to the more numerous *ghawazee*. Noteworthy, however, are his own comments on the demand for the *khawals*. He tells us that they are often employed and frequently perform at public festivals. In a subsequent chapter on private festivities, he mentions that in the morning after a child's birth, "two or three of the dancing men called Khawals, or two or three Ghazeeyehs, dance in front of the house, or in the court" (509). Male and female performers are, in other words, interchangeable, and sometimes the males are even preferred, as he mentions in the lengthy passage quoted earlier. Nonetheless, there is a note of discomfort regarding the effeminate dress and customs of the *khawals* and an obvious tone of disapproval in labeling their profession "unnatural." Lane's closing remark on "the vulgar signification" of *gink*, a remark that indicates a certain discomfort, seems to allude to these dancers' explicit availability for sexual hire (as noted in Murray 1997, 46 n. 24). Obviously, the Janissaries' enthusiasm over the dancing boys was not as openly shared, if felt at all, by either Lane or the majority of travelers to the Middle East. Sodomy, as interpreted in the West, forced the Occidental tourist to face a challenge that is often discursively construed as unsuspected or unforeseen and is, therefore, insidious as well as scandalous for the imperial subject.

On this same issue of homosexual sex, Charles S. Sonnini, a former engineer in the French navy and an intrepid traveler and naturalist, pauses in his narrative to lament: "The unnatural passion which some Thracian women punished by slaying Orpheus, who had entertained it, the inconceivable inclination which has dishonoured the Greeks and the Persians of antiquity, constitute this delight, or, more properly speaking, the infamy of Egyptians. It is not for women that their amorous sonnets are composed; it is not to them that they lavish tender caresses; no; other objects inflame their desires.... Such depravation, which to the shame of polished nations is not unknown to them, is universally spread in Egypt" (1972, 163).

This passage was written by a man who seems eager to join any army of enraged maenads to lay vengeful hands on male flesh tainted by homoerotic pleasure, this unnameable and unnatural vice. Reading the same passage, Joseph Boone finds that "a note of hysteria" infiltrates this narrative (2001, 51), a note that is remarkably strident. "Part of the horror," Boone correctly observes, "is that this 'inconceivable appetite' 'is not altogether unknown' to civilized Europe: if the Egyptian vice knows no class ('rich and poor are equally infected by it'), can it be expected to respect the boundaries of colonizer and colonized?" (52).

Particularly in the context of dance, this hysteria is exacerbated by more disconcerting and anxiety-provoking images. If the *ghawazee* provoke the Western male visitor with a voyeuristic spectacle that upsets his moral pretensions, the encounter with the *khawals* forces him into that most awkward and discomfiting space in between genders where he realizes a particularly tantalizing desire. Enclasped in this space, the imperial subject is impelled to confront a liminal identity, one that becomes the most vivid, shameless, and lurid embodiment of his taboos. The apparently great popularity of these performers (a popularity that spanned long historical periods) exacerbated the "delicate" position of the Western viewers. Even if they felt any enthusiasm over the *köçek*, the *khawals*, or the *batchas*, their enthusiasm had to be closeted in the narrative. For example, Sonnini even finds it impossible to name the act, as if to deny it entry into discourse. As a result, homosexual desire or its concomitant acts are present only through unnameability and silence, looming over the Egyptian/Oriental domain, even though they are "not unknown" to civilized, European nations.

Ironically, it is not only the European narratives that convey strong phobias as they become overwhelmed by the lurid spectacle of male performers. Writers from within the traditions also display these familiar attitudes. Metin And, a Turkish researcher writing about the dance traditions of Anatolia, details the male dancers' artistic contribution and its impact on their admirers like this:

> Their manner and dress were suited to their unnatural profession; being partly male, and partly female, they were so loved and lauded by their audiences that many poets sang their praises in verse. They praised their physical beauty as well as their skill in their art. One of the most notable poets was the famous poet, Enderunly Fazil. His *Defter-i Aşk* (meaning "Book of Love") contains 170 couplets praising the beauty and skill of the celebrated eighteenth century dancing boy, Çingene İsmail. His *Çengi-name*, a book about the famous dancing boys of the early nineteenth century, gives the names and stage names of forty-five performers. (1976, 141)

And's passage provides a good example of the frustrations involved when one wants to reconstruct an epistemology of male performers in the Orient. Their reception was so ambivalent, apparently in their own culture as well, that adequate understanding of the contradictions in the sources themselves is difficult. Two pages before the passage just quoted, And talks of the dearth of references to these dancers in Turkish literature because of their low social esteem. At this point, he tells us that there have been Turkish poets praising the male dancers' every aspect. Being a Turkish scholar, Metin And could have made a valuable contribution by focusing on this apparently significant institution of Turkish culture. He could have provided some quotations from these poets and a discussion of their work in order to clarify the social changes that elapsed between the silence of the "early" authors and the early 19th century when a Turkish poet exalted the dancing boys. But he does not. Finally, the opening of the passage here, "Their manner and dress ... being partly male, and partly female," comes from that much-quoted passage from Lane that I also include in this section. Metin And not only leaves this reference uncited, as if it forms part of his own text, but also allows it to challenge the meaning of the rest of his paragraph. In other words, he does not explain the paradox involved in an "unnatural profession" attracting such love and admiration.

Similarly, Kemal Özdemir, in his *Oriental Belly Dance*, posits with alarming confidence that modern performances of this dance are all about heterosexual intercourse. He writes that "Oriental belly dance is the artistic expression of man's innate instinct to reproduce reflected in the female's rhythmic movements," and that "when the dancer turns her back to the onlooker and swings her hips, she sends a message which can be interpreted as the call for copulation" (2000, 64). Shocking as they may seem (and at several moments quite offensive), Özdemir's interpretations try to make sense of the dance in terms of heterosexuality, while his sexism secures a safe passage for the project in the patriarchal mainstream. In a sense, Özdemir's willingness to address openly the sexuality of the dance and offer an account that is less puritan than what one often encounters is refreshing. But the package he offers does not seem intended to reform our viewing of the dance and open up possibilities of embracing homo and heteroeroticism as contexts for vital artistic expression. Rather, his text and the numerous illustrations seem geared toward a heterosexist aesthetic and intended, almost exclusively, for straight male consumption.

Therefore, his chapters on the *çengi* and the *köçek* are decidedly at odds with the general attitude, tone, and purpose of the book. Like Metin And, Kemal Özdemir seems keen on relating this part of Turkish artistic tradition (in fact, his report on the dancing boys is elaborate) but does not seem to recognize the paradoxes that his position evokes. The çengi are said to be very popular female entertainers, famous and beloved for their skilled dancing: "Young men looking for enjoyment and well-to-do womanizers clustered around such houses but it was only very seldom that chengis had a good time with men.... In short, Ottoman chengis were renowned for their unabashed lesbianism" (2000, 37–38). Similarly, the great appeal and popularity of the male dancers, the *köçek*, emerge in Özdemir's references to Evliya Çelebi, a traveler who offers an erotic and doting depiction of some of the dancing boys: "Curly-haired, doe-eyed and long-lashed Dimitraki, Neferaki and Yanaki of [the island of] Chios are the best köchecks [*sic*] who have set Istanbul on fire and spent the treasures of many an admirer, causing them to fall prey to deep poverty" (2000, 54–56). At one moment, Özdemir seems to attribute the köçeks' irresistible charm to the perfection of their drag, suggesting that spectators loved them because the dancers' true sex eluded them: "They sometimes danced fully dressed like women whereby no one could tell the difference between the sexes, and in such cases, the air would overflow with 'oh's' and 'ah's' and the wind of lust would take hold of everyone. These beautiful male coquettes drove men crazy with their seductive sighs and oriental dance" (2000, 59).

Of course, dance moves are potent because they conceal sexual codes. Özdemir's overtly heterosexual analysis, however, offers no relief for the unspeakability and taboo of sex, while female sexuality is vulgarized in his interpretation that is accompanied by a plethora of photos depicting voluptuous dancers in a variety of postures (one caption reads, "A [male] spectator dreaming of something private" [147]). Sadly, too, his information on the male dancers (and the female çengi) appears like precious, gleaming fragments against a backdrop that continuously strives to distort, obscure, or blur them.

To conclude this section on the poetics of male dancing, I will turn to another Turkish writer whose travel narrative contributes intriguing dance scenes with male performers. The author is Irfan Orga, who traveled in Turkey possibly in the late 1930s, although the year of these travels is not specified. Orga observes scenes of Turkish life with a gaze that is native but inflected by a certain morality that raises questions about his cultural influences and the audience he imagines for his narrative. The communities that Orga depicts during his travels in The Caravan Moves On have very set notions of decency and respectability, and they strictly observe social codes and hierarchies. Marriage is often not simply expected but imposed, the women have to be virgins before marriage, and the signs that denote manhood and womanhood are clear and undisputed. However, he describes a brief but overwhelming incident that makes a crucial intervention in these traditions. While visiting Konya and the surrounding region, Orga stays with Hikmet Bey, a powerful landowner of great influence, and together they visit an isolated farm owned by Hikmet Bey. At the farm, following a heavy dinner and generous consumption of raki, a locally produced alcoholic drink, Orga narrates a fascinating scene of lush eroticism that raises the specter of homosexual sex and the homoerotics of male performance. The singer who provides the first part of the after-dinner entertainment is a slender young man of about 20, with a womanish figure, who sings in a low, sweet voice that "teases" Hikmet Bey's emotions. When a young boy dances, however, the scene turns into an unexpected ritual that invokes a confounding pathos:

> For a few moments the boy stood slackly, but one felt the ripple of excitement that went through the watching men. For a little longer the boy timed his movements against the beat of the music, little hesitant movements that were suggestive of young amorous limbs. Then he began to dance, carefully, painstakingly—almost clumsily—keeping in perfect time with the quickening music. His smooth young face was as blank as a

sleepwalker's. He weaved a pattern with his feet, but his mind was somewhere else. His artistry was superb, for the movements of his body and the fluttering hands portrayed unmistakably a young girl's first reluctance to physical love, her gradual desire to experience it, finally her surrender. (Orga 2002, 51)

It is clear in the description that the sensuality of this moment is overwhelming for almost every man present: "Men sat in rapt attention.... The half-darkness was rapacious and secretive and all eyes were directed to the boy who swayed in moaning rapture, his dark shadow leaping up the wall behind him—monstrous, gigantic" (51). The fascination of the moment is clearly audible in the compelling ecstasy to which many of the men surrender, as the author tells us. The experience incites in Orga thoughts about the mysteries of life, love, and death, and the inevitability of fate. More important, however, the experience with the dancer intimates a kind of queer (in its sense of both "strange" and "homosexual") desiring fulfilled by a pained, ecstatic consummation in which Orga does not indulge. Both these processes, the desiring and the course of consummation, seem unattached to societal structures and established institutions that the author comments on in the narrative.

It would almost seem as if we as readers are invited to perceive this scene of dance and choreographed sexual and spiritual ecstasy as a site left deliberately empty so it can accommodate a kind of love and eroticism that approximate mainstream, acceptable modes but are not quite mainstream or acceptable. As Orga puts it in the previous passage, the dancer is superb not as a male dancer but because he is like a young girl about to be deflowered; his act is the same as a girl's—but not quite. Nonetheless, it is fascinating how for the others present this site seems sacred in an almost metaphysical sense. Orga does not surrender to the seduction of the dancer even though, as he puts it, "he singled me out for his attentions, standing so close in front of me that I was aware of the little pulse beating in his throat and his head outlined in flaring candlelight" (50–51). The profundity and profanity of this enchanting moment touch him deeply. Before his reader, however, he claims to remain sober enough to check his rapture and avoid falling into the trap of such "low" passions: "I found the experience of that night both moving and chilling, an experience so primitive that it could not fail to stir the blood, yet so expressive of man's lower nature, so imprisoning, that one felt brushed by the Devil himself. The room was full of *raki* fumes, of sweating humanity and the queer acrid odour of the copulations of older men. To stagger out to the sweet night air was a form of relief, for unless one has lost one's senses in drink it is impossible not to be appalled by licentiousness" (52).

In my estimation, the author employs the trope of "primitiveness" in this narrative not so much because of its explanatory potential. The term "primitive" carries an ideological charge that allows Orga to disguise the melancholy that is associated with the intense desiring manifest in this moment, and which has marked his emotions deeply. Of course, this disguise is (perhaps deliberately) diaphanous, since in the closing image of his chapter he gazes at his own spellbound reflection: "The moon was high in the sky, infinitely remote, symbol of men's dreams. Trees stood out on the horizon like a frieze. In my mind's eye I saw, as in a witch's ball, the figure of myself, spellbound" (52). Finally, in reading this scene, it is important not to lose sight of the fact that it was the young boy's choreography—a homoerotic dance performance—that opened emotive passages so that the participants could move toward the ecstatic epiphany that marks the after-dinner celebration.

Hassan el-Balbeissi

Running contrary to travel narrative orthodoxy, Flaubert does not closet his enthusiasm over the male dancers he observes in Cairo. As with Kuchuk Hanem, the experience becomes, in fact, the object of camaraderie in his correspondence with his close friend Louis Bouilhet. However, even Flaubert, a writer eager to "play openly" during his travels, cannot resolve the profound ambivalence he feels over a male performer who overwhelms him before he meets Kuchuk Hanem. In January 1850, he writes to Louis Bouilhet from Cairo describing the male dancers he has seen and identifying one of them as Hassan el-Balbeissi:

As dancers, imagine two rascals, quite ugly, but charming in their corrup-tion, in their obscene leerings and the effeminacy of their movements, dressed as women, their eyes painted with antimony.... The dancers advance and retreat, shaking the pelvis with a short convulsive movement. A quivering of the muscles is the only way to describe it; when the pelvis moves, the rest of the body is motionless; when the breast shakes, nothing else moves. In this manner they advance toward you, their arms extended, rattling brass castanets, and their faces, under the rouge and the sweat, remain more expressionless than a statue's. By that I mean they never smile. The effect is produced by the gravity of the face in contrast to the lascivious movements of the body. Sometimes they lie down flat on their backs, like a woman ready to be fucked, then rise up with a movement of the loins similar to that of a tree swinging back into place after the wind has stopped. From time to time, during the dance, the impresario, or pimp, who brought them plays around them, kissing them on the belly, the arse, and the small of the back, and making obscene remarks in an effort to put additional spice into a thing that is already quite self-evident. (Flaubert 1980, 110–11)

Evidently, Flaubert finds this performance overwhelming and even com-ments, "I doubt whether we shall find the women as good as the men; the ugliness of the latter adds greatly to the thing as art" (111). The contradictions in Flaubert's description are a sign of his disorientation, as he finds himself teased into an uncertain space signified by the performance and also by the dancers' makeup and dress. Through contraries, he struggles to circumscribe the male dancers' performance but ultimately enunciates and reiterates his own ambivalence, since the dance resists a written description in the viewer's imperial language. What Flaubert sees, evidently, is a compelling demon of the male sex luring him into realization of perverse sexual possibilities. In fact, with his behavior during the performance, the impresario turns the already lascivious dance into a profane ritual that redirects Flaubert's masculine desire onto a transgressive course. In fact, this flirtation with Egyptian sodomy inspires a homoerotic exchange with his addressee, Louis Bouilhet, "and injects into Flaubert's correspondence and diaries a stream of homoerotic banter and speculation that becomes a source of titillation and eventually the spur to experimentation without radically disturbing the writer's heterosexual self-definition" (Boone 2001, 55). The insistence on Hassan's ugliness, in fact, seems a gesture to underscore the illicitness of this entire process of watching, an attempt to mask appeal with nonappeal. Ugliness, in other words, turns into a cherished aesthetic that is meant to create a trope for the illicit desires that possess Flaubert.

In subsequent letters, however, Flaubert's sexual confidence gives way to a subliminal anxiety arising from his encounter with Near Eastern homosexuality and linked to his literary ambitions. According to Joseph Boone, "Having traveled to Egypt in search of creative inspiration, Flaubert expresses his writerly potential in metaphors of heterosexual reproduction ('but—the real thing! To ejaculate, to beget the child!') and conversely expresses his despair at not having realized his literary goals in images of non-reproductive sexual play; he subtly figures the exotic others of sexual perversion as the great threat of erasure, the negation of artistic vitality or sap, when 'the lines don't come'" (55). Although ostensibly fascinating to Flaubert, Hassan el-Balbeissi's dancing is destabilizing, an effect that Flaubert hopes to amend with his torpid affair with Kuchuk Hanem, who fulfills the stereotype of the feminine Orient that is imagined as available and must be penetrated by Western superior intellect.

Flaubert's homosexual experiences are not detailed with the same intensity. Edward Said picks up on Flaubert's heterosexual narratives and elaborates on them theoretically. In such interpretations, the *ghaziya*'s body has been read, correctly I think, as a trope for the earth that is plowed and tilled. However, Hassan el-Balbeissi's body can be neither envisioned in similar images nor allowed the same possibilities by Flaubert—a disavowal that theorists such as Said have permitted by their silence on Hassan el-Balbeissi. Flaubert is the privileged *khawadja* (the white seigneur) who never transcends his gendered longing. He boasts of homosexual sex in the baths, but it is Kuchuk he hopes to subdue through scopic conquest and sexual possession.[12]

Nerval's Dancing "Girls"

My final paradigm involves an incident that Gerard de Nerval recounts as part of his Oriental adventures. A pleasant afternoon in the finest café in the fashionable area of Mousky provides the occasion for his first experience of Cairo's famous dancing "girls" in a public performance. In his travelogue, *The Women of Cairo: Scenes of Life in the Orient,* he relates the following:

> The dancing girls appeared in a cloud of dust and tobacco smoke. . . . As their heels beat upon the ground, with a tinkle of little bells and anklets, their raised arms quivered in harmony; their hips shook with a voluptuous movement; their form seemed bare under the muslin between the little jacket and the low loose girdle, like the ceston of Venus. They twirled around so quickly that it was hard to distinguish the features of these seductive creatures, whose fingers shook little cymbals, as large as castanets, as they gestured boldly to the primitive strains of flute and tambourine. Two of them seemed particularly beautiful; they held themselves proudly: their Arab eyes were brightened by kohl, their full yet delicate cheeks were lightly painted. (1929, 64)

Nerval's description is well within the familiar colonial schema of elaborate verbal depiction. Because this is a dancing scene, however, I read these details with an interest in deciphering the complex corporealization of the objects of his gaze. They incorporate elements that are familiar from other descriptions of both male and female Eastern performers: the striking and outlandish costumes, the makeup worn by the dancers, and their finger cymbals are ubiquitous features. Here their features are enhanced by an extra touch of eroticism that the "ceston of Venus" bestows. This item of their costume acquires multivalent significance as it registers the dance moves, thus enhancing the motion, but also as it embraces the hips acting in this capacity as a material manifestation of the gaze as it circles tightly but longingly, it would seem, the same part of the body.

In fact, Nerval's account of the *khawals* forms a particularly clear exemplar of the complex dynamics of makeup, costuming adornments, and finger cymbals as worn and played by Middle Eastern dancers. Because the analysis I suggest constructs dance itself as a narrative of sorts, I regard makeup and jewelry to be indispensable components of this narrative. Along with physical movement and the sonic dimension that the finger cymbals reify, the metamorphosis of makeup and costume afford the passage that Nerval (and indeed any audience) is keen to witness. This narrative of metamorphosis is a central issue in discussions of Middle Eastern dance where, in the observer's gaze, the dancer's made-up eyes are such an arresting signifier. As the male dancers shift constantly before Nerval, their eyes *look* both transitively and intransitively, framed as they are by the black kohl.

The makeup around their eyes and on their face, the objects of self-adornment, and even the brass finger cymbals enhance the performativity of the body.

Objects of adornment and embroidered costumes afford a physical metamorphosis essential for the body, both in its preparation for and through the duration of the dance. Moreover, they serve as markers of this potentiality in the viewer's gaze, while simultaneously setting up a semiotic system that invites the gaze yet guards the body in its creative and therefore vulnerable moments. To assist and illustrate my argument, I draw from the old Cypriot dialect where a term and its meanings evoke intriguing signs. The verb *kholiazo* derives from "kohl" and means, of course, to make up oneself, but, oddly enough, it is also a word used in building and construction work. The same verb describes the process of filling up with grout the gaps between slabs or tiles laid on a floor or against a wall. Therefore, *kholiazo* clearly implies placing something in between in order to fill up space that would otherwise remain blank. The effect is one of embellishment but also strength, since grouting also secures and keeps tiles or slabs in place. Perhaps it was this quality of makeup, functioning as an emboldening and in-between agent, that scandalized and irritated but also allured Europeans. It seemed to correct the vulnerability of nature by fortifying the performer with the drama of artifice. Thus, it denied the viewer straight access to the "nature" of the subject's face while also conjuring an image that was relentlessly seductive. (I use "straight" in its puritan sense, conscious also of its heterosexual connotations, and I use the word "nature" to imply both human character and physical look or physiognomy.) All the while, this artifice in the form of makeup and adornments fills gaps in performativity, strengthens it, and keeps the artistic body in a position whose condition is both distinguished and equivocated.

Indeed, adornment and maquillage merit an examination in the same terms as dance. They come alive on the dancing body in a fashion similar to a move. They practice a choreographed intervention on the natural body that affects not only the performance of the body's movement but also its sexuality. Their sheer presence, in other words, enacts the dance itself and subjugates the gaze just as kinesthesia does. Perhaps this is where the eroticism and exoticism associated with makeup become apparent and directly relevant. Makeup is erotic because it brings about a metamorphosis that follows autoeroticism. Further, "art" and artifice here may take on sexual connotations in that the artist ritually adorns herself, enhancing the performative potential of her body and thereby its sexualness.

Transformed, the dancing body transcends the rigidity of its physical form and acquires an altered dimension that excludes Nerval and his discriminations regarding gendered makeup customs. And during this entire ritual, the viewer is invited to the spectacle, which, in a sense, owes its existence to the viewer's gaze. Nevertheless, the dancer's masquerade denies the viewer the experience of the ritual. That is, ritual is for participants, not viewers. This is confirmed by bell hooks in her definition of ritual and spectacle in her critique of Jennie Livingston's *Paris Is Burning*, a film whose black drag performances offer an intriguing parallel to Nerval's experience of the "effeminate" dancing boys: "Ritual is that ceremonial act that carries with it meaning and significance beyond what appears, while spectacle functions primarily as entertaining dramatic display. Those of us who have grown up in a segregated black setting where we participated in diverse pageants and rituals know that those elements of a given ritual that are empowering and subversive may not be readily visible to an outsider looking in. Hence it is easy for white observers to depict black rituals as spectacle" (1992, 150).

I could not suggest that dancing was indeed "empowering and subversive" for the *khawals* in this particular scene (although I have certainly experienced dance in these terms; this is, in fact, why I dance). My point here follows bell hooks, who insists that a white (or in this case Western) gaze, watching a racialized "pageant" that it cannot decipher, translates it, instead, into mere spectacle. That is, the materialization of spectacle depends, to a certain extent, on the privilege of the viewer, although, as I argue, the boundaries of this privilege do not remain fixed but are contested by dance as ritual and as spectacle.

However, the ceremony that Nerval is hosting for us does not conclude here. He informs us that his enthusiastic participation in the scene is curtailed as soon as he becomes conscious that the dancers are not female but male: "But the third, I must admit, betrayed the less gentle sex by a week-old beard; and when I looked into the matter carefully, and, the dance being ended, could better make out the features of the other two, it did not take me long to discover that the dancing girls were, in point of fact, all males" (1929, 64). Perhaps predictably, since Nerval is addressing a mainstream, bourgeois audience, the fooled viewer immediately suspends his *pothos* and shifts the mechanisms of his gaze toward these deceitful performers.[13] They have embezzled his ethics, mocked his taboos, and made him complicit through his gaze in a lubricious spectacle: "I was ready to place upon their foreheads a few pieces of gold, in accordance with the purest traditions of the Levant.... But for men dressed up as women this ceremony may well be dispensed with, and a few paras thrown to them instead" (65). It is noteworthy how Nerval stages this spectacle for himself and for his reader. Although he excitedly details the performance of these dancers, he relates only in the title of this section, "The Khowals [*sic*]"—for those who know already that this is the Arabic for male dancers—that his "dancing girls" are, in fact, dancing boys. This play might lend itself to what we would term a "queer" reading in contemporary terms. He is enamored of these boys only to be frustrated at the moment of gender recognition, yet he seems unwilling to protect his male readers from the same frustration by forewarning them. In this dissimulative restaging he has already communicated his erotic covetousness, so he could be expecting to incite it in his readers also. Along with the use of the term "queer," a further anachronism would be to call Nerval homophobic, although, according to Ramsay Burt's commentary on homosexuality and

Figure 10.2   A 19th-century lithograph of Turkish dancing boys. Many dancing boys in the Middle East wore clothing that had both male and female elements, with no attempt made to hide the fact that the dancers were male. From the Artemis Mourat collection. Used with permission.

the male dancer, the term "homophobic" might well be appropriate here, since "Western society is and has for hundreds of years been profoundly homophobic" (1995, 29).[14] Nevertheless, nothing other than fascination with these alien, dancing bodies would urge Nerval to be as whimsical with his scenario and with his reader.

Later, he engages in the deprecation we are accustomed to reading in travel narratives where the immoral East is admonished for its depravity. He cleverly substitutes the wonder of artistic epiphany—those revelations, psychic and cognitive, that a performance may induce in an audience—with the revelation of the dancers' sex and then proceeds to interpolate some imperial discourse that will further spoil the attraction of the ritual and denigrate the practice of male dancing: "Seriously, there is something very peculiar about Egyptian morality. A few years ago, the dancing girls used to go freely about the city.... Now, they are only allowed to appear in private houses and banquets, and scrupulous people consider these dances by men with effeminate features and long hair, with bare arms, figures and necks, who parody so deplorably the half-veiled attractions of the dancing girls, more respectable" (1929, 65).

Even if his intention was to be sarcastic in this description of the dancing scene, he certainly is not convincing that these boys' quivering arms, voluptuous

hips, and visible bare forms are deplorable parodies. Evidently, his pronouncements here do not attest to his depiction of the *khawals*. There is a tone of
hostility in his refusal to transgress the moral boundaries of his culture whose
morality he sees as too superior to compromise. There is something reminiscent
of Charles Sonnini's hysteria in Nerval's expression of derision. Both men
register reactions that foreclose the different kinds of contamination that
Egypt, as a nation of the potent Orient, is capable of.

Finally, this scene from Nerval's narrative supports Anthony Shay's contention that male dancers were almost always discernible from females in the
iconographic and narrative sources. Male dancers "did not specifically wear
female garb, unless playing a female role, but rather special clothing and
costumes suitable to show off their movements and to make them unique and
attractive as dancers and entertainers" (2005, 70). In colonial travel narratives,
however, the transformation afforded by makeup and jewelry, as well as henna
and opulent, flamboyant, and dramatic costumes, was feared and therefore
criticized in women of the Orient. My contrapuntal readings of these travel
narratives communicate the ways in which a dancer's makeup and personal
adornment begin to appear threatening in their defiance of hegemony. In an
effort to neutralize the effects of this transformation and the intense sexualiza-
tion of the body that results from their adoption, male travelers and writers
sought to explain them in terms of female "inconstancy" and waywardness. To
observe such demonstrations in men, however, was too taxing on European
sensibility.

Mousbah Baalbaki

Finally, I turn to the content of an article by Susan Sachs concerning a contemporary male dancer in Beirut. The article, which appeared in the *New York Times
Beirut Journal* on May 4, 2000, carried the unfortunate title "He's No Salomé,
But It's Straight from the Heart." The dancer referred to, Mousbah Baalbaki,
emerges from the article like a contemporary Hassan el-Balbeissi, gazing
through "eyes rimmed with black powder." The reference to makeup is a
necessary and, to my taste, particularly appealing and significant part of the
description, as in Nerval's description of the *khawals*. My purpose in discussing
the article is partly to trace certain enduring patterns from the past to the
present, although I do not wish to trap Mousbah, and myself, in a Romantic
vision of the same dancing figure performing unaltered through time in a
clichéd template of the "timeless Orient." There is continuation in him not in
a Romantic Orientalist sense but in the dynamics that have marked male
performances through colonial and recently postcolonial times. The reporter
finds him "sinuous and seductive ... in a gauzy black caftan over a Bedouin-
style white robe, [as] he undulated on stage with a faraway look in his eyes and a
bodyguard close at hand." The writing adopts the traditional and, sadly,

anticipated tone that ranges between sardonic and superior—an efficient and popular technique for relating information about something titillating, enticing, and "different." The same technique quells the anxiety that rises not just in the observing reporter, as is the case here, or the traveler but also in the reader. Hence the comments on the artistic components and "character" of the show: the melody of the old Arabic song sounds "lugubrious," and there is the assurance that "Mr. Baalbaki, who is 28, does not perform a transvestite show or a striptease. It is more like 'Saturday Night Fever' meets 'The Thousand and One Nights.'" These latter two productions are both Western constructs to varying degrees, which serves to leave the dancer unaccommodated and exiled between two worlds that he has had no agency in defining. Similarly, Lebanon itself is projected as a country that, "for all its worldly glitter" (i.e., capitalist "development" and therefore general approval, familiarity, and comfort with the image—something reminiscent of the Eurovision Song Contest cosmopolitanism), still has "a generous streak of religious conservatism and criminalizes homosexuality." In other words, it remains "Oriental," which here implies stubbornly backward. Beirut itself is "a paradoxical town, with European designer boutiques interspersed with the sniper-shattered buildings from the fifteen-year civil war.... But Mr. Baalbaki's public gyrations seem a step beyond the pale even for Beirut" (Sachs 2001).

It seems, however, that the journalist is not the only agent confining the male body's dance expression. Rather, in reiterating the paradox of Beirut, an "Oriental" city, the journalist is simply re-presenting the complexities of a postcolonial state of affairs, since, in its modernity, Lebanese society itself displays values and morals that seem closer to those of Europe than traditional Arab society. Thus, Mousbah's taboo performance invokes contemporary politics, national and international, and forms a most intriguing moment in postcolonial politics that is comparable to the Greek politics of Eastern dance. His body in motion becomes a crossroads where native tradition, colonialism, Lebanese class issues, and personal artistic ambition and adoration converge. "Every weekend," Mousbah claims, "I struggle with the audience." Indeed, the night Susan Sachs was at the Amor y Libertad, she noticed men "squirm and concentrate resolutely on their drinks when Mr. Baalbaki took the stage."

Baalbaki's condemnation, however, comes from within the profession as well. Although he acknowledges the struggles that professional female dancers face in a culture that is generally harsh in its judgment of dancers, his support of them remains unreciprocated by his colleague Fifi Abdou, whom Sachs calls "the leading lady of Egyptian belly dancing." In a modest estimation of her contribution to the art form, Abdou "describes herself as the only living symbol of the art" (Sachs 2001). Her charisma, prestige, and popularity are indisputable and have made her one of the wealthiest Egyptian belly dancers (it is important to allude to her elevated class status). However, what have proved her most valuable contributions to the art were her "daring" interpretations of Oriental dance, her ability to perform a sexuality and an eroticism that, in the words of Cassandra Lorius, "outwit patriarchy" (1996, 287). I agree with Lorius's assessment that, when interpreting the dance, Fifi Abdou "makes use of play, a disjunctive tactic that works against the potential closure of normative discourse" (287).[15] Despite her significant victories, however, Fifi Abdou is intent on denying Mousbah, and every male dancer, the very ability to perform this dance. She argues based on assumed biological properties of the two sexes, as she explains in Susan Sach's article: "It's impossible for a man to dance *real* belly dancing. The phrase itself describes the part from the hips to the waist, and a man lacks the energy there that a woman has. They can perform, but they can't belly-dance" (2001; my emphasis). Seemingly unconscious of the cultural weight her argument bears, Fifi Abdou—ironically a native dancer herself who, apparently, continues to fight battles on the cultural field—crystallizes in her objection the very essence of discomfort, anxiety, and allure felt by Western observers for male Oriental dancers. Even if the effort to "naturalize" the female performers achieves some limited fulfillment (realized most strongly in the sexual availability of these dancers' bodies), the effort to achieve the same with men is simply impossible to fulfill politically in Western body discourse. The male body has limitations, Fifi instructs us, and cannot perform the "real" dance—with all the problematic denotations of the term "real." The male dancer's invitation to experience an altered, othered dimension of reality and gendered space offers what is impossible to accept and therefore denied at the body, the very source of its corporeal creation.

Rerouting the East through the West

The male dancer has remained resistant to familiarization, exacerbating the anxiety felt over the male dancing body. Thus, when a dance instructor urges me, nervously and with some anxiety, not to overdo my undulations or to render my moves with machismo (they usually require sharper shoulder thrusts and less "eloquence and flair" in the hands), she is, in effect, trying to unsettle my body's resistance to normalized masculinity and hoping to reinstall something familiar, in this case a conventional masculine character, in the spectacle of the male dancer. At the same time the instructor is protecting herself and the audience. They stand on guard against the threatening opprobrium that would assault gender propriety by suggesting the unspeakable.

I am familiar with this kind of choreophobic (to use Anthony Shay's term) censorship from my native milieu in Cyprus. Here the Turkish Cypriot community of the island fostered a tradition of dancing boys called *zenne*, who caused some discomfort particularly in the Greek Cypriot community. Paradoxically, the only evidence I can trace for this discomfort is the absolute silence that exists around this cultural practice. Although one cannot assume that these young artists were available for sexual hire or that they indulged in homosexual acts, one can say with certainty that being artists, they must have inhabited a liminal space, one that permitted the artistic requirement of various transformations, indispensable in an embodied art form. The *zenne* wove their artistic activity into the fabric of (Turkish) Cypriot life, transforming audiences with movement. Such attributes signify a fluid masculinity that destabilizes imperial heterosexual equilibrium, hence the Greek Cypriots' anxious silence on the issue. The male Turkish Cypriot dancers have been forced inside the airtight closet constructed by Greek cultural epistemology. They have been filtered out of oral narratives, their existence completely annihilated by an Orientalism that excludes what does not comply with an identity set by an imperial and heterosexual canon. The dancing boys of Cyprus vanished so that Cyprus could absolve itself of its Oriental past and achieve some progress in the struggle to attain European status.

Interestingly, belly dance is now considered a hot item all over the Middle East. On the radio, on television, and in clubs in Beirut, Cairo, Alexandria, Nicosia, and Istanbul, belly dance is trendy once more with many best-selling Greek, Turkish, and Arab artists recording songs that have a distinctly Araboturkish flavor. I cannot speak for the general regard for this dance in Arab countries or in Turkey, but in Greece and Cyprus the majority of young people do not regard it as a cultural demonstration that may have some connection with Cypriot tradition. We (Greek Cypriots) claim distance and detachment from this dance. When young clubbing Cypriots shake their bodies to percussive pieces layered with a techno beat, they are oblivious to the *maqsoom* rhythm in many of these pieces, not hearing it as our traditional *arapié*. This nonchalant attitude finds some explanation in the imperial mediation of cultural sharing. Those cultural attributes that we accept to share have to be selected carefully and filtered obsessively through our nationalist and gender ideologies. In the process of cultural selection, Greek dances such as the *zeibekiko* and the *hasapiko*, dances whose names also derive from Turkish and whose popularity in Asia Minor has been great, have gained extremely high cultural currency, since they are perceived as harmonious with, in fact enhancing, the popular construction of masculine behavior. Contemplation and introspection have been saved for the *zeibekiko*, in particular, which symbolizes the male ethos and enjoys widespread recognition as the expression of an indomitable masculinity, a respected and valued disposition. Its steps reify a certain machismo that has been normalized and expected of a man. The *zeibekiko* inscribes territorial boundaries that the viewer observes with comfort, but also awe and admiration, since it ritualizes an exemplary masculinity and evokes the desire in the viewer to approve and emulate. The fact that the *çifteteli* has been designated as Oriental and feminine in the dynamic of a paternalistic society has extinguished any possibility that this dance could express something other than common female seduction and an invitation to sin. A contemplative, introspective mood of the *çifteteli*, audible in old *rebetika*, has not survived very well.

Meanwhile, the eminence of violin and lute for the rendering of traditional folk dances has seen interesting variations in the recordings of Kyriakou Pelagia, a truly intriguing artist from the popular strata who rose to stardom at an unusually mature age and quickly became a leading recorder of traditional Greek Cypriot songs. Not only do the people feel she is "one of them," but she has also given attention to a number of neglected songs and tunes that she has rendered in interesting ways with the help of Mesogios (Mediterranean), a superb group directed by Michalis Hadjimichael who is erudite in the musical styles of the Middle East. In the very popular "Eipa sou htenistou llio" ("I Asked You to Brush Your Hair a Little"), the *syrtos* (a traditional dance most often based on the *malfoof*, a rhythm very popular in Arabic and Turkish belly dance) sounds much more like the *çifteteli* than a *syrtos*, while in "Oloaspron Pezouni" ("White Pigeon") the *maqsoom* sees a very bold interpretation that enables detailed kinesthetic articulation as opposed to the more ordinary, reticent versions of standard Greek *çifteteli* songs. Moreover, "White Pigeon" (which is, significantly, a clear symbol of peace) is an old *rebetika* song and an example of a tune characteristic of Asia Minor. In Pelagia's version it is rendered with a rich orchestra featuring, among others, percussion, *qanoon*, and *oud* as well as violin.[16] Even though a number of Cypriot songs derive from Asia Minor, they are not often talked about as such unless they can be directly associated with the older Greek populations there. And when this association can be made, then these populations are talked about as if they lived and developed in total seclusion from the surrounding culture and their traditions survived pure and unadulterated through the years, a tenuous if not unsound argument motivated by nationalism and Turcophobia. Therefore, because of the risks involved in tracing the trajectory of some traditional tunes, a number of songs with potentially precarious derivation faded into obscurity. Pelagia's inclusion of songs based on Asia Minor tunes has expanded the range of what Greek Cypriot lovers of folklore can openly embrace as "theirs." Despite Pelagia's ideological limitations, conservative attachment to tradition, and the rather uneven texture of her voice (in my ears), her recordings are an intervention in Cypriot folk music that does not conform with the standard qualities of this recording genre; hence the attention to the *arapié* and the *çifteteli*.

If I can return to this article's opening paragraphs that outline certain events concerning the life of public dancers in Egypt in the 1830s, I find it intriguing how these events have been constructed as historical truth by modern dance researchers and dance enthusiasts. The information that, following Muhammad Ali's edict, there was heavier taxation to compensate for lost revenue and that the dance scene became inundated with dancing boys comes from Morroe Berger's article (1961, 30). Berger footnotes Lane as his source, yet Lane nowhere says that boys came along to replace the girls in public performances. In fact, Lane's phobia regarding the *khawals* is such that he even denies they were a large population: "the number of these male performers," he insists, "is very small"

(1963, 389). Regardless, Wendy Buonaventura reiterates that same information as Berger, presenting it as historical fact in *Serpent of the Nile* (1989, 68). These inferences and conclusions require further revision because despite being appealing in their historical tidiness, their character seems rather simplistic.

Islamic social rules, the narrative goes, prohibit women from public dancing; therefore, men do it. The head of state decided to reform his society, so he exiled the courtesans to Upper Egypt. Dancing boys came to prevail in their wake. These males were more salacious and obscene than the women. I outline these "facts" in order to point to the contradictory nature of the accounts we have been bequeathed. Also, this outline throws into relief a rather reductionist tendency toward the "Orient" itself: the notion that a few simple deductions drawn from a simple outline of events can explain away Eastern social and cultural phenomena and traditions. Meanwhile, even though the sources I have looked at hold that these events did in fact take place, they also refute them. Covel's and Schuyler's accounts indicate that male dancers belonged to a matured and highly valued tradition in the East. That they prevailed merely because female performance was interdicted by religious laws seems an unwarranted rationalization in the case of a successful and cherished cultural institution. Moreover, what lies in the imperative of explications such as Schuyler's (the boys dance because it is indecent for women to perform publicly) seems to be a need to excuse male presence in an artistic profession. Male performances were often seen as lewd and extremely improper, but, as I have tried to show in this article, this response entails emotions that were a direct corollary of imperial status. Disgust is a form of self-policing—a means to arrest desire and catch the body before it assimilates the experience of dance with any amount of pleasure. Moreover, disgust is also the feeling we register when something that is internal and invisible and expected to remain so externalizes itself. The experience of dance is visceral, and the emotion evoked by the gaze is disgust because the performing body gestures toward carnal alternatives whose very visual suggestion implicates the viewer. In the case of Middle Eastern dance, especially when performed by men or boys, viewers prefer to resist the acknowledgment of possibilities that the dancing body signifies.

The European gaze translated the experience of Eastern dance into a medium of aberrance and illicitness. In the Western imaginary, the dancer's body loomed threatening and enticing, mapping, in motion always, an intermediate zone, a threshold signifying liminality and indeterminacy, qualities often used to represent the East as a whole. Dancing women were a threat, but at least their dancing body could be subjected to symbolic Western domination through sexual intercourse. Male dancers clothed in an Eastern form of drag posed an insurmountable challenge by occupying yet a further liminal space. Marjorie Garber articulates this threat in deconstructive terms: "If transvestism offers a critique of binary sex and gender distinctions, it is not because it simply makes such distinctions reversible but because it denaturalizes, destabilizes, and de-familiarizes sex and gender *signs*" (1992, 147). The "revelation" that the dancing girls were really boys—this revelation being the moment when Nerval actually deciphered the "sign"—is the moment when Nerval has to slip from the role of mere observer into that of the imperial moralist so he will not surrender to aberrance. Imperatively, his response puts him at variance with the Janissaries, the hot-blooded sultan's soldiers, as Eastern spectators of a similar spectacle. In direct defiance of Eastern practices, he wants to throw a few *paras* to the dancers, because by throwing he will not have to take another look at them; looking could make voyeuristic indulgence in Oriental perversion a very real possibility. I should point out that this perversion may effect a two-way manifestation: the dancing boys will also look at Nerval, and their gaze will penetrate his masculinity. Perhaps their "unnaturalness" signals to him the arbitrariness of his own gender and sexuality.

The encounters with male dancers that I have examined provide some unique manifestations of the necessarily sexual performance of the look that informs both the practice and the concept of the gaze. The Orient had to become crystallized in the image of the fecund, sexually insatiable woman, even though there existed significant opportunity for Western travelers to restructure this image of the Orient. Yet, to acknowledge the male dancer as an emblem would also acknowledge him as a "designated repository of sexuality" (Shay 2005, 71) in which the Western male tourist was investing his desire. To replace the *ghawazee* with the *khawals*, *çengi*, *köçek*, or *batchas* would be representing a masculinized West that penetrates a male Orient—nothing less than an act of sodomy. Besides, much of the pleasure derived from this imaginary penetration predicated itself upon the constructed image of the Orient as a fecund, "feminized space" (McClintock 1995, 26). This image afforded a perverse and abstract but very crucial and gratifying notion of fertilization. Such was the satisfaction Flaubert needed to delude himself with. Sexual encounters with Hassan el-Balbeissi, or any other male sex partner, could not have provided the same possibility. The liminal space these male dancers occupied, a space in between genders, may have tantalized, titillated, or appalled the Western bourgeois traveler, but it never inspired an openly expressed feeling of comfort. Policed by their culture's taboos, these travelers needed a firm foothold at either the masculine or the feminine threshold, even when they relished sexual experiences with cross-dressed performers.

The dancers were not isolated in inciting curiosity and hate, attraction, and repulsion. The East as a whole generated the same emotional effects. The white European's emotions regarding the spectacle of dance—fear, shock, disgust—set in motion those mechanisms that reinstate in the traveler's gaze the superiority of European culture and its elite embodiment. The Middle Eastern male dancer, with the made-up eyes and the "lascivious" movements, posed—indeed, continues to pose—a particular threat that had to be contested and its injurious effects exorcised. However, the male dancer would not be entirely censored from the narratives, since his form, constantly shifting in the condition of dance, is necessary in the empire's constant redefining of itself against the Oriental Other. Today, a multitude of male dancers take to the dance floors of clubs in Cairo, Alexandria, Istanbul, Athens, and Beirut, performing Oriental dance movements to all the latest Arab, Turkish, and Greek hit songs that they so love and that reference strongly the sumptuous rhythms of this dance. Their choreographies negotiate gender, sexuality, and imperial standards of masculinity. However, despite the negotiation, there is so much talent, skill, and love on these dance floors that one feels that the tradition of male dancers resurrects in these rigorous and agile bodies that articulate the music with such passion that they breathe fresh life to it.

NOTES

Another version of this essay initially appeared in *Dancing Fear and Desire: Race, Sexuality, and Imperial Politics in Middle Eastern Dance* (Waterloo, ON: Wilfrid Laurier University Press, 2004).

1. For a detailed analysis of Middle Eastern dance and the sexual and gender politics of Cyprus as a postcolonial state, see my book *Dancing Fear and Desire.*

2. Paying particular attention to the visual arts, Wijdan Ali discusses the impact of Muhammad Ali's artistic reformations in Egypt in his article "Modern Painting in the Mashriq": "When Muhammad Ali became Egypt's effective ruler in 1805, after breaking away from Ottoman authority, he introduced European aesthetics to the urban Egyptian intellectual milieu" (2001, 364).

3. Sophie Lane-Poole, Edward Lane's sister, visited Egypt in 1842 with her famous brother and attended the royal wedding of Muhammad Ali's daughter Zaynab. Lane-Poole recorded her observations of the wedding in great detail. Apparently, singing and dancing were such significant parts of the ceremony that performances lasted entire days for a whole week. One of the conclusions that Kathleen Fraser reaches from Lane-Poole's narrative is that there is evidence to assume the existence of "a recognized and widely accepted dance aesthetic...in mid-19th century Egypt at all levels" (Fraser 2002, 37).

4. At this point Berger quotes a section from the same passage from Vivant Denon ([1803] 1973, 205) that I quote in the second epigraph to this essay. Berger, however, cites the wrong page for the quotation.

5. Particularly relevant here are Anthony Shay and Barbara Sellers-Young's comments in their "Introduction" to *Belly Dance: Orientalism, Transnationalism, and Harem Fantasy.* Shay and Sellers-Young comment on Wendy Buonaventura's description of belly dance as a female form of cultural expression. Following a quotation from Buonaventura's book *Serpent of the Nile,* they write: "Buonaventura conjures up a past that combines pantheism, spirituality, primitiveness.... One of the enduring beliefs that abound in the literature of the belly dancing community is that the dance has some connection with the worship and rituals connected with (usually unnamed) mother goddesses," and conclude that such theories of belly dance origins serve "to construct a

history of the dance that corresponds with their [the author's] identification with it" (2005, 17–18).

6. Andrea Deagon explores the opposing views of belly dance within feminist discourse in "Feminism and Belly Dance." Exploring the tensions between female objectification, on the one hand, and empowerment, on the other, Deagon poses the question: "Is belly dance really empowering for women, or does it simply bring 'women as sex objects' into a different range of venues than before?" (1999, 10). In response, Deagon sensitively balances these delicate issues, discussing realms of feminist inquiry that are pertinent to belly dancers: ownership of women's sexuality within patriarchy, Sartre's notion of "bad faith," and essentialism (10).

7. For a critique of the belief that the West has salvaged and given belly dance shelter, see chapter 6, "What Dancer from Which Dance?—Concluding Reflections," in my *Dancing Fear and Desire.*

8. In *Critical Terrains*, Lisa Lowe demonstrates, quite successfully I find, that Lady Mary Wortley Montague's observations on Turkish culture and society are governed by profound paradoxes. Her writings are marked by what Lowe calls "multivalence." While, on the one hand, Montague redresses many of what she insists are the misconceptions and inaccurate representations of Turkish women, propagated by male travel writers, some of her descriptions "resonate with traditional occidental imaginings of the Orient as exotic, ornate, and mysterious, imaginary qualities fundamental to eighteenth-century Anglo-Turkish relations" (Lowe 1991, 31).

9. Here I quote Andrea Deagon's translation of Martial's passage from her article "Framing the Ancient History of Oriental Dance" (2003, 38). This article is significant in offering a rare reading of Martial's epigrams with brief references to dances that are discussed in some detail, drawing insightful inferences about the dancers and their art in the latter years of the Roman Empire.

10. Metin And quotes an omitted paragraph from Dr. Covel's published diaries (the manuscript is in the British Museum) that describes a sequence of "little plays or interludes, all using the most beastly brutish language possible." These interludes represented "the damnable act of buggery in the grossest manner possible, with men, boys and beasts, whereof in show came in many…acting upon all fours" (1976, 149).

11. Hamilton's book is a compilation of various travelers' accounts that she does not always cite in detail. Although she is supposedly concerned with customs and ceremonies from the entire universe, a truly overwhelming and ambitious task, her emphasis is on sexual intrigue, scandal, and gossip from what in her day was termed "the Orient." In recent times, authors such as Carla Coco have emulated Hamilton's project. Limiting her focus to the Ottoman Empire (as opposed to Hamilton's "universe"), Coco attempts a very similar task in *Secrets of the Harem* (1997), a lavish and extravagantly illustrated volume whose sole service, it seems, is to underpin the lasting appeal of the Orientalist fantasy and the harem in particular.

12. See letter to Bouilhet, "Between Girga and Assiut, June 2, 1850," in *Letters of Gustave Flaubert* (1980, 121), and *Flaubert in Egypt* (1972, 203–4). In the latter source, Steegmuller provides an informative footnote on Jean-Paul Sartre's disbelief that Flaubert consummated homosexual experiences in the baths. Steegmuller writes: "In [Sartre's] opinion, all Flaubert's pederastic talk in his letters to Louis Bouilhet is merely a form of joking, common between him and his friends; there were no homosexual

relations between them as some have thought; and all the references to bardashes in the baths were the swank of a traveler wanting to impress a stay-at-home with his exotic experiences" (Flaubert 1972, 204). To support his position, Sartre offers to analyze various pieces of evidence, though I find that what is needed is not merely evidence testifying to the "truth" of Flaubert's sexual escapades on tour. I am particularly interested in the theoretical implications behind the imperative of such narratives and what meanings these various reconstructions of a famous, allegedly straight man's sexual behavior offer.

13. *Pothos* is a Greek term for desire. I prefer to use it here, since it signifies for me a stronger and more fervent attraction toward that which generates longing.

14. Byrne Fone's work has offered an elaborate development of Ramsay Burt's comment. Fone's *Homophobia: A History* is an ambitious and significant historical survey that demonstrates the various forms that homophobia has taken from classical Greece to the present. Most important, the book investigates the injunctions of religion, government, law, and science over same-sex sexual practice during various periods, and the consequences of these injunctions.

15. Fifi Abdou's interpretations are at times so sexually explicit that for some critics her artistic accomplishments do little more than confirm her status as a disreputable dancer. This notion holds such sway that I suspect that Edward Said has Fifi Abdou, among many others, in mind when he contrasts Tahia Carioca's talent with that of lesser dancers: "That smile has seemed to me symbolic of Tahia's distinction in a culture that featured dozens of dancers called Zouzou and Fifi, most of them treated as barely a notch above prostitutes" ("Homage to a Belly-Dancer," 349).

16. Kyriakou Pelagia and the Mesogios Musical Group, *Oloaspron Pezouni: Traditional Cypriot Folk Songs* (P. Hadjimichael, 2003).

WORKS CITED

Ahmed, Leila. 1992. *Women and Gender in Islam: Historical Roots of a Modern Debate.* New Haven, CT: Yale University Press.

And, Metin. 1976. *A Pictorial History of Turkish Dancing: From Folk Dancing to Whirling Dervishes—Belly Dancing to Ballet.* Ankara: Dost Yayinlari.

Berger, Morroe. 1961. "The Arab Danse du Ventre." *Dance Perspectives* 10: 4–43.

Boone, Joseph. 2001. "Vacation Cruises; or, The Homoerotics of Orientalism." In *Postcolonial, Queer: Theoretical Intersections*, ed. John C. Hawley, 43–78. Albany, NY: State University of New York Press.

Buonaventura, Wendy. 1989. *The Serpent of the Nile: Women and Dance in the Arab World.* London: Saqi Books.

Burt, Ramsay. 1995. *The Male Dancer: Bodies, Spectacles, Sexualities.* London: Routledge.

Coco, Carla. 1997. *Secrets of the Harem.* London: Philip Wilson.

Covel, John. 1962. "Extracts from the Diaries of Dr. John Covel, 1670–1679." In *Early Voyages and Travels in the Levant*, ed. Theodore Bent, 99–287. New York: Burt Franklin.

Deagon, Andrea. 1999. "Feminism and Belly Dance." *Habibi* 17 (4): 8–13.

———. 2003. "Framing the Ancient History of Oriental Dance." *Habibi* 19 (3): 32–41.

Denon, Vivant. [1803] 1973. *Travels in Upper and Lower Egypt, in Company with Several Divisions of the French Army, during the Campaigns of General Bonaparte in That Country.* Vol. 1. Trans. Arthur Aikin. London: Arno.

Flaubert, Gustave. 1972. *Flaubert in Egypt: A Sensibility on Tour.* Ed. Francis Steegmuller. London: Bodley Head.

————. 1980. *The Letters of Gustave Flaubert: 1830–1857.* Trans. Francis Steegmuller. Cambridge, MA: Belknap Press.

Fone, Byrne. 2000. *Homophobia: A History.* New York: Picador.

Foster, Susan Leigh. 1988. "Choreographies of Gender." *Signs: Journal of Women in Culture and Society* 24 (1): 1–33.

Fraser, Kathleen Wittick. 2002. "Public and Private Entertainment at a Royal Egyptian Wedding: 1845." *Habibi* 19 (1): 36–38.

Garber, Marjorie. 1992. *Vested Interests: Cross-Dressing and Cultural Anxiety.* New York: Harper Perennial.

Hamilton, Lady Augusta. 1822. *Marriage, Rites, Customs and Ceremonies of All Nations of the Universe.* London: Chapple and Son.

hooks, bell. 1992. *Black Looks: Race and Representation.* Toronto: Between the Lines.

Janssen, Thijs. 1992. "Transvestites and Transsexuals in Turkey." In *Sexuality and Eroticism among Males in Moslem Societies,* ed. Arno Schmitt and Jehoeda Sofer, 83–92. New York: Haworth Press.

Karayanni, Stavros Stavrou. 2004. *Dancing Fear and Desire: Race, Sexuality, and Imperial Politics in Middle Eastern Dance.* Waterloo, ON: Wilfrid Laurier University Press.

Lane, E. W. 1963. *Manners and Customs of the Modern Egyptians.* London: Everyman.

Lewis, Reina. 1996. *Gendering Orientalism: Race, Femininity and Representation.* London: Routledge.

Lorius, Cassandra. 1996. "'Oh Boy, You Salt of the Earth': Outwitting Patriarchy in *Raqs Baladi.*" *Popular Music* 15 (3): 285–98.

Lowe, Lisa. 1991. *Critical Terrains: French and British Orientalisms.* Ithaca, NY: Cornell University Press.

McClintock, Anne. 1995. *Imperial Leather: Race, Gender and Sexuality in the Colonial Contest.* London: Routledge.

Montague, Lady Mary Wortley. [1838] 1971. *Letters from the Levant during the Embassy to Constantinople 1716–18.* New York: Arno.

Murray, O. Stephen. 1997. "The Will Not to Know." In *Islamic Homosexualities: Culture, History, and Literature,* ed Stephen Murray and Will Roscoe, 14–54. New York: New York University Press.

Nerval, Gerard de. 1929. *The Women of Cairo: Scenes of Life in the Orient.* London: George Routledge; New York: AMS.

Orga, Irfan. 2002. *The Caravan Moves On: Three Weeks among Turkish Nomads.* London: Eland.

Özdemir, Kemal. 2000. *Oryantal Göbek Dansi [Oriental Belly Dance].* Istanbul: Dönence.

Sachs, Susan. 2000. "He's No Salomé, But It's Straight from the Heart." *New York Times,* May 4. www.nytimes.com/library/world/mideast/050400lebanon-bellydancer.html.

Said, Edward. 2001. "Homage to a Belly-Dancer: On Tahia Carioca." In *Reflections on Exile and Other Essays,* 346–55. Cambridge, MA: Harvard University Press.

Schuyler, Eugene. 1966. *Turkistan: Notes of a Journey in Russian Turkistan, Kokand, Bukhara and Kuldja.* Ed. Geoffrey Wheeler. New York: Praeger.

Sedgwick, Eve Kosofsky. 1985. *Between Men: English Literature and Male Homosocial Desire.* New York: Columbia University Press.

Shay, Anthony. 2002. *Choreographic Politics: State Folk Dance Companies, Representation and Power.* Middletown, CT: Wesleyan University Press.

———. 2005. "The Male Dancer in the Middle East and Central Asia." In *Belly Dance: Orientalism, Transnationalism, and Harem Fantasy,* ed. Anthony Shay and Barbara Sellers-Young, 51–84. Costa Mesa, CA: Mazda.

Shay, Anthony, and Barbara Sellers-Young. 2005. "Introduction." In *Belly Dance: Orientalism, Transnationalism, and Harem Fantasy,* ed. Anthony Shay and Barbara Sellers-Young, 1–27. Costa Mesa, CA: Mazda.

Sonnini, C. S. [1800] 1972. *Travels in Upper and Lower Egypt.* Farnborough: Gregg.

St. John, James Augustus. 1845. *Egypt and Nubia: With Illustrations.* London: Chapman and Hall.

Stokes, Martin, ed. 1994. *Ethnicity, Identity and Music: The Musical Construction of Place.* Oxford: Berg.

Widjan, Ali. 2001. "Modern Painting in the Mashriq." In *Colors of Enchantment: Theater, Dance, Music, and the Visual Arts of the Middle East,* ed. Sherifa Zuhur, 365–85. Cairo: American University in Cairo.

NAMUS ZOKHRABOV

> *Born in Baku, Azerbaijan, Zokhrabov attended the State Choreographic Institute* (koreografski institut). *He appeared for more than 20 years as a soloist with the Azerbaijan State Dance Ensemble and earned the prestigious Merited Artist of the Republic of Azerbaijan award. He was also a member of the professional Lezginka Ensemble of Daghestan and other state-supported dance companies. Today, he teaches dance, performs, and is also involved in building management in Los Angeles.*

I began to dance at the age of 11, when I met a friend on his way to a folk dance class at the Youth Palace [a huge state-run establishment in which children can pursue different extracurricular activities, including all kinds of dance—social, folk, ballet—as well as chess, sports, art, music, and other types of special interests]. I learned fast and soon became a member of the prestigious Jujehlar children's dance ensemble. It was an amazing experience. Some of the children could perform things that adults could not do. The company was run by a German woman, because at that time dance was considered to be shameful to many Azerbaijanis.[1]

Baku is a very multinational city, and attitudes toward dance varied. The many Russians, Armenians, and the old class of Persian-speaking Jews who lived in Baku admired dance.[2] Thus, it was easier for them than for the Azerbaijanis. Like the Iranians, Azerbaijanis despised dance and regarded it as a form of low behavior, despite the relatively high pay for dancers in state-supported companies, higher than for university professors, engineers, factory workers, and others. My parents, especially in the beginning, said, "Shame on you." When I began in the early 1970s, there were no Azerbaijani boys in ballet classes, they were mostly Russians.[3] The few Azerbaijani boys that were brave enough to dance were enrolled in folk dance classes. Thus, in the national company and in my early classes there were several Jewish boys and other nationality groups besides the Azerbaijani boys. Therefore, unlike the state ensembles of some of the other companies like that of Georgia or Uzbekistan, where Russians are rare, the Azerbaijan State Folk Dance Ensemble had 50 to 60 percent Russian women, although no Russian men. Rehearsals were conducted in Russian, because most of the Russians, even though they studied

Zokhrabov when he was dancing with the State Dance Ensemble of Azerbaijan in the 1980s. Used with permission.

Azeri as a second language, were never pushed to use it. The only time we used Azeri is when we were mad and wanted to swear.

The beginning was difficult because my family and boys outside were always laughing at me. They thought that I must be from a different planet. But I loved my classes and worked hard. In two years, when I was 13 to 14, I shot up to my current height of six feet two inches. Studying in the *koreografski institut* was hard work. [The *koreografski instituts* are like American high schools for the performing arts; they are found in every capital city in the former USSR and typically include grades 1 through 12]. In the morning you study what all young children study, Russian language, history, mathematics, and then in the afternoons we danced Monday through Saturday until five o'clock, sometimes later. In many ways our training resembled the military; it was rigid, and we were taught to obey.

When I graduated from the koreografski institut, I was taken on as an apprentice to the Azerbaijan State Song and Dance Ensemble. At that time there were three professional dance ensembles in Baku, and one in each of the major cities of Azerbaijan. In Baku we had the State Song and Dance Ensemble, the Rashid Beybutov Company [named for a famous vocalist], and the State Folk Dance Ensemble, the newest company, founded in 1970. Six months after working as an apprentice with no pay, Tankho Israelov saw me dancing in a rehearsal, behind the members of the company. Israelov was a former member of the Moiseyev Dance Company and the director of the Lezginka Ensemble of Daghestan, which borders Azerbaijan but is now located in the Russian Federation. Israelov, a truly knowledgeable dancer and choreographer, was one of the few individuals to truly know folk dance style because he conducted fieldwork in the various parts of Daghestan, which, although small, is home to a wide variety of ethnic groups. He asked me for my passport so I could travel with the company, and he was stunned to find out I was only 14 at the time because I was so tall, and, of course, as a minor, I didn't have one. I learned so much from him. I danced with him for 2 years, and then I received an offer from the State Folk Ensemble of Azerbaijan, which is a larger, more prestigious company with better pay, and I danced with them for over 20 years, until I was 36.

Dancing with the State Folk Dance Ensemble was hard work for a number of reasons. First, I love our Azerbaijani folk dances, and they are very complicated. For example, Georgian dance has only 8 basic movements, but Azerbaijani dance has 38. But rather than the actual folk style, the company uses the academic style.[4] We wore the *cherkes* coat for every dance.[5] None of the directors was familiar with our actual folk dances. For the Georgian company it is easier to have variation because they have definite ethnographic regions like Abkhazia, Adjaria, Ossetia, but Azerbaijan does not have those kinds of official divisions based on ethnicity.

Second, we worked long hours, and there was a great deal of competition. Twenty men would train for a choreography, but they might choose only eight dancers, and sometimes even if you were the best, you could not say anything. That was our training. Several times the second director, Afak Melikova, would say to me: "Namus, you talk too much." We had to be ready to travel at any minute. If the president went to Paris or Iraq, we had to go. Several times the president received important guests on a ship in the Caspian, and they flew us there in a helicopter to dance, and then flew us right back after it was over. Third, the directors, especially Melikova, wanted all the dancers on the stage all of the time. Unlike the Georgians, for example, where the soloists would appear and then exit as the corps danced so they could rest, we had to appear in every number. There was no rest, and I was injured from the wear and tear of rehearsals and performances, but she would not permit me to take time off to heal.

For the Azerbaijanis, dancing was no different for boys than for girls. It was shameful for both. You could be called a *mutreb* [public entertainer]. Only a few made it into the national company; the rest were either discouraged by their families, or they were not technically proficient enough. Because of this negative sentiment about dance, Azerbaijan never developed a company as brilliant as that of Georgia. In Georgia it is an honor to be a dancer—a matter of pride to represent Georgian culture, and all Georgian parents teach their kids to dance and encourage them to enter the *koreografski institut* and become a member of the national company. Azerbaijanis are natural traders and merchants—they don't understand dance and culture, only money. Dance is not valued. If you go to a wedding to dance, people interrupt you, or climb up on the stage to dance with you, and they know nothing.

Unlike the camaraderie among the dancers in some of the other folk dance companies, the Azerbaijani company was filled with jealousy and competition, and on the ensemble's anniversary, we preferred not to see one another.[6] Often in Moscow, at least every four years, all-republic festivals were held, and so we saw and met the dancers from all the other companies, and we were on good terms with them. We knew their repertoires and who the best dancers were. Of course, the Moiseyev dancers were snobs, because they were at the top of the structure, but many of the others were really nice people, and one could admire their artistry. We also saw many ballet performances. The Bolshoi, the Kirov, and other big companies came to Baku. Ballet is much more valued than folk dance. The course for ballet in the *koreografski institut* is eight years, whereas for folk dance it is only five. That is why when my wife, Olga, could no longer dance ballet, they offered her a place in the folk section as a kind of consolation prize.

When you graduated from the *koreografski institut*, you had to work for three years in whichever company selected you, and you could not receive your diploma until you had completed that time period of service. The directors of the professional dance companies came to scout for the very best dancers. When Olga was ready to graduate, she had offers from each of the three professional ensembles. The reason that you had to wait three years for your diploma was that only the few very best dancers could be selected for the national dance companies in Baku, because each year there were only a few positions open. For example, in the Azerbaijan Dance Ensemble we had 30 men and 25 women. So only the few very best dancers would get a position in Baku, and the rest had to be assigned to one of the local provincial city ensembles. Many people did not want to leave Baku to live in other cities, so if they did not accept a position there, they would not receive their diplomas. That was the way that they forced people to go to the provincial cities, or the person left without a diploma.

I also worked very hard because I was representing my culture, and it gave me great pride to do that. When I received the Merited Artist of the Republic of Azerbaijan award, at last my parents were so proud. I think that by receiving that honor, I have made it easier for boys to dance in Azerbaijan.

NOTES (Provided by Anthony Shay)

1. The Azerbaijanis are a Turkic-speaking ethnic group of the Caucasian region bordering on the western shores of the Caspian Sea. Their language is frequently referred to as Azeri. The northern portion of Azerbaijan was a former Soviet republic, now an independent nation. The southern portion of Azerbaijan constitutes two Iranian provinces, and the population is the largest ethnic group in Iran after the majority Persian population.

2. The variety of ethnicities Namus experienced is no longer evident in Azerbaijan. Soon after the breakup of the former Soviet Union, Armenia and Azerbaijan went to war. The Azerbaijanis resident in Armenia and the Armenians living in Azerbaijan fled against a background of bloodletting and ethnic enmity. Several thousand people died, and more than a million were displaced as a result of the Nagorno-Karabakh struggle (1988–94) that left Armenia occupying a considerable percentage of Azerbaijan's prewar territory, whose boundaries had been established by the USSR. Nearly all of the Azerbaijanis who had been resident in Armenia, and the Armenians resident in Azerbaijan, many of whom had lived there for generations, fled to their respective republics. Many of the Jews left for Israel.

3. Namus Zokhrabov's wife, Olga, who changed her name to Aliya in order to dance in the national ensemble, is Russian. She began as a ballet dancer and attended Krasnodarsk academy (North Caucasus region of Russia). Due to an injury after several years of ballet, she could no longer dance on pointe, and she was offered a place in the *koreografski institut* in Baku in the folk dance section. She stated that her parents were against her dancing as well, but their opposition did not stem from moral concerns, but rather because they wanted her to go to the university. Rather like many American parents who oppose their children's careers in dance, the concern was "How will you make a decent and long-lasting living?" (personal interview, July 27, 2007).

4. "Academic" style refers to the balleticized, semi-character dance style that is used throughout the former Soviet dance companies, as well as companies like Mazowsze of Poland. The government never wanted to stage actual folk dances, or even permitted them, but instead encouraged the creation of an official folklore and style that often departed radically from the folk dances and songs found in the field. (For elaboration on this topic, see the essay by Shay in this volume.)

5. The *cherkes* (from Circassian, the ethnic group with which the garment is most associated) is the well-known garment worn by many ethnic groups throughout the Caucasus. Bullet cartridges are worn across the chest of the coat, and the coat is frequently worn with a dagger. Such clothing was used for campaigning. The men throughout the region wore many other traditional garments, but the *cherkes* tends to be the only one chosen for stage use.

6. This is a very different attitude from the closeness between members of some other state folk dance ensembles. For example, during the annual gala marking the anniversary of the founding of LADO, the Croatian Ensemble of Folk Dances and Songs, many of the old members, including those living abroad, return to celebrate. Each year, many of the former and retired members participate in one or two of the dances and musical pieces in the gala performance.

11

Ibrahim Farrah

Dancer, Teacher, Choreographer, Publisher

BARBARA SELLERS-YOUNG

My Birthright is the bedrock of my aesthetics, the aesthetics that define Ibrahim Farrah, the artist.

—Ibrahim Farrah (1991)

Ibrahim Farrah's life, as a dancer, teacher, choreographer, and publisher, was a negotiation between his traditional Lebanese family life and the popular discourse that depicted Lebanon and other areas of the Middle East as a social and cultural space of unlimited sensual pleasure. Born to Lebanese immigrants in western Pennsylvania in 1939, Farrah often encountered Orientalist stereotypes of the Middle East that were maintained on the stage and in films in productions such as *Salome* and *Kismet* and, from the 1970s onward, by many participants of the belly dance community in North America.[1] Much of Ibrahim Farrah's work served to counter this popular image of the Middle East. This essay, based on a series of articles Ibrahim Farrah wrote for *Arabesque*, is an accounting of Farrah's reflections on his negotiations between the stereotypes of the dominant culture and his position as a cultural insider within the Middle Eastern community. His life (he died in 1998) provides an opportunity to consider the persistence of popular stereotypes and the methods individuals use to resist them.[2]

Early Years

Ibrahim Farrah was the fourth son of George Jacob Farrah and Abla Nassar Farrah, who emigrated in 1930 from a small village in northern Lebanon to Everson, a small town in western Pennsylvania. They were not the first Lebanese family to settle in the area. Looking for a better economic existence, Farrah's grandfather, Yaoub Gergis Farrah, immigrated to America in 1896 and worked as a peddler in Pennsylvania. Over time, he saved enough money to bring his brother to the United States. As Farrah relates in "A Dancer's Chronicle: Growing Up Lebanese," "Together they worked and saved the money to bring

Figure 11.1   Ibrahim
Farrah, courtesy of
Phyllis Saretta, Ibrahim
Farrah Archives.
Photograph by Thomas
Rodrigues.

the third brother over. With the three brothers pooling their earnings together after a few years, this first pioneer returned to Lebanon where he took a young bride. When their first son was two years old, and the wife was pregnant with their second child, the family immigrated to America. A family tradition was established: Each of the brothers traveled back to their homeland and brought back a wife. Years later, the first son of the pioneer would repeat the same pattern. The first son was my father" (1992–93, 10).

These immigrants arrived in a country in which Orientalism had already gained a strong foothold within the popular imagination through performances at fairs, carnivals, and circuses. As Lori Anne Salem writes, "The most common performances were of the Arabian acrobats, tumblers, dervishes, contortion dancers, giants, and sword swallowers who appeared in curiosity shows, dime museums, circuses, variety theaters, and other venues for popular entertainment" (1999, 273). Such entertainers were an extension of the performances of the World's Columbian Exposition of 1893, in Chicago, where entrepreneur Sol Bloom convinced the governing board to create a midway that included dancers from North Africa and the Middle East. The dancers performed as part of exhibits on the Midway Plaisance, created by the Chicago fair's Department of Ethnology. One souvenir book describes the midway as "filled with the various races of men, under the brilliant lights, and amidst the sounds of all tongues and all music" (McGovern 1894, 259). The exhibits included selected renditions of the folklore and the exotic, including versions of Austrian, Lapland, German, and Javanese villages, and the Moorish Palace. Visitors to the fair could explore the galleries of Oriental items in the Moorish Palace and walk across the street to view men and women performing the dances of Tunisia, Algeria, Egypt, Syria, and Palestine. Or they could visit the Persian Palace, which featured a group of dancers from Paris who created renditions of the fantasy Orient, based on the writings and visual representations of Flaubert, Gerome, and others. Thus, the real dances of the Middle East were performed within the same spatial frame as the fantasy Oriental version, a discursive pattern that would continue throughout the century.

The exposition's board of lady managers, wrapped tightly in their corsets, objected to the dancing, the ethnic as well as the pseudo-ethnic. In their opinion, the dancers' movement of hips, pelvis, and torso was blatantly obscene and certainly not appropriate in a venue designated as family entertainment. They requested the exhibits be shut down "for the good of public decency and morality."[3] Despite the lady managers' request, the exhibit remained open; indeed, Sol Bloom used the controversy to heighten interest in the performances, renaming them "belly dance," after the French *danse du ventre*. Among the dancers of the Midway Plaisance was Mohammed, who amazed audiences with his muscular control. The notoriety of the dancers of the Midway Plaisance soon led to imitators who billed themselves as Little Egypt and performed at carnivals and in burlesque shows across North America.

Bloom's designation was one of the many commercial representations of the Middle East that participated in the political project of Orientalism through a marketing technique that erotized the Middle East for American consumption. Despite the fact that there were both male and female dancers present at the 1893 Chicago fair, the consumption patterns of the West, fed by Orientalized images, categorized only the Middle Eastern female body as a site of sensual longing, while it erased the dancing Middle Eastern male body. Stavros Karayanni, author of *Dancing Fear and Desire*, writes: "The European gaze translated the experience of Eastern dance into a medium of aberrance and illicitness. In the Western imaginary, the dancer's body loomed threateningly and enticing, mapping in motion always an intermediate zone, a threshold signifying liminality and indeterminacy, qualities often used to represent the East as a whole. Dancing women were a threat but at least their dancing body could be subjected to symbolic Western domination through sexual intercourse" (2004, 96). Male dancers, as Anthony Shay points out in "The Male Dancer," were under colonialism eliminated in Middle Eastern countries in a form of subaltern identity reversal, in which ethnic minorities attempt to gain the acceptance of colonial elites through a denial of their cultural heritage (2005, 85–113). The result of this identity crisis was the elimination of male dancers in the public sphere while dancing by men continued as part of family celebrations. Public performances were dominated by female entertainers who had borrowed costume styles and movement vocabulary from the Hollywood film industry. Among these female performers, both in the Middle East and in the West, there were those who traced their lineage to the Middle East and others who did not.

Ibrahim Farrah grew up in a community in which people claimed their Lebanese heritage first through names; women were called Stelleni, Marianna, Yaout, Foutine, and the men Yousef, Elias, Fouad, Najib. These women and men represented a migration to the United States that started in the 1880s by Christians from what is now Lebanon but which was then part of the province of Syria in the Ottoman Empire. They left their homeland because of economic stress due to increased population and the religious oppression of the Ottoman Empire (Aswad and Bilge 1996). Michael Suleiman writes, "Under Ottoman rule, Christians in the Syrian province were not accorded equal status with their Muslim neighbors. They were subjected to many restrictions on their behavior and often suffered persecution" (1999, 2). Immigration was made more attractive to Syrian and Lebanese when sea voyages got shorter and the telephone made communication with families left behind possible. The new modes of transportation and communication kept families in close contact through periodic visits and telephone calls. In addition, the majority of Lebanese came initially as sojourners believing that they would make money in the United States that they could use to make a better life in Lebanon.

The men found jobs working the coke ovens in steel mills or else worked as peddlers, providing goods not easily attainable in rural areas. Their evenings were spent visiting the homes of male friends. The women's lives replicated village life in Lebanon, including daily visits by female friends in which they shared chores. Farrah's description provides a portrait of the women's daily life:

> There were many visitors at my home every day: The women mostly during the day and the men in the evening after work—that is, any time there was not a crisis, in which case, they received all the visitors. Though usually expected, these visits were unannounced, and it was not unusual that beginning around 11:00 in the morning until the early afternoon, the door was continually resounding with friendly knocks from our family female friends. If they came early, they usually brought a cooked dish with them which became part of our luncheon. They would never have come empty-handed. (1991a, 12)

Despite the communication problems created by World War II, Farrah's family maintained close contact with their Lebanese relatives via phone, letter, and periodic visits. Following the war, weddings and other family celebrations were often events that were accompanied by visitors from Lebanon. The majority of Lebanese had been married in Lebanon (as Ibrahim Farrah's parents were), and these celebrations in a new country symbolized the strength and continuation of the family, as well as emphasizing the family's connection to the home country. On these occasions the community would celebrate with food, music, song, and dance. Generally, dancing consisted of the *dabke* and the solo performances that Farrah's mother refers to as "the happiness dance." The *dabke* was performed in separate lines of men and women, each performing similar steps but with slight variations that highlighted their masculine or feminine identity. Ibrahim Farrah quotes his mother remembering groups of women singing and dancing the *dabke*:

> We mostly formed a circle, one of the women, you know, one with a very beautiful voice, would stand alone in the circle and sing and chant and guide us. Those of us in the circle would answer her singing with singing back to her, and we moved like this... at this moment, Mom actually began to chant and move. The movement she demonstrated had that "Eastern" flavor, as I knew it, and began like so many dances I've seen there, on the left foot. It was swaying almost—for lack of better description—spiritual-like movement done in halftime with the insinuating shifting of the body weight, two beats forward, two beats backwards which reminded me of the sinuous sway of willows in the smooth spring zephyr. This type of movement remained constant. The variations came in the subtle changes of direction and the surging and receding of vigor; with the ebb and flow of the motions. (1991b, 10)

The happiness dance provided an opportunity for each man and woman to express their joy at the changing nature of individual status represented in the communal rituals of birthdays or weddings. Ibrahim recorded his observations of his mother's illustration of the happiness dance during interviews with her:

> With her left foot flat, and the right on the ball of the foot, with loose flexible knees, though in no way bent—a placement common in all character dances—she moved forward to what she called her dance space with graceful outstretched arms. As she came to her "dance spot," she smiled and did a slow revolving turn around herself, turning left. When the turn was complete, she brought first the left hand to her head, then her right, again with amazing grace, keeping time with her feet but not moving spatially. She did a soft shoulder shake and, still smiling, she moved with a soft waving arm to greet people on all sides of the room. With the latter movement complete, the smile became serene and she lifted her head and looked up, bringing her arms to a soft second position with soft, delicate wrists and palms also upturned a very spiritual look. With this movement she said, "That's how we show people we're happy to dance." (1991c, 11)

Throughout the interview, Ibrahim's mother stressed to him the importance of the dance as an expression of personal joy and gratitude for being able to be a part of the family celebration: "Before you finish dancing, you show gratitude for the hospitality to your host. You dance around him and her and salute, always be happy [when you dance]. Sometimes you hug and kiss them and maybe bring them out to dance a little while with you. Then you move on to a friend or someone you know who dances beautifully, and pull them up to dance and then you sit down" (1991c, 11). Farrah described the male version of the "happiness dance" as falling into three categories that he labeled expressionist, conservative, and freer form. The first expressionist, he describes as follows:

> If you were to catch some of the older men who did dance on film they would look as if they were dancing in slow motion. They danced as if they were the leader of a dabke. What was especially powerful about this fascinating style, in retrospect, was the individual dancer's sense of connectedness with the earth and air simultaneously: They would stamp their feet on the ground, and one could feel the entire weight of their body and strength push through the earth. With a slow shift of weight and a wave of arms, their energy would suddenly transfer from weighing on the earth to floating in air, giving the appearance of someone about to take flight. I call this the expressionistic style, one that is quite dramatic.

In describing the second, more conservative, style of happiness dance, Farrah also explains the distinction between masculine and feminine movement:

> A second style, I would define as a more conservative approach to dance: A style with simplicity and a small vocabulary of step movements. This is a feminine rendition of the conservative style that corresponds to, and somewhat contrasts, the masculine version; examining the two in juxtaposition, it is easier to describe and visualize his masculine variant. Step patterns in the men's dance had a touch of heaviness as opposed to the light footedness of the women's style. While women shook their shoulders softly and loosely, the men's shoulders motions were those with rhythmic sharpness and more defined accents. Their shoulders would pulse up and down or thrust forward and be released in a honed fashion. Although extremely graceful, they used few decorative arm patterns, moving their arms rhythmically from pose to pose (and gesture to gesture) with a musicality and poetry that can only be described as extraordinary.

The third stylistic category, freer, includes a more expansive range of motion: "Men moved with more freedom of motion. Their dances were decorated with more turning patterns, a quick shuffling of feet that could send them scurrying across the room and through space, unconstrained: Shoulder shakes were loose; arms were more decorative; a little hip action; and an emotion of sheer exuberance" (1992–93, 15–17).

After the guests left, Farrah and his siblings would engage in danced imitations of those who attended the party. As he recalled:

After the guests departed, "Show Number Two" would begin. This was the moment when we children imitated, as near as possible (youthful carbon copies!) our elders' body gestures. My brother, whose own dancing was bouncy and a bit off rhythm, was an expert at imitating those guests whose dance bordered on the comic, reproducing their gait, posture, and even going to the extent of stuffing a pillow under his shirt to accent that particular protrusion. My presentations were quite the opposite, of course. Being the better dancer, I relished showing off that I could not only do the steps as well or better, but also I could adopt those intimate personal expressions... the idiosyncratic personality of those whom I was imitating. (1992–93, 12)

The embodied memory of dancing parents, uncles, aunts, brothers, and sisters would be a consistent reminder to Farrah of his Lebanese identity. His formal education, on the other hand, took place in what he describes as a "little red school house," in which students from different grades studied in the same class. He later attended Pennsylvania State University. Inspired by his innate curiosity and the tales of *Huckleberry Finn*, Farrah pursued an education outside the red schoolhouse that included hopping freight trains at the station that was minutes from his family home and riding them to their next stopping place and returning home by the same method. He was also fascinated by the carnivals and circuses that passed through town. He earned money by whitewashing, mowing lawns, pruning gardens, and scrubbing down porches to provide enough money to attend them. If his funds ran out, he would use his youth and look of naïveté to sneak into tents. It was through this method that he encountered his first naked woman, as well as the dance known as the "hootchie-kootchie." He was fascinated by the hootchie-kootchie dancers who were part of the sideshows, prancing and gyrating in "sequined belts and bras with a little cloth fringe hanging meagerly, and to piped music; they endeavored some sort of stomach contortion" (1993a, 16). Despite his fascination, he never associated the gyrations of hootchie-kootchie dancers with the dances that were part of family celebrations, primarily because "none of these women ever danced like my mother, my sisters, or any of my aunts. I never associated their gyrations with anything oriental or exotic, and certainly it never registered in my mind as any kind of variant, or tangent, of my own Middle Eastern background" (1993a, 16).

Ibrahim Farrah's religious tradition was Greek Orthodox, but because the nearest Orthodox Church was 45 miles away over rugged Pennsylvania hillsides, his family was not always able to attend. His mother gave him a choice of the local Catholic Church or the Evangelical United Brethren church. He decided on the Evangelical church because of the music. He found his involvement extended beyond attending Sunday church services, and eventually he became a Sunday school teacher. Although the Evangelical tradition accepted music, it had an opposite opinion of dance, in particular of men dancing.[4] As Ramsay Burt points out in *The Male Dancer*, American attitudes toward dance in the 1940s and 1950s were heavily influenced by an essentialist definition of masculinity evolved from a frontier ideal of independence, self-reliance, and strength imagined in the "gun-slinging, axe- and plough-wielding frontiersmen" (1995, 103). Throughout Ibrahim Farrah's life, this definition of masculinity would be consistently challenged by the variants found in popular culture, such as the bluesy sensuality of Elvis Presley and James Brown, yet the older-style machismo was consistently reified in films that feature action heroes played by John Wayne, Clint Eastwood, Sylvester Stallone, and others. Popular music and film, in fact, became a site for the ambivalent relationship between "frontier and urban" definitions of masculinity that mirrored the changing geopolitics of America. In his professional life, Ibrahim Farrah would challenge these dominant versions of masculinity through his performance of and research on Middle Eastern dance.

During his teenage years Farrah's life as a Sunday school teacher in a church that forbade dance created a conflict with his love of physical expression. As he phrases it: "My youthful radical fundamentalist devotion, with its prudish nature of forbidding dance began to run headlong against my natural need for freedom of self expression. Upon entering high school, this friction intensified—the two aspects of self speeding inevitably towards each other on a crash course. After dancing my heart out at high school 'hops' on Friday and Saturday nights, I would rise early and faithfully each Sunday morning to teach Sunday school" (1993b, 14). This conflict in lifestyle created in Farrah what anthropologist Gregory Bateson refers to as the "double bind," a situation in which an individual attempts to fulfill two mutually incompatible set of instructions. In this case, Farrah's involvement with the church conflicted with his love of dancing. It is a situation that could not continue indefinitely. Again, as he phrases it: "Strangely and very gradually, a typically American dilemma started to fester in the center of my being. I was experiencing a distressing polarization of two opposing and yet equally seductive pathways: The seemingly chaste and obedient nature of Puritanism coupled with the seemingly 'base' and frivolous characteristic of 'worldliness.' The Lord seemed to be coaxing me in a new direction. I could not help it: Dancing was definitely winning out" (1992b, 13).

The double-bind dilemma between church and dance was emblematic of the conflicts that often existed between Farrah's social world of his family and his identity as an American. By the age of 10, Farrah had developed preferences in popular culture that made him a full-fledged American of his generation. For example, he preferred country-and-western groups such as Abbie Neal and the Ranch Girls, a popular group of the 1940s and 1950s, to Lebanese music. His favorite movie stars were Betty Grable and Elvis Presley. This conflict between growing up in a close-knit Lebanese community and wanting to fit in with American culture would continue through his college years. Reflecting on those years, Ibrahim Farrah remarked that he would have taken the lyrics of *West Side Story*'s "I want to be in America" and replaced them with "I want to be an American" (1992b, 13). Ultimately he resolved the tensions between the two identities by accepting a hybrid identity of someone who loved being an American and also loved being Lebanese.

Dancer

Ibrahim Farrah went to college in the 1960s and then to Washington, D.C., where he started his performance career as a dancer at Club Syriannia. The decision was not made without anxiety:

> I always considered that my dance career began in Washington, D.C. in the early spring of 1964 when I was able to pay my rent and bills, buy my clothing (and costumes), feed myself (and my pets), etc. solely from dance-earned income. From the summer of 1962 to 1964 (same locale), I was, however, as so many artists are today, employed part-time in the profession. I could have gone the full-time route already by mid 1963, but that typically youthful confusion and soul-searching for the meaning and purposes of life; the discouraging reactions of my family; and a smidgen of that conventional fear of not making it, detained me. But the passion (!) to dance consumed me, and somehow I found the courage to say, "That's it. This is what I want to do; and if I fail, I am young enough to start another life." (1992–93, 8)

His performance at Club Syriannia, alongside noted performers such as the Jamal Twins, was possible because of a boom in Middle Eastern restaurants that had started with the 1952 opening of Boston's Club Zahra, a restaurant-nightclub specializing in Middle Eastern food, music, and dance. Club Zahra was an outgrowth of the ethnic identity clubs, such as the Syrian-Lebanese clubs that supported music events to raise money for less fortunate members of the community. The success of Club Zahra was followed by the opening of similar restaurants in cities across the United States, which provided an opportunity for recent immigrants from Palestine, Egypt, Syria, Iraq, Turkey, and Lebanon to meet, mingle, and converse.

Unlike those who had immigrated to the United States prior to World War II, the new immigrants came not as sojourners but with a desire to become permanent residents. As such, they were responsive to the ongoing political situation in the Middle East as it impacted their position in the United States. They were particularly humiliated by the highly publicized 1967 war and its implication that the Arabs, in losing the battle with Israel, were not strong as people or as individual nations. Consequently, there was a movement toward an increased pan-Arab identity in an attempt to counter the image of the Arab depicted by the media. As Michael Suleiman notes, there was also a move "to organize conferences and publish journals and books in defense of their cause. They [Arab Americans] wrote fiction, poetry, and memoirs declaring pride and solidarity with Arabs and Arab community in America" (1999, 14).

As the most public representative of the Arab world, Middle Eastern restaurants were the site of a complex negotiation of the popular Hollywood image of the Middle East and the Middle Eastern community's desire to meet and celebrate multiple versions of its heritage from Lebanon, Turkey, Greece, Egypt, and elsewhere via food, music, and dance. This was particularly true for second- and third-generation Arab Americans such as Farrah who found in the restaurants a site that represented a blend of their family of origin and popular culture's version of the Middle East. The clubs created this atmosphere by mixing illustrations of camels, tents, and caravans with music, musical instruments, and dance to entertain Middle Eastern and non–Middle Eastern customers.[5] Musicians played while patrons of the restaurant participated in group dances, most often the *dabke*. But there were also solo and couple versions of the Oriental dance performed by professional dancers from the Middle East, or, by the 1970s with the popularization of belly dance, dancers whose personal heritage was not Middle Eastern. As ethnomusicologist Anne Rasmussen points out, these sites held some emotional ambivalence for the musicians and other performers: "Although the trademarks of Orientalism helped these musicians to achieve success, the racist bias of this European belief system served to enhance the foreignness of these Arab and other Middle Eastern immigrants and their families, placing them in an imaginary world that was exotic—even to themselves" (1992, 345–65).

These public performances were contemporary versions of the public dancers of the 19th century in the Middle East and the 20th-century dancers of Cairo and Istanbul, made famous internationally by the Egyptian film industry.[6] In North American Middle Eastern restaurants, each dancer tended to develop her own version of Oriental dance based on traditions from the Middle Eastern country in which they grew up. This dance vocabulary was combined with the movement vocabulary the dancer picked up watching the other dancers in the restaurant. Many of the dancers also played tambourine or finger cymbals as part of the orchestra and thus added a musical element to their nightly performances. Over time, musicians and dancers integrated the folk rhythms from throughout North Africa and the Middle East, and a dancer from Egypt would be familiar with not only the 4/4 and 4/8 rhythms of Egypt but also the 9/8 rhythms of Turkey and the 6/8 rhythms of North Africa. As Rasmussen describes them, the restaurants were "adventurous, creative, polyethnic, electronic, and commercial. The music reflected interaction both with other immigrant groups and with American society and music culture as a whole" (1998, 147). The music styles and instruments of Greece, Turkey, Egypt, Lebanon, Syria, and elsewhere in the Middle East were mingled with the saxophone, electric guitar, and trap sets.

Ibrahim Farrah's personal dance style was based on the movement of the male dancers and styles he had observed as a child: expressionist, conservative, and freer. As he described it: "The simple truth is, my gait, emotions, body posture, general ambience actually came from the men I was raised with and surrounded by as a child" (1991a, 10). In 1991, Ibrahim acknowledged, "Today, when I do a specific movement, I know why. The answer is in my mind's eye; this is my grandfather Farrah ... that is Cousin Elia ... and this combination I owe to Cousin Yasmine or Uncle Sami in Lebanon" (1991a, 10). He found the term "male belly dancer" "a popular, and peculiar, appellation fostered in the West by the public and through the media" (1992–93, 8), one that did not represent the dance he performed and only created "confusion and perhaps misplaced curiosity" (10). Instead he preferred to be thought of as an Oriental dancer who, in his performances, represented an integration of the movement vocabulary of his grandfather, uncles, and cousins. However, in performing professionally, he was stepping outside of the social norm of his contemporaries in the Lebanese community in which men performed as soloists only in private family celebrations.

Farrah's performances were distinctly different from those of the other male belly dancers of his time period, such as Bert Ballandine, who had originally trained in Western dance and whose style derived from the proscenium stage rather than the movement vocabulary of a specific community. Farrah's performances relied on the technique learned from his male Lebanese relatives, and, as a consequence, his dance is the corporeal embodiment of the images of his childhood brought to life on the stage. Because Farrah was obviously male, doing what Americans recognized as a dance from the Middle East, his dancing challenged the popular American stereotype of assumed femininity of an Arab body. And, with the public nature of his performance, he also challenged Arab American social norms. On a personal level, the act of his body dancing was a performance of the tensions and related negotiations between his passion for physical expression, the assumptions of popular culture, and the role expectations of his natal family. As a second-generation Lebanese American, his performance was an enactment of elements of assimilation; in his case, he had seen in the bodies of Elvis Presley and other performers in the 1950s rock-and-roll scene who provocatively engaged their hips and torso in performance. His performances disputed popular culture's designation of Oriental dance as feminine. The synthesized unity of Farrah's hybrid identity provided an alternative image of the Arab male body for the ethnic community and for the dominant culture.

Teacher

Ibrahim Farrah's dancing career took him to cities on the East Coast, and he eventually settled in New York. He started teaching classes in response to the enormous demand for belly dance that developed in the 1970s, when it became a popular form of personal expression for women during the second phase of the feminist movement.[7] Farrah's response to the popularity of the dance was mixed. The demand for classes provided a consistent income, but the popularity of the dance created a concern in terms of the representation of the Middle East. Farrah admitted to being both shocked and stimulated by the primarily female students who, as he phrases it, approached the dance with a level of "passion, bordering on obsession" (1994a, 15). From Farrah's perspective, the passion did not make up for the lack of education in dance as a physical discipline or in knowledge of the dance as it existed in the Middle East or related diaspora. Thus, he felt the necessity to educate students not only in Oriental dance but also in the complex cultural and social values associated with it as well as related folk and ritual forms. He consistently relied on his personal experience as the basis for his teaching: "I have always credited my mother with being my first dance teacher. Surely my mother and the Lebanese community of which we were a part and all those relatives and family friends who passionately danced— be it at a family reunion; a spontaneous celebration; a wedding; a *hafla*; a *maharajan*; and a sundry of other festive occasions—gave me a solid foundation which has had a powerful and indelible impact on the way I interpret the dance and dance it" (1991a, 10). The images of his childhood were the foundation of Ibrahim Farrah's approach to teaching. He recalled, "In my role as teacher, aside from how I have grown and developed and aside from all that I have absorbed and been exposed to in a career that spans 30 years, I still find myself inserting movement images gleaned from the Lebanese community I grew up in" (1991a, 10).

Farrah taught classes in New York and weekend workshops throughout the United States and Europe. His classes were a combination of a disciplined approach to learning the dance's movement vocabulary, understanding the music's instrumentation and rhythm, and helping each student discover a personal connection to the emotionality of the dance. He accomplished the latter via a focus on each musical instrument, its emotional overtone, and the part of the body associated with it. For instance, he taught that flutes elicited a melancholic and pensive state that called on the body to be tightly controlled. Stringed instruments created an expansive feeling in the body that caused the dancer to reach upward and outward. Tambourines and cymbals engaged a dancer's complex rhythmical response, which integrated the body with the drums. The knowledge of the relationship between body and music allowed the dancer to create and improvise choreography in which the melody is expressed with the upper body, and the rhythms with the feet and lower torso. Thus engaged with the music, Ibrahim Farrah's students were noted for their dynamic and expressive performances. His students, such as Jajouka, consistently express appreciation for both "his rigorous discipline and his ability to help me discover the dancer within myself."[8]

Choreographer

In 1971, Ibrahim Farrah received a grant from the Doris Duke Foundation to, as he explained, "create a professional dance group under its jurisdiction with me as director, choreographer, and dancer; to establish a school where the indigenous dances of the Near East could be studied, and to found a library to house a collection of documentation regarding dances from the tip of North Africa to India for choreography for the Ibrahim Farrah Near East Dance Troupe" (1994a, 14). This grant would begin an intense period for Farrah that combined continued teaching and performing in New York and elsewhere with the development of his artistic vision as a choreographer and an editorial vision as publisher of *Arabesque*.

To fulfill the requirements of the Doris Duke grant, Farrah traveled to Lebanon, Syria, and Egypt in 1971 for six months and returned with renewed enthusiasm and commitment to choreography. Beyond providing the opportunity to discover new information about the context and history of dances, this trip and subsequent trips to the Middle East made him aware of the impact of globalization on the Oriental dance and the minor and major transformations of the dance's costume and movement vocabulary—for example, the wearing of a scarf around the hips. The scarf was a standard component of a professional dancer's costume, but historically it was not worn by amateur village dancers. Ibrahim attributes the transformation in the use of the scarf to images of Egyptian dancers on Lebanese television.

> This custom I knew as a child, and in my adult years when I had the opportunity to visit Lebanon, I found [the tradition of not wearing a scarf] still adhered to in my mother's village. But some modernity does seem to have permeated their lives, as I noticed on my trips to Lebanon in the late 1960s and early 70s—that on a few occasions a woman did attach a scarf to her hips while she danced. The onlookers reacted by commenting that such a display made her dance *masri* (Egyptian), as it is the practice of Egyptian women to have a scarf hugging the hips when they dance. Or they would say this is "*Beiruti*" style, somewhat pejoratively, since "city women" followed a "style" different from villagers. (1991a, 10)

During these trips Farrah had the opportunity to become acquainted with the major stars of the professional stage, including the dancer he would consider his feminine alter ego, Nadia Gamal. Gamal's performances to the classic music of the Middle East by such composers as Egyptian Mohammed Abdel Wahab combined deep emotional engagement revealed with an intricate movement vocabulary that blended seamlessly with the music. Her performances inspired Farrah and deepened his appreciation for classic Middle Eastern music. Anxious to share this vision of the dance with the U.S. community, Farrah brought Nadia Gamal to the United States to teach and wrote about her performances in

Arabesque. He quotes her on the dance: "Oriental dance is an art of subtle expression. There are delicate, shifting moods that coalesce to create feelings such as surprise, anger, shyness, fear, delight, disdain, pride and the sensuous.... a good oriental dancer must be able to depict the darker shades within man's heart as well—life and death; happiness and sorrow—all with great dignity. Oriental dance is not limited to one color, that of entertainment" (1992b, 12). Gamal's comments articulated an aspect of the dance that resonated with Farrah's experience watching his mother, sister, and other relatives dance:

> When my mother danced, I felt joy in watching her soft and graceful executions of steps, but she was not only feeling joy. It was not just the pleasure of the moment. She was also pulling feelings from a deep melancholy from her life in Lebanon; that which she left behind. My sister Janie (Heleni Tarfa), who held her body with great pride when she moved, danced, with delicacy and a beautiful smile tinged with flirtatiousness: La Coquette. My sister Peggy (Kaufah), on the other hand, the baby of the family, danced somewhat similarly to Janie, yet her gestures displayed a stronger sense of rhythm. In fact, by the age of ten, she had learned on her own how to play the drum. It seemed to me, for lack of a better metaphor, that Janie's dancing was akin to humming, while Peggy's dancing was like the art of song! Sister May (Mirianna Saudah) was the shy one. Somehow, she, like my father, refused to dance; so naturally I loved to tease her by trying to pull her out of a chair onto the dance floor. The only time I saw her do the "Happiness Dance" was at her own wedding reception. Even then it was as expected: contained, limited, rooted to one little spot, doing one tiny step, and all the while with a gentle hand movement, her eyes cast demurely upon the floor, never once glancing up to the audience: The epitome of feminine modesty. (1992b, 12)

Farrah's choreography for the Near East Dance Troupe became a means to bring the emotional variety he had witnessed in the Lebanese community to the stage. He states, "As a choreographer from the very beginning, I strived to give meaning and tell a story in my dances. Further, I sought to bring out a certain emotive content within the work and through the dancer whether for a solo performer or group choreography. The characters and the emotional qualities displayed in my works are in essence those very qualities I observed in characters I knew as a child" (1991a, 10). Jajouka, a former member of the Near East Dance Troupe, describes working with Farrah as a choreographer as "helping me to find the vocabulary for my internal emotional life and phrase it with the music."[9]

Farrah also committed himself as a choreographer to bringing to public attention an image of the complexity of the Middle East via the specificity of the dances of Lebanon, Syria, Morocco, Egypt, and elsewhere. Naming his company the Ibrahim Farrah Near East Dance Troupe was a start. Aware of the politics of the Middle East and the public view of the conflicts between Israel and Palestine, Farrah determined to separate his company from that name because, as Hicks quotes him, "it brings in an element of political conflict, and the dances of the region encompass more than these countries in conflict with one another" (Hicks, 1992, 35). Farrah preferred using the name Near East "because I think it's clearer to artistic purposes and for a comprehension of the art as it has developed through history" (35). The company's repertoire included ritual, folk, and classical dance forms from North Africa and the Near East, representing such groups as the Berbers in the ritual form *guedra*, the Lebanese and Syrians with the *dabke* folk line dance, and the Near East in general with the classical forms of the Oriental dance. Over the next decade Farrah's company was acclaimed for the quality of its performances and appeared in such venues as Lincoln Center and Carnegie Hall in New York and the Kennedy Center in Washington, D.C. In 1981, Farrah's talent was acknowledged by the dance community when he was given the Ruth St. Denis Award for choreography.

Publisher

The desire to educate the Oriental dance community about the dances of the Near East that Farrah brought to his teaching and choreography also motivated him to publish *Arabesque*, which first appeared in May 1975. In creating the journal, he joined a trend among the Arab American literary community to revise America's image of Arabs through a publication that expanded the public awareness of the breadth and diversity of Arab American heritage. With inspiration from his trips to Lebanon, his initial goal was to provide a means of educating the belly dance community in the diverse dances of the Middle East. Primarily identified as belly dancers, this community had grown, by the mid-1970s, to more than a million dancers, including those located in large cities with ethnic communities—Los Angeles, Chicago, and New York, for instance—to those in small towns such as Elmira, Oregon, which had no ethnic audience. As he phrased it in an interview with Adam Lahm: "There were books on the market, but they were more or less these 'how to' books in which I didn't want any part.... I chose a magazine format because I felt Middle Eastern dance had never been written about. Everywhere I went teachers were saying that they would be called on to lecture, go to the library for reference material, and find zilch. This lack of information was a universal problem throughout the country. I felt a magazine would offer possibilities for continual information" (Lahm, 1979, 4). Farrah was concerned that this community of dancers, with its emphasis on an Orientalist interpretation of the dance, was developing a context and aesthetic form that were separate from those of the Middle East, yet they were representing the Middle East in the popular imagination. As he suggested in an interview with Adam Lahm: "We are a society of labels. If we were to have a credible standing within the ethnic dance world, we would have to establish a more developed perspective of the total dance of the Middle East rather than just one form of it" (Lahm, 1979, 4). The popularized form of Oriental dance known as belly dance often focused more on the sensuality of the woman as opposed to a physical manifestation of community joy, and this was challenging Farrah's personal identity as a dancer/performer. He felt that the only way to counter this popular rendition of the dance was to create an alternative image.

Each issue of *Arabesque* combined information on what was happening in Middle Eastern dance in general with specific articles by those interested in dance research. Topics included the North African trance performance called the *zar*, the dances of Tunisia, Morocco, and Egypt; the social position of the *ghawazees* in Egypt; and the evolution and development of Middle Eastern dance companies such as the Reda Troupe. In addition, there were reviews of books and videos on Middle Eastern dance and dancers. Farrah wrote many of the articles and also a column titled "This and That," which focused on observations of the Middle Eastern dance scene in different parts of the United States. He also wrote specific articles on the history of the Middle Eastern dance in the United States and the Middle East, the internationalization of the dance, and accounts of his travels in the Middle East. For the dance community in the United States and for the international Middle Eastern dance community, *Arabesque* provided an opportunity to learn about the historical context of the dance and the changes that were taking place nationally and internationally. Ultimately, the magazine became the link between the Middle East and dancers around the globe until Farrah's declining health caused the demise of the publication in 1997.

In 1998 Farrah created a video that was a compilation of clips that began with Thomas Edison's film of Fatima made in 1897 and ended with a 1971 dance by Nadia Gamal. In between, there were excerpts of an early 20th-century film clip of Moroccan Berber people dancing the *guedra* and Farrah's version of the *guedra* created for his Near East Dance Troupe, as well as a long segment that featured the dances of male and female Bedouins of Lebanon. The combination of images represents Farrah's commitment to educating those involved in the belly dance community and the general public in the traditions as they are derived from the Middle East and their evolution in the United States. In an interview with Lahm, Farrah notes the multiplicity of his experiences in dance:

> I think every human being questions his commitments at some point in his life. Questioning is part of existing. I think weathering the question is a part of existing.... There are people in the dance profession who work from a scholarly perspective and that is their sole priority and commitment. There are others who work exclusively from a performing point of view, others from a choreographic one. There aren't many people who get

involved in all aspects. At times these different perspectives conflict with each other. But because I feel an inherent need and satisfaction in working in each direction of the dance, my challenge is to meet them all. (Lahm 1979, 5)

The video is an acknowledgment of the multiple influences of history, politics, family, and personal travel that helped form Farrah's approach as dancer, teacher, choreographer, and publisher.

The decision to engage all aspects of dance as publisher-writer, dancer, teacher, and choreographer allowed Farrah to intervene in, and attempt to dislocate, the dominant cultural images of Arab Americans in order to, as Homi Bhabha suggests, reinterpret and redeploy popular discourse via refocusing attention toward an "agonistic space" (2004, 181) on the borders of difference. Farrah's initial means to destabilize the stereotype was his male body in performance, a performing body that was not part of Orientalism's discursive field. He justified his performance as masculine through making public the private performance style of his male relatives both in performance and on the pages of *Arabesque*. He therefore embodied a tradition in which men articulated their hips in stately coordination with their upper torso and arms in a demonstration of sensual masculinity. Farrah countered the popular image of Middle Eastern dance as belly dance through the range of repertoire of his Near Eastern Dance Troupe. He further vindicated his performance through articles in *Arabesque* that provided an alternative history to what was presented in the popular media. All of the latter was accomplished by joining, within the realm of his sphere of influence, popular and aesthetic culture. He performed on the cabaret stages of Middle Eastern restaurants as well as the stages of major art centers such as Carnegie Hall and the Kennedy Center. As a magazine editor and publisher of *Arabesque*, he challenged the Orientalist vision of Oriental dance, while still embracing the growing global belly dance community. His life was ultimately a complex dance along the edges of alterity between self and other, with "self" defined as a Lebanese American hybrid and "other" defined via the framework of Orientalism. Within this complex dance, he was a member of the Arab American community in the later half of the 20th century, finding ways to exist in an increasingly polarized political climate. What he was *not* was a male belly dancer who identified with the growing global male belly dance movement.[10] He was instead a Lebanese American performing his artistic heritage as an Arab and American who, in the performance of this hybrid persona, challenged the Orientalist image of the Arab body.

The legacy of Ibrahim Farrah's life is the representation in his teaching, choreography, and writing of an Arab American attempting to establish a cultural space for the "happiness dance" as a creative form of aesthetic expression and in the process challenging the stereotype of the "happiness dance" that began with the imitators of the performances of the Chicago World's Faire. It is a legacy that is consistently kept alive by his students and members of the Arab American community, but constantly displaced in the popular culture by productions such as the Bellydance Superstars, an all-female company led by rock promoter Miles Copeland that currently tours in the United States and elsewhere around the globe. Despite the primacy of his standing in the general dance community, signified by honors such as the Ruth St. Denis Award for Choreography, Ibrahim Farrah was not able to eradicate the popular Orientalist representation of belly dance as primarily a sensual expression of the female body.

NOTES

1. The seminal work on Orientalism is Edward Said 's book *Orientalism* (New York: Vintage Books, 1978). Other books on the subject include Sarah Graham-Brown, *Images of Women: The Portrayal of Women in Photography of the Middle East 1860–1950* (New York: Columbia University Press, 1988); Reina Lewis, *Gendering Orientalism: Race, Femininity and Representation* (London: Routledge, 1996); Anne McClintock, *Imperial Leather: Race, Gender and Sexuality in the Colonial Context* (London: Routledge, 1995); and an article by Anthony Shay and Barbara Sellers-Young, "Belly Dance: Orientalism-Self-Exoticism," *Dance Research Journal* 34 (1): 13–37. An account of Hollywood's version of the Orient can be found in Mathew Bernstein and Gaylyn Studlar, eds., *Visions of the East: Orientalism in Film* (Piscataway, NJ: Rutgers University Press, 1997). In terms of stereotypes of Arabs, there is Jack G. Shaheen's book *Reel Bad Arabs: How Hollywood Vilifies a People* (New York: Olive Branch Press, 2001).

2. The majority of the material for this essay comes from a series of articles in *Arabesque* written by Ibrahim Farrah in the 1990s. The series of short essays were his reflections on his life, from growing up in Pennsylvania to becoming a dancer, teacher, choreographer, and publisher. To maintain his voice through this essay, I have quoted heavily from his reflections.

3. "Trouble on the Midway," *New York Times*, July 22, 1893, 1.

4. For a discussion of Islam's discomfort with the dancing body, see Anthony Shay's *Choreophobia* (Costa Mesa, CA: Mazda Press, 1999).

5. The most comprehensive discussion of Hollywood's version of the Orient can be found in Bernstein and Studlar, *Visions of the East.*

6. For more information on professional dancers in the Middle East, both male and female, see Anthony Shay's *Choreophobia* and Anthony Shay and Barbara Sellers-Young, eds., *Belly Dance: Orientalism, Transnationalism, and Harem Fantasy* (Costa Mesa, CA: Mazda Press, 2005). *Choreophobia* includes information on dance in Iran and among the large Iranian communities in California. *Belly Dance* includes articles by scholars that discuss the history of the dance in the Middle East and the United States.

7. A discussion of the feminist movement and its relationship to Middle Eastern dance is found in Shay and Sellers-Young, *Belly Dance.*

8. Personal communication, May 2000.

9. Personal communication, May 2000.

10. Male belly dancers are ever increasing in number. This includes dancers in areas of the Middle East such as Turkey and throughout the global belly dance community. This group is distinct from male dancers such as Yousry Shaif and Mahmoud Reda, who teach Oriental (*raqs sharki*) and Middle Eastern folk dances to the belly dance community but would not perform Oriental dance, belly dance, or one of its variations such as tribal belly dance.

WORKS CITED

Aswad, Barbara C., and Barbara Bilge. 1996. *Family and Gender among American Muslims.* Philadelphia: Temple University Press.

Bailey, D. A. 1988. "Re-thinking Black Representations." *Ten-8* (Winter): 36–49.

Bernstein, Mathew, and Gaylyn Studlar, eds. 1997. *Visions of the East: Orientalism in Film.* Piscataway, NJ: Rutgers University Press, 1997.

Bhabha, Homi. 2004. *Location of Culture.* New York: Routledge.

Burt, Ramsay. 1995. *The Male Dancer.* New York: Routledge.

Carlton, Donna. 1994. *Looking for Little Egypt.* Bloomington, IN: IDD Books.

Farrah, Ibrahim. 1991a. "A Dancer's Chronicle: Growing Up Lebanese." *Arabesque* 17 (4): 10–13.

———. 1991b. "A Dancer's Chronicle: The Lebanese Chapters." *Arabesque* 16 (5): 9–12.

———. 1991c. "A Dancer's Chronicle: The Lebanese Chapters." *Arabesque* 16 (6): 10–12.

———. 1991d. "A Dancer's Chronicle: The Lebanese Chapters." *Arabesque* 16 (7): 10–13.

———. 1992a. "A Dancer's Chronicle: Growing Up Lebanese." *Arabesque* 17 (5): 12–13.

———. 1992b. "A Dancer's Chronicle: Growing Up Lebanese." *Arabesque* 17 (6): 12–13.

———. 1992–93. "A Dancer's Chronicle: Growing Up in Dance, Vis a Vis the Masculine Motif, Part I." *Arabesque* 18 (1–5): 8–10.

———. 1993a. "A Dancer's Chronicle: On Developing a Primary Source." *Arabesque* 19 (4): 15–16.

———. 1993b. "A Dancer's Chronicle: The Lebanese Chapters, the Americanization of Bobby." *Arabesque* 19 (2): 14.

———. 1993c. "A Dancer's Chronicle: The Lebanese Chapters, Vis a Vis the Masculine Motif, Part II." *Arabesque* 18 (6): 15–17.

———. 1994a. "A Dancer's Chronicle: One Chapter Closes as Another Opens." *Arabesque* 19 (6): 14–15.

———. 1994b. "A Dancer's Chronicle: The Lebanese Chapters, Artistic Subsidy." *Arabesque* 19 (6): 14–15.

Fraleigh, Sondra. 2004. *Metaphysics in Motion.* Pittsburgh, PA: University of Pittsburgh Press.

Graham-Brown, Sarah. 1988. *Images of Women: The Portrayal of Women in Photography of the Middle East 1860–1950.* New York: Columbia University Press.

Hicks, Robert. 1992. "America Dances: Ibrahim Farrah." *Arabesque* 17 (5): 35.

Karayanni, Stavros Stavrou. 2004. *Dancing Fear and Desire: Race, Sexuality, and Imperial Politics in Middle Eastern Dance.* Waterloo, ON: Wilfrid Laurier University Press.

Lahm, Adam. 1979. "Ibrahim Farrah: A Commitment to Dance, a Commitment to Life." *Arabesque* 5 (2): 4–5, 21, 23.

Lewis, Reina. 1996. *Gendering Orientalism: Race, Femininity and Representation.* London: Routledge.

McClintock, Anne. 1995. *Imperial Leather: Race, Gender and Sexuality in the Colonial Context.* London: Routledge.

McGovern, John, ed. 1894. *Halligan's Illustrated World: A Portfolio of the Views of the World's Columbian Exposition.* London: Jewell N. Halligan.

Rasmussen, Anne. 1992. "An Evening in the Orient: The Middle Eastern Nightclub in America." *Asian Music* 13 (2): 345–65.

———. 1998. "The Music of Arab Americans." In *The Images of Enchantment,* ed. Sherifa Zuhur, 135–56. Cairo: American University Press.

Said, Edward. 1978. *Orientalism.* New York: Vintage Books.

Salem, Lori Anne. 1999. "Far-Off and Fascinating Things: Wadeeha Atiyeh and Images of Arabs in the American Popular Theatre, 1930–50." In *Arabs in America: Building a New Future,* ed. Michael Suleiman, 272–83. Philadelphia: Temple University Press.

Shaheen. Jack G. 2001. *Reel Bad Arabs: How Hollywood Vilifies a People.* New York: Olive Branch Press.

Shay, Anthony. 1999. *Choreophobia.* Costa Mesa, CA: Mazda Press.

———. 2005. "The Male Dancer." In *Belly Dance: Orientalism, Transnationalism, and Harem Fantasy,* ed. Anthony Shay and Barbara Sellers-Young, 85–113. Costa Mesa, CA: Mazda Press.

Shay, Anthony, and Barbara Sellers-Young. 2003. "Belly Dance: Orientalism-Self-Exoticism." *Dance Research Journal* 34 (1): 13–37.

Suleiman, Michael W. 1999. "The Arab American Experience." In *Arabs in America: Building a New Future,* ed. Michael Sulieman, 1–21. Philadelphia: Temple University Press.

SALEEM

Born and raised in Riyadh, Saudi Arabia, Saleem finished college in Dhahran, graduating in business in 1984. After earning an M.B.A. in Colorado, he has been living in Los Angeles for the past 20 years, working as both a teacher and a dancer.

I am a Middle Eastern dancer. Actually, I don't like the term "belly dance"—I prefer "Middle Eastern dance." I have been a professional dancer for the past 28 years. People ask: "How can you perform such a sensual dance?" I never studied it, I grew up with it; I watched TV. Unlike other male dancers, I don't pretend to be "a male" or wear a mask. I don't think "male" or "female." I just do the dance. It's an art, just respect the art. Some movements may seem "feminine" and others "masculine," but for me it is an expressive form of dance. I improvise by listening to the Arabic lyrics and expressing what I hear.

I never had formal dance lessons, but like most other people in the Arab world, as a child and young adult I learned my dancing by imitating what I saw on television, where they showed old Egyptian films with great dance stars like Tahia Carioca and Samia Gamal. My parents saw that I was really into it, and they let me dance around the house; they never said don't. I loved dancing so much that my mother always said jokingly that I would become a dancer. I danced at parties, which I continued to do after I came to the United States.

I actually have two professions: I teach business courses, and I dance. I had my first paying job in 1992 when the Cornerstone Theater group hired me to appear in their production that had Arab themes, in which I sang, acted, and danced. I also write plays, and in 1995 I wrote *Salam/Shalom*, which won the GLAAD award [Gay and Lesbian Alliance Against Defamation media awards]. I toured with that play for six years. In 1994, I danced at the Moun of Tunis, a restaurant on Sunset Boulevard in West Hollywood. I started it as a side gig. In 1999, I started and produced the "1001 Nights," a popular monthly evening at a local dance club in Silver Lake, and I continue to do that. It is still my expensive hobby. I don't stop, because I love the dance.

In the past three years, Leo Garcia, the artistic director of Highways, a local theater in Santa Monica that produces modern dance, asked me to produce and

Saleem carries on Middle Eastern dancing traditions: "I don't think 'male' or 'female,' I just do the dance." Photograph by Timothy Fielding. Used with permission.

direct an evening that featured all male dancers performing Oriental, solo improvised dances that are sensual and erotic from the Mediterranean region and the Middle East. I cannot tell you the problems I had gathering together a group of Middle Eastern men to perform. Some said: "I cannot perform in public." Others chose folkloric dances like the *dabka* [Levantine line dance performed as a folk dance in Iraq, Jordan, Syria, Lebanon, Palestine, and Israel]. Still others said, "I cannot perform these movements because they are feminine." Ultimately, I had to hire non-Middle Eastern dancers. I really like fusion, which I use in the concerts at Highways, because some of the dancers add in Latin American movements. I have always taken good movements and choreographic elements from Indian films and incorporated them into my dances.

But this issue of what is masculine and feminine is all ridiculous. The best belly dancers and choreographers in the Middle East are male. Dancers like Samia Gamal say that they pick up some of their best movements from the boys who work with them. It's an art. You just let your body do it. The success of the performance depends on charisma. People like and respond to a dancer who is comfortable with himself. So we sometimes encounter a gay identity issue with these guys who are afraid to show who they really are. Some are really afraid. But, I look at it like this: this show is about Middle Eastern men showing their sensuality. I don't know if I look masculine or feminine. I prefer to let the audience make that decision. All I want to do is to produce a quality show. I bring dancers who are as good as I am or better.

I like to perform at straight Arab parties the most. The Arab crowd, if they see something good, they like it. It doesn't matter if the dancer is male or female. The bottom line is: Is he good? Generally, I had luck. Most of my parties are mainstream. I perform the art I know how to perform. I don't perform an Americanized version. The most problems that I have encountered have been in Middle Eastern restaurants and nightclubs where if they hire a male dancer they would have a reputation as gay. One owner, a gay Palestinian, was afraid and canceled my shows. They won't say they don't want a male dancer, but they are afraid that their nightclub will get a reputation as a gay place. I have not been harassed or kicked out, but sometimes in a restaurant or nightclub I could feel the negative energy. I love my dance, and I choose where, when, and what I dance. I keep my job of teaching business classes because I don't want to be a slave to restaurant and nightclub owners.

I had a big fight with Miles Copeland, the producer of the big belly dance show "Bellydance Superstars and Desert Roses," which he hoped would rival Riverdance. When Jilina, one of the dancers I have performed with, made her first DVD, Copeland said, "It's a form of dance created by women for women." I said it was created by priests for God, and danced by men. It was not created by women for women.

I am self-confident. What makes me stand out is that I am neither masculine nor feminine in my dancing. I go on stage as a male Middle Eastern dancer. It is the audience's perception that determines what is "masculine" and what is "feminine."

12

From Gynemimesis to Hypermasculinity

*The Shifting Orientations of Male Performers
of South Indian Court Dance*

HARI KRISHNAN

This essay examines the central role played by colonial modernity and nationalism in the transformation of the male performer of South Indian court dance. Though it is often mistakenly represented as a form exclusively danced by women called *devadasis*, men were also involved in the cultural production of court dance in 19th-century South India not only as teachers but also as performers. The court dance repertoire itself, however, was gendered, and male performers usually employed the modality of gynemimesis in their performances.[1] In the early 20th century, when the *sadir kacheri* was reinvented as bharata natyam, gender was reimagined under colonial and upper-caste nationalist frameworks that invented the male dancer as a hypermasculine, spiritual, and patriotic icon for the emergent nation.[2]

Scholarly studies of the roles played by men in production of dance in late 19th-century and early 20th-century South India are virtually nonexistent, and the majority of essays on men in bharata natyam focus mainly on more recent, post-revival figures such as Ram Gopal (e.g., Gaston 1998). If scholars do discuss the roles of male performers in an earlier period, they usually focus on the activities of E. Krishna Iyer (1897–1968), a lawyer and dance revivalist who became infamous for his gynemimetic performances of *devadasi* repertoire in Madras city from approximately 1923 to 1929, suggesting that he was the earliest male performer of *devadasi* dance.[3]

In this essay I suggest that in late colonial South India, males were active participants in the cultural production of *devadasi* dance. They were not merely dance-masters and teachers (*nattuvanars*) for women performers but poet-composers, musicians, and even dancers in the courtly traditions of the Tamil- and Telugu-speaking regions. I suggest that the relationships between male artists and *devadasi* performers were complex and varied. My focus here is on the constitution and representation of court dance from the perspectives of

Figure 12.1   The author replicating a pose of the dancing god Shiva with his dance teacher Guru K. P. Kittappa Pillai (1913–99), a direct descendent of Ponnaiya of the Tanjavur Quartet. Photograph by Davesh Soneji.

interclass interaction, gender, and genre. Understanding the flow and exchange of repertoire and other forms of praxis across genders and classes in this period is a necessary exercise in order for us to be able to accurately analyze the same issues in 20th- and 21st-century South India.

I begin this essay with a brief overview of courtly dance called *sadir* or *sadir kacheri* in late colonial South India,[4] and then examine three instances of gynemimetic male performers of *sadir kacheri* at the Tanjavur court. These examples signal the complex histories and functions of 19th-century performers of South Indian court dance. Finally, I comment on the redefinition of masculinity in light of British colonialism and nationalism in South India. From the late 19th century onward, the dance's female *devadasi* practitioners began to disappear from public culture, and in 1948 their lifestyle was officially outlawed by independent India. They were replaced by urban middle-class performers who radically altered and resignified the *sadir kacheri*, transforming it into bharata natyam. Male performers played a significant role in this transformation, as their performances of bharata natyam came to represent the *real* gender expectations placed on men in the new nation. Although this study cannot claim to be comprehensive, I hope that it will serve as a springboard for more detailed studies on dance and masculinities in South Asia.

Gendered Spaces and the History of the *Sadir* Dance in Late Colonial South India

Before the impact of anti-*devadasi* legislation was felt in South India, hereditary female performers performed in three contexts: the temple, the court, and private functions in homes. While scholars have observed that the repertoire in each of these sites was perhaps initially distinct (Kersenboom 1987), by the end of the 19th century, the *sadir kacheri*, or concert repertoire, came to be performed in the temple, court, and home.[5]

The cultural scripting of the *sadir kacheri* and its crystallization in the 19th century is a complex process that I discuss in detail elsewhere (Krishnan 2008). By the end of the 19th century, the *sadir kacheri* repertoire throughout the Tamil- and Telugu-speaking regions of the Madras Presidency consisted of several dance genres created at the Tanjavur court, combined with popular compositions, often called "folk dances," such as those in the Tamil *kummi* genre. Scholars tell us that men were integral to these performances, usually in their capacity as *nattuvanars*, dance-masters and vocal accompanists for the *devadasi*'s *sadir kacheri*. However, my recent ethnographic work with the descendants of the Tanjavur court *nattuvanars* and documents from Tanjavur palace records seem to tell a different story when it comes to *sadir kacheri* performances in the 19th century. While the ritually consecrated female *devadasi* was the exclusive performer of the ritual dance in temples, men appear to have occasionally performed the more secular and poetic *sadir kacheri*. I turn now to three specific examples of dancing males at the Tanjavur court. Two of these males were masters—one was a *nattuvanar* and the other a composer of Telugu songs called *padams*—while the other was a performer who belonged to the Tanjavur royal family.

Three Male Dancers at the Tanjavur Court

Muvvanallur Sabhapatayya was a composer of Telugu *padams* who lived in the early part of the 19th century. Though his native home was the village of Muvvanallur in Tanjavur District, his ardent devotion to Krishna in the localized form of Rajagopalasvami enshrined in the town of Mannargudi temple earned him the nickname "Mannargudi Sabhapatayya." He was also the dance-master of a famous *devadasi* named Tiruvarur Kamalam, who lived in the early 19th century. There was once an announcement that King Serfoji II (1798–1833) would bestow special honors on the best dancer of the Tanjavur District. Sabhapatayya put on the ornaments and dress of a *devadasi* and impressed the assembled connoisseurs. All were under the impression that the dancer was a very learned and talented female. Sabhapatayya revealed his true identity, and King Serfoji II was ready to bestow upon him any honor he desired. Sabhapatayya asked to be given the image of Krishna adorning the worship hall of the

Figure 12.2   Portrait of Chinnaiya and Ponnaiya of the Tanjavur Quartet, worshipping the deity in Chidambaram, commissioned around the end of the reign of King Sivaji II. Photograph by Cylla von Tiedemann. Used with permission.

royal court and is said to have refused any financial award for his performance (Seetha 1981).

The 19th-century Tanjavur court of King Serfoji II was the site for several cultural experiments. It was here that colonial modernity interfaced with indigenous culture, and it also was here that cultural hybridities of many kinds were a part of everyday life and, indeed, were encouraged and patronized by the king himself. The Tanjavur Quartet—Chinnaiya (1802–56), Ponnaiya (1804–64), Shivanandam (1808–63), and Vadivel (1810–47)—descended from a clan of musicians who were patronized by the Tanjavur court since the seventeenth century. In the mid-19th century, the Tanjavur Quartet systematized the court dance traditions of Tanjavur, including both repertoire and the abstract dance technique. Building on preexisting court dance genres, the Tanjavur Quartet created a systematized format for the hitherto diffused and somewhat random presentation of court (or "concert") dance. The ethos of this repertoire situated itself very much within the episteme of *bhoga* (pleasure, enjoyment), with the primary agent in the lyrics of the dance compositions being the dancing woman herself. The brothers were initially patronized by King Serfoji II and later moved on to serve in the courts of Travancore and Mysore.

According to oral accounts preserved by the last living descendants of the quartet, Chinnaiya, the eldest, was known to have been an expert in *abhinaya*, or interpretive dance. He is the author of a Telugu text called *Abhinaya Lakshanamu* (The Definitive Qualities of Abhinaya). He moved from Tanjavur to Mysore when he was in his late 20s and became the court dance-master of King Krishnaraja Utaiyar III (r. 1811–68). He sometimes gave performances at the Tanjavur and Mysore courts dressed as a woman and sometimes presented his own new compositions in this manner (Sundaram 1997). He is also known to have taught men the courtly dance while in Tanjavur, and according to palace records, he had these men perform during the procession during the agricultural festival known as *matu-pongal* in the month of January (Pandither 1917, 176).[6]

The second-youngest of the Tanjavur Quartet was Shivanandam. He had two sons, Mahadevan II (1832–1904) and Sabhapati (1836–94). Mahadevan II was a great master of music and dance. He was also responsible for introducing the subtle sound of the Western clarinet into the performance of the *sadir kacheri*. He had several accomplished students. Among them was Krishnasvami Ravu Jadav, about whom not much is known (Sundaram 1997).[7] This man was trained to perform the *sadir kacheri* repertoire by Mahadevan II and was a close relative of the ruling house of the Maratha dynasty. He is known to have performed in public at the court on many occasions even after the court was officially annexed to the British in 1856.[8]

These examples of male performers challenge the claim that *devadasis* were the sole performers of *sadir kacheri* in 19th-century South India. They also help us understand that, clearly, the male performer of *sadir kacheri*, in direct opposition to the contemporary male bharata natyam dancer, was not concerned with performing some kind of a personal code of gender but rather utilized and deployed a culturally constructed and aesthetically predetermined set of signals. The very erotic nature of the *sadir kacheri* repertoire, comprising genres such as the Telugu *padam* and *javali*,[9] necessitated that the performer be able to present, in a nonlinear, sometimes nonnarrative context, the intricacies of human erotic experience. The 19th-century *sadir kacheri* was thus not about "enacting roles" as much as it was about a corporeally based poetic or textual interpretation that moved away from the realm of drama. It was not about *real* men and women but rather about reproducing idealized and culturally desired *types*. The gynemimetic performances of *sadir kacheri* given by persons like Sabhapatayya in the 19th century served to reify social and artistic perceptions of the *devadasi*, representing and reconfirming epistemological structures found in culture at large. Female impersonation in South Asia is often seen as what Kathryn Hansen calls a "theatrical compulsion resulting from the social taboo of women performing" (1999, 130). The "taboo" on women's public performances is imbricated in larger discourses surrounding the relegation of upper-class women to the private sphere, and the concurrent creation of the image of the "public woman," whose very identity was fixed in and represented through song and dance.

This approach to understanding female impersonation in South India, though recognizing some of the larger issues around Brahmanic patriarchy and women's representation, illustrates *one* aspect of what was going on at the Tanjavur court. As Hansen notes in a recent essay, men who perform female impersonation in South Asia are often too quickly dismissed as "surrogates for missing women," given the social taboo on upper-class women participating in the public domain. But in our context, a vital tradition of women performers had existed long before the advent of the Tanjavur court's male performers. Why, then, the need for men to perform the same repertoire? As Hansen explains, gynemimetic performers "were desired in their own right, as men who embodied the feminine" (2002, 164). Hansen goes on to note: "In the South Asian context, where women of status had long been secluded within private domestic spaces, masquerades of gender were productive new ways of imagining and viewing the female form. Through the transvestite performer, the external look of the 'woman' was regulated by minute attention to details of... feminine accoutrements" (169). These male performers of *devadasi* dance clearly had a place in the courtly aesthetics of colonial South India. They were part of a larger elite performance ecology in which gynemimesis was a key mode of performance. In the context of Tanjavur, we know, for example, that the court also supported religious theatrical performances by upper-caste men called Bhagavata Mela Nataka,[10] in which all the female roles would be enacted by men. However, it is important to note that these performance modes do not seem to have unsettled the heteronormativity that characterized elite society at large. There are virtually no traces of the sexuality of these performers in the archive, and it seems that figures like Krishnaswami Ravu Jadav were married, and lived with their children and extended families on the Tanjavur palace grounds. In other words, the aesthetic value of gynemimesis did not, in this case, radically alter the sexual politics or economies of the colonial royal court.

I believe, as Hansen pointed out, that these types of representations were more concerned with "imagining and viewing the female form." The reification of ideal feminine codes and their enactment in public and semipublic spaces such as those furnished for courtesan dance were a major focus for the last rulers of the Tanjavur court. Courtly records from the reign of Serfoji II mention a rigorous code of dress for female dancers, and punishments for violations of these codes.[11] The male performer's role was not so much to *substitute* for the female performer but rather to index, through a kind of mimesis, appropriate dress, conduct, and propriety for real women, as articulated and enforced by men.

The Reinvention of Gender Roles in Modern India: Gender and Male Performers of Bharata Natyam in the New Nation-Space

The emergence of the public sphere in colonial India enjoined the self-conscious reinvention of boundaries around religion, caste, and gender. The process was characterized by a complex interface of the ideologies of class struggle, anticolonial resistance, and social reform. The fixing of identities, categories, and roles related to gender and sexuality during this period was predicated on Brahmanic and colonial perceptions of propriety and obscenity (Chatterjee 1993, 116–59; Gupta 2001). In the emergent nation, sexual propriety was modeled after Victorian norms that resonated deeply with Brahmanic patriarchy "rediscovered" in the public sphere through the circulation of Orientalist publications of classical Sanskrit legal texts.[12] The emergence of the new nationalized form of dance called bharata natyam in the 1930s reflected not only a concern for sexual and aesthetic propriety on the part of its upper-class women performers (Srinivasan 1983, 1984, 1985, 1988; Meduri 1996; Natarajan 1997; Weidman 2006, 111–49) but also a parallel concern for the nurturing of a new masculine identity for its male performers. This new masculinity, a reaction to colonial constructions of South Asian men as "effeminate" (Sinha 1995), was also affected by Gandhian nationalism that was rooted in the ideas of self-control, discipline, and sexual abstinence (Katrak 1992; Alter 1994). This new, state-endorsed invention of the male performer of dance could not accommodate the slippery representations of gynemimetic performance.

The new dance and its complex modernity have been commented upon by several scholars (Meduri 1996; Allen 1997; O'Shea 2007), but what is important to note here is that in addition to resignification and reconstitution of the dance and its social order, the transformation of the *devadasi* dance into bharata natyam also involved a restructuring of gender roles and expectations. Indeed, the emphasis on devotional, narrative, and nonerotic repertoire that characterized the popularization of the art form called bharata natyam may well have been designed to allow space for the male performer. The new male performers of the 1930s such as Ram Gopal (1912–2003) became famous for their dances describing the hypermasculine icon of the god Shiva Nataraja ("King of Dance"), whom they literally "represented" onstage (Allen 1997). As Anne-Marie Gaston (1991), Matthew Allen (1997), and Padma Kaimal (1999) have pointed out, the popularization of this image of the "Dancing Shiva" was the direct result of turn-of-the-century Orientalist writings on Indian art, and the linkage of the icon to the repertoire and presentation of bharata natyam dance clearly reflected the Indian middle-class's nationalistic pride in its "great civilizational past."

In 1936, when Rukmini Devi Arundale founded the institution known today as Kalakshetra,[13] she not only selectively borrowed elements from the *sadir kacheri* performance culture and Russian ballet but also created specific aesthetic niches for her male students. By creating the famous "Kalakshetra dance-dramas, she borrowed the linear narrative form common to male-oriented performance traditions such as kathakali from Kerala, which was also taught at Kalakshetra. The *sadir kacheri* thus became resignified as "storytelling," and men took on male roles in these stories. The training of these newly invented Kalakshetra male dancers thus inevitably fell back on the histrionics of kathakali, which involved bold, strong, almost athletic movements of the face, torso,

Figure 12.3   Arun Mathai
performing *Tillana in
Behag Raga*, from
traditional bharata natyam
repertory, choreographed
by Shanta and V. P.
Dhananjayan. Photograph
by Bobby Ysias.

arms, and lower limbs. Male performers in the Kalakshetra dance-dramas thus
presented an amalgam of the newly invented bharata natyam and kathakali,
especially in terms of the interpretive aspects of the choreography or *abhinaya*.
From the period between 1940 and 1955, this new hybrid dance technique came
to be seen as the normative movement vocabulary for the male performer of
bharata natyam.

Whereas the 19th-century male performer of *sadir kacheri* reproduced an
ideal type, the contemporary performer of bharata natyam must negotiate the
tension between the performance of the new Indian masculinity, on the one
hand, and the problematic, Orientalist history of the form that circulates in the
public sphere, which represents bharata natyam as the "2,000-year-old temple
dance of the handmaids of the Hindu Gods," on the other.

Reflections

In this essay I have attempted to highlight the historical and aesthetic disjunc-
tures between the 19th-century performer of *sadir kacheri* and the contemporary male performer of bharata natyam. The larger shifts and historical ruptures

that characterize the invention of bharata natyam can be read through the reimaging of the role, nature, and aesthetic function of the male performer—repertoire is altered, movement is transformed, and social and sexual roles are embodied or represented by the dancing body. In a recent essay on South Asian masculinities, Sanjay Srivastava has argued that scholarly discussion on this subject is fundamentally rooted in the search for "core" values that explain present-day South Asian men's behaviors. Asserting that we need to move beyond the restrictive frameworks provided by postcolonial historians to understand the complexities of the present, he advocates examinations of other traditions that "are too frequently regarded as aberrations and not representative of an underlying 'truth'" about South Asian masculinities (Srivastava 2004, 15–16). Analyses of the gynemimetic Tanjavur court performer and the irony of the contemporary male bharata natyam dancer move us in this direction and open up the possibilities of discussing gender in South India in new and everexpansive ways that help us understand its multiple cultural constructions and manifestations.

NOTES

Research for this project was supported by the Department of Dance, Wesleyan University. I wish to acknowledge the help provided to me by Davesh Soneji (McGill University), whose insight has played no small part in shaping this essay. I am particularly indebted to B. M. Sundaram, whose pioneering work on dating and genealogies of 19th-century personalities has greatly aided my own work. I also wish to thank my teachers, K. P. Kittappa Pillai and R. Muttukkannammal (*devadasi* of the Murugan temple at Viralimalai), for their invaluable comments on dance history in early 20th-century South India.

1. In this essay, I have chosen to refer to the tradition of female impersonation as "gynemimesis." Though the term is generally glossed as "the imitation of women" in a very wide sense, I use it because of its links to the idea of action or performance, represented, in our context, by *abhinaya* (which I translate as "mimesis"). Technically, the word *abhinaya* consists of the prefix *abhi* (toward) added to the verbal root *ni* (to lead, guide, or carry) and thus signifies action that carries meaning toward the audience. In South Indian performance contexts, gynemimesis is referred to as *stri-vesham* (or *pomblai-vesham* in Tamil), meaning "the [assumed] appearance of a woman." Often *stri-vesham* is misrepresented as referring only to the outer appearance (dress, ornamentation, makeup) of men who perform female roles onstage. The word *vesham* comes from the verbal root *vish* (to be active, to act, do, perform). I choose to posit it as a form of total (but temporary) gender mimesis, which includes a transformation of the inner, emotional landscape as well as outer appearance. The courtly dance styles of South India revolve around the representation of idealized female types (called *nayikas*), and hence premodern male dancers of the form employed the modality of *stri-vesham* in their performances. Following the work of Davesh Soneji (2004a) on similar traditions in Andhra Pradesh, my use of the term "gynemimesis" echoes William Beeman's definition

of mimesis in the female impersonation traditions of Iranian *ru-hozi* theater: "Mimetic representation depicts women through imitation of overt gender markings with great skill, intending that the audience cannot easily determine whether the actor is a woman or not" (Beeman 1992, 18, cited in Soneji 2004b, 176).

2. Though in this essay I use the terms *sadir kacheri* and bharata natyam to mark the difference between *devadasi* performance practices and modern, national, classical reworking of these practices, I wish to point out that the term bharata natyam was not an *invention* of the so-called dance revival. Within the *devadasi* communities, dance was referred to by a range of names, including *sadir kacheri* and bharata natyam. Colonial sources dating back to 1804 refer to *devadasi* dance as bharata natyam. So in the 1930s, elite patrons and reformers did not *invent* the name but rather *chose* to intentionally foreground it from a pool of possible names that were already being used to signify the dance. Details on this issue and the early colonial sources can be found in Soneji (forthcoming).

3. E. Krishna Iyer came to the study of dance because of his involvement in amateur theater performances with a group called Suguna Vilas Sabha in Madras. He trained with Madhurantakam Jagadambal (1873–1943) a famous *devadasi* who lived in Madras until 1929 and was a disciple of the dance-master Vazhuvur Samu Nattuvanar (1844–1903). Later, Krishna Iyer trained with a Brahmin dance-master named A. P. Natesa Iyer, who practiced a form of dance-theater called Bhagavata Mela Nataka from the village of Melattur. Natesa Iyer also taught *abhinaya* to several *devadasis* in Madras.

4. The word *sadir* likely comes from the Telugu *chaduru*, which means "court, *sabha* (assembly), or throne" (Arudra 1987, 30). This is corroborated by my *devadasi* informants from the village of Ballipadu in coastal Andhra Pradesh, who occasionally refer to their performances as *chaduru*. The addition of the word *kacheri* comes from the Urdu *kachahri* (office for the transaction of any public business), also meaning "assembly" (Madras University Tamil Lexicon, vol. 2, pt. 1, 638).

5. This is clearly illustrated in the Viralimalai *devadasi* tradition. Here, the *devadasis* served in the temple to the God Murukan but were also patronized by the local *zamindars* ("little kings," or landowners) of Pudukkottai. For the past three generations, *sadir kacheri* has been performed by these women at the Murukan temple, the Pudukkottai palace, and private homes. This information was provided by my teacher R. Muttuk-kannammal, the last *devadasi* of Viralimalai, in an interview on December 20, 2004. Details of this repertoire are contained in Soneji (forthcoming).

6. Chinnaiya's training of male dancers finds mention in Abraham Pandither's famous work on music, *Karunamirtha Sagaram* (1917), in which he notes that Chinnaiya lived during the time of Sivaji II and claims that "the Maharajah [Sivaji II] introduced male dancing (especially in procession with the cows) for the first time and encouraged it." The reference to the cows points to *matu-pongal*, the annual agricultural festival in which cows are ritually processed around towns and villages.

7. Mention of Krishnasvami Ravu Jadav's training under Mahadevan II is made in the published work of B. M. Sundaram (1997). The name of a "Krishnasawmi Saheb Jado" also appears in a published document from 1879 that marks the celebrations of Queen Victoria's 60th birthday at the Tanjavur palace on May 24, 1879. This document, called *The Tanjore Palace Crown of India Remembrancer*, was published in Madras. Here, "Krishnaswami Saheb Jado" is listed as the president of the Tanjore Royal Music Society,

the Tanjore Royal Opera Society, and the Tanjore Palace Badminton Club. He also gives a speech in English and Marathi in honor of Queen Victoria. It is safe to assume that this is the same Krishnasvami Ravu Jadav who was trained in dance by Mahadevan II. I am grateful to Davesh Soneji for providing me with this reference.

8. Information (including the names of court performers) on the Tanjavur court up to the British annexation and the death of King Shivaji II in 1856 is found in the court records in Modi script, a body of which have been edited and published through the Tamil University, Tanjavur (Venkataramaiya and Vivekanandagopal 1984; Venkataramaiya 1985).

9. For a detailed analysis of the *padam* as a literary and performance genre, see Allen 1992; Ramanujan, Rao, and Shulman 1994; on the *javali*, see Soneji 2004b.

10. The Bhagavata Mela Nataka is a ritual theater piece performed by Brahmins in the Tanjavur region. It is an all-male enactment of religious narratives in the form of nightlong dramas that are punctuated by short phrases of dance. Tanjavur court records mention that in the 19th century, *devadasi* court performers and the Bhagavata Mela performers often shared technique, theory, and even costumes. Interestingly, though Bhagavata Mela shared all the classical characteristics of *devadasi* dance, it could not be accommodated as a classical art form by the state, perhaps because of its focus on gynemimetic representation. Today, it is a relatively marginalized form that is performed annually in only three villages. For details on Bhagavata Mela, see Arudra 1986; Jones 1963.

11. A major record from 1820 that describes a series of these restrictions in dress has been translated by Shelvankar (1933, 15 [bundle 3]). It provides minute details about how court dancers should dress from head to toe. Another record from 1828 describes how an exception to these restrictions was made for Sundari, the favorite concubine of King Serfoji.

12. For details on the restructuring of gender and gender roles in the nationalist movement, see Chatterjee 1993; Gupta 2001; Sarkar 2001; and Sinha 1995. Analyses of the impact of such reworkings on performance culture in South India are to be found in Meduri 1996; Natarajan 1997; and Weidman 2006.

13. For more details on Rukmini Arundale and various aspects of Kalakshetra, see the recent collection of celebratory and critical essays entitled *Rukmini Devi Arundale (1904–1986): A Visionary Architect of Indian Culture and the Performing Arts*, ed. Avanthi Meduri (2005).

WORKS CITED

Allen, Matthew Harp. 1992. "The Tamil Padam: A Dance Music Genre of South India." Ph.D. diss., Wesleyan University.

———. 1997. "Rewriting the Script for South Indian Dance." *Drama Review* 41 (3): 63–100.

Alter, Joseph. 1994. "Celibacy, Sexuality and the Transformation of Gender into Nationalism in North India." *Journal of Asian Studies* 53 (1): 45–66.

Aruda. 1986. "Bhagavata Mela: The Telugu Heritage of Tamil Nadu." *Sruti* 22: 18–28.

———. 1987. "The Renaming of an Old Dance: A Whodunit Tale of Mystery." *Sruti* 27/28, 30–31.

Beeman, William O. 1992. "Mimesis and Travesty in Iranian Traditional Theatre." In *Gender in Performance: The Presentation of Difference in the Performing Arts*, ed. Laurence Senelick, 14–25. Hanover, NH: University Press of New England.

Chatterjee, Partha. 1993. *The Nation and Its Fragments: Colonial and Postcolonial Histories*. Princeton, NJ: Princeton University Press.

Gaston, Anne-Marie. 1991. "Dance and the Hindu Woman: Bharata Natyam Re-ritualized." In *Roles and Rituals for Hindu Women*, ed. Julia Leslie, 149–71. Rutherford, NJ: Fairleigh Dickinson University Press.

———. 1998. "Men in Bharata Natyam." In *Interfacing Nations on the 50th Anniversary of India's Independence*, ed. R Chowdhari-Trembley et al., 74–85. Delhi: B. R. Publications.

Gupta, Charu. 2001. *Sexuality, Obscenity, Community: Women, Muslims, and the Hindu Public in Colonial India*. New Delhi: Permanent Black.

Hansen, Kathryn. 1999. "Making Women Visible: Race and Gender Cross-Dressing in the Parsi Theatre." *Theatre Journal* 51 (2): 127–47.

———. 2002. "A Different Desire, a Different Femininity: Theatrical Transvestism in the Parsi, Gujarati, and Marathi Theatres, 1850–1940." In *Queering India: Same-Sex Love and Eroticism in Indian Culture and Society*, ed. Ruth Vanita, 163–80. New York: Routledge.

Jones, Clifford. 1963. "Bhagavata Mela Natakam: A Traditional Dance-Drama Form." *Journal of Asian Studies* 22 (2): 193–200.

Kaimal, Padma. 1999. "Shiva Nataraja: Shifting Meanings of an Icon." *Art Bulletin* 81: 390–419.

Katrak, Ketu H. 1992. "Indian Nationalism, Gandhian 'Satyagraha,' and Representations of Female Sexuality." In *Nationalisms and Sexualities*, ed. Andrew Parker et al., 395–406. New York: Routledge.

Kersenboom, Saskia. 1987. *Nityasumangali: Devadasi Tradition in South India*. Delhi: Motilal Banarsidass.

Khokar, Mohan. 1976. "Male Dancers." *Illustrated Weekly of India*, March 7, 24–29.

Krishnan, Hari. 2008. "Inscribing Practice: Reconfigurations and Textualizations of Devadasi Repertoire in Nineteenth and Early Twentieth Century South India." In *Performing Pasts: Reinventing the Arts in South India*, ed. Indira Viswanathan Peterson and Davesh Soneji, 71–89. Delhi: Oxford University Press.

Meduri, Avanthi. 1996. "Nation, Woman, Representation: The Sutured History of the Devadasi and Her Dance." Ph.D. diss., New York University.

———, ed. 2005. *Rukmini Devi Arundale (1904–1986): A Visionary Architect of Indian Culture and the Performing Arts*. Delhi: Motilal Banarsidass.

Natarajan, Srividya. 1997. "Another Stage in the Life of the Nation: Sadir, Bharata Natyam, Feminist Theory." Ph.D. diss., University of Hyderabad.

O'Shea, Janet. 2007. *At Home in the World: Bharata Natyam on the Global Stage*. Middletown, CT: Wesleyan University Press.

Pandither, M. Abraham. 1917. *Karunamirtha Sagaram: On Srutis*. Reprint, Delhi: Asian Educational Services, 1984.

Ramanujan, A. K., Velcheru Narayana Rao, and David Shulman. 1994. *When God Is a Customer: Telugu Courtesan Songs by Ksetrayya and Others*. Berkeley: University of California Press.

Sarkar, Tanika. 2001. *Hindu Wife, Hindu Nation: Community, Religion and Cultural Nationalism*. Delhi: Permanent Black.

Seetha, S. 1981. *Tanjore as a Seat of Music (During the 17th, 18th and 19th Centuries)*. Madras: University of Madras.

Shelvankar, R. S. 1933. *A Report on the Modi Manuscripts in the Saraswati Mahal Library, Tanjore*. Madras: University of Madras.

Sinha, Mrinalini. 1995. *Colonial Masculinity: The "Manly Englishman" and the "Effeminate Bengali" in the Late Nineteenth Century*. Manchester: Manchester University Press.

Soneji, Davesh. 2004a. "Living History, Performing Memory: Devadasi Women in Telugu-Speaking South India." *Dance Research Journal* 36 (2): 30–49.

———. 2004b. "Performing Satyabhama: Text, Context, Memory and Mimesis in Telugu-Speaking South India." Ph.D. diss., McGill University.

———. Forthcoming. "Recalling a Gesture: Devadasis, Modernity and Memory in South India." Unpublished manuscript.

Srinivasan, Amrit. 1983. "The Hindu Temple Dancer: Prostitute or Nun?" *Cambridge Anthropology* 11: 73–99.

———. 1984. "Temple 'Prostitution' and Community Reform: An Examination of the Ethnographic, Historical and Textual Context of the Devadasi of Tamil Nadu, South India." Ph.D. diss., Cambridge University.

———. 1985. "Reform and Revival: The Devadasi and Her Dance." *Economic and Political Weekly* 20 (44): 1869–76.

———. 1988. "Reform or Continuity? Temple 'Prostitution' and the Community in the Madras Presidency." In *Structures of Patriarchy: State, Community and Household in Modernising Asia*, ed. Bina Agarwal, 71–89. Delhi: Kali for Women.

Srinivasan, Priya. 2003. "Performing Indian Dance in America: Interrogating Modernity, Tradition, and the Myth of Cultural Purity." Ph.D. diss., Northwestern University.

Srivastava, Sanjay. 2004. "Introduction: Semen, History, Desire and Theory." In *Sexual Sites, Seminal Attitudes: Sexualities, Masculinities and Culture in South Asia*, ed. Sanjay Srivastava, 1–20. New Delhi: Sage.

Subramanian, Lakshmi. 2006. *From the Tanjore Court to the Madras Music Academy: A Social History of Music in South India*. Delhi: Oxford University Press.

Sundaram, B. M. 1997. "Towards a Genealogy of Some Tanjavur Natyacharyas and Their Kinsfolk." *Sangeet Natak* 124: 30–41.

———. 2003. *Marapu Tanta Manikkankal* [in Tamil]. Chennai: Dr. V. Raghavan Centre for Performing Arts.

Tamil Lexicon. 1924–36. Reprinted 1982. Madras: University of Madras.

The Tanjore Palace Crown of India Remembrancer. 1879. Madras: C. Foster.

Venkataramaiya, K. M. 1985. *Tancai Marattiya Mannarkal Araciyalum Camutaya Varalkkaiyum: Administration and Social Life under the Maratha Rules of Thanjavur* [in Tamil and English]. Thanjavur: Tamil University.

Venkataramaiya, K. M., and Vivekanandagopal. 1984. *Tancai Marattiya Mannar Moti Avant Tamilakkamum Kurippuraiyum* [in Tamil]. Thanjavur: Tamil University.

Weidman, Amanda. 2006. *Singing the Classical, Voicing the Modern: The Postcolonial Politics of Music in South India*. Durham, NC: Duke University Press.

Whitehead, Judith. 1995. "Bodies Clean and Unclean: Prostitution, Sanitary Legislation, and Respectable Femininity in Colonial North India." *Gender and History* 7 (1): 41–63.

————. 1998. "Community Honor/Sexual Boundaries: A Discursive Analysis of Devadasi Criminalization in Madras, India, 1920–1947." In *Prostitution: On Whores, Hustlers, and Johns*, ed. James E. Elias et al., 91–106. New York: Prometheus Books.

————. 2001. "Measuring Women's Value: Continuity and Change in the Regulation of Prostitution in Madras Presidency, 1860–1947." In *Of Property and Propriety: The Role of Gender and Class in Imperialism and Nationalism*, ed. Himani Bannerji, Shahrzad Mojab, and Judith Whitehead, 26–42. Toronto: University of Toronto Press.

NAATYAACHAARYA V. P. DHANANJAYAN

Dhananjayan is considered a living legend in the best tradition of the esteemed dance and music conservatory Kalakshetra, founded by Rukmini Devi in Chennai. After 20 years at Kalakshetra as student, performer, and teacher, he branched off to establish Bharatakalanjali in Chennai with his stage and life partner, Shanta Dhananjayan. He has performed around the globe and choreographed and collaborated with nationally and internationally acclaimed dancers and musicians. He has won several prestigious national and international awards and participated in major dance festivals in India, Europe, the former Soviet Union, Australia, and the United States. The author of two major books on dance, he has also contributed articles to leading magazines and newspapers in India.

I am a bharata natyam dancer, performer, choreographer, and teacher. Bharata natyam is a theatrical art linked to ancient traditions in the south of India. The dance's name comes from the original name of the country, *Bharata* (the name India was given by the invaders), and *natya*, meaning "total theater art." Probably this is the only country in the world whose name is synonymous with a performing art, which is fitting, in that it is an integral part of our civilization, culture, customs, and lifestyle. The stylized and sophisticated hand gestures, combined with facial expression and body language, can communicate anything and everything. Based on the ancient text called the *Natya Shastra*, bharata natyam is meant to educate, elevate, and entertain. According to ancient tradition and practice, it was an art form mainly for male performers, but at one point in history it became associated with women. I was initiated into this *natya* in 1953 at the age of 14. Since then, I have been a practitioner of bharata natyam. I also had solid training in another male-oriented dance tradition called kathakali, which complemented my total perspective of the art form. Now I have spent nearly 60 years devoted to the theater. Luckily my wife, Shanta, is also my stage partner; we complement each other and are popularly known as the "made for each other couple."

My entry into the dancing world was sheer providence. Born in a remote village in Kerala as one of eight children of a poor schoolteacher, I was selected for the

Dhananjayan is still an active choreographer, performer, and teacher in a form often associated in the popular imagination with female dancers only. Photograph by C. P. Satyajit.

Kalakshetra school at a time when they were reviving the old tradition of boys and men playing male characters. Not aware of the rigor and struggle involved in becoming a "dancing man," I was plunged into the physical, mental, and spiritual training, feeling as if I were pushed into the deep waters of a fathomless ocean of *natya* tradition. I think that destiny had a hand in kindling the dormant artistic inclination in me, thus finally turning out a male dancer from the portals of Kalakshetra. At that time, bharata natyam was considered an art appropriate for only women, and society looked down on male dancers as effeminate and unacceptable humans. Sending me to Kalakshetra was an unusual choice for my father; it was much against the wishes of conservative kith and kin of the village, but he did it out of necessity, to reduce the burden of bringing up eight children. Initially the attitudes of my friends, relatives, and community at large were negative, but as I gained popularity and recognition nationally and internationally, that attitude changed to admiration. Those who kept a distance from me now claim proximity. Now I enjoy the respect from all classes of people and am often acclaimed as a role model for a male dancer.

Historically, starting from era of the British rule in India (Bharat), there has been a misconception among the populace throughout India that dancing is not a "real" profession. For a man, as the breadwinner of the family, a career in dancing was thought not to provide enough money to raise a family. Also, the reputation of traditional female practitioners of bharata natyam (known as *devadasi*, or servants of the Gods) had fallen into disrepute in many places, so the profession was stigmatized. It got to the point where even girls were not encouraged to practice the art, let alone the boys. When the stigma was slowly getting washed away with the Indian freedom movement during the first half of the 20th century, forward-looking educated women encouraged their daughters to learn the art as mere pastime, although boys were still being discouraged at that point. But sometimes boys with a slightly effeminate nature who were considered good for nothing else were allowed to enter the domain of the girls. Some of those boys displayed amazing talent, agility, and charm as dancers, and their public performances suggested that boys learning to dance would emulate the feminine grace and charm. This further dissuaded parents from encouraging talented boys. This kind of prejudice was directed only toward males in the bharata natyam tradition (which was then also known as *sadir* or *dasi attam*), whereas men were accepted in the kathakali and kathak traditions.

Traditionally, all our performing art forms were male-oriented, and all the scriptural evidences are in favor of this theory, culminating in the masculine icon called "Dancing Nataraja," the symbol of Indian art and culture. The prejudices against men dancing must have developed during the foreign invasion and the long spell of Mughal rule, when any sort of public performance attached to Hindu temples was discouraged. British rulers also discouraged performing arts, often misunderstanding the traditions and influencing Indian social reformers. The feudal society that patronized these male-oriented art forms also started losing its wealth, succumbing to British pressure to cut their spending on the arts. This resulted in men leaving the art form and finding other professions. Naturally, after a few generations, the attitude toward men taking up dancing as a career turned to prejudice.

We have now come a long way, and the prejudice against a man dancing like a man is slowly vanishing. Now there is a surfeit of young boys and men in the film industry talented enough to compete with the best of the female dancers. In the classical field, the trend toward more male dancers is quite encouraging, and my entry as a professional bharata natyam dancer has been a phenomenal encouragement for many to take up classical dance as a career. There are also several couples like my wife and me who are emerging on the path to stardom.

To be successful as a bharata natyam dancer (*nartaka* is the right term to denote a man dancer), I had to change the traditional female-oriented repertoire.

I had to introduce new choreographic structures to suit a man's body line and find themes suitable for both genders. I introduced more kinds of storytelling lyrics, rather than the usual maiden's love laments. Despite the initial resentment from conservative quarters, the discerning public has accepted my innovative modifications to the training system. The criticism soon died down, and all my ventures have withstood the test of time, creating a new path for the next generations to stride on.

In contrast to the Indian attitude (which over the years has changed), I am under the impression that North America always considered it "masculine" to dance, having interacted with several ballet artists of high caliber there. When I collaborated with the Ohio Ballet Company to produce *Jungle Book* as a theatrical production (combining Bharatanatyam and ballet technique), the men dancers to me appeared totally masculine in their attitude and behavior. At times, American conservatives think that male dancers are, or become, homosexuals. In India (Bharat), as far as I know, there have been no such allegations leveled at male dancers. There have been occasional cases of gender transformation (male to female), and such dancers then keep to the feminine identity in this style of dance.

The repertoire in traditional bharata natyam demands the ability to interpret sentiments of both men and women by a single person, whether male or female. Technically this type of presentation is called *eaka-aahaarya-laasya angam*—enacting or interpreting different characters while wearing a neutral costume. This technique is very unique to Indian classical dances, especially bharata natyam and kathakali. In ancient times, it was the men that used to dress and make up like women and represent different characters in a dance drama, while a woman never played the role of a man. But women have played men when accomplished male dancers were not available. It was Rukmini Devi, the founder of Kalakshetra, who revived the old tradition where men only play male roles, which encouraged boys to take up dancing and dance like men only.

To be a successful male bharata natyam artist is an extraordinarily difficult task, especially when the uninitiated, lay audience looks for glamour, colorful costumes, and jewelry and is not attracted to a simply attired male body. Earlier, if audiences did not understand or enjoy the great technicality of the classical dance, they could at least enjoy the beauty and charm of the feminine form. Therefore, the man has to compensate for the glamour with extraordinary skill as a communicative performer. There are only very few such male dancers in the bharata natyam field who have made it to the top. Those who cannot make it to the top performer level dedicate themselves to teaching and choreography, and they are able to make a good living. In India (Bharat) we find that a majority of dance teachers are men. Performing opportunities for solo male dancers are fewer than for their female counterparts. Couple dancers also have an advantage, so men who have a dancing partner are lucky in that respect. The concept of couple dancers is symbolized in the Shiva-Parvathi icons, and the legends attributed to this divine dancing couple are immortal examples to emulate. They are the inspiration for men to dance, dance, and dance.

ARUN MATHAI

Mathai grew up in California taking Indian classical dance. He now combines a career in finance with performances of traditional bharata natyam, as well as dancing and acting as assistant choreographer for blue13 dance company. The Los Angeles–based blue13 combines classical and contemporary influences and aspires to "dispel cultural stereotypes and connect diverse communities through cross-genre and multicultural classes, workshops, and live performances that inspire global unity."

I was born in 1983 in San Jose, California. My family is from Kerala, a state on the southwest coast of India, which is famous for the classical Indian dances *kathakali* and *mohini attam*. Bharata natyam, which I study and perform, did not originate in that state. It is associated with the city of Chennai (Madras), the center in South India from which it grew. Bharata natyam now has a national symbolic meaning for many Indians that reaches well beyond Chennai.

When I was very young, I would go with my mother to watch my sister, nine years my senior, attend bharata natyam classes. My parents tell me that when we returned home, I would mimic the steps I saw her guru teach my sister. While it was common for little girls to take bharata natyam classes, which were sometimes forced on them, it was not an activity common among boys. However, when my parents saw that I was interested, they were very supportive.

I began serious study of bharata natyam when I was seven at Kala Vandana Dance Center, based in San Jose. My guru is Smt. Sundara Swaminathan. When I first started studying, there was only one other boy in my dance class. He left, but soon after another one joined. And then another. And then another. At one point there were five males dancing at my school; that's a lot for a bharata natyam school in the U.S.!

I studied with Sundara Aunty (as we called her) for 10 years until I performed my *arangetram*. This is most easily described as a graduation solo dance recital. This recital takes place when the guru decides that the student has acquired all of the basic techniques of the form. As a male, performing my *arangetram* was a big deal at my school because there were, and still are, so few males who study and perform in the U.S.

Mathai with Achinta S. McDaniel (artistic director of blue13 dance company) in a "Bollywood-Tech"–style number that combines classical Indian dance and contemporary influences. Photograph by Ryuichi Oshimoto. Used with permission.

Under Sundara Aunty's tutelage I learned the Kalakshetra style of bharata natyam. This school of teaching and performing was founded by Rukmini Devi Arundale and is known for its clean lines and emphasis on technique. In the Kalakshetra tradition there are a number of differences between the way men and women perform. One example is the very first position a bharata natyam student learns. A male dancer places his hands palm down on his waist, with his fingers in an L shape. However, a female dancer places the top of her hands on her waist, with all fingers together and pointing backward. While this is a very elementary example of differences between male and female dancers, it sets the tone for differences that show up throughout the form.

The male costume, although very colorful, never made anyone comment about my masculinity. This may be because males often dance shirtless or with just a sash draped across their chest. The makeup was another thing entirely! Growing up, nearly everyone commented on the makeup I wore, and how feminine it appeared. I can't say I blame them—to see me out of context, I'm sure I looked like a drag queen in training. Bharata natyam makeup is applied heavily, with an emphasis on thickly lined eyes, blushed cheeks, and very red lips. While the teasing may have bothered me at first, eventually I just got over it.

Some people from the Malayalee community I grew up with in San Jose (people of the state of Kerala who speak the Malayalam language) thought bharata natyam was a feminine dance form, and occasionally I would get teased for taking up a "girl's dance." While the teasing most often came from kids, I'm certain some adults made comments among themselves as well. However, in the larger Indian community those who knew about and valued bharata natyam were very supportive of my participation. And while it never became a specific mission of mine, I did take satisfaction in showing Malayalees who assumed bharata natyam was a "girly dance" how powerfully masculine it could be.

Bharata natyam is received in a wide variety of ways in the Indian community abroad. For some audiences, bharata natyam works better than Ambien at putting them to sleep. For some, it is a physical expression of faith. For others it is an expressive performing art that appropriately displays the beauty of their heritage. For me it is a mix of the last two. Bharata natyam is a sublime combination of the physical, emotional, and spiritual through abstract dance and mime/storytelling that allows me to connect with and spread a small aspect of my cultural heritage. Stories are most often told using hand gestures (*hastas*) and facial expressions (*abhinaya*). Some dancers criticize literal storytelling using hand gestures. One downside to bharata natyam is that because the gestures can be so intricate and quick, they can go right over the heads of the uninitiated.

A year after I completed my *arangetram*, I graduated from high school and moved to Los Angeles to attend the University of Southern California. It was at USC that I first began to explore dance forms not native to India, including tap, jazz, and hip-hop. After graduating with a bachelor's degree in business administration, I started working full-time and began performing with a few dance companies in Southern California. The two companies I perform with most frequently are blue13 dance company and Shakti Dance Company. Shakti, led by Smt. Viji Prakash, is a bharata natyam company that regularly produces and tours bharata natyam ballets all over the U.S. and Canada. Blue13, directed by Achinta S. McDaniel, combines Bollywood, bhangra, classical Indian dance forms, and modern technique to create a signature style known as "Bollywood-Tech." There are many non-Indians in this company, and they often outnumber the dancers of Indian background.

I currently work as a financial analyst for the Los Angeles County Museum of Art. The museum is very understanding and supportive of my love of dance. My boss does everything possible to accommodate my schedule when we are preparing for a big concert or tour. My coworkers even come to support me at local shows as well. With this job I've been lucky enough to strike a fairly healthy work-life balance.

While I would love to pursue dance full-time, it is a reality that with my lack of knowledge of "Western" techniques, it is a little impractical from a purely financial perspective. From my experience, it is often the case that dancers who specialize in "foreign" dance forms often have to teach dance classes and take on regular students in order to make a living. While it is something I've considered, I don't think I have sufficient knowledge of bharata natyam theory to properly train young students. Additionally, my passion for dancing primarily manifests when I'm rehearsing and performing, so I prefer to maximize my time with that aspect of dance.

Appendix

Notes on Personal Histories

The idea to include an ethnographic component of "voices" of male practitioners originated with and was designed by Jennifer Fisher as the collection of scholarly essays were being solicited. The resulting personal histories were collaborations between the contributor and interviewer, with contributors having the final approval of their texts. On a few occasions, questions were sent to a contributor, who then provided written text, and the process of collaboration continued the same way from that point. The authors wish to thank each of the "personal history" contributors for their time and their willingness to reflect on their experiences to give us a portion of their dancing stories.

Interviewers

Jennifer Fisher interviewed David Allan and Michel Gervais, Aaron Cota, Rennie Harris, Donald McKayle, and Kristopher Wojtera. Anthony Shay interviewed Jamal (his partner and artistic associate), John Pennington, Saleem, Fred Strickler, Namus Zokhrabov, and Arun Mathai. Jill Nunes Jensen interviewed Christian Burns. Jennifer Fisher, in the editing process, further collaborated with Arun Mathai, John Pennington, and Fred Strickler; she also solicited contributions from and worked with Paul Babiak, Naatyaachaarya V. P. Dhananjayan, Hellmut Gottschild, and Seth Williams.

Choice of Contributors

The editors wanted to have a selection of practitioner contributors that covered different types of dance, as well as a variety of ages and attitudes. We started with people familiar to us, then branched out to others who were suggested or suggested themselves by being close by or who were recommended by others. It quickly became clear that virtually any and every man in dance had a story worth recounting, and our choices were based largely on interest (theirs and ours) and opportunity. These are only a sampling of the many stories there are still to tell, but we think a very good one, representative of many men in dance, while each remains unique (that is, maverick; see chapter 1).

Method

Each of this volume's coeditors has a background in ethnographic interviewing; more specifically, the process used for this project reflects methodology developed by Jennifer Fisher, a more in-depth explanation of which can be found in her essay for *Fields in Motion: Ethnography "At Home" in the Art Worlds of Dance*, edited by Dena Davida (forthcoming). In most cases, interview conversations lasted anywhere from an hour to several hours. The interviewer then edited the transcript into a first-person monologue and submitted that version to the contributor. A process of rephrasing and making additions followed, sometimes by e-mail, sometimes in conversation. The idea was to make spoken communication—which has its own logic and organization and often includes repetitions and a struggle to find the right word—into a more considered written text that accurately represented the attitudes and experiences of each contributor. Because we considered each contributor the author of this selected part of his personal history, each of them had final approval of their own texts.

Questions

Jennifer Fisher designed these guiding questions used for interviews for the "personal histories." They were adapted by each interviewer—Fisher, Anthony Shay, and Jill Nunes Jensen. Conversations were much less structured than they would have been with a formal interview schedule. The conversations were then turned into monologues, and further collaboration took place with the contributor, who had final approval.

- Where did you first get into dance?
- Tell me about your dance training.
- Tell me about your performance experience.
- What kind of dancer would you say you are?
- How did you get involved with dance?
- What do you remember from your early training?
- What were the attitudes of friends and family about your dancing?
- Do you think they thought about dance the way you did?
- Did you grow up with any stereotypes about men who dance?
- Do you think you're now surrounded by any stereotypes about men and dancing?
- Did you have role models in dance?
- What was it like to dance with a company (or dance in public, or teach, depending on circumstance)?
- Are there perceptions about men who dance that you think need changing?
- Is there anything you'd like a wider public to know about men who dance?

NOTES ON CONTRIBUTORS

Paul Babiak is currently pursuing doctoral studies at the Graduate Centre for Study of Drama, University of Toronto. Originally trained in classical acting at the Royal Academy of Dramatic Art, he has enjoyed a varied career in theater, film, and television; he is also an accomplished circus performer, playing in major venues across Canada. As playwright and director/dramaturg, he has assisted in the creation of a wide variety of new productions. His dissertation, in progress, is titled "Slapstick and Knockabout: Violent Comedy Enters the Modern Age."

Ramsay Burt is professor of dance history at De Montfort University. His publications include *The Male Dancer: Bodies, Spectacle, Sexualities* (1995), *Alien Bodies: Representations of Modernity, "Race" and Nation in Early Modern Dance* (1998), and *The Judson Dance Theater: Performative Traces* (2007). In 1999 he was Visiting Professor at the Department of Performance Studies, New York University. With Professor Susan Foster, he is founder and editor of *Discourses in Dance.*

Jennifer Fisher is an associate professor in the dance department of the University of California, Irvine, and the author of *Nutcracker Nation: How an Old World Ballet Became a Christmas Tradition in the New World* (2003), which won the 2004 de la Torre Bueno special citation. She has previously contributed dance writing to the *Los Angeles Times* and the *New York Times,* as well as many dance publications and scholarly journals. She holds the distinction of being the only ballet coroner who holds regular inquests into the death of Giselle.

Yvonne Hardt is an assistant professor in the Department of Theater, Dance, and Performance Studies at the University of California, Berkeley. After her modern dance education, she studied history and theater at the Free University of Berlin and in Montreal and wrote her dissertation on the political dimensions of modern dance in the Weimar Republic. She has also continuously choreographed her own works for her company, BodyAttacksWord.

Jill Nunes Jensen is a lecturer in the dance departments of California State University, Long Beach, and Loyola Marymount University. She also teaches dance history courses for Saint Mary's College Liberal Education for Arts Professionals (LEAP) program in Los Angeles. While remaining an active ballet practitioner, she received a master's degree in dance from the University of California, Los Angeles, and a Ph.D. in dance history and theory from the University of California, Riverside. She has presented work at several dance scholarship conferences and is currently working on a monograph about Alonzo King's LINES Ballet of San Francisco.

Stephen Johnson is the director of the Graduate Centre for Study of Drama at the University of Toronto. He is the author of *The Roof Gardens of Broadway Theatres* and has published articles in a variety of journals, including *Nineteenth Century Theatre Research, Drama Review, Theatre Topics, Canadian Theatre Review,* and *Theatre Research in Canada,* which he also edited for 10 years. His online database and Web site detailing blackface minstrelsy in Britain from 1842 to 1852, funded by the Social Sciences and Humanities Research Council of Canada, is available at http://link.library.utoronto.ca/minstrels/. He is a member of the Playwrights Guild of Canada, and the Writers Union of Canada.

John Bryce Jordan received a Ph.D. in dance history and theory from the University of California, Riverside, and has presented conference papers on the topic of his dissertation, "Light in the Heels: The Emergence of the Effeminate Male Dancer in Eighteenth-Century English History" (2001). He is a lecturer in the Department of Theatre Arts at California State University, Fresno.

Stavros Stavrou Karayanni was born in Cyprus and pursued English studies in Canada on a Commonwealth scholarship. He has published widely on culture, gender, and sexuality in the Middle East, with belly dance as the main focus of his intellectual interest. His book *Dancing Fear and Desire: Race, Sexuality and Imperial Politics in Middle Eastern Dance* (2004) won the European Society for the Study of English book award in cultural studies. The United Kingdom Alliance of Professional Teachers of Dancing has made him an honorary fellow. He teaches English literature and cultural theory in the School of Social Sciences and Humanities at Cyprus College.

Maura Keefe is a dance writer and historian. She is a scholar-in-residence at Jacob's Pillow Dance Festival and has led audience programs at Princeton University, UCLA, and the Goethe Institut, as well as for the Paul Taylor Dance Company and the Martha Graham Dance Company. She has traveled with Dance/USA to lead seminars for regional artists. Her current research investigates the relationships between dance and sports. She has an M.F.A. in choreography and performance from Smith College and a Ph.D. in dance history and theory from the University of California, Riverside. She is an assistant professor of dance at the State University of New York, Brockport.

Hari Krishnan is World Dance Artist in Residence at Wesleyan University and artistic director of the Toronto-based company inDANCE. Trained by hereditary dance-masters, including K. P. Kittappa Pillai and R. Muttukkannammal, Krishnan received his M.A. degree in dance from York University. For close to a decade, he has been involved with the documentation, translation, and analysis of the last vestiges of hereditary systems of dance in South India. Specializing in *devadasi* dance and contemporary abstractions of bharata natyam in performance, he integrates for his research the disciplines of dance studies, anthropology, history, and gender studies.

Doug Risner is professor of dance at Wayne State University, Detroit, Michigan. He has an M.F.A. in choreography and performance and a Ph.D. in curriculum and teaching with cultural studies specialization from the University of North Carolina at Greensboro. Risner is editor-in-chief of the *Journal of Dance Education* and has served the National Dance Education Organization as Secretary and is currently on its board of directors. He presents his research nationally and internationally and contributes to *Research in Dance Education, Dance Research Journal, Arts Education Policy Review, Selected Research in Dance,* and *Chronicle of Higher Education.* His forthcoming book, *When Boys Dance: Rehearsing Heterosexuality in Dance Education,* will be published in 2009.

Barbara Sellers-Young is dean of the Faculty of Fine Arts at York University in Toronto. For many years, she was in the Department of Theatre and Dance at the University of California, Davis. Her research projects on the intersections of dance, body, and globalization have taken place in Sudan, Egypt, Nepal, China, England, and Australia. She is the author of three books: *Teaching Personality with Gracefulness* (1993), a discussion of Kanriye Fujima's life and teaching of Nihon Buyo in the United States; *Breathing, Movement, Exploration: A Movement Text for Actors* (2001); and an edited volume with Anthony Shay on the globalization of belly dance, *Belly Dance: Orientalism, Transnationalism, and Harem Fantasy* (2005).

Anthony Shay is an assistant professor in the Department of Theatre and Dance at Pomona College. He is the author of *Choreophobia: Solo Improvised Dance in the Iranian World* (1999); *Choreographic Politics: State Folk Dance Companies, Representation, and Power* (2002), which was honored as the Outstanding Scholarly Dance Publication in 2003 by the Congress on Research in Dance; *Choreographing Identities: Folk Dance, Ethnicity and Festival in the United States and Canada* (2006); and *Dancing across Borders: Americans and Exotic Dances* (2008). He is editor of *Balkan Dance: Essays on Characteristics, Performance, and*

Teaching (2007), and (with Barbara Sellers-Young) *Belly Dance: Orientalism, Transnationalism, and Harem Fantasy.* He is a James Irvine Foundation Choreographic Fellow and has received a Lifetime Achievement Award from the California Arts Council. In 2007 he received the Distinguished Scholar award from the Association of Professors and Scholars of Iranian Heritage.

INDEX

LaVergne, TN USA
28 May 2010
184383LV00001B/2/P